THE EUSTACE DIAMONDS

ANTHONY TROLLOPE'S
PALLISER NOVELS

General Editor: W. J. Mc Cormack

CAN YOU FORGIVE HER? (1864–5)

Introduced by Kate Flint and edited by Andrew Swarbrick,
with a Preface by Norman St. John-Stevas

PHINEAS FINN (1869)

Introduced and edited by Jacques Berthoud

THE EUSTACE DIAMONDS (1873)

Introduced and edited by W. J. Mc Cormack

PHINEAS REDUX (1874)

Introduced by F. S. L. Lyons and edited by John C. Whale

THE PRIME MINISTER (1876)

Introduced by John McCormick and edited by Jennifer Uglow

THE DUKE'S CHILDREN (1880)

Introduced and edited by Hermione Lee

ANTHONY TROLLOPE
The Eustace Diamonds

EDITED WITH AN INTRODUCTION BY
W. J. Mc CORMACK

WITH ILLUSTRATIONS BY
BLAIR HUGHES-STANTON

OXFORD UNIVERSITY PRESS
Oxford   New York

Oxford University Press

Oxford New York Toronto
Delhi Bombay Calcutta Madras Karachi
Petaling Jaya Singapore Hong Kong Tokyo
Nairobi Dar es Salaam Cape Town
Melbourne Auckland

and associated companies in
Berlin Ibadan

Introduction, Bibliography and Chronology
© W.J. McCormack 1983

This edition first published 1983 as a World's Classics paperback

This cloth edition issued in 1991 by Oxford University Press, Inc.
200 Madison Avenue, New York, New York 10016

Oxford is a registered trademark of Oxford University Press

British Library Cataloguing in Publication Data
Trollope, Anthony
The Eustace diamonds.—(The World's classics)
I. Title. II. McCormack, W.J.
823'8[F] PR5684
ISBN 0-19-281588-1

Library of Congress Cataloging in Publication Data
Trollope, Anthony, 1815-1882.
The Eustace diamonds. (The World's classics)
Bibliography: p.
I. McCormack, W.J. II. Title. III. Series.
PR5684.E7 1983 823.'8 82-14348
ISBN 0-19-281588-1 (pbk.)
ISBN 0-19-520897-8

CONTENTS

INTRODUCTION

THE MYTH OF ENGLAND

To accelerate the social development in Europe, you must push on the catastrophe of official England. To do so, you must attack her in Ireland. That's her weakest point. Ireland lost, the British 'Empire' is gone, and the class war in England, till now somnolent and chronic, will assume acute forms. But England is the metropolis of landlordism and capitalism all over the world.[1]

I

Trollope was a liberal Tory, and *The Eustace Diamonds* was the least political of the Palliser series upon which his reputation as a political novelist largely depends. Here are two reasons, it would seem, for ignoring the quotation from Karl Marx with which I have begun. However, Marx's letter to Paul and Laura Lafargue renders explicit connections between England and Ireland, between England and the rest of the world, which are, in my view, deeply embedded in Trollope's fiction. The trouble is that the politics of the novels has never been considered at any level other than that of uncomplicated representation.[2] Parliamentary elections and prime ministers are not the be-all and end-all of politics; on the contrary they are often only the symbolic paraphernalia behind which political reality operates. In introducing and

[1] Karl Marx to Paul and Laura Lafargue, 5 March 1870. Karl Marx and Frederic Engels, *Ireland and the Irish Question*, Progress Publishers, Moscow, 1971, p. 290. Laura Lafargue was Marx's daughter who in 1868 married one of the founders of the French Workers' Party.

[2] The principal studies of the politics of Trollope's fiction are listed in the Select Bibliography (p. xxxv); Kate Flint's Introduction to *Can You Forgive Her?* (The World's Classics, Oxford, 1982), 'Trollope and Sexual Politics', deals with an important aspect of the fiction which can only be briefly treated here.

vii

annotating *The Eustace Diamonds* I am particularly concerned with this dimension of the fiction.

Of course, in life, Trollope was a Liberal. It was under those colours that he stood for election at Beverley in 1868. However, the attitudes officially displayed in the novels and in the autobiography are more properly associated with the kind of literary Toryism which links Samuel Johnson and F. R. Leavis. But just as Trollope's fiction has been read too literally for its political content so his life and social experience have been oversimplified and assimilated into neat and misleading categories. The Marxist critic Terry Eagleton, for example, places him in conventional pigeon-holes with a resultant distortion and rigidity:

> The major fiction of Victorian society was the product of the petty bourgeoisie. The Brontës, Dickens, Eliot, Hardy: it is with them, rather than with Thackeray, Trollope, Disraeli, Bulwer Lytton, that the finest achievements of nineteenth-century realism are to be found. Ambiguously placed within the social formation, the petty bourgeoisie was able on the whole to encompass a richer, more significant range of experience than those writers securely lodged within a single class.[3]

There is no doubt that the latter group of novelists were, so to speak, better-born than the former, but it could be energetically contested whether Trollope's place in the class system was always secure and George Eliot's always ambiguous. As for 'a richer, more significant range of experience', I would immediately concede that Trollope wrote nothing to compare with *Our Mutual Friend* or *Dombey and Son*. I would add, however, that any comparison between Dickens and Trollope requires points of reference additional to those implied in Dr. Eagleton's analysis.

To an extent unrivalled by any of his mid-Victorian contemporaries, Trollope is *the* imperial novelist. (Doubtless, Thackeray and *Vanity Fair* deserve consideration here, but

[3] Terry Eagleton, *Criticism and Ideology*, New Left Books, London, 1976, p. 125.

Trollope's sheer volume is, so to speak, symbolic of the imperialist credo.) This claim may seem extravagant, indeed perverse, to those readers of his who have been nursed on (and in some cases never weaned from) the Barsetshire novels, with their highly localized and quintessentially native settings. Yet the *paruchia* of early Trollope is an allegory of that most extensive and pervasive institution—the state church. And, to be strictly accurate, the very early Trollope's setting was Ireland, repeatedly Ireland, the most central and sublimated of imperial themes in the nineteenth century.

Ireland and Barsetshire are not simply marginal to a central world that is directly evoked in, say, *The Way We Live Now*. Trollope's fiction is not organized by means of microcosmic symbols or metaphors, by which we translate deanery squabbles into national issues or moral universals. On the contrary, Trollope is always expansive rather than intensive, or to put it in terms more recently fashionable, metonymic and not metaphoric. His novels exist cheek by jowl with each other, extending or encroaching upon the territory of each other, with a few characters occasionally straying across the frontier without a visa and without difficulty. *The Warden*, we might remind ourselves, was written in Belfast. In *The Eustace Diamonds*, the Pallisers themselves are marginal.

To appreciate the real complexity of Trollope as imperial novelist, and the insecurity of his position in British society (at least during the first half of his life), we need to pursue simultaneously the course of his career and the expanding dossier of his writings. Embarrassed at school by his father's financial troubles, and the resultant uncertainty of pocket money, Trollope entered the domestic civil service rather than the more prestigious overseas administration. His apprenticeship in adult life is served in Ireland and not India or Whitehall, and his home remained in Ireland until 1859, by which time he had published eight novels. As he progressed in his official career his incessant travels came more

directly to feed his novel-writing, to feed his insatiable appe-
tite for writing generally. Unlike Dickens, for whom America
was both in life and in art a splendid convenience, Trollope's
journeys to the United States, the West Indies, Australia,
New Zealand, and South Africa (with *en route* visits to India
and Ceylon) are immediately turned into copy. This is not to
suggest that *The American Senator*, and even less so *The New
Zealander*, should replace *The Last Chronicle* or *The Way We Live
Now* in the reader's estimate. Nevertheless, the co-existence
of such titles as *The Prime Minister* and *The West Indies and the
Spanish Main*, the projected *Guide to Ireland* and *The Macdermots
of Ballycloran*—tourism or tragedy, it's all writing—indicates
the range of Trollope's awareness of the British global
presence in the nineteenth century. One is obliged to say that
George Eliot remains his superior in the moral analysis of
provincial manners, but her perception of the British as
distinct from the English perspective is strictly limited. And
while in Dickens's late fiction we are shown with ferocious
intensity how a man's changing his mind in the Australian
settlements has its causes and consequences in London and
London's surrounding marshes, in Trollope the treatment of
the settlements, the colonies, the empire is extensive. Of
course he is no documentary reporter of penal conditions,
but inevitably the raw-red parts of the globe are admitted.

To twentieth-century readers heavily indoctrinated by a
.riticism in which symbolic integration (emotionally expressed as intensity) is all-in-all, this side of Trollope's achievement seems less deserving of comment than the moral symmetry of *Doctor Thorne* or the sympathetic humour of the
Barsetshire novels generally. Then, to such twentieth-
century readers, Trollope has always seemed if not marginal,
at least marginally second-rank. I suggest, therefore, that
our revaluation of Trollope will begin by emphasizing the
extensive mosaic of his writing, its cheek-by-jowlness. Forty-
seven novels, together with tales and travel-books, translations and hack-work, constitute a very large mosaic. Its
organizing structure is loose but elaborate: one piece of work

(itself large) touches upon three or four others on their congruent sides, and each of those three or four has as many neighbouring books. Mosaic, one might say, is the composition of a representing whole from non-representing fragments. Its dynamics are based both on congruity of tone, of scale, of configuration, and on decisive disjunctions of these. It radiates alternately by means of its composed colours and shapes and by means of the bounding extrusions which hold these—*apart*. That the pieces of this vast mosaic are frankly mimetic, imitative of social life and manners as Trollope saw them and sought to understand them, only serves to make the mosaic all the more remarkable. By the dual aura of the mosaic, the meaning of the individual part may be radically transcended by the entire composition, the whole *oeuvre*; and, conversely, the ostensible unity and determined achievement of the whole thing revealingly jeopardized by the manifestation of the mimetic fragment. Mosaic, the unity achieved by fragmentation, creation preceded and rendered possible by destruction or at least reduction, is an art of contradictions.

By comparison, Dickens writes the same novel over again, proceeding from sentimental resolution and the individual's reunion with respectable society to a fiercely controlled despair at the chains which bind him to society's outer walls, neither allowing him *in* or *away*. The contradictions of Dickens's fiction may be found in embryo even in the early novels, and we prefer the later ones largely because we have been taught the merits of symbolic intensity. But in Trollope the contradictions are extensive, juxtaposing the quiet-watered texture of an ecclesiastical setting with the sexual perversity of a central character in a neighbouring novel. Both setting and character are then placed against an exotic excursion to that empire of which Barchester never ceases to be a part and in which even the heroine of *The Small House at Allington* is embroiled.

II

The very title of *The Eustace Diamonds* seems to signal a departure from the landscape and characterization of the typical Trollope fiction. Yet why do we jump to this conclusion; does not that use of family name as adjective subtly tell us that we are among the possessing classes? To the Victorian reader, however, 'diamonds' not only connoted wealth but ostentatious, guarded wealth, wealth which might be stolen. Trollope quite deliberately drew his reader's attention to the sensational–forensic novels of Wilkie Collins and Charles Reade when he named his new novel. Here we have a titular emphasis, not on moral judgment (cf. *Can You Forgive Her?*), nor on human identities and roles (cf. *Phineas Finn* and *The Prime Minister*). Here, as rarely in Trollope, *things* get the credit they deserve. It is ironic that the novel which gives prominence to the power objects have over human beings should be considered the least political of the Palliser series: the manner in which men and women in Victorian society are held in thrall by the objects they valorize is clearly not outmoded. On several occasions in the course of the novel, we are told how the diamonds were like a weight tied round Lizzie's neck, and the literalness of the metaphor (if indeed metaphor it really is) gives one a rare opportunity to see through the normally protected and decorated accounts of wealth and its connotations.[1] Yet, as the title once again emphasizes, this is not simply a tale of the struggle of an individual with tainted wealth: it is a narrative of specifically hereditable wealth, family (not just private) property. The legal notion of heirloom, so central to the plot, depends upon a theory of society in which the identity of different generations of the same family predominates over other, lateral, claims. The heirloom, whether it is a picture or a sword or a kitchen utensil, is not in Mr. Wemmick's sense

[1] Compare the phrase 'the bosom of Society' used frequently in connection with Mrs. Merdle's jewellery in Dickens's *Little Dorrit* (1855–7), The World's Classics, Oxford, 1982.

fully portable property. It cannot be disposed of freely, and when Trollope tells us that it hangs like a weight round Lady Eustace's neck he ironically indicates its attachment to her. But the legal knot at the heart of the plot is this—can jewels *be* heirlooms?—a knot which the narrative ultimately does not unravel.

It would take a robust obscurantism to insist that such questions are non-political. After all, the altering forms of wealth experienced throughout the nineteenth century—the 'abstraction' capital replacing land but bringing with it alienable tokens such as those encapsulated in Trollope's title here—are accompanied by the gradual modification of aristocratic behaviour to a bourgeois code. Here one might compare the styles of Sir Florian and John Eustace. Both these developments are reflected also in the growth of administration which affects the older social relations of landed estate. (Fawn's role as junior minister rather than proprietor is significant, just as Greystock's career is subordinated to systematic requirements as well as individualist ambitions.)

Recently, a lawyer commenting on the appropriation of certain official insignia by Sir John Coleridge in 1873 pointed to a resemblance to the plot of *The Eustace Diamonds*. The time-table of the novel's publication makes it difficult to accept that Trollope utilized the retiring Attorney-General's conduct, for the novel was already in serialization prior to Coleridge's retirement and his retention of the insignia. Nevertheless, the network of half-allusions and hints in the novel is well described in the lawyer's analysis:

It will be recalled that much turned upon whether the diamond necklace in Lady Eustace's possession was an heirloom and as such was claimable by the trustees of the Eustace Estate or whether it belonged to Lady Eustace absolutely by virtue of her husband's gift. The trustees sought the opinion of Mr. 'Turtle' Dove ... Mr. Dove's opinion is printed in full in Chapter XXV. The most interesting paragraph of the opinion reads thus:

'Certain chattels may undoubtedly be held and claimed as being in the nature of heirlooms—as swords, pennons of honour, garter and Collar of SS. See the case of the Earl of Northumberland; and that of the Pusey Horn—*Pusey v. Pusey.*'

The latter case sheds no light upon the Collar of SS, but the *Earl of Northumberland's Case* (1583) . . . is interesting. The Earl of Northumberland had devised his jewels by will to his wife. He died possessing, in addition to certain jewellery, 'a Collar of Esses'. The question was whether the collar passed to the widow by virtue of the devise of the jewels . . . this decision suggests that in the late sixteenth century, and presumably thereafter, a Collar of Esses was treated as an heirloom, and thus transmitted down a family, generation after generation.

It is interesting to speculate how Trollope came to write about the Collar of SS. In Chapter LXXII of *Eustace Diamonds*, Mr. Dove refers to an intrigue concerning the promotion of 'a somewhat unpopular Attorney-General' to the Bench, the question being whether he should succeed to the Woolsack or to a vacant Lord Justiceship, or whether a 'Second-class Chief Justice' should be persuaded to resign from 'a certain Second-class Chief Justiceship' to make way for the unpopular Attorney-General . . . It is not unreasonable to guess that the 'Second-class Chief Justiceship' was that of the Common Pleas. Now according to the Dictionary of National Biography *Eustace Diamonds* was first published in 1873, the year in which Sir John Coleridge (then Attorney-General) was appointed . . . Chief Justice of the Common Pleas. Lord Justice MacKinnon says in his note that Sir John Coleridge acquired his predecessor's Collar of SS upon his appointment.[5]

The note by MacKinnon referred to here establishes one or two further factors we should take into account in considering this intrigue as a source for *The Eustace Diamonds*:

On the death of Cockburn in November, 1880, Coleridge became Lord Chief Justice of the King's Bench, and he then received Cockburn's Collar pursuant to his trust. He had no successor as Chief Justice of the Common Pleas. So apparently he persuaded himself that it was right and proper to appropriate the old Common

[5] Eustace Roskill, 'Gold Collar of SS', *Law Quarterly Review*, vol. 62, 1946, pp. 27–8.

Pleas Collar as his private property. It is now [1943] in the possession of his grandson.[6]

Strictly speaking then, Coleridge did not arrogate to himself the Collar of SS until 1880, seven years after Trollope's novel referring to unpopular Attorney-Generals, their promotion, and to the possible status of Collars of SS as heirlooms. It is possible that the subject of Coleridge's intentions was rumoured in 1873, but the chapters (25 and 72) referring to such topics appeared in serial form in the *Fortnightly Review* in January 1872 and December 1872 respectively. Moreover, the novel had been completed in manuscript by August 1870, and from May till October 1871 Trollope was either at sea *en route* for Australia or travelling in the antipodes. As he returned to Britain via the United States and arrived finally on 20 December 1872, he was remote from sources of Whitehall rumour throughout the period the novel was serialized. We can conclude therefore that the Coleridge business was not directly employed in the composition of *The Eustace Diamonds*.

At first sight it seems that this scrutiny of the timetable deals a blow to the argument that the novel has a significant political stratum, for we have cut it off from a promising link with the acquisitive behaviour of important law officers. However, a *roman-à-clef* in which Lizzie Eustace stands in for Sir John Coleridge would be an embarrassing trophy—and not a very good novel either. What is striking in Trollope's depiction of the jewels' transactions between family and possessor is not its specific mimesis of an individual intrigue but its partial and general resemblance to a broader structure of legal and social behaviour. For, if the Coleridge business lies some years ahead of *The Eustace Diamonds*, there is another case which predates it in a suggestive manner. In 1868 Edward Shelley and his mother Elizabeth Shelley (widow of John Shelley) went to law to establish who was

---

[6] F. D. MacKinnon, loc. cit., vol. 59, 1943, p. 32. See also R. A. Riches 'The Gold Collar of SS', loc. cit., vol. 59, 1943, pp. 120–21.

entitled to certain jewels left to the late John Shelley by his aunt, Mrs. Helen Parker. When Mrs. Parker had died in 1838 she left these jewels to her nephew *as heirlooms* with directions to him that he should ensure their perpetuation as heirlooms. In the event, the court ruled that the will of Mrs. Parker created a good executory trust which should be executed. The bearing of the case upon Mr. Dove's opinion on the question of jewels as heirlooms is perhaps less than central, and the precise legal position is not our immediate concern. The *Law Reports (Equity)*, in recording the case, include a passage of Sir W. Page Wood's which is significant:

Now, it is quite settled that there is a mode of executing a trust of this description, subject to an observation—which was made in the exhaustive argument addressed to the Court—that the bulk of the authorities [i.e. legal cases cited as precedent etc.] are those in which real estate has first been limited, and then a direction has come that the personal estate should follow the limitations of the real, subject to the mode in which heirlooms are ordinarily limited with reference to the possession of family estates.[7]

Mrs. Parker, it was noted, had no real estate, and herein lay some novelty in the case, for it centred upon the future movement of objects of personal property, valorized as heirlooms, within a world in which real estate (land) no longer was the overwhelming index of wealth or social status. *Shelley v. Shelley* was available to Trollope, and its implications impinge directly upon the plot of *The Eustace Diamonds*. In the novel, of course, Mr. Dove does not cite it. On the other hand, Lady Eustace reads Shelley, Mrs. Parker's nephew.

What we have done is to burst the balloon which is inflated by vaporous opinions as to the non-political nature of *The Eustace Diamonds* by placing it in a historically alert series of comparisons to other narratives. For, the sequence of events recited in court also forms a narrative, though at the outset it

[7] See *Law Reports (Equity)*, vol. 6, 1868, pp. 540–50. The Mrs. Parker referred to was a sister of Sir Timothy Shelley, Bart., and so was the poet's aunt.

is a narrative either unresolved or formulated in rival versions. It is not for nothing that the criminal lawyer and the novelist share the word 'plot', and the mediator between them is theatre. What is crucial in Trollope's fiction is the limitation he imposes upon the application of plot in its political context, a limitation which is itself part of the political content of the novels. Lucy Morris has no interest in politics, but she knows that her lover, the Tory MP is right. (One determinant of her certainty is that he is a Tory, another that he is a man.) Lizzie Eustace's defence of her jewels by means of a simulated theft is not *immoral*, but representative of all defences of property in the novel. And here we reach a further level of Trollope's political intelligence, if also his political evasion, his inclusion of evidence which explodes the idea of England as the self-contained stage of the Victorian novel.

III

In 1872, as *The Eustace Diamonds* was appearing serially in the *Fortnightly Review*, its author was travelling in Australia. In the inevitable book which followed, Trollope commented on the pessimism of Tasmanian politicians:

That such a belief as to one's country should not be accompanied by any personal act evincing despair has been the case in all national panics. English country gentlemen have very often been sure of England's ruin; but I have never heard of the country gentleman who, in consequence of his belief, sold his estate and went to live elsewhere.[8]

As the editors of *Australia* note, that quirk of the Tory mentality crops up elsewhere in Trollope's writings, most adjacently in the fourth chapter of the present novel where a long list of political disasters is advanced. 'A huge, living, daily increasing grievance that does one no palpable harm, is the

[8] Trollope, *Australia*, ed. P. D. Edwards and R. B. Joyce, St. Lucia: University of Queensland, 1967, p. 540.

happiest possession that a man can have.'[9] The function of
Trollope's travel-books was, basically, to demonstrate the
admirable viability of the colonial venture. Australian towns
are not as bad as reported; it is easier to paddle in the sea at
Sydney than at any comparable city back home—with the
possible exception of Dublin. And this comparative method
is all important—Melbourne's Chinatown is compared to
that of several European and American cities in breathless
approval of Australian cleanliness. Irish prisoners in Tas-
mania are interviewed, though the criminal past of a West
Hobart politician is delicately suppressed—the editors here
speculate that Trollope had known the man's family during
his eighteen-year residence in Ireland. The Trollopian eye
for detail, even detail which is tactfully elided from the
official proceedings, is active in the fiction also. Indeed, it is
one of the features of his immense mosaic which renders it
intelligible—the tendency to include things which are
scarcely recorded by the conscious, composing mind, things
which are detonatingly representative of the writer's attitudes. Two sentences from *Australia* may give advance notice
of what is possible in analysing the fiction:

One cannot walk about Melbourne without being struck by all that
has been done for the welfare of the people generally. There is no
squalor to be seen,—though there are quarters of the town in which
the people no doubt are squalid.[10]

In terms of *The Eustace Diamonds*'s conventional reputation
one could argue, by the same doubtful logic, that it is the
least political of Trollope's political novels—that is, there is
virtually no politics *to be seen*. On further investigation,
however, we discover the concealed psychic ghettoes to
which politics has been assigned in the novel. And this
'non-political' appearance of the book is its most political
characteristic.

[9] Trollope, *The Eustace Diamonds*, The World's Classics, Oxford, 1983,
p. 1.34.
[10] Trollope, *Australia*, p. 375.

Frank Greystock is a Tory, of course, and Lord Fawn a Whig with a minor post in the Government. These political identifications are undeniable, but little force is given to their implementation. Greystock and Fawn disagree in Parliament, but surely it is hard to read ironically the narrator's dismissal of these issues involving the Sawab of Mygawb:

Lady Linlithgow's visit to her niece had been made on a Thursday, and on that same evening Frank Greystock had asked his question in the House of Commons,—or rather had made his speech about the Sawab of Mygawb. We all know the meaning of such speeches. Had not Frank belonged to the party that was out, and had not the resistance of the Sawab's claim come from the party that was in, Frank would not probably have cared much about the Prince. We may be sure that he would not have troubled himself to read a line of that very dull and long pamphlet of which he had to make himself master before he could venture to stir in the matter, had not the road of opposition been open to him in that direction . . . Frank made his speech, and made it very well. It was just the case for a lawyer, admitting the kind of advocacy which it is a lawyer's business to practise. The Indian minister of the day, Lord Fawn's chief, had determined, after much anxious consideration, that it was his duty to resist the claim; and then, for resisting it he was attacked. Had he yielded to the claim, the attack would have been as venomous, and very probably would have come from the same quarter. No blame by such an assertion is cast upon the young Conservative aspirant for party honours. It is thus the war is waged.[11]

It is difficult to invest any faith in an ironic interpretation of this. After all, the jousting between Greystock and Fawn is rapidly translated into a consideration of the merits of Lucy Morris and Lizzie Eustace as potential wives. And the title of the chapter—'Mr. Burke's Speeches'—while it has an ironic perspective, doesn't direct us to reverse this translation and see the marriage contract as some 'symbol' of a political meaning. Lucy knows who Burke was, but she hasn't read and doesn't intend to read him. It is made agonizingly

[11] Trollope, *The Eustace Diamonds*, p. 1.61.

obvious to the reader that Lucy is just the right kind of girl to marry Frank, and that right marriage is the thing Frank must manage if he is to deserve the sympathy Trollope has heaped on him.

What we are witnessing here is a local incident in the mosaic. Trollope is concerned with manners and marriage, but the social setting of his plot obliges him to' nod in the direction of politics. So politics is placed side by side with the brighter and more radiant theme, and generations of readers have obligingly focussed their attention on the brightly lit, nominal, theme—the diamonds. The rigorous pattern of mosaic, however, insists on incorporating that political theme by associating it in a manner which—like squalor in Melbourne—need not be seen. The Sawab has been robbed, or at least makes a claim to this effect. The Eustace family claim Lizzie has robbed them. In his *Autobiography* Trollope was unguarded enough to cite Wilkie Collins as the man who could resolve the mysteries of *The Eustace Diamonds* at a stroke. And there, if we look, is the solution indeed—the gem of Collins's novel is originally stolen at the storming of Seringapatam during the Sepoy wars. Trollope's debt to Collins is significant critically in that *The Eustace Diamonds* is more tightly organized and emotionally taut than Trollope novels generally are, and the influence of the sensation-cum-detective plot of *The Moonstone* is undeniable. However, the comparison also suddenly throws light on that apparently dismissive political passage about the Sawab. India has been the subject of many of 'Mr. Burke's Speeches', and the robbery of India at that too. To appreciate the deep coloration of that fragment in the mosaic, its sombre and dark shades flashily overawed by the brilliance of the marriage theme, one has to be prepared to see an allusion to Warren Hastings and a structural debt to Wilkie Collins not as disparate and unrelated things but as integral parts of a larger pattern. The Sawab of Mygawb, a non-character if ever there was one, nevertheless produces a shattering of that butter-wouldn't-melt-in-her-mouth heroine, Lucy Morris.

Defending her man against the Fawns Lucy simply reduces the defrauded prince to a racial object:

> To think that Mr. Greystock should be so mean as to bear malice about a thing like that wild Indian because he takes his own cousin's part![12]

The Indian, for all his non-existence in the plot, has the effect of revealing the heroine's priorities—blood is thicker than water, and English blood is thicker than Indian justice.

In a manner which no other Victorian novel attempted *The Eustace Diamonds* tosses off these insights into the immediacy with which England becomes Britain. The purity with which George Eliot reflects the Englishness of England is in fact the gravest defect in her fiction considered as a mimesis of Victorian life. If *Daniel Deronda* suggests some limitation of this criticism, then the relevant correction is Edward Said's analysis of British Zionism in George Eliot.[13] Half the effects which Trollope achieves in reflecting the reality of a Greater Britain were unplanned and unintended, but given his compositional method—minute observation combined with swiftness of execution—the traces are there willy-nilly. It only requires the reader to move slightly from the conventional position he reverently gazes from, and the patterns of the fiction are thrown into a new kind of order, or at least reveal elements not previously noted. The Palliser novels are noted for their incorporation of the Irish MP, Phineas Finn, in the political framework of the entire fiction. Yet *The Eustace Diamonds* (in which Finn does not appear) offers two other revealing Irish references which are usually passed over in silence. Lord Fawn, outlining his rather insecure circumstances to Lizzie Eustace on the occasion of his proposing marriage, explains to her that the family title was an Irish one until Lord Melbourne elevated Fawn's father to the English peerage. Fawn has property in Ireland, in

[12] Trollope, *The Eustace Diamonds*, p. 1.246.
[13] Edward W. Said, *The Question of Palestine*, Vintage Books, New York, 1980, pp. 60–68.

County Tipperary to be exact, but there is no house on it, and in any case it only produces £5,000 a year in rents. Fawn's financial insecurity, together with his government post, motivates his approach to Lizzie Eustace, but his need is specified in a manner which reveals the complex historical circumstances which determine a man's position. Fawn is not Irish, he is not an outsider like Finn who has to be 'incorporated'; but his family's honours had not evidently merited a full-scale English peerage at the time of the original creation. An Irish peerage was a second-class reward which had the added advantage (for the British authorities) of imposing no burden or clutter on *the* peerage. It was said of George II that, in refusing a Welsh baronet permission to build an avenue near St. James's Park, he softened the blow with an offer of an Irish peerage. In *The Eustace Diamonds*, Fawn is by now a fully blown British peer but he still is constricted by the remoteness and primitive condition of his estates in Ireland, a condition he simultaneously regrets and sustains.

The second Irish allusion to which I want to draw the attention of readers who insist on this novel's non-political nature concerns Lord George de Bruce Carruthers. An attorney's apprentice who fabulously inherited a title from his third cousin, Lord George is presented in a neat cameo:

He always had horses, but never had a home. When in London he lodged in a single room, and dined at his club. He was a Colonel of Volunteers, having got up the regiment known as the Long Shore Riflemen,—the roughest regiment of Volunteers in all England—and was reputed to be a bitter Radical. He was suspected even of republican sentiments, and ignorant young men about London hinted that he was the grand centre of the British Fenians. He had been invited to stand for the Tower Hamlets, but had told the deputation which waited upon him that he knew a thing worth two of that. Would they guarantee his expenses, and then give him a salary? The deputation doubted its ability to promise so much. 'I more than doubt it,' said Lord George; and then the deputation went away.[14]

[14] Trollope, *The Eustace Diamonds*, pp. 1.332–3.

This is Trollope introducing his character, one of those paragraphs in which the action is briefly suspended while the character is paraded before us. Now, the action will very immediately be fox-hunting, so the remark about horses is to the point. Ultimately Lord George will see through Lizzie Eustace and rescue himself from entanglement, so the Tower Hamlets anecdote serves an anticipatory purpose. But what is the 'thing worth two of that'? We don't know and we are not told. The prospect which is twice as valuable as a seat in Parliament is never specified; its function in the passage is rhetorical, though I use the term 'rhetorical' without any of its frequent pejorative connotations. The passage has a distinctive, Trollopian rhythm in which a degree of humorous delight at Lord George's anomalies participates. Sentences run from a pattern of the most obvious associations—Colonel of Volunteers . . . roughest regiment of Volunteers—into a pattern of syncopation—dined at his club . . . Colonel . . . bitter Radical. But the least harmoniously modulated of these citations is that Lord George was 'the grand centre of the British Fenians'. This extraordinary rumour, admittedly the work of ignorant young men about town, requires some distracting and yet undemanding blur of context in which it can be swallowed, and so we get the waffle about 'a thing worth two of that'. The strategy is to follow up the impudent claim with what looks like a clue to some subsequent action. After all, in a political novel nominations, especially for Tower Hamlets, *ought* to be significant. I describe all this as Trollope's strategy, though in fact I believe he was scarcely aware of what happens within such passages as these: his rapid assimilation of the mood of Victorian Britain was such that he transmitted these richly contradictory effects before they registered with him.

The Eustace Diamonds appeared serially between 1871 and 1873. As we have seen, the author was in Australia for part of that time. While he was in Victoria, the Prime Minister of that province fell from power, an incident that Trollope commented on in his Australian travel-book. The Prime

Minister was Charles Gavan Duffy, who in the late 1840s led an advanced wing of the Irish nationalist movement. Trollope was in Ireland in those days, and the Fenian rebellion (with explosive side-effects in Britain) occurred as a direct consequence of Duffy's failure. Everything in Trollope fits into a tightly packed, chessboard-like pattern: Lord George Carruthers goes to press as the pre-Fenian falls from power in the colonies: the agitations which inform Trollope's last novel, *The Landleaguers*, were effectively launched by the same Gavan Duffy in the early 1850s, just before he departed from Australia. Every stroke of Trollope's pen concedes the existence of a world beyond that of his official operation, and it is little wonder that New Critics have had no time for him (while at the same time resembling strongly some of his more introspective characters). The *text* of a Trollope novel extrudes between the canonical limitations to touch upon the history of the Anglo-Irish tension or the echoes of Indian colonial policy. Most characteristic of all are the authorial self-allusions in which the transcendent merits of the pillar-box (invented by Trollope) vie with satirical allusions to a bad play called *The Noble Jilt* (which the same inventive mind contrived)—*The Eustace Diamonds* provides examples of both. What is critically significant, however, is the manner in which the Trollope novel leaves itself open to interpretation, allows one to bring to it cognate material from other 'disciplines'.

IV

This revised view of the novel's basic character naturally has implications for an assessment of the plot. A recent critic has set up a parallel between *The Eustace Diamonds* and Spenser's *Faerie Queene* according to which Miss Morris is a modern Una, an embodiment of light (*lux* = 'light' in Latin) and truth. The evidence for this is Frank Greystock's declaration 'You are truth itself'. This abysmal surrender to Greystock's point of view is all the more deplorable when we remember Greystock's notions of truth in the Sawab's affairs. Moreover, Lucy under pressure shows herself to be equally capable of racist eloquence and logical argument. The truth is, of course, that the heroine of the novel is Lady Elizabeth Eustace. In a world of officially sanctioned theft and expropriation, Lizzie has little alternative but to hang on to what wealth she has and to manoeuvre in the marriage stakes to her best advantage. In all this she has to contend with the unrelenting hostility of the narrator:

Thoughts of a second marriage had, of course, crossed Lady Eustace's mind, and they were by no means the worst thoughts that found a place there. She had a grand idea,—this selfish, hard-fisted little woman, who could not bring herself to abandon the plunder on which she had laid her hand,—a grand idea of surrendering herself and all her possessions to a great passion.[15]

Trollope might be accused in his presentation of Lizzie's personality of relying too much on description and not enough on narrative. We are earnestly advised to note the wickedness of the lady, we are less often *shown* how she is what she is. The first chapter, indeed the first sentence, specifies her governing Vice, and nothing that follows seeks to *understand* that condition. Whenever we see Lizzie in action, with the narrator's moralisms held temporarily in abeyance, she is witty and alluring. It is not just that Trollope succeeds in persuading us that she is beautiful, we recognize the sexual attraction of the woman in her speech, the shapes of her behaviour. The psychological realism of the contorted relationship between Lucinda Roanoke and Sir Griffin Tewett has been noted: Lucinda is the beautiful woman considered 'purely' as object, polystyrene sexuality. (With reference to Lucinda, *lux* evidently does not mean 'light'.) Trapped into an engagement, she literally breaks—goes mad. Lucinda's is the repressed neurotic behaviour with which Lizzie is more successfully dealing. For Lizzie's

---

[15] Trollope, *The Eustace Diamonds*, p. 1.43.

position, the position Trollope declines to understand, is that she comes to a kind of sexual consciousness in a society where female consciousness is taboo. It is not enough to say that she is a coquette, her problem is far more radical and tragic than that: she must think her feelings, possess them in pure intellectuality; conversely, she is only allowed to think by means of tangible and palpable strategies. The narrator wants us to label this as falseness, but the narrator is a simple-minded fellow compared to the novelist who admits so much evidence against the grain.

Instead of seeing the novel as an eternal struggle between light and darkness, Lucy and Lizzie, we should recognize Lucinda's emblematic role. Lucinda is beyond the world of remedial reflection because she is ultimately mad, and Lucy is perhaps the counterbalancing extreme on the other side. Uncertainty, and hence the possibility of insight, lies with Lizzie at the centre of the spectrum. To Lizzie are drawn all those evidences of the world beyond England, a world in which England is ubiquitous but self-effacingly so. Lucy Morris is indeed the epitome of English virtues—patient, trusting, true—and England does not exist. If you acknowledge and approve the imperial venture, then you should logically concede that Lizzie is your heroine.

'A huge, living, daily increasing grievance that does one no palpable harm, is the happiest possession that a man can have.' This Trollopian statement of the English Tory psychology points in the direction of the epigram cited in George Meredith's *The Ordeal of Richard Feverel* (1859)—'Sentimentalists . . . are they who seek to enjoy Reality, without incurring the Immense Debtorship for a thing done.' In time, Stephen Dedalus will polish Meredith's phrase and telegram it to Buck Mulligan. (Joyce was born some months before Trollope died.) It is true that Trollope intends an ironic reading of his analysis of gentlemanly complaint, but true also that his fiction cleaves to a similar sentimentality. Having bravely shown Lizzie to be a courageous breaker of new territory, and Lucy a dish of blancmange, he then marries Lucy and Frank to each other. Trollope's novels faithfully employed the happy ending in its nuptial form, but the conclusion to *The Eustace Diamonds* is particularly significant in its sentimentality. By relegating imperial, striving Lizzie and elevating her placid, native rival, he enacts the most strategic feature of nineteenth-century British feeling—the notion that England survives unaltered amid the expansive and violent gestures of its global presence. It is to destroy this powerful illusion that Stephen Dedalus must specify with an ungentlemanly precision his opposition to both 'the imperial British state' and 'the holy Roman catholic and apostolic church'. Trollopian irony is uncertain in that it never quite articulates the balance between its study of imperialism and its manifestation of imperialism, but then it is not the function of irony to absorb the reader's immense debtorship for the thing done.

'Theoretically a member of the ruling class, and sharing its insistent myth and ideology of "England", he and men like him were in practice on the outer edge of the system, in several ways. Owning no land or substantial property, they were dependent on their professional salaries which were in turn dependent on accepting the definitions of "profession" and "service" which the system as a whole had created.'[16] Raymond Williams's account of George Orwell might be momentarily taken over to qualify and extend Terry Eagleton's insistent placing of Trollope 'securely lodged within a single class'. Such a static notion of class is consistent with what Marx mockingly termed 'official England'. To concentrate on a single setting of Trollope's, or to take as one the narrator and the novelist, is to reduce the mosaic of his composition to monochrome. If Dr. Leavis and his followers to right and left insist on associating Trollope with Mrs. Gaskell and leaving the argument unspoken, it conveniently follows that his work does not feature among 'the finest achievements of nineteenth-century realism'. But then one of

---

[16] Raymond Williams, *Orwell*, Fontana, 1971, pp. 18–19.

the recurring principles of bourgeois realism is its myth of England, an illusion which the fragmentary aura of *The Eustace Diamonds*, with its subversive admissions, successfully jeopardizes.

NOTE ON THE TEXT

T ROLLOPE wrote *The Eustace Diamonds* between 4 December 1869 and 25 August 1870. Serialization in the *Fortnightly Review* (published monthly) began on 1 July 1871; there were twenty instalments, each of four chapters, the last appearing on 1 February 1873. In keeping with the format of the magazine, there were no illustrations.

As was customary, the three-volume book edition was published before the serial was concluded in order to catch Christmas sales in December 1872. It is however dated 1873. An American edition published in one volume by Harper of New York had appeared in October 1872. *The Eustace Diamonds* was not included in Tauschnitz's British Authors series; continental publication was effected through the rival Asher series.

In keeping with the principles outlined in the General Introduction to this Centenary Edition, the text here reproduced is that of the Oxford Trollope. Edited by Michael Sadleir and Frederick Page, this text was first published in 1950.

SELECT BIBLIOGRAPHY

THERE is a daily increase in the critical material written about Trollope, and a note such as this can only be useful by being highly selective. Readers should consult George H. Ford, *Victorian Fiction: a Second Guide to Research* (Modern Language Association of America, New York, 1978), and the bibliographies published annually in *Victorian Studies*.

Michael Sadleir's *Trollope: a Commentary* (Oxford University Press, 3rd edn, 1961) is still the best biography, though it has been augmented by James Pope Hennessy, *Anthony Trollope* (Little, Brown, Boston, 1971) and C. P. Snow, *Trollope: His Life and Art* (Macmillan, 1975). In *Trollope: A Bibliography* (Dawson, 2nd edn, 1964) Sadleir also provides an account of Trollope's original publications. Donald Smalley, *Trollope; the Critical Heritage* (Routledge, 1969) and David Skilton, *Anthony Trollope and his Contemporaries* (Longman, 1972) very fully document his reception.

Of the many general studies recently published, the following should be noted—A. O. J. Cockshut, *Anthony Trollope: a Critical Study* (Collins, 1955); Ruth apRoberts, *Trollope: Artist and Moralist* (Chatto & Windus, 1971); James R. Kincaid, *The Novels of Anthony Trollope* (Clarendon Press, 1977). Robert Tracy's *Trollope's Later Novels* (University of California Press, Berkeley, 1978), though it does not deal with any of the Palliser novels at length, is also recommended.

The most important studies to deal specifically with the political fiction are Arthur Pollard, *Trollope's Political Novels* (University of Hull, 1968), which argues that the author's own political engagement is the root of his power in these novels; John Halperin's *Trollope and Politics: A Study of the Pallisers* (Macmillan, 1977) and Juliet McMaster's *Trollope's Palliser Novels: Theme and Pattern* (Macmillan, 1978). Halperin takes a conventional view of politics, while McMaster is inclined to depoliticize the fiction even as to content as well as form.

One or two more marginal books deserve notice. *A Guide to*

SELECT BIBLIOGRAPHY

Trollope, by W. G. and J. T. Gerould (Oxford University Press, 1948) is a dictionary which can aid those who have not memorized every character in the forty-seven novels. John W. Clark, *Language and Style of Anthony Trollope* (Deutsch, 1975), scandalously lacks an index but is otherwise excellent. In *Trollope and his Illustrators* (Macmillan, 1980) N. John Hall discusses two of the Palliser novels—*Can You Forgive Her?* and *Phineas Finn*—and by reproducing illustrations by Hablot K. Browne and J. E. Millais amongst others provides evidence of how contemporary readers were directed to visualize the fiction.

Critical articles in journals and elsewhere are legion. For an historical context, see J. A. Banks 'The Way They Lived Then: Anthony Trollope and the 1870s', *Victorian Studies*, 12, 1968, pp. 177–200. A useful foreign perspective is present in Ludwig Borinski, 'Trollope's Palliser Novels', *Die Neueren Sprachen*, 12, 1963, pp. 389–407. For *The Eustace Diamonds* as presented in this edition, two items are particularly relevant—Henry Miley, '*The Eustace Diamonds* and *The Moonstone*', *Studies in Philology*, 26, 1939, pp. 651–63; and the first chapter (pp. 46–73) of Donald D. Stone, *The Romantic Impulse in Victorian Fiction* (Harvard University Press, 1980).

A CHRONOLOGY OF
ANTHONY TROLLOPE

Virtually all Trollope's fiction appeared first in serial form, with book production timed to coincide with the final instalment of the serial. In this chronology the titles are dated as on the title-page of the first book edition. On a very few occasions the book edition appeared in December of the year previous to that indicated on the title-page, so as to catch the Christmas sales.

1815   (24 Apr.) Born at 6 Keppel Street, Bloomsbury, the fourth son of Thomas and Frances Trollope.

1822   To Harrow as a day-boy.

1825   To a private school at Sunbury.

1827   To school at Winchester.

1830   Removed from Winchester and returned to Harrow.

1834   The family move to Bruges.
       (Autumn) He accepts a junior clerkship in the General Post Office.

1841   (Aug.) Deputy Postal Surveyor at Banagher, King's County, Ireland.

1843   (Autumn) Begins work on his first novel, *The Macdermots of Ballycloran*.

1844   (11 June) Marries Rose Heseltine.
       Transferred to Clonmel, County Tipperary.

1845   Promoted to the office of Surveyor, and transferred to Mallow, County Cork.

1845–7 Famine and epidemic throughout Ireland, especially the south and west with which Trollope was familiar.

1847   *The Macdermots of Ballycloran*, published in 3 vols. (Newby).

1848   Rebellion in Ireland, concentrated in Cork and Tipperary. *The Kellys and the O'Kellys; or Landlords and Tenants* 3 vols. (Colburn).

1850   Writes *The Noble Jilt* (published 1923).
       La Vendée; an Historical Romance 3 vols. (Colburn).

1851   Transferred to England.

1853   Returns to Ireland; completes *The Warden* (the first of the Barsetshire novels) in Belfast.

1854   (Autumn) Leaves Belfast and settles outside Dublin at Donnybrook.

1855   *The Warden* 1 vol. (Longman).

1857   *Barchester Towers* 3 vols. (Longman).
       (Sept.) Visits his mother in Florence.

1858   *Doctor Thorne* 3 vols. (Chapman & Hall).
       The Three Clerks 3 vols. (Bentley).
       (Feb.) Departs for Egypt on Post Office business.
       (Mar.) Removes from Egypt to Palestine.
       (Apr.–May) Returns via Malta, Gibraltar and Spain.
       (May–July) Visits Scotland and north of England on business.
       (Aug.–Oct.) At home in Ireland.
       (Nov.) On Post Office business in the West Indies.

1859   *The Bertrams* 3 vols. (Chapman & Hall).
       The West Indies and the Spanish Main 1 vol. (Chapman & Hall).
       (Sept.) Holiday in the Pyrenees.
       (Dec.) Leaves Ireland; settles at Waltham Cross.

1860   *Castle Richmond* 3 vols. (Chapman & Hall).
       (Oct.) With his wife he visits his mother and brother in Florence; makes the acquaintance of Kate Field, a beautiful twenty-year-old American with whom he falls in love.

1861   *Framley Parsonage* 3 vols. (Smith, Elder).
       Tales of All Countries—first series, 1 vol. (Chapman & Hall).
       (Spring) Elected a member of the Garrick Club; some two years later is elected to the committee to fill the vacancy caused by Thackeray's death.
       (Aug.) To America on official business.

1862   *Orley Farm* 2 vols. (Chapman & Hall).
       North America 2 vols. (Chapman & Hall).
       The Struggles of Brown, Jones and Robinson; by One of the Firm 1 vol. (New York, Harper—an American piracy).
       (Spring) Returns home from America.

1863   *Rachel Ray* 2 vols. (Chapman & Hall).
       Tales of All Countries—second series 1 vol. (Chapman & Hall).
       (6 Oct.) Death of his mother, Mrs. Frances Trollope.
       (Dec.) Death of W. M. Thackeray.

1864   *The Small House at Allington* 2 vols. (Smith, Elder).
       Can You Forgive Her? 2 vols. (Chapman & Hall).
       (Summer) Elected a member of the Athenaeum Club.

1865   *Miss Mackenzie* 1 vol. (Chapman & Hall).
       Hunting Sketches 1 vol. (Chapman & Hall).

1866   *The Belton Estate* 3 vols. (Chapman & Hall).

Travelling Sketches 1 vol. (Chapman & Hall).
Clergymen of the Church of England 1 vol. (Chapman & Hall).

1867   *Nina Balatka* 2 vols. (Blackwood).
The Last Chronicle of Barset 2 vols. (Smith, Elder).
The Claverings 2 vols. (Smith, Elder).
Lotta Schmidt and Other Stories 1 vol. (Strahan).
(1 Sept.) Resigns from the Civil Service.

1868   *Linda Tressel* 2 vols. (Blackwood).
(Mar.) Leaves London for the United States on business involving copyright, in touch again with Kate Field.
(July) Returns from America.
(Nov.) Stands unsuccessfully as Liberal candidate for Beverley, Yorkshire, losing £2,000 in the enterprise.

1869   *Phineas Finn; the Irish Member* 2 vols. (Virtue & Co.).
He Knew He was Right 2 vols. (Strahan).
Did He Steal It? A Comedy in Three Acts—a version of *The Last Chronicle of Barset* 1 vol. (printed by Virtue & Co.).

1870   *The Vicar of Bullhampton* 1 vol. (Bradbury, Evans).
An Editor's Tales 1 vol. (Strahan).
The Commentaries of Caesar 1 vol. (Blackwood).

1871   *Sir Harry Hotspur of Humblethwaite* 1 vol. (Hurst & Blackett).
Ralph the Heir 3 vols. (Hurst & Blackett).
(Apr.) Gives up house at Waltham Cross.
(May) Sails to Australia to visit his son.
(20 July) Arrives at Melbourne.

1872   *The Golden Lion of Granpere* 1 vol. (Tinsley).
(Jan.–Oct.) Travelling in Australia and New Zealand.
(Apr.) A dramatized (and pirated) version of *Ralph the Heir* produced by Charles Reade.
(Dec.) Returns via the United States, and settles in Montagu Square, London.

1873   *The Eustace Diamonds* 3 vols. (Chapman & Hall).
Australia and New Zealand 2 vols. (Chapman & Hall).
(Winter) Hunting actively.

1874   *Phineas Redux* 2 vols. (Chapman & Hall).
Lady Anna 2 vols. (Chapman & Hall).
Harry Heathcote of Gangoil; a Tale of Australian Bush Life 1 vol. (Sampson Low).

1875   *The Way We Live Now* 2 vols. (Chapman & Hall).
(Feb.) Travels to Ceylon via Brindisi and the Suez Canal, once again on the way to Australia.
(Mar.–Apr.) In Ceylon.

(June) Arrives in Australia.
(Aug.–Oct.) Sailing homewards.
(Oct.) Begins work on his *Autobiography*.

1876   *The Prime Minister* 4 vols. (Chapman & Hall).

1877   *The American Senator* 3 vols. (Chapman & Hall).
Christmas at Thompson Hall 1 vol. (New York, Harper).
(June) Leaves London for South Africa.
(Dec.) Sails for home.

1878   *Is He Popenjoy?* 3 vols. (Chapman & Hall).
South Africa 2 vols. (Chapman & Hall).
How the 'Mastiffs' Went to Iceland 1 vol. (Virtue & Co.).
(June–July) Travels to Iceland in the yacht 'Mastiff'.

1879   *An Eye for an Eye* 2 vols. (Chapman & Hall).
John Caldigate 3 vols. (Chapman & Hall).
Cousin Henry 2 vols. (Chapman & Hall).
Thackeray 1 vol. (Macmillan).

1880   *The Duke's Children* 3 vols. (Chapman & Hall).
(July) Settles at Harting Grange, near Petersfield.

1881   *Dr. Wortle's School* 2 vols. (Chapman & Hall).
Ayala's Angel 3 vols. (Chapman & Hall).

1882   *Why Frau Frohmann Raised Her Prices; and Other Stories* 1 vol. (Isbister).
Kept in the Dark 2 vols. (Chatto & Windus).
Marion Fay 3 vols. (Chapman & Hall).
The Fixed Period 2 vols. (Blackwood).
Palmerston 1 vol. (Isbister).
(May) Visits Ireland to collect material for a new Irish novel.
(Aug.) Returns to Ireland a second time.
(Sept.) Moves to London for the winter.
(6 Dec.) Dies in London.

1883   *Mr. Scarborough's Family* 3 vols. (Chatto & Windus).
The Landleaguers (unfinished) 3 vols. (Chatto & Windus).
An Autobiography 2 vols. (Blackwood).

1884   *An Old Man's Love* 2 vols. (Blackwood).

1923   *The Noble Jilt* (a play) 1 vol. (Constable).

1927   *London Tradesmen* 1 vol. (Elkin Mathews).

1972   *The New Zealander* 1 vol. (Oxford University Press.)

CONTENTS
Volume I

CONTENTS

CONTENTS

Volume II

CONTENTS

THE EUSTACE DIAMONDS

VOLUME I

CHAPTER I
Lizzie Greystock

IT was admitted by all her friends, and also by her enemies,
—who were in truth the more numerous and active body of
the two,—that Lizzie Greystock had done very well with herself. We will tell the story of Lizzie Greystock from the
beginning, but we will not dwell over it at great length, as
we might do if we loved her. She was the only child of old
Admiral Greystock, who in the latter years of his life was
much perplexed by the possession of a daughter. The admiral
was a man who liked whist, wine,—and wickedness in general
we may perhaps say, and whose ambition it was to live every
day of his life up to the end of it. People say that he succeeded,
and that the whist, wine, and wickedness were there, at the
side even of his dying bed. He had no particular fortune, and

1

yet his daughter, when she was little more than a child, went about everywhere with jewels on her fingers, and red gems hanging round her neck, and yellow gems pendent from her ears, and white gems shining in her black hair. She was hardly nineteen when her father died and she was taken home by that dreadful old termagant,* her aunt Lady Linlithgow. Lizzie would have sooner gone to any other friend or relative, had there been any other friend or relative to take her possessed of a house in town. Her uncle, Dean Greystock, of Bobsborough, would have had her, and a more good-natured old soul than the dean's wife did not exist,—and there were three pleasant, good-tempered girls in the deanery who had made various little efforts at friendship with their cousin Lizzie; but Lizzie had higher ideas for herself than life in the deanery at Bobsborough. She hated Lady Linlithgow. During her father's lifetime, when she hoped to be able to settle herself before his death, she was not in the habit of concealing her hatred for Lady Linlithgow. Lady Linlithgow was not indeed amiable or easily managed. But when the admiral died, Lizzie did not hesitate for a moment in going to the old 'vulturess,' as she was in the habit of calling the countess in her occasional correspondence with the girls at Bobsborough.

The admiral died greatly in debt;—so much so that it was a marvel how tradesmen had trusted him. There was literally nothing left for anybody,—and Messrs. Harter and Benjamin of Old Bond Street*condescended to call at Lady Linlithgow's house in Brook Street,* and to beg that the jewels supplied during the last twelve months might be returned. Lizzie protested that there were no jewels,—nothing to signify, nothing worth restoring. Lady Linlithgow had seen the diamonds, and demanded an explanation. They had been 'parted with,' by the admiral's orders,—so said Lizzie,—for the payment of other debts. Of this Lady Linlithgow did not believe a word, but she could not get at any exact truth. At that moment the jewels were in very truth pawned for money which had been necessary for Lizzie's needs. Certain things must be paid for, —one's own maid for instance; and one must have some money in one's pocket for railway-trains and little nicknacks which cannot be had on credit. Lizzie when she was nineteen knew how to do without money as well as most girls; but there were calls which she could not withstand, debts which even she must pay.

She did not, however, drop her acquaintance with Messrs. Harter and Benjamin. Before her father had been dead eight months, she was closeted with Mr. Benjamin, transacting a little business with him. She had come to him, she told him, the moment she was of age, and was willing to make herself responsible for the debt, signing any bill, note, or document which the firm might demand from her, to that effect. Of course she had nothing of her own, and never would have anything. That Mr. Benjamin knew. As for payment of the debt by Lady Linlithgow, who for a countess was as poor as Job, Mr. Benjamin, she was quite sure, did not expect anything of the kind. But—— Then Lizzie paused, and Mr. Benjamin, with the sweetest and wittiest of smiles, suggested that perhaps Miss Greystock was going to be married. Lizzie, with a pretty maiden blush, admitted that such a catastrophe was probable. She had been asked in marriage by Sir Florian Eustace. Now Mr. Benjamin knew, as all the world knew, that Sir Florian Eustace was a very rich man indeed; a man in no degree embarrassed, and who could pay any amount of jewellers' bills for which claim might be made upon him. Well; what did Miss Greystock want? Mr. Benjamin did not suppose that Miss Greystock was actuated simply by a desire to have her old bills paid by her future husband. Miss Greystock wanted a loan sufficient to take the jewels out of pawn. She would then make herself responsible for the full amount due. Mr. Benjamin said that he would make a few inquiries. 'But you won't betray me,' said Lizzie, 'for the match might be off.' Mr. Benjamin promised to be more than cautious.

There was not so much of falsehood as might have been expected in the statement which Lizzie Greystock made to the jeweller. It was not true that she was of age, and therefore no future husband would be legally liable for any debt

which she might then contract. And it was not true that Sir
Florian Eustace had asked her in marriage. Those two little
blemishes in her statement must be admitted. But it was
true that Sir Florian was at her feet; and that by a proper
use of her various charms,—the pawned jewels included,—
she might bring him to an offer. Mr. Benjamin made his
inquiries, and acceded to the proposal. He did not tell Miss
Greystock that she had lied to him in that matter of her age,
though he had discovered the lie. Sir Florian would no doubt
pay the bill for his wife without any arguments as to the
legality of the claim. From such information as Mr. Benjamin
could acquire he thought that there would be a marriage, and
that the speculation was on the whole in his favour. Lizzie
recovered her jewels and Mr. Benjamin was in possession of a
promissory note purporting to have been executed by a person
who was no longer a minor. The jeweller was ultimately
successful in his views,—and so was the lady.

Lady Linlithgow saw the jewels come back, one by one,
ring added to ring on the little taper fingers, the rubies for the
neck, and the pendent yellow earrings. Though Lizzie was
in mourning for her father, still these things were allowed to
be visible. The countess was not the woman to see them
without inquiry, and she inquired vigorously. She threatened,
stormed, and protested. She attempted even a raid upon the
young lady's jewel-box. But she was not successful. Lizzie
snapped and snarled and held her own,—for at that time the
match with Sir Florian was near its accomplishment, and the
countess understood too well the value of such a disposition
of her niece to risk it at the moment by any open rupture.
The little house in Brook Street,—for the house was very
small and very comfortless,—a house that had been squeezed
in, as it were, between two others without any fitting space
for it,—did not contain a happy family. One bedroom, and
that the biggest, was appropriated to the Earl of Linlithgow,
the son of the countess, a young man who passed perhaps five
nights in town during the year. Other inmate there was none
besides the aunt and the niece and the four servants,—of

whom one was Lizzie's own maid. Why should such a countess have troubled herself with the custody of such a niece? Simply because the countess regarded it as a duty. Lady Linlithgow was worldly, stingy, ill-tempered, selfish, and mean. Lady Linlithgow would cheat a butcher out of a mutton-chop, or a cook out of a month's wages, if she could do so with some slant of legal wind in her favour. She would tell any number of lies to carry a point in what she believed to be social success. It was said of her that she cheated at cards. In backbiting no venomous old woman between Bond Street and Park Lane could beat her,—or, more wonderful still, no venomous old man at the clubs. But nevertheless she recognised certain duties,—and performed them, though she hated them. She went to church, not merely that people might see her there,—as to which in truth she cared nothing,—but because she thought it was right. And she took in Lizzie Greystock, whom she hated almost as much as she did sermons, because the admiral's wife had been her sister, and she recognised a duty. But, having thus bound herself to Lizzie,—who was a beauty,—of course it became the first object of her life to get rid of Lizzie by a marriage. And, though she would have liked to think that Lizzie would be tormented all her days, though she thoroughly believed that Lizzie deserved to be tormented, she set her heart upon a splendid match. She would at any rate be able to throw it daily in her niece's teeth that the splendour was of her doing. Now a marriage with Sir Florian Eustace would be very splendid, and therefore she was unable to go into the matter of the jewels with that rigour which in other circumstances she would certainly have displayed.

The match with Sir Florian Eustace,—for a match it came to be,—was certainly very splendid. Sir Florian was a young man about eight-and-twenty, very handsome, of immense wealth, quite unencumbered, moving in the best circles, popular, so far prudent that he never risked his fortune on the turf or in gambling-houses, with the reputation of a gallant soldier, and a most devoted lover. There were two facts concerning him which might, or might not, be taken as objections. He was vicious, and—he was dying. When a friend, intending to be kind, hinted the latter circumstance to Lady Linlithgow, the countess blinked and winked and nodded, and then swore that she had procured medical advice on the subject. Medical advice declared that Sir Florian was not more likely to die than another man,—if only he would get married; all of which statement on her ladyship's part was a lie. When the same friend hinted the same thing to Lizzie herself, Lizzie resolved that she would have her revenge upon that friend. At any rate the courtship went on.

We have said that Sir Florian was vicious;—but he was not altogether a bad man, nor was he vicious in the common sense of the word. He was one who denied himself no pleasure, let the cost be what it might in health, pocket, or morals. Of sin or wickedness he had probably no distinct idea. In virtue, as an attribute of the world around him, he had no belief. Of honour he thought very much, and had conceived a somewhat noble idea that because much had been given to him much was demanded of him. He was haughty, polite,—and very generous. There was almost a nobility even about his vices. And he had a special gallantry of which it is hard to say whether it is or is not to be admired. They told him that he was like to die,—very like to die, if he did not change his manner of living. Would he go to Algiers*for a period? Certainly not. He would do no such thing. If he died, there was his brother John left to succeed him. And the fear of death never cast a cloud over that grandly beautiful brow. They had all been short-lived,—the Eustaces. Consumption had swept a hecatomb*of victims from the family. But still they were grand people, and never were afraid of death.

And then Sir Florian fell in love. Discussing this matter with his brother, who was perhaps his only intimate friend, he declared that if the girl he loved would give herself to him, he would make what atonement he could to her for his own early death by a princely settlement. John Eustace, who was somewhat nearly concerned in the matter, raised no objection to this proposal. There was ever something grand about these

Eustaces. Sir Florian was a grand gentleman; but surely he must have been dull of intellect, slow of discernment, bleareyed in his ways about the town, when he took Lizzie Greystock,—of all the women whom he could find in the world,—to be the purest, the truest, and the noblest. It has been said of Sir Florian that he did not believe in virtue. He freely expressed disbelief in the virtue of women around him,—in the virtue of women of all ranks. But he believed in his mother and sisters as though they were heaven-born; and he was one who could believe in his wife as though she were the queen of heaven. He did believe in Lizzie Greystock, thinking that intellect, purity, truth, and beauty, each perfect in its degree, were combined in her. The intellect and beauty were there;—but, for the purity and truth——; how could it have been that such a one as Sir Florian Eustace should have been so blind!

Sir Florian was not, indeed, a clever man; but he believed himself to be a fool. And believing himself to be a fool, he desired, nay painfully longed, for some of those results of cleverness which might, he thought, come to him, from contact with a clever woman. Lizzie read poetry well, and she read verses to him,—sitting very near to him, almost in the dark, with a shaded lamp throwing its light on her book. He was astonished to find how sweet a thing was poetry. By himself he could never read a line, but as it came from her lips it seemed to charm him. It was a new pleasure, and one which, though he had ridiculed it, he had so often coveted! And then she told him of such wondrous thoughts,—such wondrous joys in the world which would come from thinking! He was proud, I have said, and haughty; but he was essentially modest and humble in his self-estimation. How divine was this creature, whose voice to him was as that of a goddess!

Then he spoke out to her, with his face a little turned from her. Would she be his wife? But, before she answered him, let her listen to him. They had told him that an early death must probably be his fate. He did not himself feel that it

7

must be so. Sometimes he was ill,—very ill; but often he was well. If she would run the risk with him he would endeavour to make her such recompense as might come from his wealth. The speech he made was somewhat long, and as he made it he hardly looked into her face.

But it was necessary to him that he should be made to know by some signal from her how it was going with her feelings. As he spoke of his danger, there came a gurgling little trill of wailing from her throat, a soft, almost musical sound of woe, which seemed to add an unaccustomed eloquence to his words. When he spoke of his own hope the sound was somewhat changed, but it was still continued. When he alluded to the disposition of his fortune, she was at his feet. 'Not that,' she said; 'not that!' He lifted her, and with his arm round her waist he tried to tell her what it would be his duty to do for her. She escaped from his arm and would not listen to him. But,—but—! When he began to talk of love again, she stood with her forehead bowed against his bosom. Of course the engagement was then a thing accomplished.

But still the cup might slip from her lips. Her father was now dead but ten months, and what answer could she make, when the common pressing petition for an early marriage was poured into her ear? This was in July, and it would never do that he should be left, unmarried, to the rigour of another winter. She looked into his face and knew that she had cause for fear. Oh, heavens! if all these golden hopes should fall to the ground, and she should come to be known only as the girl who had been engaged to the late Sir Florian! But he himself pressed the marriage on the same ground. 'They tell me,' he said, 'that I had better get a little south by the beginning of October. I won't go alone. You know what I mean;—eh, Lizzie?' Of course she married him in September.

They spent a honeymoon of six weeks at a place he had in Scotland, and the first blow came upon him as they passed through London, back from Scotland, on their way to Italy. Messrs. Harter and Benjamin sent in their little bill, which amounted to something over £400, and other little bills were sent in. Sir Florian was a man by whom such bills would certainly be paid, but by whom they would not be paid without his understanding much and conceiving more as to their cause and nature. How much he really did understand she was never quite aware;—but she did know that he detected her in a positive falsehood. She might certainly have managed the matter better than she did; and had she admitted everything there might probably have been but few words about it. She did not, however, understand the nature of the note she had signed, and thought that simply new bills would be presented by the jewellers to her husband. She gave a false account of the transaction, and the lie was detected. I do not know that she cared very much. As she was utterly devoid of true tenderness, so also was she devoid of conscience. They went abroad, however; and by the time the winter was half over in Naples, he knew what his wife was;—and before the end of the spring he was dead.

She had so far played her game well, and had won her stakes. What regrets, what remorse she suffered when she knew that he was going from her,—and then knew that he was gone, who can say? As man is never strong enough to take unmixed delight in good, so may we presume also that he cannot be quite so weak as to find perfect satisfaction in evil. There must have been qualms as she looked at his dying face, soured with the disappointment she had brought upon him, and listened to the harsh querulous voice that was no longer eager in the expressions of love. There must have been some pang when she reflected that the cruel wrong which she had inflicted on him had probably hurried him to his grave. As a widow, in the first solemnity of her widowhood, she was wretched and would see no one. Then she returned to England and shut herself up in a small house at Brighton. Lady Linlithgow offered to go to her, but she begged that she might be left to herself. For a few short months the awe arising from the rapidity with which it had all occurred did afflict her. Twelve months since she had hardly known the man who was to be her husband. Now she was a widow,—a widow very richly endowed,—and she bore beneath her bosom the fruit of her husband's love.

But, even in these early days, friends and enemies did not hesitate to say that Lizzie Greystock had done very well with herself; for it was known by all concerned that in the settlements made she had been treated with unwonted generosity.

CHAPTER II
Lady Eustace

THERE were circumstances in her position which made it impossible that Lizzie Greystock,—or Lady Eustace, as we must now call her,—should be left altogether to herself in the modest widow's retreat which she had found at Brighton. It was then April, and it was known that if all things went well with her, she would be a mother before the summer was over. On what the Fates might ordain in this matter immense interests were dependent. If a son should be born he would inherit everything, subject, of course, to his mother's settlement. If a daughter, to her would belong the great personal wealth which Sir Florian had owned at the time of his death. Should there be no son, John Eustace, the brother, would inherit the estates in Yorkshire which had been the backbone of the Eustace wealth. Should no child be born, John Eustace would inherit everything that had not been settled upon or left to the widow. Sir Florian had made a settlement immediately before his marriage, and a will immediately afterwards. Of what he had done then, nothing had been altered in those sad Italian days. The settlement had been very generous. The whole property in Scotland was to belong to Lizzie for her life,—and after her death was to go to a second son, if such second son there should be. By the will money was left to her, more than would be needed for any possible temporary emergency. When she knew how it was all arranged,—as far as she did know it,—she was aware that she was a rich woman.

10

For so clever a woman she was infinitely ignorant as to the possession and value of money and land and income,—though, perhaps, not more ignorant than are most young girls under twenty-one. As for the Scotch property,—she thought that it was her own, for ever, because there could not now be a second son,—and yet was not quite sure whether it would be her own at all if she had no son. Concerning that sum of money left to her, she did not know whether it was to come out of the Scotch property or be given to her separately,—and whether it was to come annually or to come only once. She had received, while still in Naples, a letter from the family lawyer, giving her such details of the will as it was necessary that she should know, and now she longed to ask questions, to have her belongings made plain to her, and to realise her wealth. She had brilliant prospects; and yet, through it all, there was a sense of loneliness that nearly killed her. Would it not have been much better if her husband had lived, and still worshipped her, and still allowed her to read poetry to him? But she had read no poetry to him after that affair of Messrs. Harter and Benjamin.

The reader has, or will have, but little to do with these days, and may be hurried on through the twelve, or even twenty-four months which followed the death of poor Sir Florian. The question of the heirship, however, was very grave, and early in the month of May Lady Eustace was visited by her husband's uncle, Bishop Eustace, of Bobsborough. The bishop had been the younger brother of Sir Florian's father,—was at this time a man about fifty, very active and very popular,—and was one who stood high in the world, even among bishops. He suggested to his niece-in-law that it was very expedient that, during her coming hour of trial, she should not absent herself from her husband's family, and at last persuaded her to take up her residence at the palace at Bobsborough till such time as the event should be over. Lady Eustace was taken to the palace, and in due time a son was born. John, who was now the uncle of the heir, came down, and, with the frankest good-humour, declared that he would devote himself to the little head of the family. He had been left as guardian, and the management of the great family estates was to be in his hands. Lizzie had read no poetry to him, and he had never liked her, and the bishop did not like her, and the ladies of the bishop's family disliked her very much, and it was thought by them that the dean's people,—the Dean of Bobsborough was Lizzie's uncle,—were not very fond of Lizzie since Lizzie had so raised herself in the world as to want no assistance from them. But still they were bound to do their duty by her as the widow of the late and the mother of the present baronet. And they did not find much cause of complaining as to Lizzie's conduct in these days. In that matter of the great family diamond necklace,—which certainly should not have been taken to Naples at all, and as to which the jeweller had told the lawyer and the lawyer had told John Eustace that it certainly should not now be detained among the widow's own private property,—the bishop strongly recommended that nothing should be said at present. The mistake, if there was a mistake, could be remedied at any time. And nothing in those very early days was said about the great Eustace necklace, which afterwards became so famous.

Why Lizzie should have been so generally disliked by the Eustaces, it might be hard to explain. While she remained at the palace she was very discreet,—and perhaps demure. It may be said they disliked her expressed determination to cut her aunt, Lady Linlithgow;—for they knew that Lady Linlithgow had been, at any rate, a friend to Lizzie Greystock. There are people who can be wise within a certain margin, but beyond that commit great imprudences. Lady Eustace submitted herself to the palace people for that period of her prostration, but she could not hold her tongue as to her future intentions. She would, too, now and then ask of Mrs. Eustace, and even of her daughter, an eager, anxious question about her own property. 'She is dying to handle her money,' said Mrs. Eustace to the bishop. 'She is only like the rest of the world in that,' said the bishop. 'If she would be really open,

I wouldn't mind it,' said Mrs. Eustace. None of them liked her,—and she did not like them.

She remained at the palace for six months, and at the end of that time she went to her own place in Scotland. Mrs. Eustace had strongly advised her to ask her aunt, Lady Linlithgow, to accompany her, but in refusing to do this, Lizzie was quite firm. She had endured Lady Linlithgow for that year between her father's death and her marriage; she was now beginning to dare to hope for the enjoyment of the good things which she had won, and the presence of the dowager-countess,—'the vulturess,'—was certainly not one of these good things. In what her enjoyment was to consist, she had not as yet quite formed a definite conclusion. She liked jewels. She liked admiration. She liked the power of being arrogant to those around her. And she liked good things to eat. But there were other matters that were also dear to her. She did like music,—though it may be doubted whether she would ever play it or even listen to it alone. She did like reading, and especially the reading of poetry,—though even in this she was false and pretentious, skipping, pretending to have read, lying about books, and making up her market of literature for outside admiration at the easiest possible cost of trouble. And she had some dream of being in love, and would take delight even in building castles in the air, which she would people with friends and lovers whom she would make happy with the most open-hearted benevolence. She had theoretical ideas of life which were not bad,—but in practice, she had gained her objects, and she was in a hurry to have liberty to enjoy them.

There was considerable anxiety in the palace in reference to the future mode of life of Lady Eustace. Had it not been for that baby-heir, of course there would have been no cause for interference; but the rights of that baby were so serious and important that it was almost impossible not to interfere. The mother, however, gave some little signs that she did not intend to submit to much interference, and there was no real reason why she should not be as free as air. But did she really intend to go down to Portray Castle*all alone;—that is, with her baby and nurses? This was ended by an arrangement, in accordance with which she was accompanied by her eldest cousin, Ellinor Greystock, a lady who was just ten years her senior. There could hardly be a better woman than Ellinor Greystock,—or a more good-humoured, kindly being. After many debates in the deanery and in the palace,—for there was much friendship between the two ecclesiastical establishments—the offer was made and the advice given. Ellinor had accepted the martyrdom on the understanding that if the advice were accepted she was to remain at Portray Castle for three months. After a long discussion between Lady Eustace and the bishop's wife the offer was accepted, and the two ladies went to Scotland together.

During those three months the widow still bided her time. Of her future ideas of life she said not a word to her companion. Of her infant she said very little. She would talk of books,—choosing such books as her cousin did not read; and she would interlard her conversation with much Italian, because her cousin did not know the language. There was a carriage kept by the widow, and they had themselves driven out together. Of real companionship there was none. Lizzie was biding her time, and at the end of the three months Miss Greystock thankfully, and, indeed, of necessity, returned to Bobsborough. 'I've done no good,' she said to her mother, 'and have been very uncomfortable.' 'My dear,' said her mother, 'we have disposed of three months out of a two years' period of danger. In two years from Sir Florian's death she will be married again.'

When this was said Lizzie had been a widow nearly a year, and had bided her time upon the whole discreetly. Some foolish letters she had written,—chiefly to the lawyer about her money and property; and some foolish things she had said,—as when she told Ellinor Greystock that the Portray property was her own for ever, to do what she liked with it. The sum of money left to her by her husband had by that time been paid into her own hands, and she had opened a banker's account. The revenues from the Scotch estate,—some £4,000 a year—were clearly her own for life. The family diamond-necklace was still in her possession, and no answer had been given by her to a postscript to a lawyer's letter in which a little advice had been given respecting it. At the end of another year, when she had just reached the age of twenty-two, and had completed her second year of widowhood, she was still Lady Eustace, thus contradicting the prophecy made by the dean's wife. It was then spring, and she had a house of her own in London. She had broken openly with Lady Linlithgow. She had opposed, though not absolutely refused, all overtures of brotherly care from John Eustace. She had declined a further invitation, both for herself and for her child, to the palace. And she had positively asserted her intention of keeping the diamonds. Her late husband, she said, had given the diamonds to her. As they were supposed to be worth £10,000, and were really family diamonds, the matter was felt by all concerned to be one of much importance. And she was oppressed by a heavy load of ignorance, which became serious from the isolation of her position. She had learned to draw cheques, but she had no other correct notion as to business. She knew nothing as to spending money, saving it, or invest-ing it. Though she was clever, sharp, and greedy, she had no idea what her money would do, and what it would not; and there was no one whom she would trust to tell her. She had a young cousin a barrister,—a son of the dean's, whom she perhaps liked better than any other of her relations,—but she declined advice even from her friend the barrister. She would have no dealings on her own behalf with the old family solici-tor of the Eustaces,—the gentleman who had now applied very formally for the restitution of the diamonds; but had appointed other solicitors to act for her. Messrs. Mowbray and Mopus were of opinion that as the diamonds had been given into her hands by her husband without any terms as to their surrender, no one could claim them. Of the manner in which the diamonds had been placed in her hands, no one knew more than she chose to tell.

But when she started with her house in town,—a modest

little house in Mount Street, near the park,*—just two years after her husband's death, she had a large circle of acquaintances. The Eustace people, and the Greystock people, and even the Linlithgow people, did not entirely turn their backs on her. The countess, indeed, was very venomous, as she well might be; but then the countess was known for her venom. The dean and his family were still anxious that she should be encouraged to discreet living, and, though they feared many things, thought that they had no ground for open complaint. The Eustace people were forbearing, and hoped the best. 'D—— the necklace!' John Eustace had said, and the bishop unfortunately had heard him say it! 'John,' said the prelate, 'whatever is to become of the bauble, you might express your opinion in more sensible language.' 'I beg your lordship's pardon,' said John, 'I only mean to say that I think we shouldn't trouble ourselves about a few stones.' But the family lawyer, Mr. Camperdown, would by no means take this view of the matter. It was, however, generally thought that the young widow opened her campaign more prudently than had been expected.

And now as so much has been said of the character and fortune and special circumstances of Lizzie Greystock, who became Lady Eustace as a bride, and Lady Eustace as a widow and a mother, all within the space of twelve months, it may be as well to give some description of her person and habits, such as they were at the period in which our story is supposed to have its commencement. It must be understood in the first place that she was very lovely;—much more so, indeed, now than when she had fascinated Sir Florian. She was small, but taller than she looked to be,—for her form was perfectly symmetrical. Her feet and hands might have been taken as models by a sculptor. Her figure was lithe, and soft, and slim, and slender. If it had a fault it was this,—that it had in it too much of movement. There were some who said that she was almost snake-like in her rapid bendings and the almost too easy gestures of her body; for she was much given to action, and to the expression of her thought by the motion of her limbs. She might certainly have made her way as an actress, had fortune called upon her to earn her bread in that fashion. And her voice would have suited the stage. It was powerful when she called upon it for power; but, at the same time, flexible and capable of much pretence at feeling. She could bring it to a whisper that would almost melt your heart with tenderness,—as she had melted Sir Florian's, when she sat near to him reading poetry; and then she could raise it to a pitch of indignant wrath befitting a Lady Macbeth when her husband ventured to rebuke her. And her ear was quite correct in modulating these tones. She knew,—and it must have been by instinct, for her culture in such matters was small,—how to use her voice so that neither its tenderness nor its wrath should be misapplied. There were pieces in verse that she could read,—things not wondrously good in themselves,—so that she would ravish you; and she would so look at you as she did it that you would hardly dare either to avert your eyes or to return her gaze. Sir Florian had not known whether to do the one thing or the other, and had therefore seized her in his arms. Her face was oval,—some-what longer than an oval,—with little in it, perhaps nothing in it, of that brilliancy of colour which we call complexion. And yet the shades of her countenance were ever changing between the softest and most transparent white, and the richest, mellowest shades of brown. It was only when she simulated anger,—she was almost incapable of real anger,—that she would succeed in calling the thinnest streak of pink from her heart, to show that there was blood running in her veins. Her hair, which was nearly black,—but in truth with more of softness and of lustre than ever belong to hair that is really black,—she wore bound tight round her perfect fore-head, with one long love-lock hanging over her shoulder. The form of her head was so good that she could dare to carry it without a chignon,* or any adventitious adjuncts from an artiste's shop. Very bitter was she in consequence when speaking of the head-gear of other women. Her chin was per-fect in its round, not over long,—as is the case with so many

17

such faces, utterly spoiling the symmetry of the countenance. But it lacked a dimple, and therefore lacked feminine tenderness. Her mouth was perhaps faulty in being too small, or, at least, her lips were too thin. There was wanting from the mouth that expression of eager-speaking truthfulness which full lips will often convey. Her teeth were without flaw or blemish, even, small, white, and delicate; but perhaps they were shown too often. Her nose was small, but struck many as the prettiest feature of her face, so exquisite was the moulding of it, and so eloquent and so graceful the slight inflations of the transparent nostrils. Her eyes, in which she herself thought that the lustre of her beauty lay, were blue and clear, bright as cerulean*waters. They were long large eyes,—but very dangerous. To those who knew how to read a face, there was danger plainly written in them. Poor Sir Florian had not known. But, in truth, the charm of her face did not lie in her eyes. This was felt by many even who could not read the book fluently. They were too expressive, too loud in their demands for attention, and they lacked tenderness. How few there are among women, few perhaps also among men, who know that the sweetest, softest, tenderest, truest eyes which a woman can carry in her head are green in colour! Lizzie's eyes were not tender,—neither were they true. But they were surmounted by the most wonderfully pencilled eyebrows that ever nature unassisted planted on a woman's face.

We have said that she was clever. We must add that she had in truth studied much. She spoke French, understood Italian, and read German. She played well on the harp, and moderately well on the piano. She sang, at least in good taste and in tune. Of things to be learned by reading she knew much, having really taken diligent trouble with herself. She had learned much poetry by heart, and could apply it. She forgot nothing, listened to everything, understood quickly, and was desirous to show not only as a beauty but as a wit. There were men at this time who declared that she was simply the cleverest and the handsomest woman in England. As an independent young woman she was perhaps one of the richest.

CHAPTER III
Lucy Morris

Although the first two chapters of this new history have been devoted to the fortunes and personal attributes of Lady Eustace, the historian begs his readers not to believe that that opulent and aristocratic Becky Sharp* is to assume the dignity of heroine in the forthcoming pages. That there shall be any heroine the historian will not take upon himself to assert; but if there be a heroine, that heroine shall not be Lady Eustace. Poor Lizzie Greystock!—as men double her own age, and who had known her as a forward, capricious, spoilt child in her father's lifetime, would still call her. She did so many things, made so many efforts, caused so much suffering to others, and suffered so much herself throughout the scenes with which we are about to deal, that the story can hardly be told without giving her that prominence of place which has been assigned to her in the last two chapters.

Nor does the chronicler dare to put forward Lucy Morris as a heroine. The real heroine, if it be found possible to arrange her drapery for her becomingly, and to put that part which she enacted into properly heroic words, shall stalk in among us at some considerably later period of the narrative, when the writer shall have accustomed himself to the flow of words, and have worked himself up to a state of mind fit for the reception of noble acting and noble speaking. In the meantime, let it be understood that poor little Lucy Morris was a governess in the house of old Lady Fawn, when our beautiful young widow established herself in Mount Street.

Lady Eustace and Lucy Morris had known each other for many years,—had indeed been children together,—there having been some old family friendship between the Greystocks and the Morrises. When the admiral's wife was living, Lucy had, as a little girl of eight or nine, been her guest. She had often been a guest at the deanery. When Lady Eustace had gone down to the bishop's palace at Bobsborough, in order that an heir to the Eustaces might be born under an auspicious roof, Lucy Morris was with the Greystocks. Lucy, who was a year younger than Lizzie, had at that time been an orphan for the last four years. She too had been left penniless, but no such brilliant future awaited her as that which Lizzie had earned for herself. There was no countess-aunt to take her into her London house. The dean and the dean's wife and the dean's daughter had been her best friends, but they were not friends on whom she could be dependent. They were in no way connected with her by blood. Therefore, at the age of eighteen, she had gone out to be a child's governess. Then old Lady Fawn had heard of her virtues,—Lady Fawn, who had seven unmarried daughters running down from seven-and-twenty to thirteen, and Lucy Morris had been hired to teach English, French, German, and something of music to the two youngest Miss Fawns.

During that visit at the deanery, when the heir of the Eustaces was being born, Lucy was undergoing a sort of probation for the Fawn establishment. The proposed engagement with Lady Fawn was thought to be a great thing for her. Lady Fawn was known as a miracle of Virtue, Benevolence, and Persistency. Every good quality that she possessed was so marked as to be worthy of being expressed with a capital. But her virtues were of that extraordinarily high character that there was no weakness in them,—no getting over them, no perverting them with follies or even exaggerations. When she heard of the excellencies of Miss Morris from the dean's wife. and then, after minutest investigation, learned the exact qualities of the young lady, she expressed herself willing to take Lucy into her house on special conditions. She must be able to teach music up to a certain point. 'Then it's all over,' said Lucy to the dean with her pretty smile,—that smile which caused all the old and middle-aged men to fall in love with her. 'It's not over at all,' said the dean. 'You've got four months. Our organist is about as good a teacher as there is in England. You are clever and quick, and he shall teach you.' So Lucy went to Bobsborough, and was afterwards accepted by Lady Fawn.

While she was at the deanery there sprung up a renewed friendship between her and Lizzie. It was, indeed, chiefly a one-sided friendship; for Lucy, who was quick and unconsciously capable of reading that book to which we alluded in a previous chapter, was somewhat afraid of the rich widow. And when Lizzie talked to her of their old childish days, and quoted poetry, and spoke of things romantic,—as she was much given to do,—Lucy felt that the metal did not ring true. And then Lizzie had an ugly habit of abusing all her other friends behind their backs. Now Lucy did not like to hear the Greystocks abused, and would say so. 'That's all very well, you little minx,' Lizzie would say playfully, 'but you know that they are all asses!' Lucy by no means thought that the Greystocks were asses, and was very strongly of opinion that one of them was as far removed from being an ass as any human being she had ever known. This one was Frank Greystock, the barrister. Of Frank Greystock some special but, let it be hoped, very short description must be given by-and-by. For the present it will be sufficient to declare that, during that short Easter holiday which he spent at his father's house in Bobsborough, he found Lucy Morris to be a most agreeable companion.

'Remember her position,' said Mrs. Dean to her son.

'Her position! Well;—and what is her position mother?'

'You know what I mean, Frank. She is as sweet a girl as ever lived, and a perfect lady. But with a governess, unless you mean to marry her, you should be more careful than with another girl, because you may do her such a world of mischief.'

'I don't see that at all.'

'If Lady Fawn knew that she had an admirer, Lady Fawn would not let her come into her house.'

'Then Lady Fawn is an idiot. If a girl be admirable, of course she will be admired. Who can hinder it?'

'You know what I mean, Frank.'

'Yes—I do; well. I don't suppose I can afford to marry

Lucy Morris. At any rate, mother, I will never say a word to raise a hope in her,—if it would be a hope——'

'Of course it would be a hope.'

'I don't know that at all. But I will never say any such word to her,—unless I make up my mind that I can afford to marry her.'

'Oh, Frank, it would be impossible!' said Mrs. Dean.

Mrs. Dean was a very good woman, but she had aspirations in the direction of filthy lucre*on behalf of her children, or at least on behalf of this special child, and she did think it would be very nice if Frank would marry an heiress. This, however, was a long time ago, nearly two years ago; and many grave things had got themselves transacted since Lucy's visit to the deanery. She had become quite an old and an accustomed member of Lady Fawn's family. The youngest Fawn girl was not yet fifteen, and it was understood that Lucy was to remain with the Fawns for some quite indefinite time to come. Lady Fawn's eldest daughter, Mrs. Hittaway, had a family of her own, having been married ten or twelve years, and it was quite probable that Lucy might be transferred. Lady Fawn fully appreciated her treasure, and was, and ever had been, conscientiously anxious to make Lucy's life happy. But she thought that a governess should not be desirous of marrying, at any rate till a somewhat advanced period of life. A governess, if she were given to falling in love, could hardly perform her duties in life. No doubt, not to be a governess, but a young lady free from the embarrassing necessity of earning bread, free to have a lover and a husband, would be upon the whole nicer. So it is nicer to be born to £10,000 a year*than to have to wish for £500. Lady Fawn could talk excellent sense on this subject by the hour, and always admitted that much was due to a governess who knew her place and did her duty. She was very fond of Lucy Morris, and treated her dependant with affectionate consideration;—but she did not approve of visits from Mr. Frank Greystock. Lucy, blushing up to the eyes, had once declared that she desired to have no personal visitors at Lady Fawn's house; but that, as regarded her own friendships, the matter was one for her own bosom. 'Dear Miss Morris,' Lady Fawn had said, 'we understand each other so perfectly, and you are so good, that I am quite sure everything will be as it ought to be.' Lady Fawn lived down at Richmond, all the year through, in a large old-fashioned house with a large old-fashioned garden, called Fawn Court. After that speech of hers to Lucy, Frank Greystock did not call again at Fawn Court for many months, and it is possible that her ladyship had said a word also to him. But Lady Eustace, with her pretty little pair of grey ponies, would sometimes drive down to Richmond to see her 'dear little old friend' Lucy, and her visits were allowed. Lady Fawn had expressed an opinion among her daughters that she did not see any harm in Lady Eustace. She thought that she rather liked Lady Eustace. But then Lady Fawn hated Lady Linlithgow as only two old women can hate each other;—and she had not heard the story of the diamond necklace.

Lucy Morris certainly was a treasure,—a treasure though no heroine. She was a sweetly social, genial little human being whose presence in the house was ever felt to be like sunshine. She was never forward, but never bashful. She was always open to familiar intercourse without ever putting herself forward. There was no man or woman with whom she would not so talk as to make the man or woman feel that the conversation was remarkably pleasant,—and she could do the same with any child. She was an active, mindful, bright, energetic little thing to whom no work ever came amiss. She had catalogued the library,—which had been collected by the late Lord Fawn with peculiar reference to the Christian theology of the third and fourth centuries. She had planned the new flower-garden,—though Lady Fawn thought that she had done that herself. She had been invaluable during Clara Fawn's long illness. She knew every rule at croquet, and could play piquet.* When the girls got up charades they had to acknowledge that everything depended on Miss Morris. They were good-natured, plain, unattractive girls, who spoke of her to her face as one who could easily do anything to which she might put her hand. Lady Fawn did really love her. Lord Fawn, the eldest son, a young man of about thirty-five, a Peer of Parliament and an Under-Secretary of State,*— very prudent and very diligent,—of whom his mother and sisters stood in great awe, consulted her frequently and made no secret of his friendship. The mother knew her awful son well, and was afraid of nothing wrong in that direction. Lord Fawn had suffered a disappointment in love, but he had consoled himself with blue-books,* and mastered his passion by incessant attendance at the India Board.* The lady he had loved had been rich, and Lord Fawn was poor; but nevertheless he had mastered his passion. There was no fear that his feelings towards the governess would become too warm;—nor was it likely that Miss Morris should encounter danger in regard to him. It was quite an understood thing in the family that Lord Fawn must marry money.

Lucy Morris was indeed a treasure. No brighter face ever looked into another to seek sympathy there, either in mirth or woe. There was a gleam in her eyes that was almost magnetic, so sure was she to obtain by it that community of interest which she desired,—though it were but for a moment. Lord Fawn was pompous, slow, dull, and careful; but even he had given way to it at once. Lady Fawn too was very careful, but she had owned to herself long since that she could not bear to look forward to any permanent severance. Of course Lucy would be made over to the Hittaways, whose mother lived in Warwick Square, and whose father was Chairman of the Board of Civil Appeals.* The Hittaways were the only grandchildren with whom Lady Fawn had as yet been blessed, and of course Lucy must go to the Hittaways.

She was but a little thing;—and it cannot be said of her, as of Lady Eustace, that she was a beauty. The charm of her face consisted in the peculiar, watery brightness of her eyes, —in the corners of which it would always seem that a diamond of a tear was lurking whenever any matter of excitement was afoot. Her light-brown hair was soft and smooth and pretty. As hair it was very well, but it had no speciality. Her mouth was somewhat large, but full of ever-varying expression. Her forehead was low and broad, with prominent temples, on which it was her habit to clasp tightly her little outstretched fingers as she sat listening to you. Of listeners she was the very best, for she would always be saying a word or two, just to help you,—the best word that could be spoken, and then again she would be hanging on your lips. There are listeners who show by their mode of listening that they listen as a duty, —not because they are interested. Lucy Morris was not such a one. She would take up your subject, whatever it was, and make it her own. There was forward just then a question as to whether the Sawab of Mygawb* should have twenty millions of rupees paid to him and placed upon a throne, or whether he should be kept in prison all his life. The British world generally could not be made to interest itself about the Sawab, but Lucy positively mastered the subject, and almost got Lord Fawn into a difficulty by persuading him to stand up against his chief on behalf of the injured prince.

What else can be said of her face or personal appearance that will interest a reader? When she smiled, there was the daintiest little dimple on her cheek. And when she laughed, that little nose, which was not as well-shaped a nose as it might have been, would almost change its shape and cock itself up in its mirth. Her hands were very thin and long, and so were her feet,—by no means models as were those of her friend Lady Eustace. She was a little, thin, quick, graceful creature, whom it was impossible that you should see without wishing to have near you. A most unselfish little creature she was, but one who had a well-formed idea of her own identity. She was quite resolved to be somebody among her fellow-creatures,—not somebody in the way of marrying a lord or a rich man, or somebody in the way of being a beauty, or some-body as a wit; but somebody as having a purpose and a use in life. She was the humblest little thing in the world in regard to any possible putting of herself forward or needful putting of herself back; and yet, to herself, nobody was her superior. What she had was her own, whether it was the old grey silk dress which she had bought with the money she had earned, or the wit which nature had given her. And Lord Fawn's title was his own, and Lady Fawn's rank her own. She coveted no man's possessions,—and no woman's; but she was minded to hold by her own. Of present advantages or disadvantages,— whether she had the one or suffered from the other,—she thought not at all. It was her fault that she had nothing of feminine vanity. But no man or woman was ever more anxious to be effective, to persuade, to obtain belief, sympathy, and co-operation;—not for any result personal to herself, but because, by obtaining these things, she could be effective in the object then before her, be it what it might.

One other thing may be told of her. She had given her heart,—for good and all, as she owned to herself,—to Frank Greystock. She had owned to herself that it was so, and had owned to herself that nothing could come of it. Frank was becoming a man of mark,—but was becoming a man of mark without much money. Of all men he was the last who could afford to marry a governess. And then, moreover, he had never said a word to make her think that he loved her. He had called on her once or twice at Fawn Court,—as why should he not? Seeing that there had been friendship between the families for so many years, who could complain of that? Lady Fawn, however, had,—not complained, but just said a word. A word in season, how good is it? Lucy did not much regard the word spoken to herself; but when she reflected that a word must also have been spoken to Mr. Greystock,—otherwise how should it have been that he never came again?—that she did not like.

In herself she regarded this passion of hers as a healthy man regards the loss of a leg or an arm. It is a great nuisance, a loss that maims the whole life,—a misfortune to be much regretted. But because a leg is gone, everything is not gone. A man with a wooden leg may stump about through much action, and may enjoy the keenest pleasures of humanity. He has his eyes left to him, and his ears, and his intellect. He will not break his heart for the loss of that leg. And so it was with Lucy Morris. She would still stump about and be very active. Eyes, ears, and intellect were left to her. Looking at her position, she told herself that a happy love could hardly have been her lot in life. Lady Fawn, she thought, was right. A governess should make up her mind to do without a lover. She had given away her heart, and yet she would do without a lover. When, on one dull, dark afternoon, as she was thinking of all this, Lord Fawn suddenly put into her hands a cruelly long printed document respecting the Sawab, she went to work upon it immediately. As she read it, she could not refrain from thinking how wonderfully Frank Greystock would plead the cause of the Indian prince, if the privilege of pleading it could be given to him.

The spring had come round, with May and the London butterflies, at the time at which our story begins, and during six months Frank Greystock had not been at Fawn Court. Then one day Lady Eustace came down with her ponies, and her footman, and a new dear friend of hers, Miss Macnulty. While Miss Macnulty was being honoured by Lady Fawn, Lizzie had retreated to a corner with her old dear friend Lucy Morris. It was pretty to see how so wealthy and fashionable a woman as Lady Eustace could show so much friendship to a governess. 'Have you seen Frank, lately?' said Lady Eustace, referring to her cousin the barrister.

'Not for ever so long,' said Lucy, with her cheeriest smile.

'He is not going to prove a false knight?' asked Lady Eustace, in her lowest whisper.

'I don't know that Mr. Greystock is much given to knighthood at all,' said Lucy,—'unless it is to being made Sir Francis by his party.'

'Nonsense, my dear; as if I didn't know. I suppose Lady Fawn has been interfering—like an old cat as she is.'

'She is not an old cat, Lizzie! and I won't hear her called so. If you think so, you shouldn't come here. And she hasn't interfered. That is, she has done nothing that she ought not to have done.'

'Then she has interfered,' said Lady Eustace, as she got up and walked across the room, with a sweet smile to the old cat.

CHAPTER IV
Frank Greystock

FRANK GREYSTOCK the barrister was the only son of the Dean of Bobsborough. Now the dean had a family of daughters, —not quite so numerous indeed as that of Lady Fawn, for there were only three of them,—and was by no means a rich man. Unless a dean have a private fortune, or has chanced to draw the happy lot of Durham in the lottery of deans, he can hardly be wealthy. At Bobsborough the dean was endowed with a large, rambling, picturesque, uncomfortable house, and with £1,500 a year. In regard to personal property it may be asserted of all the Greystocks that they never had any. They were a family of which the males would surely come to be deans and admirals, and the females would certainly find husbands. And they lived on the good things of the world, and mixed with wealthy people. But they never had any money. The Eustaces always had money, and the Bishop of Bobsborough was wealthy. The dean was a man very different from his brother the admiral, who had never paid anybody anything. The dean did pay; but he was a little slow in his payments, and money with him was never very plentiful. In these circumstances it became very expedient that Frank Greystock should earn his bread early in life.

Nevertheless, he had chosen a profession which is not often lucrative at first. He had been called to the Bar, and had gone,—and was still going,—the circuit in which lies the cathedral city of Bobsborough. Bobsborough is not much of a town, and was honoured with the judges' visits only every other circuit. Frank began pretty well, getting some little work in London, and perhaps nearly enough to pay the cost of his circuit out of the county in which the cathedral was situated. But he began life after that impecunious fashion for which the Greystocks have been noted. Tailors, robemakers, and booksellers gave him trust, and did believe that they would get their money. And any persistent tradesman did get it. He did not actually hoist the black flag of impecuniosity, and proclaim his intention of preying generally upon the retail dealers, as his uncle the admiral had done. But he became known as a young man with whom money was 'tight.' All this had been going on for three or four years before he had met Lucy Morris at the deanery. He was then eight-and-twenty, and had been four years called. He was thirty when old Lady Fawn hinted to him that he had better not pay any more visits at Fawn Court.

But things had much altered with him of late. At the time of that visit to the deanery he had made a sudden start in his profession. The Corporation of the City of London had brought an action against the Bank of England with reference to certain alleged encroachments, of which action, considerable as it was in all its interests, no further notice need be taken here than is given by the statement that a great deal of money in this cause had found its way among the lawyers. Some of it penetrated into the pocket of Frank Greystock, but he earned more than money, better than money, out of that affair. It was attributed to him by the attorneys that the Bank of England was saved from the necessity of reconstructing all its bullion-cellars, and he had made his character for industry. In the year after that the Bobsborough people were rather driven into a corner in search of a clever young conservative candidate for the borough, and Frank Greystock was invited to stand. It was not thought that there was much chance of success, and the dean was against it. But Frank liked the honour and glory of the contest, and so did Frank's mother. Frank Greystock stood, and at the time in which he was warned away from Fawn Court had been nearly a year in Parliament. 'Of course it does interfere with one's business,' he had said to his father, 'but then it brings one business also. A man with a seat in Parliament who shows that he means work will always get nearly as much work as he can do.' Such was Frank's exposition to his father. It may perhaps not be found to hold water in all cases. Mrs. Dean was of course delighted with her son's success, and so were the girls. Women like to feel that the young men belonging to them are doing something in the world, so that a reflected glory may be theirs. It was pleasant to talk of Frank as member for the city. Brothers do not always care much for a brother's success, but a sister is generally sympathetic. If Frank would only marry money, there was nothing he might not achieve. That he would live to sit on the woolsack was now almost a certainty to the dear old lady. But in order that he might sit there comfortably it was necessary that he should at least abstain from marrying a poor wife. For there was fear at the deanery also in regard to Lucy Morris.

'That notion of marrying money as you call it,' Frank said to his second sister Margaret, 'is the most disgusting idea in the world.'

'It is as easy to love a girl who has something as one who has nothing,' said Margaret.

'No,—it is not; because the girls with money are scarce, and those without it are plentiful,—an argument of which I don't suppose you see the force.' Then Margaret for the moment was snubbed and retired.

'Indeed, Frank, I think Lady Fawn was right,' said the mother.

'And I think she was quite wrong. If there be anything in it, it won't be expelled by Lady Fawn's interference. Do you think I should allow Lady Fawn to tell me not to choose such or such a woman for my wife?'

'It's the habit of seeing her, my dear. Nobody loves Lucy Morris better than I do. We all like her. But, dear Frank, would it do for you to make her your wife?'

Frank Greystock was silent for a moment, and then he answered his mother's question. 'I am not quite sure whether it would or would not. But I do think this—that if I were bold enough to marry now, and to trust all to the future, and could get Lucy to be my wife, I should be doing a great thing. I doubt, however, whether I have the courage.' All of which made the dean's wife uneasy.

The reader, who has read so far, will perhaps think that

Frank Greystock was in love with Lucy as Lucy was in love with him. But such was not exactly the case. To be in love, as an absolute, well-marked, acknowledged fact, is the condition of a woman more frequently and more readily than of a man. Such is not the common theory on the matter, as it is the man's business to speak, and the woman's business to be reticent. And the woman is presumed to have kept her heart free from any load of love, till she may accept the burthen with an assurance that it shall become a joy and a comfort to her. But such presumptions, though they may be very useful for the regulation of conduct, may not be always true. It comes more within the scope of a woman's mind, than that of a man's, to think closely and decide sharply on such a matter. With a man it is often chance that settles the question for him. He resolves to propose to a woman, or proposes without resolving, because she is close to him. Frank Greystock ridiculed the idea of Lady Fawn's interference in so high a matter as his love,—or abstinence from love. Nevertheless, had he been made a welcome guest at Fawn Court, he would undoubtedly have told his love to Lucy Morris. He was not a welcome guest, but had been banished; and, as a consequence of that banishment, he had formed no resolution in regard to Lucy, and did not absolutely know whether she was necessary to him or not. But Lucy Morris knew all about it.

Moreover, it frequently happens with men that they fail to analyse these things, and do not make out for themselves any clear definition of what their feelings are or what they mean. We hear that a man has behaved badly to a girl, when the behaviour of which he has been guilty has resulted simply from want of thought. He has found a certain companionship to be agreeable to him, and he has accepted the pleasure without inquiry. Some vague idea has floated across his brain that the world is wrong in supposing that such friendship cannot exist without marriage, or question of marriage. It is simply friendship. And yet were his friend to tell him that she intended to give herself in marriage elsewhere, he would suffer all the pangs of jealousy, and would imagine himself to be

31

horribly ill-treated! To have such a friend,—a friend whom he cannot or will not make his wife,—is no injury to him. To him it is simply a delight, an excitement in life, a thing to be known to himself only and not talked of to others, a source of pride and inward exultation. It is a joy to think of when he wakes, and a consolation in his little troubles. It dispels the weariness of life, and makes a green spot of holiday within his daily work. It is, indeed, death to her;—but he does not know it. Frank Greystock did think that he could not marry Lucy Morris without making an imprudent plunge into deep water, and yet he felt that Lady Fawn was an ill-natured old woman for hinting to him that he had better not, for the present, continue his visits to Fawn Court. 'Of course you understand me, Mr. Greystock,' she had said, meaning to be civil. 'When Miss Morris has left us,—should she ever leave us,—I should be most happy to see you.' 'What on earth would take me to Fawn Court, if Lucy were not there!' he said to himself,—not choosing to appreciate Lady Fawn's civility.

Frank Greystock was at this time nearly thirty years old. He was a good-looking, but not strikingly handsome man; thin, of moderate height, with sharp grey eyes, a face clean shorn with the exception of a small whisker, with wiry, strong dark hair, which was already beginning to show a tinge of grey;—the very opposite in appearance to his late friend Sir Florian Eustace. He was quick, ready-witted, self-reliant, and not over scrupulous in the outward things of the world. He was desirous of doing his duty to others,* but he was specially desirous that others should do their duty to him. He intended to get on in the world, and believed that happiness was to be achieved by success. He was certainly made for the profession which he had adopted. His father, looking to certain morsels of Church patronage which occasionally came in his way, and to the fact that he and the bishop were on most friendly terms, had wished his son to take orders. But Frank had known himself and his own qualities too well to follow his father's advice. He had chosen to be a barrister, and now, at thirty, he was in Parliament.

He had been asked to stand for Bobsborough in the conservative interest, and as a Conservative he had been returned. Those who invited him knew probably but little of his own political beliefs or feelings,—did not probably know whether he had any. His father was a fine old Tory of the ancient school, who thought that things were going from bad to worse, but was able to live happily in spite of his anticipations. The dean was one of those old-world politicians,—we meet them every day, and they are generally pleasant people,—who enjoy the politics of the side to which they belong without any special belief in them. If pressed hard they will almost own that their so-called convictions are prejudices. But not for worlds would they be rid of them. When two or three of them meet together, they are as freemasons,* who are bound by a pleasant bond which separates them from the outer world. They feel among themselves that everything that is being done is bad,—even though that everything is done by their own party. It was bad to interfere with Charles, bad to endure Cromwell, bad to banish James, bad to put up with William. The House of Hanover was bad. All interference with prerogative has been bad. The Reform bill was very bad. Encroachment on the estates of the bishops was bad. Emancipation of Roman Catholics was the worst of all. Abolition of corn-laws, church-rates, and oaths and tests were all bad. The meddling with the Universities has been grievous. The treatment of the Irish Church has been Satanic. The overhauling of schools is most injurious to English education. Education bills and Irish land bills were all bad. Every step taken has been bad. And yet to them old England is of all countries in the world the best to live in, and is not at all the less comfortable because of the changes that have been made.* These people are ready to grumble at every boon conferred on them, and yet to enjoy every boon. They know too their privileges, and, after a fashion, understand their position. It is picturesque, and it pleases them. To have been always in the right and yet always on the losing side; always being ruined, always under persecution from a wild spirit of republicandemagogism,—and yet never to lose anything, not even position or public esteem, is pleasant enough. A huge, living, daily increasing grievance that does one no palpable harm, is the happiest possession that a man can have. There is a large body of such men in England, and, personally, they are the very salt of the nation. He who said that all Conservatives are stupid did not know them. Stupid Conservatives there may be, —and there certainly are very stupid Radicals. The well-educated, widely-read Conservative, who is well assured that all good things are gradually being brought to an end by the voice of the people, is generally the pleasantest man to be met. But he is a Buddhist, possessing a religious creed which is altogether dark and mysterious to the outer world. Those who watch the ways of the advanced Buddhist hardly know whether the man does believe himself in his hidden god, but men perceive that he is respectable, self-satisfied, and a man of note. It is of course from the society of such that Conservative candidates are to be sought; but, alas, it is hard to indoctrinate young minds with the old belief, since new theories of life have become so rife!

Nevertheless Frank Greystock, when he was invited to stand for Bobsborough in the Conservative interest, had not for a moment allowed any political heterodoxy on his own part to stand in the way of his advancement. It may, perhaps, be the case that a barrister is less likely to be influenced by personal convictions in taking his side in politics than any other man who devotes himself to public affairs. No slur on the profession is intended by this suggestion. A busy, clever, useful man, who has been at work all his life, finds that his own progress towards success demands from him that he shall become a politician. The highest work of a lawyer can only be reached through political struggle. As a large-minded man of the world, peculiarly conversant with the fact that every question has two sides, and that as much may often be said on one side as on the other, he has probably not become violent in his feelings as a political partisan. Thus he sees that there is an opening here or an opening there, and the

offence in either case is not great to him. With Frank Greystock the matter was very easy. There certainly was no
apostacy.* He had now and again attacked his father's ultra-
Toryism, and rebuked his mother and sisters when they spoke
of Gladstone as Apollyon,* and called John Bright the Abomination of Desolation.* But it was easy to him to fancy himself
a Conservative, and as such he took his seat in the House
without any feeling of discomfort.

During the first four months of his first session he had not
spoken,—but he had made himself useful. He had sat on one
or two Committees, though as a barrister he might have excused himself, and had done his best to learn the forms of the
House. But he had already begun to find that the time which
he devoted to Parliament was much wanted for his profession.
Money was very necessary to him. Then a new idea was
presented to him.

John Eustace and Greystock were very intimate,—as also
had been Sir Florian and Greystock. 'I tell you what I wish
you'd do, Greystock,' Eustace said to him one day, as they
were standing idly together in the lobby of the House. For
John Eustace was also in Parliament.

'Anything to oblige you, my friend.'

'It's only a trifle,' said Eustace. 'Just to marry your cousin,
my brother's widow.'

'By Jove,—I wish I had the chance!'

'I don't see why you shouldn't. She is sure to marry somebody, and at her age so she ought. She's not twenty-three
yet. We could trust you,—with the child and all the rest of it.
As it is, she is giving us a deal of trouble.'

'But, my dear fellow——'

'I know she's fond of you. You were dining there last
Sunday.'

'And so was Fawn. Lord Fawn is the man to marry Lizzie.
You see if he doesn't. He was uncommonly sweet on her the
other night, and really interested her about the Sawab.'

'She'll never be Lady Fawn,' said John Eustace. 'And to tell
the truth, I shouldn't care to have to deal with Lord Fawn. He

would be infinitely troublesome; and I can hardly wash my hands of her affairs. She's worth nearly £5,000 a year as long as she lives, and I really don't think that she's much amiss.'

'Much amiss! I don't know whether she's not the prettiest woman I ever saw,' said Greystock.

'Yes;—but I mean in conduct, and all that. She is making herself queer; and Camperdown, our lawyer, means to jump upon her; but it's only because she doesn't know what she ought to be at, and what she ought not. You could tell her.'

'It wouldn't suit me at all to have to quarrel with Camperdown,' said the barrister, laughing.

'You and he would settle everything in five minutes, and it would save me a world of trouble,' said Eustace.

'Fawn is your man;—take my word for it,' said Greystock, as he walked back into the House.

.   .   .   .

Dramatists, when they write their plays, have a delightful privilege of prefixing a list of their personages;—and the dramatists of old used to tell us who was in love with whom, and what were the blood relationships of all the persons. In such a narrative as this, any proceeding of that kind would be unusual,—and therefore the poor narrator has been driven to expend his first four chapters in the mere task of introducing his characters. He regrets the length of these introductions, and will now begin at once the action of his story.

CHAPTER V
The Eustace Necklace

JOHN EUSTACE, Lady Eustace's brother-in-law, had told his friend Greystock, the lady's cousin, that Mr. Camperdown the lawyer intended to 'jump upon' that lady. Making such allowance and deduction from the force of these words as the slang expression requires, we may say that John Eustace was right. Mr. Camperdown was in earnest, and did intend to obtain the restoration of those jewels. Mr. Camperdown was a gentleman of about sixty, who had been lawyer to Sir Florian's father, and whose father had been lawyer to Sir Florian's grandfather. His connection with the property and with the family was of a nature to allow him to take almost any liberty with the Eustaces. When therefore John Eustace, in regard to those diamonds, had pleaded that the heir in his long minority would obtain ample means of buying more diamonds, and of suggesting that the plunder for the sake of tranquillity should be allowed, Mr. Camperdown took upon himself to say that he'd 'be——if he'd put up with it!' 'I really don't know what you are to do,' said John Eustace.

'I'll file a bill in Chancery if it's necessary,' said the old lawyer. 'Heaven on earth! as trustee how are you to reconcile yourself to such a robbery? They represent £500 a year for ever, and she is to have them simply because she chooses to take them!'

'I suppose Florian could have given them away. At any rate he could have sold them.'

'I don't know that,' said Mr. Camperdown. 'I have not looked as yet, but I think that this necklace has been made an heirloom. At any rate it represents an amount of property that shouldn't and couldn't be made over legally without some visible evidence of transfer. It's as clear a case of stealing as I ever knew in my life, and as bad a case. She hadn't a farthing, and she has got the whole of the Ayrshire property for her life. She goes about and tells everybody that it's hers to sell to-morrow if she pleases to sell it! No, John;—' Mr. Camperdown had known Eustace when he was a boy, and had watched him become a man, and hadn't yet learned to drop the name by which he had called the boy,—'we mustn't allow it. What do you think of her applying to me for an income to support her child,—a baby not yet two years old?' Mr. Camperdown had been very adverse to all the circumstances of Sir Florian's marriage, and had subjected himself to Sir Florian's displeasure for expressing his opinion. He had tried to explain that as the lady brought no money into the family she was not entitled to such a jointure as Sir Florian was determined to lavish upon her. But Sir Florian had been obstinate,—both in regard to the settlement and the will. It was not till after Sir Florian's death that this terrible matter of the jewels had even suggested itself to Mr. Camperdown. The jewellers in whose custody the things had been since the death of the late Lady Eustace had mentioned the affair to him immediately on the young widow's return from Naples. Sir Florian had withdrawn, not all the jewels, but by far the most valuable of them, from the jewellers' care on his return to London from their marriage tour to Scotland, and this was the result. The jewellers were at that time without any doubt as to the date at which the necklace was taken from them.

Mr. Camperdown's first attempt was made by a most courteous and even complimentary note, in which he suggested to Lady Eustace that it would be for the advantage of all parties that the family jewels should be kept together. Lizzie as she read this note smiled, and said to herself that she did not exactly see how her own interests would be best served by such an arrangement. She made no answer to Mr. Camperdown's note. Some months after this, when the heir was born, and as Lady Eustace was passing through London on her journey from Bobsborough to Portray, a meeting had been arranged between her and Mr. Camperdown. She had endeavoured by all the wiles she knew to avoid this meeting, but it had been forced upon her. She had been almost given to understand that unless she submitted to it, she would not be able to draw her income from the Portray property. Messrs. Mowbray and Mopus had advised her to submit. 'My husband gave me a necklace, and they want me to give it back,' she had said to Mr. Mopus. 'Do nothing of the kind,' Mr. Mopus had replied. 'If you find it necessary refer Mr. Camperdown to us. We will answer him.' The interview had taken place, during which Mr. Camperdown took the trouble to explain very plainly and more than once that the income from the Portray property belonged to Lady Eustace for her life only. It would after her death be rejoined, of necessity, to the rest of the Eustace property. This was repeated to

Lady Eustace in the presence of John Eustace; but she made no remark on being so informed. 'You understand the nature of the settlement, Lady Eustace?' Mr. Camperdown had said. 'I believe I understand everything,' she replied. Then just at the close of the interview, he asked a question about the jewels. Lady Eustace at first made no reply. 'They might as well be sent back to Messrs. Garnett's,' said Mr. Camperdown. 'I don't know that I have any to send back,' she answered; and then she escaped before Mr. Camperdown was able to arrange any further attack. 'I can manage with her better by letter than I can personally,' he said to John Eustace.

Lawyers such as Mr. Camperdown are slow, and it was three or four months after that when he wrote a letter in his own name to Lady Eustace, explaining to her, still courteously, that it was his business to see that the property of the Eustace family was placed in fit hands, and that a certain valuable necklace of diamonds, which was an heirloom of the family, and which was undeniably the property of the heir, was believed to be in her custody. As such property was peculiarly subject to risks, would she have the kindness to make arrangements for handing over the necklace to the custody of Messrs. Garnett? To this letter Lizzie made no answer whatever, nor did she to a second note, calling attention to the first. When John Eustace told Greystock that Camperdown intended to 'jump on' Lady Eustace, the following further letter had been written by the firm;—but up to that time Lizzie had not replied to it:

'62, New Square, Lincoln's Inn,
May 5, 186—.

'MADAM,

'It is our duty as attorneys acting on behalf of the estate of your late husband Sir Florian Eustace, and in the interest of your son his heir, to ask for restitution of a certain valuable diamond necklace which is believed to be now in the possession of your ladyship. Our senior partner, Mr. Camperdown, has written to your ladyship more than once on the subject, but has not been honoured with any reply. Doubtless had there been any mistake as to the necklace being in your hands we should have been so informed. The diamonds were withdrawn from Messrs. Garnett's, the jewellers, by Sir Florian soon after his marriage, and were, no doubt, entrusted to your keeping. They are appanages*of the family which should not be in your hands as the widow of the late baronet, and they constitute an amount of property which certainly cannot be alienated from the family without inquiry or right, as might any trifling article either of use or ornament. The jewels are valued at over £10,000.

'We are reluctantly compelled, by the fact of your having left unanswered three letters from Mr. Camperdown Senior, on the subject, to explain to you that if attention be not paid to this letter, we shall be obliged, in the performance of our duty, to take legal steps for the restitution of the property.

> 'We have the honour to be,
> 'Madam,
> 'Your ladyship's most obedient servants,
> 'CAMPERDOWN & SON.

'To Lady Eustace.'
  &c. &c.

A few days after it was sent old Mr. Camperdown got the letter-book of the office and read the letter to John Eustace.

'I don't see how you're to get them,' said Eustace.

'We'll throw upon her the burthen of showing that they have become legally her property. She can't do it.'

'Suppose she sold them?'

'We'll follow them up. £10,000, my dear John! God bless my soul! it's a magnificent dowry for a daughter,—an ample provision for a younger son. And she is to be allowed to filch it, as other widows filch china cups, and a silver teaspoon or two! It's quite a common thing, but I never heard of such a haul as this.'

'It will be very unpleasant,' said Eustace.

'And then she still goes about everywhere declaring that the Portray property is her own. She's a bad lot. I knew it from the first. Of course we shall have trouble.' Then Mr. Eustace explained to the lawyer that their best way out of it all would be to get the widow married to some respectable husband. She was sure to marry sooner or later,—so John Eustace said, —and any 'decently decent' fellow would be easier to deal with than she herself. 'He must be very indecently indecent if he is not,' said Mr. Camperdown. But Mr. Eustace did not name Frank Greystock the barrister as the probable future decent husband.

When Lizzie first got the letter, which she did on the day after the visit at Fawn Court of which mention has been made, she put it by unread for a couple of days. She opened it, not knowing the clerk's handwriting, but read only the first line and the signature. For two days she went on with the ordinary affairs and amusements of her life, as though no such letter had reached her; but she was thinking of it all the time. The diamonds were in her possession, and she had had them valued by her old friend Mr. Benjamin—of the firm of Harter and Benjamin. Mr. Benjamin had suggested that stones of such a value should not be left to the risk of an ordinary London house; but Lizzie had felt that if Mr. Benjamin got them into his hands, Mr. Benjamin might perhaps not return them. Messrs. Camperdown and Garnett between them might form a league with Mr. Benjamin. Where would she be, should Mr. Benjamin tell her that under some legal sanction he had given the jewels up to Mr. Camperdown? She hinted to Mr. Benjamin that she would perhaps sell them if she got a good offer. Mr. Benjamin, who was very familiar with her, hinted that there might be a little family difficulty. 'Oh, none in the least,' said Lizzie;—'but I don't think I shall part with them.' Then she gave Mr. Benjamin an order for a strong box, which was supplied to her. The strong box, which was so heavy that she could barely lift it herself, was now in her London bedroom.

On the morning of the third day she read the letter. Miss Macnulty was staying with her, but she had not said a word to Miss Macnulty about the letter. She read it up in her own bedroom, and then sat down to think about it. Sir Florian, as he had handed to her the stones for the purpose of a special dinner party which had been given to them when passing through London, had told her that they were family jewels. 'That setting was done for my mother,' he said, 'but it is already old. When we are at home again they shall be reset.' Then he had added some little husband's joke as to a future daughter-in-law who should wear them. Nevertheless she was not sure whether the fact of their being so handed to her did not make them her own. She had spoken a second time to Mr. Mopus, and Mr. Mopus had asked her whether there existed any family deed as to the diamonds. She had heard of no such deed, nor did Mr. Camperdown mention such a deed. After reading the letter once she read it a dozen times; and then, like a woman, made up her mind that her safest course would be not to answer it.

But yet she felt sure that something unpleasant would come of it. Mr. Camperdown was not a man to take up such a question and to let it drop. Legal steps! What did legal steps mean, and what could they do to her? Would Mr. Camperdown be able to put her in prison,—or to take away from her the estate of Portray? She could swear that her husband had given them to her, and could invent any form of words she pleased as accompanying the gift. No one else had been near them then. But she was, and felt herself to be absolutely, alarmingly ignorant, not only of the laws, but of custom in such matters. Messrs. Mowbray and Mopus and Mr. Benjamin were the allies to whom she looked for guidance; but she was wise enough to know that Mowbray and Mopus, and Harter and Benjamin were not trustworthy, whereas Camperdown and Son and the Messrs. Garnett were all as firm as rocks and as respectable as the Bank of England. Circumstances,— unfortunate circumstances,—drove her to Harter and Benjamin and to Mowbray and Mopus, while she would have taken so much delight in feeling the strong honesty of the other people to be on her side! She would have talked to her friends about Mr. Camperdown and the people at Garnett's with so much satisfaction! But ease, security, and even respectability may be bought too dearly. Ten thousand pounds! Was she prepared to surrender such a sum as that? She had, indeed, already realised the fact that it might be very difficult to touch the money. When she had suggested to Mr. Benjamin that he should buy the jewels, that worthy tradesman had by no means jumped at the offer. Of what use to her would be a necklace always locked up in an iron box, which box, for aught she knew, myrmidons from Mr. Camperdown might carry off during her absence from the house? Would it not be better to come to terms and surrender? But then what should the terms be?

If only there had been a friend whom she could consult; a friend whom she could consult on a really friendly footing!—not a simply respectable, off-handed, high-minded friend, who would advise her as a matter of course to make restitution. Her uncle the dean, or her cousin Frank, or old Lady Fawn, would be sure to give her such advice as that. There are people who are so very high-minded when they have to deal with the interests of their friends! What if she were to ask Lord Fawn?

Thoughts of a second marriage had, of course, crossed Lady Eustace's mind, and they were by no means the worst thoughts that found a place there. She had a grand idea,—this selfish, hard-fisted little woman, who could not bring herself to abandon the plunder on which she had laid her hand,—a grand idea of surrendering herself and all her possessions to a great passion. For Florian Eustace she had never cared. She had sat down by his side, and looked into his handsome face, and read poetry to him,—because of his wealth, and because it had been indispensable to her to settle herself well. And he had been all very well,—a generous, open-hearted, chivalrous, irascible, but rather heavy-minded gentleman; but she had never been in love with him. Now she desired to be so in love that she could surrender everything to her love. There was as yet nothing of such love in her bosom. She had seen no one who had so touched her. But she was alive to the romance of the thing, and was in love with the idea of being in love. 'Ah,' she would say to herself in her moments of solitude, 'if I had a Corsair of my own, how I would sit on watch for my lover's boat by the sea-shore!'*And she believed it of herself, that she could do so.

But it would also be very nice to be a peeress,—so that she might, without any doubt, be one of the great ladies of London. As a baronet's widow with a large income, she was already almost a great lady; but she was quite alive to a suspicion that she was not altogether strong in her position. The bishop's people and the dean's people did not quite trust her. The Camperdowns and Garnetts utterly distrusted her. The Mopuses and Benjamins were more familiar than they would be with a really great lady. She was sharp enough to understand all this. Should it be Lord Fawn or should it be a Corsair? The worst of Lord Fawn was the undoubted fact that he was not himself a great man. He could, no doubt, make his wife a peeress; but he was poor, encumbered with a host of sisters, dull as a blue-book, and possessed of little beyond his peerage to recommend him. If she could only find a peer, unmarried, with a dash of the Corsair about him! In the meantime, what was she to do about the jewels?

There was staying with her at this time a certain Miss Macnulty, who was related, after some distant fashion, to old Lady Linlithgow, and who was as utterly destitute of possessions or means of existence as any unfortunate, well-born, and moderately-educated, middle-aged woman in London. To live upon her friends, such as they might be, was the only mode of life within her reach. It was not that she had chosen such dependence; nor, indeed, had she endeavoured to reject it. It had come to her as a matter of course,—either that or the poor-house. As to earning her bread, except by that attendance which a poor friend gives,—the idea of any possibility that way had never entered her head. She could do nothing,—except dress like a lady with the smallest possible cost, and endeavour to be obliging. Now, at this moment, her condition was terribly precarious. She had quarrelled with Lady Linlithgow, and had been taken in by her old friend Lizzie,—her old enemy might, perhaps, be a truer expression,—because of that quarrel. But a permanent home had not even been promised to her; and poor Miss Macnulty was aware that even a permanent home with Lady Eustace would not be an unmixed blessing. In her way, Miss Macnulty was an honest woman.

They were sitting together one May afternoon in the little back drawing-room in Mount Street. They had dined early, were now drinking tea, and intended to go to the opera. It was six o'clock, and was still broad day, but the thick coloured blind was kept across the single window, and the folding doors of the room were nearly closed, and there was a feeling of evening in the room. The necklace during the whole day had been so heavy on Lizzie's heart, that she had been unable to apply her thoughts to the building of that castle in the air in which the Corsair was to reign supreme, but not alone. 'My dear,' she said,—she generally called Miss Macnulty my dear, —'you know that box I had made by the jewellers.'

'You mean the safe.'

'Well,—yes; only it isn't a safe. A safe is a great big thing. I had it made especially for the diamonds Sir Florian gave me.'

'I supposed it was so.'

'I wonder whether there's any danger about it?'

'If I were you, Lady Eustace, I wouldn't keep them in the house. I should have them kept where Sir Florian kept them. Suppose anybody should come and murder you!'

'I'm not a bit afraid of that,' said Lizzie.

'I should be. And what will you do with it when you go to Scotland?'

'I took them with me before;—in my own care. I know that wasn't safe. I wish I knew what to do with them!'

'There are people who keep such things,' said Miss Macnulty.

Then Lizzie paused a moment. She was dying for counsel and for confidence. 'I cannot trust them anywhere,' she said. 'It is just possible there may be a lawsuit about them.'

'How a lawsuit?'

'I cannot explain it all, but I am very unhappy about it.

They want me to give them up;—but my husband gave them to me, and for his sake I will not do so. When he threw them round my neck he told me that they were my own;—so he did. How can a woman give up such a present,—from a husband,— who is dead? As to the value, I care nothing. But I won't do it.' By this time Lady Eustace was in tears, and had so far succeeded as to have produced some amount of belief in Miss Macnulty's mind.

'If they are your own, they can't take them from you,' said Miss Macnulty.

'They sha'n't. They shall find that I've got some spirit left.' Then she reflected that a real Corsair lover would protect her jewels for her;—would guard them against a score of Camperdowns. But she doubted whether Lord Fawn would do much in that way. Then the door was opened, and Lord Fawn was announced. It was not at all unusual with Lord Fawn to call on the widow at this hour. Mount Street is not exactly in the way from the India Office to the House of Lords; but a Hansom cab can make it almost in the way. Of neglect of official duty Lord Fawn was never guilty; but a half hour for private business or for relaxation between one stage of duty and another,—can any Minister grudge so much to an indefatigable follower? Lady Eustace had been in tears as he was announced, but the light of the room was so low that the traces of them could hardly be seen. She was in her Corsair state of mind, divided between her jewels and her poetry, and caring not very much for the increased rank which Lord Fawn could give her. 'The Sawab's case is coming on in the House of Commons this very night,' he said, in answer to a question from Miss Macnulty. Then he turned to Lady Eustace. 'Your cousin, Mr. Greystock, is going to ask a question in the House.'

'Shall you be there to answer him?' asked Miss Macnulty innocently.

'Oh dear, no. But I shall be present. A peer can go,* you know.' Then Lord Fawn, at considerable length, explained to the two ladies the nature and condition of the British Parliament. Miss Macnulty experienced an innocent pleasure in having such things told to her by a lord. Lady Eustace knew that this was the way in which Lord Fawn made love, and thought that from him it was as good as any other way. If she were to marry a second time simply with the view of being a peeress, of having a respected husband, and making good her footing in the world, she would as lief listen to parliamentary details and the prospects of the Sawab as to any other matters. She knew very well that no Corsair propensities would be forthcoming from Lord Fawn. Lord Fawn had just worked himself round to the Sawab again, when Frank Greystock entered the room. 'Now we have both the Houses represented,' said Lady Eustace, as she welcomed her cousin.

'You intend to ask your question about the Sawab tonight?' asked Lord Fawn, with intense interest, feeling that, had it been his lot to perform that task before he went to his couch, he would at this moment have been preparing his little speech.

But Frank Greystock had not come to his cousin's house to talk of the Prince of the Mygawb territory. When his friend Eustace had suggested to him that he should marry the widow, he had ridiculed the idea;—but nevertheless he had thought of it a good deal. He was struggling hard, working diligently, making for himself a character in Parliament, succeeding,—so said all his friends,—as a barrister. He was a rising young man, one of those whose names began to be much in the mouths of other men;—but still he was poor. It seemed to himself that among other good gifts that of economy had not been bestowed upon him. He owed a little money, and though he owed it, he went on spending his earnings. He wanted just such a lift in the world as a wife with an income would give him. As for looking about for a girl whom he could honestly love, and who should have a fortune of her own as well as beauty, birth, and all the other things,—that was out of his reach. If he talked to himself of love, if he were ever to acknowledge to himself that love was to have sway over him, then must Lucy

Morris be the mistress of his heart. He had come to know enough about himself to be aware of that;—but he knew also that he had said nothing binding him to walk in that path. It was quite open to him to indulge a discreet ambition without dishonour. Therefore he also had come to call upon the beautiful widow. The courtship with her he knew need not be long. He could ask her to marry him to-morrow,—as for that matter to-day,—without a feeling of hesitation. She might accept him or might reject him; but, as he said to himself, in neither case would any harm be done.

An idea of the same kind flitted across Lizzie's mind as she sat and talked to the two gentlemen. She knew that her cousin Frank was poor, but she thought that she could fall in love with him. He was not exactly a Corsair;—but he was a man who had certain Corsair propensities. He was bold and dashing, unscrupulous and clever, a man to make a name for himself, and one to whom a woman could endure to be obedient. There could be no question as to choice between him and Lord Fawn, if she were to allow herself to choose by liking. And she thought that Frank Greystock would keep the necklace, if he himself were made to have an interest in the necklace; whereas Lord Fawn would undoubtedly surrender it at once to Mr. Camperdown.

Lord Fawn had some slight idea of waiting to see the cousin go; but as Greystock had a similar idea, and as he was the stronger of the two, of course Lord Fawn went. He perhaps remembered that the Hansom cab was at the door,— costing sixpence every fifteen minutes,—and that he wished to show himself in the House of Lords before the peers rose. Miss Macnulty also left the room, and Frank was alone with the widow. 'Lizzie,' said he, 'you must be very solitary here.'

'I am solitary.'

'And hardly happy.'

'Anything but happy, Frank. I have things that make me very unhappy;—one thing that I will tell you if you will let me.' Frank had almost made up his mind to ask her on the spot to give him permission to console all her sorrows, when there came a clattering double-knock at the door. 'They know I shall be at home to nobody else now,' said Lady Eustace. But Frank Greystock had hardly regained his self-possession when Miss Macnulty hurried into the room, and with a look almost of horror declared that Lady Linlithgow was in the parlour.

CHAPTER VI
Lady Linlithgow's Mission

'LADY LINLITHGOW!'—said Frank Greystock, holding up both his hands.

'Yes, indeed!' said Miss Macnulty. 'I did not speak to her, but I saw her. She has sent her——love to Lady Eustace, and begs that she will see her.'

Lady Eustace had been so surprised by the announcement that hitherto she had not spoken a word. The quarrel between her and her aunt had been of such a nature that it had seemed to be impossible that the old countess should come to Mount Street. Lizzie had certainly behaved very badly to her aunt;—about as badly as a young woman could behave to an old woman. She had accepted bread, and shelter, and the very clothes on her back from her aunt's bounty, and had rejected even the hand of her benefactress the first moment that she had bread, and shelter, and clothes of her own. And here was Lady Linlithgow down-stairs in the parlour, and sending up her love to her niece! 'I won't see her!' said Lizzie.

'You had better see her,' said Frank.

'I can't see her!' said Lizzie. 'Good gracious, my dear— what has she come for?'

'She says it's very important,' said Miss Macnulty.

'Of course you must see her,' said Frank. 'Let me get out of the house, and then tell the servant to show her up at once. Don't be weak now, Lizzie, and I'll come and find out all about it to-morrow.'

'Mind you do,' said Lizzie. Then Frank took his departure, and Lizzie did as she was bidden. 'You remain in here, Julia,' she said,—'so as to be near if I want you. She shall come into the front room.' Then, absolutely shaking with fear of the approaching evil, she took her seat in the largest drawing-room. There was still a little delay. Time was given to Frank Greystock to get away, and to do so without meeting Lady Linlithgow in the passage. The message was conveyed by Miss Macnulty to the servant, and the same servant opened the front door for Frank before he delivered it. Lady Linlithgow, too, though very strong, was old. She was slow, or perhaps it might more properly be said she was stately in her movements. She was one of those old women who are undoubtedly old women,—who in the remembrance of younger people seem always to have been old women,—but on whom old age appears to have no debilitating effects. If the hand of Lady Linlithgow ever trembled, it trembled from anger;—if her foot ever faltered, it faltered for effect. In her way Lady Linlithgow was a very powerful human being. She knew nothing of fear, nothing of charity, nothing of mercy, and nothing of the softness of love. She had no imagination. She was worldly, covetous, and not unfrequently cruel. But she meant to be true and honest, though she often failed in her meaning;—and she had an idea of her duty in life. She was not self-indulgent. She was as hard as an oak post,—but then she was also as trustworthy. No human being liked her;—but she had the good word of a great many human beings. At great cost to her own comfort she had endeavoured to do her duty to her niece, Lizzie Greystock, when Lizzie was homeless. Undoubtedly Lizzie's bed, while it had been spread under her aunt's roof, had not been one of roses; but such as it had been she had endured to occupy it while it served her needs. She had constrained herself to bear her aunt;—but from the moment of her escape she had chosen to reject her aunt altogether. Now her aunt's heavy step was heard upon the stairs! Lizzie also was a brave woman after a certain fashion. She could dare to incur a great danger for an adequate object. But she was too young as yet to have become mistress of that persistent courage which was Lady Linlithgow's peculiar possession.

When the countess entered the drawing-room Lizzie rose upon her legs, but did not come forward from her chair. The old woman was not tall;—but her face was long, and at the same time large, square at the chin and square at the forehead, and gave her almost an appearance of height. Her nose was very prominent, not beaked, but straight and strong, and broad at the bridge, and of a dark-red colour. Her eyes were sharp and grey. Her mouth was large, and over it there was almost beard enough for a young man's moustache. Her chin was firm, and large, and solid. Her hair was still brown, and was only just grizzled in parts. Nothing becomes an old woman like grey hair, but Lady Linlithgow's hair would never be grey. Her appearance on the whole was not prepossessing, but it gave one an idea of honest, real strength. What one saw was not buckram, whalebone, paint, and false hair. It was all human,—hardly feminine, certainly not angelic, with perhaps a hint in the other direction,—but a human body, and not a thing of pads and patches. Lizzie, as she saw her aunt, made up her mind for the combat. Who is there that has lived to be a man or woman, and has not experienced a moment in which a combat has impended, and a call for such sudden courage has been necessary? Alas!—sometimes the combat comes, and the courage is not there. Lady Eustace was not at her ease as she saw her aunt enter the room. 'Oh, come ye in peace, or come ye in war?' she would have said had she dared. Her aunt had sent up her love,—if the message had been delivered aright; but what of love could there be between the two? The countess dashed at once to the matter in hand, making no allusion to Lizzie's ungrateful conduct to herself. 'Lizzie,' she said, 'I've been asked to come to you by Mr. Camperdown. I'll sit down, if you please.'

'Oh, certainly, Aunt Penelope. Mr. Camperdown!'

'Yes;—Mr. Camperdown. You know who he is. He has been with me because I am your nearest relation. So I am, and therefore I have come. I don't like it, I can tell you.'

'As for that, Aunt Penelope, you've done it to please yourself,' said Lizzie, in a tone of insolence with which Lady Linlithgow had been familiar in former days.

'No, I haven't, miss. I haven't come for my own pleasure at all. I have come for the credit of the family, if any good can be done towards saving it. You've got your husband's diamonds locked up somewhere, and you must give them back.'

'My husband's diamonds were my diamonds,' said Lizzie stoutly.

'They are family diamonds, Eustace diamonds, heirlooms, —old property belonging to the Eustaces, just like their estates. Sir Florian didn't give 'em away, and couldn't, and wouldn't if he could. Such things ain't given away in that fashion. It's all nonsense, and you must give them up.'

'Who says so?'

'I say so.'

'That's nothing, Aunt Penelope.'

'Nothing, is it? You'll see. Mr. Camperdown says so. All the world will say so. If you don't take care, you'll find yourself brought into a court of law, my dear, and a jury will say so. That's what it will come to. What good will they do you? You can't sell them;—and as a widow you can't wear 'em. If you marry again, you wouldn't disgrace your husband by going about showing off the Eustace diamonds! But you don't know anything about "proper feelings."'

'I know every bit as much as you do, Aunt Penelope, and I don't want you to teach me.'

'Will you give up the jewels to Mr. Camperdown?'

'No—I won't.'

'Or to the jewellers?'

'No; I won't. I mean to—keep them—for—my child.' Then there came forth a sob, and a tear, and Lizzie's handkerchief was held to her eyes.

'Your child! Wouldn't they be kept properly for him, and for the family, if the jewellers had them? I don't believe you care about your child.'

'Aunt Penelope, you had better take care.'

'I shall say just what I think, Lizzie. You can't frighten me. The fact is, you are disgracing the family you have married into, and as you are my niece——'

'I'm not disgracing anybody. You are disgracing everybody.'

'As you are my niece, I have undertaken to come to you and to tell you that if you don't give 'em up within a week from this time, they'll proceed against you for—stealing 'em!' Lady Linlithgow, as she uttered this terrible threat, bobbed her head at her niece in a manner calculated to add very much to the force of her words. The words, and tone, and gesture combined were, in truth, awful.

'I didn't steal them. My husband gave them to me with his own hands.'

'You wouldn't answer Mr. Camperdown's letters, you know. That alone will condemn you. After that there isn't a word to be said about it;—not a word. Mr. Camperdown is the family lawyer, and when he writes to you letter after letter you take no more notice of him than a—dog!' The old woman was certainly very powerful. The way in which she pronounced that last word did make Lady Eustace ashamed of herself. 'Why didn't you answer his letters, unless you knew you were in the wrong? Of course you knew you were in the wrong.'

'No; I didn't. A woman isn't obliged to answer everything that is written to her.'

'Very well! You just say that before the judge! for you'll have to go before a judge. I tell you, Lizzie Greystock, or Eustace, or whatever your name is, it's downright picking and stealing.* I suppose you want to sell them.'

'I won't stand this, Aunt Penelope!' said Lizzie, rising from her seat.

'You must stand it:—and you'll have to stand worse than that. You don't suppose Mr. Camperdown got me to come here for nothing. If you don't want to be made out to be a thief before all the world——'

'I won't stand it!' shrieked Lizzie. 'You have no business to come here and say such things to me. It's my house.'

'I shall say just what I please.'

'Miss Macnulty, come in.' And Lizzie threw open the door, hardly knowing how the very weak ally whom she now invoked could help her, but driven by the stress of the combat to seek assistance somewhere. Miss Macnulty, who was seated near the door, and who had necessarily heard every word of the conversation, had no alternative but to appear. Of all human beings Lady Linlithgow was to her the most terrible, and yet, after a fashion, she loved the old woman. Miss Macnulty was humble, cowardly, and subservient; but she was not a fool, and she understood the difference between truth and falsehood. She had endured fearful things from Lady Linlithgow; but she knew that there might be more of sound protection in Lady Linlithgow's real wrath than in Lizzie's pretended affection.

'So you àre there, are you?' said the countess.

'Yes;—I am here, Lady Linlithgow.'

'Listening, I suppose. Well;—so much the better. You know well enough, and you can tell her. You ain't a fool, though I suppose you'll be afraid to open your mouth.'

'Julia,' said Lady Eustace, 'will you have the kindness to see that my aunt is shown to her carriage. I cannot stand her violence, and I will go up-stairs.' So saying she made her way very gracefully into the back drawing-room, whence she could escape to her bed-room.

But her aunt fired a last shot at her. 'Unless you do as you're bid, Lizzie, you'll find yourself in prison as sure as eggs!' Then, when her niece was beyond hearing, she turned to Miss Macnulty. 'I suppose you've heard about these diamonds, Macnulty?'

'I know she's got them, Lady Linlithgow.'

'She has no more right to them than you have. I suppose you're afraid to tell her so, lest she should turn you out;—but it's well she should know it. I've done my duty. Never mind about the servant. I'll find my way out of the house.' Neverthe-

less the bell was rung, and the countess was shown to her
carriage with proper consideration.

The two ladies went to the opera, and it was not till after
their return, and just as they were going to bed, that anything
further was said about either the necklace or the visit. Miss
Macnulty would not begin the subject, and Lizzie purposely
postponed it. But not for a moment had it been off Lady
Eustace's mind. She did not care much for music, though she
professed to do so,—and thought that she did. But on this
night, had she at other times been a slave to St. Cecilia, she
would have been free from that thraldom. The old woman's
threats had gone into her very heart's blood. Theft, and
prison, and juries, and judges had been thrown at her head so
violently that she was almost stunned. Could it really be the
case that they would prosecute her for stealing? She was
Lady Eustace, and who but Lady Eustace should have these
diamonds or be allowed to wear them? Nobody could say
that Sir Florian had not given them to her. It could not,
surely, be brought against her as an actual crime that she had
not answered Mr. Camperdown's letters? And yet she was
not sure. Her ideas about law and judicial proceedings were
very vague. Of what was wrong and what was right she
had a distinct notion. She knew well enough that she was
endeavouring to steal the Eustace diamonds; but she did not
in the least know what power there might be in the law to
prevent, or to punish her for the intended theft. She knew
well that the thing was not really her own; but there were, as
she thought, so many points in her favour, that she felt it to
be a cruelty that any one should grudge her the plunder. Was
not she the only Lady Eustace living? As to these threats
from Mr. Camperdown and Lady Linlithgow, she felt certain
they would be used against her whether they were true or
false. She would break her heart should she abandon her
prey and afterwards find that Mr. Camperdown would have
been wholly powerless against her had she held on to it. But
then who would tell her the truth? She was sharp enough to
understand, or at any rate suspicious enough to believe, that

Mr. Mopus would be actuated by no other desire in the matter than that of running up a bill against her. 'My dear,' she said to Miss Macnulty, as they went up-stairs after the opera, 'come into my room a moment. You heard all that my aunt said?'

'I could not help hearing. You told me to stay there, and the door was ajar.'

'I wanted you to hear. Of course what she said was the greatest nonsense in the world.'

'I don't know.'

'When she talked about my being taken to prison for not answering a lawyer's letter, that must be nonsense?'

'I suppose that was.'

'And then she is such a ferocious old termagant,—such an old vulturess. Now isn't she a ferocious old termagant?' Lizzie paused for an answer, desirous that her companion should join her in her enmity against her aunt, but Miss Macnulty was unwilling to say anything against one who had been her protectress, and might, perhaps, be her protectress again. 'You don't mean to say you don't hate her?' said Lizzie. 'If you didn't hate her after all she has done to you, I should despise you. Don't you hate her?'

'I think she's a very upsetting old woman,' said Miss Macnulty.

'Oh, you poor creature! Is that all you dare to say about her?'

'I'm obliged to be a poor creature,' said Miss Macnulty, with a red spot on each of her cheeks.

Lady Eustace understood this, and relented. 'But you needn't be afraid,' she said, 'to tell me what you think.'

'About the diamonds, you mean?'

'Yes; about the diamonds.'

'You have enough without them. I'd give 'em up for peace and quiet.' That was Miss Macnulty's advice.

'No;—I haven't enough;—or nearly enough. I've had to buy ever so many things since my husband died. They've done all they could to be hard to me. They made me pay for

56

the very furniture at Portray.' This wasn't true; but it was true that Lizzie had endeavoured to palm off on the Eustace estate bills for new things which she had ordered for her own country-house. 'I haven't near enough. I am in debt already. People talked as though I were the richest woman in the world; but when it comes to be spent, I ain't rich. Why should I give them up if they're my own?'

'Not if they're your own.'

'If I give you a present and then die, people can't come and take it away afterwards because I didn't put it into my will. There'd be no making presents like that at all.' This Lizzie said with an evident conviction in the strength of her argument.

'But this necklace is so very valuable.'

'That can't make a difference. If a thing is a man's own he can give it away;—not a house, or a farm, or a wood, or anything like that; but a thing that he can carry about with him,—of course he can give it away.'

'But perhaps Sir Florian didn't mean to give it for always,' suggested Miss Macnulty.

'But perhaps he did. He told me that they were mine, and I shall keep them. So that's the end of it. You can go to bed now.' And Miss Macnulty went to bed.

Lizzie, as she sat thinking of it, owned to herself that no help was to be expected in that quarter. She was not angry with Miss Macnulty, who was, almost of necessity, a poor creature. But she was convinced more strongly than ever that some friend was necessary to her who should not be a poor creature. Lord Fawn, though a peer, was a poor creature. Frank Greystock she believed to be as strong as a house.

CHAPTER VII
*Mr. Burke's Speeches**

LUCY MORRIS had been told by Lady Fawn that,—in point of fact that, being a governess, she ought to give over falling in love with Frank Greystock, and she had not liked it. Lady Fawn no doubt had used words less abrupt,—had probably used but few words, and had expressed her meaning chiefly by little winks, and shakings of her head, and small gestures of her hands, and had ended by a kiss,—in all of which she had intended to mingle mercy with justice,* and had, in truth, been full of love. Nevertheless, Lucy had not liked it. No girl likes to be warned against falling in love, whether the warning be needed or not needed. In this case Lucy knew very well that the caution was too late. It might be all very well for Lady Fawn to decide that her governess should not receive visits from a lover in her house;—and then the governess

58

might decide whether, in those circumstances, she would remain or go away; but Lady Fawn could have no right to tell her governess not to be in love. All this Lucy said to herself over and over again, and yet she knew that Lady Fawn had treated her well. The old woman had kissed her, and purred over her, and praised her, and had really loved her. As a matter of course, Lucy was not entitled to have a lover. Lucy knew that well enough. As she walked alone among the shrubs she made arguments in defence of Lady Fawn as against herself. And yet at every other minute she would blaze up into a grand wrath, and picture to herself a scene in which she would tell Lady Fawn boldly that as her lover had been banished from Fawn Court, she, Lucy, would remain there no longer. There were but two objections to this course. The first was that Frank Greystock was not her lover; and the second, that on leaving Fawn Court she would not know whither to betake herself. It was understood by everybody that she was never to leave Fawn Court till an unexceptionable home should be found for her, either with the Hittaways or elsewhere. Lady Fawn would no more allow her to go away, depending for her future on the mere chance of some promiscuous engagement, than she would have turned one of her own daughters out of the house in the same forlorn condition. Lady Fawn was a tower of strength to Lucy. But then a tower of strength may at any moment become a dungeon.

Frank Greystock was not her lover. Ah,—there was the worst of it all! She had given her heart and had got nothing in return. She conned it all over in her own mind, striving to ascertain whether there was any real cause for shame to her in her own conduct. Had she been unmaidenly? Had she been too forward with her heart? Had it been extracted from her, as women's hearts are extracted, by efforts on the man's part; or had she simply chucked it away from her to the first comer? Then she remembered certain scenes at the deanery, words that had been spoken, looks that had been turned upon her, a pressure of the hand late at night, a little whisper, a ribbon that had been begged, a flower that had been given;—

and once, once——; then there came a burning blush upon her cheek that there should have been so much, and yet so little that was of avail. She had no right to say to any one that the man was her lover. She had no right to assure herself that he was her lover. But she knew that some wrong was done her in that he was not her lover.

Of the importance of her own self as a living thing with a heart to suffer and a soul to endure, she thought enough. She believed in herself, thinking of herself, that should it ever be her lot to be a man's wife, she would be to him a true, loving friend and companion, living in his joys, and fighting, if it were necessary, down to the stumps of her nails in his interests. But of what she had to give over and above her heart and intellect she never thought at all. Of personal beauty she had very little appreciation even in others. The form and face of Lady Eustace, which indeed were very lovely, were distasteful to her; whereas she delighted to look upon the broad, plain, colourless countenance of Lydia Fawn, who was endeared to her by frank good humour and an unselfish disposition. In regard to men she had never asked herself the question whether this man was handsome or that man ugly. Of Frank Greystock she knew that his face was full of quick intellect; and of Lord Fawn she knew that he bore no outward index of mind. One man she not only loved, but could not help loving; the other man, as regarded that sort of sympathy which marriage should recognise, must always have been worlds asunder from her. She knew that men demand that women shall possess beauty, and she certainly had never thought of herself as beautiful; but it did not occur to her that on that account she was doomed to fail. She was too strong-hearted for any such fear. She did not think much of these things, but felt herself to be so far endowed as to be fit to be the wife of such a man as Frank Greystock. She was a proud, stout, self-confident, but still modest, little woman, too fond of truth to tell lies of herself even to herself. She was possessed of a great power of sympathy, genial, very social, greatly given to the mirth of conversation,—though in talking she would listen much and say but little. She was keenly alive to humour, and had at her command a great fund of laughter, which would illumine her whole face without producing a sound from her mouth. She knew herself to be too good to be a governess for life;—and yet how could it be otherwise with her?

Lady Linlithgow's visit to her niece had been made on a Thursday, and on that same evening Frank Greystock had asked his question in the House of Commons,—or rather had made his speech about the Sawab of Mygawb. We all know the meaning of such speeches. Had not Frank belonged to the party that was out, and had not the resistance to the Sawab's claim come from the party that was in, Frank would not probably have cared much about the prince. We may be sure that he would not have troubled himself to read a line of that very dull and long pamphlet of which he had to make himself master before he could venture to stir in the matter, had not the road of Opposition been open to him in that direction. But what exertion will not a politician make with the view of getting the point of his lance within the joints of his enemies' harness? Frank made his speech, and made it very well. It was just the case for a lawyer, admitting that kind of advocacy which it is a lawyer's business to practise. The Indian minister of the day, Lord Fawn's chief, had determined, after much anxious consideration, that it was his duty to resist the claim; and then, for resisting it he was attacked. Had he yielded to the claim, the attack would have been as venomous, and very probably would have come from the same quarter. No blame by such an assertion is cast upon the young Conservative aspirant for party honours. It is thus the war is waged. Frank Greystock took up the Sawab's case, and would have drawn mingled tears and indignation from his hearers, had not his hearers all known the conditions of the contest. On neither side did the hearers care much for the Sawab's claims, but they felt that Greystock was making good his own claims to some future reward from his party. He was very hard upon the minister,—and he was hard also upon Lord Fawn, stating that the cruelty of Government ascendancy had never been put forward as a doctrine in plainer terms than those which had been used in 'another place' in reference to the wrongs of this poor ill-used native chieftain. This was very grievous to Lord Fawn, who had personally desired to favour the ill-used chieftain;—and harder again because he and Greystock were intimate with each other. He felt the thing keenly, and was full of his grievance when, in accordance with his custom, he came down to Fawn Court on the Saturday evening.

The Fawn family, which consisted entirely of women, dined early. On Saturdays, when his lordship would come down, a dinner was prepared for him alone. On Sundays they all dined together at three o'clock. On Sunday evening Lord Fawn would return to town to prepare himself for his Monday's work. Perhaps, also, he disliked the sermon which Lady Fawn always read to the assembled household at nine o'clock on Sunday evening. On this Saturday he came out into the grounds after dinner, where the oldest unmarried daughter, the present Miss Fawn, was walking with Lucy Morris. It was almost a summer evening;—so much so, that some of the party had been sitting on the garden benches, and four of the girls were still playing croquet on the lawn, though there was hardly light enough to see the balls. Miss Fawn had already told Lucy that her brother was very angry with Mr. Greystock. Now, Lucy's sympathies were all with Frank and the Sawab. She had endeavoured, indeed, and had partially succeeded, in perverting the Under-Secretary. Nor did she now intend to change her opinions, although all the Fawn girls, and Lady Fawn, were against her. When a brother or a son is an Under-Secretary of State, sisters and mothers will constantly be on the side of the Government, so far as that Under-Secretary's office is concerned.

'Upon my word, Frederic,' said Augusta Fawn, 'I do think Mr. Greystock was too bad.'

'There's nothing these fellows won't say or do,' exclaimed Lord Fawn. 'I can't understand it myself. When I've been in opposition, I never did that kind of thing.'

'I wonder whether it was because he is angry with mamma,' said Miss Fawn. Everybody who knew the Fawns knew that Augusta Fawn was not clever, and that she would occasionally say the very thing that ought not to be said.

'Oh, dear no,' said the Under-Secretary, who could not endure the idea that the weak women-kind of his family should have, in any way, an influence on the august doings of Parliament.

'You know mamma did——'

'Nothing of that kind at all,' said his lordship, putting down his sister with great authority. 'Mr. Greystock is simply not an honest politician. That is about the whole of it. He chose to attack me because there was an opportunity. There isn't a man in either House who cares for such things, personally, less than I do;'—had his lordship said 'more than he did,' he might, perhaps, have been correct;—'but I can't bear the feeling. The fact is, a lawyer never understands what is and what is not fair fighting.'

Lucy felt her face tingling with heat, and was preparing to say a word in defence of that special lawyer, when Lady Fawn's voice was heard from the drawing-room window. 'Come in, girls. It's nine o'clock.' In that house Lady Fawn reigned supreme, and no one ever doubted, for a moment, as to obedience. The clicking of the balls ceased, and those who were walking immediately turned their faces to the drawing-room window. But Lord Fawn, who was not one of the girls, took another turn by himself, thinking of the wrongs he had endured.

'Frederic is so angry about Mr. Greystock,' said Augusta, as soon as they were seated.

'I do feel that it was provoking,' said the second sister.

'And considering that Mr. Greystock has so often been here, I don't think it was kind,' said the third.

Lydia did not speak, but could not refrain from glancing her eyes at Lucy's face. 'I believe everything is considered fair in Parliament,' said Lady Fawn.

Then Lord Fawn, who had heard the last words, entered

through the window. 'I don't know about that, mother,' said he. 'Gentleman-like conduct is the same everywhere. There are things that may be said and there are things which may not. Mr. Greystock has altogether gone beyond the usual limits, and I shall take care that he knows my opinion.'

'You are not going to quarrel with the man?' asked the mother.

'I am not going to fight him, if you mean that; but I shall let him know that I think that he has transgressed.' This his lordship said with that haughty superiority which a man may generally display with safety among the women of his own family.

Lucy had borne a great deal, knowing well that it was better that she should bear such injury in silence;—but there was a point beyond which she could not endure it. It was intolerable to her that Mr. Greystock's character as a gentleman should be impugned before all the ladies of the family, every one of whom did, in fact, know her liking for the man. And then it seemed to her that she could rush into the battle, giving a side blow at his lordship on behalf of his absent antagonist, but appearing to fight for the Sawab. There had been a time when the poor Sawab was in favour at Fawn Court. 'I think Mr. Greystock was right to say all he could for the prince. If he took up the cause, he was bound to make the best of it.' She spoke with energy and with a heightened colour; and Lady Fawn hearing her, shook her head at her.

'Did you read Mr. Greystock's speech, Miss Morris?' asked Lord Fawn.

'Every word of it, in the "Times."'

'And you understood his allusion to what I had been called upon to say in the House of Lords on behalf of the Government?'

'I suppose I did. It did not seem to be difficult to understand.'

'I do think Mr. Greystock should have abstained from attacking Frederic,' said Augusta.

'It was not—not quite the thing that we are accustomed to,' said Lord Fawn.

'Of course I don't know about that,' said Lucy. 'I think the prince is being used very ill,—that he is being deprived of his own property,—that he is kept out of his rights, just because he is weak, and I am very glad that there is some one to speak up for him.'

'My dear Lucy,' said Lady Fawn, 'if you discuss politics with Lord Fawn, you'll get the worst of it.'

'I don't at all object to Miss Morris's views about the Sawab,' said the Under-Secretary generously. 'There is a great deal to be said on both sides. I know of old that Miss Morris is a great friend of the Sawab.'

'You used to be his friend too,' said Lucy.

'I felt for him,—and do feel for him. All that is very well. I ask no one to agree with me on the question itself. I only say that Mr. Greystock's mode of treating it was unbecoming.'

'I think it was the very best speech I ever read in my life,' said Lucy, with headlong energy and heightened colour.

'Then, Miss Morris, you and I have very different opinions about speeches,' said Lord Fawn, with severity. 'You have, probably, never read Burke's speeches.'

'And I don't want to read them,' said Lucy.

'That is another question,' said Lord Fawn; and his tone and manner were very severe indeed.

'We are talking about speeches in Parliament,' said Lucy. Poor Lucy! She knew quite as well as did Lord Fawn that Burke had been a House of Commons orator; but in her impatience, and from absence of the habit of argument, she omitted to explain that she was talking about the speeches of the day.

Lord Fawn held up his hands, and put his head a little on one side. 'My dear Lucy,' said Lady Fawn, 'you are showing your ignorance. Where do you suppose that Mr. Burke's speeches were made?'

'Of course I know they were made in Parliament,' said Lucy, almost in tears.

'If Miss Morris means that Burke's greatest efforts were not made in Parliament,—that his speech to the electors of

Bristol, for instance, and his opening address on the trial of Warren Hastings,* were, upon the whole, superior to——'

'I didn't mean anything at all,' said Lucy.'

'Lord Fawn is trying to help you, my dear,' said Lady Fawn.

'I don't want to be helped,' said Lucy. 'I only mean that I thought Mr. Greystock's speech as good as it could possibly be. There wasn't a word in it that didn't seem to me to be just what it ought to be. I do think that they are ill-treating that poor Indian prince, and I am very glad that somebody has had the courage to get up and say so.'

No doubt it would have been better that Lucy should have held her tongue. Had she simply been upholding against an opponent a political speaker whose speech she had read with pleasure, she might have held her own in the argument against the whole Fawn family. She was a favourite with them all, and even the Under-Secretary would not have been hard upon her. But there had been more than this for poor Lucy to do. Her heart was so truly concerned in the matter, that she could not refrain herself from resenting an attack on the man she loved. She had allowed herself to be carried into superlatives, and had almost been uncourteous to Lord Fawn. 'My dear,' said Lady Fawn, 'we won't say anything more upon the subject.' Lord Fawn took up a book. Lady Fawn busied herself in her knitting. Lydia assumed a look of unhappiness, as though something very sad had occurred. Augusta addressed a question to her brother in a tone which plainly indicated a feeling on her part that her brother had been ill-used and was entitled to special consideration. Lucy sat silent and still, and then left the room with a hurried step. Lydia at once rose to follow her, but was stopped by her mother. 'You had better leave her alone just at present, my dear,' said Lady Fawn.

'I did not know that Miss Morris was so particularly interested in Mr. Greystock,' said Lord Fawn.

'She has known him since she was a child,' said his mother.

About an hour afterwards Lady Fawn went up-stairs and found Lucy sitting all alone in the still so-called school-room.

She had no candle, and had made no pretence to do anything since she had left the room downstairs. In the interval family prayers had been read, and Lucy's absence was unusual and contrary to rule. 'Lucy, my dear, why are you sitting here?' said Lady Fawn.

'Because I am unhappy.'

'What makes you unhappy, Lucy?'

'I don't know. I would rather you didn't ask me. I suppose I behaved badly down-stairs.'

'My son would forgive you in a moment if you asked him.'

'No;—certainly not. I can beg your pardon, Lady Fawn, but not his. Of course I had no right to talk about speeches, and politics, and this prince in your drawing-room.'

'Lucy, you astonish me.'

'But it is so. Dear Lady Fawn, don't look like that. I know how good you are to me. I know you let me do things which other governesses mayn't do;—and say things; but still I am a governess, and I know I misbehaved—to you.' Then Lucy burst into tears.

Lady Fawn, in whose bosom there was no stony corner or morsel of hard iron, was softened at once. 'My dear, you are more like another daughter to me than anything else.'

'Dear Lady Fawn!'

'But it makes me unhappy when I see your mind engaged about Mr. Greystock. There is the truth, Lucy. You should not think of Mr. Greystock. Mr. Greystock is a man who has his way to make in the world, and could not marry you, even if, under other circumstances, he would wish to do so. You know how frank I am with you, giving you credit for honest, sound good sense. To me and to my girls, who know you as a lady, you are as dear a friend as though you were,—were anything you may please to think. Lucy Morris is to us our own dear, dear little friend Lucy. But Mr. Greystock, who is a Member of Parliament, could not marry a governess.'

'But I love him so dearly,' said Lucy, getting up from her chair, 'that his slightest word is to me more than all the words of all the world beside! It is no use, Lady Fawn. I do love him, and I don't mean to try to give it up!' Lady Fawn stood silent for a moment, and then suggested that it would be better for them both to go to bed. During that minute she had been unable to decide what she had better say or do in the present emergency.

CHAPTER VIII
The conquering hero comes

THE reader will perhaps remember that when Lizzie Eustace was told that her aunt was down-stairs Frank Greystock was with her, and that he promised to return on the following day to hear the result of the interview. Had Lady Linlithgow not come at that very moment Frank would probably have asked his rich cousin to be his wife. She had told him that she was solitary and unhappy; and after that what else could he have done but ask her to be his wife? The old countess, however, arrived, and interrupted him. He went away abruptly, promising to come on the morrow;—but on the morrow he never came. It was a Friday, and Lizzie remained at home for him the whole morning. When four o'clock was passed she knew that he would be at the House. But still she did not stir. And she contrived that Miss Macnulty should be absent the entire day. Miss Macnulty was even made to go to the play by herself in the evening. But her absence was of no service. Frank Greystock came not; and at eleven at night Lizzie swore to herself that should he ever come again, he should come in vain. Nevertheless, through the whole of Saturday she expected him with more or less of confidence, and on the Sunday morning she was still well-inclined towards him. It might be that he would come on that day. She could understand that a man with his hands so full of business, as were those of her cousin Frank, should find himself unable to keep an appointment. Nor would there be fair ground for permanent anger with such a one, even should he forget an appointment.

But surely he would come on the Sunday! She had been quite sure that the offer was about to be made when that odious old harridan had come in and disturbed everything. Indeed, the offer had been all but made. She had felt the premonitory flutter, had asked herself the important question,—and had answered it. She had told herself that the thing would do. Frank was not the exact hero that her fancy had painted,—but he was sufficiently heroic. Everybody said that he would work his way up to the top of the tree, and become a rich man. At any rate she had resolved;—and then Lady Linlithgow had come in! Surely he would come on the Sunday.

He did not come on the Sunday, but Lord Fawn did come. Immediately after morning church Lord Fawn declared his intention of returning at once from Fawn Court to town. He was very silent at breakfast, and his sisters surmised that he was still angry with poor Lucy. Lucy, too, was unlike herself, —was silent, sad, and oppressed. Lady Fawn was serious, and almost solemn;—so that there was little even of holy mirth at Fawn Court on that Sunday morning. The whole family, however, went to church, and immediately on their return Lord Fawn expressed his intention of returning to town. All the sisters felt that an injury had been done to them by Lucy. It was only on Sundays that their dinner-table was graced by the male member of the family, and now he was driven away. 'I am sorry that you are going to desert us, Frederic,' said Lady Fawn. Lord Fawn muttered something as to absolute necessity, and went. The afternoon was very dreary at Fawn Court. Nothing was said on the subject; but there was still the feeling that Lucy had offended. At four o'clock on that Sunday afternoon Lord Fawn was closeted with Lady Eustace.

The 'closeting' consisted simply in the fact that Miss Macnulty was not present. Lizzie fully appreciated the pleasure, and utility, and general convenience of having a companion, but she had no scruple whatever in obtaining absolute freedom for herself when she desired it. 'My dear,' she would say, 'the best friends in the world shouldn't always be together; should they? Wouldn't you like to go to the Horticultural?'

Then Miss Macnulty would go to the Horticultural,—or else up into her own bed-room. When Lizzie was beginning to wax wrathful again because Frank Greystock did not come Lord Fawn made his appearance. 'How kind this is,' said Lizzie. 'I thought you were always at Richmond on Sundays.'

'I have just come up from my mother's,' said Lord Fawn, twiddling his hat. Then Lizzie, with a pretty eagerness, asked after Lady Fawn and the girls, and her dear little friend Lucy Morris. Lizzie could be very prettily eager when she pleased. She leaned forward her face as she asked her questions, and threw back her loose lustrous lock of hair, with her long lithe fingers covered with diamonds,—the diamonds, these, which Sir Florian had really given her, or which she had procured from Mr. Benjamin in the clever manner described in the opening chapter. 'They are all quite well, thank you,' said Lord Fawn. 'I believe Miss Morris is quite well, though she was a little out of sorts last night.'

'She is not ill, I hope,' said Lizzie, bringing the lustrous lock forward again.

'In her temper, I mean,' said Lord Fawn.

'Indeed! I hope Miss Lucy is not forgetting herself. That would be very sad, after the great kindness she has received.' Lord Fawn said that it would be very sad, and then put his hat down upon the floor. It came upon Lizzie at that moment, as by a flash of lightning,—by an electric message delivered to her intellect by that movement of the hat,—that she might be sure of Lord Fawn if she chose to take him. On Friday she might have been sure of Frank,—only that Lady Linlithgow came in the way. But now she did not feel at all sure of Frank. Lord Fawn was at any rate a peer. She had heard that he was a poor peer,—but a peer, she thought, can't be altogether poor. And though he was a stupid owl,—she did not hesitate to acknowledge to herself that he was as stupid as an owl,—he had a position. He was one of the Government, and his wife would, no doubt, be able to go anywhere. It was becoming essential to her that she should marry. Even though her husband should give up the diamonds, she would not in such case incur the disgrace of surrendering them herself. She would have kept them till she had ceased to be a Eustace. Frank had certainly meant it on that Thursday afternoon;— but surely he would have been in Mount Street before this if he had not changed his mind. We all know that a bird in the hand is worth two in the bush.* 'I have been at Fawn Court once or twice,' said Lizzie, with her sweetest grace, 'and I always think it a model of real family happiness.'

'I hope you may be there very often,' said Lord Fawn.

'Ah, I have no right to intrude myself often on your mother, Lord Fawn.'

There could hardly be a better opening than this for him had he chosen to accept it. But it was not thus that he had arranged it,—for he had made his arrangements. 'There would be no feeling of that kind, I am sure,' he said. And then he was silent. How was he to deploy himself on the ground before him so as to make the strategy which he had prepared answer the occasion of the day? 'Lady Eustace,' he said, 'I don't know what your views of life may be.'

'I have a child, you know, to bring up.'

'Ah, yes;—that gives a great interest, of course.'

'He will inherit a very large fortune, Lord Fawn;—too large, I fear, to be of service to a youth of one-and-twenty; and I must endeavour to fit him for the possession of it. That is,—and always must be the chief object of my existence.' Then she felt that she had said too much. He was just the man who would be fool enough to believe her. 'Not but what it is hard to do it. A mother can of course devote herself to her child;—but when a portion of the devotion must be given to the preservation of material interests there is less of tenderness in it. Don't you think so?'

'No doubt,' said Lord Fawn;—'no doubt.' But he had not followed her, and was still thinking of his own strategy. 'It's a comfort, of course, to know that one's child is provided for.'

'Oh, yes;—but they tell me the poor little dear will have forty thousand a year when he's of age; and when I look at him in his little bed, and press him in my arms, and think of all that money, I almost wish that his father had been a poor plain gentleman.' Then the handkerchief was put to her eyes, and Lord Fawn had a moment in which to collect himself.

'Ah!—I myself am a poor man;—for my rank I mean.'

'A man with your position, Lord Fawn, and your talents and genius for business, can never be poor.'

'My father's property was all Irish,* you know.'

'Was it indeed?'

'And he was an Irish peer,* till Lord Melbourne gave him an English peerage.'

'An Irish peer, was he?' Lizzie understood nothing of this, but presumed that an Irish peer was a peer who had not sufficient money to live upon. Lord Fawn, however, was endeavouring to describe his own history in as few words as possible.

'He was then made Lord Fawn of Richmond, in the peerage of the United Kingdom. Fawn Court, you know, belonged to my mother's father before my mother's marriage. The property in Ireland is still mine, but there's no place on it.'*

'Indeed!'

'There was a house, but my father allowed it to tumble down. It's in Tipperary;*—not at all a desirable country to live in.'

'Oh, dear, no! Don't they murder the people?'

'It's about five thousand a year, and out of that my mother has half for her life.'

'What an excellent family arrangement,' said Lizzie. There was so long a pause made between each statement that she was forced to make some reply.

'You see, for a peer, the fortune is very small indeed.'

'But then you have a salary;—don't you?'

'At present I have;—but no one can tell how long that may last.'

'I'm sure it's for everybody's good that it should go on for ever so many years,' said Lizzie.

'Thank you,' said Lord Fawn. 'I'm afraid, however, there

are a great many people who don't think so. Your cousin Greystock would do anything on earth to turn us out.'

'Luckily, my cousin Frank has not much power,' said Lizzie. And in saying it she threw into her tone, and into her countenance, a certain amount of contempt for Frank as a man and as a politician, which was pleasant to Lord Fawn.

'Now,' said he, 'I have told you everything about myself which I was bound, as a man of honour, to tell before—I—I—I——. In short you know what I mean.'

'Oh, Lord Fawn!'

'I have told you everything. I owe no money, but I could not afford to marry a wife without an income. I admire you more than any woman I ever saw. I love you with all my heart.' He was now standing upright before her, with the fingers of his right hand touching his left breast, and there was something almost of dignity in his gesture and demeanour. 'It may be that you are determined never to marry again. I can only say that if you will trust yourself to me,—yourself and your child,—I will do my duty truly by you both, and will make your happiness the chief object of my existence.' When she had listened to him thus far, of course she must accept him; but he was by no means aware of that. She sat silent, with her hands folded on her breast, looking down upon the ground; but he did not as yet attempt to seat himself by her. 'Lady Eustace,' he continued, 'may I venture to entertain a hope?'

'May I not have an hour to think of it?' said Lizzie, just venturing to turn a glance of her eye upon his face.

'Oh, certainly. I will call again whenever you may bid me.'

Now she was silent for two or three minutes, during which he still stood over her. But he had dropped his hand from his breast, and had stooped, and picked up his hat ready for his departure. Was he to come again on Monday, or Tuesday, or Wednesday? Let her tell him that and he would go. He doubtless reflected that Wednesday would suit him best, because there would be no House. But Lizzie was too magnanimous for this. 'Lord Fawn,' she said, rising, 'you have paid me the greatest compliment that a man can pay a woman.

Coming from you it is doubly precious; first, because of your character; and secondly——'

'Why secondly?'

'Secondly, because I can love you.' This was said in her lowest whisper, and then she moved towards him gently, and almost laid her head upon his breast. Of course he put his arm round her waist,—but it was first necessary that he should once more disembarrass himself of his hat,—and then her head was upon his breast. 'Dearest Lizzie!' he said.

'Dearest Frederic!' she murmured.

'I shall write to my mother to-night,' he said.

'Do, do;—dear Frederic.'

'And she will come to you at once, I am sure.'

'I will receive her and love her as a mother,' said Lizzie, with all her energy. Then he kissed her again,—her forehead and her lips,—and took his leave, promising to be with her at any rate on Wednesday.

'Lady Fawn!' she said to herself. The name did not sound so well as that of Lady Eustace. But it is much to be a wife; and more to be a peeress.

CHAPTER IX

Showing what the Miss Fawns said, and what
Mrs. Hittaway thought

In the way of duty Lord Fawn was a Hercules,—not, indeed, 'climbing trees in the Hesperides,*' but achieving enterprises which, to other men, if not impossible, would have been so unpalatable as to have been put aside as impracticable. On the Monday morning, after he was accepted by Lady Eustace, he was with his mother at Fawn Court before he went down to the India Office.

He had at least been very honest in the description he had given of his own circumstances to the lady whom he intended to marry. He had told her the exact truth; and though she, with all her cleverness, had not been able to realise the facts when related to her so suddenly, still enough had been said to make it quite clear that, when details of business should here-after be discussed in a less hurried manner, he would be able to say that he had explained all his circumstances before he had made his offer. And he had been careful, too, as to her affairs. He had ascertained that her late husband had certainly settled upon her for life an estate worth four thousand a year. He knew, also, that eight thousand pounds had been left her, but of that he took no account. It might be probable that she had spent it. If any of it were left, it would be a godsend. Lord Fawn thought a great deal about money. Being a poor man, filling a place fit only for rich men, he had been driven to think of money, and had become self-denying and parsi-monious,—perhaps we may say hungry and close-fisted. Such a condition of character is the natural consequence of such a position. There is, probably, no man who becomes naturally so hard in regard to money as he who is bound to live among rich men, who is not rich himself, and who is yet honest. The weight of the work of life in these circumstances is so crushing, requires such continued thought, and makes itself so continually felt, that the mind of the sufferer is never free from the contamination of sixpences. Of such a one it is not fair to judge as of other men with similar incomes. Lord Fawn had declared to his future bride that he had half five thousand a year to spend,—or the half, rather, of such actual income as might be got in from an estate presumed to give five thousand a year,—and it may be said that an unmarried gentleman ought not to be poor with such an income. But Lord Fawn unfortunately was a lord, unfortunately was a landlord, unfortunately was an Irish landlord. Let him be as careful as he might with his sixpences, his pounds would fly from him, or, as might, perhaps, be better said, could not be made to fly to him. He was very careful with his sixpences, and was always thinking, not exactly how he might make two ends meet, but how to reconcile the strictest personal economy with the proper bearing of an English nobleman.

Such a man almost naturally looks to marriage as an

assistance in the dreary fight. It soon becomes clear to him that he cannot marry without money, and he learns to think that heiresses have been invented exactly to suit his case. He is conscious of having been subjected to hardship by Fortune, and regards female wealth as his legitimate mode of escape from it. He has got himself, his position, and, perhaps, his title to dispose of, and they are surely worth so much per annum. As for giving anything away, that is out of the question. He has not been so placed as to be able to give. But, being an honest man, he will, if possible, make a fair bargain. Lord Fawn was certainly an honest man, and he had been endeavouring for the last six or seven years to make a fair bargain. But then it is so hard to decide what is fair. Who is to tell a Lord Fawn how much per annum he ought to regard himself as worth? He had, on one or two occasions, asked a high price, but no previous bargain had been made. No doubt he had come down a little in his demand in suggesting a matrimonial arrangement to a widow with a child, and with only four thousand a year. Whether or no that income was hers in perpetuity, or only for life, he had not positively known when he made his offer. The will made by Sir Florian Eustace did not refer to the property at all. In the natural course of things, the widow would only have a life-interest in the income. Why should Sir Florian make away, in perpetuity, with his family property? Nevertheless, there had been a rumour abroad that Sir Florian had been very generous; that the Scotch estate was to go to a second son in the event of there being a second son;—but that otherwise it was to be at the widow's own disposal. No doubt, had Lord Fawn been persistent, he might have found out the exact truth. He had, however, calculated that he could afford to accept even the life-income. If more should come of it, so much the better for him. He might, at any rate, so arrange the family matters, that his heir, should he have one, should not at his death be called upon to pay something more than half the proceeds of the family property to his mother,—as was now done by himself.

Lord Fawn breakfasted at Fawn Court on the Monday, and his mother sat at the table with him, pouring out his tea. 'Oh, Frederic,' she said, 'it is so important!'

'Just so;—very important indeed. I should like you to call and see her either to-day or to-morrow.'

'That's of course.'

'And you had better get her down here.'

'I don't know that she'll come. Ought I to ask the little boy?'

'Certainly,' said Lord Fawn, as he put a spoonful of egg into his mouth; 'certainly.'

'And Miss Macnulty?'

'No; I don't see that at all. I'm not going to marry Miss Macnulty. The child, of course, must be one of us.'

'And what is the income, Frederic?'

'Four thousand a year. Something more, nominally, but four thousand to spend.'

'You are sure about that?'

'Quite sure.'

'And for ever?'

'I believe so. Of that I am not sure.'

'It makes a great difference, Frederic.'

'A very great difference indeed. I think it is her own. But, at any rate, she is much younger than I am, and there need be no settlement out of my property. That is the great thing. Don't you think she's—nice?'

'She is very lovely.'

'And clever?'

'Certainly very clever. I hope she is not self-willed, Frederic.'

'If she is, we must try and balance it,' said Lord Fawn, with a little smile. But, in truth, he had thought nothing about any such quality as that to which his mother now referred. The lady had an income. That was the first and most indispensable consideration. She was fairly well-born, was a lady, and was beautiful. In doing Lord Fawn justice, we must allow that, in all his attempted matrimonial speculations, some amount of feminine loveliness had been combined with feminine wealth. He had for two years been a suitor of Violet Effingham, who was the acknowledged beauty of the day,—of Violet Effingham who, at the present time, was the wife of Lord Chiltern; and he had offered himself thrice to Madame Max Goesler, who was reputed to be as rich as she was beautiful. In either case, the fortune would have been greater than that which he would now win, and the money would certainly have been for ever. But in these attempts he had failed; and Lord Fawn was not a man to think himself ill-used because he did not get the first good thing for which he asked.

'I suppose I may tell the girls?' said Lady Fawn.

'Yes;—when I am gone. I must be off now, only I could not bear not to come and see you.'

'It was so like you, Frederic.'

'And you'll go to-day?'

'Yes; if you wish it,—certainly.'

'Go up in the carriage, you know, and take one of the girls with you. I would not take more than one. Augusta will be the best. You'll see Clara, I suppose.' Clara was the married sister, Mrs. Hittaway.

'If you wish it.'

'She had better call too,—say on Thursday. It's quite as well that it should be known. I sha'n't choose to have more delay than can be avoided. Well;—I believe that's all.'

'I hope she'll be a good wife to you, Frederic.'

'I don't see why she shouldn't. Good-bye, mother. Tell the girls I will see them next Saturday.' He didn't see why this woman he was about to marry should not be a good wife to him! And yet he knew nothing about her, and had not taken the slightest trouble to make inquiry. That she was pretty he could see; that she was clever he could understand; that she lived in Mount Street was a fact; her parentage was known to him;—that she was the undoubted mistress of a large income was beyond dispute. But, for aught he knew, she might be afflicted by every vice to which a woman can be subject. In truth, she was afflicted by so many, that the addition of all the others could hardly have made her worse than she was. She had never sacrificed her beauty to a lover,—she had never sacrificed anything to anybody,—nor did she drink. It would be difficult, perhaps, to say anything else in her favour; and yet Lord Fawn was quite content to marry her, not having seen any reason why she should not make a good wife! Nor had Sir Florian seen any reason;—but she had broken Sir Florian's heart.

When the girls heard the news, they were half frightened and half delighted. Lady Fawn and her daughters lived very much out of the world. They also were poor rich people,—if such a term may be used,—and did not go much into society. There was a butler kept at Fawn Court, and a boy in buttons, and two gardeners, and a man to look after the cows, and a carriage and horses, and a fat coachman. There was a cook and a scullery maid, and two lady's maids,—who had to make the dresses,—and two housemaids and a dairymaid. There was a large old brick house to be kept in order, and handsome grounds with old trees. There was, as we know, a governess, and there were seven unmarried daughters. With such encumbrances, and an income altogether not exceeding three thousand pounds per annum, Lady Fawn could not be rich. And yet who would say that an old lady and her daughters could be poor with three thousand pounds a year to spend? It may be taken almost as a rule by the unennobled ones of this country, that the sudden possession of a title would at once raise the price of every article consumed twenty per cent. Mutton that before cost ninepence would cost tenpence a pound, and the mouths to be fed would demand more meat. The chest of tea would run out quicker. The labourer's work, which for the farmer is ten hours a day, for the squire nine, is for the peer only eight. Miss Jones, when she becomes Lady de Jongh, does not pay less than threepence apiece for each 'my lady' with which her ear is tickled. Even the baronet when he becomes a lord has to curtail his purchases, because of increased price, unless he be very wide awake to the affairs of the world. Old Lady Fawn, who would not on any account have owed a shilling which she could not pay, and who, in the midst of her economies, was not close-fisted, knew very well what she could do and what she could not. The old family carriage and the two lady's maids were there,—as necessaries of life; but London society was not within her reach. It was, therefore, the case that they had not heard very much about Lizzie Eustace. But they had heard something. 'I hope she won't be too fond of going out,' said Amelia, the second girl.

'Or extravagant,' said Georgina, the third.

'There was some story of her being terribly in debt when she married Sir Florian Eustace,' said Diana, the fourth.

'Frederic will be sure to see to that,' said Augusta, the eldest.

'She is very beautiful,' said Lydia, the fifth.

'And clever,' said Cecilia, the sixth.

'Beauty and cleverness won't make a good wife,' said Amelia, who was the wise one of the family.

'Frederic will be sure to see that she doesn't go wrong,' said Augusta, who was not wise.

Then Lucy Morris entered the room with Nina, the cadette of the family. 'Oh, Nina, what do you think?' said Lydia.

'My dear!' said Lady Fawn, putting up her hand and stopping further indiscreet speech.

'Oh, mamma, what is it?' asked the cadette.

'Surely Lucy may be told,' said Lydia.

'Well, yes; Lucy may be told certainly. There can be no reason why Lucy should not know all that concerns our family;—and the more so as she has been for many years intimate with the lady. My dear, my son is going to be married to Lady Eustace.'

'Lord Fawn going to marry Lizzie!' said Lucy Morris, in a tone which certainly did not express unmingled satisfaction.

'Unless you forbid the banns,'*said Diana.

'Is there any reason why he should not?' said Lady Fawn.

'Oh no;—only it seems so odd. I didn't know that they knew each other;—not well, that is. And then——'

'Then what, my dear?'

'It seems odd;—that's all. It's all very nice, I dare say, and I'm sure I hope they will be happy.' Lady Fawn, however, was displeased, and did not speak to Lucy again before she started with Augusta on the journey to London.

The carriage first stopped at the door of the married daughter in Warwick Square. Now, Mrs. Hittaway, whose husband was chairman of the Board of Civil Appeals and who was very well known at all Boards and among official men generally, heard much more about things that were going on than did her mother. And, having been emancipated from maternal control for the last ten or twelve years, she could express herself before her mother with more confidence than would have become the other girls. 'Mamma,' she said, 'you don't mean it!'

'I do mean it, Clara. Why should I not mean it?'

'She is the greatest vixen in all London.'

'Oh, Clara!' said Augusta.

'And such a liar,' said Mrs. Hittaway.

There came a look of pain across Lady Fawn's face, for Lady Fawn believed in her eldest daughter. But yet she intended to fight her ground on a matter so important to her as was this. 'There is no word in the English language,' she said, 'which conveys to me so little of defined meaning as that word vixen. If you can, tell me what you mean, Clara.'

'Stop it, mamma.'

'But why should I stop it,—even if I could?'

'You don't know her, mamma.'

'She has visited at Fawn Court, more than once. She is a friend of Lucy's.'

'If she is a friend of Lucy Morris, mamma, Lucy Morris shall never come here.'

'But what has she done? I have never heard that she has behaved improperly. What does it all mean? She goes out everywhere. I don't think she has had any lovers. Frederic would be the last man in the world to throw himself away upon an ill-conditioned young woman.'

'Frederic can see just as far as some other men, and not a bit farther. Of course she has an income,—for her life.'

'I believe it is her own altogether, Clara.'

'She says so, I don't doubt. I believe she is the greatest liar about London. You find out about her jewels before she married poor Sir Florian, and how much he had to pay for her; or rather, I'll find out. If you want to know, mamma, you just ask her own aunt, Lady Linlithgow.'

'We all know, my dear, that Lady Linlithgow quarrelled with her.'

'It's my belief that she is over head and ears in debt again. But I'll learn. And when I have found out, I shall not scruple to tell Frederic. Orlando will find out all about it.' Orlando was the Christian name of Mrs. Hittaway's husband. 'Mr. Camperdown, I have no doubt, knows all the ins and outs of her story. The long and the short of it is this, mamma, that I've heard quite enough about Lady Eustace to feel certain that Frederic would live to repent it.'

'But what can we do?' said Lady Fawn.

'Break it off,' said Mrs. Hittaway.

Her daughter's violence of speech had a most depressing effect upon poor Lady Fawn. As has been said, she did believe in Mrs. Hittaway. She knew that Mrs. Hittaway was conversant with the things of the world, and heard tidings daily which never found their way down to Fawn Court. And yet her son went about quite as much as did her daughter. If Lady Eustace was such a reprobate as was now represented, why had not Lord Fawn heard the truth? And then she had already given in her own adhesion,* and had promised to call. 'Do you mean that you won't go to her?' said Lady Fawn.

'As Lady Eustace,—certainly not. If Frederic does marry her, of course I must know her. That's a different thing. One has to make the best one can of a bad bargain. I don't doubt they'd be separated before two years were over.'

'Oh, dear, how dreadful!' exclaimed Augusta.

Lady Fawn, after much consideration, was of opinion that

she must carry out her intention of calling upon her son's intended bride in spite of all the evil things that had been said. Lord Fawn had undertaken to send a message to Mount Street, informing the lady of the honour intended for her. And in truth Lady Fawn was somewhat curious now to see the household of the woman, who might perhaps do her the irreparable injury of ruining the happiness of her only son. Perhaps she might learn something by looking at the woman in her own drawing-room. At any rate she would go. But Mrs. Hittaway's words had the effect of inducing her to leave Augusta where she was. If there were contamination, why should Augusta be contaminated? Poor Augusta! She had looked forward to the delight of embracing her future sister-in-law;—and would not have enjoyed it the less, perhaps, because she had been told that the lady was false, profligate, and a vixen. As, however, her position was that of a girl, she was bound to be obedient,—though over thirty years old,—and she obeyed.

Lizzie was of course at home, and Miss Macnulty was of course visiting the Horticultural Gardens or otherwise engaged. On such an occasion Lizzie would certainly be alone. She had taken great pains with her dress, studying not so much her own appearance as the character of her visitor. She was very anxious, at any rate for the present, to win golden opinions from Lady Fawn. She was dressed richly, but very simply. Everything about her room betokened wealth; but she had put away the French novels,* and had placed a Bible on a little table, not quite hidden, behind her own seat. The long lustrous lock was tucked up, but the diamonds were still upon her fingers. She fully intended to make a conquest of her future mother-in-law and sister-in-law;—for the note which had come up to her from the India Office had told her that Augusta would accompany Lady Fawn. 'Augusta is my favourite sister,' said the enamoured lover, 'and I hope that you two will always be friends.' Lizzie, when she had read this, had declared to herself that of all the female oafs she had ever seen, Augusta Fawn was the greatest oaf. When she found that Lady Fawn was alone, she did not betray herself, or ask for the beloved friend of the future. 'Dear, dear Lady Fawn!' she said, throwing herself into the arms and nestling herself against the bosom of the old lady, 'this makes my happiness perfect.' Then she retreated a little, still holding the hand she had grasped between her own, and looking up into the face of her future mother-in-law. 'When he asked me to be his wife, the first thing I thought of was whether you would come to me at once.' Her voice as she thus spoke was perfect. Her manner was almost perfect. Perhaps there was a little too much of gesture, too much gliding motion, too violent an appeal with the eyes, too close a pressure of the hand. No suspicion, however, of all this would have touched Lady Fawn had she come to Mount Street without calling in Warwick Square on the way. But those horrible words of her daughter were ringing in her ears, and she did not know how to conduct herself.

'Of course I came as soon as he told me,' she said.

'And you will be a mother to me?' demanded Lizzie.

Poor Lady Fawn! There was enough of maternity about her to have enabled her to undertake the duty for a dozen sons' wives,—if the wives were women with whom she could feel sympathy. And she could feel sympathy very easily; and was a woman not at all prone to inquire too curiously as to the merits of a son's wife. But what was she to do after the caution she had received from Mrs. Hittaway? How was she to promise maternal tenderness to a vixen and a liar? By nature she was not a deceitful woman. 'My dear,' she said, 'I hope you will make him a good wife.'

It was not very encouraging, but Lizzie made the best of it. It was her desire to cheat Lady Fawn into a good opinion, and she was not disappointed when no good opinion was expressed at once. It is seldom that a bad person expects to be accounted good. It is the general desire of such a one to conquer the existing evil impression; but it is generally presumed that the evil impression is there. 'Oh, Lady Fawn!' she said, 'I will so strive to make him happy. What is it that he likes? What

84

would he wish me to do and to be? You know his noble nature, and I must look to you for guidance.'

Lady Fawn was embarrassed. She had now seated herself on the sofa, and Lizzie was close to her, almost enveloped within her mantle. 'My dear,' said Lady Fawn, 'if you will endeavour to do your duty by him, I am sure he will do his by you.'

'I know it. I am sure of it. And I will; I will. You will let me love you, and call you mother?' A peculiar perfume came up from Lizzie's hair which Lady Fawn did not like. Her own girls, perhaps, were not given to the use of much perfumery. She shifted her seat a little, and Lizzie was compelled to sit upright, and without support. Hitherto Lady Fawn had said very little, and Lizzie's part was one difficult to play. She had heard of that sermon read every Sunday evening at Fawn Court, and she believed that Lady Fawn was peculiarly religious. 'There,' she said, stretching out her hand backwards and clasping the book which lay upon the small table,—'there; that shall be my guide. That will teach me how to do my duty by my noble husband.'

Lady Fawn in some surprise took the book from Lizzie's hand, and found that it was the Bible. 'You certainly can't do better, my dear, than read your Bible,' said Lady Fawn,— but there was more of censure than of eulogy in the tone of her voice. She put the Bible down very quietly, and asked Lady Eustace when it would suit her to come down to Fawn Court. Lady Fawn had promised her son to give the invitation, and could not now, she thought, avoid giving it.

'Oh, I should like it so much!' said Lizzie. 'Whenever it will suit you, I will be there at a minute's notice.' It was then arranged that she should be at Fawn Court on that day week, and stay for a fortnight. 'Of all things that which I most desire now,' said Lizzie, 'is to know you and the dear girls,—and to be loved by you all.'

Lady Eustace, as soon as she was alone in the room, stood in the middle of it, scowling,—for she could scowl. 'I'll not go near them,' she said to herself,—'nasty, stupid, dull, puritanical drones. If he don't like it, he may lump it. After all it's no such great catch.' Then she sat down to reflect whether it was or was not a catch. As soon as ever Lord Fawn had left her after the engagement was made, she had begun to tell herself that he was a poor creature, and that she had done wrong. 'Only five thousand a year!' she said to herself;—for she had not perfectly understood that little explanation which he had given respecting his income. 'It's nothing for a lord.' And now again she murmured to herself, 'It's my money he's after. He'll find out that I know how to keep what I've got in my own hands.' Now that Lady Fawn had been cold to her, she thought still less of the proposed marriage. But there was this inducement for her to go on with it. If they, the Fawn women, thought that they could break it off, she would let them know that they had no such power.

'Well, mamma, you've seen her?' said Mrs. Hittaway.

'Yes, my dear; I've seen her. I had seen her two or three times before, you know.'

'And you are still in love with her?'

'I never said that I was in love with her, Clara.'

'And what has been fixed?'

'She is to come down to Fawn Court next week, and stay a fortnight with us. Then we shall find out what she is.'

'That will be best, mamma,' said Augusta.

'Mind, mamma; you understand me. I shall tell Frederic plainly just what I think. Of course he will be offended, and if the marriage goes on, the offence will remain,—till he finds out the truth.'

'I hope he'll find out no such truth,' said Lady Fawn. She was, however, quite unable to say a word in behalf of her future daughter-in-law. She said nothing as to that little scene with the Bible, but she never forgot it.

CHAPTER X
Lizzie and her Lover

DURING the remainder of that Monday and all the Tuesday, Lizzie's mind was, upon the whole, averse to matrimony. She had told Miss Macnulty of her prospects, with some amount of exultation; and the poor dependant, though she knew that she must be turned out into the street, had congratulated her patroness. 'The Vulturess will take you in again, when she knows you've nowhere else to go,' Lizzie had said,—displaying, indeed, some accurate discernment of her aunt's character. But after Lady Fawn's visit she spoke of the marriage in a different tone. 'Of course, my dear, I shall have to look very close after the settlement.'

'I suppose the lawyers will do that,' said Miss Macnulty.

'Yes;—lawyers! That's all very well. I know what lawyers are. I'm not going to trust any lawyer to give away my property. Of course we shall live at Portray, because his place is in Ireland;—and nothing shall take me to Ireland. I told him that from the very first. But I don't mean to give up my own income. I don't suppose he'll venture to suggest such a thing.' And then again she grumbled. 'It's all very well being in the Cabinet——!'

'Is Lord Fawn in the Cabinet?' asked Miss Macnulty, who in such matters was not altogether ignorant.

'Of course he is,' said Lizzie, with an angry gesture. It may seem unjust to accuse her of being stupidly unacquainted with circumstances, and a liar at the same time; but she was both. She said that Lord Fawn was in the Cabinet because she had heard some one speak of him as not being a Cabinet Minister, and in so speaking appear to slight his political position. Lizzie did not know how much her companion knew, and Miss Macnulty did not comprehend the depth of the ignorance of her patroness. Thus the lies which Lizzie told were amazing to Miss Macnulty. To say that Lord Fawn was in the Cabinet, when all the world knew that he was an Under-

Secretary! What good could a woman get from an assertion so plainly, so manifestly false? But Lizzie knew nothing of Under-Secretaries. Lord Fawn was a lord, and even Commoners were in the Cabinet. 'Of course he is,' said Lizzie; 'but I sha'n't have my drawing-room made a Cabinet. They sha'n't come here.' And then again on the Tuesday evening she displayed her independence. 'As for those women down at Richmond, I don't mean to be overrun by them, I can tell you. I said I would go there, and of course I shall keep my word.'

'I think you had better go,' said Miss Macnulty.

'Of course, I shall go. I don't want anybody to tell me where I'm to go, my dear, and where I'm not. But it'll be about the first and the last visit. And as for bringing those dowdy girls out in London, it's the last thing I shall think of doing. Indeed, I doubt whether they can afford to dress themselves.' As she went up to bed on the Tuesday evening, Miss Macnulty doubted whether the match would go on. She never believed her friend's statements; but if spoken words might be supposed to mean anything, Lady Eustace's words on that Tuesday betokened a strong dislike to everything appertaining to the Fawn family. She had even ridiculed Lord Fawn himself, declaring that he understood nothing about anything beyond his office.

And, in truth, Lizzie almost had made up her mind to break it off. All that she would gain did not seem to weigh down with sufficient preponderance all that she would lose. Such were her feelings on the Tuesday night. But on the Wednesday morning she received a note which threw her back violently upon the Fawn interest. The note was as follows: 'Messrs. Camperdown and Son present their compliments to Lady Eustace. They have received instructions to proceed by law for the recovery of the Eustace diamonds, now in Lady Eustace's hands, and will feel obliged to Lady Eustace if she will communicate to them the name and address of her attorney. 62, New Square, May 30, 186—.' The effect of this note was to drive Lizzie back upon the Fawn interest. She was frightened about the diamonds, and was, nevertheless, almost

determined not to surrender them. At any rate, in such a
strait she would want assistance, either in keeping them or in
giving them up. The lawyer's letter afflicted her with a sense
of weakness, and there was strength in the Fawn connexion.
As Lord Fawn was so poor, perhaps he would adhere to the
jewels. She knew that she could not fight Mr. Camperdown
with no other assistance than what Messrs. Mowbray and
Mopus might give her, and therefore her heart softened
towards her betrothed. 'I suppose Frederic will be here to-day,'
she said to Miss Macnulty, as they sat at breakfast together
about noon. Miss Macnulty nodded. 'You can have a cab, you
know, if you like to go anywhere.' Miss Macnulty said she
thought she would go to the National Gallery. 'And you can
walk back, you know,' said Lizzie. 'I can walk there and back
too,' said Miss Macnulty,—in regard to whom it may be said
that the last ounce would sometimes almost break the horse's
back.

'Frederic' came and was received very graciously. Lizzie
had placed Mr. Camperdown's note on the little table behind
her, beneath the Bible, so that she might put her hand upon it
at once, if she could make an opportunity of showing it to her
future husband. 'Frederic' sat himself beside her, and the
intercourse for awhile was such as might be looked for between
two lovers of whom one was a widow, and the other an Under-
Secretary of State from the India Office. They were loving,
but discreetly amatory, talking chiefly of things material,
each flattering the other, and each hinting now and again at
certain little circumstances of which a more accurate knowledge
seemed to be desirable. The one was conversant with things
in general, but was slow; the other was quick as a lizard in
turning hither and thither, but knew almost nothing. When
she told Lord Fawn that the Ayrshire estate was 'her own, to
do what she liked with,' she did not know that he would
certainly find out the truth from other sources before he
married her. Indeed, she was not quite sure herself whether
the statement was true or false, though she would not have
made it so frequently had her idea of the truth been a fixed

idea. It had all been explained to her;—but there had been something about a second son, and there was no second son. Perhaps she might have a second son yet,—a future little Lord Fawn, and he might inherit it. In regard to honesty, the man was superior to the woman, because his purpose was declared, and he told no lies;—but the one was as mercenary as the other. It was not love that had brought Lord Fawn to Mount Street.

'What is the name of your place in Ireland?' she asked.

'There is no house, you know.'

'But there was one, Frederic?'

'The town-land where the house used to be, is called Killeagent.* The old demesne is called Killaud.'

'What pretty names! and—and——; does it go a great many miles?' Lord Fawn explained that it did run a good many miles up into the mountains. 'How beautifully romantic!' said Lizzie. 'But the people live on the mountain and pay rent?'

Lord Fawn asked no such inept questions respecting the Ayrshire property, but he did inquire who was Lizzie's solicitor. 'Of course there will be things to be settled,' he said, 'and my lawyer had better see yours. Mr. Camperdown is a——'

'Mr. Camperdown!' almost shrieked Lizzie. Lord Fawn then explained, with some amazement, that Mr. Camperdown was his lawyer. As far as his belief went, there was not a more respectable gentleman in the profession. Then he inquired whether Lizzie had any objection to Mr. Camperdown. 'Mr. Camperdown was Sir Florian's lawyer,' said Lizzie.

'That will make it all the easier, I should think,' said Lord Fawn.

'I don't know how that may be,' said Lizzie, trying to bring her mind to work upon the subject steadily. 'Mr. Camperdown has been very uncourteous to me;—I must say that; and, as I think, unfair. He wishes to rob me now of a thing that is quite my own.'

'What sort of a thing?' asked Lord Fawn slowly.

'A very valuable thing. I'll tell you all about it, Frederic. Of course I'll tell you everything now. I never could keep back anything from one that I loved. It's not my nature. There; you might as well read that note.' Then she put her hand back and brought Mr. Camperdown's letter from under the Bible. Lord Fawn read it very attentively, and as he read it there came upon him a great doubt. What sort of woman was this to whom he had engaged himself because she was possessed of an income? That Mr. Camperdown should be in the wrong in such a matter was an idea which never occurred to Lord Fawn. There is no form of belief stronger than that which the ordinary English gentleman has in the discretion and honesty of his own family lawyer. What his lawyer tells him to do, he does. What his lawyer tells him to sign, he signs. He buys and sells in obedience to the same direction, and feels perfectly comfortable in the possession of a guide who is responsible and all but divine. 'What diamonds are they?' asked Lord Fawn in a very low voice.

'They are my own,—altogether my own. Sir Florian gave them to me. When he put them into my hands, he said that they were to be my own for ever and ever. "There," said he, —"those are yours to do what you choose with them." After that they oughtn't to ask me to give them back,—ought they? If you had been married before, and your wife had given you a keepsake,—to keep for ever and ever, would you give it up to a lawyer? You would not like it;—would you, Frederic?' She had put her hand on his, and was looking up into his face as she asked the question. Again, perhaps, the acting was a little overdone; but there were the tears in her eyes, and the tone of her voice was perfect.

'Mr. Camperdown calls them Eustace diamonds,—family diamonds,' said Lord Fawn. 'What do they consist of? What are they worth?'

'I'll show them to you,' said Lizzie, jumping up and hurrying out of the room. Lord Fawn, when he was alone, rubbed his hands over his eyes and thought about it all. It would be a very harsh measure, on the part of the Eustace family and

of Mr. Camperdown, to demand from her the surrender of
any trinket which her late husband might have given her in the
manner she had described. But it was, to his thinking, most
improbable that the Eustace people or the lawyer should be
harsh to a widow bearing the Eustace name. The Eustaces
were by disposition lavish, and old Mr. Camperdown was not
one who would be strict in claiming little things for rich
clients. And yet here was his letter, threatening the widow of
the late baronet with legal proceedings for the recovery of
jewels which had been given by Sir Florian himself to his wife
as a keepsake! Perhaps Sir Florian had made some mistake,
and had caused to be set in a ring or brooch for his bride some
jewel which he had thought to be his own, but which had, in
truth, been an heirloom. If so, the jewel should, of course, be
surrendered,—or replaced by one of equal value. He was
making out some such solution, when Lizzie returned with the
morocco case in her hand. 'It was the manner in which he
gave it to me,' said Lizzie, as she opened the clasp, 'which
makes its value to me.'

Lord Fawn knew nothing about jewels, but even he knew
that if the circle of stones which he saw, with a Maltese cross*
appended to it, was constituted of real diamonds, the thing
must be of great value. And it occurred to him at once that
such a necklace is not given by a husband even to a bride in
the manner described by Lizzie. A ring, or brooch, or perhaps
a bracelet, a lover or a loving lord may bring in his pocket.
But such an ornament as this on which Lord Fawn was now
looking, is given in another sort of way. He felt sure that it
was so, even though he was entirely ignorant of the value of
the stones. 'Do you know what it is worth?' he asked.

Lizzie hesitated a moment, and then remembered that
'Frederic,' in his present position in regard to herself, might
be glad to assist her in maintaining the possession of a substantial property, 'I think they say its value is about—ten
thousand pounds,' she replied.

'Ten—thousand—pounds!' Lord Fawn riveted his eyes
upon them.

'That's what I am told,—by a jeweller.'

'By what jeweller?'

'A man had to come and see them,—about some repairs,— or something of that kind. Poor Sir Florian wished it. And he said so.'

'What was the man's name?'

'I forget his name,' said Lizzie, who was not quite sure whether her acquaintance with Mr. Benjamin would be considered respectable.

'Ten thousand pounds! You don't keep them in the house; —do you?'

'I have an iron case up-stairs for them;—ever so heavy.'

'And did Sir Florian give you the iron case?'

Lizzie hesitated for a moment. 'Yes,' said she. 'That is,— no. But he ordered it to be made; and then it came,—after he was—dead.'

'He knew their value, then?'

'Oh, dear, yes. Though he never named any sum. He told me, however, that they were very—very valuable.'

Lord Fawn did not immediately recognise the falseness of every word that the woman said to him, because he was slow and could not think and hear at the same time. But he was at once involved in a painful maze of doubt and almost of dismay. An action for the recovery of jewels brought against the lady whom he was engaged to marry, on behalf of the family of her late husband, would not suit him at all. To have his hands quite clean, to be above all evil report, to be respectable, as it were, all round, was Lord Fawn's special ambition. He was a poor man, and a greedy man, but he would have abandoned his official salary at a moment's notice, rather than there should have fallen on him a breath of public opinion hinting that it ought to be abandoned. He was especially timid, and lived in a perpetual fear lest the newspapers should say something hard of him. In that matter of the Sawab he had been very wretched, because Frank Greystock had accused him of being an administrator of tyranny. He would have liked his wife to have ten thousand pounds' worth of diamonds very well; but he would rather go without a wife for ever,—and without a wife's fortune,—than marry a woman subject to an action for claiming diamonds not her own. 'I think,' said he, at last, 'that if you were to put them into Mr. Camperdown's hands——'

'Into Mr. Camperdown's hands!'

'And then let the matter be settled by arbitration——'

'Arbitration? That means going to law?'

'No, dearest,—that means not going to law. The diamonds would be entrusted to Mr. Camperdown. And then some one would be appointed to decide whose property they were.'

'They're my property,' said Lizzie.

'But he says they belong to the family.'

'He'll say anything,' said Lizzie.

'My dearest girl, there can't be a more respectable man than Mr. Camperdown. You must do something of the kind, you know.'

'I sha'n't do anything of the kind,' said Lizzie. 'Sir Florian Eustace gave them to me, and I shall keep them.' She did not look at her lover as she spoke; but he looked at her, and did not like the change which he saw on her countenance. And he did not like the circumstances in which he found himself placed. 'Why should Mr. Camperdown interfere?' continued Lizzie. 'If they don't belong to me, they belong to my son;—and who has so good a right to keep them for him as I have? But they belong to me.'

'They should not be kept in a private house like this at all, if they are worth all that money.'

'If I were to let them go, Mr. Camperdown would get them. There's nothing he wouldn't do to get them. Oh, Frederic, I hope you'll stand to me, and not see me injured. Of course I only want them for my darling child.'

'Frederic's' face had become very long, and he was much disturbed in his mind. He could only suggest that he himself would go and see Mr. Camperdown, and ascertain what ought to be done. To the last, he adhered to his assurance that Mr. Camperdown could do no evil;—till Lizzie, in her wrath, asked him whether he believed Mr. Camperdown's word before hers. 'I think he would understand a matter of business better than you,' said the prudent lover.

'He wants to rob me,' said Lizzie, 'and I shall look to you to prevent it.'

When Lord Fawn took his leave,—which he did not do till he had counselled her again and again to leave the matter in Mr. Camperdown's hands,—the two were not in good accord together. It was his fixed purpose, as he declared to her, to see Mr. Camperdown; and it was her fixed purpose,—so, at least, she declared to him,—to keep the diamonds, in spite of Mr. Camperdown. 'But, my dear, if it's decided against you ——' said Lord Fawn gravely.

'It can't be decided against me, if you stand by me as you ought to do.'

'I can do nothing,' said Lord Fawn, in a tremor. Then Lizzie looked at him,—and her look, which was very eloquent, called him a poltroon*as plain as a look could speak. Then they parted, and the signs of affection between them were not satisfactory.

The door was hardly closed behind him before Lizzie began to declare to herself that he shouldn't escape her. It was not yet twenty-four hours since she had been telling herself that she did not like the engagement and would break it off; and now she was stamping her little feet, and clenching her little hands, and swearing to herself by all her gods, that this wretched, timid lordling should not get out of her net. She did, in truth, despise him because he would not clutch the jewels. She looked upon him as mean and paltry because he was willing to submit to Mr. Camperdown. But still she was prompted to demand all that could be demanded from her engagement,—because she thought that she perceived a something in him which might produce in him a desire to be relieved from it. No! he should not be relieved. He should marry her. And she would keep the key of that iron box with the diamonds, and he should find what sort of a noise she would make, if he attempted to take it from her. She closed the morocco case, ascended with it to her bed-room, locked it up in the iron safe, deposited the little patent key in its usual place round her neck, and then seated herself at her desk, and wrote letters to her various friends, making known to them her engagement. Hitherto she had told no one but Miss Macnulty, —and, in her doubts, had gone so far as to desire Miss Macnulty not to mention it. Now she was resolved to blazon forth her engagement before all the world.

The first 'friend' to whom she wrote was Lady Linlithgow. The reader shall see two or three of her letters, and that to the countess shall be the first.

'MY DEAR AUNT,

'When you came to see me the other day, I cannot say that you were very kind to me, and I don't suppose you care very much what becomes of me. But I think it right to let you know that I am going to be married. I am engaged to Lord Fawn, who, as you know, is a peer, and a member of Her Majesty's Government, and a nobleman of great influence. I do not suppose that even you can say anything against such an alliance.

'I am, your affectionate niece,
'ELI. EUSTACE.'

Then she wrote to Mrs. Eustace, the wife of the Bishop of Bobsborough. Mrs. Eustace had been very kind to her in the first days of her widowhood, and had fully recognised her as the widow of the head of her husband's family. Lizzie had liked none of the Bobsborough people. They were, according to her ideas, slow, respectable, and dull. But they had not found much open fault with her, and she was aware that it was for her interest to remain on good terms with them. Her letter, therefore, to Mrs. Eustace was somewhat less acrid than that written to her aunt Linlithgow.

'MY DEAR MRS. EUSTACE,

'I hope you will be glad to hear from me, and will not be sorry to hear my news. I am going to be married again. Of course I am not about to take a step which is in every way so very important without thinking about it a great deal. But I am sure it will be better for my darling little Florian in every way; and as for myself, I have felt for the last two years how unfitted I have been to manage everything myself. I have therefore accepted an offer made to me by Lord Fawn, who is, as you know, a peer of Parliament, and a most distinguished member of Her Majesty's Government; and he is, too, a nobleman of very great influence in every respect, and has a property in Ireland, extending over ever so many miles, and running up into the mountains. His mansion there is called Killmage, but I am not sure that I remember the name quite rightly. I hope I may see you there some day, and the dear bishop. I look forward with delight to doing something to make those dear Irish happier. The idea of rambling up into our own mountains charms me, for nothing suits my disposition so well as that kind of solitude.

'Of course Lord Fawn is not so rich a man as Sir Florian, but I have never looked to riches for my happiness. Not but what Lord Fawn has a good income from his Irish estates; and then, of course, he is paid for doing Her Majesty's Government;—so there is no fear that he will have to live upon my jointure, which, of course, would not be right. Pray tell the dear bishop and dear Margaretta all this, with my love. You will be happy, I know, to hear that my little Flo is quite well. He is already so fond of his new papa!'—Lizzie's turn for lying was exemplified in this last statement, for, as it happened, Lord Fawn had never yet seen the child.

'Believe me to be always your most affectionate niece,
                                        ELI. EUSTACE.'

There were two other letters,—one to her uncle, the dean, and the other to her cousin Frank. There was great doubt in her mind as to the expediency of writing to Frank Greystock; but at last she decided that she would do it. The letter to the dean need not be given in full, as it was very similar to that written to the bishop's wife. The same mention was made of her intended husband's peerage, and the same allusion to Her Majesty's Government,—a phrase which she had heard from Lord Fawn himself. She spoke of the Irish property, but in terms less glowing than she had used in writing to the lady, and ended by asking for her uncle's congratulation—and blessing. Her letter to Frank was as follows, and, doubtless, as she wrote it, there was present to her mind a remembrance of the fact that he himself might have offered to her, and have had her if he would.

'MY DEAR COUSIN,

'As I would rather that you should hear my news from myself than from any one else, I write to tell you that I am going to be married to Lord Fawn. Of course I know that there are certain matters as to which you and Lord Fawn do not agree,—in politics, I mean; but still I do not doubt but you will think that he is quite able to take care of your poor little cousin. It was only settled a day or two since, but it has been coming on ever so long. You understand all about that;—don't you? Of course you must come to my wedding, and be very good to me,—a kind of brother, you know; for we have always been friends;—haven't we? And if the dean doesn't come up to town, you must give me away. And you must come and see me ever so often; for I have a sort of feeling that I have no one else belonging to me that I call really my own, except you. And you must be great friends with Lord Fawn, and must give up saying that he doesn't do his work properly. Of course he does everything better than anybody else could possibly do it,—except Cousin Frank.

'I am going down next week to Richmond. Lady Fawn has insisted on my staying there for a fortnight. Oh, dear, what shall I do all the time? You must positively come down and see me,—and see somebody else too! Only, you naughty coz! you mustn't break a poor girl's heart.

'Your affectionate cousin,
'ELI. EUSTACE.'

Somebody, in speaking on Lady Eustace's behalf, and making the best of her virtues, had declared that she did not have lovers. Hitherto that had been true of her;—but her mind had not the less dwelt on the delight of a lover. She still thought of a possible Corsair who would be willing to give up all but his vices for her love, and for whose sake she would be willing to share even them. It was but a dream, but nevertheless it pervaded her fancy constantly. Lord Fawn,—peer of Parliament, and member of Her Majesty's Government, as he was,—could not have been such a lover to her. Might it not be possible that there should exist something of romance between her and her cousin Frank? She was the last woman in the world to run away with a man, or to endanger her position by a serious indiscretion; but there might, perhaps, be a something between her and her cousin,—a *liaison* quite correct in its facts, a secret understanding, if nothing more,— a mutual sympathy, which should be chiefly shown in the abuse of all their friends,—and in this she could indulge her passion for romance and poetry.

CHAPTER XI
Lord Fawn at his Office

THE news was soon all about London,—as Lizzie had intended. She had made a sudden resolve that Lord Fawn should not escape her, and she had gone to work after the fashion we have seen. Frank Greystock had told John Eustace, and John Eustace had told Mr. Camperdown before Lord Fawn himself, in the slow prosecution of his purpose, had consulted the lawyer about the necklace. 'God bless my soul;— —Lord Fawn!' the old lawyer had said when the news was communicated to him. 'Well,—yes;—he wants money. I don't envy him; that's all. We shall get the diamonds now, John. Lord Fawn isn't the man to let his wife keep what doesn't belong to her.' Then, after a day or two, Lord Fawn had himself gone to Mr. Camperdown's chambers. 'I believe I am to congratulate you, my lord,' said the lawyer. 'I'm told you are going to marry——; well, I mustn't really say another of my clients, but the widow of one of them. Lady Eustace is a very beautiful woman, and she has a very pretty income too. She has the whole of the Scotch property for her life.'

'It's only for her life, I suppose?' said Lord Fawn.

'Oh, no, no;—of course not. There's been some mistake on her part;—at least, so I've been told. Women never understand. It's all as clear as daylight. Had there been a second son, the second son would have had it. As it is, it goes with the rest of the property—just as it ought to do, you know. Four thousand a year isn't so bad, you know, considering that she isn't more than a girl yet, and that she hadn't sixpence of her own. When the admiral died, there wasn't sixpence, Lord Fawn.'

'So I have heard.'

'Not sixpence. It's all Eustace money. She had six or eight thousand pounds, or something like that, besides. She's as lovely a young widow as I ever saw,—and very clever.'

'Yes;—she is clever.'

'By-the-bye, Lord Fawn, as you have done me the honour of calling,—there's a stupid mistake about some family diamonds.'

'It is in respect to them that I've come,' said Lord Fawn. Then Mr. Camperdown, in his easy, off-hand way, imputing no blame to the lady in the hearing of her future husband, and declaring his opinion that she was doubtless unaware of its value, explained the matter of the necklace. Lord Fawn listened, but said very little. He especially did not say that Lady Eustace had had the stones valued. 'They're real, I suppose?' he asked. Mr. Camperdown assured him that no diamonds more real had ever come from Golconda,* or passed through Mr. Garnett's hands. 'They are as well known as any family diamonds in England,' said Mr. Camperdown. 'She has got into bad hands,'—continued Mr. Camperdown. 'Mowbray and Mopus;—horrible people; sharks, that make one blush for one's profession; and I was really afraid there would have been trouble. But, of course, it'll be all right now;—and if she'll only come to me, tell her I'll do everything I can to make things straight and comfortable for her. If she likes to have another lawyer, of course, that's all right. Only make her understand who Mowbray and Mopus are. It's quite out of the question, Lord Fawn, that your wife should have anything to do with Mowbray and Mopus.' Every word that Mr. Camperdown said was gospel to Lord Fawn.

And yet, as the reader will understand, Mr. Camperdown had by no means expressed his real opinion in this interview. He had spoken of the widow in friendly terms,—declaring that she was simply mistaken in her ideas as to the duration of her interest in the Scotch property, and mistaken again about the diamonds;—whereas in truth he regarded her as a dishonest, lying, evil-minded harpy. Had Lord Fawn consulted him simply as a client, and not have come to him an engaged lover, he would have expressed his opinion quite frankly; but it is not the business of a lawyer to tell his client evil things of the lady whom that client is engaged to marry. In regard to the property he spoke the truth, and he spoke what he believed to be the truth when he said that the whole thing would no doubt now be easily arranged. When Lord Fawn took his leave, Mr. Camperdown again declared to himself that as regarded money the match was very well for his lordship; but that, as regarded the woman, Lizzie was dear at the price. 'Perhaps he doesn't mind it,' said Mr. Camperdown to himself, 'but I wouldn't marry such a woman myself, though she owned all Scotland.'

There had been much in the interview to make Lord Fawn unhappy. In the first place, that golden hope as to the perpetuity of the property was at an end. He had never believed that it was so; but a man may hope without believing. And he was quite sure that Lizzie was bound to give up the diamonds,—and would ultimately be made to give them up. Of any property in them, as possibly accruing to himself, he had not thought much;—but he could not abstain from thinking of the woman's grasp upon them. Mr. Camperdown's plain statement, which was gospel to him, was directly at variance with Lizzie's story. Sir Florian certainly would not have given such diamonds in such a way. Sir Florian would not have ordered a separate iron safe for them, with a view that they might be secure in his wife's bed-room. And then she had had them valued, and manifestly was always thinking of her treasure. It was very well for a poor, careful peer to be always thinking of his money, but Lord Fawn was well aware that a young woman such as Lady Eustace should have her thoughts elsewhere. As he sat signing letters at the India Board, relieving himself when he was left alone between each batch by standing up with his back to the fire-place, his mind was full of all this. He could not unravel truth quickly, but he could grasp it when it came to him. She was certainly greedy, false, and dishonest. And,—worse than all this,—she had dared to tell him to his face that he was a poor creature because he would not support her in her greed, and falsehoods, and dishonesty! Nevertheless, he was engaged to marry her! Then he thought of one Violet Effingham whom he had loved, and then came over him some suspicion of a fear that he himself was hard and selfish. And yet what was such a one as he to do? It was of course necessary for the maintenance of the very constitution of his country that there should be future Lord Fawns. There could be no future Lord Fawns unless he married;—and how could he marry without money? 'A peasant can marry whom he pleases,' said Lord Fawn, pressing his hand to his brow, and dropping one flap of his coat, as he thought of his own high and perilous destiny, standing with his back to the fire-place, while a huge pile of letters lay there before him waiting to be signed.

It was a Saturday evening, and as there was no House*there was nothing to hurry him away from the office. He was the occupier for the time of a large, well-furnished official room, looking out into St. James's Park, and as he glanced round it he told himself that his own happiness must be there, and not in the domesticity of a quiet home. The House of Lords, out of which nobody could turn him, and official life,—as long as he could hold to it,—must be all in all to him. He had engaged himself to this woman, and he must—marry her. He did not think that he could now see any way of avoiding that event. Her income would supply the needs of her home, and then there might probably be a continuation of Lord Fawns. The world might have done better for him,—had he been able to find favour in Violet Effingham's sight. He was a man capable of love,—and very capable of constancy to a woman true to him. Then he wiped away a tear as he sat down to sign the huge batch of letters. As he read some special letter in which instructions were conveyed as to the insufficiency of the Sawab's claims, he thought of Frank Greystock's attack upon him, and of Frank Greystock's cousin. There had been a time in which he had feared that the two cousins would become man and wife. At this moment he uttered a malediction against the member for Bobsborough, which might perhaps have been spared had the member been now willing to take the lady off his hands. Then the door was opened, and the messenger told him that Mrs. Hittaway was in the waiting-room. Mrs. Hittaway was, of course, at once made welcome to the Under-Secretary's own apartment.

Mrs. Hittaway was a strong-minded woman,—the strong-est-minded probably of the Fawn family,—but she had now come upon a task which tasked all her strength to the utmost. She had told her mother that she would tell 'Frederic' what she thought about his proposed bride, and she had now come to carry out her threat. She had asked her brother to come and dine with her, but he had declined. His engagements hardly admitted of his dining with his relatives. She had called upon him at the rooms he occupied in Victoria Street,—but of course she had not found him. She could not very well go to his club;—so now she had hunted him down at his office. From the very commencement of the interview Mrs. Hittaway was strong-minded. She began the subject of the marriage, and did so without a word of congratulation. 'Dear Frederic,' she said, 'you know that we have all got to look up to you.'

'Well, Clara,—what does that mean?'

'It means this,—that you must bear with me, if I am more anxious as to your future career than another sister might be.'

'Now I know you are going to say something unpleasant.'

'Yes, I am, Frederic. I have heard so many bad things about Lady Eustace!'

The Under-Secretary sat silent for awhile in his great arm-chair. 'What sort of evil things do you mean, Clara?' he asked at last. 'Evil things are said of a great many people,—as you know. I am sure you would not wish to repeat slanders.'

Mrs. Hittaway was not to be silenced after this fashion. 'Not slanders, certainly, Frederic. But when I hear that you intend to raise this lady to the rank and position of your wife, then of course the truth or falsehood of these reports becomes a matter of great moment to us all. Don't you think you had better see Mr. Camperdown?'

'I have seen him.'

'And what does he say?'

'What should he say? Lady Eustace has, I believe, made some mistake about the condition of her property, and people who have heard it have been good-natured enough to say that the error has been wilful. That is what I call slander, Clara.'

'And have you heard about her jewels?' Mrs. Hittaway was alluding here to the report which had reached her as to Lizzie's debt to Harter and Benjamin when she married Sir Florian; but Lord Fawn of course thought of the diamond necklace.

'Yes;' said he, 'I have heard all about them. Who told you?'

'I have known it ever so long. Sir Florian never got over it.' Lord Fawn was again in the dark, but he did not choose to commit himself by asking further questions. 'And then her treatment of Lady Linlithgow, who was her only friend before she married, was something quite unnatural. Ask the dean's people what they think of her. I believe even they would tell you.'

'Frank Greystock desired to marry her himself.'

'Yes,—for her money, perhaps;—because he has not got a farthing in the world. Dear Frederic, I only wish to put you on your guard. Of course this is very unpleasant, and I shouldn't do it if I didn't think it my duty. I believe she is artful and very false. She certainly deceived Sir Florian Eustace about her debts;—and he never held up his head after he found out what she was. If she has told you falsehoods, of course you can break it off. Dear Frederic, I hope you won't be angry with me.'

'Is that all?' he asked.

'Yes;—that is all.'

'I'll bear it in mind,' he said. 'Of course it isn't very pleasant.'

'No;—I know it is not pleasant,' said Mrs. Hittaway rising, and taking her departure with an offer of affectionate sisterly greeting, which was not accepted with cordiality.

It was very unpleasant. That very morning Lord Fawn had received letters from the Dean and the Bishop of

Bobsborough congratulating him on his intended marriage,— both those worthy dignitaries of the Church having thought it expedient to verify Lizzie's statements. Lord Fawn was, therefore, well aware that Lady Eustace had published the engagement. It was known to everybody, and could not be broken off without public scandal.

CHAPTER XII
'I only thought of it'

THERE was great perturbation down at Fawn Court. On the day fixed, Monday, June 5, Lizzie arrived. Nothing further had been said by Lady Fawn to urge the invitation; but, in accordance with the arrangement already made, Lady Eustace, with her child, her nurse, and her own maid, was at Fawn Court by four o'clock. A very long letter had been received from Mrs. Hittaway that morning,—the writing of which must have seriously interfered with the tranquillity of her Sunday afternoon. Lord Fawn did not make his appearance at Richmond on the Saturday evening,—nor was he seen on the Sunday. That Sunday was, we may presume, chiefly devoted to reflection. He certainly did not call upon his future wife. His omission to do so no doubt increased Lizzie's urgency in the matter of her visit to Richmond. Frank Greystock had written to congratulate her. 'Dear Frank,' she had said in reply, 'a woman situated as I am has so many things to think of. Lord Fawn's position will be of service to my child. Mind you come and see me at Fawn Court. I count so much on your friendship and assistance.'

Of course she was expected at Richmond,—although throughout the morning Lady Fawn had entertained almost a hope that she wouldn't come. 'He was only lukewarm in defending her,' Mrs. Hittaway had said in her letter, 'and I still think that there may be an escape.' Not even a note had come from Lord Fawn himself,—nor from Lady Eustace. Possibly something violent might have been done, and Lady

Eustace would not appear. But Lady Eustace did appear,—and, after a fashion, was made welcome at Fawn Court.

The Fawn ladies were not good hypocrites. Lady Fawn had said almost nothing to her daughters of her visit to Mount Street, but Augusta had heard the discussion in Mrs. Hittaway's drawing-room as to the character of the future bride. The coming visit had been spoken of almost with awe, and there was a general conviction in the dovecote that an evil thing had fallen upon them. Consequently, their affection to the new-comer, though spoken in words, was not made evident by signs and manners. Lizzie herself took care that the position in which she was received should be sufficiently declared. 'It seems so odd that I am to come among you as a sister,' she said. The girls were forced to assent to the claim, but they assented coldly. 'He has told me to attach myself especially to you,' she whispered to Augusta. The unfortunate chosen one, who had but little strength of her own, accepted the position, and then, as the only means of escaping the embraces of her newly-found sister, pleaded the violence of a headache. 'My mother!' said Lizzie to Lady Fawn. 'Yes, my dear,' said Lady Fawn. 'One of the girls had perhaps better go up and show you your room.' 'I am very much afraid about it,' said Lady Fawn to her daughter Amelia. Amelia replied only by shaking her head.

On the Tuesday morning there came a note from Lord Fawn to his lady-love. Of course the letter was not shown, but Lizzie received it at the breakfast table, and read it with many little smiles and signs of satisfaction. And then she gave out various little statements as having been made in that letter. He says this, and he says that, and he is coming here, and going there, and he will do one thing, and he won't do the other. We have often seen young ladies crowing over their lovers' letters, and it was pleasant to see Lizzie crowing over hers. And yet there was but very little in the letter. Lord Fawn told her that what with the House and what with the Office, he could not get down to Richmond before Saturday; but that on Saturday he would come. Then he signed himself 'yours affectionately,

Fawn.' Lizzie did her crowing very prettily. The outward show of it was there to perfection,—so that the Fawn girls really believed that their brother had written an affectionate lover's letter. Inwardly, Lizzie swore to herself, as she read the cold words with indignation, that the man should not escape her.

The days went by very tediously. On the Wednesday and the Friday Lady Eustace made an excuse of going up to town, and insisted on taking the unfortunate Augusta with her. There was no real reason for these journeys to London,— unless that glance which on each occasion was given to the contents of the iron case was a real reason. The diamonds were safe, and Miss Macnulty was enjoying herself. On the Friday Lizzie proposed to Augusta that they should jointly make a raid upon the member of Her Majesty's Government at his office; but Augusta positively refused to take such a step. 'I know he would be angry,' pleaded Augusta. 'Psha! who cares for his anger?' said Lizzie. But the visit was not made.

On the Saturday,—the Saturday which was to bring Lord Fawn down to dinner,—another most unexpected visitor made his appearance. At about three o'clock Frank Greystock was at Fawn Court. Now it was certainly understood that Mr. Greystock had been told not to come to Fawn Court as long as Lucy Morris was there. 'Dear Mr. Greystock, I'm sure you will take what I say as I mean it,' Lady Fawn had whispered to him. 'You know how attached we all are to our dear little Lucy. Perhaps you know——.' There had been more of it; but the meaning of it all was undoubtedly this,— that Frank was not to pay visits to Lucy Morris at Fawn Court. Now he had come to see his cousin Lizzie Eustace.

On this occasion Lady Fawn, with Amelia and two of the other girls, were out in the carriage. The unfortunate Augusta had been left at home with her bosom friend;—while Cecilia and Nina were supposed to be talking French with Lucy Morris. They were all out in the grounds, sitting upon the benches, and rambling among the shrubberies, when of a sudden Frank

Greystock was in the midst of them. Lizzie's expression of joy at seeing her cousin was almost as great as though he had been in fact a brother. She ran up to him and grasped his hand, and hung on his arm, and looked up into his face, and then burst into tears. But the tears were not violent tears. There were just three sobs, and two bright eyes full of water, and a lace handkerchief,—and then a smile. 'Oh, Frank,' she said, 'it does make one think so of old times!' Augusta had by this time been almost persuaded to believe in her,—though the belief by no means made the poor young woman happy. Frank thought that his cousin looked very well, and said something as to Lord Fawn being 'the happiest fellow going.' 'I hope I shall make him happy,' said Lizzie, clasping her hands together.

Lucy meanwhile was standing in the circle with the others. It never occurred to her that it was her duty to run away from the man she loved. She had shaken hands with him, and felt something of affection in his pressure. She did believe that his visit was made entirely to his cousin, and had no idea at the moment of disobeying Lady Fawn. During the last few days she had been thrown very much with her old friend Lizzie, and had been treated by the future peeress with many signs of almost sisterly affection. 'Dear Lucy,' Lizzie had said, 'you can understand me. These people,—oh, they are so good, but they can't understand me.' Lucy had expressed a hope that Lord Fawn understood her. 'Oh, Lord Fawn,—well; yes; perhaps;—I don't know. It so often happens that one's husband is the last person to understand one.'

'If I thought so, I wouldn't marry him,' said Lucy.

'Frank Greystock will understand you,' said Lizzie. It was indeed true that Lucy did understand something of her wealthy friend's character, and was almost ashamed of the friendship. With Lizzie Greystock she had never sympathised, and Lizzie Eustace had always been distasteful to her. She already felt that the less she should see of Lizzie Fawn the better she should like it.

Before an hour was over, Frank Greystock was walking

round the shrubberies with Lucy,—and was walking with
Lucy alone. It was undoubtedly the fact that Lady Eustace
had contrived that it should be so. The unfitness of the thing
recommended it to her. Frank could hardly marry a wife without a shilling. Lucy would certainly not think at all of shillings.
Frank,—as Lizzie knew,—had been almost at her feet within
the last fortnight, and might, in some possible emergency, be
there again. In the midst of such circumstances nothing could
be better than that Frank and Lucy should be thrown together.
Lizzie regarded all this as romance. Poor Lady Fawn, had she
known it all, would have called it diabolical wickedness and
inhuman cruelty.

'Well, Lucy;—what do you think of it?' Frank Greystock
said to her.

'Think of what, Mr. Greystock?'

'You know what I mean;—this marriage?'

'How should I be able to think? I have never seen them
together. I suppose Lord Fawn isn't very rich. She is rich.
And then she is very beautiful. Don't you think her very
beautiful?'

'Sometimes exquisitely lovely.'

'Everybody says so;—and I am sure it is the fact. Do you
know;—but perhaps you'll think I am envious.'

'If I thought you envious of Lizzie, I should have to think
you very foolish at the same time.'

'I don't know what that means;'—she did know well enough
what it meant;—'but sometimes to me she is almost frightful
to look at.'

'In what way?'

'Oh, I can't tell you. She looks like a beautiful animal that
you are afraid to caress for fear it should bite you;—an animal
that would be beautiful if its eyes were not so restless, and its
teeth so sharp and so white.'

'How very odd.'

'Why odd, Mr. Greystock?'

'Because I feel exactly in the same way about her. I am not
in the least afraid that she'll bite me; and as for caressing the

110

animal,—that kind of caressing which you mean,—it seems to me to be just what she's made for. But, I do feel sometimes, that she is like a cat.'

'Something not quite so tame as a cat,' said Lucy.

'Nevertheless she is very lovely,—and very clever. Sometimes I think her the most beautiful woman I ever saw in the world.'

'Do you indeed?'

'She will be immensely run after as Lady Fawn. When she pleases she can make her own house quite charming. I never knew a woman who could say pretty things to so many people at once.'

'You are making her out to be a paragon of perfection, Mr. Greystock.'

'And when you add to all the rest that she has four thousand a year, you must admit that Lord Fawn is a lucky man.'

'I have said nothing against it.'

'Four thousand a year is a very great consideration, Lucy.'

Lucy for a while said nothing. She was making up her mind that she would say nothing;—that she would make no reply indicative of any feeling on her part. But she was not sufficiently strong to keep her resolution. 'I wonder, Mr. Greystock,' she said, 'that you did not attempt to win the great prize yourself. Cousins do marry.'

He had thought of attempting it, and at this moment he would not lie to her. 'The cousinship had nothing to do with it,' he said.

'Perhaps you did think of it.'

'I did, Lucy. Yes, I did. Thank God, I only thought of it.' She could not refrain herself from looking up into his face and clasping her hands together. A woman never so dearly loves a man as when he confesses that he has been on the brink of a great crime,—but has refrained, and has not committed it. 'I did think of it. I am not telling you that she would have taken me. I have no reason whatever for thinking so.'

'I am sure she would,' said Lucy, who did not in the least know what words she was uttering.

'It would have been simply for her money,—her money and her beauty. It would not have been because I love her.'

'Never,—never ask a girl to marry you, unless you love her, Mr. Greystock.'

'Then there is only one that I can ever ask,' said he. There was nothing of course that she could say to this. If he did not choose to go further, she was not bound to understand him. But would he go further? She felt at the moment that an open declaration of his love to herself would make her happy for ever, even though it should be accompanied by an assurance that he could not marry her. If they only knew each other,— that it was so between them,—that, she thought, would be enough for her. And as for him—if a woman could bear such a position, surely he might bear it. 'Do you know who that one is?' he asked.

'No,' she said,—shaking her head.

'Lucy, is that true?'

'What does it matter?'

'Lucy;—look at me, Lucy,' and he put his hand upon her arm.

'No,—no,—no!' she said.

'I love you so well, Lucy, that I never can love another. I have thought of many women, but could never even think of one, as a woman to love, except you. I have sometimes fancied I could marry for money and position,—to help myself on in the world by means of a wife,—but when my mind has run away with me, to revel amidst ideas of feminine sweetness, you have always—always been the heroine of the tale, as the mistress of the happy castle in the air.'

'Have I?' she asked.

'Always,—always. As regards this,'—and he struck himself on the breast,—'no man was ever more constant. Though I don't think much of myself as a man, I know a woman when I see her.' But he did not ask her to be his wife;—nor did he wait at Fawn Court till Lady Fawn had come back with the carriage.

CHAPTER XIII
Showing what Frank Greystock did

FRANK GREYSTOCK escaped from the dovecote before Lady Fawn had returned. He had not made his visit to Richmond with any purpose of seeing Lucy Morris, or of saying to her when he did see her anything special,—of saying anything that should, or anything that should not, have been said. He had gone there, in truth, simply because his cousin had asked him, and because it was almost a duty on his part to see his cousin on the momentous occasion of this new engagement. But he had declared to himself that old Lady Fawn was a fool, and that to see Lucy again would be very pleasant. 'See her; —of course I'll see her,' he had said. 'Why should I be prevented from seeing her?' Now he had seen her, and as he returned by the train to London, he acknowledged to himself that it was no longer in his power to promote his fortune by marriage. He had at last said that to Lucy which made it impossible for him to offer his hand to any other woman. He had not, in truth, asked her to be his wife; but he had told her that he loved her, and could never love any other woman. He had asked for no answer to this assurance, and then he had left her.

In the course of that afternoon he did question himself as to his conduct to this girl, and subjected himself to some of the rigours of a cross-examination. He was not a man who could think of a girl as the one human being whom he loved above all others, and yet look forward with equanimity to the idea of doing her an injury. He could understand that a man unable to marry should be reticent as to his feelings,—supposing him to have been weak enough to have succumbed to a passion which could only mar his own prospects. He was frank enough in owning to himself that he had been thus weak. The weakness had come upon himself early in life,—and was there, an established fact. The girl was to him unlike any

113

other girl;—or any man. There was to him a sweetness in her companionship which he could not analyse. She was not beautiful. She had none of the charms of fashion. He had never seen her well-dressed,—according to the ideas of dress which he found to be prevailing in the world. She was a little thing, who, as a man's wife, could attract no attention by figure, form, or outward manner,—one who had quietly submitted herself to the position of a governess, and who did not seem to think that in doing so she obtained less than her due. But yet he knew her to be better than all the rest. For him, at any rate, she was better than all the rest. Her little hand was cool and sweet to him. Sometimes when he was heated and hard at work, he would fancy how it would be with him if she were by him, and would lay it on his brow. There was a sparkle in her eye that had to him more of sympathy in it than could be conveyed by all the other eyes in the world. There was an expression in her mouth when she smiled, which was more eloquent to him than any sound. There were a reality and a truth about her which came home to him, and made themselves known to him as firm rocks which could not be shaken. He had never declared to himself that deceit or hypocrisy in a woman was especially abominable. As a rule he looked for it in women, and would say that some amount of affectation was necessary to a woman's character. He knew that his cousin Lizzie was a little liar,—that she was, as Lucy had said, a pretty animal that would turn and bite;—and yet he liked his cousin Lizzie. He did not want women to be perfect,—so he would say. But Lucy Morris, in his eyes, was perfect; and when he told her that she was ever the queen who reigned in those castles in the air which he built,—as others build them, he told her no more than the truth.

He had fallen into these feelings and could not now avoid them, or be quit of them;—but he could have been silent respecting them. He knew that in former days, down at Bobsborough, he had not been altogether silent. When he had first seen her at Fawn Court he had not been altogether silent. But he had been warned away from Fawn Court, and in that very warning there was conveyed, as it were, an absolution from the effect of words hitherto spoken. Though he had called Lady Fawn an old fool, he had known that it was so,—had, after a fashion, perceived her wisdom,—and had regarded himself as a man free to decide, without disgrace, that he might abandon ideas of ecstatic love and look out for a rich wife. Presuming himself to be reticent for the future in reference to his darling Lucy, he might do as he pleased with himself. Thus there had come a moment in which he had determined that he would ask his rich cousin to marry him. In that little project he had been interrupted, and the reader knows what had come of it. Lord Fawn's success had not in the least annoyed him. He had only half resolved in regard to his cousin. She was very beautiful no doubt, and there was her income;—but he also knew that those teeth would bite and that those claws would scratch. But Lord Fawn's success had given a turn to his thoughts, and had made him think, for a moment, that if a man loved, he should be true to his love. The reader also knows what had come of that,—how at last he had not been reticent. He had not asked Lucy to be his wife; but he had said that which made it impossible that he should marry any other woman without dishonour.

As he thought of what he had done himself, he tried to remember whether Lucy had said a word expressive of affection for himself. She had in truth spoken very few words, and he could remember almost every one of them. 'Have I?'—she had asked, when he told her that she had ever been the princess reigning in his castles. And there had been a joy in the question which she had not attempted to conceal. She had hesitated not at all. She had not told him that she loved him. But there had been something sweeter than such protestation in the question she had asked him. 'Is it indeed true,' she had said, 'that I have been placed there where all my joy and all my glory lies?' It was not in her to tell a lie to him, even by a tone. She had intended to say nothing of her love, but he knew that it had all been told. 'Have I?'—he repeated the words to himself a dozen times, and as he did so, he could hear her voice. Certainly there never was a voice that brought home to the hearer so strong a sense of its own truth!

Why should he not at once make up his mind to marry her? He could do it. There was no doubt of that. It was possible for him to alter the whole manner of his life, to give up his clubs,—to give up even Parliament, if the need to do so was there,—and to live as a married man on the earnings of his profession. There was no need why he should regard himself as a poor man. Two things, no doubt, were against his regarding himself as a rich man. Ever since he had commenced life in London he had been more or less in debt; and then, unfortunately, he had acquired a seat in Parliament at a period of his career in which the dangers of such a position were greater than the advantages. Nevertheless he could earn an income on which he and his wife, were he to marry, could live in all comfort; and as to his debts, if he would set his shoulder to the work they might be paid off in a twelvemonth. There was nothing in the prospect which would frighten Lucy, though there might be a question whether he possessed the courage needed for so violent a change.

He had chambers in the Temple;*he lived in rooms which he hired from month to month in one of the big hotels at the West-end; and he dined at his club, or at the House, when he was not dining with a friend. It was an expensive and a luxurious mode of life,—and one from the effects of which a man is prone to drift very quickly into selfishness. He was by no means given to drinking,—but he was already learning to like good wine. Small economies in reference to cab-hire, gloves, umbrellas, and railway fares were unknown to him. Sixpences and shillings were things with which, in his mind, it was grievous to have to burden the thoughts. The Greystocks had all lived after that fashion. Even the dean himself was not free from the charge of extravagance. All this Frank knew, and he did not hesitate to tell himself, that he must make a great change if he meant to marry Lucy Morris. And he was wise enough to know that the change would become more difficult every day that it was postponed. Hitherto the

question had been an open question with him. Could it now
be an open question any longer? As a man of honour, was he
not bound to share his lot with Lucy Morris?

That evening,—that Saturday evening,—it so happened
that he met John Eustace at a club to which they both belonged; and they dined together. They had long known each
other, and had been thrown into closer intimacy by the marriage between Sir Florian and Lizzie. John Eustace had never
been fond of Lizzie, and now, in truth, liked her less than
ever; but he did like Lizzie's cousin, and felt that possibly
Frank might be of use to him in the growing difficulty of
managing the heir's property and looking after the heir's
interests. 'You've let the widow slip through your fingers,'
he said to Frank, as they sat together at the table.

'I told you Lord Fawn was to be the lucky man,' said Frank.

'I know you did. I hadn't seen it. I can only say I wish it
had been the other way.'

'Why so? Fawn isn't a bad fellow.'

'No;—not exactly a bad fellow. He isn't, you know, what
I call a good fellow. In the first place, he is marrying her
altogether for her money.'

'Which is just what you advised me to do.'

'I thought you really liked her. And then Fawn will be
always afraid of her,—and won't be in the least afraid of us.
We shall have to fight him, and he won't fight her. He's a
cantankerous fellow,—is Fawn,—when he's not afraid of his
adversary.'

'But why should there be any fighting?'

Eustace paused a minute, and rubbed his face and considered the matter before he answered. 'She is troublesome,
you know,' he said.

'What; Lizzie?'

'Yes;—and I begin to be afraid she'll give us as much as
we know how to do. I was with Camperdown to-day. I'm
blessed if she hasn't begun to cut down a whole side of a forest
at Portray. She has no more right to touch the timber, except
for repairs about the place, than you have.'

'And if she lived for fifty years,' asked Greystock, 'is none to be cut?'

'Yes;—by consent. Of course the regular cutting for the year is done, year by year. That's as regular as the rents, and the produce is sold by the acre. But she is marking the old oaks. What the deuce can she want money for?'

'Fawn will put all that right.'

'He'll have to do it,' said Eustace. 'Since she has been down with the old Lady Fawn, she has written a note to Camperdown,—after leaving all his letters unanswered for the last twelvemonth,—to tell him that Lord Fawn is to have nothing to do with her property, and that certain people, called Mowbray and Mopus, are her lawyers. Camperdown is in an awful way about it.'

'Lord Fawn will put it all right,' said Frank.

'Camperdown is afraid that he won't. They've met twice since the engagement was made, and Camperdown says that, at the last meeting, Fawn gave himself airs, or was, at any rate, unpleasant. There were words about those diamonds.'

'You don't mean to say that Lord Fawn wants to keep your brother's family jewels?'

'Camperdown didn't say that exactly;—but Fawn made no offer of giving them up. I wasn't there, and only heard what Camperdown told me. Camperdown thinks he's afraid of her.'

'I shouldn't wonder at that in the least,' said Frank.

'I know there'll be trouble,' continued Eustace, 'and Fawn won't be able to help us through it. She's a strong-willed, cunning, obstinate, clever little creature. Camperdown swears he'll be too many for her, but I almost doubt it.'

'And therefore you wish I were going to marry her?'

'Yes, I do. You might manage her. The money comes from the Eustace property, and I'd sooner it should go to you than a half-hearted, numb-fingered, cold-blooded Whig, like Fawn.'

'I don't like cunning women,' said Frank.

'As bargains go, it wouldn't be a bad one,' said Eustace.

'She's very young, has a noble jointure, and is as handsome as she can stand. It's too good a thing for Fawn;—too good for any Whig.'

When Eustace left him, Greystock lit his cigar and walked with it in his mouth from Pall Mall to the Temple. He often worked there at night when he was not bound to be in the House, or when the House was not sitting,—and he was now intent on mastering the mysteries of some much-complicated legal case which had been confided to him, in order that he might present it to a jury enveloped in increased mystery. But, as he went, he thought rather of matrimony than of law;—and he thought especially of matrimony as it was about to affect Lord Fawn. Could a man be justified in marrying for money, or have rational ground for expecting that he might make himself happy by doing so? He kept muttering to himself as he went, the Quaker's advice to the old farmer, 'Doan't thou marry for munny, but goa where munny is!'* But he muttered it as condemning the advice rather than accepting it.

He could look out and see two altogether different kinds of life before him, both of which had their allurements. There was the Belgrave-cum-Pimlico life,* the scene of which might extend itself to South Kensington, enveloping the parks and coming round over Park Lane, and through Grosvenor Square and Berkeley Square back to Piccadilly. Within this he might live with lords and countesses and rich folk generally, going out to the very best dinner-parties, avoiding stupid people, having everything the world could give, except a wife and family and home of his own. All this he could achieve by the work which would certainly fall in his way, and by means of that position in the world which he had already attained by his wits. And the wife, with the family and house of his own, might be forthcoming, should it ever come in his way to form an attachment with a wealthy woman. He knew how dangerous were the charms of such a life as this to a man growing old among the flesh-pots, without any one to depend upon him. He had seen what becomes of the man who is always dining out at sixty. But he might avoid that. 'Doan't thou marry for munny, but goa where munny is.' And then there was that other outlook, the scene of which was laid somewhere north of Oxford Street,* and the glory of which consisted in Lucy's smile, and Lucy's hand, and Lucy's kiss, as he returned home weary from his work.

There are many men, and some women, who pass their lives without knowing what it is to be or to have been in love. They not improbably marry,—the men do, at least,—and make good average husbands. Their wives are useful to them, and they learn to feel that a woman, being a wife, is entitled to all the respect, protection, and honour which a man can give, or procure for her. Such men, no doubt, often live honest lives, are good Christians, and depart hence with hopes as justifiable as though they had loved as well as Romeo.* But yet, as men, they have lacked a something, the want of which has made them small and poor and dry. It has never been felt by such a one that there would be triumph in giving away every-thing belonging to him for one little whispered, yielding word, in which there should be acknowledgment that he had suc-ceeded in making himself master of a human heart. And there are other men,—very many men,—who have felt this love, and have resisted it, feeling it to be unfit that Love should be Lord of all. Frank Greystock had told himself, a score of times, that it would be unbecoming in him to allow a passion to obtain such mastery of him as to interfere with his ambition. Could it be right that he who, as a young man, had already done so much, who might possibly have before him so high and great a career, should miss that, because he could not resist a feeling which a little chit of a girl had created in his bosom,—a girl without money, without position, without even beauty; a girl as to whom, were he to marry her, the world would say, 'Oh, heaven!—there has Frank Greystock gone and married a little governess out of old Lady Fawn's nur-sery!' And yet he loved her with all his heart, and to-day he had told her of his love. What should he do next?

The complicated legal case received neither much ravelling

or unravelling from his brains that night; but before he left his chambers he wrote the following letter:—

'Midnight, Saturday,
'All among my books and papers,
'2, Bolt Court, Middle Temple.

'DEAR, DEAR LUCY,

'I told you to-day that you had ever been the Queen who reigned in those palaces which I have built in Spain. You did not make me much of an answer; but such as it was,—only just one muttered doubtful-sounding word,—it has made me hope that I may be justified in asking you to share with me a home which will not be palatial. If I am wrong——? But no; —I will not think I am wrong, or that I can be wrong. No sound coming from you is really doubtful. You are truth itself, and the muttered word would have been other than it was, if you had not——! may I say,—had you not already learned to love me?

'You will feel, perhaps, that I ought to have said all this to you then, and that a letter in such a matter is but a poor substitute for a spoken assurance of affection. You shall have the whole truth. Though I have long loved you, I did not go down to Fawn Court with the purpose of declaring to you my love. What I said to you was God's truth; but it was spoken without thought at the moment. I have thought of it much since;— and now I write to ask you to be my wife. I have lived for the last year or two with this hope before me; and now—— Dear, dear Lucy, I will not write in too great confidence; but I will tell you that all my happiness is in your hands.

'If your answer is what I hope it may be, tell Lady Fawn at once. I shall immediately write to Bobsborough, as I hate secrets in such matters. And if it is to be so,—then I shall claim the privilege of going to Fawn Court as soon and as often as I please.

'Yours ever and always,—if you will have me,—
'F. G.'

He sat for an hour at his desk, with his letter lying on the table, before he left his chambers,—looking at it. If he should decide on posting it, then would that life in Belgravia-cum-Pimlico,—of which in truth he was very fond,—be almost closed for him. The lords and countesses, and rich county members, and leading politicians, who were delighted to welcome him, would not care for his wife; nor could he very well take his wife among them. To live with them as a married man, he must live as they lived;—and must have his own house in their precincts. Later in life, he might possibly work up to this;—but for the present he must retire into dim domestic security and the neighbourhood of Regent's Park. He sat looking at the letter, telling himself that he was now, at this moment, deciding his own fate in life. And he again muttered the Quaker's advice, 'Doan't thou marry for munny, but goa where munny is!' It may be said, however, that no man ever writes such a letter, and then omits to send it. He walked out of the Temple with it in his hand, and dropped it into a pillar letter-box just outside the gate. As the envelope slipped through his fingers, he felt that he had now bound himself to his fate.

CHAPTER XIV
'Doan't thou marry for munny'

As that Saturday afternoon wore itself away, there was much excitement at Fawn Court. When Lady Fawn returned with the carriage, she heard that Frank Greystock had been at Fawn Court; and she heard also, from Augusta, that he had been rambling about the grounds alone with Lucy Morris. At any exhibition of old ladies, held before a competent jury, Lady Fawn would have taken a prize on the score of good humour. No mother of daughters was ever less addicted to scold and to be fretful. But just now she was a little unhappy. Lizzie's visit had not been a success, and she looked forward to her son's marriage with almost unmixed dismay. Mrs. Hittaway had written daily, and in all Mrs. Hittaway's letters some addition was made to the evil things already known. In her last letter Mrs. Hittaway had expressed her opinion that even yet 'Frederic' would escape. All this Lady Fawn had, of course, not told to her daughters generally. To the eldest, Augusta, it was thought expedient to say nothing, because Augusta had been selected as the companion of the, alas! too probable future Lady Fawn. But to Amelia something did leak out, and it became apparent that the household was uneasy. Now,—as an evil added to this,—Frank Greystock had been there in Lady Fawn's absence, walking about the grounds alone with Lucy Morris. Lady Fawn could hardly restrain herself. 'How could Lucy be so very wrong?' she said, in the hearing both of Augusta and Amelia.

Lizzie Eustace did not hear this; but knowing very well that a governess should not receive a lover in the absence of the lady of the house, she made her little speech about it. 'Dear Lady Fawn,' she said, 'my cousin Frank came to see me while you were out.'

'So I hear,' said Lady Fawn.

'Frank and I are more like brother and sister than anything else. I had so much to say to him;—so much to ask him to do! I have no one else, you know, and I had especially told him to come here.'

'Of course he was welcome to come.'

'Only I was afraid you might think that there was some little lover's trick,—on dear Lucy's part, you know.'

'I never suspect anything of that kind,' said Lady Fawn, bridling up. 'Lucy Morris is above any sort of trick. We don't have any tricks here, Lady Eustace.' Lady Fawn herself might say that Lucy was 'wrong,' but no one else in that house should even suggest evil of Lucy. Lizzie retreated smiling. To have 'put Lady Fawn's back up,' as she called it, was to her an achievement and a pleasure.

But the great excitement of the evening consisted in the expected coming of Lord Fawn. Of what nature would be the meeting between Lord Fawn and his promised bride? Was there anything of truth in the opinion expressed by Mrs.

Hittaway that her brother was beginning to become tired of his bargain? That Lady Fawn was tired of it herself,—that she disliked Lizzie, and was afraid of her, and averse to the idea of regarding her as a daughter-in-law,—she did not now attempt to hide from herself. But there was the engagement, known to all the world, and how could its fulfilment now be avoided? The poor dear old woman began to repeat to herself the first half of the Quaker's advice, 'Doan't thou marry for munny.'

Lord Fawn was to come down only in time for a late dinner. An ardent lover, one would have thought, might have left his work somewhat earlier on a Saturday, so as to have enjoyed with his sweetheart something of the sweetness of the Saturday summer afternoon;—but it was seven before he reached Fawn Court, and the ladies were at that time in their rooms dressing. Lizzie had affected to understand all his reasons for being so late, and had expressed herself as perfectly satisfied. 'He has more to do than any of the others,' she had said to Augusta. 'Indeed, the whole of our vast Indian empire may be said to hang upon him, just at present:'—which was not complimentary to Lord Fawn's chief, the Right Honourable Legge Wilson,* who at the present time represented the interests of India in the Cabinet. 'He is terribly overworked, and it is a shame;—but what can one do?'

'I think he likes work.' Augusta had replied.

'But I don't like it,—not so much of it; and so I shall make him understand, my dear. But I don't complain. As long as he tells me everything, I will never really complain.' Perhaps it might some day be as she desired; perhaps as a husband he would be thoroughly confidential and communicative; perhaps when they two were one flesh*he would tell her everything about India;—but as yet he certainly had not told her much.

'How had they better meet?' Amelia asked her mother.

'Oh;—I don't know;—anyhow; just as they like. We can't arrange anything for her. If she had chosen to dress herself early, she might have seen him as he came in; but it was impossible to tell her so.' No arrangement was therefore made, and as all the other ladies were in the drawing-room before Lizzie came down, she had to give him his welcome in the midst of the family circle. She did it very well. Perhaps she had thought of it, and made her arrangements. When he came forward to greet her, she put her cheek up, just a little, so that he might see that he was expected to kiss it;—but so little, that should he omit to do so, there might be no visible awkwardness. It must be acknowledged on Lizzie's behalf, that she could always avoid awkwardness. He did touch her cheek with his lips, blushing as he did so. She had her ungloved hand in his, and, still holding him, returned into the circle. She said not a word; and what he said was of no moment;—but they had met as lovers, and any of the family who had allowed themselves to imagine that even yet the match might be broken, now unconsciously abandoned that hope. 'Was he always such a truant, Lady Fawn?'—Lizzie asked, when it seemed to her that no one else would speak a word.

'I don't know that there is much difference,' said Lady Fawn. 'Here is dinner. Frederic, will you give——Lady Eustace your arm?' Poor Lady Fawn! It often came to pass that she was awkward.

There were no less than ten females sitting round the board, at the bottom of which Lord Fawn took his place. Lady Fawn had especially asked Lucy to come in to dinner, and with Lucy had come the two younger girls. At Lord Fawn's right hand sat Lizzie, and Augusta at his left. Lady Fawn had Amelia on one side and Lucy on the other. 'So Mr. Greystock was here to-day,' Lady Fawn whispered into Lucy's ear.

'Yes; he was here.'

'Oh, Lucy!'

'I did not bid him come, Lady Fawn.'

'I am sure of that, my dear;—but—but——' Then there was no more to be said on that subject on that occasion.

During the whole of the dinner the conversation was kept up at the other end of the table by Lizzie talking to Augusta across her lover. This was done in such a manner as to seem to include Lord Fawn in every topic discussed. Parliament,

India, the Sawab, Ireland, the special privileges of the House of Lords, the ease of a bachelor life, and the delight of having at his elbow just such a rural retreat as Fawn Court,—these were the fruitful themes of Lizzie's eloquence. Augusta did her part at any rate with patience; and as for Lizzie herself, she worked with that superhuman energy which women can so often display in making conversation under unfavourable circumstances. The circumstances were unfavourable, for Lord Fawn himself would hardly open his mouth; but Lizzie persevered, and the hour of dinner passed over without any show of ill humour, or of sullen silence. When the hour was over, Lord Fawn left the room with the ladies, and was soon closeted with his mother, while the girls strolled out upon the lawn. Would Lizzie play croquet? No; Lizzie would not play croquet. She thought it probable that she might catch her lover and force him to walk with her through the shrubberies; but Lord Fawn was not seen upon the lawn that evening, and Lizzie was forced to content herself with Augusta as a companion. In the course of the evening, however, her lover did say a word to her in private. 'Give me ten minutes to-morrow between breakfast and church, Lizzie.' Lizzie promised that she would do so, smiling sweetly. Then there was a little music, and then Lord Fawn retired to his studies.

'What is he going to say to me?' Lizzie asked Augusta the next morning. There existed in her bosom a sort of craving after confidential friendship,—but with it there existed something that was altogether incompatible with confidence. She thoroughly despised Augusta Fawn, and yet would have been willing,—in want of a better friend,—to press Augusta to her bosom, and swear that there should ever be between them the tenderest friendship. She desired to be the possessor of the outward shows of all those things of which the inward facts are valued by the good and steadfast ones of the earth. She knew what were the aspirations,—what the ambition, of an honest woman; and she knew, too, how rich were the probable rewards of such honesty. True love, true friendship, true benevolence, true tenderness, were beautiful to her,—qualities

on which she could descant almost with eloquence; and therefore she was always shamming love and friendship and benevolence and tenderness. She could tell you, with words most
appropriate to the subject, how horrible were all shams, and
in saying so would be not altogether insincere;—yet she knew
that she herself was ever shamming, and she satisfied herself
with shams. 'What is he going to say to me?' she asked
Augusta, with her hands clasped, when she went up to put
her bonnet on after breakfast.

'To fix the day, I suppose,' said Augusta.

'If I thought so, I would endeavour to please him. But it
isn't that. I know his manner so well! I am sure it is not that.
Perhaps it is something about my boy. He will not wish to
separate a mother from her child.'

'Oh dear no,' said Augusta. 'I am sure Frederic will not
want to do that.'

'In anything else I will obey him,' said Lizzie, again clasping her hands. 'But I must not keep him waiting,—must I?
I fear my future lord is somewhat impatient.' Now, if among
Lord Fawn's merits one merit was more conspicuous than
another, it was that of patience. When Lizzie descended he
was waiting for her in the hall without a thought that he was
being kept too long. 'Now, Frederic! I should have been with
you two whole minutes since, if I had not had just a word to
say to Augusta. I do so love Augusta.'

'She is a very good girl,' said Lord Fawn.

'So true and genuine,—and so full of spirit. I will come on
the other side because of my parasol and the sun. There, that
will do. We have an hour nearly before going to church;—
haven't we? I suppose you will go to church.'

'I intend it,' said Lord Fawn.

'It is so nice to go to church,' said Lizzie. Since her widowhood had commenced, she had compromised matters with the
world. One Sunday she would go to church, and the next she
would have a headache and a French novel and stay in bed.
But she was prepared for stricter conduct during at least the
first months of her newly-married life.

'My dear Lizzie,' began Lord Fawn, 'since I last saw you I have been twice with Mr. Camperdown.'

'You are not going to talk about Mr. Camperdown to-day?'

'Well;—yes. I could not do so last night, and I shall be back in London either to-night or before you are up to-morrow morning.'

'I hate the very name of Mr. Camperdown,' said Lizzie.

'I am sorry for that, because I am sure you could not find an honester lawyer to manage your affairs for you. He does everything for me, and so he did for Sir Florian Eustace.'

'That is just the reason why I employ some one else,' she answered.

'Very well. I am not going to say a word about that. I may regret it, but I am, just at present, the last person in the world to urge you upon that subject. What I want to say is this. You must restore those diamonds.'

'To whom shall I restore them?'

'To Mr. Garnett, the silversmith, if you please,—or to Mr. Camperdown;—or, if you like it better, to your brother-in-law, Mr. John Eustace.'

'And why am I to give up my own property?'

Lord Fawn paused for some seconds before he replied. 'To satisfy my honour,' he then said. As she made him no immediate answer, he continued,—'It would not suit my views that my wife should be seen wearing the jewels of the Eustace family.'

'I don't want to wear them,' said Lizzie.

'Then why should you desire to keep them?'

'Because they are my own. Because I do not choose to be put upon. Because I will not allow such a cunning old snake as Mr. Camperdown to rob me of my property. They are my own, and you should defend my right to them.'

'Do you mean to say that you will not oblige me by doing what I ask you?'

'I will not be robbed of what is my own,' said Lizzie.

'Then I must declare—;' and now Lord Fawn spoke very slowly;—'then I must declare that under these circumstances, let the consequences be what they may, I must retreat from the enviable position which your favour has given me.' The words were cold and solemn, and were ill-spoken; but they were deliberate, and had been indeed actually learned by heart.

'What do you mean?' said Lizzie, flashing round upon him.

'I mean what I say,—exactly. But perhaps it may be well that I should explain my motives more clearly.'

'I don't know anything about motives, and I don't care anything about motives. Do you mean to tell me that you have come here to threaten me with deserting me?'

'You had better hear me.'

'I don't choose to hear a word more after what you have said,—unless it be in the way of an apology, or retracting your most injurious accusation.'

'I have said nothing to retract,' said Lord Fawn solemnly.

'Then I will not hear another word from you. I have friends, and you shall see them.'

Lord Fawn, who had thought a great deal upon the subject, and had well understood that this interview would be for him one of great difficulty, was very anxious to induce her to listen to a few further words of explanation. 'Dear Lizzie——' he began.

'I will not be addressed, sir, in that way by a man who is treating me as you are doing,' she said.

'But I want you to understand me.'

'Understand you! You understand nothing yourself that a man ought to understand. I wonder that you have the courage to be so insolent. If you knew what you were doing, you would not have the spirit to do it.'

Her words did not quite come home to him, and much of her scorn was lost upon him. He was now chiefly anxious to explain to her that though he must abide by the threat he had made, he was quite willing to go on with his engagement if she would oblige him in the matter of the diamonds. 'It was necessary that I should explain to you that I could not allow that necklace to be brought into my house.'

'No one thought of taking it to your house.'

'What were you to do with it, then?'

'Keep it in my own,' said Lizzie stoutly. They were still walking together, and were now altogether out of sight of the house. Lizzie in her excitement had forgotten church, had forgotten the Fawn women,—had forgotten everything except the battle which it was necessary that she should fight for herself. She did not mean to allow the marriage to be broken off,—but she meant to retain the necklace. The manner in which Lord Fawn had demanded its restitution,—in which there had been none of that mock tenderness by which she might have permitted herself to be persuaded,—had made her, at any rate for the moment, as firm as steel on this point. It was inconceivable to her that he should think himself at liberty to go back from his promise, because she would not render up property which was in her possession, and which no one could prove not to be legally her own! She walked on full of fierce courage,—despising him, but determined that she would marry him.

'I am afraid we do not understand each other,' he said at last.

'Certainly I do not understand you, sir.'

'Will you allow my mother to speak to you on the subject?'

'No. If I told your mother to give up her diamonds, what would she say?'

'But they are not yours, Lady Eustace, unless you will submit that question to an arbitrator.'

'I will submit nothing to anybody. You have no right to speak on such a subject till after we are married.'

'I must have it settled first, Lady Eustace.'

'Then, Lord Fawn, you won't have it settled first. Or rather it is settled already. I shall keep my own necklace, and Mr. Camperdown may do anything he pleases. As for you,—if you ill-treat me, I shall know where to go to.' They had now come out from the shrubbery upon the lawn, and there was the carriage at the door, ready to take the elders of the family to church. Of course in such a condition of affairs it would be understood that Lizzie was one of the elders. 'I shall not go to church now,' she said, as she advanced across the lawn towards the hall door. 'You will be pleased, Lord Fawn, to let your mother know that I am detained. I do not suppose that you will dare to tell her why.' Then she sailed round at the back of the carriage and entered the hall, in which several of the girls were standing. Among them was Augusta, waiting to take her seat among the elders;—but Lizzie passed on through them all, without a word, and marched up to her bed-room.

'Oh, Frederic, what is the matter?' asked Augusta, as soon as her brother entered the house.

'Never mind. Nothing is the matter. You had better go to church. Where is my mother?'

At this moment Lady Fawn appeared at the bottom of the stairs, having passed Lizzie as she was coming down. Not a syllable had then been spoken, but Lady Fawn at once knew that much was wrong. Her son went up to her and whispered a word in her ear. 'Oh, certainly,' she said, desisting from the operation of pulling on her gloves. 'Augusta, neither your brother nor I will go to church.'

'Nor—Lady Eustace?'

'It seems not,' said Lady Fawn.

'Lady Eustace will not go to church,' said Lord Fawn.

'And where is Lucy?' asked Lydia.

'She will not go to church either,' said Lady Fawn. 'I have just been with her.'

'Nobody is going to church,' said Nina. 'All the same, I shall go by myself.'

'Augusta, my dear, you and the girls had better go. You can take the carriage of course.' But Augusta and the girls chose to walk, and the carriage was sent round into the yard.

'There's a rumpus already between my lord and the young missus,' said the coachman to the groom;—for the coachman had seen the way in which Lady Eustace had returned to the house. And there certainly was a rumpus. During the whole morning Lord Fawn was closeted with his mother, and then he went away to London without saying a word to any one of the family. But he left this note for Lady Eustace.

'DEAREST LIZZIE,

'Think well of what I have said to you. It is not that I desire to break off our engagement; but that I cannot allow my wife to keep the diamonds which belong of right to her late husband's family. You may be sure that I should not be thus urgent had I not taken steps to ascertain that I am right in my judgment. In the meantime you had better consult my mother.

'Yours affectionately,
'FAWN.'

CHAPTER XV
'I'll give you a Hundred Guinea Brooch'

THERE had been another 'affair' in the house that morning, though of a nature very different to the 'rumpus' which had occurred between Lord Fawn and Lady Eustace. Lady Fawn had been closeted with Lucy, and had expressed her opinion of the impropriety of Frank Greystock's visit. 'I suppose he came to see his cousin,' said Lady Fawn, anxious to begin with some apology for such conduct.

'I cannot tell,' said Lucy. 'Perhaps he did. I think he said so. I think he cared more to see me.' Then Lady Fawn was obliged to express her opinion, and she did so, uttering many words of wisdom. Frank Greystock, had he intended to sacrifice his prospects by a disinterested marriage, would have spoken out before now. He was old enough to have made up his mind on such a subject, and he had not spoken out. He did not mean marriage. That was quite evident to Lady Fawn;— and her dear Lucy was revelling in hopes which would make her miserable. If Lucy could only have known of the letter, which was already her own property though lying in the pillar letter-box*in Fleet Street, and which had not already been sent down and delivered simply because it was Sunday morning! But she was very brave. 'He does love me,' she said. 'He told me so.'

'Oh, Lucy;—that is worse and worse. A man to tell you that he loves you, and yet not ask you to be his wife!'

'I am contented,' said Lucy. That assertion, however, could hardly have been true.

'Contented! And did you tell him that you returned his love?'

'He knew it without my telling him,' said Lucy. It was so hard upon her that she should be so interrogated while that letter was lying in the iron box!

'Dear Lucy, this must not be,' said Lady Fawn. 'You are preparing for yourself inexpressible misery.'

'I have done nothing wrong, Lady Fawn.'

'No, my dear;—no. I do not say you have been wrong. But I think he is wrong,—so wrong! I call it wicked. I do indeed. For your own sake you should endeavour to forget him.'

'I will never forget him!' said Lucy. 'To think of him is everything to me. He told me I was his Queen, and he shall be my King. I will be loyal to him always.' To poor Lady Fawn this was very dreadful. The girl persisted in declaring her love for the man, and yet did not even pretend to think that the man meant to marry her! And this, too, was Lucy Morris,—of whom Lady Fawn was accustomed to say to her intimate friends that she had altogether ceased to look upon her as a governess. 'Just one of ourselves, Mrs. Winslow,—and almost as dear as one of my own girls!' Thus, in the warmth of her heart, she had described Lucy to a neighbour within the last week. Many more words of wisdom she spoke, and then she left poor Lucy in no mood for church. Would she have been in a better mood for the morning service had she known of the letter in the iron post?

Then Lady Fawn had put on her bonnet and gone down into the hall, and the 'rumpus' had come. After that, everybody in the house knew that all things were astray. When the girls came home from church, their brother was gone. Half an hour before dinner Lady Fawn sent the note up to Lizzie, with a message to say that they would dine at three,—it being Sunday. Lizzie sent down word that as she was unwell, she would ask to have just a cup of tea and 'something' sent to her own room. If Lady Fawn would allow her, she would remain upstairs with her child. She always made use of her child when troubles came.

The afternoon was very sad and dreary. Lady Fawn had an interview with Lady Eustace, but Lizzie altogether refused to listen to any advice on the subject of the necklace. 'It is an affair,' she said haughtily, 'in which I must judge for myself, —or with the advice of my own particular friends. Had Lord Fawn waited until we were married; then indeed——!'

'But that would have been too late,' said Lady Fawn severely.

'He is at any rate premature now in laying his commands upon me,' said Lizzie. Lady Fawn, who was perhaps more anxious that the marriage should be broken off than that the jewels should be restored, then withdrew; and as she left the room Lizzie clasped her boy to her bosom. 'He, at any rate, is left to me,' she said. Lucy and the Fawn girls went to evening church, and afterwards Lizzie came down among them when they were at tea. Before she went to bed Lizzie declared her intention of returning to her own house in Mount Street on the following day. To this Lady Fawn of course made no objection.

On the next morning there came an event which robbed Lizzie's departure of some of the importance which might otherwise have been attached to it. The post-office, with that accuracy in the performance of its duties for which it is conspicuous among all offices,* caused Lucy's letter to be delivered to her while the members of the family were sitting round the breakfast table. Lizzie, indeed, was not there. She had expressed her intention of breakfasting in her own room, and had requested that a conveyance might be ready to take her to the 11.30 train. Augusta had been with her, asking whether anything could be done for her. 'I care for nothing now, except my child,' Lizzie had replied. As the nurse and the lady's maid were both in the room, Augusta, of course, could say nothing further. That occurred after prayers, and while the tea was being made. When Augusta reached the breakfast-room, Lucy was cutting up the loaf of bread, and at the same moment the old butler was placing a letter immediately under her eyes. She saw the handwriting and recognised it, but yet she finished cutting the bread. 'Lucy, do give me that hunchy bit,' said Nina.

'Hunchy is not in the dictionary,' said Cecilia.

'I want it in my plate, and not in the dictionary,' said Nina.

Lucy did as she was asked, but her hand trembled as she gave the hunch, and Lady Fawn saw that her face was crimson. She took the letter and broke the envelope, and as she drew out the sheet of paper, she looked up at Lady Fawn. The fate of her whole life was in her hands, and there she was standing with all their eyes fixed upon her. She did not even know how to sit down, but, still standing, she read the first words, and at the last, 'Dear, dear Lucy,'—'Yours ever and always, if you will have me, F. G.' She did not want to read any more of it then. She sat down slowly, put the precious paper back into its envelope, looked round upon them all, and knew that she was crimson to the roots of her hair, blushing like a guilty thing.

'Lucy, my dear,' said Lady Fawn,—and Lucy at once turned her face full upon her old friend,—'you have got a letter that agitates you.'

'Yes,—I have,' she said.

'Go into the book-room. You can come back to breakfast when you have read it, you know.' Thereupon Lucy rose from her seat, and retired with her treasure into the book-room. But even when she was there she could not at once read her letter. When the door was closed and she knew that she was alone she looked at it, and then clasped it tight between her hands. She was almost afraid to read it lest the letter itself should contradict the promise which the last words of it had seemed to convey to her. She went up to the window and stood there gazing out upon the gravel road, with her hand containing the letter pressed upon her heart. Lady Fawn had told her that she was preparing for herself inexpressible misery;— and now there had come to her joy so absolutely inexpressible! 'A man to tell you that he loves you, and yet not ask you to be his wife!' She repeated to herself Lady Fawn's words,— and then those other words, 'Yours ever and always, if you will have me!' Have him, indeed! She threw from her, at once, as vain and wicked and false, all idea of coying her love. She would leap at his neck if he were there, and tell him that for years he had been, almost, her god. And of course he knew it. 'If I will have him! Traitor!' she said to herself, smiling through her tears. Then she reflected that after all it would be well that she should read the letter. There might be conditions;—though what conditions could he propose with which she would not comply? However, she seated herself in a corner of the room and did read the letter. As she read it, she hardly understood it all;—but she understood what she wanted to understand. He asked her to share with him his home. He had spoken to her that day without forethought;— but mustn't such speech be the truest and the sweetest of all speeches? 'And now I write to you to ask you to be my wife.' Oh, how wrong some people can be in their judgments! How wrong Lady Fawn had been in hers about Frank Greystock! 'For the last year or two I have lived with this hope before me.' 'And so have I,' said Lucy. 'And so have I;—with that and no other.' 'Too great confidence! Traitor,' she said again, smiling and weeping, 'yes, traitor; when of course you knew it.' 'Is his happiness in my hands? Oh,—then he shall be happy.' 'Of course I will tell Lady Fawn at once;—instantly. Dear Lady Fawn! But yet she has been so wrong. I suppose she will let him come here. But what does it matter, now that I know it?' 'Yours ever and always,—if you will have me.— F. G.' 'Traitor, traitor, traitor!' Then she got up and walked about the room, not knowing what she did, holding the letter now between her hands, and then pressing it to her lips.

She was still walking about the room when there came a low

tap at the door, and Lady Fawn entered. 'There is nothing
the matter, Lucy?' Lucy stood stock still, with her treasure
still clasped, smiling, almost laughing, while the tears ran
down her cheeks. 'Won't you eat your breakfast, my dear?'
said Lady Fawn.

'Oh, Lady Fawn—oh, Lady Fawn!' said Lucy, rushing into
her friend's arms.

'What is it Lucy? I think our little wise one has lost her
wits.'

'Oh, Lady Fawn, he has asked me!'

'Is it Mr. Greystock?'

'Yes;—Mr. Greystock. He has asked me. He has asked me
to be his wife. I thought he loved me. I hoped he did, at least.
Oh, dear, I did so hope it! And he does!'

'Has he proposed to you?'

'Yes, Lady Fawn. I told you what he said to me. And then
he went and wrote this. Is he not noble and good,—and so
kind? You shall read it,—but you'll give it me back, Lady
Fawn?'

'Certainly I'll give it you back. You don't think I'd rob you
of your lover's letter?'

'Perhaps you might think it right.'

'If it is really an offer of marriage——,' said Lady Fawn
very seriously.

'It couldn't be more of an offer if he had sat writing it for
ever,' said Lucy as she gave up her letter with confidence.
Lady Fawn read it with leisurely attention, and smiled as she
put the paper back into the envelope. 'All the men in the world
couldn't say it more plainly,' said Lucy, nodding her head
forward.

'I don't think they could,' said Lady Fawn. 'I never read
anything plainer in my life. I wish you joy with all my heart,
Lucy. There is not a word to be said against him.'

'Against him!' said Lucy, who thought that this was very
insufficient praise.

'What I mean is, that when I objected to his coming here
I was only afraid that he couldn't afford,—or would think,

137

you know, that in his position he couldn't afford to marry a wife without a fortune.'

'He may come now, Lady Fawn?'

'Well,—yes; I think so. I shall be glad just to say a word to him. Of course you are in my hands, and I do love you so dearly, Lucy! I could not bear that anything but good should happen to you.'

'This is good,' said Lucy.

'It won't be good, and Mr. Greystock won't think you good, if you don't come and eat your breakfast.' So Lucy was led back into the parlour, and sipped her tea and crunched her toast, while Lydia came and stood over her.

'Of course it is from him?' whispered Lydia. Lucy again nodded her head while she was crunching her toast.

The fact that Mr. Greystock had proposed in form to Lucy Morris was soon known to all the family, and the news certainly did take away something from the importance which would otherwise have been attached to Lizzie's departure. There was not the same awe of the ceremony, the same dread of some scene, which but for Frank Greystock's letter would have existed. Of course, Lord Fawn's future matrimonial prospects were to them all an affair of more moment than those of Lucy; but Lord Fawn himself had gone, and had already quarrelled with the lady before he went. There was at present nothing more to be done by them in regard to Lizzie, than just to get rid of her. But Lucy's good fortune, so unexpected, and by her so frankly owned as the very best fortune in the world that could have befallen her, gave an excitement to them all. There could be no lessons that morning for Nina, and the usual studies of the family were altogether interrupted. Lady Fawn purred, and congratulated, and gave good advice, and declared that any other home for Lucy before her marriage would now be quite out of the question. 'Of course it wouldn't do for you to go even to Clara,' said Lady Fawn,—who seemed to think that there still might be some delay before Frank Greystock would be ready for his wife. 'You know, my dear, that he isn't rich;—not for a member of Parliament. I suppose he makes a good income, but I have always heard that he was a little backward when he began. Of course, you know, nobody need be in a hurry.' Then Lucy began to think that if Frank should wish to postpone his marriage,—say for three or four years,—she might even yet become a burthen on her friend. 'But don't you be frightened,' continued Lady Fawn; 'you shall never want a home as long as I have one to give you. We shall soon find out what are Mr. Greystock's ideas; and unless he is very unreasonable we'll make things fit.'

Then there came a message to Lucy from Lady Eustace. 'If you please, miss, Lady Eustace will be glad to see you for a minute up in her room before she starts.' So Lucy was torn away from the thoughts of her own happiness, and taken up-stairs to Lady Eustace. 'You have heard that I am going?' said Lizzie.

'Yes;—I heard you were to go this morning.'

'And you have heard why? I'm sure you will not deceive me, Lucy. Where am I to look for truth, if not to an old old friend like you?'

'Why should I deceive you, Lizzie?'

'Why, indeed? only that all people do. The world is so false, so material, so worldly! One gives out one's heart and gets in return nothing but dust and ashes,—nothing but ashes and dust. Oh, I have been so disappointed in Lady Fawn!'

'You know she is my dearest friend,' said Lucy.

'Psha! I know that you have worked for her like a slave, and that she gives you but a bare pittance.'

'She has been more like a mother to me than anything else,' said Lucy angrily.

'Because you have been tame. It does not suit me to be tame. It is not my plan to be tame. Have you heard the cause of the disagreement between Lord Fawn and me?'

'Well,—no.'

'Tell the truth, Lucy.'

'How dare you tell me to tell the truth? Of course, I tell the truth. I believe it is something about some property which he wants you to give back to somebody; but I don't know any more.'

'Yes, my dear husband, Sir Florian, who understood me,—whom I idolized,—who seemed to have been made for me,—gave me a present. Lord Fawn is pleased to say that he does not approve of my keeping any gift from my late lord. Considering that he intends to live upon the wealth which Sir Florian was generous enough to bestow upon me, this does seem to be strange! Of course, I resented such interference. Would not you have resented it?'

'I don't know,' said Lucy, who thought that she could bring herself to comply with any request made to her by Frank Greystock.

'Any woman who had a spark of ¬pirit would resent it, and I have resented it. I have told Lord Fawn that I will, on no account, part with the rich presents which my adored Florian showered upon me in his generosity. It is not for their richness that I keep them, but because they are, for his sake, so inexpressibly dear to me. If Lord Fawn chooses to be jealous of a necklace, he must be jealous.' Lucy, who had, in truth, heard but a small fragment of the story,—just so much of it as Lydia had learned from the discreet Amelia, who herself had but a very hazy idea of the facts,—did not quite know how much of the tale, as it was now told to her, might be true and how much false. After a certain fashion she and Lizzie Eustace called themselves friends. But she did not believe her friend to be honest, and was aware that in some matters her friend would condescend—to fib. Lizzie's poetry, and romance, and high feelings, had never had the ring of true soundness in Lucy's ears. But her imagination was not strong enough to soar to the altitude of the lies which Lizzie was now telling. She did believe that the property which Lizzie was called upon to restore was held to be objectionable by Lord Fawn simply because it had reached Lizzie from the hands of her late husband. 'What do you think of such conduct as that?' asked Lady Eustace.

'Won't it do if you lock them up instead of wearing them?' asked Lucy.

'I have never dreamed of wearing them.'

'I don't understand about such things,' said Lucy, determined not to impute any blame to one of the Fawn family.

'It is tyranny, sheer tyranny,' continued the other, 'and he will find that I am not the woman to yield to it. No. For love I could give up everything;—but nothing from fear. He has told me in so many words that he does not intend to go on with his engagement!'

'Has he indeed?'

'But I intend that he shall. If he thinks that I am going to be thrown over because he takes ideas of that kind into his head, he's mistaken. He shall know that I'm not to be made a plaything of like that. I'll tell you what you can do for me, Lucy.'

'What can I do for you?'

'There is no one in the world I trust more thoroughly than I do you,' said Lizzie,—'and hardly any one that I love so well. Think how long we have known each other! And you may be sure of this;—I always have been, and always will be, your friend with my cousin Frank.'

'I don't want anything of that kind,' said Lucy,—'and never did.'

'Nobody has so much influence with Frank as I. Just do you write to me to-morrow, and the next day,—and the day after,—a mere line, you know, to tell me how the land lies here.'

'There would be nothing to tell.'

'Yes, there will; ever so much. They will be talking about me every hour. If you'll be true to me, Lucy, in this business, I'll make you the handsomest present you ever saw in your life. I'll give you a hundred guinea brooch;—I will, indeed. You shall have the money, and buy it yourself.'

'A what!' said Lucy.

'A hundred guineas to do what you please with!'

'You mean thing!' said Lucy. 'I didn't think there was a woman so mean as that in the world. I'm not surprised now at Lord Fawn. Pick up what I hear, and send it you in letters, —and then be paid money for it!'

'Why not? It's all to do good.'

'How can you have thought to ask me to do such a thing? How can you bring yourself to think so badly of people? I'd sooner cut my hand off; and as for you, Lizzie——I think you are mean and wicked to conceive such a thing. And now good-bye.' So saying, she left the room, giving her dear friend no time for further argument.

Lady Eustace got away that morning, not in time, indeed, for the 11.30 train, but at such an hour as to make it unnecessary that she should appear at the early dinner. The saying of farewell was very cold and ceremonious. Of course, there was no word as to any future visit,—no word as to any future events whatever. They all shook hands with her, and special injunctions were given to the coachman to drive her safely to the station. At this ceremony Lucy was not present. Lydia had asked her to come down and say good-bye; but Lucy refused. 'I saw her in her own room,' said Lucy.

'And was it all very affectionate?' Lydia asked.

'Well—no; it was not affectionate at all.' This was all that Lucy said, and thus Lady Eustace completed her visit to Fawn Court.

The letters were taken away for the post at eight o'clock in the evening, and before that time it was necessary that Lucy should write to her lover. 'Lady Fawn,' she said in a whisper, 'may I tell him to come here?'

'Certainly, my dear. You had better tell him to call on me. Of course he'll see you, too, when he comes.'

'I think he'd want to see me,' said Lucy, 'and I'm sure I should want to see him!' Then she wrote her answer to Frank's letter. She allowed herself an hour for the happy task; but though the letter, when written, was short, the hour hardly sufficed for the writing of it.

'DEAR MR. GREYSTOCK;'—there was matter for her of great consideration before she could get even so far as this; but, after biting her pen for ten minutes, during which she pictured to herself how pleasant it would be to call him Frank

142

when he should have told her to do so, and had found, upon repeated whispered trials, that of all names it was the pleasantest to pronounce, she decided upon refraining from writing it now—'Lady Fawn has seen your letter to me,—the dearest letter that ever was written, and she says that you may call upon *her*. But you mustn't go away without seeing *me too*.' Then there was great difficulty as to the words to be used by her for the actual rendering herself up to him as his future wife. At last the somewhat too Spartan simplicity of his nature prevailed, and the words were written, very plain and very short. 'I love you better than all the world, and I will be your wife. It shall be the happiness of my life to try to deserve you.

'I am, with all my heart,

'Most affectionately your own

'LUCY.'

When it was written it did not content her. But the hour was over, and the letters must go. 'I suppose it'll do,' she said to herself. 'He'll know what it means.' And so the letter was sent.

CHAPTER XVI
Certainly an Heirloom

THE burden of his position was so heavy on Lord Fawn's mind that, on the Monday morning after leaving Fawn Court, he was hardly as true to the affairs of India as he himself would have wished. He was resolved to do what was right,—if only he could find out what would be the right thing in his present difficulty. Not to break his word, not to be unjust, not to deviate by a hair's breadth from that line of conduct which would be described as 'honourable' in the circle to which he belonged, not to give his political enemies an opportunity for calumny,—this was all in all to him. The young widow was very lovely and very rich, and it would have suited him well to marry her. It would still suit him well to do so, if she would make herself amenable to reason and the laws. He had assured himself that he was very much in love with her, and had already, in his imagination, received the distinguished heads of his party at Portray Castle. But he would give all this up,—love, income, beauty, and castle, without a doubt, rather than find himself in the mess of having married a wife who had stolen a necklace, and who would not make restitution. He might marry her, and insist on giving it up afterwards; but he foresaw terrible difficulties in the way of such an arrangement. Lady Eustace was self-willed, and had already told him that she did not intend to keep the jewels in his house,—but in her own! What should he do, so that no human being,—not the most bigoted Tory that ever expressed scorn for a Whig lord,—should be able to say that he had done wrong? He was engaged to the lady, and could not simply change his mind and give no reason. He believed in Mr. Camperdown; but he could hardly plead that belief, should he hereafter be accused of heartless misconduct. For aught he knew, Lady Eustace might bring an action against him for breach of promise, and obtain a verdict and damages, and annihilate him as an Under-Secretary. How should he keep his hands quite clean?

Frank Greystock was, as far as he knew, Lizzie's nearest relative in London. The dean was her uncle, but then the dean was down at Bobsborough. It might be necessary for him to go down to Bobsborough;—but in the meantime he would see Frank Greystock. Greystock was as bitter a Tory as any in England. Greystock was the very man who had attacked him, Lord Fawn, in the House of Commons respecting the Sawab,—making the attack quite personal,—and that without a shadow of a cause! Within the short straight grooves of Lord Fawn's intellect the remembrance of this supposed wrong was always running up and down, renewing its own soreness. He regarded Greystock as an enemy who would lose no opportunity of injuring him. In his weakness and littleness he was quite unable to judge of other men by himself. He would not go a hair's breadth astray, if he knew it; but because Greystock had, in debate, called him timid and tyrannical, he believed that Greystock would stop short of nothing that might injure him. And yet he must appeal to Greystock? He did appeal, and in answer to his appeal Frank came to him at the India House. But Frank, before he saw Lord Fawn, had, as was fitting, been with his cousin.

Nothing was decided at this interview. Lord Fawn became more than ever convinced that the member of Bobsborough was his determined enemy, and Frank was more convinced than ever that Lord Fawn was an empty, stiff-necked, self-sufficient prig.

Greystock, of course, took his cousin's part. He was there to do so; and he himself really did not know whether Lizzie was or was not entitled to the diamonds. The lie which she had first fabricated for the benefit of Mr. Benjamin when she had the jewels valued, and which she had since told with different degrees of precision to various people,—to Lady Linlithgow, to Mr. Camperdown, to Lucy, and to Lord Fawn, —she now repeated with increased precision to her cousin. Sir Florian, in putting the trinket into her hands, had explained to her that it was very valuable, and that she was to regard it as her own peculiar property. 'If it was an heirloom he couldn't do it,' Frank had said, with all the confidence of a practising barrister.

'He made it over as an heirloom to me,' said Lizzie, with plaintive tenderness.

'That's nonsense, dear Lizzie.' Then she smiled sweetly on him, and patted the back of his hand with hers. She was very gentle with him, and bore his assumed superiority with pretty meekness. 'He could not make it over as an heirloom to you. If it was his to give, he could give it you.'

'It was his,—certainly.'

'That is just what I cannot tell as yet, and what must be found out. If the diamonds formed part of an heirloom, and there is evidence that it is so,—you must give them up. Sir Florian could only give away what was his own to give.'

'But Lord Fawn had no right to dictate.'

145

'Certainly not,' said Frank; and then he made a promise, which he knew to be rash, that he would stand by his pretty cousin in this affair. 'I don't see why you should assume that Lady Eustace is keeping property that doesn't belong to her,' he said to Lord Fawn.

'I go by what Camperdown tells me,' said Lord Fawn.

'Mr. Camperdown is a very excellent attorney, and a most respectable man,' said Greystock. 'I have nothing on earth to say against Mr. Camperdown. But Mr. Camperdown isn't the law and the prophets, nor yet can we allow him to be judge and jury in such a case as this.'

'Surely, Mr. Greystock, you wouldn't wish it to go before a jury..'

'You don't understand me, Lord Fawn. If any claim be really made for these jewels by Mr. John Eustace on the part of the heir, or on behalf of the estate, a statement had better be submitted to counsel. The family deeds must be inspected, and no doubt counsel would agree in telling my cousin, Lady Eustace, what she should, or what she should not do. In the meantime, I understand that you are engaged to marry her?'

'I was engaged to her, certainly,' said Lord Fawn.

'You can hardly mean to assert, my lord, that you intend to be untrue to your promise, and to throw over your own engagement because my cousin has expressed her wish to retain property which she believes to be her own!' This was said in a tone which made Lord Fawn surer than ever that Greystock was his enemy to the knife. Personally, he was not a coward; and he knew enough of the world to be quite sure that Greystock would not attempt any personal encounter.* But, morally, Lord Fawn was a coward, and he did fear that the man before him would work him some bitter injury. 'You cannot mean that,' continued Frank, 'and you will probably allow me to assure my cousin that she misunderstood you in the matter.'

'I'd sooner see Mr. Camperdown again before I say anything.'

'I cannot understand, Lord Fawn, that a gentleman should

require an attorney to tell him what to do in such a case as this.' They were standing now, and Lord Fawn's countenance was heavy, troubled, and full of doubt. He said nothing, and was probably altogether unaware how eloquent was his face. 'My cousin, Lady Eustace,' continued Frank, 'must not be kept in this suspense. I agree on her behalf that her title to these trinkets must be made the subject of inquiry by persons adequate to form a judgment. Of course, I, as her relative, shall take no part in that inquiry. But, as her relative, I must demand from you an admission that your engagement with her cannot in any way be allowed to depend on the fate of those jewels. She has chosen to accept you as her future husband, and I am bound to see that she is treated with good faith, honour, and fair observance.'

Frank made his demand very well, while Lord Fawn was looking like a whipped dog. 'Of course,' said his lordship, 'all I want is, that the right thing should be done.'

'The right thing will be done. My cousin wishes to keep nothing that is not her own. I may tell her, then, that she will receive from you an assurance that you have had no intention of departing from your word?' After this, Lord Fawn made some attempt at a stipulation that this assurance to Lizzie was to be founded on the counter-assurance given to him that the matter of the diamonds should be decided by proper legal authority; but Frank would not submit to this, and at last the Under-Secretary yielded. The engagement was to remain in force. Counsel were to be employed. The two lovers were not to see each other just at present. And when the matter had been decided by the lawyers, Lord Fawn was to express his regret for having suspected his lady-love! That was the verbal agreement, according to Frank Greystock's view of it. Lord Fawn, no doubt, would have declared that he had never consented to the latter stipulation.

About a week after this there was a meeting at Mr. Camperdown's chambers. Greystock, as his cousin's friend, attended to hear what Mr. Camperdown had to say in the presence of Lord Fawn and John Eustace. He, Frank, had, in the meantime, been down to Richmond, had taken Lucy to his arms as his future bride, and had been closeted with Lady Fawn. As a man who was doing his duty by Lucy Morris, he was welcomed and made much of by her ladyship; but it had been

impossible to leave Lizzie's name altogether unmentioned, and Frank had spoken as the champion of his cousin. Of course, there had arisen something of ill-feeling between the two. Lady Fawn had taught herself to hate Lizzie, and was desirous that the match should be over, diamonds or no diamonds. She could not quite say this to her visitor, but she showed her feeling very plainly. Frank was courteous, cold, and resolute in presuming, or pretending to presume, that as a matter of course the marriage would take place. Lady Fawn intended to be civil, but she could not restrain her feeling; and though she did not dare to say that her son would have nothing more to do with Lizzie Eustace, she showed very plainly that she intended to work with that object. Of course, the two did not part as cordial friends, and of course poor Lucy perceived that it was so.

Before the meeting took place, Mr. Camperdown had been at work, looking over old deeds. It is undoubtedly the case that things often become complicated which, from the greatness of their importance, should have been kept clear as running water. The diamonds in question had been bought, with other jewels, by Sir Florian's grandfather, on the occasion of his marriage with the daughter of a certain duke,— on which occasion old family jewels, which were said to have been heirlooms, were sold or given in exchange as part value for those then purchased. This grandfather, who had also been Sir Florian in his time, had expressly stated in his will that these jewels were to be regarded as an heirloom in the family, and had as such left them to his eldest son, and to that son's eldest son, should such a child be born. His eldest son had possessed them, but not that son's son. There was such an Eustace born, but he had died before his father. The younger son of that old Sir Florian had then succeeded, as Sir Thomas, and he was the father of that Florian who had married Lizzie Eustace. That last Sir Florian had therefore been the fourth in succession from the old Sir Florian by whom the will had been made, and who had directed that these jewels should be regarded as heirlooms in the family. The two intermediate baronets had made no allusion to the diamonds in any deeds executed by them. Indeed, Sir Florian's father had died without a will. There were other jewels, larger but much less valuable than the diamonds, still in the hands of Messrs. Garnett, as to which no question was raised. The late Sir Florian had, by his will, left all the property in his house at Portray to his widow, but all property elsewhere to his heir. This was what Mr. Camperdown had at last learned, but he had been forced to admit to himself, while learning this, that there was confusion.

He was confident enough, however, that there was no difficulty in the matter. The Messrs. Garnett were able to say that the necklace had been in their keeping, with various other jewels still in their possession, from the time of the death of the late Lady Eustace, up to the marriage of the late Sir Florian, her son. They stated the date on which the jewels were given up, to be the 24th of September, which was the day after Sir Florian's return from Scotland with his bride. Lizzie's first statement had coincided with this entry in the Messrs. Garnett's books; but latterly she had asserted that the necklace had been given to her in Scotland. When Mr. Camperdown examined the entry himself in the jewellers' book, he found the figures to be so blotted that they might represent either the 4th or 24th September. Now, the 4th September had been the day preceding Sir Florian's marriage. John Eustace only knew that he had seen the necklace worn in Scotland by his mother. The bishop only knew that he had often seen them on the neck of his sister-in-law when, as was very often the case, she appeared in full-blown society. Mr. Camperdown believed that he had traced two stories to Lizzie, —one, repeated more than once, that the diamonds had been given to her in London, and a second, made to himself, that they had been given to her at Portray. He himself believed that they had never been in Scotland since the death of the former Lady Eustace; but he was quite confident that he could trust altogether to the disposition made of them by the old Sir Florian. There could be no doubt as to these being the diamonds there described, although the setting had been altered. Old Mr. Garnett stated that he would swear to them if he saw the necklace.

'You cannot suppose that Lady Eustace wishes to keep anything that is not her own,' said Frank Greystock.

'Of course not,' said John Eustace.

'Nobody imagines it,' said Mr. Camperdown. Lord Fawn, who felt that he ought not to be there, and who did not know whether he might with a better grace take Lizzie's part or a part against her, said nothing. 'But,' continued Mr. Camperdown, 'there is luckily no doubt as to the facts. The diamonds in question formed a part of a set of most valuable ornaments settled in the family by Sir Florian Eustace in 1799.

The deed was drawn up by my grandfather, and is now here. I do not know how we are to have further proof. Will you look at the deed, Mr. Greystock, and at the will?' Frank suggested that, as it might probably be expedient to take advice on the subject professionally, he had rather not look at the deed. Anything which he might say, on looking at the document now, could have no weight. 'But why should any advice be necessary,' said Mr. Camperdown, 'when the matter is so clear?'

'My dear sir,' said Frank, 'my cousin, Lady Eustace, is strong in her confidence that her late husband intended to give them to her as her own, and that he would not have done this without the power of doing so.' Now, Mr. Camperdown was quite sure that Lizzie was lying in this, and could therefore make no adequate answer. 'Your experience must probably have told you,' continued Frank, 'that there is considerable difficulty in dealing with the matter of heirlooms.'

'I never heard of any such difficulty,' said Mr. Camperdown.

'People generally understand it all so clearly,' said Lord Fawn.

'The late Sir Florian does not appear to have understood it very clearly,' said Frank.

'Let her put them into the hands of any indifferent*person or firm till the matter is decided,' said Mr. Camperdown. 'They will be much safer so than in her keeping.'

'I think they are quite safe,' said Frank.

And this was all that took place at that meeting. As Mr. Camperdown said to John Eustace, it was manifest enough that she meant 'to hang on to them.' 'I only hope Lord Fawn will not be fool enough to marry her,' said Mr. Camperdown. Lord Fawn himself was of the same way of thinking;—but then how was he to clear his character of the charge which would be brought against him; and how was he to stand his ground before Frank Greystock?

CHAPTER XVII
The Diamonds are seen in Public

LET it not be supposed that Lady Eustace, during these summer weeks, was living the life of a recluse. The London season was in its full splendour, and she was by no means a recluse. During the first year of her widowhood she had been every inch a widow,—as far as crape would go, and a quiet life either at Bobsborough or Portray Castle. During this year her child was born,—and she was in every way thrown upon her good behaviour, living with bishops' wives and deans' daughters. Two years of retreat from the world is generally thought to be the proper thing for a widow. Lizzie had not quite accomplished her two years before she re-opened the campaign in Mount Street with very small remnants of weeds, and with her crape brought down to a minimum;—but she was young and rich, and the world is aware that a woman of twenty-two can hardly afford to sacrifice two whole years. In the matter of her widowhood Lizzie did not encounter very much reproach. She was not shunned, or so ill spoken of as to have a widely-spread bad name among the streets and squares in which her carriage-wheels rolled. People called her a flirt, held up their hands in surprise at Sir Florian's foolish genero- sity,—for the accounts of Lizzie's wealth were greatly exag- gerated,—and said that of course she would marry again.

The general belief which often seizes upon the world in re- gard to some special falsehood is very surprising. Everybody on a sudden adopts an idea that some particular man is over head and ears in debt, so that he can hardly leave his house for fear of the bailiffs;—or that some ill-fated woman is cruelly-used by her husband;—or that some eldest son has ruined his father; whereas the man doesn't owe a shilling, the woman never hears a harsh word from her lord, and the eldest son in question has never succeeded in obtaining a shilling beyond his allowance. One of the lies about London this season was founded on the extent of Lady Eustace's jointure.* Indeed, the lie went on to state that the jointure was more than a jointure. It was believed that the property in Ayrshire was her own, to do what she pleased with it. That the property in Ayrshire was taken at double its value was a matter of course. It had been declared, at the time of his marriage, that Sir Florian had been especially generous to his penniless wife, and the generosity was magnified in the ordinary way. No doubt Lizzie's own diligence had done much to propagate the story as to her positive ownership of Portray. Mr. Camperdown had been very busy denying this. John Eustace had denied it whenever occasion offered. The bishop in his quiet way had denied it. Lady Linlithgow had denied it. But the lie had been set on foot and had thriven, and there was hardly a man about town who didn't know that Lady Eustace had eight or nine thousand a year, altogether at her own disposal, down in Scotland. Of course a woman so endowed, so rich, so beautiful, so clever, so young, would marry again, and would marry well. No doubt, added to this there was a feeling that 'Lizzie,' as she was not uncommonly called by people who had hardly ever seen her,—had something amiss with it all. 'I don't know where it is she's lame,'*said that very clever man, Captain Boodle, who had lately reappeared among his military friends at his club, 'but she don't go flat all round.'*

'She has the devil of a temper, no doubt,' said Lieutenant Griggs.

'No mouth, I should say,' said Boodle. It was thus that Lizzie was talked about at the clubs; but she was asked to dinners and balls, and gave little dinners herself, and to a certain extent was the fashion. Everybody had declared that of course she would marry again, and now it was known everywhere that she was engaged to Lord Fawn.

'Poor dear Lord Fawn!' said Lady Glencora Palliser to her dear friend Madame Max Goesler; 'do you remember how violently he was in love with Violet Effingham two years ago?'

'Two years is a long time, Lady Glencora; and Violet Effingham has chosen another husband.'

'But isn't this a fall for him? Violet was the sweetest

girl out, and at one time I really thought she meant to take him.'

'I thought she meant to take another man whom she did not take,' said Madame Goesler, who had her own recollections, who was a widow herself, and who, at the period to which Lady Glencora was referring, had thought that perhaps she might cease to be a widow. Not that she had ever suggested to herself that Lord Fawn might be her second husband.

'Poor Lord Fawn!' continued Lady Glencora. 'I suppose he is terribly in want of money.'

'But surely Lady Eustace is very pretty.'

'Yes;—she is very pretty; nay more, she is quite lovely to look at. And she is clever,—very. And she is rich,—very. But——'

'Well, Lady Glencora. What does your "but" mean?'

'Who ever explains a "but"? You're a great deal too clever, Madame Goesler, to want any explanation. And I couldn't explain it. I can only say I'm sorry for poor Lord Fawn,—who is a gentleman, but will never set the Thames on fire.'

'No, indeed. All the same, I like Lord Fawn extremely, said Madame Goesler, 'and I think he's just the man to marry Lady Eustace. He's always at his office or at the House.'

'A man may be a great deal at his office, and a great deal more at the House than Lord Fawn,' said Lady Glencora laughing, 'and yet think about his wife, my dear.' For of all men known, no man spent more hours at the House or in his office than did Lady Glencora's husband, Mr. Palliser, who at this time, as he had now for more than two years, filled the high place of Chancellor of the Exchequer.

This conversation took place in Madame Goesler's little drawing-room in Park Lane; but, three days after this, the same two ladies met again at the house then occupied by Lady Chiltern in Portman Square,—Lady Chiltern, with whom, as Violet Effingham, poor Lord Fawn had been much in love. 'I think it is the nicest match in the world for him,' Lady Chiltern had said to Madame Goesler.

'But have you heard of the diamonds?' asked Lady Glencora.

'What diamonds?' 'Whose diamonds?' Neither of the others had heard of the diamonds, and Lady Glencora was able to tell her story. Lady Eustace had found all the family jewels belonging to the Eustace family in the strong plate room at Portray Castle, and had taken possession of them as property found in her own house. John Eustace and the bishop had combined in demanding them on behalf of the heir, and a lawsuit had then commenced! The diamonds were the most costly belonging to any Commoner*in England, and had been valued at twenty-four thousand pounds! Lord Fawn had retreated from his engagement the moment he heard that any doubt was thrown on Lady Eustace's right to their possession! Lady Eustace had declared her intention of bringing an action against Lord Fawn,—and had also secreted the diamonds! The reader will be aware that this statement was by no means an accurate history of the difficulty as far as it had as yet progressed. It was, indeed, absolutely false in every detail; but it sufficed to show that the matter was becoming public. 'You don't mean to say that Lord Fawn is off?' asked Madame Goesler.

'I do,' said Lady Glencora.

'Poor Lord Fawn!' exclaimed Lady Chiltern. 'It really seems as though he never would be settled.'

'I don't think he has courage enough for such conduct as that,' said Madame Goesler.

'And besides, Lady Eustace's income is quite certain,' said Lady Chiltern, 'and poor dear Lord Fawn does want money so badly.'

'But it is very disagreeable,' said Lady Glencora, 'to believe that your wife has got the finest diamonds in England, and then to find that she has only——stolen them. I think Lord Fawn is right. If a man does marry for money he should have the money. I wonder she ever took him. There is no doubt about her beauty, and she might have done better.'

'I won't hear Lord Fawn be-littled,' said Lady Chiltern.

'Done better!' said Madame Goesler. 'How could she have

done better? He is a peer, and her son would be a peer. I don't think she could have done better.' Lady Glencora in her time had wished to marry a man who had sought her for her money. Lady Chiltern in her time had refused to be Lady Fawn. Madame Goesler in her time had declined to marry an English peer. There was, therefore, something more of interest in the conversation to each of them than was quite expressed in the words spoken. 'Is she to be at your party on Friday, Lady Glencora?' asked Madame Goesler.

'She has said she would come,—and so has Lord Fawn, for that matter. Lord Fawn dines with us. She'll find that out, and then she'll stay away.'

'Not she,' said Lady Chiltern. 'She'll come for the sake of the bravado. She's not the woman to show the white feather.'

'If he's ill-using her she's quite right,' said Madame Goesler.

'And wear the very diamonds in dispute,' said Lady Chiltern. It was thus that the matter was discussed among ladies in the town.

'Is Fawn's marriage going on?' This question was asked of Mr. Legge Wilson by Barrington Erle. Mr. Legge Wilson was the Secretary of State for India, and Barrington Erle was in the Government.

'Upon my word I don't know,' said Mr. Wilson. 'The work goes on at the office;—that's all I know about Fawn. He hasn't told me of his marriage, and therefore I haven't spoken to him about it.'

'He hasn't made it official?'

'The papers haven't come before me yet,' said Mr. Wilson.

'When they do they'll be very awkward papers, as far as I hear,' said Barrington Erle. 'There is no doubt they were engaged, and I believe there is no doubt that he has declared off, and refused to give any reason.'

'I suppose the money is not all there,' suggested Mr. Wilson.

'There's a queer story going about as to some diamonds. No one knows whom they belong to, and they say that Fawn has accused her of stealing them. He wants to get hold of them, and she won't give them up. I believe the lawyers are to have a shy at it. I'm sorry for Fawn. It'll do him a deal of mischief.'

'You'll find he won't come out much amiss,' said Mr. Legge Wilson. 'He's as cautious a man as there is in London. If there is anything wrong——'

'There is a great deal wrong,' said Barrington Erle.

'You'll find it will be on her side.'

'And you'll find also that she'll contrive that all the blame shall lie upon him. She's clever enough for anything. Who's to be the new bishop?'

'I have not heard Gresham say as yet; Jones, I should think,' said Mr. Wilson.

'And who is Jones?'

'A clergyman, I suppose,—of the safe sort. I don't know that anything else is necessary.' From which it will be seen that Mr. Wilson had his own opinion about church matters, and also that people very high up in the world were concerning themselves about poor Lizzie's affairs.

Lady Eustace did go to Lady Glencora's evening party, in spite of Mr. Camperdown and all her difficulties. Lady Chiltern had been quite right in saying that Lizzie was not the woman to show the white feather. She went, knowing that she would meet Lord Fawn, and she did wear the diamonds. It was the first time that they had been round her neck since the occasion in respect to which Sir Florian had placed them in her hands, and it had not been without much screwing up of her courage that she had resolved to appear on this occasion with the much-talked-of ornament upon her person. It was now something over a fortnight since she had parted with Lord Fawn at Fawn Court; and, although they were still presumed to be engaged to marry each other, and were both living in London, she had not seen him since. A sort of message had reached her, through Frank Greystock, to the effect that Lord Fawn thought it as well that they should not meet till the matter was settled. Stipulations had been made by

Frank on her behalf, and this had been inserted among them. She had received the message with scorn,—with a mixture of scorn and gratitude,—of scorn in regard to the man who had promised to marry her, and of affectionate gratitude to the cousin who had made the arrangement. 'Of course I shall not wish to see him while he chooses to entertain such an idea,' she had said, 'but I shall not keep out of his way. You would not wish me to keep out of his way, Frank?' When she received a card for Lady Glencora's party very soon after this, she was careful to answer it in such a manner as to impress Lady Glencora with a remembrance of her assent. Lord Fawn would probably be there,—unless he remained away in order to avoid her. Then she had ten days in which to make up her mind as to wearing the diamonds. Her courage was good, but then her ignorance was so great! She did not know whether Mr. Camperdown might not contrive to have them taken by violence from her neck, even on Lady Glencora's stairs. Her best security,—so she thought,—would be in the fact that Mr. Camperdown would not know of her purpose. She told no one,—not even Miss Macnulty; but she appeared before that lady, arrayed in all her glory, just as she was about to descend to her carriage. 'You've got the necklace on!' said Miss Macnulty. 'Why should I not wear my own necklace?' she asked, with assumed anger.

Lady Glencora's rooms were already very full when Lizzie entered them, but she was without a gentleman, and room was made for her to pass quickly up the stairs. The diamonds had been recognised by many before she had reached the drawing-room;—not that these very diamonds were known, or that there was a special memory for that necklace;—but the subject had been so generally discussed, that the blaze of the stones immediately brought it to the minds of men and women. 'There she is, with poor Eustace's twenty thousand pounds round her neck,' said Laurence Fitzgibbon to his friend Barrington Erle. 'And there is Lord Fawn going to look after them,' replied the other.

Lord Fawn thought it right, at any rate, to look after his

bride. Lady Glencora had whispered into his ear before they went down to dinner that Lady Eustace would be there in the evening, so that he might have the option of escaping or remaining. Could he have escaped without any one knowing that he had escaped, he would not have gone up-stairs after dinner; but he knew that he was observed; he knew that people were talking about him; and he did not like it to be said that he had run away. He went up, thinking much of it all, and, as soon as he saw Lady Eustace, he made his way to her and accosted her. Many eyes were upon them, but no ear probably heard how infinitely unimportant were the words which they spoke to each other. Her manner was excellent. She smiled and gave him her hand,—just her hand without the slightest pressure,—and spoke a half-whispered word, looking into his face, but betraying nothing by her look. Then he asked her whether she would dance. Yes;—she would stand up for a quadrille;*and they did stand up for a quadrille. As she danced with no one else, it was clear that she treated Lord Fawn as her lover. As soon as the dance was done she took his arm and moved for a few minutes about the room with him. She was very conscious of the diamonds, but she did not show the feeling in her face. He also was conscious of them, and he did show it. He did not recognise the necklace, but he knew well that this was the very bone of contention. They were very beautiful, and seemed to him to outshine all other jewellery in the room. And Lady Eustace was a woman of whom it might almost be said that she ought to wear diamonds. She was made to sparkle, to be bright with outside garniture,*—to shine and glitter, and be rich in apparel. The only doubt might be whether paste diamonds might not better suit her character. But these were not paste, and she did shine and glitter and was very rich. It must not be brought as an accusation against Lady Glencora's guests that they pressed round to look at the necklace. Lady Glencora's guests knew better than to do that. But there was some slight ferment,— slight, but still felt both by Lord Fawn and by Lady Eustace. Eyes were turned upon the diamonds, and there were whispers here and there. Lizzie bore it very well; but Lord Fawn was uncomfortable.

'I like her for wearing them,' said Lady Glencora to Lady Chiltern.

'Yes;—if she means to keep them. I don't pretend, however, to know anything about it. You see the match isn't off.'

'I suppose not. What do you think I did? He dined here, you know, and, before going down-stairs, I told him that she was coming. I thought it only fair.'

'And what did he say?'

'I took care that he shouldn't have to say anything; but, to tell the truth, I didn't expect him to come up.'

'There can't be any quarrel at all,' said Lady Chiltern.

'I'm not sure of that,' said Lady Glencora. 'They are not so very loving.'

Lady Eustace made the most of her opportunity. Soon after the quadrille was over she asked Lord Fawn to get her carriage for her. Of course he got it, and of course he put her into it, passing up and down-stairs twice in his efforts on her behalf. And of course all the world saw what he was doing. Up to the last moment not a word had been spoken between them that might not have passed between the most ordinary acquaintance, but, as she took her seat, she put her face forward and did say a word. 'You had better come to me soon,' she said.

'I will,' said Lord Fawn.

'Yes; you had better come soon. All this is wearing me,— perhaps more than you think.'

'I will come soon,' said Lord Fawn, and then he returned among Lady Glencora's guests, very uncomfortable. Lizzie got home in safety and locked up her diamonds in the iron box.

CHAPTER XVIII
'And I Have nothing to give'

IT was now the end of June, and Frank Greystock had been as yet but once at Fawn Court since he had written to Lucy Morris asking her to be his wife. That was three weeks since, and as the barrier against him at Fawn Court had been removed by Lady Fawn herself, the Fawn girls thought that as a lover he was very slack; but Lucy was not in the least annoyed. Lucy knew that it was all right; for Frank, as he took his last walk round the shrubbery with her during that visit, had given her to understand that there was a little difference between him and Lady Fawn in regard to Lizzie Eustace. 'I am her only relative in London,' Frank had said.

'Lady Linlithgow,' suggested Lucy.

'They have quarrelled, and the old woman is as bitter as gall. There is no one else to stand up for her, and I must see that she isn't ill-used. Women do hate each other so virulently, and Lady Fawn hates her future daughter-in-law.' Lucy did not in the least grudge her lover's assistance to his cousin. There was nothing of jealousy in her feeling. She thought that Lizzie was unworthy of Frank's goodness, but on such an occasion as this she would not say so. She told him nothing of the bribe that had been offered her, nor on that subject had she said a word to any of the Fawns. She understood, too, that as Frank had declared his purpose of supporting Lizzie, it might be as well that he should see just at present as little of Lady Fawn as possible. Not a word, however, had Lady Fawn said to Lucy disparaging her lover for his conduct. It was quite understood now at Fawn Court, by all the girls, and no doubt by the whole establishment, that Lizzie Eustace was to be regarded as an enemy. It was believed by them all that Lord Fawn had broken off the match—or, at least, that he was resolved to break it; but various stratagems were to be used, and terrible engines of war were to be brought up, if necessary, to prevent an alliance which was now thought to be disreputable. Mrs. Hittaway had been hard at work, and had found out something very like truth in regard to the whole transaction with Mr. Benjamin. Perhaps Mrs. Hittaway had found out more than was quite true as to poor Lizzie's former sins; but what she did find out she used with all her skill, communicating her facts to her mother, to Mr. Camperdown, and to her brother. Her brother had almost quarrelled with her, but still she continued to communicate her facts.

At this period Frank Greystock was certainly somewhat unreasonable in regard to his cousin. At one time, as the reader will remember, he had thought of asking her to be his wife;—because she was rich; but even then he had not thought well of her, had hardly believed her to be honest, and had rejoiced when he found that circumstances rather than his own judgment had rescued him from that evil. He had professed to be delighted when Lord Fawn was accepted,—as being happy to think that his somewhat dangerous cousin was provided with so safe a husband; and, when he had first heard of the necklace, he had expressed an opinion that of course it would be given up. In all this then he had shown no strong loyalty to his cousin, no very dear friendship, nothing to make those who knew him feel that he would buckle on armour in her cause. But of late,—and that, too, since his engagement with Lucy,—he had stood up very stoutly as her friend, and the armour was being buckled on. He had not scrupled to say that he meant to see her through this business with Lord Fawn, and had somewhat astonished Mr. Camperdown by raising a doubt on the question of the necklace. 'He can't but know that she has no more right to it than I have,' Mr. Camperdown had said to his son with indignation. Mr. Camperdown was becoming unhappy about the necklace, not quite knowing how to proceed in the matter.

In the meantime Frank had obeyed his better instincts, and had asked Lucy Morris to be his wife. He had gone to Fawn Court in compliance with a promise to Lizzie Eustace, that he

would call upon her there. He had walked with Lucy because
he was at Fawn Court: And he had written to Lucy because
of the words he had spoken during the walk. In all this the
matter had arranged itself as such matters do, and there was
nothing, in truth, to be regretted. He really did love the girl
with all his heart. It may, perhaps, be said that he had never
in truth loved any other woman. In the best humours of his
mind he would tell himself,—had from old times told himself
often,—that unless he married Lucy Morris he could never
marry at all. When his mother, knowing that poor Lucy was
penniless, had, as mothers will do, begged him to beware, he
had spoken up for his love honestly, declaring to her that in
his eyes there was no woman living equal to Lucy Morris.
The reader has seen him with the words almost on his
tongue with which to offer his hand to his cousin, Lizzie
Eustace, knowing as he did so that his heart had been given
to Lucy,—knowing also that Lucy's heart had been given
to him! But he had not done it, and the better humour had
prevailed.

Within the figure and frame and clothes and cuticle, within
the bones and flesh of many of us, there is but one person,—a
man or woman, with a preponderance either of good or evil,
whose conduct in any emergency may be predicted with some
assurance of accuracy by any one knowing the man or woman.
Such persons are simple, single, and, perhaps, generally, safe.
They walk along lines in accordance with certain fixed instincts or principles, and are to-day as they were yesterday,
and will be to-morrow as they are to-day. Lady Eustace was
such a person, and so was Lucy Morris. Opposite in their
characters as two poles, they were, each of them, a simple
entity; and any doubt or error in judging of the future conduct
of either of them would come from insufficient knowledge of
the woman. But there are human beings who, though of
necessity single in body, are dual in character;—in whose
breasts not only is evil always fighting against good,—but to
whom evil is sometimes horribly, hideously evil, but is sometimes also not hideous at all. Of such men it may be said that

Satan obtains an intermittent grasp, from which, when it is released, the rebound carries them high amidst virtuous resolutions and a thorough love of things good and noble. Such men,—or women,—may hardly, perhaps, debase themselves with the more vulgar vices. They will not be rogues, or thieves, or drunkards,—or, perhaps, liars; but ambition, luxury, self-indulgence, pride, and covetousness will get a hold of them, and in various moods will be to them virtues in lieu of vices. Such a man was Frank Greystock, who could walk along the banks of the quiet, trout-giving Bob, at Bobsborough, whipping the river with his rod, telling himself that the world lost for love would be a bad thing well lost for a fine purpose; and who could also stand, with his hands in his trousers pockets, looking down upon the pavement, in the purlieus of the courts at Westminster, and swear to himself that he would win the game, let the cost to his heart be what it might. What must a man be who would allow some undefined feeling,—some inward ache which he calls a passion and cannot analyse, some desire which has come of instinct and not of judgment,—to interfere with all the projects of his intellect, with all the work which he has laid out for his accomplishment? Circumstances had thrown him into a path of life for which, indeed, his means were insufficient, but which he regarded as, of all paths, the noblest and the manliest. If he could be true to himself,—with such truth as at these moments would seem to him to be the truest truth,—there was nothing in rank, nothing in ambition, which might not be within his reach. He might live with the highest, the best-educated, and the most beautiful; he might assist in directing national councils by his intelligence; and might make a name for himself which should be remembered in his country, and of which men would read the records in the histories written in after ages. But to do this, he must walk warily. He, an embarrassed man, a man already in debt, a man with no realised property coming to him in reversion, was called upon to live, and to live as though at his ease, among those who had been born to wealth. And, indeed, he had so cleverly

learned the ways of the wealthy, that he hardly knew any
longer how to live at his ease among the poor.

But had he walked warily when he went down to Richmond,
and afterwards, sitting alone in the obscurity of his chamber,
wrote the letter which had made Lucy Morris so happy? It
must be acknowledged that he did, in truth, love the girl,—
that he was capable of a strong feeling. She was not beautiful,
—hardly even pretty, small, in appearance almost insignificant, quite penniless, a governess! He had often asked himself what it was that had so vanquished him. She always wore
a pale grey frock,—with, perhaps, a grey ribbon,—never
running into any bright form of clothing. She was educated,
very well-educated; but she owned no great accomplishment.
She had not sung his heart away, or ravished him with the
harp. Even of her words she was sparing, seeming to care
more to listen than to speak; a humble little thing to look at,—
one of whom you might say that she regarded herself as well-
placed if left in the background. Yet he had found her out,
and knew her. He had recognised the treasure, and had greatly
desired to possess it. He had confessed to himself that, could
splendour and ambition be laid aside, that little thing would
be all the world to him. As he sat in court, or in the House,
patient from practice as he half-listened to the ponderous
speeches of advocates or politicians, he would think of the
sparkle in her eye, of the dimple in her chin, of the lines of
the mouth which could plead so eloquently, though with few
words. To sit on some high seat among his countrymen, and
also to marry Lucy Morris,—that would be a high ambition.
He had chosen his way now, and she was engaged to be his
wife.

As he thought of it after he had done it, it was not all happiness, all contentment, with him. He did feel that he had
crippled himself,—impeded himself in running the race, as it
were, with a log round his leg. He had offered to marry her,
and he must do so at once, or almost at once, because she
could now find no other home but his. He knew, as well as
did Lady Fawn, that she could not go into another family as

governess; and he knew also that she ought not to remain in Lady Fawn's house an hour longer than she would be wanted there. He must alter his plan of living at once, give up the luxury of his rooms at the Grosvenor, take a small house somewhere, probably near the Swiss Cottage,* come up and down to his chambers by the underground railway, and, in all probability, abandon Parliament altogether. He was not sure whether, in good faith, he should not at once give notice of his intended acceptance of the Chiltern Hundreds to the electors of Bobsborough. Thus meditating, under the influence of that intermittent evil grasp, almost angry with himself for the open truth which he had spoken,—or rather written, and perhaps thinking more of Lizzie and her beauty than he should have done, in the course of three weeks he had paid but one visit to Fawn Court. Then, of a sudden, finding himself one afternoon relieved from work, he resolved to go there. The days were still almost at their longest, and he did not scruple to present himself before Lady Fawn between eight and nine in the evening. They were all at tea, and he was welcomed kindly. Lucy, when he was announced, at once got up, and met him almost at the doorway, sparkling, with just a tear of joy in her eye, with a look in her face, and a loving manner, which for the moment made him sure that the little house near the Swiss Cottage would, after all, be the only Elysium*upon earth. If she spoke a word he hardly heard it, but her hand was in his, so cool and soft, almost trembling in its grasp, with no attempt to withdraw itself, frank, loving, and honest. There was a perfect satisfaction in her greeting which at once told him that she had no discontented thoughts, —had had no such thought,—because he had been so long without coming. To see him was a great joy. But every hour of her life was a joy to her, knowing, as she did know, that he loved her.

Lady Fawn was gracious, the girls were hospitable, and he found himself made very welcome amidst all the women at the tea-table. Not a word was said about Lizzie Eustace. Lady Fawn talked about Parliament, and professed to pity a poor lover who was so bound to his country that he could not see his mistress above once a fortnight. 'But there'll be a good time coming next month,' she said;—for it was now July. 'Though the girls can't make their claims felt, the grouse can.'*

'It isn't the House altogether that rules me with a rod of iron, Lady Fawn,' said Frank, 'but the necessity of earning daily bread by the sweat of my brow. A man who has to sit in court all day must take the night,—or, indeed, any time that he can get,—to read up his cases.'

'But the grouse put a stop to all work,' said Lady Fawn. 'My gardener told me just now that he wanted a day or two in August. I don't doubt but that he is going to the moors. Are you going to the moors, Mr. Greystock?'

As it happened, Frank Greystock did not quite know whether he was going to the moors or not. The Ayrshire grouse-shooting is not the best in Scotland;—but there is grouse-shooting in Ayrshire; and the shooting on the Portray mountains is not the worst shooting in the county. The castle at Portray overhangs the sea, but there is a wild district attached to it stretching far back inland, in regard to which Lizzie Eustace was very proud of talking of 'her shooting.' Early in the spring of the present year she had asked her cousin Frank to accept the shooting for the coming season,— and he had accepted it. 'I shall probably be abroad,' she said, 'but there is the old castle.' She had offered it as though he had been her brother, and he had said that he would go down for a couple of weeks,—not to the castle, but to a little lodge some miles up from the sea, of which she told him when he declined the castle. When this invitation was given there was no engagement between her and Lord Fawn. Since that date, within the last day or two, she had reminded him of it. 'Won't his lordship be there?' he had said laughingly. 'Certainly not,' she had answered with serious earnestness. Then she had explained that her plan of going abroad had been set aside by circumstances. She did mean to go down to Portray. 'I couldn't have you at the castle,' she said smiling; 'but even an Othello*couldn't object to a first cousin at a little cottage ever so many miles off.' It wasn't for him to suggest what objections might rise to the brain of a modern Othello; but after some hesitation he said that he would be there. He had promised the trip to a friend, and would like to keep his promise. But, nevertheless, he almost thought that he ought to avoid Portray. He intended to support his cousin as far as he might do so honestly; but he was not quite minded to stand by her through good report and evil report. He did not desire to be specially known as her champion, and yet he felt that that position would be almost forced upon him. He foresaw danger,—and consequently he was doubting about his journey to Scotland.

'I hardly know whether I am or not,' said Frank,—and he almost felt that he was blushing.

'I hope you are,' said Lucy. 'When a man has to work all day and nearly all night he should go where he may get fresh air.'

'There's very good air without going to Scotland for it,' said Lady Fawn, who kept up an excellent house at Richmond, but who, with all her daughters, could not afford autumn trips. The Fawns lived at Fawn Court all the year round, and consequently Lady Fawn thought that air was to be found in England sufficiently good for all purposes of vitality and recreation.

'It's not quite the same thing,' said Lucy;—'at least, not for a man.'

After that she was allowed to escape into the grounds with her lover, and was made happy with half-an-hour of unalloyed bliss. To be alone with the girl to whom he is not engaged is a man's delight;—to be alone with the man to whom she is engaged is the woman's. When the thing is settled there is always present to the man something of a feeling of clipped wings; whereas the woman is conscious of a new power of expanding her pinions. The certainty of the thing is to him repressive. He has done his work, and gained his victory,— and by conquering has become a slave. To her the certainty of the thing is the removal of a restraint which has hitherto always been on her. She can tell him everything, and be told everything,—whereas her previous confidences, made with those of her own sex, have been tame, and by comparison valueless. He has no new confidence to make,—unless when he comes to tell her he likes his meat well done, and wants his breakfast to be punctual. Lucy now not only promised herself, but did actually realise a great joy. He seemed to her all that her heart desired. He was a man whose manner was naturally caressing and demonstrative, and she was to him, of all women, the sweetest, the dearest, the most perfect,—and all his own. 'But, Frank,'—she had already been taught to call him Frank when they were alone together,—'what will come of all this about Lizzie Eustace?'

'They will be married,—of course.'

'Do you think so? I am sure Lady Fawn doesn't think so.'

'What Lady Fawn thinks on such a matter cannot be helped. When a man asks a woman to marry him, and she accepts, the natural consequence is that they will be married. Don't you think so?'

'I hope so,—sometimes,' said Lucy, with her two hands joined upon his arm, and hanging to it with all her little weight.

'You really do hope it?' he said.

'Oh, I do; you know I do. Hope it! I should die if I didn't hope it.'

'Then why shouldn't she?' He asked his question with a quick, sharp voice, and then turned upon her for an answer.

'I don't know,' she said, very softly, and still clinging to him. 'I sometimes think there is a difference in people.'

'There is a difference; but, still, we hardly judge of people sufficiently by our own feelings. As she accepted him, you may be sure that she wishes to marry him. She has more to give than he has.'

'And I have nothing to give,' she said.

'If I thought so, I'd go back even now,' he answered. 'It is because you have so much to give,—so much more than most others,—that I have thought of you, dreamed of you as my wife, almost ever since I first knew you.'

'I have nothing left to give,' she said. 'What I ever had is all given. People call it the heart. I think it is heart, and brain, and mind, and body,—and almost soul. But, Frank, though Lizzie Eustace is your cousin, I don't want to be likened to her. She is very clever, and beautiful,—and has a way with her that I know is charming;—but——'

'But what, Lucy?'

'I don't think she cares so much as some people. I dare say she likes Lord Fawn very well, but I do not believe she loves him as I love you.'

'They're engaged,' said Frank, 'and the best thing they can do is to marry each other. I can tell you this, at any rate,'—and his manner again became serious,—'if Lord Fawn behaves ill to her, I, as her cousin, shall take her part.'

'You don't mean that you'll—fight him!'

'No, my darling. Men don't fight each other now-a-days;—not often, at least, and Fawn and I are not of the fighting sort. I can make him understand what I mean and what others will mean without fighting him. He is making a paltry excuse.'

'But why should he want to excuse himself—without reason?'

'Because he is afraid. People have got hold of him and told him lies, and he thinks there will be a scrape about this necklace, and he hates a scrape. He'll marry her at last, without a doubt, and Lady Fawn is only making trouble for herself by trying to prevent it. You can't do anything.'

'Oh no;—I can't do anything. When she was here it became at last quite disagreeable. She hardly spoke to them, and I'm sure that even the servants understood that there was a quarrel.' She did not say a word of Lizzie's offer of the brooch to herself, nor of the stories which by degrees were reaching her ears as to the old debts, and the diamonds, and the young bride's conduct to Lady Linlithgow as soon as she married her grand husband, Sir Florian. She did think badly of Lizzie, and could not but regret that her own noble, generous Frank should have to expend his time and labour on a friend unworthy of his friendship; but there was no shade of jealousy in her feeling, and she uttered no word against Lizzie more bitter than that in which she declared that there was a difference between people.

And then there was something said as to their own prospects in life. Lucy at once and with vehemence declared that she did not look for or expect an immediate marriage. She did not scruple to tell him that she knew well how difficult was the task before him, and that it might be essential for his interest that he should remain as he was for a year or two. He was astonished to find how completely she understood his position, and how thoroughly she sympathised with his interests. 'There is only one thing I couldn't do for you,' she said.

'And what is the one thing?'

'I couldn't give you up. I almost thought that I ought to refuse you because I can do nothing,—nothing to help you. But there will always come a limit to self-denial. I couldn't do that! Could I?'

The reader will know how this question was answered, and will not want to be told of the long, close, clinging, praiseworthy kiss with which the young barrister assured her that would have been on her part an act of self-denial which would to him have been absolutely ruinous. It was agreed, however, between them, that Lady Fawn should be told that they did not propose to marry till some time in the following year, and that she should be formally asked to allow Lucy to have a home at Fawn Court in the interval.

CHAPTER XIX
'As my Brother'

LORD FAWN had promised, as he put Lizzie into her carriage,
that he would come to her soon,—but he did not come
soon. A fortnight passed and he did not show himself. Nothing
further had been done in the matter of the diamonds, except
that Mr. Camperdown had written to Frank Greystock, explaining how impossible it was that the question of their
possession should be referred to arbitration. According to him
they belonged to the heir, as did the estate; and no one would
have the power of accepting an arbitration respecting them,—
an arbitration which might separate them from the estate of

which an infant was the owner for his life,—any more than such arbitration could be accepted as to the property of the estate itself. 'Possession is nine points of the law,' said Frank to himself, as he put the letter aside,—thinking at the same time that possession in the hands of Lizzie Eustace included certainly every one of those nine points. Lizzie wore her diamonds again and then again. There may be a question whether the possession of the necklace and the publicity of their history,—which, however, like many other histories, was most inaccurately told,—did not add something to her reputation as a lady of fashion. In the meantime, Lord Fawn did not come to see her. So she wrote to him. 'My dear Frederic, had you not better come to me? Yours affectionately,—L. I go to the North at the end of this month.'

But Frank Greystock did visit her,—more than once. On the day after the above letter was written he came to her. It was on Sunday afternoon, when July was more than half over, and he found her alone. Miss Macnulty had gone to church, and Lizzie was lying listlessly on a sofa with a volume of poetry in her hand. She had in truth been reading the book, and in her way enjoying it. It told her the story of certain knights of old, who had gone forth in quest of a sign from heaven, which sign, if verily seen by them, might be taken to signify that they themselves were esteemed holy, and fit for heavenly joy. One would have thought that no theme could have been less palatable to such a one as Lizzie Eustace; but the melody of the lines had pleased her ear, and she was always able to arouse for herself a false enthusiasm on things which were utterly outside herself in life. She thought that she too could have travelled in search of that holy sign, and have borne all things, and abandoned all things, and have persevered,—and of a certainty have been rewarded. But as for giving up a string of diamonds, in common honesty,—that was beyond her.

'I wonder whether men ever were like that,' she said, as she allowed her cousin to take the book from her hands.

'Let us hope not.'

'Oh, Frank!'

'They were, no doubt, as fanatic and foolish as you please. If you will read to the end——'

'I have read it all,—every word of it,' said Lizzie enthusiastically.

'Then you know that Arthur did not go on the search, because he had a job of work to do, by the doing of which the people around him might perhaps be somewhat benefited.'

'I like Launcelot better than Arthur,' said Lizzie.

'So did the Queen,' replied Frank.

'Your useful, practical man, who attends vestries, and sits at Boards, and measures out his gifts to others by the ounce, never has any heart. Has he, Frank?'

'I don't know what heart means. I sometimes fancy that it is a talent for getting into debt, and running away with other men's wives.'

'You say that on purpose to make me quarrel with you. You don't run away with other men's wives, and you have heart.'

'But I get into debt, unfortunately; and as for other men's wives, I am not sure that I may not do even that some day. Has Lord Fawn been here?' She shook her head. 'Or written?' Again she shook her head. As she did so the long curl waved and was very near to him, for he was sitting close to the sofa, and she had raised herself so that she might look into his face and speak to him almost in a whisper. 'Something should be settled, Lizzie, before you leave town.'

'I wrote to him, yesterday,—one line, and desired him to come. I expected him here to-day, but you have come instead. Shall I say that I am disappointed?'

'No doubt you are so.'

'Oh, Frank, how vain you men are! You want me to swear to you that I would sooner have you with me than him. You are not content with—thinking it, unless I tell you that it is so. You know that it is so. Though he is to be my husband,—I suppose he will be my husband,—his spirit is not congenial to mine as is yours.'

'Had you not loved him you would not have accepted him.'

'What was I to do, Frank? What am I to do? Think how desolate I am, how unfriended, how much in want of some one whom I can call a protector! I cannot have you always with me. You care more for the little finger of that prim piece of propriety down at the old dowager's than you do for me and all my sorrows.' This was true, but Frank did not say that it was true. 'Lord Fawn is at any rate respectable. At least, I thought he was so when I accepted his offer.'

'He is respectable enough.'

'Just that;—isn't it?—and nothing more. You do not blame me for saying that I would be his wife? If you do, I will unsay it, let it cost me what it may. He is treating me so badly that I need not go far for an excuse.' Then she looked into his face with all the eagerness of her gaze, clearly implying that she expected a serious answer. 'Why do you not answer me, Frank?'

'What am I to say? He is a timid, cautious man. They have frightened him about this trumpery necklace, and he is behaving badly. But he will make a good husband. He is not a spendthrift. He has rank. All his people are respectable. As Lady Fawn, any house in England will be open to you. He is not rich, but together you will be rich.'

'What is all that without love?'

'I do not doubt his love. And when you are his own he will love you dearly.'

'Ah, yes;—as he would a horse or a picture. Is there anything of the rapture of love in that? Is that your idea of love? Is it so you love your Miss Demure?'

'Don't call names, Lizzie.'

'I shall say what I please of her. You and I are to be friends, and I may not speak? No;—I will have no such friendship! She is demure. If you like it, what harm is there in my saying it? I am not demure. I know that. I do not, at least, pretend to be other than I am. When she becomes your wife, I wonder whether you will like her ways?' He had not yet told her that

175

she was to be his wife, nor did he so tell her now. He thought for a moment that he had better tell her, but he did not do so. It would, he said to himself, add an embarrassment to his present position. And as the marriage was to be postponed for a year, it might be better, perhaps, for Lucy that it should not be declared openly. It was thus he argued with himself, but yet, no doubt, he knew well that he did not declare the truth because it would take away something of its sweetness from this friendship with his cousin Lizzie.

'If ever I do marry,' he said, 'I hope I shall like my wife's ways.'

'Of course you will not tell me anything. I do not expect confidence from you. I do not think a man is ever able to work himself up to the mark of true confidence with his friend. Men together, when they like each other, talk of politics, or perhaps of money; but I doubt whether they ever really tell their thoughts and longings to each other.'

'Are women more communicative?'

'Yes;—certainly. What is there that I would not tell you if you cared to hear it? Every thought I have is open to you if you chose to read it. I have that feeling regarding you that I would keep nothing back from you. Oh, Frank, if you understood me, you could save me,—I was going to say from all unhappiness.'

She did it so well that he would have been more than man had he not believed some of it. She was sitting almost upright now, though her feet were still on the sofa, and was leaning over towards him, as though imploring him for his aid, and her eyes were full of tears, and her lips were apart as though still eager with the energy of expression, and her hands were clasped together. She was very lovely, very attractive, almost invincible. For such a one as Frank Greystock opposition to her in her present mood was impossible. There are men by whom a woman, if she have wit, beauty, and no conscience, cannot be withstood. Arms may be used against them, and a sort of battle waged, against which they can raise no shield,— from which they can retire into no fortress,—in which they

can parry no blow. A man so weak and so attacked may sometimes run; but even the poor chance of running is often cut off
from him. How unlike she was to Lucy! He believed her,—
in part; and yet that was the idea that occurred to him. When
Lucy was much in earnest, in her eye, too, a tear would
sparkle, the smallest drop, a bright liquid diamond that never
fell; and all her face would be bright and eloquent with feeling;
—but how unlike were the two! He knew that the difference
was that between truth and falsehood;—and yet he partly
believed the falsehood! 'If I knew how to save you from an
hour's uneasiness I would do it,' he said.

'No;—no;—no;' she murmured.

'Would I not? You do not know me then.' He had nothing
further to say, and it suited her to remain silent for the moment, while she dried her eyes, and recovered her composure,
and prepared herself to carry on the battle with a smile. She
would carry on the battle, using every wile she knew, strain-
ing every nerve to be victorious, encountering any and all
dangers, and yet she had no definite aim before her. She herself did not know what she would be at. At this period of her
career she did not want to marry her cousin,—having resolved that she would be Lady Fawn. Nor did she intend that
her cousin should be her lover,—in the ordinary sense of love.
She was far too wary in the pursuit of the world's goods to
sacrifice herself to any such wish as that. She did want him to
help her about the diamonds,—but such help as that she might
have, as she knew well, on much easier terms. There was
probably an anxiety in her bosom to cause him to be untrue
to Lucy Morris; but the guiding motive of her conduct was
the desire to make things seem to be other than they were. To
be always acting a part rather than living her own life was to
her everything. 'After all we must come to facts,' he said,
after a while. 'I suppose it will be better that you should marry
Lord Fawn.'

'If you wish it.'

'Nay;—I cannot have that said. In this matter you must
rule yourself by your own judgment. If you are averse to

it——' She shook her head. 'Then you will own that it had better be so.' Again she shook her head. 'Lizzie, for your sake and my own I must declare, that if you have no opinion in this matter, neither will I have any. You shall never have to say that I pressed you into this marriage or debarred you from marrying. I could not bear such an accusation.'

'But you might tell me what I ought to do.'

'No;—certainly not.'

'Think how young I am, and—by comparison,—how old you are. You are eight years older than I am. Remember;— after all that I have gone through, I am but twenty-two. At my age other girls have their friends to tell them. I have no one,—unless you will tell me.'

'You have accepted him?'

'Yes.'

'I suppose he is not altogether indifferent to you?'

She paused, and again shook her head. 'Indeed, I do not know. If you mean, do I love him, as I could love some man whose heart was quite congenial to my own, certainly I do not.' She continued to shake her head very sadly. 'I esteemed him,—when he asked me.'

'Say at once that, having made up your mind, you will go through with it.'

'You think that I ought?'

'You think so,—yourself.'

'So be it, Frank. I will. But, Frank, I will not give up my property. You do not wish me to do that. It would be weak, now;—would it not? I am sure that it is my own.'

'His faith to you should not depend on that.'

'No; of course not; that is just what I mean. He can have no right to interfere. When he asked me to be his wife, he said nothing about that. But if he does not come to me, what shall I do?'

'I suppose I had better see him,'—said Frank slowly.

'Will you? That will be so good of you. I feel that I can leave it all so safely in your hands. I shall go out of town, you know, on the thirtieth. I feel that I shall be better away, and

I am sick of all the noise, and glitter, and worldliness of London. You will come on the twelfth?'

'Not quite so soon as that,' he said, after a pause.

'But you will come?'

'Yes;—about the twentieth.'

'And, of course, I shall see you?'

'Oh, yes.'

'So that I may have some one to guide me that I can trust. I have no brother, Frank; do you ever think of that?' She put out her hand to him, and he clasped it, and held it tight in his own; and then, after a while, he pulled her towards him. In a moment she was on the ground, kneeling at his feet, and his arm was round her shoulder, and his hand was on her back, and he was embracing her. Her face was turned up to him, and he pressed his lips upon her forehead. 'As my brother,' she said, stretching back her head and looking up into his face. 'Yes;—as your brother.'

They were sitting, or rather acting their little play together, in the back drawing-room, and the ordinary entrance to the two rooms was from the landing-place into the larger apartment;—of which fact Lizzie was probably aware, when she permitted herself to fall into a position as to which a moment or two might be wanted for recovery. When, therefore, the servant in livery opened the door, which he did, as Frank thought somewhat suddenly, she was able to be standing on her legs before she was caught. The quickness with which she sprung from her position, and the facility with which she composed not her face only, but the loose lock of her hair and all her person, for the reception of the coming visitor, was quite marvellous. About her there was none of the look of having been found out which is so very disagreeable to the wearer of it; whereas Frank, when Lord Fawn was announced, was aware that his manner was awkward, and his general appearance flurried. Lizzie was no more flurried than if she had stepped that moment from out of the hands of her tire-woman.* She greeted Lord Fawn very prettily, holding him by the hand long enough to show that she had more claim to do so than could any other woman, and then she just murmured her cousin's name. The two men shook hands—and looked at each other as men do who know that they are not friends, and think that they may live to be enemies. Lord Fawn, who rarely forgot anything, had certainly not forgotten the Sawab; and Frank was aware that he might soon be called on to address his lordship in anything but friendly terms. They said, however, a few words about Parliament and the weather, and the desirability of escaping from London.

'Frank,' said Lady Eustace, 'is coming down in August to shoot my three annual grouse at Portray. He would keep one for you, my lord, if he thought you would come for it.'

'I'll promise Lord Fawn a fair third, at any rate,' said Frank.

'I cannot visit Portray this August, I'm afraid,' said his lordship, 'much as I might wish to do so. One of us must remain at the India Office——'

'Oh, that weary India Office!' exclaimed Lizzie.

'I almost think you official men are worse off than we barristers,' said Frank. 'Well, Lizzie, good-bye. I dare say I shall see you again before you start.'

'Of course you will,' said Lizzie. And then the two lovers were left together. They had met once, at Lady Glencora's ball, since the quarrel at Fawn Court, and there, as though by mutual forbearance, had not alluded to their troubles. Now he had come, especially to speak of the matter that concerned them both so deeply. As long as Frank Greystock was in the room, his work was comparatively easy, but he had known beforehand that he would not find it at all easy should he be left alone with her. Lizzie began. 'My lord,' she said, 'considering all that has passed between us, you have been a truant.'

'Yes;—I admit it—but——'

'With me, my lord, a fault admitted is a fault forgiven.' Then she took her old seat on the sofa, and he placed himself on the chair which Frank Greystock had occupied. He had not intended to own a fault, and certainly not to accept forgiveness; but she had been too quick for him; and now he could not find words by which to express himself. 'In truth,' she continued, 'I would always rather remember one kindness than a dozen omissions on the part of a friend.'

'Lady Eustace, I have not willingly omitted anything.'

'So be it. I will not give you the slightest excuse for saying that you have heard a reproach from me. You have come at last, and you are welcome. Is that enough for you?'

He had much to say to her about the diamonds, and, when he was entering the room, he had not a word to say to her about anything else. Since that, another subject had sprung up before him. Whether he was, or was not, to regard himself as being at this moment engaged to marry Lady Eustace was a matter to him of much doubt;—but of this he was sure, that if she were engaged to him as his wife, she ought not to be entertaining her cousin Frank Greystock down at Portray Castle, unless she had some old lady, not only respectable in life, but high in rank also, to see that everything was right. It was almost an insult to him that such a visit should have been arranged without his sanction or cognizance. Of course, if he were bound by no engagement,—and he had been persuaded by his mother and sister to wish that he were not bound,—then the matter would be no affair of his. If, however, the diamonds were abandoned, then the engagement was to be continued;—and in that case it was out of the question that his elected bride should entertain another young man,—even though she was a widow and the young man was her cousin. Of course, he should have spoken of the diamonds first; but the other matter had obtruded itself upon him, and he was puzzled. 'Is Mr. Greystock to accompany you into Scotland?' he asked.

'Oh dear no. I go on the thirtieth of this month. I hardly know when he means to be there.'

'He follows you to Portray?'

'Yes;—he follows me, of course. "The king himself has followed her, When she has gone before." '*Lord Fawn did not remember the quotation, and was more puzzled than ever. 'Frank will follow me, just as the other shooting men will follow me.'

'He goes direct to Portray Castle?'

'Neither directly nor indirectly. Just at present, Lord Fawn, I am in no mood to entertain guests,—not even one that I love so well as my cousin Frank. The Portray mountains are somewhat extensive, and at the back of them there is a little shooting-lodge.'

'Oh, indeed,' said Lord Fawn, feeling that he had better dash at once at the diamonds.

'If you, my lord, could manage to join us for a day, my cousin and his friend would, I am sure, come over to the castle, so that you should not suffer from being left alone with me and Miss Macnulty.'

'At present it is impossible,' said Lord Fawn;—and then he paused. 'Lady Eustace, the position in which you and I stand to each other is one not altogether free from trouble.'

'You cannot say that it is of my making,' she said, with a smile. 'You once asked,—what men think a favour from me; and I granted it,—perhaps too easily.'

'I know how greatly I am indebted to your goodness, Lady Eustace——' And then again he paused.

'Lord Fawn!'

'I trust you will believe that nothing can be further from me than that you should be harassed by any conduct of mine.'

'I am harassed, my lord.'

'And so am I. I have learned that you are in possession of certain jewels which I cannot allow to be held by my wife.'

'I am not your wife, Lord Fawn.' As she said this, she rose from her reclining posture and sat erect.

'That is true. You are not. But you said you would be.'

'Go on, sir.'

'It was the pride of my life to think that I had attained to so much happiness. Then came this matter of the diamonds.'

'What business have you with my diamonds,—more than any other man?'

'Simply that I am told that they are not yours.'

'Who tells you so?'

'Various people. Mr. Camperdown.'

'If you, my lord, intend to take an attorney's word against mine, and that on a matter as to which no one but myself can know the truth, then you are not fit to be my husband. The diamonds are my own, and should you and I become man and wife, they must remain so by special settlement. While I choose to keep them they will be mine,—to do with them as I please. It will be my pleasure, when my boy marries, to hang them round his bride's neck.' She carried herself well, and spoke her words with dignity.

'What I have got to say is this,' began Lord Fawn;—'I must consider our engagement as at an end unless you will give them up to Mr. Camperdown.'

'I will not give them up to Mr. Camperdown.'

'Then,—then,—then,——'

'And I make bold to tell you, Lord Fawn, that you are not behaving to me like a man of honour. I shall now leave the matter in the hands of my cousin, Mr. Greystock.' Then she sailed out of the room, and Lord Fawn was driven to escape from the house as he might. He stood about the room for five minutes with his hat in his hand, and then walked down and let himself out of the front door.

CHAPTER XX
The Diamonds become Troublesome

THE thirtieth of July came round, and Lizzie was prepared for her journey down to Scotland. She was to be accompanied by Miss Macnulty and her own maid and her own servants, and to travel, of course, like a grand lady. She had not seen Lord Fawn since the meeting recorded in the last chapter, but had seen her cousin Frank nearly every other day. He, after much consideration, had written a long letter to Lord Fawn, in which he had given that nobleman to understand that some explanation was required as to conduct which Frank described as being to him 'at present unintelligible.' He then went, at considerable length, into the matter of the diamonds, with the object of proving that Lord Fawn could have no possible right to interfere in the matter. And though he had from the first wished that Lizzie would give up the trinket, he made various points in her favour. Not only had they been given to his cousin by her late husband;—even had they not been so given, they would have been hers by will. Sir Florian had left her everything that was within the walls of Portray Castle, and the diamonds had been at Portray at the time of Sir Florian's death. Such was Frank's statement,— untrue indeed, but believed by him to be true. This was one of Lizzie's lies, forged as soon as she understood that some subsidiary claim might be made upon them on the ground that they formed a portion of property left by will away from her; —some claim subsidiary to the grand claim, that the necklace was a family heirloom. Lord Fawn was not in the least shaken in his conviction that Lizzie had behaved, and was behaving, badly, and that, therefore, he had better get rid of her, but he knew that he must be very wary in the reasons he would give for jilting her. He wrote, therefore, a very short note to Greystock, promising that any explanation needed should be given as soon as circumstances should admit of his forming a decision. In the meantime, the 30th of July came, and Lady Eustace was ready for her journey.

There is, or there was, a train leaving London for Carlisle at 11 a.m., by which Lizzie proposed to travel, so that she might sleep in that city and go on through Dumfries to Portray the next morning. This was her scheme; but there was another part of her scheme as to which she had felt much doubt. Should she leave the diamonds, or should she take them with her? The iron box in which they were kept was small, and so far portable that a strong man might carry it without much trouble. Indeed, Lizzie could move it from one part of the room to the other, and she had often done so. But it was so heavy that it could not be taken with her without attracting attention. The servant would know what it was, and the porter would know, and Miss Macnulty would know. That her own maid should know was a matter of course; but even to her own maid the journey of the jewels would be remarkable because of the weight of the box, whereas if they went with her other jewels in her dressing-case, there would be nothing remarkable. She might even have taken them in her pocket,—had she dared. But she did not dare. Though she was intelligent and courageous, she was wonderfully ignorant as to what might and what might not be done for the recovery of the necklace by Mr. Camperdown. She did not dare to take them without the iron box, and at last she decided that the box should go. At a little after ten, her own carriage,—the job-carriage, which was now about to perform its last journey in her service, —was at the door, and a cab was there for the servants. The luggage was brought down, and with the larger boxes was brought the iron case with the necklace. The servant, certainly making more of the weight than he need have done, deposited it as a foot-stool for Lizzie, who then seated herself, and was followed by Miss Macnulty. She would have it placed in the same way beneath her feet in the railway carriage, and again brought into her room at the Carlisle hotel. What though the porter did know! There was nothing illegal in travelling about with a heavy iron box full of diamonds, and the risk would be less this way, she thought, than were she to leave them behind her in London. The house in Mount Street, which she had taken for the season, was to be given up; and whom could she trust in London? Her very bankers, she feared, would have betrayed her, and given up her treasure to Mr. Camperdown. As for Messrs. Harter and Benjamin, she felt sure that they would be bribed by Mr. Camperdown. She once thought of asking her cousin to take the charge of them, but she could not bring herself to let them out of her own hands. Ten thousand pounds! If she could only sell them and get the money, from what a world of trouble would she be relieved. And the sale, for another reason, would have been convenient; for Lady Eustace was already a little in debt. But she could not sell them, and therefore when she got into the carriage there was the box under her feet.

At that very moment who should appear on the pavement,

standing between the carriage and the house-door, but Mr.
Camperdown! And with Mr. Camperdown there was another
man,—a very suspicious-looking man,—whom Lizzie at once
took to be a detective officer of police. 'Lady Eustace!' said
Mr. Camperdown, taking off his hat. Lizzie bowed across
Miss Macnulty, and endeavoured to restrain the tell-tale
blood from flying to her cheeks. 'I believe,' said Mr. Camperdown 'that you are now starting for Scotland.'

'We are, Mr. Camperdown;—and we are very late.'

'Could you allow me two minutes' conversation with you
in the house?'

'Oh dear no. We are late, I tell you. What a time you
have chosen for coming, Mr. Camperdown!'

'It is an awkward hour, Lady Eustace. I only heard this
morning that you were going so soon, and it is imperative that
I should see you.'

'Had you not better write, Mr. Camperdown?'

'You will never answer my letters, madam.'

'I—I—I really cannot see you now. William, the coachman must drive on. We cannot allow ourselves to lose the
train. I am really very sorry, Mr. Camperdown; but we must
not lose the train.'

'Lady Eustace,' said Mr. Camperdown, putting his hand on
the carriage-door, and so demeaning himself that the coachman did not dare to drive on, 'I must ask you a question.' He
spoke in a low voice, but he was speaking across Miss Macnulty. That lady, therefore, heard him, and so did William,
the servant, who was standing close to the door. 'I must insist
on knowing where are the Eustace diamonds.' Lizzie felt the
box beneath her feet and, without showing that she did so,
somewhat widened her drapery.

'I can tell you nothing now. William, make the coachman
drive on.'

'If you will not answer me, I must tell you that I shall be
driven in the execution of my duty to obtain a search-warrant,
in order that they may be placed in proper custody. They are
not your property, and must be taken out of your hands.'

Lizzie looked at the suspicious man with a frightened gaze. The suspicious man was, in fact, a very respectable clerk in Mr. Camperdown's employment, but Lizzie for a moment felt that the search was about to begin at once. She had hardly understood the threat, and thought that the attorney was already armed with the powers of which he spoke. She glanced for a moment at Miss Macnulty, and then at the servant. Would they betray her? If they chose to use force to her, the box certainly might be taken from her. 'I know I shall lose the train,' she said. 'I know I shall. I must insist that you let my servant drive on.' There was now a little crowd of a dozen persons on the pavement, and there was nothing to cover her diamonds but the skirt of her travelling-dress.

'Are they in this house, Lady Eustace?'

'Why doesn't he go on?' shouted Lizzie. 'You have no right, sir, to stop me. I won't be stopped.'

'Or have you got them with you?'

'I shall answer no questions. You have no right to treat me in this way.'

'Then I shall be forced, on behalf of the family, to obtain a search-warrant, both here and in Ayrshire, and proceedings will be taken also against your ladyship personally.' So saying, Mr. Camperdown withdrew, and at last the carriage was driven on.

As it happened, there was time enough for catching the train,—and to spare. The whole affair in Mount Street had taken less than ten minutes. But the effect upon Lizzie was very severe. For a while she could not speak, and at last she burst out into hysteric tears,—not a sham fit,—but a true convulsive agony of sobbing. All the world of Mount Street, including her own servants, had heard the accusation against her. During the whole morning she had been wishing that she had never seen the diamonds; but now it was almost impossible that she should part with them. And yet they were like a load upon her chest, a load as heavy as though she were compelled to sit with the iron box on her lap day and night. In her sobbing she felt the thing under her feet, and knew that she could not get rid of it. She hated the box, and yet she must cling to it now. She was thoroughly ashamed of the box, and yet she must seem to take a pride in it. She was horribly afraid of the box, and yet she must keep it in her own very bed-room. And what should she say about the box now to Miss Macnulty, who sat by her side, stiff and scornful, offering her smelling-bottles, but not offering her sympathy? 'My dear,' she said at last, 'that horrid man has quite upset me.'

'I don't wonder that you should be upset,' said Miss Macnulty.

'And so unjust, too,—so false,—so—so—so———. They are my own as much as that umbrella is yours, Miss Macnulty.'

'I don't know,' said Miss Macnulty.

'But I tell you,' said Lizzie.

'What I mean is, that it is such a pity there should be a doubt.'

'There is no doubt,' said Lizzie;—'how dare you say there is a doubt? My cousin, Mr. Greystock, says that there is not the slightest doubt. He is a barrister,* and must know better than an attorney* like that Mr. Camperdown.' By this time they were at the Euston Square station, and then there was more trouble with the box. The footman struggled with it into the waiting-room, and the porter struggled with it from the waiting-room to the carriage. Lizzie could not but look at the porter as he carried it, and she felt sure that the man had been told of its contents and was struggling with the express view of adding to her annoyance. The same thing happened at Carlisle, where the box was carried up into Lizzie's bedroom by the footman, and where she was convinced that her treasure had become the subject of conversation for the whole house. In the morning people looked at her as she walked down the long platform with the box still struggling* before her. She almost wished that she had undertaken its carriage herself, as she thought that even she could have managed with less outward show of effort. Her own servants seemed to be in league against her, and Miss Macnulty had never before been so generally unpleasant. Poor Miss Macnulty, who had a conscientious idea of doing her duty, and who always attempted to give an adequate return for the bread she ate, could not so far overcome the effect of Mr. Camperdown's visit, as to speak on any subject without being stiff and hard. And she suffered, too, from the box,—to such a degree that she turned over in her mind the thought of leaving Lizzie, if any other possible home might be found for her. Who would willingly live with a woman who always travelled about with a diamond necklace worth ten thousand pounds, locked up in an iron safe,—and that necklace not her own property.

But at last Lady Eustace, and Miss Macnulty, and the servants,—and the iron box,—reached Portray Castle in safety.

CHAPTER XXI

'Ianthe's soul'

LADY EUSTACE had been rather cross on the journey down to Scotland, and had almost driven the unfortunate Macnulty to think that Lady Linlithgow or the workhouse would be better than this young tyrant; but on her arrival at her own house she was for awhile all smiles and kindness. During the journey she had been angry without thought, but was almost entitled to be excused for her anger. Could Miss Macnulty have realised the amount of oppression inflicted on her patroness by the box of diamonds she would have forgiven anything. Hitherto there had been some secrecy, or at any rate some privacy attached to the matter; but now that odious lawyer had discussed the matter aloud, in the very streets, in the presence of the servants, and Lady Eustace had felt that it was discussed also by every porter on the railway from London down to Troon,* the station in Scotland at which her own carriage met her to take her to her own castle. The night at Carlisle had been terrible to her, and the diamonds had never been for a moment off her mind. Perhaps the worst of it all was that her own man-servant and maid-servant had heard the claim which had been so violently made by Mr. Camperdown. There are people, in that respect very fortunately circumstanced, whose servants, as a matter of course, know all their affairs, have an interest in their concerns, sympathise with their demands, feel their wants, and are absolutely at one with them. But in such cases the servants are really known, and are almost as completely a part of the family as the sons and daughters. There may be disruptions and quarrels; causes may arise for ending the existing condition of things; but while this condition lasts, the servants in such households are, for the most part, only too well inclined to fight the battles of their employers. Mr. Binns, the butler, would almost foam at the mouth if it were suggested to him that the plate at Silvercup Hall was not the undoubted property of the old squire; and Mrs. Pouncebox could not be made to believe, by any amount of human evidence, that the jewels which her lady has worn for the last fifteen years are not her ladyship's very own. Binns would fight for the plate, and so would Pouncebox for the jewels, almost till they were cut to pieces. The preservation of these treasures on behalf of those who paid them their wages, and fed them, who occasionally scolded them but always succoured them, would be their point of honour. No torture would get the key of the cellar from Binns; no threats extract from Pouncebox a secret of the toilet. But poor Lizzie Eustace had no Binns and no Pouncebox. They are plants that grow slowly. There was still too much of the mushroom about Lady Eustace to permit of her possessing such treasures. Her footman was six feet high, was not bad looking, and was called Thomas. She knew no more about him, and was far too wise to expect sympathy from him, or other aid than the work for which she paid him. Her own maid was somewhat nearer to her; but not much nearer. The girl's name was Patience Crabstick, and she could do hair well. Lizzie knew but little more of her than that.

Lizzie considered herself still to be engaged to be married to Lord Fawn,—but there was no sympathy to be had in that quarter. Frank Greystock might be induced to sympathise with her;—but hardly after the fashion which Lizzie desired. And then sympathy in that direction would be so dangerous, should she decide upon going on with the Fawn marriage. For the present she had quarrelled with Lord Fawn;—but the very bitterness of that quarrel, and the decision with which her betrothed had declared his intention of breaking off the match, made her the more resolute that she would marry him. During her journey to Portray she had again determined that he should be her husband—and, if so, advanced sympathy,—sympathy that would be pleasantly tender with her cousin Frank, would be dangerous. She would be quite willing to accept even Miss Macnulty's sympathy, if that humble lady would give it to her of the kind she wanted. She declared to herself that she could pour herself out on Miss Macnulty's bosom, and mingle her tears even with Miss Macnulty's, if only Miss Macnulty would believe in her. If Miss Macnulty would be enthusiastic about the jewels, enthusiastic as to the wickedness of Lord Fawn, enthusiastic in praising Lizzie herself, Lizzie, —so she told herself,—would have showered all the sweets of female friendship even on Miss Macnulty's head. But Miss Macnulty was as hard as a deal board. She did as she was bidden, thereby earning her bread. But there was no tenderness in her;—no delicacy;—no feeling;—no comprehension. It was thus that Lady Eustace judged her humble companion; and in one respect she judged her rightly. Miss Macnulty did not believe in Lady Eustace, and was not sufficiently gifted to act up to a belief which she did not entertain.

Poor Lizzie! The world, in judging of people who are false and bad and selfish and prosperous to outward appearances, is apt to be hard upon them, and to forget the punishments which generally accompany such faults. Lizzie Eustace was very false and bad and selfish,—and, we may say, very prosperous also; but in the midst of all she was thoroughly uncomfortable. She was never at ease. There was no green spot*in her life with which she could be contented. And though, after a fashion, she knew herself to be false and bad, she was thoroughly convinced that she was ill-used by everybody about her. She was being very badly treated by Lord Fawn;—but she flattered herself that she would be able to make Lord Fawn know more of her character before she had done with him.

Portray Castle was really a castle,—not simply a country mansion so called, but a stone edifice with battlements and a round tower at one corner, and a gate which looked as if it might have had a portcullis, and narrow windows in a portion of it, and a cannon mounted up on a low roof, and an excavation called the moat,—but which was now a fantastic and somewhat picturesque garden,—running round two sides of it. In very truth, though a portion of the castle was undoubtedly old, and had been built when strength was needed for defence and probably for the custody of booty,—the battlements, and the round tower, and the awe-inspiring gateway had all been added by one of the late Sir Florians. But the castle looked like a castle, and was interesting. As a house it was not particularly eligible, the castle form of domestic architecture being exigeant in its nature, and demanding that space, which in less ambitious houses can be applied to comfort, shall be surrendered to magnificence. There was a great hall, and a fine dining-room with plate-glass windows looking out upon the sea; but the other sitting-rooms were insignificant, and the bedrooms were here and there, and were for the most part small and dark. That, however, which Lizzie had appropriated to her own use was a grand chamber, looking also out upon the open sea.

The castle stood upon a bluff of land, with a fine prospect of the Firth of Clyde, and with a distant view of the Isle of Arran. When the air was clear, as it often is clear there, the Arran hills could be seen from Lizzie's window, and she was proud of talking of the prospect. In other respects, perhaps, the castle was somewhat desolate. There were a few stunted trees around it, but timber had not prospered there. There was a grand kitchen garden,—or rather a kitchen garden which had been intended to be grand;—but since Lizzie's reign had been commenced, the grandeur had been neglected. Grand kitchen gardens are expensive, and Lizzie had at once been firm in reducing the under-gardeners from five men to one and a boy. The head-gardener had of course left her at once; but that had not broken her heart, and she had hired a modest man at a guinea a week instead of a scientific artist, who was by no means modest, with a hundred and twenty pounds a year and coals, house, milk, and all other horticultural luxuries. Though Lizzie was prosperous and had a fine income, she was already aware that she could not keep up a town and country establishment and be a rich woman on four thousand a year. There was a flower garden and small shrubbery within the so-called moat; but, otherwise, the grounds of Portray Castle were not alluring. The place was sombre, exposed, and, in winter, very cold; and, except that the expanse of sea beneath the hill on which stood the castle was fine and open, it had no great claim to praise on the score of scenery. Behind the castle, and away from the sea, the low mountains belonging to the estate stretched for some eight or ten miles; and towards the further end of them, where stood a shooting-lodge, called always The Cottage, the landscape became rough and grand. It was in this cottage that Frank Greystock was to be sheltered with his friend, when he came down to shoot what Lady Eustace had called her three annual grouse.

She ought to have been happy and comfortable. There will, of course, be some to say that a young widow should not be happy and comfortable,—that she should be weeping her lost lord, and subject to the desolation of bereavement. But as the world goes now, young widows are not miserable; and there is, perhaps, a growing tendency in society to claim from them year by year still less of any misery that may be avoidable. Suttee*propensities of all sorts, from burning alive down to bombazine*and hideous forms of clothing, are becoming less and less popular among the nations, and women are beginning to learn that, let what misfortunes will come upon them, it is well for them to be as happy as their nature will allow them to be. A woman may thoroughly respect her husband, and mourn him truly, honestly, with her whole heart, and yet enjoy thoroughly the good things which he has left behind for her use. It was not, at any rate, sorrow for the lost Sir Florian that made Lady Eustace uncomfortable. She had her child. She had her income. She had her youth and beauty. She had Portray Castle. She had a new lover,—and, if she chose to be quit of him, not liking him well enough for the purpose, she might undoubtedly have another whom she would like better. She had hitherto been thoroughly successful in her life. And yet she was unhappy. What was it that she wanted?

She had been a very clever child,—a clever, crafty child; and now she was becoming a clever woman. Her craft remained with her; but so keen was her outlook upon the world, that she was beginning to perceive that craft, let it be never so crafty, will in the long run miss its own object. She actually envied the simplicity of Lucy Morris, for whom she delighted to find evil names, calling her demure, a prig, a sly puss, and so on. But she could see,—or half see,—that Lucy with her simplicity was stronger than was she with her craft. She had nearly captivated Frank Greystock with her wiles, but without any wiles Lucy had captivated him altogether. And a man captivated by wiles was only captivated for a time, whereas a man won by simplicity would be won for ever,—if he himself were worth the winning. And this, too, she felt,—that let her success be what it might, she could not be happy unless she could win a man's heart. She had won Sir Florian's, but that had been but for an hour,—for a month or two. And then Sir Florian had never really won hers. Could not she be simple? Could not she act simplicity so well that the thing acted could be as powerful as the thing itself;—perhaps even more powerful? Poor Lizzie Eustace! In thinking over all this, she saw a great deal. It was wonderful that she should see so much and tell herself so many home truths. But there was one truth she could not see, and therefore could not tell it to herself. She had not a heart to give. It had become petrified during those lessons of early craft in which she had taught herself how to get the better of Messrs. Harter and Benjamin, of Sir Florian Eustace, of Lady Linlithgow, and of Mr. Camperdown.

Her ladyship had now come down to her country house,

leaving London and all its charms before the end of the season, actuated by various motives. In the first place, the house in Mount Street was taken, furnished, by the month, and the servants were hired after the same fashion, and the horses jobbed.* Lady Eustace was already sufficiently intimate with her accounts to know that she would save two hundred pounds by not remaining another month or three weeks in London, and sufficiently observant of her own affairs to have perceived that such saving was needed. And then it appeared to her that her battle with Lord Fawn could be better fought from a distance than at close quarters. London, too, was becoming absolutely distasteful to her. There were many things there that tended to make her unhappy, and so few that she could enjoy! She was afraid of Mr. Camperdown, and ever on the rack lest some dreadful thing should come upon her in respect of the necklace,—some horrible paper served upon her from a magistrate, ordering her appearance at Newgate,* or perhaps before the Lord Chancellor,* or a visit from policemen, who would be empowered to search for and carry off the iron box. And then there was so little in her London life to gratify her! It is pleasant to win in a fight;—but to be always fighting is not pleasant. Except in those moments, few and far between, in which she was alone with her cousin Frank,—and perhaps in those other moments in which she wore her diamonds,—she had but little in London that she enjoyed. She still thought that a time would come when it would be otherwise. Under these influences she had actually made herself believe that she was sighing for the country, and for solitude; for the wide expanse of her own bright waves,—as she had called them,—and for the rocks of dear Portray. She had told Miss Macnulty and Augusta Fawn that she thirsted for the breezes of Ayrshire, so that she might return to her books and her thoughts. Amidst the whirl of London it was impossible either to read or to think. And she believed it, too,—herself. She so believed it, that on the first morning of her arrival she took a little volume in her pocket, containing Shelley's 'Queen Mab,' and essayed to go down upon the rocks. She had actually breakfasted at nine, and was out in the sloping grounds below the castle before ten, having made some boast to Miss Macnulty about the morning air.

She scrambled down,—not very far down, but a little way beneath the garden gate, to a spot on which a knob of rock cropped out from the scanty herbage of the incipient cliff. Fifty yards lower, the real rocks began; and, though the real rocks were not very rocky, not precipitous or even bold, and were partially covered with salt-fed mosses, down almost to the sea, nevertheless they justified her in talking about her rock-bound shore. The shore was hers,—for her life, and it was rock-bound. This knob she had espied from her windows;—and, indeed, had been thinking of it for the last week, as a place appropriate to solitude and Shelley. She had stood on it before, and had stretched her arms with enthusiasm towards the just-visible mountains of Arran. On that occasion the weather, perhaps, had been cool; but now a blazing sun was overhead, and when she had been seated half a minute, and 'Queen Mab' had been withdrawn from her pocket, she found that it would not do. It would not do, even with the canopy she could make for herself with her parasol. So she stood up and looked about herself for shade;—for shade in some spot in which she could still look out upon 'her dear wide ocean, with its glittering smile.' For it was thus that she would talk about the mouth of the Clyde. Shelter near her there was none. The scrubby trees lay nearly half a mile to the right,—and up the hill, too. She had once clambered down to the actual shore, and might do so again. But she doubted that there would be shelter even there; and the clambering up on that former occasion had been a nuisance and would be a worse nuisance now. Thinking of all this, and feeling the sun keenly, she gradually retraced her steps to the garden within the moat, and seated herself, Shelley in hand, within the summer-house. The bench was narrow, hard, and broken; and there were some snails which discomposed her;—but, nevertheless, she would make the best of it. Her darling 'Queen Mab' must be read without the coarse, inappropriate, every-day surround-

ings of a drawing-room; and it was now manifest to her that,
unless she could get up much earlier in the morning, or come
out to her reading after sunset, the knob of rock would not
avail her.

She began her reading, resolved that she would enjoy her
poetry in spite of the narrow seat. She had often talked of
'Queen Mab,' and perhaps she thought she had read it. This,
however, was in truth her first attempt at that work. 'How
wonderful is Death! Death and his brother, Sleep!' Then she
half-closed the volume, and thought that she enjoyed the idea.
Death,—and his brother Sleep! She did not know why they
should be more wonderful than Action, or Life, or Thought;
—but the words were of a nature which would enable her to
remember them, and they would be good for quoting. 'Sudden
arose Ianthe's soul; it stood all-beautiful in naked purity.' The
name of Ianthe suited her exactly. And the antithesis conveyed
to her mind by naked purity struck her strongly, and she determined to learn the passage by heart. Eight or nine lines were
printed separately, like a stanza, and the labour would not be
great, and the task, when done, would be complete. 'Instinct
with inexpressible beauty and grace, Each stain of earthliness
Had passed away, it reassumed Its native dignity, and stood
Immortal amid ruin.'*Which was instinct with beauty,—the
stain or the soul, she did not stop to inquire, and may be
excused for not understanding. 'Ah,'—she exclaimed to herself, 'how true it is; how one feels it; how it comes home to
one!—"Sudden arose Ianthe's soul!" ' And then she walked
about the garden, repeating the words to herself, and almost
forgetting the heat. ' "Each stain of earthliness had passed
away." Ha;—yes. They will pass away, and become instinct
with beauty and grace.' A dim idea came upon her that when
this happy time should arrive, no one would claim her necklace from her, and that the man at the stables would not be so
disagreeably punctual in sending in his bill. ' "All-beautiful
in naked purity!" '*What a tawdry world was this, in which
clothes and food and houses are necessary! How perfectly
that boy-poet had understood it all! ' "Immortal amid ruin!" '

She liked the idea of the ruin almost as well as that of the immortality, and the stains quite as well as the purity. As immortality must come, and as stains were instinct with grace, why be afraid of ruin? But then, if people go wrong,—at least women,—they are not asked out any where! ' "Sudden arose Ianthe's soul; it stood all-beautiful——" ' And so the piece was learned, and Lizzie felt that she had devoted her hour to poetry in a quite rapturous manner. At any rate she had a bit to quote; and though in truth she did not understand the exact bearing of the image, she had so studied her gestures, and so modulated her voice, that she knew that she could be effective. She did not then care to carry her reading further, but returned with the volume into the house. Though the passage about Ianthe's soul comes very early in the work, she was now quite familiar with the poem, and when, in after days, she spoke of it as a thing of beauty that she had made her own by long study, she actually did not know that she was lying. As she grew older, however, she quickly became wiser, and was aware that in learning one passage of a poem, it is expedient to select one in the middle, or at the end. The world is so cruelly observant now-a-days, that even men and women who have not themselves read their 'Queen Mab', will know from what part of the poem a morsel is extracted, and will not give you credit for a page beyond that from which your passage comes.

After lunch Lizzie invited Miss Macnulty to sit at the open window of the drawing-room and look out upon the 'glittering waves.' In giving Miss Macnulty her due, we must acknowledge that, though she owned no actual cleverness herself, had no cultivated tastes, read but little, and that little of a colourless kind, and thought nothing of her hours but that she might get rid of them and live,—yet she had a certain power of insight, and could see a thing. Lizzie Eustace was utterly powerless to impose upon her. Such as Lizzie was, Miss Macnulty was willing to put up with her and accept her bread. The people whom she had known had been either worthless— as had been her own father, or cruel—like Lady Linlithgow, or false—as was Lady Eustace. Miss Macnulty knew that worth-lessness, cruelty, and falseness had to be endured by such as she. And she could bear them without caring much about them;—not condemning them, even within her own heart, very heavily. But she was strangely deficient in this,—that she could not call these qualities by other names, even to the owners of them. She was unable to pretend to believe Lizzie's rhapsodies. It was hardly conscience or a grand spirit of truth that actuated her, as much as a want of the courage needed for lying. She had not had the face to call old Lady Linlithgow kind, and therefore old Lady Linlithgow had turned her out of the house. When Lady Eustace called on her for sympathy, she had not courage enough to dare to attempt the bit of acting which would be necessary for sympathetic expression. She was like a dog or a child, and was unable not to be true. Lizzie was longing for a little mock sympathy,—was longing to show off her Shelley, and was very kind to Miss Macnulty when she got the poor old lady into the recess of the window. 'This is nice;—is it not?' she said, as she spread her hand out through the open space towards the 'wide expanse of glittering waves.'

'Very nice,—only it glares so,' said Miss Macnulty.

'Ah, I love the full warmth of the real summer. With me it always seems that the sun is needed to bring to true ripe-ness the fruit of the heart.' Nevertheless she had been much troubled both by the heat and by the midges when she tried to sit on the stone. 'I always think of those few glorious days which I passed with my darling Florian at Naples;—days too glorious because they were so few.' Now Miss Macnulty knew some of the history of those days and of their glory,—and knew also how the widow had borne her loss.

'I suppose the bay of Naples is fine,' she said.

'It is not only the bay. There are scenes there which ravish you, only it is necessary that there should be some one with you that can understand you. "Soul of Ianthe!" ' she said, meaning to apostrophise that of the deceased Sir Florian. 'You have read "Queen Mab?" '

'I don't know that I ever did. If I have, I have forgotten it.'

'Ah,—you should read it. I know nothing in the English language that brings home to one so often one's own best feelings and aspirations. "It stands all beautiful in naked purity," ' she continued, still alluding to poor Sir Florian's soul, ' "Instinct with inexpressible beauty and grace, Each stain of earthliness had passed away." I can see him now in all his manly beauty, as we used to sit together by the hour, looking over the waters. Oh, Julia, the thing itself has gone, —the earthly reality; but the memory of it will live for ever!'

'He was a very handsome man, certainly,' said Miss Macnulty, finding herself forced to say something.

'I see him now,' she went on, still gazing out upon the shining water, ' "It reassumed its native dignity, and stood Primeval amid ruin." Is not that a glorious idea, gloriously worded?' She had forgotten one word and used a wrong epithet; but it sounded just as well. Primeval seemed to her to be a very poetical word.

'To tell the truth,' said Miss Macnulty, 'I never understand poetry when it is quoted unless I happen to know the passage beforehand. I think I'll go away from this, for the light is too much for my poor old eyes.' Certainly Miss Macnulty had fallen into a profession for which she was not suited.

CHAPTER XXII
Lady Eustace procures a Pony for the use of her Cousin

LADY EUSTACE could make nothing of Miss Macnulty in the way of sympathy, and could not bear her disappointment with patience. It was hardly to be expected that she should do so. She paid a great deal for Miss Macnulty. In a moment of rash generosity, and at a time when she hardly knew what money meant, she had promised Miss Macnulty seventy pounds for the first year, and seventy for the second, should the arrangement last longer than a twelvemonth. The second year had been now commenced, and Lady Eustace was beginning to think that seventy pounds was a great deal of money, when so very little was given in return. Lady Linlithgow had paid her dependant no fixed salary. And then there was the lady's 'keep,' and first-class travelling when they went up and down to Scotland, and cab-fares in London when it was desirable that Miss Macnulty should absent herself. Lizzie, reckoning all up, and thinking that for so much her friend ought to be ready to discuss Ianthe's soul, or any other kindred subject, at a moment's warning, would become angry, and would tell herself that she was being swindled out of her money. She knew how necessary it was that she should have some companion at the present emergency of her life, and therefore could not at once send Miss Macnulty away; but she would sometimes become very cross, and would tell poor Macnulty that she was—a fool. Upon the whole, however, to be called a fool was less objectionable to Miss Macnulty than were demands for sympathy which she did not know how to give.

Those first ten days of August went very slowly with Lady Eustace. 'Queen Mab' got itself poked away, and was heard of no more. But there were other books. A huge box full of novels had come down, and Miss Macnulty was a great devourer of novels. If Lady Eustace would talk to her about the sorrows of the poorest heroine that ever saw her lover murdered before her eyes, and then come to life again with ten thousand pounds a year,—for a period of three weeks, or till another heroine, who had herself been murdered, obliterated the former horrors from her plastic mind,—Miss Macnulty could discuss the catastrophe with the keenest interest. And Lizzie, finding herself to be, as she told herself, unstrung, fell also into novel-reading. She had intended during this vacant time to master the 'Fairy Queen;' but the 'Fairy Queen' fared even worse than 'Queen Mab;'—and the studies of Portray Castle were confined to novels. For poor Macnulty, if she could only be left alone, this was well enough. To have her meals, and her daily walk, and her fill of novels, and to be left alone, was all that she asked of the gods. But it was not so with Lady Eustace. She asked much more than that, and was now thoroughly discontented with her own idleness. She was sure that she could have read Spenser from sunrise to sundown, with no other break than an hour or two given to Shelley,—if only there had been some one to sympathise with her in her readings. But there was no one, and she was very cross. Then there came a letter to her from her cousin,—which for that morning brought some life back to the castle. 'I have seen Lord Fawn,' said the letter, 'and I have also seen Mr. Camperdown. As it would be very hard to explain what took place at these interviews by letter, and as I shall be at Portray Castle on the 20th,—I will not make the attempt. We shall go down by the night train, and I will get over to you as soon as I have dressed and had my breakfast. I suppose I can find some kind of a pony for the journey. The "we" consists of myself and my friend, Mr. Herriot,—a man whom I think you will like, if you will condescend to see him, though he is a barrister like myself. You need express no immediate condescension in his favour, as I shall of course come over alone on Wednesday morning. Yours always affectionately, F. G.'

The letter she received on the Sunday morning, and as the Wednesday named for Frank's coming was the next Wednesday, and was close at hand, she was in rather a better humour than she had displayed since the poets had failed her. 'What a blessing it will be,' she said, 'to have somebody to speak to!'

This was not complimentary, but Miss Macnulty did not want compliments. 'Yes, indeed,' she said. 'Of course you will be glad   see your cousin.'

'I shall be glad to see anything in the shape of a man. I declare that I have felt almost inclined to ask the minister from Craigie to elope with me.'

'He has got seven children,' said Miss Macnulty.

'Yes, poor man, and a wife, and not more than enough to live upon. I daresay he would have come. By-the-bye, I wonder whether there's a pony about the place.'

'A pony!' Miss Macnulty of course supposed that it was needed for the purpose of the suggested elopement.

'Yes;—I suppose you know what a pony is? Of course there ought to be a shooting pony at the cottage for these men. My poor head has so many things to work upon that I had forgotten it; and you're never any good at thinking of things.'

'I didn't know that gentlemen wanted ponies for shooting.'

'I wonder what you do know? Of course there must be a pony.'

'I suppose you'll want two?'

'No, I sha'n't. You don't suppose that men always go riding about. But I want one. What had I better do?' Miss Macnulty suggested that Gowran should be consulted. Now, Gowran was the steward and bailiff and manager and factotum about the place, who bought a cow or sold one if occasion required, and saw that nobody stole anything, and who knew the boundaries of the farms, and all about the tenants, and looked after the pipes when frost came, and was an honest, domineering, hard-working, intelligent Scotchman, who had been brought up to love the Eustaces, and who hated his present mistress with all his heart. He did not leave her service, having an idea in his mind that it was now the great duty of his life to save Portray from her ravages. Lizzie fully returned the compliment of the hatred, and was determined to rid herself of Andy Gowran's services as soon as possible. He had been called Andy by the late Sir Florian, and, though every one else about the place called him Mr. Gowran, Lady Eustace thought it became her, as the man's mistress, to treat him as he had been treated by the late master. So she called him Andy. But she was resolved to get rid of him,—as soon as she should dare. There were things which it was essential that somebody about the place should know, and no one knew them but Mr. Gowran. Every servant in the castle might rob her, were it not for the protection afforded by Mr. Gowran. In that affair of the garden it was Mr. Gowran who had enabled her to conquer the horticultural Leviathian who had oppressed her, and who, in point of wages, had been a much bigger man than Mr. Gowran himself. She trusted Mr. Gowran, and hated him,—whereas Mr. Gowran hated her, and did not trust her. 'I believe you think that nothing can be done at Portray except by that man,' said Lady Eustace.

'He'll know how much you ought to pay for the pony.'

'Yes,—and get some brute not fit for my cousin to ride, on purpose, perhaps, to break his neck.'

'Then I should ask Mr. Macallum, the postmaster of Troon, for I have seen three or four very quiet-looking ponies standing in the carts at his door.'

'Macnulty, if there ever was an idiot you are one!' said Lady Eustace, throwing up her hands. 'To think that I should get a pony for my cousin Frank out of one of the mail carts.'

'I daresay I am an idiot,' said Miss Macnulty, resuming her novel.

Lady Eustace was, of course, obliged to have recourse to Gowran, to whom she applied on the Monday morning. Not even Lizzie Eustace, on behalf of her cousin Frank, would have dared to disturb Mr. Gowran with considerations respecting a pony on the Sabbath. On the Monday morning she found Mr. Gowran superintending four boys and three old women, who were making a bit of her ladyship's hay on the ground above the castle. The ground about the castle was poor and exposed, and her ladyship's hay was apt to be late. 'Andy,' she said, 'I shall want to get a pony for the gentlemen who are coming to the Cottage. It must be there by Tuesday evening.'

'A pownie, my leddie?'

'Yes;—a pony. I suppose a pony may be purchased in Ayrshire,—though of all places in the world it seems to have the fewest of the comforts of life.'

'Them as find it like that, my leddie, needn't bide there.'

'Never mind. You will have the kindness to have a pony purchased and put into the stables of the Cottage on the Tuesday afternoon. There are stables, no doubt.'

'Oh, ay,—there's shelter, na doubt, for mair pownies than they'll ride. When the Cottage was biggit, my leddie, there was nae cause for sparing nowt.' Andy Gowran was continually throwing her comparative poverty in poor Lizzie's teeth, and there was nothing he could do which displeased her more.

'And I needn't spare my cousin the use of a pony,' she said grandiloquently, but feeling as she did so that she was exposing herself before the man. 'You'll have the goodness to procure one for him on Tuesday.'

'But there ain't aits nor yet fother, nor nowt for bedding down. And wha's to tent the pownie? There's mair in keeping a pownie than your leddyship thinks. It'll be a matter of auchteen*and saxpence a week,—will a pownie.' Mr. Gowran, as he expressed his prudential scruples, put a very strong emphasis indeed on the sixpence.

'Very well. Let it be so.'

'And there'll be the beastie to buy, me leddie. He'll be—— a lump of money, my leddie. Pownies ain't to be had for nowt in Ayrshire, as was ance, my leddie.'

'Of course I must pay for him.'

'He'll be a matter of——ten pound, my leddie.'

'Very well.'

'Or may be—twal; just as likely.' And Mr. Gowran shook his head at his mistress in a most uncomfortable way. It was not surprising that she should hate him.

'You must give the proper price,—of course.'

'There ain't no proper prices for pownies,—as there is for jew'ls and sich like.' If this was intended for sarcasm upon Lady Eustace in regard to her diamonds, Mr. Gowran ought to have been dismissed on the spot. In such a case no English jury would have given him his current wages. 'And he'll be to sell again, my leddie?'

'We shall see about that afterwards.'

'Ye'll never let him eat his head off there a' the winter! He'll be to sell. And the gentles'll*ride him, may be, ance across the hillside, out and back. As to the grouse, they can't cotch them with the pownie, for there ain't none to cotch.' There had been two keepers on the mountains,—men who were paid five or six shillings a week to look after the game in addition to their other callings, and one of these had been sent away, actually in obedience to Gowran's advice;—so that this blow was cruel and unmanly. He made it, too, as severe as he could by another shake of his head.

'Do you mean to tell me that my cousin cannot be supplied with an animal to ride upon?'

'My leddie, I've said nowt o' the kind. There ain't no useful animal as I kens the name and nature of as he can't have in Ayrshire,—for paying for it, my leddie;—horse, pownie, or ass, just whichever you please, my leddie. But there'll be a seddle*——'

'A what?'

There can be no doubt that Gowran purposely slurred the word so that his mistress should not understand him. 'Seddles don't come for nowt, my leddie, though it be Ayrshire.'

'I don't understand what it is that you say, Andy.'

'A seddle, my leddie,'—said he, shouting the word at her at the top of his voice,—'and a briddle* I suppose as your leddyship's cousin don't ride bare-back up in Lunnon?'

'Of course there must be the necessary horse-furniture,' said Lady Eustace, retiring to the castle. Andy Gowran had certainly ill-used her, and she swore that she would have revenge. Nor when she was informed on the Tuesday that an adequate pony had been hired for eighteen pence a day, saddle, bridle, groom, and all included, was her heart at all softened towards Mr. Gowran.

CHAPTER XXIII
Frank Greystock's first visit to Portray

H AD Frank Greystock known all that his cousin endured for his comfort, would he have been grateful? Women, when they are fond of men, do think much of men's comfort in small matters, and men are apt to take the good things provided almost as a matter of course. When Frank Greystock and Herriot reached the cottage about nine o'clock in the morning, having left London over night by the limited mail train, the pony at once presented itself to them. It was a little shaggy, black beast, with a boy almost as shaggy as itself, but they were both good of their kind. 'Oh, you're the laddie with the pownie, are you?' said Frank, in answer to an announcement made to him by the boy. He did at once perceive that Lizzie had taken notice of the word in his note, in which he had suggested that some means of getting over to Portray would be needed, and he learned from the fact that she was thinking of him and anxious to see him.

His friend was a man a couple of years younger than himself, who had hitherto achieved no success at the Bar, but who was nevertheless a clever, diligent, well-instructed man. He was what the world calls penniless, having an income from his father just sufficient to keep him like a gentleman. He was not much known as a sportsman, his opportunities for shooting not having been great; but he dearly loved the hills and fresh air, and the few grouse which were,—or were not,—on Lady Eustace's mountains would go as far with him as they would with any man. Before he had consented to come with Frank, he had especially inquired whether there was a game-keeper, and it was not till he had been assured that there was no officer attached to the estate worthy of such a name, that he had consented to come upon his present expedition. 'I don't clearly know what a gillie*is,' he said, in answer to one of Frank's explanations. 'If a gillie means a lad without any breeches on, I don't mind; but I couldn't stand a severe man got up in well-made velveteens, who would see through my ignorance in a moment, and make known by comment the fact that he had done so.' Greystock had promised that there should be no severity, and Herriot had come. Greystock brought with him two guns, two fishing rods, a man-servant, and a huge hamper from Fortnum and Mason's.* Arthur Herriot, whom the attorneys had not yet loved, brought some very thick boots, a pair of knickerbockers, together with Stone and Toddy's 'Digest of the Common Law.'*The best of the legal profession consists in this;—that when you get fairly at work you may give over working. An aspirant must learn everything; but a man may make his fortune at it, and know almost nothing. He may examine a witness with judgment, see through a case with precision, address a jury with eloquence,—and yet be altogether ignorant of law. But he must be believed to be a very pundit before he will get a chance of exercising his judgment, his precision, or his eloquence. The men whose names are always in the newspapers never look at their Stone and Toddy,—care for it not at all,—have their Stone and Toddy got up for them by their juniors when cases require that reference shall be made to precedents. But till that blessed time has come, a barrister who means success should carry his Stone and Toddy with him everywhere. Greystock never thought of the law now, unless he had some special case in hand; but Herriot could not afford to go out on his holiday without two volumes of Stone and Toddy's Digest in his portmanteau.

'You won't mind being left alone for the first morning?' said Frank, as soon as they had finished the contents of one of the pots from Fortnum and Mason.

'Not in the least. Stone and Toddy will carry me through.'

'I'd go on the mountain if I were you, and get into a habit of steady loading.'

'Perhaps I will take a turn,—just to find out how I feel in the knickerbockers. At what time shall I dine if you don't come back?'

'I shall certainly be here to dinner,' said Frank, 'unless the pony fails me or I get lost on the mountain.' Then he started, and Herriot at once went to work on Stone and Toddy, with a pipe in his mouth. He had travelled all night, and it is hardly necessary to say that in five minutes he was fast asleep.

So also had Frank travelled all night, but the pony and the fresh air kept him awake. The boy had offered to go with him, but that he had altogether refused;—and, therefore, to his other cares was added that of finding his way. The sweep of the valleys, however, is long and not abrupt, and he could hardly miss his road if he would only make one judicious turn through a gap in a certain wall which lay half way between the cottage and the castle. He was thinking of the work in hand, and he found the gap without difficulty. When through that he ascended the hill for two miles, and then the sea was before him, and Portray Castle, lying, as it seemed to him at that distance, close upon the sea-shore. 'Upon my word, Lizzie has not done badly for herself,' he said almost aloud, as he looked down upon the fair sight beneath him, and round upon the mountains, and remembered that, for her life at least, it was all hers, and after her death would belong to her son. What more does any human being desire of such a property than that?

He rode down to the great doorway,—the mountain track which fell on to the road about half a mile from the castle having been plain enough, and there he gave up the pony into the hands of no less a man than Mr. Gowran himself. Gowran had watched the pony coming down the mountain-side, and had desired to see of what like was 'her leddyship's' cousin. In telling the whole truth of Mr. Gowran, it must be acknowledged that he thought that his late master had made a very great mistake in the matter of his marriage. He could not imagine bad things enough of Lady Eustace, and almost believed that she was not now, and hadn't been before her marriage, any better than she should be. The name of Admiral Greystock, as having been the father of his mistress, had indeed reached his ears; but Andy Gowran was a suspicious man, and felt no confidence even in an admiral,—in regard to whom he heard nothing of his having, or having had, a wife. 'It's my fer-rm opeenion she's jist naebody—and waur,' he had said more than once to his own wife, nodding his head with great emphasis at the last word. He was very anxious, therefore, to see 'her leddyship's' cousin. Mr. Gowran thought that he knew a gentleman when he saw one. He thought, also, that he knew a lady, and that he didn't see one when he was engaged with his mistress. Cousin, indeed! 'For the matter o' that, ony man that comes the way may be ca'ed a coosin.' So Mr. Gowran was on the grand sweep before the garden gate, and took the pony from Frank's hand. 'Is Lady Eustace at home?' Frank asked. Mr. Gowran perceived that Frank was a gentleman, and was disappointed. And Frank didn't come as a man comes who calls himself by a false name, and pretends to be an honest cousin when in fact he is something,—oh, ever so wicked! Mr. Gowran, who was a stern moralist, was certainly disappointed at Frank's appearance.

Lizzie was in a little sitting-room, reached by a long passage with steps in the middle, at some corner of the castle which seemed a long way from the great door. It was a cheerful little room, with chintz curtains, and a few shelves laden with brightly-bound books, which had been prepared for Lizzie immediately on her marriage. It looked out upon the sea, and she had almost taught herself to think that here she had sat with her adored Florian, gazing in mutual ecstasy upon the 'wide expanse of glittering waves.' She was lying back in a low arm-chair as her cousin entered, and she did not rise to receive him. Of course she was alone, Miss Macnulty having received a suggestion that it would be well that she should do a little gardening in the moat. 'Well, Frank?' she said, with her sweetest smile, as she gave him her hand. She felt and understood the extreme intimacy which would be implied by her not rising to receive him. As she could not rush into his arms there was no device by which she could more clearly show to him how close she regarded his friendship.

'So I am at Portray Castle at last,' he said, still holding her hand.

'Yes,—at the dullest, dreariest, deadliest spot in all Christendom, I think,——if Ayrshire be Christendom. But never mind about that now. Perhaps, as you are at the other side of the mountain at the Cottage, we shall find it less dull here at the castle.'

'I thought you were to be so happy here.'

'Sit down and we'll talk it all over by degrees. What will you have,—breakfast or lunch?'

'Neither, thank you.'

'Of course you'll stay to dinner?'

'No, indeed. I've a man there at the Cottage with me who would cut his throat in his solitude.'

'Let him cut his throat;—but never mind now. As for being happy, women are never happy without men. I needn't tell any lies to you, you know. What makes me sure that this fuss about making men and women all the same must be wrong, is just the fact that men can get along without women, and women can't without men. My life has been a burthen to me. But never mind. Tell me about my lord;—my lord and master.'

'Lord Fawn?'

'Who else? What other lord and master? My bosom's own; my heart's best hope; my spot of terra firma; my cool running brook of fresh water; my rock; my love; my lord; my all! Is he always thinking of his absent Lizzie? Does he still toil at Downing Street? Oh, dear; do you remember, Frank, when he told us that——"one of us must remain in town?"'

'I have seen him.'

'So you wrote me word.'

'And I have seen a very obstinate, pig-headed, but nevertheless honest and truth-speaking gentleman.'

'Frank, I don't care twopence for his honesty and truth. If he ill-treats me——' Then she paused; looking into his face she had seen at once by the manner in which he had taken her badinage, without a smile, that it was necessary that she should be serious as to her matrimonial prospects. 'I suppose I had better let you tell your story,' she said, 'and I will sit still and listen.'

'He means to ill-treat you.'

'And you will let him?'

'You had better listen, as you promised, Lizzie. He declares that the marriage must be off at once unless you will send those diamonds to Mr. Camperdown or to the jewellers.'

'And by what law or rule does he justify himself in a decision so monstrous? Is he prepared to prove that the property is not my own?'

'If you ask me my opinion as a lawyer, I doubt whether any such proof can be shown. But as a man and a friend I do advise you to give them up.'

'Never!'

'You must, of course, judge for yourself;—but that is my advice. You had better, however, hear my whole story.'

'Certainly,' said Lizzie. Her whole manner was now changed. She had extricated herself from the crouching position in which her feet, her curl, her arms, her whole body had been so arranged as to combine the charm of her beauty with the charm of proffered intimacy. Her dress was such as a woman would wear to receive her brother, and yet it had been studied. She had no gems about her but what she might well wear in her ordinary life, and yet the very rings on her fingers had not been put on without reference to her cousin Frank. Her position had been one of lounging ease, such as a woman might adopt when all alone, giving herself all the luxuries of solitude;—but she had adopted it in special reference to cousin Frank. Now she was in earnest, with business before her; and though it may be said of her that she could never forget her appearance in presence of a man whom she desired to please, her curl, and rings, and attitude were for the moment in the background. She had seated herself on a common chair, with her hands upon the table, and was looking into Frank's face with eager, eloquent, and combative eyes. She would take his law, because she believed in it; but, as far as she could see as yet, she would not take his advice unless it were backed by his law.

'Mr. Camperdown,' continued Greystock, 'has consented to prepare a case for opinion, though he will not agree that the Eustace estate shall be bound by that opinion.'

'Then what's the good of it?'

'We shall at least know, all of us, what is the opinion of some lawyer qualified to understand the circumstances of the case.'

'Why isn't your opinion as good as that of any lawyer?'

'I couldn't give an opinion;—not otherwise than as a private friend to you, which is worth nothing, unless for your private guidance. Mr. Camperdown——'

'I don't care one straw for Mr. Camperdown.'

'Just let me finish.'

'Oh, certainly;—and you mustn't be angry with me, Frank. The matter is so much to me; isn't it?'

'I won't be angry. Do I look as if I were angry? Mr. Camperdown is right.'

'I daresay he may be,—what you call right. But I don't care about Mr. Camperdown a bit.'

'He has no power, nor has John Eustace any power to decide that the property which may belong to a third person shall be jeopardised by any arbitration. The third person could not be made to lose his legal right by any such arbitration, and his claim, if made, would still have to be tried.'

'Who is the third person, Frank?'

'Your own child at present.'

'And will not he have it any way?'

'Camperdown and John Eustace say that it belongs to him at present. It is a point that, no doubt, should be settled.'

'To whom do you say that it belongs?'

'That is a question I am not prepared to answer.'

'To whom do you think that it belongs?'

'I have refused to look at a single paper on the subject, and my opinion is worth nothing. From what I have heard in conversation with Mr. Camperdown and John Eustace, I cannot find that they make their case good.'

'Nor can I,' said Lizzie.

'A case is to be prepared for Mr. Dove.'

'Who is Mr. Dove?'

'Mr. Dove is a barrister, and no doubt a very clever fellow. If his opinion be such as Mr. Camperdown expects, he will at once proceed against you at law for the immediate recovery of the necklace.'

'I shall be ready for him,' said Lizzie, and as she spoke all her little feminine softnesses were for the moment laid aside.

'If Mr. Dove's opinion be in your favour,——'

'Well,' said Lizzie,—'what then?'

'In that case Mr. Camperdown, acting on behalf of John Eustace and young Florian——'

'How dreadful it is to hear of my bitterest enemy acting on behalf of my own child!' said Lizzie, holding up her hands piteously. 'Well?'

'In that case Mr. Camperdown will serve you with some notice that the jewels are not yours,—to part with them as you may please.'

'But they will be mine.'

'He says not;—but in such case he will content himself with taking steps which may prevent you from selling them.'

'Who says that I want to sell them?' demanded Lizzie indignantly.

'Or from giving them away,—say to a second husband.'

'How little they know me!'

'Now I have told you all about Mr. Camperdown.'

'Yes.'

'And the next thing is to tell you about Lord Fawn.'

'That is everything. I care nothing for Mr. Camperdown; nor yet for Mr. Dove,—if that is his absurd name. Lord Fawn is of more moment to me,—though, indeed, he has given me but little cause to say so.'

'In the first place I must explain to you that Lord Fawn is very unhappy.'

'He may thank himself for it.'

'He is pulled this way and that, and is half distraught; but he has stated with as much positive assurance as such a man can assume, that the match must be regarded as broken off unless you will at once restore the necklace.'

'He does?'

'He has commissioned me to give you that message;—and it is my duty, Lizzie, as your friend, to tell you my conviction that he repents his engagement.'

She now rose from her chair and began to walk about the room. 'He shall not go back from it. He shall learn that I am not a creature at his own disposal in that way. He shall find that I have some strength,—if you have none.'

'What would you have had me do?'

'Taken him by the throat,' said Lizzie.

'Taking by the throat in these days seldom forwards any object,—unless the taken one be known to the police. I think Lord Fawn is behaving very badly, and I have told him so. No doubt he is under the influence of others,—mothers and sisters,—who are not friendly to you.'

'False-faced idiots!' said Lizzie.

'He himself is somewhat afraid of me,—is much afraid of you;—is afraid of what people will say of him; and,—to give him his due,—is afraid also of doing what is wrong. He is timid, weak, conscientious, and wretched. If you have set your heart upon marrying him——'

'My heart!' said Lizzie scornfully.

'Or your mind,—you can have him by simply sending the diamonds to the jewellers. Whatever may be his wishes, in that case he will redeem his word.'

'Not for him or all that belongs to him! It wouldn't be much. He's just a pauper with a name.'

'Then your loss will be so much the less.'

'But what right has he to treat me so? Did you ever before hear of such a thing? Why is he to be allowed to go back,—without punishment,—more than another?'

'What punishment would you wish?'

'That he should be beaten within an inch of his life;—and if the inch were not there I should not complain.'

'And I am to do it,—to my absolute ruin, and to your great injury?'

'I think I could almost do it myself.' And Lizzie raised her hand as though there were some weapon in it. 'But, Frank, there must be something. You wouldn't have me sit down and bear it. All the world has been told of the engagement. There must be some punishment.'

'You would not wish to have an action brought,—for breach of promise?'

'I would wish to do whatever would hurt him most,—without hurting myself,' said Lizzie.

'You won't give up the necklace?' said Frank.

'Certainly not,' said Lizzie. 'Give it up for his sake,—a man that I have always despised.'

'Then you had better let him go.'

'I will not let him go. What,—to be pointed at as the woman that Lord Fawn had jilted? Never! My necklace should be nothing more to him than this ring.' And she drew from her finger a little circlet of gold with a stone, for which she had owed Messrs. Harter and Benjamin five-and-thirty pounds till Sir Florian had settled that account for her. 'What cause can he give for such treatment?'

'He acknowledges that there is no cause which he can state openly.'

'And I am to bear it? And it is you that tell me so? Oh, Frank!'

'Let us understand each other, Lizzie. I will not fight him,—that is, with pistols; nor will I attempt to thrash him. It would be useless to argue whether public opinion is right or wrong; but public opinion is now so much opposed to that kind of thing, that it is out of the question. I should injure your position and destroy my own. If you mean to quarrel with me on that score, you had better say so.'

Perhaps at that moment he almost wished that she would quarrel with him, but she was otherwise disposed. 'Oh, Frank,' she said, 'do not desert me?'

'I will not desert you.'

'You feel that I am ill-used, Frank?'

'I do. I think that his conduct is inexcusable.'

'And there is to be no punishment?' she asked, with that strong indignation at injustice which the unjust always feel when they are injured.

'If you carry yourself well,—quietly and with dignity,— the world will punish him.'

'I don't believe a bit of it. I am not a Patient Grizel,* who can content myself with heaping benefits on those who injure me, and then thinking that they are coals of fire. Lucy Morris is one of that sort.' Frank ought to have resented the attack, but he did not. 'I have no such tame virtues. I'll tell him to his face what he is. I'll lead him such a life that he shall be sick of the very name of necklace.'

'You cannot ask him to marry you.'

'I will. What, not ask a man to keep his promise when you are engaged to him? I am not going to be such a girl as that.'

'Do you love him, then?'

'Love him! I hate him. I always despised him, and now I hate him.'

'And yet you would marry him?'

'Not for worlds, Frank. No. Because you advised me, I thought that I would do so. Yes, you did, Frank. But for you I would never have dreamed of taking him. You know, Frank, how it was,—when you told me of him and wouldn't come to me yourself.' Now again she was sitting close to him and had her hand upon his arm. 'No, Frank; even to please you I could not marry him now. But I'll tell you what I'll do. He shall ask me again. In spite of those idiots at Richmond he shall kneel at my feet,—necklace or no necklace; and then, —then I'll tell him what I think of him. Marry him! I would not touch him with a pair of tongs.' As she said this, she was holding her cousin fast by the hand.

CHAPTER XXIV
Showing what Frank Greystock thought about marriage

It had not been much after noon when Frank Greystock reached Portray Castle, and it was very nearly five when he left it. Of course he had lunched with the two ladies, and as the conversation before lunch had been long and interesting, they did not sit down till near three. Then Lizzie had taken him out to show him the grounds and garden, and they had clambered together down to the sea-beach. 'Leave me here,' she had said, when he insisted on going because of his friend at the Cottage. When he suggested that she would want help to climb back up the rocks to the castle, she shook her head,

217

as though her heart was too full to admit of a consideration so trifling. 'My thoughts flow more freely here with the surge of the water in my ears, than they will with that old woman droning to me. I come here often, and know every rock and every stone.' That was not exactly true, as she had never been down but once before. 'You mean to come again?' He told her that of course he should come again. 'I will name neither day nor hour. I have nothing to take me away. If I am not at the castle I shall be at this spot. Good-bye, Frank.' He took her in his arms and kissed her,—of course as a brother; and then he clambered up, got on his pony, and rode away. 'I dinna ken just what to mak' o' him,' said Gowran to his wife. 'May be he is her coosin; but coosins are nae that sib that a weedow is to be hailed aboot jist ane as though she were ony quean at a fair.' From which it may be inferred that Mr. Gowran had watched the pair as they were descending together towards the shore.

Frank had so much to think of, riding back to the Cottage, that when he came to the gap, instead of turning round along the wall down the valley, he took the track right on across the mountain and lost his way. He had meant to be back at the Cottage by three or four, and yet had made his visit to the castle so long, that without any losing of his way he could not have been there before seven. As it was, when that hour arrived, he was up on the top of a hill, and could again see Portray Castle clustering down close upon the sea, and the thin belt of trees, and the shining water beyond;—but of the road to the Cottage he knew nothing. For a moment he thought of returning to Portray, till he had taught himself to perceive that the distance was much greater than it had been from the spot at which he had first seen the castle in the morning;—and then he turned his pony round and descended on the other side.

His mind was very full of Lizzie Eustace, and full also of Lucy Morris. If it were to be asserted here that a young man may be perfectly true to a first young woman while he is falling in love with a second, the readers of this story would probably be offended. But undoubtedly many men believe themselves to be quite true while undergoing this process, and many young women expect nothing else from their lovers. If only he will come right at last, they are contented. And if he don't come right at all,—it is the way of the world, and the game has to be played over again. Lucy Morris, no doubt, had lived a life too retired for the learning of such useful forbearance, but Frank Greystock was quite a proficient. He still considered himself to be true to Lucy Morris, with a truth seldom found in this degenerate age,— with a truth to which he intended to sacrifice some of the brightest hopes of his life,—with a truth which, after much thought, he had generously preferred to his ambition. Perhaps there was found some shade of regret to tinge the merit which he assumed on this head, in respect of the bright things which it would be necessary that he should abandon; but, if so, the feeling only assisted him in defending his present conduct from any aspersions his conscience might bring against it. He intended to marry Lucy Morris,—without a shilling, without position, a girl who had earned her bread as a governess, simply because he loved her. It was a wonder to himself that he, a lawyer, a man of the world, a member of Parliament, one who had been steeped up to his shoulders in the ways of the world, should still be so pure as to be capable of such a sacrifice. But it was so; and the sacrifice would undoubtedly be made,—some day. It would be absurd in one conscious of such high merit to be afraid of the ordinary social incidents of life. It is the debauched broken drunkard who should become a teetotaller, and not the healthy hard-working father of a family who never drinks a drop of wine till dinner-time. He need not be afraid of a glass of champagne when, on a chance occasion, he goes to a picnic. Frank Greystock was now going to his picnic; and, though he meant to be true to Lucy Morris, he had enjoyed his glass of champagne with Lizzie Eustace under the rocks. He was thinking a good deal of his champagne when he lost his way.

What a wonderful woman was his cousin Lizzie;—and so unlike any other girl he had ever seen! How full she was of energy, how courageous, and, then, how beautiful! No doubt her special treatment of him was sheer flattery. He told himself that it was so. But, after all, flattery is agreeable. That she did like him better than anybody else was probable. He could have no feeling of the injustice he might do to the heart of a woman who at the very moment that she was expressing her partiality for him, was also expressing her anger that another man would not consent to marry her. And then women who have had one husband already are not like young girls, in respect to their hearts. So at least thought Frank Greystock. Then he remembered the time at which he had intended to ask Lizzie to be his wife,—the very day on which he would have done so had he been able to get away from that early division at the House,—and he asked himself whether he felt any regret on that score. It would have been very nice to come down to Portray Castle as to his own mansion after the work of the courts and of the session. Had Lizzie become his wife, her fortune would have helped him to the very highest steps beneath the throne. At present he was almost nobody;—because he was so poor, and in debt. It was so, undoubtedly; but what did all that matter in comparison with the love of Lucy Morris? A man is bound to be true. And he would be true. Only, as a matter of course, Lucy must wait.

When he had first kissed his cousin up in London, she suggested that the kiss was given as by a brother, and asserted that it was accepted as by a sister. He had not demurred, having been allowed the kiss. Nothing of the kind had been said under the rocks to-day;—but then that fraternal arrangement, when once made and accepted, remains, no doubt, in force for a long time. He did like his cousin Lizzie. He liked to feel that he could be her friend, with the power of domineering over her. She, also, was fond of her own way, and loved to domineer herself; but the moment that he suggested to her that there might be a quarrel, she was reduced to a prayer that he would not desert her. Such a friendship has charms for a young man, especially if the lady be pretty. As to Lizzie's prettiness, no man or woman could entertain a doubt. And she had a way of making the most of herself, which it was very hard to resist. Some young women, when they clamber over rocks, are awkward, heavy, unattractive, and troublesome. But Lizzie had at one moment touched him as a fairy might have done; had sprung at another from stone to stone, requiring no help; and then, on a sudden, had become so powerless that he had been forced almost to carry her in his arms. That, probably, must have been the moment which induced Mr. Gowran to liken her to a quean at a fair.

But, undoubtedly, there might be trouble. Frank was sufficiently experienced in the ways of the world to know that trouble would sometimes come from young ladies who treat young men like their brothers, when those young men are engaged to other young ladies. The other young ladies are apt to disapprove of brothers who are not brothers by absolute right of birth. He knew also that all the circumstances of his cousin's position would make it expedient that she should marry a second husband. As he could not be that second husband,—that matter was settled, whether for good or bad,—was he not creating trouble, both for her and for himself? Then there arose in his mind a feeling, very strange, but by no means uncommon, that prudence on his part would be mean, because by such prudence he would be securing safety for himself as well as for her. What he was doing was not only imprudent,—but wrong also. He knew that it was so. But Lizzie Eustace was a pretty young woman; and, when a pretty young woman was in the case, a man is bound to think neither of what is prudent, nor of what is right. Such was,—perhaps his instinct rather than his theory. For her sake, if not for his own, he should have abstained. She was his cousin; and was so placed in the world as specially to require some strong hand to help her. He knew her to be, in truth, heartless, false, and greedy; but she had so lived that even yet her future life might be successful. He had called himself her friend as well as cousin, and was bound to protect her from evil, if protection were possible. But he was adding to all her difficulties, because she pretended to be in love with him. He knew that it was pretence; and yet, because she was pretty, and because he was a man, he could not save her from herself. 'It doesn't do to be wiser than other men,' he said to himself as he looked round about on the bare hill-side. In the meantime he had altogether lost his way.

It was between nine and ten when he reached the Cottage. 'Of course you have dined?' said Herriot.

'Not a bit of it. I left before five, being sure that I could get here in an hour and a half. I have been riding up and down these dreary hills for nearly five hours. You have dined?'

'There was a neck of mutton and a chicken. She said the neck of mutton would keep hot best, so I took the chicken. I hope you like lukewarm neck of mutton?'

'I'm hungry enough to eat anything;—not but what I had a first-rate luncheon. What have you done all day?'

'Stone and Toddy,' said Herriot.

'Stick to that. If anything can pull you through, Stone and Toddy will. I lived upon them for two years.'

'Stone and Toddy,—with a little tobacco, have been all my comfort. I began, however, by sleeping for a few hours. Then I went upon the mountains.'

'Did you take a gun?'

'I took it out of the case, but it didn't come right, and so I left it. A man came to me and said he was the keeper.'

'He'd have put the gun right for you.'

'I was too bashful for that. I persuaded him that I wanted to go out alone and see what birds there were, and at last I induced him to stay here with the old woman. He's to be at the Cottage at nine to-morrow. I hope that is all right.'

In the evening, as they smoked and drank whisky and water,—probably supposing that to be correct in Ayrshire,*— they were led on by the combined warmth of the spirit, the tobacco, and their friendship, to talk about women. Frank, some month or six weeks since, in a moment of soft confidence, had told his friend of his engagement with Lucy

Morris. Of Lizzie Eustace he had spoken only as of a cousin whose interests were dear to him. Her engagement with Lord Fawn was known to all London, and was, therefore, known to Arthur Herriot. Some distant rumour, however, had reached him that the course of true-love was not running quite smooth, and therefore on that subject he would not speak, at any rate till Greystock should first mention it. 'How odd it is to find two women living all alone in a great house like that,' Frank had said.

'Because so few women have the means to live in large houses, unless they live with fathers or husbands.'

'The truth is,' said Frank, 'that women don't do well alone. There is always a savour of misfortune,—or, at least, of melancholy,—about a household which has no man to look after it. With us, generally, old maids don't keep houses, and widows marry again. No doubt it was an unconscious appreciation of this feeling which brought about the burning of Indian widows. There is an unfitness in women for solitude. A female Prometheus, even without a vulture, would indicate cruelty worse even than Jove's. A woman should marry,—once, twice, and thrice if necessary.'

'Women can't marry without men to marry them.'

Frank Greystock filled his pipe as he went on with his lecture. 'That idea as to the greater number of women is all nonsense. Of course we are speaking of our own kind of men and women, and the disproportion of the numbers in so small a division of the population amounts to nothing. We have no statistics to tell us whether there be any such disproportion in classes where men do not die early from overwork.'

'More females are born than males.'

'That's more than I know. As one of the legislators of the country I am prepared to state that statistics are always false. What we have to do is to induce men to marry. We can't do it by statute.'

'No, thank God.'

'Nor yet by fashion.'

'Fashion seems to be going the other way,' said Herriot.

'It can be only done by education and conscience. Take men of forty all round,—men of our own class,—you believe that the married men are happier than the unmarried? I want an answer, you know, just for the sake of the argument.'

'I think the married men are the happier. But you speak as the fox who had lost his tail;*—or, at any rate, as a fox in the act of losing it.'

'Never mind my tail. If morality in life and enlarged affections are conducive to happiness it must be so.'

'Short commons*and unpaid bills are conducive to misery. That's what I should say if I wanted to oppose you.'

'I never came across a man willing to speak the truth who did not admit that, in the long run, married men are the happier. As regards women, there isn't even ground for an argument. And yet men don't marry.'

'They can't.'

'You mean there isn't food enough in the world.'

'The man fears that he won't get enough of what there is for his wife and family.'

'The labourer with twelve shillings a week has no such fear. And if he did marry the food would come. It isn't that. The man is unconscientious and ignorant as to the sources of true happiness, and won't submit himself to cold mutton and three clean shirts a week,—not because he dislikes mutton and dirty linen himself,—but because the world says they are vulgar. That's the feeling that keeps you from marrying, Herriot.'

'As for me,' said Herriot, 'I regard myself as so placed that I do not dare to think of a young woman of my own rank except as a creature that must be foreign to me. I cannot make such a one my friend as I would a man, because I should be in love with her at once. And I do not dare to be in love because I would not see a wife and children starve. I regard my position as one of enforced monasticism, and myself as a monk under the cruellest compulsion. I often wish that I had been brought up as a journeyman hatter.'

'Why a hatter?'

'I'm told it's an active sort of life. You're fast asleep, and I was just now, when you were preaching. We'd better go to bed. Nine o'clock for breakfast, I suppose?'

CHAPTER XXV
Mr. Dove's opinion

MR. THOMAS DOVE, familiarly known among club-men, attorneys' clerks, and, perhaps, even among judges when very far from their seats of judgment, as Turtle Dove, was a counsel learned in the law. He was a counsel so learned in the law, that there was no question within the limits of an attorney's capability of putting to him, that he could not answer with the aid of his books. And when he had once given an opinion, all Westminster*could not move him from it,—nor could Chancery Lane*and Lincoln's Inn*and the Temple*added to Westminster. When Mr. Dove had once been positive, no man on earth was more positive. It behoved him, therefore, to be right when he was positive; and though, whether wrong or right, he was equally stubborn, it must be acknowledged that he was seldom proved to be wrong. Consequently the attorneys believed in him, and he prospered. He was a thin man, over fifty years of age, very full of scorn and wrath, impatient of a fool, and thinking most men to be fools; afraid of nothing on earth,—and, so his enemies said, of nothing elsewhere; eaten up by conceit; fond of law, but fonder, perhaps, of dominion; soft as milk to those who acknowledged his power, but a tyrant to all who contested it; conscientious, thoughtful, sarcastic, bright-witted, and laborious. He was a man who never spared himself. If he had a case in hand, though the interest to himself in it was almost nothing, he would rob himself of rest for a week should a point arise which required such labour. It was the theory of Mr. Dove's life that he would never be beaten. Perhaps it was some fear in this respect that had kept him from Parliament and confined him to the courts and the company of attorneys. He was, in truth, a married man with a family; but they who knew him as the terror of opponents and as the divulger of legal opinion, heard nothing of his wife and children. He kept all such matters quite to himself, and was not given to much social intercourse with those among whom his work lay. Out at Streatham,* where he lived, Mrs. Dove probably had her circle of acquaintance;—but Mr. Dove's domestic life and his forensic life were kept quite separate.

At the present moment Mr. Dove is interesting to us solely as being the learned counsel in whom Mr. Camperdown trusted,—to whom Mr. Camperdown was willing to trust for an opinion in so grave a matter as that of the Eustace diamonds. A case was made out and submitted to Mr. Dove immediately after that scene on the pavement in Mount Street, at which Mr. Camperdown had endeavoured to induce Lizzie to give up the necklace; and the following is the opinion which Mr. Dove gave:—

'There is much error about heirlooms. Many think that any chattel may be made an heirloom by any owner of it.

This is not the case. The law, however, does recognise heirlooms;—as to which the Exors. or Admors.* are excluded in favour of the Successor; and when there are such heirlooms they go to the heir by special custom. Any devise of an heirloom is necessarily void, for the will takes place after death; and the heirloom is already vested in the heir by custom. We have it from Littleton,* that law prefers custom to devise.

'Brooke* says, that the best thing of every sort may be an heirloom,—such as the best bed, the best table, the best pot or pan.

'Coke* says, that heirlooms are so by custom, and not by law.

'Spelman* says, in defining an heirloom, that it may be "Omne utensil robustius;"*which would exclude a necklace.

'In the "Termes de Ley,"*it is defined as "Ascun parcel des ustensiles."*

'We are told in "Coke upon Littleton,"*that Crown jewels are heirlooms, which decision,—as far as it goes,—denies the right to other jewels.

'Certain chattels may undoubtedly be held and claimed as being in the nature of heirlooms,—as swords, pennons* of honour, garter and collar of S. S.* See case of the Earl of Northumberland;* and that of the Pusey horn,*—Pusey v. Pusey.* The journals of the House of Lords, delivered officially to peers, may be so claimed. See Upton v. Lord Ferrers.*

'A devisor may clearly devise or limit the possession of chattels, making them inalienable by devisees in succession. But in such cases they will become the absolute possession of the first person seized in tail,—even though an infant, and in case of death without will, would go to the Exors. Such arrangement, therefore, can only hold good for lives in existence and for 21 years afterwards. Chattels so secured would not be heirlooms. See Carr v. Lord Errol,* 14 Vesey,* and Rowland v. Morgan.*

'Lord Eldon* remarks, that such chattels held in families are "rather favourites of the court." This was in the Ormonde case.* Executors, therefore, even when setting aside any claim as for heirlooms, ought not to apply such property in payment of debts unless obliged.

'The law allows of claims for paraphernalia*for widows, and, having adjusted such claims, seems to show that the claim may be limited.

'If a man deliver cloth to his wife, and die, she shall have it, though she had not fashioned it into the garment intended.

'Pearls and jewels, even though only worn on state occasions, may go to the widow as paraphernalia,—but with a limit. In the case of Lady Douglas*, she being the daughter of an Irish Earl and widow of the King's Sergeant (temp. Car. I.), it was held that £370 was not too much, and she was allowed a diamond and a pearl chain to that value.

'In 1674, Lord Keeper Finch*declared that he would never allow paraphernalia, except to the widow of a nobleman.

'But in 1721 Lord Macclesfield*gave Mistress Tipping paraphernalia to the value of £200,—whether so persuaded by law and precedent, or otherwise, may be uncertain.

'Lord Talbot*allowed a gold watch as paraphernalia.

'Lord Hardwicke* went much further, and decided that Mrs. Northey was entitled to wear jewels to the value of £3000,—saying that value made no difference; but seems to have limited the nature of her possession in the jewels by declaring her to be entitled to wear them only when full-dressed.

'It is, I think, clear that the Eustace estate cannot claim the jewels as an heirloom. They are last mentioned, and, as far as I know, only mentioned as an heirloom, in the will of the great-grandfather of the present baronet,—if these be the diamonds then named by him. As such, he could not have devised them to the present claimant, as he died in 1820, and the present claimant is not yet two years old.

'Whether the widow could claim them as paraphernalia is more doubtful. I do not know that Lord Hardwicke's ruling would decide the case; but, if so, she would, I think, be debarred from selling, as he limits the use of jewels of lesser value than these, to the wearing of them when full-dressed.

The use being limited, possession with power of alienation cannot be intended.

'The lady's claim to them as a gift from her husband amounts to nothing. If they are not hers by will,—and it seems that they are not so,—she can only hold them as paraphernalia belonging to her station.

'I presume it to be capable of proof that the diamonds were not in Scotland when Sir Florian made his will or when he died. The former fact might be used as tending to show his intention when the will was made. I understand that he did leave to his widow by will all the chattels in Portray Castle.

'15 August, 18—'   'J. D.'

When Mr. Camperdown had thrice read this opinion, he sat in his chair an unhappy old man. It was undoubtedly the case that he had been a lawyer for upwards of forty years, and had always believed that any gentleman could make any article of value an heirloom in his family. The title-deeds of vast estates had been confided to his keeping, and he had had much to do with property of every kind; and now he was told that, in reference to property of a certain description,—property which, by its nature, could only belong to such as they who were his clients,—he had been long without any knowledge whatsoever. He had called this necklace an heirloom to John Eustace above a score of times; and now he was told by Mr. Dove, not only that the necklace was not an heirloom, but that it couldn't have been an heirloom. He was a man who trusted much in a barrister,—as was natural with an attorney; but he was now almost inclined to doubt Mr. Dove. And he was hardly more at ease in regard to the other clauses of the opinion. Not only could not the estate claim the necklace as an heirloom, but that greedy syren, that heartless snake, that harpy of a widow,—for it was thus that Mr. Camperdown in his solitude spoke to himself of poor Lizzie, perhaps throwing in a harder word or two,—that female swindler could claim it as—paraphernalia!

There was a crumb of comfort for him in the thought that he could force her to claim that privilege from a decision of the Court of Queen's Bench, and that her greed would be exposed should she do so. And she could be prevented from selling the diamonds. Mr. Dove seemed to make that quite clear. But then there came that other question, as to the inheritance of the property under the husband's will. That Sir Florian had not intended that she should inherit the necklace, Mr. Camperdown was quite certain. On that point he suffered no doubt. But would he be able to prove that the diamonds had never been in Scotland since Sir Florian's marriage? He had traced their history from that date with all the diligence he could use, and he thought that he knew it. But it might be doubtful whether he could prove it. Lady Eustace had first stated—had so stated before she had learned the importance of any other statement,—that Sir Florian had given her the diamonds in London, as they passed through London from Scotland to Italy, and that she had carried them thence to Naples where Sir Florian had died. If this were so they could not have been at Portray Castle till she took them there as a widow, and they would undoubtedly be regarded as a portion of that property which Sir Florian habitually kept in London. That this was so Mr. Camperdown entertained no doubt. But now the widow alleged that Sir Florian had given the necklace to her in Scotland, whither they had gone immediately after their marriage, and that she herself had brought them up to London. They had been married on the 5th of September; and by the jewellers' books it was hard to tell whether the trinket had been given up to Sir Florian on the 4th or 24th of September. On the 24th Sir Florian and his young bride had undoubtedly been in London. Mr. Camperdown anathematised the carelessness of everybody connected with Messrs. Garnett's establishment. 'Those sort of people have no more idea of accuracy than,—than——' than he had had of heirlooms, his conscience whispered to him, filling up the blank.

Nevertheless he thought he could prove that the necklace

was first put into Lizzie's hands in London. The middle-aged and very discreet man at Messrs. Garnett's, who had given up the jewel-case to Sir Florian, was sure that he had known Sir Florian to be a married man when he did so. The lady's maid who had been in Scotland with Lady Eustace, and who was now living in Turin, having married a courier, had given evidence before an Italian man of law, stating that she had never seen the necklace till she came to London. There were, moreover, the probabilities of the case. Was it likely that Sir Florian should take such a thing down in his pocket to Scotland? And there was the statement as first made by Lady Eustace herself to her cousin Frank, repeated by him to John Eustace, and not to be denied by any one. It was all very well for her now to say that she had forgotten; but would any one believe that on such a subject she could forget?

But still the whole thing was very uncomfortable. Mr. Dove's opinion, if seen by Lady Eustace and her friends, would rather fortify them than frighten them. Were she once to get hold of that word, paraphernalia, it would be as a tower of strength to her. Mr. Camperdown specially felt this,—that whereas he had hitherto believed that no respectable attorney would take up such a case as that of Lady Eustace, he could not now but confess to himself that any lawyer seeing Mr. Dove's opinion, would be justified in taking it up. And yet he was as certain as ever that the woman was robbing the estate which it was his duty to guard, and that should he cease to be active in the matter, the necklace would be broken up and the property sold and scattered before a year was out, and then the woman would have got the better of him! 'She shall find that we have not done with her yet,' he said to himself, as he wrote a line to John Eustace.

But John Eustace was out of town, as a matter of course; —and on the next day Mr. Camperdown himself went down and joined his wife and family at a little cottage which he had at Dawlish.* The necklace, however, interfered much with his holiday.

CHAPTER XXVI
Mr. Gowran is very funny

FRANK GREYSTOCK certainly went over to Portray too often, —so often that the pony was proved to be quite necessary. Miss Macnulty held her tongue and was gloomy,—believing that Lady Eustace was still engaged to Lord Fawn, and feeling that in that case there should not be so many visits to the rocks. Mr. Gowran was very attentive, and could tell on any day, to five minutes, how long the two cousins were sitting together on the sea-shore. Arthur Herriot, who cared nothing for Lady Eustace, but who knew that his friend had promised to marry Lucy Morris, was inclined to be serious on the subject; but,—as is always the case with men,—was not willing to speak about it.

Once, and once only, the two men dined together at the castle,—for the doing of which it was necessary that a gig* should be hired all the way from Prestwick.* Herriot had not been anxious to go over, alleging various excuses,—the absence of dress clothes, the calls of Stone and Toddy, his bashfulness, and the absurdity of paying fifteen shillings for a gig. But he went at last, constrained by his friend, and a very dull evening he passed. Lizzie was quite unlike her usual self, —was silent, grave, and solemnly courteous; Miss Macnulty had not a word to say for herself; and even Frank was dull. Arthur Herriot had not tried to exert himself, and the dinner had been a failure.

'You don't think much of my cousin, I daresay,' said Frank, as they were driving back.

'She is a very pretty woman.'

'And I should say that she does not think much of you.'

'Probably not.'

'Why on earth wouldn't you speak to her? I went on making speeches to Miss Macnulty on purpose to give you a chance. Lizzie generally talks about as well as any young woman I know; but you had not a word to say to her, nor she to you.'

'Because you devoted yourself to Miss Mac——whatever her name is.'

'That's nonsense,' said Frank; 'Lizzie and I are more like brother and sister than anything else. She has no one else belonging to her, and she has to come to me for advice, and all that sort of thing. I wanted you to like her.'

'I never like people, and people never like me. There is an old saying that you should know a man seven years before you poke his fire. I want to know a person seven years before I can ask them how they do. To take me out to dine in this way was of all things the most hopeless.'

'But you do dine out,—in London.'

'That's different. There's a certain routine of conversation going, and one falls into it. At such affairs as that this evening one has to be intimate, or it is a bore. I don't mean to say anything against Lady Eustace. Her beauty is undeniable, and I don't doubt her cleverness.'

'She is sometimes too clever,' said Frank.

'I hope she is not becoming too clever for you. You've got to remember that you're due elsewhere;—eh, old fellow?' This was the first word that Herriot had said on the subject, and to that word Frank Greystock made no answer. But it had its effect, as also did the gloomy looks of Miss Macnulty, and the not unobserved presence of Mr. Andy Gowran on various occasions.

Between them they shot more grouse,—so the keeper swore,—than had ever been shot on these mountains before. Herriot absolutely killed one or two himself, to his own great delight, and Frank, who was fairly skilful, would get four or five in a day. There were excursions to be made, and the air of the hills was in itself a treat to both of them. Though Greystock was so often away at the castle, Herriot did not find the time hang heavy on his hands, and was sorry when his fortnight was over. 'I think I shall stay a couple of days longer,' Frank said, when Herriot spoke of their return. 'The truth is I must see Lizzie again. She is bothered by business, and I have to see her about a letter that came this morning. You needn't pull such a long face. There's nothing of the kind you're thinking of.'

'I thought so much of what you once said to me about another girl that I hope she at any rate may never be in trouble.'

'I hope she never may,—on my account,' said Frank. 'And what troubles she may have,—as life will be troublesome, I trust that I may share and lessen.'

On that evening Herriot went, and on the next morning Frank Greystock again rode over to Portray Castle; but when he was alone after Herriot's departure, he wrote a letter to Lucy Morris. He had expressed a hope that he might never be a cause of trouble to Lucy Morris, and he knew that his silence would trouble her. There could be no human being less inclined to be suspicious than Lucy Morris. Of that Frank was sure. But there had been an express stipulation with Lady Fawn that she should be allowed to receive letters from him, and she would naturally be vexed when he did not write to her. So he wrote.

'Portray Cottage, 3 Sept., 18—.
'DEAREST LUCY,

'We have been here for a fortnight, shooting grouse, wandering about the mountains, and going to sleep on the hill-sides. You will say that there never was a time so fit for the writing of letters, but that will be because you have not learned yet that the idler people are, the more inclined they are to be idle. We hear of Lord Chancellors writing letters to their mothers every day of their lives; but men who have nothing on earth to do cannot bring themselves to face a sheet of paper. I would promise that when I am Lord Chancellor I would write to you every day, were it not that when that time comes I shall hope to be always with you.

'And, in truth, I have had to pay constant visits to my cousin, who lives in a big castle on the sea-side, ten miles from here, over the mountains, and who is in a peck of troubles;*—in spite of her prosperity, one of the unhappiest women I should say that you could meet anywhere. You know so much of her affairs that, without breach of trust, I may say so much. I wish she had a father or a brother to manage her matters for her; but she has none, and I cannot desert her. Your Lord Fawn is behaving badly to her; and so, as far as I can see, are the people who manage the Eustace property. Lizzie, as you know, is not the most tractable of women, and altogether I have more to do in the matter than I like. Riding ten miles backwards and forwards so often over the same route on a little pony is not good fun, but I am almost glad the distance is not less. Otherwise I might have been always there. I know you don't quite like Lizzie, but she is to be pitied.

'I go up to London on Friday, but shall only be there for one or two days,—that is, for one night. I go almost entirely on her business, and must, I fear, be here again, or at the castle, before I can settle myself either for work or happiness. On Sunday night I go down to Bobsborough,—where, indeed, I ought to have been earlier. I fear I cannot go to Richmond on the Saturday, and on the Sunday Lady Fawn would hardly make me welcome. I shall be at Bobsborough for about three weeks, and there, if you have commands to give, I will obey them.

'I may, however, tell you the truth at once,—though it is a truth you must keep very much to yourself. In the position in which I now stand as to Lord Fawn,—being absolutely forced to quarrel with him on Lizzie's behalf,—Lady Fawn could hardly receive me with comfort to herself. She is the best of women; and, as she is your dear friend, nothing is further from me than any idea of quarrelling with her; but of course she takes her son's part, and I hardly know how all allusion to the subject could be avoided.

'This, however, dearest, need ruffle no feather between you and me, who love each other better than we love either the Fawns or the Lizzies. Let me find a line at my chambers to say that it is so, and always shall be so.

'God bless my own darling,

'Ever and always your own,

'F. G.'

On the following day he rode over to the castle. He had received a letter from John Eustace, who had found himself forced to run up to London to meet Mr. Camperdown. The lawyer had thought to postpone further consideration of the whole matter till he and everybody else would be naturally in London,—till November that might be, or, perhaps, even till after Christmas. But his mind was ill at ease; and he knew that so much might be done with the diamonds in four months! They might even now be in the hands of some Benjamin or of some Harter, and it might soon be beyond the power either of lawyers or of policemen to trace them. He therefore went up from Dawlish, and persuaded John Eustace to come from Yorkshire. It was a great nuisance, and Eustace freely anathematised the necklace. 'If only some one would steal it, so that we might hear no more of the thing!' he said. But, as Mr. Camperdown had frequently remarked, the value was too great for trifling, and Eustace went up to London. Mr. Camperdown put into his hands the Turtle Dove's opinion, explaining that it was by no means expedient that it should be shown to the other party. Eustace thought that the opinion should be common to them all. 'We pay for it,' said Mr. Camperdown, 'and they can get their opinion from any other barrister if they please.' But what was to be done? Eustace declared that as to the present whereabouts of the necklace, he did not in the least doubt that he could get the truth from Frank Greystock. He therefore wrote to Greystock, and with that letter in his pocket, Frank rode over to the castle for the last time.

He, too, was heartily sick of the necklace;—but unfortunately he was not equally sick of her who held it in possession. And he was, too, better alive to the importance of the value of the trinket than John Eustace, though not so keenly as was Mr. Camperdown. Lady Eustace was out somewhere among the cliffs, the servant said. He regretted this as he followed her, but he was obliged to follow her. Half way down to the sea-shore, much below the knob on which she had attempted to sit with her Shelley, but yet not below the need of assistance, he found her seated in a little ravine. 'I knew you would come,' she said. Of course she had known that he would come. She did not rise, or even give him her hand, but there was a spot close beside her on which it was to be presumed that he would seat himself. She had a volume of Byron*in her hand,—the Corsair, Lara, and the Giaour,—a kind of poetry which was in truth more intelligible to her than Queen Mab. 'You go to-morrow?'

'Yes;—I go to-morrow.'

'And Lubin*has gone?' Arthur Herriot was Lubin.

'Lubin has gone. Though why Lubin, I cannot guess. The normal Lubin to me is a stupid fellow always in love. Herriot is not stupid and is never in love.'

'Nevertheless, he is Lubin if I choose to call him so. Why did he twiddle his thumbs instead of talking? Have you heard anything of Lord Fawn?'

'I have had a letter from your brother-in-law.'

'And what is John the Just pleased to say?'

'John the Just, which is a better name for the man than the other, has been called up to London, much against his will, by Mr. Camperdown.'

'Who is Samuel the Unjust.' Mr. Camperdown's name was Samuel.

'And now wants to know where this terrible necklace is at this present moment.' He paused a moment, but Lizzie did not answer him. 'I suppose you have no objection to telling me where it is.'

'None in the least:—or to giving it you to keep for me, only that I would not so far trouble you. But I have an objection to telling them. They are my enemies. Let them find out.'

'You are wrong, Lizzie. You do not want, or at any rate, should not want, to have any secret in the matter.'

'They are here,—in the castle; in the very place in which Sir Florian kept them when he gave them to me. Where should my own jewels be, but in my own house? What does that Mr. Dove say, who was to be asked about them? No doubt they can pay a barrister to say anything.'

'Lizzie, you think too hardly of people.'

'And do not people think too hardly of me? Does not all this amount to an accusation against me that I am a thief? Am I not persecuted among them? Did not this impudent attorney stop me in the public street and accuse me of theft before my very servants? Have they not so far succeeded in misrepresenting me, that the very man who is engaged to be my husband betrays me? And now you are turning against me? Can you wonder that I am hard?'

'I am not turning against you.'

'Yes; you are. You take their part, and not mine, in everything. I tell you what, Frank;—I would go out in that boat that you see yonder, and drop the bauble into the sea, did I not know that they'd drag it up again with their devilish ingenuity. If the stones would burn, I would burn them. But the worst of it all is, that you are becoming my enemy!' Then she burst into violent and almost hysteric tears.

'It will be better that you should give them into the keeping of some one whom you can both trust, till the law has decided to whom they belong.'

'I will never give them up. What does Mr. Dove say?'

'I have not seen what Mr. Dove says. It is clear that the necklace is not an heirloom.'

'Then how dare Mr. Camperdown say so often that it was?'

'He said what he thought,' pleaded Frank.

'And he is a lawyer!'

'I am a lawyer, and I did not know what is or what is not an heirloom. But Mr. Dove is clearly of opinion that such a property could not have been given away, simply by word of mouth.' John Eustace in his letter had made no allusion to that complicated question of paraphernalia.

'But it was,' said Lizzie. 'Who can know but I myself, when no one else was present?'

'The jewels are here now?'

'Not in my pocket. I do not carry them about with me. They are in the castle.'

'And will they go back with you to London?'

'Was ever lady so interrogated? I do not know yet that I shall go back to London. Why am I asked such questions? As to you, Frank;—I would tell you everything,—my whole heart, if only you cared to know it. But why is John Eustace to make inquiry as to personal ornaments which are my own property? If I go to London, I will take them there, and wear them at every house I enter. I will do so in defiance of Mr. Camperdown and Lord Fawn. I think, Frank, that no woman was ever so ill-treated as I am.'

He himself thought that she was ill-treated. She had so pleaded her case, and had been so lovely in her tears and her indignation, that he began to feel something like true sympathy for her cause. What right had he, or had Mr. Camperdown, or any one, to say that the jewels did not belong to her? And if her claim to them was just, why should she be persuaded to give up the possession of them? He knew well that were she to surrender them with the idea that they should be restored to her if her claim were found to be just, she would not get them back very soon. If once the jewels were safe, locked up in Mr. Garnett's strong box, Mr. Camperdown would not care how long it might be before a jury or a judge should have decided on the case. The burthen of proof would then be thrown upon Lady Eustace. In order that she might recover her own property she would have to thrust herself forward as a witness, and appear before the world a claimant, greedy for rich ornaments. Why should he advise her to give them up? 'I am only thinking,' said he, 'what may be the best for your own peace.'

'Peace!'—she exclaimed. 'How am I to have peace? Remember the condition in which I find myself! Remember the manner in which that man is treating me, when all the world has been told of my engagement to him! When I think of it my heart is so bitter that I am inclined to throw, not the diamonds, but myself from off the rocks. All that remains to me is the triumph of getting the better of my enemies. Mr. Camperdown shall never have the diamonds. Even if they

could prove that they did not belong to me, they should find
them—gone.'

'I don't think they can prove it.'

'I'll flaunt them in the eyes of all of them till they do; and
then—they shall be gone. And I'll have such revenge on Lord
Fawn before I have done with him, that he shall know that it
may be worse to have to fight a woman than a man. Oh,
Frank, I do not think that I am hard by nature, but these
things make a woman hard.' As she spoke she took his hand
in hers, and looked up into his eyes through her tears. 'I
know that you do not care for me, and you know how much
I care for you.'

'Not care for you, Lizzie?'

'No;—that little thing at Richmond is everything to you.
She is tame and quiet,—a cat that will sleep on the rug before
the fire, and you think that she will never scratch. Do not
suppose that I mean to abuse her. She was my dear friend
before you had ever seen her. And men, I know, have tastes
which we women do not understand. You want what you
call—repose.'

'We seldom know what we want, I fancy. We take what
the gods send us.' Frank's words were perhaps more true
than wise. At the present moment the gods had clearly sent
Lizzie Eustace to him, and unless he could call up some increased strength of his own, quite independent of the gods,—
or of what we may perhaps call chance,—he would have to
put up with the article sent.

Lizzie had declared that she would not touch Lord Fawn
with a pair of tongs, and in saying so had resolved that she
could not and would not now marry his lordship even were
his lordship in her power. It had been decided by her as
quickly as thoughts flash, but it was decided. She would
torture the unfortunate lord, but not torture him by becoming his wife. And, so much being fixed as the stars in
heaven, might it be possible that she should even yet induce
her cousin to take the place that had been intended for Lord
Fawn? After all that had passed between them she need

hardly hesitate to tell him of her love. And with the same flashing thoughts she declared to herself that she did love him, and that therefore this arrangement would be so much better than that other one which she had proposed to herself. The reader, perhaps, by this time, has not a high opinion of Lady Eustace, and may believe that among other drawbacks on her character there is especially this,—that she was heartless. But that was by no means her own opinion of herself. She would have described herself,—and would have meant to do so with truth,—as being all heart. She probably thought that an over-amount of heart was the malady under which she specially suffered. Her heart was overflowing now towards the man who was sitting by her side. And then it would be so pleasant to punish that little chit who had spurned her gift and had dared to call her mean! This man, too, was needy, and she was wealthy. Surely, were she to offer herself to him, the generosity of the thing would make it noble. She was still dissolved in tears and was still hysteric. 'Oh, Frank!' she said, and threw herself upon his breast.

Frank Greystock felt his position to be one of intense difficulty, but whether his difficulty was increased or diminished by the appearance of Mr. Andy Gowran's head over a rock at the entrance of the little cave in which they were sitting, it might be difficult to determine. But there was the head. And it was not a head that just popped itself up and then retreated, as a head would do that was discovered doing that which made it ashamed of itself. The head, with its eyes wide open, held its own, and seemed to say,—'Ay,—I've caught you, have I?' And the head did speak, though not exactly in those words. 'Coosins!' said the head; and then the head was wagged. In the meantime Lizzie Eustace, whose back was turned to the head, raised her own, and looked up into Greystock's eyes for love. She perceived at once that something was amiss, and, starting to her feet, turned quickly round. 'How dare you intrude here?' she said to the head. 'Coosins!' replied the head, wagging itself.

It was clearly necessary that Greystock should take some

steps, if only with the object of proving to the impudent factotum that he was not altogether overcome by the awkwardness of his position. That he was a good deal annoyed, and that he felt not altogether quite equal to the occasion, must be acknowledged. 'What is it that the man wants?' he said, glaring at the head. 'Coosins!' said the head, wagging itself again. 'If you don't take yourself off, I shall have to thrash you,' said Frank. 'Coosins!' said Andy Gowran, stepping from behind the rock and showing his full figure. Andy was a man on the wrong side of fifty, and therefore, on the score of age, hardly fit for thrashing. And he was compact, short, broad, and as hard as flint;—a man bad to thrash, look at it from what side you would. 'Coosins!' he said yet again. 'Ye're mair couthie than coosinly, I'm thinking.'

'Andy Gowran, I dismiss you my service for your impertinence,' said Lady Eustace.

'It's ae ane to Andy Gowran for that, my leddie. There's timber and a warld o' things aboot the place as wants proteection on behalf o' the heir. If your leddieship is minded to be quit o' my sarvices, I'll find a maister in Mr. Camperdoon, as'll nae alloo me to be thrown out o' employ. Coosins!'

'Walk off from this!' said Frank Greystock, coming forward and putting his hand upon the man's breast. Mr. Gowran repeated the objectionable word yet once again, and then retired.

Frank Greystock immediately felt how very bad for him was his position. For the lady, if only she could succeed in her object, the annoyance of the interruption would not matter much after its first absurdity had been endured. When she had become the wife of Frank Greystock there would be nothing remarkable in the fact that she had been found sitting with him in a cavern by the sea-shore. But for Frank the difficulty of extricating himself from his dilemma was great, not in regard to Mr. Gowran, but in reference to his cousin Lizzie. He might, it was true, tell her that he was engaged to Lucy Morris;—but then why had he not told her so before? He had not told her so;—nor did he tell her on this occasion.

When he attempted to lead her away up the cliff, she insisted on being left where she was. 'I can find my way alone,' she said, endeavouring to smile through her tears. 'The man has annoyed me by his impudence,—that is all. Go,—if you are going.'

Of course he was going; but he could not go without a word of tenderness. 'Dear, dear Lizzie,' he said, embracing her.

'Frank, you'll be true to me?'

'I will be true to you.'

'Then go now,' she said. And he went his way up the cliff, and got his pony, and rode back to the cottage, very uneasy in his mind.

CHAPTER XXVII
Lucy Morris misbehaves

LUCY MORRIS got her letter and was contented. She wanted some demonstration of love from her lover, but very little sufficed for her comfort. With her it was almost impossible that a man should be loved and suspected at the same time. She could not have loved the man, or at any rate confessed her love, without thinking well of him; and she could not think good and evil at the same time. She had longed for some word from him since she last saw him; and now she had got a word. She had known that he was close to his fair cousin,—the cousin whom she despised, and whom, with womanly instinct, she had almost regarded as a rival. But to her the man had spoken out; and though he was far away from her, living close to the fair cousin, she would not allow a thought of trouble on that score to annoy her. He was her own, and let Lizzie Eustace do her worst, he would remain her own. But she had longed to be told that he was thinking of her, and at last the letter had come. She answered it that same night with the sweetest, prettiest little letter, very short, full of love and full of confidence. Lady Fawn, she said, was the dearest of women;—but what was Lady Fawn to her, or all the Fawns, compared with her lover? If he could come to Richmond without disturbance to himself, let him come; but if he felt that, in the present unhappy condition of affairs between him and Lord Fawn, it was better that he should stay away, she had not a word to say in the way of urging him. To see him would be a great delight. But had she not the greater delight of knowing that he loved her? That was quite enough to make her happy. Then there was a little prayer that God might bless him, and an assurance that she was in all things his own, own Lucy. When she was writing her letter she was in all respects a happy girl.

But on the very next day there came a cloud upon her happiness,—not in the least, however, affecting her full confidence in her lover. It was a Saturday, and Lord Fawn came down to Richmond. Lord Fawn had seen Mr. Greystock in London on that day, and the interview had been by no means pleasant to him. The Under-Secretary of State for India was as dark as a November day when he reached his mother's house, and there fell upon every one the unintermittent cold drizzling shower of his displeasure from the moment in which he entered the house. There was never much reticence among the ladies at Richmond in Lucy's presence, and since the completion of Lizzie's unfortunate visit to Fawn Court, they had not hesitated to express open opinions adverse to the prospects of the proposed bride. Lucy herself could say but little in defence of her old friend, who had lost all claim upon that friendship since the offer of the bribe had been made,—so that it was understood among them all that Lizzie was to be regarded as a black sheep;—but hitherto Lord Fawn himself had concealed his feelings before Lucy. Now unfortunately he spoke out, and in speaking was especially bitter against Frank. 'Mr. Greystock has been most insolent,' he said, as they were all sitting together in the library after dinner. Lady Fawn made a sign to him and shook her head. Lucy felt the hot blood fly into both her cheeks, but at the moment she did not speak. Lydia Fawn put out her hand beneath the table and took hold of Lucy's. 'We must all remember that he is her cousin,' said Augusta.

'His relationship to Lady Eustace cannot justify ungentle-manlike impertinence to me,' said Lord Fawn. 'He has dared to use words to me which would make it necessary that I should call him out,* only——'

'Frederic, you shall do nothing of the kind!' said Lady Fawn, jumping up from her chair.

'Oh, Frederic, pray, pray don't!' said Augusta, springing on to her brother's shoulder.

'I am sure Frederic does not mean that,' said Amelia.

'Only that nobody does call any body out now,' added the pacific lord. 'But nothing on earth shall ever induce me to speak again to a man who is so little like a gentleman.' Lydia now held Lucy's hand still tighter, as though to prevent her rising. 'He has never forgiven me,' continued Lord Fawn, 'because he was so ridiculously wrong about the Sawab.'

'I am sure that had nothing to do with it,' said Lucy.

'Miss Morris, I shall venture to hold my own opinion,' said Lord Fawn.

'And I shall hold mine,' said Lucy bravely. 'The Sawab of Mygawb had nothing to do with what Mr. Greystock may have said or done about his cousin. I am quite sure of it.'

'Lucy, you are forgetting yourself,' said Lady Fawn.

'Lucy, dear, you shouldn't contradict my brother,' said Augusta.

'Take my advice, Lucy, and let it pass by,' said Amelia.

'How can I hear such things said and not notice them?' demanded Lucy. 'Why does Lord Fawn say them when I am by?'

Lord Fawn had now condescended to be full of wrath against his mother's governess. 'I suppose I may express my own opinion, Miss Morris, in my mother's house.'

'And I shall express mine,' said Lucy. 'Mr. Greystock is a gentleman. If you say that he is not a gentleman, it is not true.' Upon hearing these terrible words spoken, Lord Fawn rose from his seat and slowly left the room. Augusta followed him with both her arms stretched out. Lady Fawn covered her face with her hands, and even Amelia was dismayed.

'O Lucy! why could you not hold your tongue?' said Lydia.

'I won't hold my tongue!' said Lucy, bursting out into tears. 'He is a gentleman.'

Then there was great commotion at Fawn Court. After a few moments Lady Fawn followed her son without having said a word to Lucy, and Amelia went with her. Poor Lucy was left with the younger girls, and was no doubt very unhappy. But she was still indignant, and would yield nothing. When Georgina, the fourth daughter, pointed out to her that, in accordance with all rules of good breeding, she should have abstained from asserting that her brother had spoken an untruth, she blazed up again. 'It was untrue,' she said.

'But, Lucy, people never accuse each other of untruth. No lady should use such a word to a gentleman.'

'He should not have said so. He knows that Mr. Greystock is more to me than all the world.'

'If I had a lover,' said Nina, 'and anybody were to say a word against him, I know I'd fly at them. I don't know why Frederic is to have it all his own way.'

'Nina, you're a fool,' said Diana.

'I do think it was very hard for Lucy to bear,' said Lydia.

'And I won't bear it!' exclaimed Lucy. 'To think that Mr. Greystock should be so mean as to bear malice about a thing like that wild Indian because he takes his own cousin's part! Of course I'd better go away. You all think that Mr. Greystock is an enemy now; but he never can be an enemy to me.'

'We think that Lady Eustace is an enemy,' said Cecilia, 'and a very nasty enemy, too.'

'I did not say a word about Lady Eustace,' said Lucy. 'But Mr. Greystock is a gentleman.'

About an hour after this Lady Fawn sent for Lucy, and the two were closeted together for a long time. Lord Fawn was very angry, and had hitherto altogether declined to overlook the insult offered. 'I am bound to tell you,' declared Lady

Fawn, with much emphasis, 'that nothing can justify you in having accused Lord Fawn of telling an untruth. Of course, I was sorry that Mr. Greystock's name should have been mentioned in your presence; but as it was mentioned, you should have borne what was said with patience.'

'I couldn't be patient, Lady Fawn.'

'That is what wicked people say when they commit murder, and then they are hung for it.'

'I'll go away, Lady Fawn——'

'That is ungrateful, my dear. You know that I don't wish you to go away. But if you behave badly, of course I must tell you of it.'

'I'd sooner go away. Everybody here thinks ill of Mr. Greystock. But I don't think ill of Mr. Greystock, and I never shall. Why did Lord Fawn say such very hard things about him?'

It was suggested to her that she should be down-stairs early the next morning, and apologise to Lord Fawn for her rudeness; but she would not, on that night, undertake to do any such thing. Let Lady Fawn say what she might, Lucy thought that the injury had been done to her, and not to his lordship. And so they parted hardly friends. Lady Fawn gave her no kiss as she went, and Lucy, with obstinate pride, altogether refused to own her fault. She would only say that she had better go, and when Lady Fawn over and over again pointed out to her that the last thing that such a one as Lord Fawn could bear was to be accused of an untruth, she would continue to say that in that case he should be careful to say nothing that was untrue. All this was very dreadful, and created great confusion and unhappiness at Fawn Court. Lydia came into her room that night, and the two girls talked the matter over for hours. In the morning Lucy was up early, and found Lord Fawn walking in the grounds. She had been told that he would probably be found walking in the grounds, if she were willing to tender to him any apology.

Her mind had been very full of the subject,—not only in reference to her lover, but as it regarded her own conduct.

One of the elder Fawn girls had assured her that under no circumstances could a lady be justified in telling a gentleman that he had spoken an untruth, and she was not quite sure but that the law so laid down was right. And then she could not but remember that the gentleman in question was Lord Fawn, and that she was Lady Fawn's governess. But Mr. Greystock was her affianced lover, and her first duty was to him. And then, granting that she herself had been wrong in accusing Lord Fawn of untruth, she could not refrain from asking herself whether he had not been much more wrong in saying in her hearing that Mr. Greystock was not a gentleman? And his offence had preceded her offence, and had caused it! She hardly knew whether she did or did not owe an apology to Lord Fawn, but she was quite sure that Lord Fawn owed an apology to her.

She walked straight up to Lord Fawn, and met him beneath the trees. He was still black and solemn, and was evidently brooding over his grievance; but he bowed to her, and stood still as she approached him. 'My lord,' said she, 'I am very sorry for what happened last night.'

'And so was I,—very sorry, Miss Morris.'

'I think you know that I am engaged to marry Mr. Greystock?'

'I cannot allow that that has anything to do with it.'

'When you think that he must be dearer to me than all the world, you will acknowledge that I couldn't hear hard things said of him without speaking.' His face became blacker than ever, but he made no reply. He wanted an abject begging of unconditional pardon from the little girl who loved his enemy. If that were done, he would vouchsafe his forgiveness; but he was too small by nature to grant it on other terms. 'Of course, continued Lucy, 'I am bound to treat you with special respect in Lady Fawn's house.' She looked almost beseechingly into his face as she paused for a moment.

'But you treated me with especial disrespect,' said Lord Fawn.

'And how did you treat me, Lord Fawn?'

'Miss Morris, I must be allowed, in discussing matters with

my mother, to express my own opinions in such language as I may think fit to use. Mr. Greystock's conduct to me was,—was,—was altogether most ungentlemanlike.'

'Mr. Greystock is a gentleman.'

'His conduct was most offensive, and most,—most ungentle-manlike. Mr. Greystock disgraced himself.'

'It isn't true!' said Lucy. Lord Fawn gave one start, and then walked off to the house as quick as his legs could carry him.

CHAPTER XXVIII
Mr. Dove in his Chambers

THE scene between Lord Fawn and Greystock had taken place in Mr. Camperdown's chambers, and John Eustace had also been present. The lawyer had suffered considerable annoyance, before the arrival of the two first-named gentle-men, from reiterated assertions made by Eustace that he would take no further trouble whatsoever about the jewels. Mr. Camperdown had in vain pointed out to him that a plain duty lay upon him as executor and guardian to protect the property on behalf of his nephew, but Eustace had asserted that, though he himself was comparatively a poor man, he would sooner replace the necklace out of his own property, than be subject to the nuisance of such a continued quarrel. 'My dear John; ten thousand pounds!' Mr. Camperdown had said. 'It is a fortune for a younger son.'

"The boy is only two years old, and will have time enough to make fortunes for his own younger sons, if he does not squander everything. If he does, the ten thousand pounds will make no difference.'

'But the justice of the thing, John!'

'Justice may be purchased too dearly.'

'Such a harpy as she is, too!' pleaded the lawyer. Then Lord Fawn had come in, and Greystock had followed immediately afterwards.

'I may as well say at once,' said Greystock, 'that Lady Eustace is determined to maintain her right to the property; and that she will not give up the diamonds till some adequate court of law shall have decided that she is mistaken in her views. Stop one moment, Mr. Camperdown. I feel myself bound to go further than that, and express my own opinion that she is right.'

'I can hardly understand such an opinion as coming from you,' said Mr. Camperdown.

'You have changed your mind, at any rate,' said John Eustace.

'Not so, Eustace. Mr. Camperdown, you'll be good enough to understand that my opinion expressed here is that of a friend, and not that of a lawyer. And you must understand, Eustace,' continued Greystock, 'that I am speaking now of my cousin's right to the property. Though the value be great, I have advised her to give up the custody of it for a while, till the matter shall be clearly decided. That has still been my advice to her, and I have in no respect changed my mind. But she feels that she is being cruelly used, and with a woman's spirit will not, in such circumstances, yield anything. Mr. Camperdown actually stopped her carriage in the street.'

'She would not answer a line that anybody wrote to her,' said the lawyer.

'And I may say plainly,—for all here know the circumstances,—that Lady Eustace feels the strongest possible indignation at the manner in which she is being treated by Lord Fawn.'

'I have only asked her to give up the diamonds till the question should be settled,' said Lord Fawn.

'And you backed your request, my lord, by a threat! My cousin is naturally most indignant; and, my lord, you must allow me to tell you that I fully share the feeling.'

'There is no use in making a quarrel about it,' said Eustace.

'The quarrel is ready made,' replied Greystock. 'I am here to tell Lord Fawn in your presence, and in the presence of Mr. Camperdown, that he is behaving to a lady with ill-usage, which he would not dare to exercise did he not know that her position saves him from legal punishment, as do the present usages of society from other consequences.'

'I have behaved to her with every possible consideration,' said Lord Fawn.

'That is a simple assertion,' said the other. 'I have made one assertion, and you have made another. The world will have to judge between us. What right have you to take upon yourself to decide whether this thing or that belongs to Lady Eustace, or to any one else?'

'When the thing was talked about I was obliged to have an opinion,' said Lord Fawn, who was still thinking of words in which to reply to the insult offered him by Greystock without injury to his dignity as an Under-Secretary of State.

'Your conduct, sir, has been altogether inexcusable.' Then Frank turned to the attorney. 'I have been given to understand that you are desirous of knowing where this diamond necklace is at present. It is at Lady Eustace's house in Scotland;—at Portray Castle.' Then he shook hands with John Eustace, bowed to Mr. Camperdown, and succeeded in leaving the room before Lord Fawn had so far collected his senses as to be able to frame his anger into definite words.

'I will never willingly speak to that man again,' said Lord Fawn. But as it was not probable that Greystock would greatly desire any further conversation with Lord Fawn, this threat did not carry with it any powerful feeling of severity.

Mr. Camperdown groaned over the matter with thorough vexation of spirit. It seemed to him as though the harpy, as he called her, would really make good her case against him,—at any rate, would make it seem to be good for so long a time that all the triumph of success would be hers. He knew that she was already in debt, and gave her credit for a propensity to fast living which almost did her an injustice. Of course, the jewels would be sold for half their value, and the harpy would triumph. Of what use to him or to the estate would be a decision of the courts in his favour, when the diamonds should have been broken up and scattered to the winds of heaven? Ten thousand pounds! It was, to Mr. Camperdown's mind, a thing quite terrible that, in a country which boasts of its laws and of the execution of its laws, such an impostor as was this widow should be able to lay her dirty, grasping fingers on so great an amount of property, and that there should be no means of punishing her. That Lizzie Eustace had stolen the diamonds, as a pickpocket steals a watch, was a fact as to which Mr. Camperdown had in his mind no shadow of a doubt. And, as the reader knows, he was right. She had stolen them. Mr. Camperdown knew that she had stolen them, and was a wretched man. From the first moment of the late Sir Florian's infatuation about this woman, she had worked woe for Mr. Camperdown. Mr. Camperdown had striven hard,—to the great and almost permanent offence of Sir Florian,—to save Portray from its present condition of degradation; but he had striven in vain. Portray belonged to the harpy for her life; and moreover he himself had been forced to be instrumental in paying over to the harpy a large sum of Eustace money almost immediately on her becoming a widow. Then had come the affair of the diamonds;—an affair of ten thousand pounds!—as Mr. Camperdown would exclaim to himself, throwing his eyes up to the ceiling. And now it seemed that she was to get the better of him even in that, although there could not be a shadow of doubt as to her falsehood and fraudulent dishonesty! His luck in the matter was so bad! John Eustace had no backbone, no spirit, no proper feeling as to his own family. Lord Fawn was as weak as water, and almost disgraced the cause by the accident of his adherence to it. Greystock, who would have been a tower of strength, had turned against him, and was now prepared to maintain that the harpy was right. Mr. Camperdown knew that the harpy was wrong,—that she was a harpy, and he would not abandon the cause; but the difficulties in his way were great, and the annoyance to which he was subjected was excessive. His wife and daughters were still at Dawlish, and he was up in town in September, simply because the harpy had the present possession of these diamonds.

Mr. Camperdown was a man turned sixty, handsome, grey-haired, healthy, somewhat florid, and carrying in his face and person external signs of prosperity and that kind of self-assertion which prosperity always produces. But they who knew him best were aware that he did not bear trouble well. In any trouble, such as was this about the necklace, there would come over his face a look of weakness which betrayed the want of real inner strength. How many faces one sees which, in ordinary circumstances, are comfortable, self-asserting, sufficient, and even bold; the lines of which, under difficulties, collapse and become mean, spiritless, and insignificant. There are faces which, in their usual form, seem to bluster with prosperity, but which the loss of a dozen points at whist will reduce to that currish*aspect which reminds one of a dog-whip. Mr. Camperdown's countenance, when Lord Fawn and Mr. Eustace left him, had fallen away into this meanness of appearance. He no longer carried himself as a man owning a dog-whip, but rather as the hound that feared it.

A better attorney, for the purposes to which his life was devoted, did not exist in London than Mr. Camperdown. To say that he was honest, is nothing. To describe him simply as zealous, would be to fall very short of his merits. The interests of his clients were his own interests, and the legal rights of the properties of which he had the legal charge, were as dear to him as his own blood. But it could not be said of him that he was a learned lawyer. Perhaps in that branch of a solicitor's profession in which he had been called upon to work, experience goes further than learning. It may be doubted, indeed, whether it is not so in every branch of every profession. But it might, perhaps, have been better for Mr. Camperdown had he devoted more hours of his youth to reading books on convey-ancing. He was now too old for such studies, and could trust only to the reading of other people. The reading, however, of other people was always at his command, and his clients were rich men who did not mind paying for an opinion. To have an opinion from Mr. Dove, or some other learned gentleman, was the every-day practice of his life; and when he obtained, as he often did, little coigns of legal vantage*and subtle definitions as to property which were comfortable to him, he would rejoice to think that he could always have a Dove at his hand to tell him exactly how far he was justified in going in defence of his clients' interests. But now there had come to him no comfort from his corner of legal knowledge. Mr. Dove had taken extraordinary pains in the matter, and had simply succeeded in throwing over his employer. 'A necklace can't be an heirloom!' said Mr. Camperdown to himself, telling off on his fingers half-a-dozen instances in which he had either known or had heard that the head of a family had so arranged the future possession of the family jewels. Then he again read Mr. Dove's opinion; and actually took a law-book off his shelves with the view of testing the correctness of the barrister in reference to some special assertion. A pot or a pan might be an heirloom, but not a necklace! Mr. Camperdown could hardly bring himself to believe that this was law. And then as to paraphernalia! Up to this moment, though he had been called upon to arrange great dealings in reference to widows, he had never as yet heard of a claim made by a widow for paraphernalia. But then the widows with whom he had been called upon to deal, had been ladies quite content to accept the good things settled upon them by the liberal prudence of their friends and husbands,—not greedy, bloodsucking harpies such as this Lady Eustace. It was quite terrible to Mr. Camperdown that one of his clients should have fallen into such a pit. Mors omnibus est communis.* But to have left such a widow behind one!

'John,' he said, opening his door. John was his son and partner, and John came to him, having been summoned by a clerk from another room. 'Just shut the door. I've had such a scene here;—Lord Fawn and Mr. Greystock almost coming to blows about that horrid woman.'

'The Upper House would have got the worst of it, as it usually does,' said the younger attorney.

'And there is John Eustace, cares no more what becomes of the property than if he had nothing to do with it;—absolutely talks of replacing the diamonds out of his own pocket; a man whose personal interest in the estate is by no means equal to her own.'

'He wouldn't do it, you know,' said Camperdown Junior, who did not know the family.

'It's just what he would do,' said the father, who did. 'There's nothing they wouldn't give away, when once the idea takes them. Think of that woman having the whole Portray estate, perhaps for the next sixty years,—nearly the fee-simple of the property,—just because she made eyes to Sir Florian!'

'That's done and gone, father.'

'And here's Dove tells us that a necklace can't be an heir-loom, unless it belongs to the Crown.'

'Whatever he says, you'd better take his word for it.'

'I'm not so sure of that. It can't be. I'll tell you what I'll do. I'll go over and see him. We can file a bill in Chancery, I don't doubt, and prove that the property belongs to the family and must go by the will. But she'll sell them before we can get the custody of them.'

'Perhaps she has done that already.'

'Greystock says they are at Portray, and I believe they are. She was wearing them in London only in July,—a day or two before I saw her as she was leaving town. If anybody like a jeweller had been down at the castle, I should have heard of it. She hasn't sold 'em yet, but she will.'

'She could do that just the same if they were an heirloom.'

'No, John. I think not. We could have acted much more quickly, and have frightened her.'

'If I were you, father, I'd drop the matter altogether, and let John Eustace replace them if he pleases. We all know that he would never be called on to do anything of the kind. It isn't our sort of business.'

'Not ten thousand pounds!' said Camperdown Senior, to whom the magnitude of the larceny almost ennobled the otherwise mean duty of catching the thief. Then Mr. Camperdown rose, and slowly walked across the New Square,

Lincoln's Inn, under the low archway, by the entrance to the old court in which Lord Eldon used to sit, to the Old Square, in which the Turtle Dove had built his legal nest on a first floor, close to the old gateway.

Mr. Dove was a gentleman who spent a very great portion of his life in this somewhat gloomy abode of learning. It was not now term time, and most of his brethren were absent from London, recruiting their strength among the Alps, or drinking in vigours*for fresh campaigns with the salt sea breezes of Kent and Sussex, or perhaps shooting deer in Scotland, or catching fish in Connemara.* But Mr. Dove was a man of iron, who wanted no such recreation. To be absent from his law-books and the black, littered, ink-stained old table on which he was wont to write his opinions, was, to him, to be wretched. The only exercise necessary to him was that of putting on his wig and going into one of the courts that were close to his chambers;—but even that was almost distasteful to him. He preferred sitting in his old arm-chair, turning over his old books in search of old cases, and producing opinions which he would be prepared to back against all the world of Lincoln's Inn. He and Mr. Camperdown had known each other intimately for many years, and though the rank of the two men in their profession differed much, they were able to discuss questions of law without any appreciation of that difference among themselves. The one man knew much, and the other little; the one was not only learned, but possessed also of great gifts, while the other was simply an ordinary clear-headed man of business; but they had sympathies in common which made them friends; they were both honest and unwilling to sell their services to dishonest customers; and they equally entertained a deep-rooted contempt for that portion of mankind who thought that property could be managed and protected without the intervention of lawyers. The outside world to them was a world of pretty, laughing, ignorant children; and lawyers were the parents, guardians, pastors and masters by whom the children should be protected from the evils incident to their childishness.

'Yes, sir; he's here,' said the Turtle Dove's clerk. 'He is talking of going away, but he won't go. He's told me I can have a week, but I don't know that I like to leave him. Mrs. Dove and the children are down at Ramsgate, and he's here all night. He hadn't been out so long that when he wanted to go as far as the Temple yesterday, we couldn't find his hat.' Then the clerk opened the door, and ushered Mr. Camperdown into the room. Mr. Dove was the younger man by five or six years, and his hair was still black. Mr. Camperdown's was nearer white than grey; but, nevertheless, Mr. Camperdown looked as though he were the younger man. Mr. Dove was a long, thin man, with a stoop in his shoulders, with deep-set, hollow eyes, and lanthorn cheeks, and sallow complexion, with long, thin hands, who seemed to acknowledge by every movement of his body and every tone of his voice that old age was creeping on him,—whereas the attorney's step was still elastic, and his speech brisk. Mr. Camperdown wore a blue frock-coat, and a coloured cravat, and a light waistcoat. With Mr. Dove every visible article of his raiment was black, except his shirt, and he had that peculiar blackness which a man achieves when he wears a dress-coat over a high black waistcoat in the morning.

'You didn't make much, I fear, of what I sent you about heirlooms,' said Mr. Dove, divining the purport of Mr. Camperdown's visit.

'A great deal more than I wanted, I can assure you, Mr. Dove.'

'There is a common error about heirlooms.'

'Very common, indeed, I should say. God bless my soul! when one knows how often the word occurs in family deeds, it does startle one to be told that there isn't any such thing.'

'I don't think I said quite so much as that. Indeed, I was careful to point out that the law does acknowledge heirlooms.'

'But not diamonds,' said the attorney.

'I doubt whether I went quite so far as that.'

'Only the Crown diamonds.'

'I don't think I ever debarred all other diamonds. A

diamond in a star of honour might form a part of an heirloom; but I do not think that a diamond itself could be an heirloom.'

'If in a star of honour, why not in a necklace?' argued Mr. Camperdown almost triumphantly.

'Because a star of honour, unless tampered with by fraud, would naturally be maintained in its original form. The setting of a necklace will probably be altered from generation to generation. The one, like a picture or a precious piece of furniture,——'

'Or a pot or a pan,' said Mr. Camperdown, with sarcasm.

'Pots and pans may be precious, too,' replied Mr. Dove. 'Such things can be traced, and can be held as heirlooms without imposing too great difficulties on their guardians. The Law is generally very wise and prudent, Mr. Camperdown;—much more so often than are they who attempt to improve it.'

'I quite agree with you there, Mr. Dove.'

'Would the Law do a service, do you think, if it lent its authority to the special preservation in special hands of trinkets only to be used for vanity and ornament? Is that a kind of property over which an owner should have a power of disposition more lasting, more autocratic, than is given him even in regard to land? The land, at any rate, can be traced. It is a thing fixed and known. A string of pearls is not only alterable, but constantly altered, and cannot easily be traced.'

'Property of such enormous value should, at any rate, be protected,' said Mr. Camperdown indignantly.

'All property is protected, Mr. Camperdown;—although, as we know too well, such protection can never be perfect. But the system of heirlooms, if there can be said to be such a system, was not devised for what you and I mean when we talk of protection of property.'

'I should have said that that was just what it was devised for.'

'I think not. It was devised with the more picturesque idea of maintaining chivalric associations.* Heirlooms have become so, not that the future owners of them may be assured of so much wealth, whatever the value of the thing so settled may be,—but that the son or grandson or descendant may enjoy

258

the satisfaction which is derived from saying, my father or my grandfather or my ancestor sat in that chair, or looked as he now looks in that picture, or was graced by wearing on his breast that very ornament which you now see lying beneath the glass. Crown jewels are heirlooms in the same way, as representing not the possession of the sovereign, but the time-honoured dignity of the Crown. The Law, which, in general, concerns itself with our property or lives and our liberties, has in this matter bowed gracefully to the spirit of chivalry and has lent its aid to romance;—but it certainly did not do so to enable the discordant heirs of a rich man to settle a simple dirty question of money, which, with ordinary prudence, the rich man should himself have settled before he died.'

The Turtle Dove had spoken with emphasis and had spoken well, and Mr. Camperdown had not ventured to interrupt him while he was speaking. He was sitting far back on his chair, but with his neck bent and with his head forward, rubbing his long thin hands slowly over each other, and with his deep bright eyes firmly fixed on his companion's face. Mr. Camperdown had not unfrequently heard him speak in the same fashion before, and was accustomed to his manner of unravelling the mysteries and searching into the causes of Law with a spirit which almost lent poetry to the subject. When Mr. Dove would do so, Mr. Camperdown would not quite understand the words spoken, but he would listen to them with an undoubting reverence. And he did understand them in part, and was conscious of an infusion of a certain amount of poetic spirit into his own bosom. He would think of these speeches afterwards, and would entertain high but somewhat cloudy ideas of the beauty and the majesty of Law. Mr. Dove's speeches did Mr. Camperdown good, and helped to preserve him from that worst of all diseases,—a low idea of humanity.

'You think, then, we had better not claim them as heirlooms?' he asked.

'I think you had better not.'

'And you think that she could claim them—as paraphernalia.'

'That question has hardly been put to me,—though I

allowed myself to wander into it. But for my intimacy with you, I should hardly have ventured to stray so far.'

'I need hardly say how much obliged we are. But we will submit one or two other cases to you.'

'I am inclined to think the court would not allow them to her as paraphernalia, seeing that their value is excessive as compared with her income and degree; but if it did, it would do so in a fashion that would guard them from alienation.'*

'She would sell them—under the rose.'*

'Then she would be guilty of stealing them,—which she would hardly attempt, even if not restrained by honesty, knowing, as she would know, that the greatness of the value would almost assuredly lead to detection. The same feeling would prevent buyers from purchasing.'

'She says, you know, that they were given to her, absolutely.'

'I should like to know the circumstances.'

'Yes;—of course.'

'But I should be disposed to think that in equity no allegation by the receiver of such a gift, unsubstantiated either by evidence or by deed, would be allowed to stand. The gentleman left behind him a will, and regular settlements. I should think that the possession of these diamonds,—not, I presume, touched on in the settlements——'

'Oh dear no;—not a word about them.'

'I should think, then, that, subject to any claim for paraphernalia, the possession of the diamonds would be ruled by the will.' Mr. Camperdown was rushing into the further difficulty of the chattels in Scotland and those in England, when the Turtle Dove stopped him, declaring that he could not venture to discuss matters as to which he knew none of the facts.

'Of course not;—of course not,' said Mr Camperdown. 'We'll have cases prepared. I'd apologise for coming at all, only that I get so much from a few words.'

'I'm always delighted to see you, Mr. Camperdown,' said the Turtle Dove, bowing.

CHAPTER XXIX
'I had better go away'

WHEN Lord Fawn gave a sudden jump and stalked away towards the house on that Sunday morning before breakfast, Lucy Morris was a very unhappy girl. She had a second time accused Lord Fawn of speaking an untruth. She did not quite understand the usages of the world in the matter; but she did know that the one offence which a gentleman is supposed never to commit is that of speaking an untruth. The offence may be one committed oftener than any other by gentlemen,—as also by all other people; but, nevertheless, it is regarded by the usages of society as being the one thing which a gentleman never does. Of all this Lucy understood something. The word 'lie' she knew to be utterly abominable. That Lizzie Eustace was a little liar had been acknowledged between herself and the Fawn girls very often,—but to have told Lady Eustace that any word spoken by her was a lie, would have been a worse crime than the lie itself. To have brought such an accusation, in that term, against Lord Fawn, would have been to degrade herself for ever. Was there any difference between a lie and an untruth? That one must be, and that the other need not be, intentional, she did feel; but she felt also that the less offensive word had come to mean a lie,—the world having been driven so to use it because the world did not dare to talk about lies; and this word, bearing such a meaning in common parlance, she had twice applied to Lord Fawn. And yet, as she was well aware, Lord Fawn had told no lie. He had himself believed every word that he had spoken against Frank Greystock. That he had been guilty of unmanly cruelty in so speaking of her lover in her presence, Lucy still thought, but she should not therefore have accused him of falsehood. 'It was untrue all the same,' she said to herself, as she stood still on the gravel walk, watching the rapid disappearance of Lord Fawn, and endeavouring to think what she had better now do with herself. Of course Lord

Fawn, like a great child, would at once go and tell his mother what that wicked governess had said to him.

In the hall she met her friend Lydia. 'Oh, Lucy, what is the matter with Frederic?' she asked.

'Lord Fawn is very angry indeed.'

'With you?'

'Yes;—with me. He is so angry that I am sure he would not sit down to breakfast with me. So I won't come down. Will you tell your mamma? If she likes to send to me, of course I'll go to her at once.'

'What have you done, Lucy?'

'I've told him again that what he said wasn't true.'

'But why?'

'Because—Oh, how can I say why? Why does any person do everything that she ought not to do? It's the fall of Adam, I suppose.'

'You shouldn't make a joke of it, Lucy.'

'You can have no conception how unhappy I am about it. Of course, Lady Fawn will tell me to go away. I went out on purpose to beg his pardon for what I said last night, and I just said the very same thing again.'

'But why did you say it?'

'And I should say it again and again and again, if he were to go on telling me that Mr. Greystock isn't a gentleman. I don't think he ought to have done it. Of course, I have been very wrong; I know that. But I think he has been wrong too. But I must own it, and he needn't. I'll go up now and stay in my own room till your mamma sends for me.'

'And I'll get Jane to bring you some breakfast.'

'I don't care a bit about breakfast,' said Lucy.

Lord Fawn did tell his mother, and Lady Fawn was perplexed in the extreme. She was divided in her judgment and feelings between the privilege due to Lucy as a girl possessed of an authorised lover,—a privilege which no doubt existed, but which was not extensive,—and the very much greater privilege which attached to Lord Fawn as a man, as a peer, as an Under-Secretary of State,—but which attached to him especially as the head and only man belonging to the Fawn family. Such a one, when, moved by filial duty, he condescends to come once a week to his mother's house, is entitled to say whatever he pleases, and should on no account be contradicted by any one. Lucy no doubt had a lover,—an authorised lover; but perhaps that fact could not be taken as more than a balancing weight against the inferiority of her position as a governess. Lady Fawn was of course obliged to take her son's part, and would scold Lucy. Lucy must be scolded very seriously. But it would be a thing so desirable if Lucy could be induced to accept her scolding and have done with it, and not to make matters worse by talking of going away! 'You don't mean that she came out into the shrubbery, having made up her mind to be rude to you?' said Lady Fawn to her son.

'No;—I do not think that. But her temper is so ungovernable, and she has, if I may say so, been so spoilt among you here,—I mean by the girls, of course,—that she does not know how to restrain herself.'

'She is as good as gold, you know, Frederic.' He shrugged his shoulders, and declared that he had not a word more to say about it. He could, of course, remain in London till it should suit Mr. Greystock to take his bride. 'You'll break my heart if you say that!' exclaimed the unhappy mother. 'Of course, she shall leave the house if you wish it.'

'I wish nothing,' said Lord Fawn. 'But I peculiarly object to be told that I am a—liar.' Then he stalked away along the corridor and went down to breakfast, as black as a thundercloud.

Lady Fawn and Lucy sat opposite to each other in church, but they did not speak till the afternoon. Lady Fawn went to church in the carriage and Lucy walked, and as Lucy retired to her room immediately on her return to the house, there had not been an opportunity even for a word. After lunch Amelia came up to her, and sat down for a long discussion. 'Now, Lucy, something must be done, you know,' said Amelia.

'I suppose so.'

'Of course, mamma must see you. She can't allow things to

go on in this way. Mamma is very unhappy, and didn't eat a morsel of breakfast.' By this latter assertion Amelia simply intended to imply that her mother had refused to be helped a second time to fried bacon, as was customary.

'Of course, I shall go to her the moment she sends for me. Oh,—I am so unhappy!'

I don't wonder at that, Lucy. So is my brother unhappy. These things make people unhappy. It is what the world calls—temper, you know, Lucy.'

'Why did he tell me that Mr. Greystock isn't a gentleman? Mr. Greystock is a gentleman. I meant to say nothing more than that.'

'But you did say more, Lucy.'

'When he said that Mr. Greystock wasn't a gentleman, I told him it wasn't true. Why did he say it? He knows all about it. Everybody knows. Would you think it wise to come and abuse him to me, when you know what he is to me? I can't bear it, and I won't. I'll go away to-morrow, if your mamma wishes it.' But that going away was just what Lady Fawn did not wish.

'I think, you know, Lucy, you should express your deep sorrow at what has passed.'

'To your brother?'

'Yes.'

'Then he would abuse Mr. Greystock again, and it would all be as bad as ever. I'll beg Lord Fawn's pardon if he'll promise beforehand not to say a word about Mr. Greystock.'

'You can't expect him to make a bargain like that, Lucy.'

'I suppose not. I daresay I'm very wicked, and I must be left wicked. I'm too wicked to stay here. That's the long and the short of it.'

'I'm afraid you're proud, Lucy.'

'I suppose I am. If it wasn't for all that I owe to everybody here, and that I love you all so much, I should be proud of being proud;—because of Mr. Greystock. Only it kills me to make Lady Fawn unhappy.'

Amelia left the culprit, feeling that no good had been done, and Lady Fawn did not see the delinquent till late in the afternoon. Lord Fawn had, in the meantime, wandered out along the river all alone to brood over the condition of his affairs. It had been an evil day for him in which he had first seen Lady Eustace. From the first moment of his engagement to her he had been an unhappy man. Her treatment of him, the stories which reached his ears from Mrs. Hittaway and others, Mr. Camperdown's threats of law in regard to the diamonds, and Frank Greystock's insults, altogether made him aware that he could not possibly marry Lady Eustace. But yet he had no proper and becoming way of escaping from the bonds of his engagement. He was a man with a conscience, and was made miserable by the idea of behaving badly to a woman. Perhaps it might have been difficult to analyse his misery, and to decide how much arose from the feeling that he was behaving badly, and how much from the conviction that the world would accuse him of doing so; but, between the two, he was wretched enough. The punishment of the offence had been commenced by Greystock's unavenged insults;—and it now seemed to him that this girl's conduct was a continuation of it. The world was already beginning to treat him with that want of respect which he so greatly dreaded. He knew that he was too weak to stand up against a widely-spread expression of opinion that he had behaved badly. There are men who can walk about the streets with composed countenances, take their seats in Parliament if they happen to have seats, work in their offices, or their chambers, or their counting-houses with diligence, and go about the world serenely, even though everybody be saying evil of them behind their backs. Such men can live down temporary calumny, and almost take a delight in the isolation which it will produce. Lord Fawn knew well that he was not such a man. He would have described his own weakness as caused, perhaps, by a too thin-skinned sensitiveness. Those who knew him were inclined to say that he lacked strength of character, and, perhaps, courage.

He had certainly engaged himself to marry this widow, and he was most desirous to do what was right. He had said that he would not marry her unless she would give up the necklace, and he was most desirous to be true to his word. He had been twice insulted, and he was anxious to support these injuries with dignity. Poor Lucy's little offence against him rankled in his mind with the other great offences. That this humble friend of his mother's should have been insolent was a terrible thing to him. He was not sure even whether his own sisters did not treat him with scantier reverence than of yore. And yet he was so anxious to do right, and do his duty in that state of life to which it had pleased God to call him! As to much he was in doubt; but of two things he was quite sure,—that Frank Greystock was a scoundrel, and that Lucy Morris was the most impertinent young woman in England.

'What would you wish to have done, Frederic?' his mother said to him on his return.

'In what respect, mother?'

'About Lucy Morris? I have not seen her yet. I have thought it better that she should be left to herself for a while before I did so. I suppose she must come down to dinner. She always does.'

'I do not wish to interfere with the young lady's meals.'

'No;—but about meeting her? If there is to be no talking it will be so very unpleasant. It will be unpleasant to us all, but I am thinking chiefly of you.'

'I do not wish anybody to be disturbed for my comfort.' A young woman coming down to dinner as though in disgrace, and not being spoken to by any one, would, in truth, have had rather a soothing effect upon Lord Fawn, who would have felt that the general silence and dulness had been produced as a sacrifice in his honour. 'I can, of course, insist that she should apologise; but if she refuses, what shall I do then?'

'Let there be no more apologies, if you please, mother.'

'What shall I do then, Frederic?'

'Miss Morris's idea of an apology is a repetition of her offence with increased rudeness. It is not for me to say what you should do. If it be true that she is engaged to that man——'

'It is true, certainly.'

'No doubt that will make her quite independent of you, and I can understand that her presence here in such circumstances must be very uncomfortable to you all. No doubt she feels her power.'

'Indeed, Frederic, you do not know her.'

'I can hardly say that I desire to know her better. You cannot suppose that I can be anxious for further intimacy with a young lady who has twice given me the lie*in your house. Such conduct is, at least, very unusual; and as no absolute punishment can be inflicted, the offender can only be avoided. It is thus and thus only that such offences can be punished. I shall be satisfied if you will give her to understand that I should prefer that she should not address me again.'

Poor Lady Fawn was beginning to think that Lucy was right in saying that there was no remedy for all these evils but that she should go away. But whither was she to go? She had no home but such home as she could earn for herself by her services as a governess, and in her present position it was almost out of the question that she should seek another place. Lady Fawn, too, felt that she had pledged herself to Mr. Greystock that till next year Lucy should have a home at Fawn Court. Mr. Greystock, indeed, was now an enemy to the family; but Lucy was not an enemy, and it was out of the question that she should be treated with real enmity. She might be scolded, and scowled at, and put into a kind of drawing-room Coventry*for a time,—so that all kindly intercourse with her should be confined to school-room work and bed-room conferences. She could be generally 'sat upon,' as Nina would call it. But as for quarrelling with her,—making a real enemy of one whom they all loved, one whom Lady Fawn knew to be 'as good as gold,' one who had become so dear to the old lady that actual extrusion from their family affections would be like the cutting off of a limb,—that was simply impossible. 'I suppose I had better go and see her,' said Lady Fawn,—'and I have got such a headache.'

'Do not see her on my account,' said Lord Fawn. The duty,

however, was obligatory, and Lady Fawn with slow steps sought Lucy in the school-room.

'Lucy,' she said, seating herself, 'what is to be the end of all this?'

Lucy came up to her and knelt at her feet. 'If you knew how unhappy I am, because I have vexed you!'

'I am unhappy, my dear, because I think you have been betrayed by warm temper into misbehaviour.'

'I know I have.'

'Then why do you not control your temper?'

'If anybody were to come to you, Lady Fawn, and make horrible accusations against Lord Fawn, or against Augusta, would not you be angry? Would you be able to stand it?'

Lady Fawn was not clear-headed; she was not clever; nor was she even always rational. But she was essentially honest. She knew that she would fly at anybody who should in her presence say such bitter things of any of her children as Lord Fawn had said of Mr. Greystock in Lucy's hearing;—and she knew also that Lucy was entitled to hold Mr. Greystock as dearly as she held her own sons and daughters. Lord Fawn, at Fawn Court, could not do wrong. That was a tenet by which she was obliged to hold fast. And yet Lucy had been subjected to great cruelty. She thought awhile for a valid argument. 'My dear,' she said, 'your youth should make a difference.'

'Of course it should.'

'And though to me and to the girls you are as dear as any friend can be, and may say just what you please—— Indeed, we all live here in such a way that we all do say just what we please,—young and old together. But you ought to know that Lord Fawn is different.'

'Ought he to say that Mr. Greystock is not a gentleman to me?'

'We are, of course, very sorry that there should be any quarrel. It is all the fault of that—nasty, false young woman.'

'So it is, Lady Fawn. Lady Fawn, I have been thinking about it all the day, and I am quite sure that I had better not stay here while you and the girls think badly of Mr. Greystock.

It is not only about Lord Fawn, but because of the whole thing.
I am always wanting to say something good about Mr. Greystock, and you are always thinking something bad about him.
You have been to me,—oh, the very best friend that a girl
ever had. Why you should have treated me so generously I
never could know.'

'Because we have loved you.'

'But when a girl has got a man whom she loves, and has
promised to marry, he *must* be her best friend of all. Is it not
so, Lady Fawn?' The old woman stooped down and kissed the
girl who had got the man. 'It is not ingratitude to you that
makes me think most of him; is it?'

'Certainly not, dear.'

'Then I had better go away.'

'But where will you go, Lucy?'

'I will consult Mr. Greystock.'

'But what can he do, Lucy? It will only be a trouble to him.
He can't find a home for you.'

'Perhaps they would have me at the deanery,' said Lucy
slowly. She had evidently been thinking much of it all. 'And,
Lady Fawn, I will not go down-stairs while Lord Fawn is
here; and when he comes,—if he does come again while I am
here,—he shall not be troubled by seeing me. He may be sure
of that. And you may tell him that I don't defend myself, only
I shall always think that he ought not to have said that Mr.
Greystock wasn't a gentleman before me.' When Lady Fawn
left Lucy the matter was so far settled that Lucy had neither
been asked to come down to dinner, nor had she been for-
bidden to seek another home.

CHAPTER XXX
Mr. Greystock's Troubles

FRANK GREYSTOCK stayed the Sunday in London and went down to Bobsborough on the Monday. His father and mother and sister all knew of his engagement to Lucy, and they had heard also that Lady Eustace was to become Lady Fawn. Of the necklace they had hitherto heard very little, and of the quarrel between the two lovers they had heard nothing. There had been many misgivings at the deanery, and some regrets about these marriages. Mrs. Greystock, Frank's mother, was, as we are so wont to say of many women, the best woman in the world. She was unselfish, affectionate, charitable, and thoroughly feminine. But she did think that her son Frank, with all his advantages,—good looks, cleverness, general popularity, and seat in Parliament,—might just as well marry an heiress as a little girl without twopence in the world. As for herself, who had been born a Jackson, she could do with very little; but the Greystocks were all people who wanted money. For them there was never more than ninepence in a shilling, if so much. They were a race who could not pay their way with moderate incomes. Even the dear dean, who really had a conscience about money, and who hardly ever left Bobsborough, could not be kept quite clear of debt, let her do what she would. As for the admiral, the dean's elder brother, he had been notorious for insolvency; and Frank was a Greystock all over. He was the very man to whom money with a wife was almost a necessity of existence.

And his pretty cousin, the widow, who was devoted to him, and would have married him at a word, had ever so many thousands a year! Of course, Lizzie Eustace was not just all that she should be;—but then who is? In one respect, at any rate, her conduct had always been proper. There was no rumour against her as to lovers or flirtations. She was very young, and Frank might have moulded her as he pleased. Of course there were regrets. Poor dear little Lucy Morris was as good as gold. Mrs. Greystock was quite willing to admit that. She was not good-looking;—so at least Mrs. Greystock said. She never would allow that Lucy was good-looking. And she didn't see much in Lucy, who, according to her idea, was a little chit of a thing. Her position was simply that of a governess. Mrs. Greystock declared to her daughter that no one in the whole world had a higher respect for governesses than had she. But a governess is a governess;—and for a man in Frank's position such a marriage would be simply suicide.

'You shouldn't say that, mamma, now; for it's fixed,' said Ellinor Greystock.

'But I do say it, my dear. Things sometimes are fixed which must be unfixed. You know your brother.'

'Frank is earning a large income, mamma.'

'Did you ever know a Greystock who didn't want more than his income?'

'I hope I don't, mamma, and mine is very small.'

'You're a Jackson. Frank is Greystock to the very backbone. If he marries Lucy Morris he must give up Parliament. That's all.'

The dean himself was more reticent, and less given to interference than his wife; but he felt it also. He would not for the world have hinted to his son that it might be well to marry money; but he thought that it was a good thing that his son should go where money was. He knew that Frank was apt to spend his guineas faster than he got them. All his life long the dean had seen what came of such spending. Frank had gone out into the world and had prospered,—but he could hardly continue to prosper unless he married money. Of course, there had been regrets when the news came of that fatal engagement with Lucy Morris. 'It can't be for the next ten years, at any rate,' said Mrs. Greystock.

'I thought at one time that he would have made a match with his cousin,' said the dean.

'Of course;—so did everybody,' replied Mrs. Dean.

Then Frank came among them. He had intended staying some weeks,—perhaps for a month, and great preparations were made for him; but immediately on his arrival he announced the necessity that was incumbent on him of going down again to Scotland in ten days. 'You've heard about Lizzie, of course?' he said. They had heard that Lizzie was to become Lady Fawn, but beyond that they had heard nothing. 'You know about the necklace?' asked Frank. Something of a tale of a necklace had made its way even down to quiet Bobsborough. They had been informed that there was a dispute between the widow and the executors of the late Sir Florian about some diamonds. 'Lord Fawn is behaving about it in the most atrocious manner,' continued Frank, 'and the long and the short of it is that there will be no marriage!'

'No marriage!' exclaimed Mrs. Greystock.

'And what is the truth about the diamonds?' asked the dean.

'Ah;—it will give the lawyers a job before they decide that. They're very valuable;—worth about ten thousand pounds, I'm told; but the most of it will go among some of my friends at the Chancery bar. It's a pity that I should be out of the scramble myself.'

'But why should you be out?' asked his mother with tender regrets,—not thinking of the matter as her son was thinking of it, but feeling that when there was so much wealth so very near him, he ought not to let it all go past him.

'As far as I can see,' continued Frank, 'she has a fair claim to them. I suppose they'll file a bill in Chancery, and then it will be out of my line altogether. She says her husband gave them to her,—absolutely put them on her neck himself, and told her that they were hers. As to their being an heirloom, that turns out to be impossible. I didn't know it, but it seems you can't make diamonds an heirloom. What astonishes me is, that Fawn should object to the necklace. However, he has objected, and has simply told her that he won't marry her unless she gives them up.'

'And what does she say?'

'Storms and raves,—as of course any woman would. I don't think she is behaving badly. What she wants is, to reduce him to obedience, and then to dismiss him. I think that is no more than fair. Nothing on earth would make her marry him now.'

'Did she ever care for him?'

'I don't think she ever did. She found her position to be troublesome, and she thought she had better marry. And then he's a lord,—which always goes for something.'

'I am sorry you should have so much trouble,' said Mrs. Greystock. But in truth the mother was not sorry. She did not declare to herself that it would be a good thing that her son should be false to Lucy Morris, in order that he might marry his rich cousin; but she did feel it to be an advantage that he should be on terms of intimacy with so large an income as that belonging to Lady Eustace. 'Doan't thou marry for munny, but goa where munny is.' Mrs. Greystock would have repudiated the idea of mercenary marriages in any ordinary conversation, and would have been severe on any gentleman who was false to a young lady. But it is so hard to bring one's general principles to bear on one's own conduct or in one's own family;—and then the Greystocks were so peculiar a people! When her son told her that he must go down to Scotland again very shortly, she reconciled herself to his loss. Had he left Bobsborough for the sake of being near Lucy at Richmond, she would have felt it very keenly.

Days passed by, and nothing was said about poor Lucy. Mrs. Greystock had made up her mind that she would say nothing on the subject. Lucy had behaved badly in allowing herself to be loved by a man who ought to have loved money, and Mrs. Greystock had resolved that she would show her feelings by silence. The dean had formed no fixed determination, but he had thought that it might be, perhaps, as well to drop the subject. Frank himself was unhappy about it; but from morning to evening, and from day to day, he allowed it to pass by without a word. He knew that it should not be so, that such silence was in truth treachery to Lucy;—but he did. What had he meant when, as he left Lizzie Eustace among the rocks at Portray,—in that last moment,—he had assured her that he would be true to her? And what had been Lizzie's meaning? He was more sure of Lizzie's meaning than he was of his own. 'It's a very rough world to live in,' he said to himself in these days as he thought of his difficulties.

But when he had been nearly a week at the deanery, and when the day of his going was so near as to be a matter of concern, his sister did at last venture to say a word about Lucy. 'I suppose there is nothing settled about your own marriage, Frank?'

'Nothing at all.'

'Nor will be for some while?'

'Nor will be,—for some while.' This he said in a tone which he himself felt to be ill-humoured and almost petulant. And he felt also that such ill-humour on such a subject was unkind, not to his sister, but to Lucy. It seemed to imply that the matter of his marriage was distasteful to him. 'The truth is,' he said, 'that nothing can be fixed. Lucy understands that as well as I do. I am not in a position at once to marry a girl who has nothing. It's a pity, perhaps, that one can't train oneself to like some girl best that has got money; but as I haven't, there must be some delay. She is to stay where she is,—at any rate, for a twelvemonth.'

'But you mean to see her?'

'Well; yes; I hardly know how I can see her, as I have quarrelled to the knife*with Lord Fawn; and Lord Fawn is recognised by his mother and sisters as the one living Jupiter upon earth.'

'I like them for that,' said Ellinor.

'Only it prevents my going to Richmond;—and poor Fawn himself is such an indifferent Jupiter.'

That was all that was said about Lucy at Bobsborough, till there came a letter from Lucy to her lover acquainting him with the circumstances of her unfortunate position at Richmond. She did not tell him quite all the circumstances. She did not repeat the strong expressions which Lord Fawn had used, nor did she clearly explain how wrathful she had been herself. 'Lord Fawn has been here,' she said, 'and there has been ever so much unpleasantness. He is very angry with you about Lady Eustace, and, of course, Lady Fawn takes his part. I need not tell you whose part I take. And so there have been what the servants call,—just a few words. It is very dreadful, isn't it? And, after all, Lady Fawn has been as kind as possible. But the upshot of it is, that I am not to stay here. You mustn't suppose that I'm to be turned out at twelve hours' notice. I am to stay till arrangements have been made, and everybody will be kind to me. But what had I better do? I'll try and get another situation at once if you think it best, only I suppose I should have to explain how long I could stay. Lady Fawn knows that I am writing to you to ask you what you think best.'

On receipt of this, Greystock was very much puzzled. What a little fool Lucy had been, and yet what a dear little fool! Who cared for Lord Fawn and his hard words? Of course, Lord Fawn would say all manner of evil things of him, and would crow valiantly in his own farm-yard; but it would have been so much wiser on Lucy's part to have put up with the crowing, and to have disregarded altogether the words of a man so weak and insignificant! But the evil was done, and he must make some arrangement for poor Lucy's comfort. Had he known exactly how matters stood, that the proposition as to Lucy's departure had come wholly from herself, and that at the present time all the ladies at Fawn Court,—of course, in the absence of Lord Fawn,—were quite disposed to forgive Lucy if Lucy would only be forgiven, and hide herself when Lord Fawn should come;—had Frank known all this, he might, perhaps, have counselled her to remain at Richmond. But he believed that Lady Fawn had insisted on Lucy's departure; and of course, in such a case, Lucy must depart. He showed the letter to his sister, and asked for advice. 'How very unfortunate!' said Ellinor.

'Yes; is it not?'

'I wonder what she said to Lord Fawn.'

'She would speak out very plainly.'

'I suppose she has spoken out plainly, or otherwise they would never have told her to go away. It seems so unlike what I have always heard of Lady Fawn.'

'Lucy can be very headstrong if she pleases,' said Lucy's

lover. 'What on earth had I better do for her? I don't suppose she can get another place that would suit.'

'If she is to be your wife, I don't think she should go into another place. If it is quite fixed,——' she said, and then she looked into her brother's face.

'Well; what then?'

'If you are sure you mean it——'

'Of course I mean it.'

'Then she had better come here. As for her going out as a governess, and telling the people that she is to be your wife in a few months, that is out of the question. And it would, I think, be equally so that she should go into any house and not tell the truth. Of course, this would be the place for her.' It was at last decided that Ellinor should discuss the matter with her mother.

When the whole matter was unfolded to Mrs. Greystock, that lady was more troubled than ever. If Lucy were to come to the deanery, she must come as Frank's affianced bride, and must be treated as such by all Bobsborough. The dean would be giving his express sanction to the marriage, and so would Mrs. Greystock herself. She knew well that she had no power of refusing her sanction. Frank must do as he pleased about marrying. Were Lucy once his wife, of course she would be made welcome to the best the deanery could give her. There was no doubt about Lucy being as good as gold;—only that real gold, vile as it is, was the one thing that Frank so much needed. The mother thought that she had discovered in her son something which seemed to indicate a possibility that this very imprudent match might at last be abandoned; and if there were such possibility, sure Lucy ought not now to be brought to the deanery. Nevertheless, if Frank were to insist upon her coming,—she must come.

But Mrs. Greystock had a plan. 'Oh, mamma,' said Ellinor, when the plan was proposed to her, 'do not you think that would be cruel?'

'Cruel, my dear! no; certainly not cruel.'

'She is such a virago.'

'You think that because Lizzie Eustace has said so. I don't know that she's a virago at all. I believe her to be a very good sort of woman.'

'Do you remember, mamma, what the admiral used to say of her?'

'The admiral, my dear, tried to borrow her money, as he did everybody's, and when she wouldn't give him any, then he said severe things. The poor admiral was never to be trusted in such matters.'

'I don't think Frank would like it,' said Ellinor. The plan was this. Lady Linlithgow, who, through her brother-in-law, the late Admiral Greystock, was connected with the dean's family, had made known her desire to have a new companion for six months. The lady was to be treated like a lady, but was to have no salary. Her travelling expenses were to be paid for her, and no duties were to be expected from her, except that of talking and listening to the countess.

'I really think it's the very thing for her,' said Mrs. Greystock. 'It's not like being a governess. She's not to have any salary.

'I don't know whether that makes it better, mamma.'

'It would just be a visit to Lady Linlithgow. It is that which makes the difference, my dear.'

Ellinor felt sure that her brother would not hear of such an engagement,—but he did hear of it, and, after various objections, gave a sort of sanction to it. It was not to be pressed upon Lucy if Lucy disliked it. Lady Linlithgow was to be made to understand that Lucy might leave whenever she pleased. It was to be an invitation, which Lucy might accept if she were so minded. Lucy's position as an honourable guest was to be assured to her. It was thought better that Lady Linlithgow should not be told of Lucy's engagement unless she asked questions;—or unless Lucy should choose to tell her. Every precaution was to be taken, and then Frank gave his sanction. He could understand, he said, that it might be inexpedient that Lucy should come at once to the deanery, as,—were she to do so,—she must remain there till her marriage, let the time be ever so long. 'It might be two years,' said the mother. 'Hardly so long as that,' said the son. 'I don't think it would be—quite fair—to papa,' said the mother. It was well that the argument was used behind the dean's back, as, had it been made in his hearing, the dean would have upset it at once. The dean was so short-sighted and imprudent, that he would have professed delight at the idea of having Lucy Morris as a resident at the deanery. Frank acceded to the argument,—and was ashamed of himself for acceding. Ellinor did not accede, nor did her sisters, but it was necessary that they should yield. Mrs. Greystock at once wrote to Lady Linlithgow, and Frank wrote by the same post to Lucy Morris. 'As there must be a year's delay,' he wrote, 'we all here think it best that your visit to us should be postponed for a while. But if you object to the Linlithgow plan, say so at once. You shall be asked to do nothing disagreeable.' He found the letter very difficult to write. He knew that she ought to have been welcomed at once to Bobsborough. And he knew, too, the reason on which his mother's objection was founded. But it might be two years before he could possibly marry Lucy Morris;—or it might be three. Would it be proper that she should be desired to make the deanery her home for so long and so indefinite a time? And when an engagement was for so long, could it be well that everybody should know it,—as everybody would, if Lucy were to take up her residence permanently at the deanery? Some consideration, certainly, was due to his father.

And, moreover, it was absolutely necessary that he and Lizzie Eustace should understand each other as to that mutual pledge of truth which had passed between them.

In the meantime he received the following letter from Messrs. Camperdown:—

'62, New Square, Lincoln's Inn,
15 September, 18—

'DEAR SIR,

'After what passed in our chambers the other day, we think it best to let you know that we have been instructed by the executor of the late Sir Florian Eustace to file a bill in Chancery against the widow, Lady Eustace, for the recovery of valuable diamonds. You will oblige us by making the necessary communication to her ladyship, and will perhaps tell us the names of her ladyship's solicitors.

> 'We are, dear sir,
>
> 'Your very obedient servants,
>
> 'CAMPERDOWN & SON.

'F. Greystock, Esq., M.P.'

A few days after the receipt of this letter Frank started for Scotland.

CHAPTER XXXI
Frank Greystock's Second Visit to Portray

ON this occasion Frank Greystock went down to Portray Castle with the intention of staying at the house during the very short time that he would remain in Scotland. He was going there solely on his cousin's business,—with no view to grouse-shooting or other pleasure, and he purposed remaining but a very short time,—perhaps only one night. His cousin, moreover, had spoken of having guests with her, in which case there could be no tinge of impropriety in his doing so. And whether she had guests, or whether she had not, what difference could it really make? Mr. Andrew Gowran had already seen what there was to see, and could do all the evil that could be done. He could, if he were so minded, spread reports in the neighbourhood, and might, perhaps, have the power of communicating what he had discovered to the Eustace faction,—John Eustace, Mr. Camperdown, and Lord Fawn. That evil, if it were an evil, must be encountered with absolute indifference. So he went direct to the castle, and was received quietly, but very graciously, by his cousin Lizzie.

There were no guests then staying at Portray; but that very distinguished lady, Mrs. Carbuncle, with her niece, Miss Roanoke, had been there; as had also that very well-known nobleman, Lord George de Bruce Carruthers. Lord George and Mrs. Carbuncle were in the habit of seeing a good deal of each other, though, as all the world knew, there was nothing between them but the simplest friendship. And Sir Griffin Tewett had also been there, a young baronet who was supposed to be enamoured of that most gorgeous of beauties, Lucinda Roanoke. Of all these grand friends,—friends with whom Lizzie had become acquainted in London,—nothing further need be said here, as they were not at the castle when Frank arrived. When he came, whether by premeditated plan or by the chance of circumstances, Lizzie had no one with her at Portray,—except the faithful Macnulty.

'I thought to have found you with all the world here,' said Frank,—the faithful Macnulty being then present.

'Well,—we have had people, but only for a couple of days. They are all coming again, but not till November. You hunt; —don't you, Frank?'

'I have no time for hunting. Why do you ask?'

'I'm going to hunt. It's a long way to go,—ten or twelve miles generally; but almost everybody hunts here. Mrs. Carbuncle is coming again, and she is about the best lady in England after hounds;—so they tell me. And Lord George is coming again.'

'Who is Lord George?'

'You remember Lord George Carruthers, whom we all knew in London?'

'What,—the tall man with the hollow eyes and the big whiskers, whose life is a mystery to every one. Is he coming?'

'I like him, just because he isn't a ditto to every man one meets. And Sir Griffin Tewett is coming.'

'Who is a ditto to everybody.'

Well;—yes; poor Sir Griffin! The truth is, he is awfully smitten with Mrs. Carbuncle's niece.'

'Don't you go match-making, Lizzie,' said Frank. 'That Sir Griffin is a fool, we will all allow; but it's my belief he has wit enough to make himself pass off as a man of fortune, with very little to back it. He's at law with his mother, at law with his sisters, and at law with his younger brother.'

'If he were at law with his great-grandmother, it would be nothing to me, Frank. She has her aunt to take care of her, and Sir Griffin is coming with Lord George.'

'You don't mean to put up all their horses, Lizzie?'

'Well, not all. Lord George and Sir Griffin are to keep theirs at Troon, or Kilmarnock, or somewhere. The ladies will bring two apiece, and I shall have two of my own.'

'And carriage-horses and hacks?'

'The carriage-horses are here,—of course.'

'It will cost you a great deal of money, Lizzie.'

'That's just what I tell her,' said Miss Macnulty.

'I've been living here, not spending one shilling for the last two months,' said Lizzie, 'and all for the sake of economy; yet people think that no woman was ever left so rich. Surely I can afford to see a few friends for one month in the year. If I find I can't afford so much as that, I shall let the place, and go and live abroad somewhere. It's too much to suppose that a woman should shut herself up here for six or eight months and see nobody all the time.'

On that, the day of Frank's arrival, not a word was said about the necklace, nor of Lord Fawn, nor of that mutual pledge which had been taken and given down among the rocks. Frank, before dinner, went out about the place, that he might see how things were going on, and observe whether the widow was being ill-treated and unfairly eaten up by her dependants. He was, too, a little curious as to a matter as to which his curiosity was soon relieved. He had hardly reached the out-buildings which lay behind the kitchen-gardens on his way to the Portray woods, before he encountered Andy Gowran. That faithful adherent of the family raised his hand to his cap and bobbed his head, and then silently, and with renewed diligence, applied himself to the job which he had in hand. The gate of the little yard in which the cowshed stood was off its hinges, and Andy was resetting the post and making the fence tight and tidy. Frank stood a moment watching him, and then asked after his health. ' 'Deed am I nae that to boost about in the way of bodily heelth, Muster Greystock. I've just o'er mony things to tent to, to tent to my ain sell as a prudent mon ought. It's airly an' late wi' me, Muster Greystock; and the lumbagy just a' o'er a mon, isn't the pleasantest freend in the warld.' Frank said that he was sorry to hear so bad an account of Mr. Gowran's health, and passed on. It was not for him to refer to the little scene in which Mr. Gowran had behaved so badly and had shaken his head. If the misbehaviour had been condoned by Lady Eustace, the less that he said about it the better. Then he went on through the woods, and was well aware that Mr. Gowran's fostering care had not been abated by his disapproval of his mistress. The fences had been re-paired since Frank was there, and stones had been laid on the road or track over which was to be carried away the under-wood*which it would be Lady Eustace's privilege to cut during the coming winter.

Frank was not alone for one moment with his cousin during

that evening, but in the presence of Miss Macnulty all the circumstances of the necklace were discussed. 'Of course it is my own,' said Lady Eustace, standing up,—'my own to do just what I please with. If they go on like this with me, they will almost tempt me to sell it for what it will fetch,—just to prove to them that I can do so. I have half a mind to sell it, and then send them the money, and tell them to put it by for my little Flory. Would not that serve them right Frank?'

'I don't think I'd do that, Lizzie.'

'Why not? You always tell me what not to do, but you never say what I ought?'

'That is because I am so wise and prudent. If you were to attempt to sell the diamonds they would stop you, and would not give you credit for the generous purpose afterwards.'

'They wouldn't stop you if you sold the ring you wear.' The ring had been given to him by Lucy, after their engagement, and was the only present she had ever made him. It had been purchased out of her own earnings, and had been put on his finger by her own hand. Either from accident or craft he had not worn it when he had been before at Portray, and Lizzie had at once observed it as a thing she had never seen before. She knew well that he would not buy such a ring. Who had given him the ring? Frank almost blushed as he looked down at the trinket, and Lizzie was sure that it had been given by that sly little creeping thing, Lucy. 'Let me look at the ring,' she said. 'Nobody could stop you if you chose to sell this to me.'

'Little things are always less troublesome than big things,' he said.

'What is the price?' she asked.

'It is not in the market, Lizzie. Nor should your diamonds be there. You must be content to let them take what legal steps they may think fit, and defend your property. After that you can do as you please; but keep them safe till the thing is settled. If I were you I would have them at the bankers.'

'Yes;—and then when I asked for them be told that they couldn't be given up to me, because of Mr. Camperdown or the Lord Chancellor. And what's the good of a thing locked up? You wear your ring;—why shouldn't I wear my necklace?'

'I have nothing to say against it.'

'It isn't that I care for such things. Do I, Julia?'

'All ladies like them, I suppose,' said that stupidest and most stubborn of all humble friends, Miss Macnulty.

'I don't like them at all, and you know I don't. I hate them. They have been the misery of my life. Oh, how they have tormented me! Even when I am asleep I dream about them, and think that people steal them. They have never given me one moment's happiness. When I have them on I am always fearing that Camperdown and Son are behind me and are going to clutch them. And I think too well of myself to believe that anybody will care more for me because of a necklace. The only good they have ever done me has been to save me from a man who I now know never cared for me. But they are mine;—and therefore I choose to keep them. Though I am only a woman I have an idea of my own rights, and will defend them as far as they go. If you say I ought not to sell them, Frank, I'll keep them; but I'll wear them as commonly as you do that gage d'amour which you carry on your finger. Nobody shall ever see me without them. I won't go to any old dowager's tea-party without them. Mr. John Eustace has chosen to accuse me of stealing them.'

'I don't think John Eustace has ever said a word about them,' said Frank.

'Mr. Camperdown then;—the people who choose to call themselves the guardians and protectors of my boy, as if I were not his best guardian and protector! I'll show them at any rate that I'm not ashamed of my booty. I don't see why I should lock them up in a musty old bank. Why don't you send your ring to the bank?' Frank could not but feel that she did it all very well. In the first place she was very pretty in the display of her half-mock indignation. Though she used some strong words she used them with an air that carried them off and left no impression that she had been either vulgar or violent. And then, though the indignation was half mock, it

was also, half real, and her courage and spirit were attractive.
Greystock had at last taught himself to think that Mr. Camperdown was not justified in the claim which he made, and
that in consequence of that unjust claim Lizzie Eustace had
been subjected to ill-usage. 'Did you ever see this bone of contention,' she asked;—'this fair Helen for which Greeks and
Romans are to fight?'

'I never saw the necklace, if you mean that.'

'I'll fetch it. You ought to see it as you have to talk about
it so often.'

'Can I get it?' asked Miss Macnulty.

'Heaven and earth! To suppose that I should ever keep
them under less than seven keys, and that there should be
any of the locks that anybody should be able to open except
myself!'

'And where are the seven keys?' asked Frank.

'Next to my heart,' said Lizzie, putting her hand on her
left side. 'And when I sleep they are always tied round my
neck in a bag, and the bag never escapes from my grasp. And
I have such a knife under my pillow, ready for Mr. Camperdown, should he come to seize them!' Then she ran out of the
room, and in a couple of minutes returned with the necklace,
hanging loose in her hand. It was part of her little play to show
by her speed that the close locking of the jewels was a joke,
and that the ornament, precious as it was, received at her
hands no other treatment than might any indifferent feminine
bauble. Nevertheless within those two minutes she had contrived to unlock the heavy iron case which always stood
beneath the foot of her bed. 'There,' she said, chucking the
necklace across the table to Frank, so that he was barely able
to catch it. 'There is ten thousand pounds' worth, as they tell
me. Perhaps you will not believe me when I say that I should
have the greatest satisfaction in the world in throwing them
out among those blue waves yonder, did I not think that
Camperdown and Son would fish them up again.'

Frank spread the necklace on the table, and stood up to look
at it, while Miss Macnulty came and gazed at the jewels

over his shoulder. 'And that is worth ten thousand pounds,' said he.

'So people say.'

'And your husband gave it you just as another man gives a trinket that costs ten shillings!'

'Just as Lucy Morris gave you that ring.'

He smiled, but took no other notice of the accusation. 'I am so poor a man,' said he, 'that this string of stones, which you throw about the room like a child's toy, would be the making of me.'

'Take it and be made,' said Lizzie.

'It seems an awful thing to me to have so much value in my hands,' said Miss Macnulty, who had lifted the necklace off the table. 'It would buy an estate; wouldn't it?'

'It would buy the honourable estate of matrimony if it belonged to many women,' said Lizzie,—'but it hasn't had just that effect with me;—has it, Frank?'

'You haven't used it with that view yet.'

'Will you have it, Frank?' she said. 'Take it with all its encumbrances, and weight of cares. Take it with all the burthen of Messrs. Camperdown's lawsuits upon it. You shall be as welcome to it as flowers were ever welcomed in May.'

'The encumbrances are too heavy,' said Frank.

'You prefer a little ring.'

'Very much.'

'I don't doubt but you're right,' said Lizzie. 'Who fears to rise will hardly get a fall. But there they are for you to look at, and there they shall remain for the rest of the evening.' So saying, she clasped the string round Miss Macnulty's throat. 'How do you feel, Julia, with an estate upon your neck? Five hundred acres at twenty pounds an acre. Let us call it five hundred pounds a year. That's about it.' Miss Macnulty looked as though she did not like it, but she stood for a time bearing the precious burthen, while Frank explained to his cousin that she could hardly buy land to pay her five per cent. They were then taken off and left lying on the table till Lady Eustace took them with her as she went to bed. 'I do feel so like some naughty person in the "Arabian Nights," '*she said, 'who has got some great treasure that always brings him into trouble; but he can't get rid of it, because some spirit has given it to him. At last, some morning it turns into slate stones, and then he has to be a water-carrier, and is happy ever afterwards, and marries the king's daughter. What sort of a king's son will there be for me when this turns into slate stones? Good night, Frank.' Then she went off with her diamonds and her bed-candle.

On the following day Frank suggested that there should be a business conversation. 'That means that I am to sit silent and obedient while you lecture me,' she said. But she submitted, and they went together into the little sitting-room which looked out over the sea,—the room where she kept her Shelley and her Byron, and practised her music and did water-colours, and sat, sometimes, dreaming of a Corsair. 'And now, my gravest of Mentors, what must a poor ignorant female Telemachus do, so that the world may not trample on her too heavily?'*He began by telling her what had happened between himself and Lord Fawn, and recommended her to write to that unhappy nobleman, returning any present that she might have received from him, and expressing, with some mild but intelligible sarcasm, her regret that their paths should have crossed each other. 'I've worse in store for his lordship than that,' said Lizzie.

'Do you mean by any personal interview?'

'Certainly.'

'I think you are wrong, Lizzie.'

'Of course you do. Men have become so soft themselves, that they no longer dare to think even of punishing those who behave badly, and they expect women to be softer and more fainéant*than themselves. I have been ill-used.'

'Certainly you have.'

'And I will be revenged. Look here, Frank; if your view of these things is altogether different from mine, let us drop the subject. Of all living human beings you are the one that is most to me now. Perhaps you are more than any other ever was.

But, even for you, I cannot alter my nature. Even for you I would not alter it if I could. That man has injured me, and all the world knows it. I will have my revenge, and all the world shall know that. I did wrong;—I am sensible enough of that.'

'What wrong do you mean?'

'I told a man whom I never loved that I would marry him. God knows that I have been punished.'

'Perhaps, Lizzie, it is better as it is.'

'A great deal better. I will tell you now that I could never induce myself to go into church with that man as his bride. With a man I didn't love I might have done so, but not with a man I despised.'

'You have been saved, then, from a greater evil.'

'Yes;—but not the less is his injury to me. It is not because he despises me that he rejects me;—nor is it because he thought that I had taken property that was not my own.'

'Why then?'

'Because he was afraid the world would say that I had done so. Poor shallow creature! But he shall be punished.'

'I do not know how you can punish him.'

'Leave that to me. I have another thing to do much more difficult.' She paused, looking for a moment up into his face, and then turning her eyes upon the ground. As he said nothing, she went on. 'I have to excuse myself to you for having accepted him.'

'I have never blamed you.'

'Not in words. How should you? But if you have not blamed me in your heart, I despise you. I know you have. I have seen it in your eyes when you have counselled me, either to take the poor creature or to leave him. Speak out, now, like a man. Is it not so?'

'I never thought you loved him.'

'Loved him! Is there anything in him or about him that a woman could love? Is he not a poor social stick;—a bit of half-dead wood, good to make a post of, if one wants a post? I did want a post so sorely then!'

'I don't see why.'

'You don't?'

'No, indeed. It was natural that you should be inclined to marry again.'

'Natural that I should be inclined to marry again! And is that all? It is hard sometimes to see whether men are thick-witted, or hypocrites so perfect that they seem to be so. I cannot bring myself to think you thick-witted, Frank.'

'Then I must be the perfect hypocrite,—of course.'

'You believe I accepted Lord Fawn because it was natural that I should wish to marry again! Frank, you believed nothing of the kind. I accepted him in my anger, in my misery, in my despair, because I had expected you to come to me,—and you had not come!'—She had thrown herself now into a chair, and sat looking at him. 'You had told me that you would come, and you had stayed away. It was you, Frank, that I wanted to punish then;—but there was no punishment in it for you. When is it to be, Frank?'

'When is what to be?' he asked, in a low voice, all but dumb-founded. How was he to put an end to this conversation, and what was he to say to her?

'Your marriage with that little wizened thing who gave you the ring—that prim morsel of feminine propriety who has been clever enough to make you believe that her morality would suffice to make you happy.'

'I will not hear Lucy Morris abused, Lizzie.'

'Is that abuse? Is it abuse to say that she is moral and proper? But, sir, I shall abuse her. I know her for what she is, while your eyes are sealed. She is wise and moral, and decorous and prim; but she is a hypocrite; and has no touch of real heart in her composition. Not abuse her when she has robbed me of all,—all,—all that I have in the world! Go to her. You had better go at once. I did not mean to say all this, but it has been said, and you must leave me. I, at any rate, cannot play the hypocrite;—I wish I could.' He rose and came to her, and attempted to take her hand, but she flung away from him. 'No!' she said—'never again; never, unless you will tell me that the promise you made me when we were down on the sea-shore was a true promise. Was that truth, sir, or was it a—lie?'

'Lizzie, do not use such a word as that to me.'

'I cannot stand picking my words when the whole world is going round with me, and my very brain is on fire. What is it to me what my words are? Say one syllable to me, and every word I utter again while breath is mine shall be spoken to do you pleasure. If you cannot say it, it is nothing to me what you or any one may think of my words. You know my secret, and I care not who else knows it. At any rate, I can die!' Then she paused a moment, and after that stalked steadily out of the room.

That afternoon Frank took a long walk by himself over the mountains, nearly to the Cottage and back again; and on his return was informed that Lady Eustace was ill, and had gone to bed. At any rate, she was too unwell to come down to dinner. He, therefore, and Miss Macnulty sat down to dine, and passed the evening together without other companionship. Frank had resolved during his walk that he would leave Portray the next day; but had hardly resolved upon anything else. One thing, however, seemed certain to him. He was engaged to marry Lucy Morris, and to that engagement he must be true. His cousin was very charming,—and had never looked so lovely in his eyes as when she had been confessing her love for him. And he had wondered at and admired her courage, her power of language, and her force. He could not quite forget how useful would be her income to him. And, added to this, there was present to him an unwholesome feeling,—ideas absolutely at variance with those better ideas which had prompted him when he was writing his offer to Lucy Morris in his chambers,—that a woman such as was his cousin Lizzie was fitter to be the wife of a man thrown, as he must be, into the world, than a dear, quiet, domestic little girl such as Lucy Morris. But to Lucy Morris he was engaged, and therefore there was an end of it.

The next morning he sent his love to his cousin, asking whether he should see her before he went. It was still necessary that he should know what attorneys to employ on her behalf if the threatened bill were filed by Messrs. Camperdown. Then he suggested a firm in his note. Might he put the case into the hands of Mr. Townsend, who was a friend of his own? There came back to him a scrap of paper, an old envelope, on which were written the names of Mowbray and Mopus;— Mowbray and Mopus in a large scrawling hand, and with pencil. He put the scrap of paper into his pocket, feeling that he could not remonstrate with her at this moment, and was prepared to depart; when there came a message to him. Lady Eustace was still unwell, but had risen; and if it were not giving him too much trouble, would see him before he went. He followed the messenger to the same little room, looking out upon the sea, and then found her, dressed indeed, but with a white morning wrapper on, and with hair loose over her shoulders. Her eyes were red with weeping, and her face was pale, and thin, and woe-begone. 'I am so sorry that you are ill, Lizzie,' he said.

'Yes; I am ill;—sometimes very ill; but what does it matter? I did not send for you, Frank, to speak of aught so trivial as that. I have a favour to ask.'

'Of course I will grant it.'

'It is your forgiveness for my conduct yesterday.'

'Oh, Lizzie!'

'Say that you forgive me. Say it!'

'How can I forgive where there has been no fault?'

'There has been fault. Say that you forgive me.' And she stamped her foot as she demanded his pardon.

'I do forgive you,' he said.

'And now, one farewell.' She then threw herself upon his breast and kissed him. 'Now, go,' she said; 'Go, and come no more to me, unless you would see me mad. May God Almighty bless you, and make you happy!' As she uttered this prayer she held the door in her hand, and there was nothing for him but to leave her.

CHAPTER XXXII
Mr. and Mrs. Hittaway in Scotland

A GREAT many people go to Scotland in the autumn. When you have your autumn holiday in hand to dispose of it, there is nothing more aristocratic that you can do than go to Scotland. Dukes are more plentiful there than in Pall Mall, and you will meet an earl or at least a lord on every mountain. Of course, if you merely travel about from inn to inn, and neither have a moor of your own or stay with any great friend, you don't quite enjoy the cream of it; but to go to Scotland in August and stay there, perhaps, till the end of September, is about the most certain step you can take towards autumnal fashion. Switzerland and the Tyrol, and even Italy, are all redolent of Mr. Cook,* and in those beautiful lands you become subject at least to suspicion.

By no persons was the duty of adhering to the best side of society more clearly appreciated than by Mr. and Mrs. Hittaway of Warwick Square. Mr. Hittaway was Chairman of the Board of Civil Appeals, and was a man who quite understood that there are chairmen—and chairmen. He could name to you three or four men holding responsible permanent official positions quite as good as that he filled in regard to salary,—which, as he often said of his own, was a mere nothing, just a poor two thousand pounds a yea., not as much as a grocer would make in a decent business,—but they were simply head clerks and nothing more. Nobody knew anything of them. They had no names. You did not meet them anywhere. Cabinet ministers never heard of them; and nobody out of their own offices ever consulted them. But there are others, and Mr. Hittaway felt greatly conscious that he was one of them, who moved altogether in a different sphere. One minister of State would ask another whether Hittaway had been consulted on this or on that measure;—so at least the Hittawayites were in the habit of reporting. The names of Mr. and Mrs. Hittaway were constantly in the papers. They were invited to evening gatherings at the houses of both the alternate Prime Ministers.* They were to be seen at fashionable gatherings up the river. They attended concerts at Buckingham Palace. Once a year they gave a dinner-party which was inserted in the 'Morning Post'.* On such occasions at least one Cabinet Minister always graced the board. In fact, Mr. Hittaway, as Chairman of the Board of Civil Appeals, was somebody; and Mrs. Hittaway, as his wife and as sister to a peer, was somebody also. The reader will remember that Mrs. Hittaway had been a Fawn before she married.

There is this drawback upon the happy condition which Mr. Hittaway had achieved,—that it demands a certain expenditure. Let nobody dream that he can be somebody without having to pay for that honour;—unless, indeed, he be a clergyman. When you go to a concert at Buckingham Palace you pay nothing, it is true, for your ticket; and a Cabinet Minister dining with you does not eat or drink more than your old friend Jones the attorney. But in some insidious unforeseen manner,—in a way that can only be understood after much experience,—these luxuries of fashion do make a heavy pull on a modest income. Mrs. Hittaway knew this thoroughly, having much experience, and did make her fight bravely. For Mr. Hittaway's income was no more than modest. A few thousand pounds he had of his own when he married, and his Clara had brought to him the unpretending sum of fifteen hundred. But, beyond that, the poor official salary,—which was less than what a decent grocer would make,—was their all. The house in Warwick Square they had prudently purchased on their marriage,—when houses in Warwick Square were cheaper than they are now,—and there they carried on their battle, certainly with success. But two thousand a year does not go very far in Warwick Square, even though you sit rent free, if you have a family and absolutely must keep a carriage. It therefore resulted that when Mr. and Mrs. Hittaway went to Scotland, which they would endeavour to do every year, it was very important that they should accomplish their aristocratic holiday as visitors at the house of some aristocratic friend. So well had they played their cards in this respect, that they seldom failed altogether. In one year they had been the guests of a great marquis quite in the north, and that had been a very glorious year. To talk of Stackallan*was, indeed, a thing of beauty.* But in that year Mr. Hittaway had made himself very useful in London. Since that they had been at delicious shooting lodges in Ross and Inverness-shire, had visited a millionaire at his palace amidst the Argyle mountains, had been fêted in a western island, had been bored by a Dundee dowager, and put up with a Lothian laird. But the thing had been almost always done, and the Hittaways were known as people that went to Scotland. He could handle a gun, and was clever enough never to shoot a keeper. She could read aloud, could act a little, could talk or hold her tongue; and let her hosts be who they would and as mighty as you please, never caused them trouble by seeming to be out of their circle, and on that account requiring peculiar attention.

On this occasion Mr. and Mrs. Hittaway were the guests of old Lady Pierrepoint, in Dumfries. There was nothing special to recommend Lady Pierrepoint except that she had a large house and a good income, and that she liked to have people with her of whom everybody knew something. So far was Lady Pierrepoint from being high in the Hittaway world, that Mrs. Hittaway felt herself called upon to explain to her friends that she was forced to go to Dumdum House by the duties of old friendship. Dear old Lady Pierrepoint had been insisting on it for the last ten years. And there was this advantage, that Dumfriesshire is next to Ayrshire, that Dumdum was not very far,—some twenty or thirty miles,—from Portray, and that she might learn something about Lizzie Eustace in her country house.

It was nearly the end of August when the Hittaways left London to stay an entire month with Lady Pierrepoint. Mr. Hittaway had very frequently explained his defalcation*as to fashion,—in that he was remaining in London for three weeks after Parliament had broken up,—by the peculiar exigencies of the Board of Appeals in that year. To one or two very intimate friends Mrs. Hittaway had hinted that everything must be made to give way to this horrid business of Fawn's marriage. 'Whatever happens, and at whatever cost, that must be stopped,' she had ventured to say to Lady Glencora Palliser, —who, however, could hardly be called one of her very intimate friends. 'I don't see it at all,' said Lady Glencora. 'I think Lady Eustace is very nice. And why shouldn't she marry Lord Fawn if she's engaged to him?' 'But you have heard of the necklace, Lady Glencora?' 'Yes, I've heard of it. I wish anybody would come to me and try and get my diamonds! They should hear what I would say.' Mrs. Hittaway greatly admired Lady Glencora, but not the less was she determined to persevere.

Had Lord Fawn been altogether candid and open with his family at this time, some trouble might have been saved; for he had almost altogether resolved that, let the consequences be what they might, he would not marry Lizzie Eustace. But he was afraid to say this even to his own sister. He had promised to marry the woman, and he must walk very warily, or the objurgations*of the world would be too many for him. 'It must depend altogether on her conduct, Clara,' he had said when last his sister had persecuted him on the subject. She was not, however, sorry to have an opportunity of learning something of the lady's doings. Mr. Hittaway had more than once called on Mr. Camperdown. 'Yes,' Mr. Camperdown had said in answer to a question from Lord Fawn's brother-in-law; 'she would play old gooseberry*with the property, if we hadn't some one to look after it. There's a fellow named Gowran who has lived there all his life, and we depend very much upon him.'

It is certainly true, that as to many points of conduct, women are less nice than men. Mr. Hittaway would not probably have condescended himself to employ espionage, but Mrs. Hittaway was less scrupulous. She actually went down to Troon and had an interview with Mr. Gowran, using freely the names of Mr. Camperdown and of Lord Fawn; and some ten days afterwards Mr. Gowran travelled as far as Dumfries, and Dumdum, and had an interview with Mrs. Hittaway. The result of all this, and of further inquiries, will be shown by the following letter from Mrs. Hittaway to her sister Amelia;—

'Dumdum, 9th September, 18—.
'My DEAR AMELIA,

'Here we are, and here we have to remain to the end of the month. Of course it suits, and all that; but it is awfully dull. Richmond for this time of the year is a paradise to it; and as for coming to Scotland every autumn, I am sick of it. Only what is one to do if one lives in London? If it wasn't for Orlando and the children, I'd brazen it out, and let people say what they pleased. As for health, I'm never so well as at home, and I do like having my own things about me. Orlando has literally nothing to do here. There is no shooting, except pheasants, and that doesn't begin till October.

'But I'm very glad I've come as to Frederic, and the more so, as I have learned the truth as to that Mr. Greystock. She, Lady Eustace, is a bad creature in every way. She still pretends that she is engaged to Frederic, and tells everybody that the marriage is not broken off, and yet she has her cousin with her, making love to him in the most indecent way. People used to say in her favour that at any rate she never flirted. I never quite know what people mean when they talk of flirting. But you may take my word for it that she allows her cousin to embrace her, and *embraces him*. I would not say it if I could not prove it. It is horrible to think of it, when one remembers that she is almost justified in saying that Frederic is engaged to her.

'No doubt he was engaged to her. It was a great misfortune, but, thank God, is not yet past remedy. He has some foolish feeling of what he calls honour; as if a man can be bound in honour to marry a woman who has deceived him in every point? She still sticks to the diamonds,—if she has not sold them, as I believe she has; and Mr. Camperdown is going to bring an action against her in the High Court of Chancery. But still Frederic will not absolutely declare the thing off. I feel, therefore, that it is my duty to let him know what I have learned. I should be the last to stir in such a matter unless I was sure I could prove it. But I don't quite like to write to Frederic. Will mamma see him, and tell him what I say? Of course you will show this letter to mamma. If not, I must postpone it till I am in town;—but I think it would come better from mamma. Mamma may be sure that she is a bad woman.

'And now what do you think of your Mr. Greystock? As sure as I am here he was seen with his arm round his cousin's waist, sitting out of doors,—*kissing her!* I was never taken in by that story of his marrying Lucy Morris. He is the last man in the world to marry a governess. He is over head and ears in debt, and if he marries at all, he must marry some one with money. I really think that mamma, and you, and all of you have been soft about that girl. I believe she has been a good governess,—that is, good after mamma's easy fashion; and I don't for a moment suppose that she is doing anything underhand. But a governess with a lover never does suit, and I'm sure it won't suit in this case. If I were you I would tell her. I think it would be the best charity. Whether they mean to marry I can't tell,—Mr. Greystock, that is, and this woman; *but they ought to mean it*;—that's all.

'Let me know at once whether mamma will see Frederic, and speak to him openly. She is quite at liberty to use my name; only nobody but mamma should see this letter.

'Love to them all,

'Your most affectionate sister,

'CLARA HITTAWAY.'

In writing to Amelia instead of to her mother, Mrs. Hittaway was sure that she was communicating her ideas to at least two persons at Fawn Court, and that therefore there would be discussion. Had she written to her mother, her mother might probably have held her peace, and done nothing.

CHAPTER XXXIII
'It won't be True'

Mrs. greystock, in making her proposition respecting Lady Linlithgow, wrote to Lady Fawn, and by the same post Frank wrote to Lucy. But before those letters reached Fawn Court there had come that other dreadful letter from Mrs. Hittaway. The consternation caused at Fawn Court in respect to Mr. Greystock's treachery almost robbed of its importance the suggestion made as to Lord Fawn. Could it be possible that this man, who had so openly and in so manly a manner engaged himself to Lucy Morris, should now be proposing to himself a marriage with his rich cousin? Lady Fawn did not believe that it was possible. Clara had not seen those horrid things with her own eyes, and other people might be liars. But Amelia shook her head. Amelia evidently believed that all manner of iniquities were possible to man. 'You see, mamma, the sacrifice he was making was so very great!' 'But he made it!' pleaded Lady Fawn. 'No, mamma, he said he would make it. Men do these things. It is very horrid, but I think they do them more now than they used to. It seems to me that nobody cares now what he does, if he's not to be put into prison.' It was resolved between these two wise ones that nothing at the present should be said to Lucy or to any one of the family. They would wait awhile, and in the meantime they attempted,—as far as it was possible to make the attempt without express words,—to let Lucy understand that she might remain at Fawn Court if she pleased. While this was going on, Lord Fawn did come down once again, and on that occasion Lucy simply absented herself from the dinner-table and from the family circle for that evening. 'He's coming in, and you've got to go to prison again,' Nina said to her, with a kiss.

The matter to which Mrs. Hittaway's letter more specially alluded was debated between the mother and daughter at great length. They, indeed, were less brave and less energetic than was the married daughter of the family; but as they saw Lord Fawn more frequently, they knew better than Mrs. Hittaway the real state of the case. They felt sure that he was already sufficiently embittered against Lady Eustace, and thought that therefore the peculiarly unpleasant task assigned to Lady Fawn need not be performed. Lady Fawn had not the advantage of living so much in the world as her daughter, and was oppressed by, perhaps, a squeamish delicacy. 'I really could not tell him about her sitting and—and kissing the man. Could I, my dear?' 'I couldn't,' said Amelia;—'but Clara would.'

'And to tell the truth,' continued Lady Fawn, 'I shouldn't care a bit about it if it was not for poor Lucy. What will become of her if that man is untrue to her?'

'Nothing on earth would make her believe it, unless it came from himself,' said Amelia,—who really did know something of Lucy's character. 'Till he tells her, or till she knows that he's married, she'll never believe it.'

Then, after a few days, there came those other letters from Bobsborough,—one from the dean's wife and the other from Frank. The matter there proposed it was necessary that they should discuss with Lucy, as the suggestion had reached Lucy as well as themselves. She at once came to Lady Fawn with her lover's letter, and with a gentle merry laughing face declared that the thing would do very well. 'I am sure I should get on with her, and I should know that it wouldn't be for long,' said Lucy.

'The truth is, we don't want you to go at all,' said Lady Fawn.

'Oh, but I must,' said Lucy in her sharp, decided tone. 'I must go. I was bound to wait till I heard from Mr. Greystock, because it is my first duty to obey him. But of course I cannot stay here after what has passed. As Nina says, it is simply going to prison when Lord Fawn comes here.'

'Nina is an impertinent little chit,' said Amelia.

'She is the dearest little friend in all the world,' said Lucy, 'and always tells the exact truth. I do go to prison, and when he comes I feel that I ought to go to prison. Of course, I must go away. What does it matter? Lady Linlithgow won't be exactly like you,'—and she put her little hand upon Lady Fawn's fat arm caressingly, 'and I shan't have you all to spoil me; but I shall be simply waiting till he comes. Everything now must be no more than waiting till he comes.'

If it was to be that the 'he' would never come, this was very dreadful. Amelia clearly thought that 'he' would never come, and Lady Fawn was apt to think her daughter wiser than herself. And if Mr. Greystock were such as Mrs. Hittaway had described him to be,—if there were to be no such coming as that for which Lucy fondly waited,—then there would be reason ten-fold strong why she should not leave Fawn Court and go to Lady Linlithgow. In such case,—when that blow should fall,—Lucy would require very different treatment than might be expected for her from the hands of Lady Linlithgow. She would fade and fall to the earth like a flower with an insect at its root. She would be like a wounded branch, into which no sap would run. With such misfortune and wretchedness possibly before her, Lady Fawn could not endure the idea that Lucy should be turned out to encounter it all beneath the cold shade of Lady Linlithgow's indifference. 'My dear,' she said, 'let bygones be bygones. Come down and meet Lord Fawn. Nobody will say anything. After all, you were provoked very much, and there has been quite enough about it.'

This, from Lady Fawn, was almost miraculous,—from Lady Fawn, to whom her son had ever been the highest of human beings! But Lucy had told the tale to her lover, and her lover approved of her going. Perhaps there was acting upon her mind some feeling, of which she was hardly conscious, that as long as she remained at Fawn Court she would not see her lover. She had told him that she could make herself supremely happy in the simple knowledge that he loved her. But we all know how far such declarations should be taken as true. Of course, she was longing to see him. 'If he would only pass by the road,' she would say to herself, 'so that I might peep at him through the gate!' She had no formed idea in her own mind that she would be able to see him should she go to Lady Linlithgow, but still, there would be the chances of her altered life! She would tell Lady Linlithgow the truth, and why should Lady Linlithgow refuse her so rational a pleasure? There was, of course, a reason why Frank should not come to Fawn Court; but the house in Bruton Street*need not be closed to him. 'I hardly know how to love you enough,' she said to Lady Fawn, 'but indeed I must go. I do so hope the time may come when you and Mr. Greystock may be friends. Of course, it will come. Shall it not?'

'Who can look into the future?' said the wise Amelia.

'Of course, if he is your husband, we shall love him,' said the less wise Lady Fawn.

'He is to be my husband,' said Lucy, springing up. 'What do you mean? Do you mean anything?' Lady Fawn, who was not at all wise, protested that she meant nothing.

What were they to do? On that special day they merely stipulated that there should be a day's delay before Lady Fawn answered Mrs. Greystock's letter,—so that she might sleep upon it. The sleeping on it meant that further discussion which was to take place between Lady Fawn and her second daughter in her ladyship's bed-room that night. During all this period the general discomfort of Fawn Court was increased by a certain sullenness on the part of Augusta, the elder daughter, who knew that letters had come and that consultations were being held,—but who was not admitted to those consultations. Since the day on which poor Augusta had been handed over to Lizzie Eustace as her peculiar friend in the family, there had always existed a feeling that she, by her position, was debarred from sympathising in the general desire to be quit of Lizzie; and then, too, poor Augusta was never thoroughly trusted by that great guide of the family, Mrs. Hittaway. 'She couldn't keep it to herself if you'd give her gold to do it,' Mrs. Hittaway would say. Consequently Augusta was sullen and conscious of ill-usage. 'Have you fixed upon anything?' she said to Lucy that evening.

'Not quite;—only I am to go away.'

'I don't see why you should go away at all. Frederic doesn't come here so very often, and when he does come he doesn't say much to any one. I suppose it's all Amelia's doings.'

'Nobody wants me to go, only I feel that I ought. Mr. Greystock thinks it best.'

'I suppose he's going to quarrel with us all.'

'No, dear. I don't think he wants to quarrel with any one; —but above all he must not quarrel with me. Lord Fawn has quarrelled with him, and that's a misfortune,—just for the present.'

'And where are you going?'

'Nothing has been settled yet; but we are talking of Lady Linlithgow,—if she will take me.'

'Lady Linlithgow! Oh dear!'

'Won't it do?'

'They say she is the most dreadful old woman in London. Lady Eustace told such stories about her.'

'Do you know, I think I shall rather like it.'

But things were very different with Lucy the next morning. That discussion in Lady Fawn's room was protracted till midnight, and then it was decided that just a word should be said to Lucy, so that, if possible, she might be induced to remain at Fawn Court. Lady Fawn was to say the word, and on the following morning she was closeted with Lucy. 'My dear,' she began, 'we all want you to do us a particular favour.' As she said this, she held Lucy by the hand, and no one looking at them would have thought that Lucy was a governess and that Lady Fawn was her employer.

'Dear Lady Fawn, indeed it is better that I should go.'

'Stay just one month.'

'I couldn't do that, because then this chance of a home would be gone. Of course, we can't wait a month before we let Mrs. Greystock know.'

'We must write to her, of course.'

'And then, you see, Mr. Greystock wishes it.' Lady Fawn knew that Lucy could be very firm, and had hardly hoped that anything could be done by simple persuasion. They had long been accustomed among themselves to call her obstinate, and knew that even in her acts of obedience she had a way of obeying after her own fashion. It was as well, therefore, that the thing to be said should be said at once.

'My dear Lucy, has it ever occurred to you that there may be a slip between the cup and the lip?'

'What do you mean, Lady Fawn?'

'That sometimes engagements take place which never become more than engagements. Look at Lord Fawn and Lady Eustace.'

'Mr. Greystock and I are not like that,' said Lucy proudly.

'Such things are very dreadful, Lucy, but they do happen.'

'Do you mean anything;—anything real, Lady Fawn?'

'I have so strong a reliance on your good sense, that I will tell you just what I do mean. A rumour has reached me that Mr. Greystock is—paying more attention than he ought to do to Lady Eustace.'

'His own cousin!'

'But people marry their cousins, Lucy.'

'To whom he has always been just like a brother! I do think that is the cruellest thing. Because he sacrifices his time and his money and all his holidays to go and look after her affairs, this is to be said of him! She hasn't another human being to look after her, and, therefore, he is obliged to do it. Of course he has told me all about it. I do think, Lady Fawn,—I do think that is the greatest shame I ever heard!'

'But if it should be true——?'

'It isn't true.'

'But just for the sake of showing you, Lucy——; if it was to be true.'

'It won't be true.'

'Surely I may speak to you as your friend, Lucy. You needn't be so abrupt with me. Will you listen to me, Lucy?'

'Of course I will listen;—only nothing that anybody on earth could say about that would make me believe a word of it.'

'Very well! Now just let me go on. If it were to be so——'

'Oh-h, Lady Fawn!'

'Don't be foolish, Lucy. I will say what I've got to say. If—— if—— Let me see. Where was I? I mean just this. You had better remain here till things are a little more settled. Even if it be only a rumour,—and I'm sure I don't believe it's anything more,—you had better hear about it with us,—with friends round you, than with a perfect stranger like Lady Linlithgow. If anything were to go wrong there, you wouldn't know where to go for comfort. If anything were wrong with you here, you could come to me as though I were your mother. —Couldn't you, now?'

'Indeed, indeed I could! And I will;—I always will. Lady Fawn, I love you and the dear darling girls better than all the world—except Mr. Greystock. If anything like that were to happen, I think I should creep here and ask to die in your house. But it won't. And just now it will be better that I should go away.'

It was found at last that Lucy must have her way, and letters were written both to Mrs. Greystock and to Frank, requesting that the suggested overtures might at once be made to Lady Linlithgow. Lucy, in her letter to her lover, was more than ordinarily cheerful and jocose. She had a good deal to say about Lady Linlithgow that was really droll, and not a word to say indicative of the slightest fear in the direction of Lady Eustace. She spoke of poor Lizzie, and declared her conviction that that marriage never could come off now. 'You mustn't be angry when I say that I can't break my heart for them, for I never did think that they were very much in love. As for Lord Fawn, of course he is my—ENEMY!' And she wrote the word in big letters. 'And as for Lizzie,—she's your cousin, and all that. And she's ever so pretty, and all that. And she's as rich as Crœsus,* and all that. But I don't think she'll break her own heart. I would break mine; only,—only,— only—— You will understand the rest. If it should come to pass, I wonder whether "the duchess" would ever let a poor creature see a friend of hers in Bruton Street?' Frank had once called Lady Linlithgow the duchess, after a certain popular

picture in a certain popular book, and Lucy never forgot anything that Frank had said.

It did come to pass. Mrs. Greystock at once corresponded
with Lady Linlithgow, and Lady Linlithgow, who was at
Ramsgate for her autumn vacation, requested that Lucy Morris
might be brought to see her at her house in London on the
2nd of October. Lady Linlithgow's autumn holiday always
ended on the last day of September. On the 2nd of October
Lady Fawn herself took Lucy up to Bruton Street, and Lady
Linlithgow appeared. 'Miss Morris,' said Lady Fawn, 'thinks
it right that you should be told that she's engaged to be
married.' 'Who to?' demanded the countess. Lucy was as red
as fire, although she had especially made up her mind that she
would not blush when the communication was made. 'I don't
know that she wishes me to mention the gentleman's name,
just at present; but I can assure you that he is all that he ought
to be.' 'I hate mysteries,' said the countess. 'If Lady Linlithgow——' began Lucy. 'Oh, it's nothing to me,' continued the
old woman. 'It won't come off for six months I suppose?' Lucy
gave a mute assurance that there would be no such difficulty as
that. 'And he can't come here, Miss Morris.' To this Lucy
said nothing. Perhaps she might win over even the countess,
and if not, she must bear her six months of prolonged exclu-
sion from the light of day. And so the matter was settled. Lucy
was to be taken back to Richmond, and to come again on the
following Monday. 'I don't like this parting at all, Lucy,' Lady
Fawn said on her way home.

'It is better so, Lady Fawn.'

'I hate people going away; but, somehow, you don't feel it
as we do.'

'You wouldn't say that if you really knew what I do feel.'

'There was no reason why you should go. Frederic was
getting not to care for it at all. What's Nina to do now? I
can't get another governess after you. I hate all these sudden
breaks up. And all for such a trumpery thing. If Frederic
hasn't forgotten all about it, he ought.'

'It hasn't come altogether from him, Lady Fawn.'

'How has it come, then?'

'I suppose it is because of Mr. Greystock. I suppose when a girl has engaged herself to marry a man she must think more of him than of anything else.'

'Why couldn't you think of him at Fawn Court?'

'Because,—because things have been unfortunate. He isn't your friend,—not as yet. Can't you understand, Lady Fawn, that, dear as you all must be to me, I must live in his friendships, and take his part when there is a part?'

'Then I suppose that you mean to hate all of us?' Lucy could only cry at hearing this;—whereupon Lady Fawn also burst into tears.

On the Sunday before Lucy took her departure, Lord Fawn was again at Richmond. 'Of course, you'll come down,—just as if nothing had happened,' said Lydia. 'We'll see,' said Lucy. 'Mamma will be very angry if you don't,' said Lydia.

But Lucy had a little plot in her head, and her appearance at the dinner-table on that Sunday must depend on the manner in which her plot was executed. After church, Lord Fawn would always hang about the grounds for awhile before going into the house; and on this morning Lucy also remained outside. She soon found her opportunity, and walked straight up to him, following him on the path. 'Lord Fawn,' she said, 'I have come to beg your pardon.'

He had turned round hearing footsteps behind him, but still was startled and unready. 'It does not matter at all,' he said.

'It matters to me, because I behaved badly.'

'What I said about Mr. Greystock wasn't intended to be said to you, you know.'

'Even if it was it would make no matter. I don't mean to think of that now. I beg your pardon because I said what I ought not to have said.'

'You see, Miss Morris, that as the head of this family——'

'If I had said it to Juniper, I would have begged his pardon.' Now Juniper was the gardener, and Lord Fawn did not quite like the way in which the thing was put to him. The cloud came across his brow, and he began to fear that she would again insult him. 'I oughtn't to accuse anybody of an untruth,—not in that way; and I am very sorry for what I did, and I beg your pardon.' Then she turned as though she were going back to the house.

But he stopped her. 'Miss Morris, if it will suit you to stay with my mother, I will never say a word against it.'

'It is quite settled that I am to go to-morrow, Lord Fawn. Only for that I would not have troubled you again.'

Then she did turn towards the house, but he recalled her. 'We will shake hands, at any rate,' he said, 'and not part as enemies.' So they shook hands, and Lucy came down and sat in his company at the dinner-table.

CHAPTER XXXIV
Lady Linlithgow at Home

LUCY, in her letter to her lover, had distinctly asked whether she might tell Lady Linlithgow the name of her future husband, but had received no reply when she was taken to Bruton Street. The parting at Richmond was very painful, and Lady Fawn had declared herself quite unable to make another journey up to London with the ungrateful runagate.* Though there was no diminution of affection among the Fawns, there was a general feeling that Lucy was behaving badly. That obstinacy of hers was getting the better of her. Why should she have gone? Even Lord Fawn had expressed his desire that she should remain. And then, in the breasts of the wise ones, all faith in the Greystock engagement had nearly vanished. Another letter had come from Mrs. Hittaway, who now declared that it was already understood about Portray that Lady Eustace intended to marry her cousin. This was described as a terrible crime on the part of Lizzie, though the antagonistic crime of a remaining desire to marry Lord Fawn was still imputed to her. And, of course, the one crime heightened the other. So that words from the eloquent pen of Mrs. Hittaway failed to make dark enough the blackness of poor Lizzie's character. As for Mr. Greystock, he was simply a heartless man of the world, wishing to feather his nest. Mrs. Hittaway did not, for a moment, believe that he had ever dreamed of marrying Lucy Morris. Men always have three or four little excitements of that kind going on for the amusement of their leisure hours,—so, at least, said Mrs. Hittaway. 'The girl had better be told at once.' Such was her decision about poor Lucy. 'I can't do more than I have done,' said Lady Fawn to Augusta. 'She'll never get over it, mamma; never,' said Augusta.

Nothing more was said, and Lucy was sent off in the family carriage. Lydia and Nina were sent with her, and though there was some weeping on the journey, there was also much laughing. The character of the 'duchess' was discussed very much at large, and many promises were made as to long letters. Lucy, in truth, was not unhappy. She would be nearer to Frank; and then it had been almost promised her that she should go to the deanery, after a residence of six months with Lady Linlithgow. At the deanery of course she would see Frank; and she also understood that a long visit to the deanery would be the surest prelude to that home of her own of which she was always dreaming.

'Dear me;—sent you up in the carriage, has she? Why shouldn't you have come by the railway?'

'Lady Fawn thought the carriage best. She is so very kind.'

'It's what I call twaddle, you know. I hope you ain't afraid of going in a cab.'

'Not in the least, Lady Linlithgow.'

'You can't have the carriage to go about here. Indeed, I never have a pair of horses till after Christmas. I hope you know that I'm as poor as Job '*

'I didn't know.'

'I am, then. You'll get nothing beyond wholesome food with me. And I'm not sure it is wholesome always. The butchers are scoundrels, and the bakers are worse. What used you to do at Lady Fawn's?'

'I still did lessons with the two youngest girls.'

'You won't have any lessons to do here, unless you do 'em with me. You had a salary there?'

'Oh yes.'

'Fifty pounds a year, I suppose.'

'I had eighty.'

'Had you, indeed; eighty pounds;—and a coach to ride in!'

'I had a great deal more than that, Lady Linlithgow.'

'How do you mean?'

'I had downright love and affection. They were just so many dear friends. I don't suppose any governess was ever so treated before. It was just like being at home. The more I laughed, the better every one liked it.'

'You won't find anything to laugh at here; at least, I don't. If you want to laugh, you can laugh up-stairs, or down in the parlour.'

'I can do without laughing for a while.'

'That's lucky, Miss Morris. If they were all so good to you, what made you come away? They sent you away, didn't they?'

'Well;—I don't know that I can explain it just all. There were a great many things together. No;—they didn't send me away. I came away because it suited.'

'It was something to do with your having a lover, I suppose.' To this Lucy thought it best to make no answer, and the conversation for a while was dropped.

Lucy had arrived at about half-past three, and Lady Linlithgow was then sitting in the drawing-room. After the first series of questions and answers, Lucy was allowed to go up to her room, and on her return to the drawing-room, found the countess still sitting upright in her chair. She was now busy with accounts, and at first took no notice of Lucy's return. What were to be the companion's duties? What tasks in the house were to be assigned to her? What hours were to be her own; and what was to be done in those of which the countess would demand the use? Up to the present moment nothing had been said of all this. She had simply been told that she was to be Lady Linlithgow's companion,—without salary, indeed, —but receiving shelter, guardianship, and bread and meat in return for her services. She took up a book from the table and sat with it for ten minutes. It was Tupper's great poem,* and she attempted to read it. Lady Linlithgow sat, totting up her figures, but said nothing. She had not spoken a word since Lucy's return to the room; and as the great poem did not at first fascinate the new companion,—whose mind not unnaturally was somewhat disturbed,—Lucy ventured upon a question. 'Is there anything I can do for you, Lady Linlithgow?'

'Do you know about figures?'

'Oh, yes. I consider myself quite a ready-reckoner.'

'Can you make two and two come to five on one side of the sheet, and only come to three on the other?'

'I'm afraid I can't do that, and prove it afterwards.'

'Then you ain't worth anything to me.' Having so declared, Lady Linlithgow went on with her accounts, and Lucy relapsed into her great poem.

'No, my dear,' said the countess, when she had completed her work. 'There isn't anything for you to do. I hope you haven't come here with that mistaken idea. There won't be any sort of work of any kind expected from you. I poke my own fires, and I carve my own bit of mutton. And I haven't got a nasty little dog to be washed. And I don't care two-pence about worsted work. I have a maid to darn my stockings, and because she has to work, I pay her wages. I don't like being alone, so I get you to come and live with me. I breakfast at nine, and if you don't manage to be down by that time, I shall be cross.'

'I'm always up long before that.'

'There's lunch at two,—just bread and butter and cheese, and perhaps a bit of cold meat. There's dinner at seven;— and very bad it is, because they don't have any good meat in London. Down in Fifeshire the meat's a deal better than it is here, only I never go there now. At half-past ten I go to bed. It's a pity you're so young, because I don't know what you'll do about going out. Perhaps, as you ain't pretty, it won't signify.'

'Not at all, I should think,' said Lucy.

'Perhaps you consider yourself pretty. It's all altered now since I was young. Girls make monsters of themselves, and I'm told the men like it;—going about with unclean, frowzy structures on their head,* enough to make a dog sick. They used to be clean and sweet and nice,—what one would like to kiss. How a man can like to kiss a face with a dirty horse's tail all whizzing about it, is what I can't at all understand. I don't think they do like it, but they have to do it.'

'I haven't even a pony's tail,' said Lucy.

'They do like to kiss you, I daresay.'

'No, they don't,' ejaculated Lucy, not knowing what answer to make.

'I haven't hardly looked at you, but you didn't seem to me to be a beauty.'

'You're quite right about that, Lady Linlithgow.'

'I hate beauties. My niece, Lizzie Eustace, is a beauty; and I think that, of all the heartless creatures in the world, she is the most heartless.'

'I know Lady Eustace very well.'

'Of course you do. She was a Greystock, and you know the Greystocks. And she was down staying with old Lady Fawn at Richmond. I should think old Lady Fawn had a time with her;—hadn't she?'

'It didn't go off very well.'

'Lizzie would be too much for the Fawns, I should think. She was too much for me, I know. She's about as bad as anybody ever was. She's false, dishonest, heartless, cruel, irreligious, ungrateful, mean, ignorant, greedy, and vile!'

'Good gracious, Lady Linlithgow!'

'She's all that, and a great deal worse. But she is handsome. I don't know that I ever saw a prettier woman. I generally go out in a cab at three o'clock, but I shan't want you to go with me. I don't know what you can do. Macnulty used to walk round Grosvenor Square and think that people mistook her for a lady of quality. You musn't go and walk round Grosvenor Square by yourself, you know. Not that I care.'

'I'm not a bit afraid of anybody,' said Lucy.

'Now you know all about it. There isn't anything for you to do. There are Miss Edgeworth's novels*down-stairs, and "Pride and Prejudice"*in my bed-room. I don't subscribe to Mudie's*because when I asked for "Adam Bede,"*they always sent me the "Bandit Chief."*Perhaps you can borrow books from your friends at Richmond. I daresay Mrs. Greystock has told you that I'm very cross.'

'I havn't seen Mrs. Greystock for ever so long.'

'Then Lady Fawn has told you,—or somebody. When the wind is east, or north-east, or even north, I am cross, for I have the lumbago. It's all very well talking about being good-humoured. You can't be good-humoured with the lumbago. And I have the gout sometimes in my knee. I'm cross enough then, and so you'd be. And, among 'em all, I don't get much above half what I ought to have out of my jointure. That makes me very cross. My teeth are bad, and I like to have the meat tender. But it's always tough, and that makes me cross. And when people go against the grain with me, as Lizzie Eustace always did, then I'm very cross.'

'I hope you won't be very bad with me,' said Lucy.

'I don't bite, if you mean that,' said her ladyship.

'I'd sooner be bitten than barked at,—sometimes,' said Lucy.

'Humph!' said the old woman, and then she went back to her accounts.

Lucy had a few books of her own, and she determined to ask Frank to send her some. Books are cheap things*and she would not mind asking him for magazines, and numbers, and perhaps for the loan of a few volumes. In the meantime she did read Tupper's poem, and 'Pride and Prejudice,' and one of Miss Edgeworth's novels,—probably for the third time. During the first week in Bruton Street she would have been comfortable enough, only that she had not received a line from Frank. That Frank was not specially good at writing letters she had already taught herself to understand. She was inclined to believe that but few men of business do write letters willingly, and that, of all men, lawyers are the least willing to do so. How reasonable it was that a man who had to perform a great part of his daily work with a pen in his hand, should loathe a pen when not at work. To her the writing of letters was perhaps the most delightful occupation of her life, and the writing of letters to her lover was a foretaste of heaven; but then men, as she knew, are very different from women. And she knew this also,—that of all her immediate duties, no duty could be clearer than that of abstaining from all jealousy, petulance, and impatient expectation of little attentions. He loved her, and had told her so, and had promised her that she should be his wife, and that ought to be enough for her. She was longing for a letter, because she was very anxious to know whether she might mention his name to Lady Linlithgow;—but she would abstain from any idea of blaming him because the letter did not come.

On various occasions the countess showed some little curiosity about the lover; and at last, after about ten days, when she found herself beginning to be intimate with her new companion, she put the question point-blank. 'I hate mysteries,' she said. 'Who is the young man you are to marry?'

'He is a gentleman I've known a long time.'

'That's no answer.'

'I don't want to tell his name quite yet, Lady Linlithgow.'

'Why shouldn't you tell his name, unless it's something improper. Is he a gentleman?'

'Yes;—he is a gentleman.'

'And how old?'

'Oh, I don't know;—perhaps thirty-two.'

'And has he any money?'

'He has his profession.'

'I don't like these kind of secrets, Miss Morris. If you won't say who he is, what was the good of telling me that you were engaged at all? How is a person to believe it?'

'I don't want you to believe it.'

'Highty, tighty!'

313

'I told you my own part of the affair, because I thought you ought to know it as I was coming into your house. But I don't see that you ought to know his part of it. As for not believing, I suppose you believed Lady Fawn.'

'Not a bit better than I believe you. People don't always tell truth because they have titles, nor yet because they've grown old. He don't live in London;—does he?'

'He generally lives in London. He is a barrister.'

'Oh,—oh; a barrister is he. They're always making a heap of money, or else none at all. Which is it with him?'

'He makes something.'

'As much as you could put in your eye and see none the worse.' To see the old lady, as she made this suggestion, turn sharp round upon Lucy, was as good as a play.* 'My sister's nephew, the dean's son, is one of the best of the rising ones, I'm told.' Lucy blushed up to her hair, but the dowager's back was turned, and she did not see the blushes. 'But he's in Parliament, and they tell me he spends his money faster than he makes it. I suppose you know him?'

'Yes;—I knew him at Bobsborough.

'It's my belief that after all this fuss about Lord Fawn, he'll marry his cousin, Lizzie Eustace. If he's a lawyer, and as sharp as they say, I suppose he could manage her. I wish he would.'

'And she so bad as you say she is!'

'She'll be sure to get somebody, and why shouldn't he have her money as well as another. There never was a Greystock who didn't want money. That's what it will come to;—you'll see.'

'Never,' said Lucy decidedly.

'And why not?'

'What I mean is that Mr. Greystock is,—at least, I should think so from what I hear,—the very last man in the world to marry for money.'

'What do you know of what a man would do?'

'It would be a very mean thing;—particularly if he does not love her.'

'Bother!' said the countess. 'They were very near it in town last year before Lord Fawn came up at all. I knew as much as that. And it's what they'll come to before they've done.'

'They'll never come to it,' said Lucy.

Then a sudden light flashed across the astute mind of the countess. She turned round in her chair, and sat for awhile silent, looking at Lucy. Then she slowly asked another question. 'He isn't your young man;—is he?' To this Lucy made no reply. 'So that's it; is it,' said the dowager. 'You've done me the honour of making my house your home till my own sister's nephew shall be ready to marry you?'

'And why not?' said Lucy, rather roughly.

'And dame Greystock, from Bobsborough, has sent you here to keep you out of her son's way. I see it all. And that old frump at Richmond has passed you over to me because she did not choose to have such goings on under her own eye.'

'There have been no goings on,' said Lucy.

'And he's to come here, I suppose, when my back's turned?'

'He is not thinking of coming here. I don't know what you mean. Nobody has done anything wrong to you. I don't know why you say such cruel things.'

'He can't afford to marry you, you know.'

'I don't know anything about it. Perhaps we must wait ever so long;—five years. That's nobody's business but my own.'

'I found it all out;—didn't I?'

'Yes;—you found it out.'

'I'm thinking of that sly old dame Greystock at Bobsborough,—sending you here!' Neither on that nor on the two following days did Lady Linlithgow say a word further to Lucy about her engagement.

CHAPTER XXXV
Too Bad for Sympathy

WHEN Frank Greystock left Bobsborough to go to Scotland, he had not said that he would return, nor had he at that time made up his mind whether he would do so or no. He had promised to go and shoot in Norfolk, and had half undertaken to be up in London with Herriot working. Though it was holiday-time, still there was plenty of work for him to do,—various heavy cases to get up,* and papers to be read, if only he could settle himself down to the doing of it. But the scenes down in Scotland had been of a nature to make him unfit for steady labour. How was he to sail his bark through the rocks by which his present voyage was rendered so dangerous? Of course, to the reader, the way to do so seems to be clear enough. To work hard at his profession; to explain to his cousin that she had altogether mistaken his feelings;

and to be true to Lucy Morris was so manifestly his duty, that to no reader will it appear possible that to any gentleman there could be a doubt. Instead of the existence of a difficulty, there was a flood of light upon his path,—so the reader will think;—a flood so clear that not to see his way was impossible. A man carried away by abnormal appetites, and wickedness, and the devil, may of course commit murder, or forge bills, or become a fraudulent director of a bankrupt company. And so may a man be untrue to his troth,—and leave true love in pursuit of tinsel, and beauty, and false words, and a large income. But why should one tell the story of creatures so base? One does not willingly grovel in gutters, or breathe fetid atmospheres, or live upon garbage. If we are to deal with heroes and heroines, let us, at any rate, have heroes and heroines who are above such meanness as falsehood in love. This Frank Greystock must be little better than a mean villain, if he allows himself to be turned from his allegiance to Lucy Morris for an hour by the seductions and money of such a one as Lizzie Eustace.

We know the dear old rhyme;—

> 'It is good to be merry and wise,
> It is good to be honest and true,
> It is good to be off with the old love
> Before you are on with the new.'*

There was never better truth spoken than this, and if all men and women could follow the advice here given there would be very little sorrow in the world. But men and women do not follow it. They are no more able to do so than they are to use a spear, the staff of which is like a weaver's beam, or to fight with the sword Excalibur.* The more they exercise their arms the nearer will they get to using the giant's weapon,—or even the weapon that is divine. But as things are at present their limbs are limp and their muscles soft, and over-feeding impedes their breath. They attempt to be merry without being wise, and have theories about truth and honesty with which they desire to shackle others, thinking that freedom from such trammels may be good for themselves. And in that matter of love,—though love is very potent,—treachery will sometimes seem to be prudence, and a hankering after new delights will often interfere with real devotion.

It is very easy to depict a hero,—a man absolutely stainless, perfect as an Arthur,—a man honest in all his dealings, equal to all trials, true in all his speech, indifferent to his own prosperity, struggling for the general good, and, above all, faithful in love. At any rate, it is as easy to do that as to tell of the man who is one hour good and the next bad, who aspires greatly, but fails in practice, who sees the higher, but too often follows the lower course. There arose at one time a school of art, which delighted to paint the human face as perfect in beauty; and from that time to this we are discontented unless every woman is drawn for us as a Venus, or, at least, a Madonna. I do not know that we have gained much by this untrue portraiture, either in beauty or in art. There may be made for us a pretty thing to look at, no doubt;—but we know that that pretty thing is not really visaged as the mistress whom we serve, and whose lineaments we desire to perpetuate on the canvas. The winds of heaven, or the fleshpots of Egypt, or the midnight gas,—passions, pains, and, perhaps, rouge and powder, have made her something different. But there still is the fire of her eye, and the eager eloquence of her mouth, and something, too, perhaps, left of the departing innocence of youth, which the painter might give us without the Venus or the Madonna touches. But the painter does not dare to do it. Indeed, he has painted so long after the other fashion that he would hate the canvas before him, were he to give way to the rouge-begotten roughness or to the fleshpots,—or even to the winds. And how, my lord, would you, who are giving hundreds, more than hundreds, for this portrait of your dear one, like to see it in print from the art critic of the day, that she is a brazen-faced hoyden who seems to have had a glass of wine too much, or to have been making hay?

And so also has the reading world taught itself to like best the characters of all but divine men and women. Let the man who paints with pen and ink give the gaslight, and the fleshpots, the passions and pains, the prurient prudence and the rouge-pots and pounce-boxes of the world as it is, and he will be told that no one can care a straw for his creations. With whom are we to sympathise? says the reader, who not un-naturally imagines that a hero should be heroic. Oh, thou, my reader, whose sympathies are in truth the great and only aim of my work, when you have called the dearest of your friends round you to your hospitable table, how many heroes are there sitting at the board? Your bosom friend,—even if he be a knight without fear, is he a knight without reproach? The Ivanhoe*that you know, did he not press Rebecca's hand? Your Lord Evandale*,—did he not bring his coronet into play when he strove to win his Edith Bellenden?*Was your Tresilian*still true and still forbearing when truth and forbearance could avail him nothing? And those sweet girls whom you know, do they never doubt between the poor man they think they love, and the rich man whose riches they know they covet?

Go into the market, either to buy or sell, and name the thing you desire to part with or to get, as it is, and the market is closed against you. Middling oats are the sweepings of the granaries. A useful horse is a jade gone at every point. Good sound port is sloe juice. No assurance short of A 1* betokens even a pretence to merit. And yet in real life we are content with oats that are really middling, are very glad to have a useful horse, and know that if we drink port at all we must drink some that is neither good nor sound. In those delinea-tions of life and character which we call novels a similarly superlative vein is desired. Our own friends around us are not always merry and wise, nor, alas! always honest and true. They are often cross and foolish, and sometimes treacherous and false. They are so, and we are angry. Then we forgive them, not without a consciousness of imperfection on our own part. And we know—or, at least, believe,—that though they be sometimes treacherous and false, there is a balance of good. We cannot have heroes to dine with us. There are none. And were these heroes to be had, we should not like them. But neither are our friends villains,—whose every aspiration is for evil, and whose every moment is a struggle for some achievement worthy of the devil.

The persons whom you cannot care for in a novel, because they are so bad, are the very same that you so dearly love in your life, because they are so good. To make them and ourselves somewhat better,—not by one spring heavenwards to perfection, because we cannot so use our legs,—but by slow climbing, is, we may presume, the object of all teachers, leaders, legislators, spiritual pastors, and masters. He who writes tales such as this, probably also has, very humbly, some such object distantly before him. A picture of surpassing godlike nobleness,—a picture of a King Arthur among men, may perhaps do much. But such pictures cannot do all. When such a picture is painted, as intending to show what a man should be, it is true. If painted to show what men are, it is false. The true picture of life as it is, if it could be adequately painted, would show men what they are, and how they might rise, not, indeed, to perfection, but one step first, and then another on the ladder.

Our hero, Frank Greystock, falling lamentably short in his heroism, was not in a happy state of mind when he reached Bobsborough. It may be that he returned to his own borough and to his mother's arms because he felt, that were he to determine to be false to Lucy, he would there receive sympathy in his treachery. His mother would, at any rate, think that it was well, and his father would acknowledge that the fault committed was in the original engagement with poor Lucy, and not in the treachery. He had written that letter to her in his chambers one night in a fit of ecstasy; and could it be right that the ruin of a whole life should be the consequence?

It can hardly be too strongly asserted that Lizzie Greystock did not appear to Frank as she has been made to appear to the reader. In all this affair of the necklace he was beginning to believe that she was really an ill-used woman; and as to other traits in Lizzie's character,—traits which he had seen, and which were not of a nature to attract,—it must be remembered that beauty reclining in a man's arms does go far towards washing white the lovely blackamoor. Lady Linlithgow, upon whom Lizzie's beauty could have no effect of that kind, had nevertheless declared her to be very beautiful. And this loveliness was of a nature that was altogether pleasing, if once the beholder of it could get over the idea of falseness which certainly Lizzie's eye was apt to convey to the beholder. There was no unclean horse's tail. There was no get up of flounces, and padding, and paint, and hair, with a dorsal excrescence appended with the object surely of showing in triumph how much absurd ugliness women can force men to endure. She was lithe, and active, and bright,—and was at this moment of her life at her best. Her growing charms had as yet hardly reached the limits of full feminine loveliness,—which, when reached, have been surpassed. Luxuriant beauty had with her not as yet become comeliness; nor had age or the good things of the world added a pound to the fairy lightness of her footstep. All this had been tendered to Frank,—and with it that worldly wealth which was so absolutely necessary to his career. For though Greystock would not have said to any man or woman that nature had intended him to be a spender of much money and a consumer of many good things, he did undoubtedly so think of himself. He was a Greystock, and to what miseries would he not reduce his Lucy if, burthened by such propensities, he were to marry her and then become an aristocratic pauper!

The offer of herself by a woman to a man is, to us all, a thing so distasteful that we at once declare that the woman must be abominable. There shall be no whitewashing of Lizzie Eustace. She was abominable. But the man to whom the offer is made hardly sees the thing in the same light. He is disposed to believe that, in his peculiar case, there are circumstances by which the woman is, if not justified, at least excused. Frank did put faith in his cousin's love for himself. He did credit her when she told him that she had accepted Lord Fawn's offer in pique, because he had not come to her when he had promised that he would come. It did seem natural to him that she should have desired to adhere to her engagement when he would not advise her to depart from it. And then her jealousy about Lucy's ring, and her abuse of Lucy, were proofs to him of her love. Unless she loved him, why should she care to marry him? What was his position that she should desire to share it;—unless she so desired because he was dearer to her than aught beside? He had not eyes clear enough to perceive that his cousin was a witch whistling for a wind, and ready to take the first blast that would carry her and her broomstick somewhere into the sky. And then, in that matter of the offer, which in ordinary circumstances certainly should not have come from her to him, did not the fact of her wealth and of his comparative poverty cleanse her from such stain as would, in usual circumstances, attach to a woman who is so forward? He had not acceded to her proposition. He had not denied his engagement to Lucy. He had left her presence without a word of encouragement, because of that engagement. But he believed that Lizzie was sincere. He believed, now, that she was genuine; though he had previously been all but sure that falsehood and artifice were second nature to her.

At Bobsborough he met his constituents, and made them the normal autumn speech. The men of Bobsborough were well pleased and gave him a vote of confidence. As none but those of his own party attended the meeting, it was not wonderful that the vote was unanimous. His father, mother, and sister all heard his speech, and there was a strong family feeling that Frank was born to set the Greystocks once more upon their legs. When a man can say what he likes with the certainty that every word will be reported, and can speak to those around him as one manifestly their superior, he always looms large. When the Conservatives should return to their proper place at the head of affairs, there could be no doubt that Frank Greystock would be made Solicitor-General. There were not wanting even ardent admirers who conceived that, with such claims and such talents as his, the ordinary steps in political promotion would not be needed, and that he would become Attorney-General at once. All men began to say all good things to the dean, and to Mrs. Greystock it seemed that the woolsack, or at least the Queen's Bench with a peerage, was hardly an uncertainty. But then,—there must be no marriage with a penniless governess. If he would only marry his cousin one might say that the woolsack was won.

Then came Lucy's letter; the pretty, dear, joking letter about the 'duchess,' and broken hearts. 'I would break my heart, only—only, only——' Yes, he knew very well what she meant. I shall never be called upon to break my heart, because you are not a false scoundrel. If you were a false scoundrel,—instead of being, as you are, a pearl among men, —then I should break my heart. That was what Lucy meant. She could not have been much clearer, and he understood it perfectly. It is very nice to walk about one's own borough and be voted unanimously worthy of confidence, and be a great man; but if you are a scoundrel, and not used to being a scoundrel, black care is apt to sit very close behind you as you go caracolling*along the streets.

Lucy's letter required an answer, and how should he answer it? He certainly did not wish her to tell Lady Linlithgow of her engagement, but Lucy clearly wished to be allowed to tell, and on what ground could he enjoin her to be silent? He knew, or he thought he knew, that till he answered the letter, she would not tell his secret,—and therefore from day to day he put off the answer. A man does not write a love-letter easily when he is in doubt himself whether he does or does not mean to be a scoundrel.

Then there came a letter to 'Dame' Greystock from Lady Linlithgow, which filled them all with amazement.

'MY DEAR MADAM,'—began the letter,—

'Seeing that your son is engaged to marry Miss Morris,—at least she says so,—you ought not to have sent her here without telling me all about it. She says you know of the match, and she says that I can write to you if I please. Of course, I can do that without her leave. But it seems to me that if you know all about it, and approve the marriage, your house and not mine would be the proper place for her.

'I'm told that Mr. Greystock is a great man. Any lady being with me as my companion can't be a great woman. But perhaps you wanted to break it off;—else you would have told me. She shall stay here six months, but then she must go.

'Yours truly,

SUSANNA LINLITHGOW.'

It was considered absolutely necessary that this letter should be shown to Frank. 'You see,' said his mother, 'she told the old lady at once.'

'I don't see why she shouldn't.' Nevertheless Frank was annoyed. Having asked for permission, Lucy should at least have waited for a reply.

'Well; I don't know,' said Mrs. Greystock. 'It is generally considered that young ladies are more reticent about such things. She has blurted it out and boasted about it at once.'

'I thought girls always told of their engagements,' said Frank, 'and I can't for the life of me see that there was any boasting in it.' Then he was silent for a moment. 'The truth is, we are, all of us, treating Lucy very badly.'

'I cannot say that I see it,' said his mother.

'We ought to have had her here.'

'For how long, Frank?'

'For as long as a home was needed by her.'

'Had you demanded it, Frank, she should have come, of course. But neither I nor your father could have had pleasure in receiving her as your future wife. You, yourself, say that it cannot be for two years at least.'

'I said one year.'

'I think, Frank, you said two. And we all know that such a marriage would be ruinous to you. How could we make her welcome? Can you see your way to having a house for her to live in within twelve months?'

'Why not a house? I could have a house to-morrow.'

'Such a house as would suit you in your position? And, Frank, would it be a kindness to marry her and then let her find that you were in debt?'

'I don't believe she'd care, if she had nothing but a crust to eat.'

'She ought to care, Frank.'

'I think,' said the dean to his son, on the next day, 'that in our class of life an imprudent marriage is the one thing that should be avoided. My marriage has been very happy, God knows; but I have always been a poor man, and feel it now when I am quite unable to help you. And yet your mother had some fortune. Nobody, I think, cares less for wealth than I do. I am content almost with nothing.'—The nothing with which the dean had hitherto been contented had always included every comfort of life, a well-kept table, good wine, new books, and canonical habiliments*with the gloss still on; but as the Bobsborough tradesmen had, through the agency of Mrs. Greystock, always supplied him with these things as though they came from the clouds, he really did believe that he had never asked for anything.—'I am content almost with nothing. But I do feel that marriage cannot be adopted as the ordinary form of life by men in our class as it can be by the rich or by the poor. You, for instance, are called upon to live with the rich, but are not rich. That can only be done by wary walking, and is hardly consistent with a wife and children.'

'But men in my position do marry, sir.'

'After a certain age,—or else they marry ladies with money. You see, Frank, there are not many men who go into Parliament with means so moderate as yours; and they who do perhaps have stricter ideas of economy.' The dean did not say a word about Lucy Morris, and dealt entirely with generalities.

In compliance with her son's advice,—or almost command, —Mrs. Greystock did not answer Lady Linlithgow's letter. He was going back to London, and would give personally, or by letter written there, what answer might be necessary. 'You will then see Miss Morris?' asked his mother.

'I shall certainly see Lucy. Something must be settled.' There was a tone in his voice as he said this which gave some comfort to his mother.

CHAPTER XXXVI
Lizzie's Guests

TRUE to their words, at the end of October, Mrs. Carbuncle and Miss Roanoke, and Lord George de Bruce Carruthers, and Sir Griffin Tewett, arrived at Portray Castle. And for a couple of days there was a visitor whom Lizzie was very glad to welcome, but of whose good nature on the occasion Mr. Camperdown thought very ill indeed. This was John Eustace. His sister-in-law wrote to him in very pressing language; and as,—so he said to Mr. Camperdown,—he did not wish to seem to quarrel with his brother's widow as long as such seeming might be avoided, he accepted the invitation. If there was to be a lawsuit about the diamonds, that must be Mr. Camperdown's affair. Lizzie had never entertained her friends in style before. She had had a few people to dine with her in London, and once or twice had received company on an evening. But in all her London doings there had been the trepidation of fear,—to be accounted for by her youth and widowhood; and it was at Portray,—her own house at Portray,—that it would best become her to exercise hospitality. She had bided her time even there, but now she meant to show her friends that she had got a house of her own.

She wrote even to her husband's uncle, the bishop, asking him down to Portray. He could not come, but sent an affectionate answer, and thanked her for thinking of him. Many people she asked who, she felt sure, would not come,— and one or two of them accepted her invitation. John Eustace promised to be with her for two days. When Frank had left her, going out of her presence in the manner that has been described, she actually wrote to him, begging him to join her party. This was her note.

'Come to me, just for a week,' she said, 'when my people are here, so that I may not seem to be deserted. Sit at the bottom of my table, and be to me as a brother might. I shall expect you to do so much for me.' To this he had replied that he would come during the first week in November.

And she got a clergyman down from London, the Rev. Joseph Emilius, of whom it was said that he was born a Jew in Hungary, and that his name in his own country had been Mealyus. At the present time he was among the most eloquent of London preachers, and was reputed by some to have reached such a standard of pulpit-oratory, as to have had no equal within the memory of living hearers. In regard to his reading it was acknowledged that no one since Mrs. Siddons had touched him. But he did not get on very well with any particular bishop, and there was doubt in the minds of some people whether there was or was not any—Mrs. Emilius. He had come up quite suddenly within the last season, and had made church-going quite a pleasant occupation to Lizzie Eustace.

On the last day of October, Mr. Emilius and Mr. John Eustace came each alone. Mrs. Carbuncle and Miss Roanoke came over with post-horses from Ayr,—as also did Lord George and Sir Griffin about an hour after them. Frank was not yet expected. He had promised to name a day and had not yet named it.

'Varra weel; varra weel,' Gowran had said when he was told of what was about to occur, and was desired to make preparations necessary in regard to the outside plenishing of the house; 'nae doobt she'll do with her ain, what pleases her ainself. The mair ye poor out, the less there'll be left in. Mr. Jo-ohn coming? I'll be glad then to see Mr. Jo-ohn. Oo, ay; aits,—there'll be aits eneuch. And anither coo? You'll want twa ither coos. I'll see to the coos.' And Andy Gowran, in spite of the internecine warfare which existed between him and his mistress, did see to the hay, and the cows, and the oats, and the extra servants that were wanted both inside and outside the house. There was enmity between him and Lady Eustace, and he didn't care who knew it;—but he took her wages and he did her work.

Mrs. Carbuncle was a wonderful woman. She was the wife
of a man with whom she was very rarely seen, whom nobody
knew, who was something in the City, but somebody who
never suceeded in making money; and yet she went everywhere. She had at least the reputation of going everywhere,
and did go to a great many places. Carbuncle had no money,—
so it was said; and she had none. She was the daughter of a
man who had gone to New York and had failed there. Of her
own parentage no more was known. She had a small house in
one of the very small Mayfair streets, to which she was wont
to invite her friends for five o'clock tea. Other receptions she
never attempted. During the London seasons she always kept
a carriage, and during the winters she always had hunters.
Who paid for them no one knew or cared. Her dress was
always perfect,—as far as fit and performance went. As to
approving Mrs. Carbuncle's manner of dress,—that was a
question of taste. Audacity may, perhaps, be said to have been
the ruling principle of her toilet;—not the audacity of in-
decency, which, let the satirists say what they may, is not
efficacious in England, but audacity in colour, audacity in
design, and audacity in construction. She would ride in the
park in a black and yellow habit, and appear at the opera in
white velvet without a speck of colour. Though certainly
turned thirty, and probably nearer to forty, she would wear
her jet-black hair streaming down her back, and when June
came would drive about London in a straw hat. But yet it was
always admitted that she was well dressed. And then would
arise that question, Who paid the bills?

Mrs. Carbuncle was certainly a handsome woman. She was
full-faced,—with bold eyes, rather far apart, perfect black eyebrows, a well-formed broad nose, thick lips, and regular teeth.
Her chin was round and short, with, perhaps, a little bearing
towards a double chin. But though her face was plump and
round, there was a power in it, and a look of command of
which it was, perhaps, difficult to say in what features was the
seat. But in truth the mind will lend a tone to every feature,
and it was the desire of Mrs. Carbuncle's heart to command.

But perhaps the wonder of her face was its complexion. People said,—before they knew her, that, as a matter of course, she had been made beautiful for ever. But, though that too brilliant colour was almost always there, covering the cheeks but never touching the forehead or the neck, it would at certain moments shift, change, and even depart. When she was angry, it would vanish for a moment and then return intensified. There was no chemistry on Mrs. Carbuncle's cheek; and yet it was a tint so brilliant and so little transparent, as almost to justify a conviction that it could not be genuine. There were those who declared that nothing in the way of complexion so beautiful as that of Mrs. Carbuncle's had been seen on the face of any other woman in this age, and there were others who called her an exaggerated milkmaid. She was tall, too, and had learned so to walk as though half the world belonged to her.

Her niece, Miss Roanoke, was a lady of the same stamp, and of similar beauty, with those additions and also with those drawbacks which belong to youth. She looked as though she were four-and-twenty, but in truth she was no more than eighteen. When seen beside her aunt, she seemed to be no more than half the elder lady's size; and yet her proportions were not insignificant. She, too, was tall, and was as one used to command, and walked as though she were a young Juno.* Her hair was very dark,—almost black,—and very plentiful. Her eyes were large and bright, though too bold for a girl so young. Her nose and mouth were exactly as her aunt's, but her chin was somewhat longer, so as to divest her face of that plump roundness, which, perhaps, took something from the majesty of Mrs. Carbuncle's appearance. Miss Roanoke's complexion was certainly marvellous. No one thought that she had been made beautiful for ever, for the colour would go and come and shift and change with every word and every thought;—but still it was there, as deep on her cheeks as on her aunt's, though somewhat more transparent, and with more delicacy of tint as the bright hues faded away and became merged in the almost marble whiteness of her skin. With Mrs.

Carbuncle there was no merging and fading. The red and white bordered one another on her cheek without any merging, as they do on a flag.

Lucinda Roanoke was undoubtedly a very handsome woman. It probably never occurred to man or woman to say that she was lovely. She had sat for her portrait during the last winter, and her picture had caused much remark in the Exhibition. Some said that she might be a Brinvilliers,* others a Cleopatra,* and others again a Queen of Sheba.* In her eyes as they were limned there had been nothing certainly of love, but they who likened her to the Egyptian queen believed that Cleopatra's love had always been used simply to assist her ambition. They who took the Brinvilliers side of the controversy were men so used to softness and flattery from women as to have learned to think that a woman silent, arrogant, and hard of approach, must be always meditating murder. The disciples of the Queen of Sheba school, who formed, perhaps, the more numerous party, were led to their opinion by the majesty of Lucinda's demeanour rather than by any clear idea in their own minds of the lady who visited Solomon. All men, however, agreed in this, that Lucinda Roanoke was very handsome, but that she was not the sort of girl with whom a man would wish to stray away through the distant beech-trees at a picnic.

In truth she was silent, grave, and, if not really haughty, subject to all the signs of haughtiness. She went everywhere with her aunt, and allowed herself to be walked out at dances, and to be accosted when on horseback, and to be spoken to at parties; but she seemed hardly to trouble herself to talk,— and as for laughing, flirting, or giggling, one might as well expect such levity from a marble Minerva.* During the last winter she had taken to hunting with her aunt, and already could ride well to hounds. If assistance were wanted at a gate, or in the management of a fence, and the servant who attended the two ladies were not near enough to give it, she would accept it as her due from the man nearest to her; but she rarely did more than bow her thanks, and, even by young lords, or hard-riding handsome colonels, or squires of undoubted thousands, she could hardly ever be brought to what might be called a proper hunting-field conversation. All of which things were noted, and spoken of, and admired. It must be presumed that Lucinda Roanoke was in want of a husband, and yet no girl seemed to take less pains to get one. A girl ought not to be always busying herself to bring down a man, but a girl ought to give herself some charm. A girl so handsome as Lucinda Roanoke, with pluck enough to ride like a bird, dignity enough for a duchess, and who was undoubtedly clever, ought to put herself in the way of taking such good things as her charms and merits would bring her;—but Lucinda Roanoke stood aloof and despised everybody. So it was that Lucinda was spoken of when her name was mentioned; and her name was mentioned a good deal after the opening of the exhibition of pictures.

There was some difficulty about her,—as to who she was. That she was an American was the received opinion. Her mother, as well as Mrs. Carbuncle, had certainly been in New York. Carbuncle was a London man; but it was supposed that Mr. Roanoke was, or had been, an American. The received opinion was correct. Lucinda had been born in New York, had been educated there till she was sixteen, had then been taken to Paris for nine months, and from Paris had been brought to London by her aunt. Mrs. Carbuncle always spoke of Lucinda's education as having been thoroughly Parisian. Of her own education and antecedents, Lucinda never spoke at all. 'I'll tell you what it is,' said a young scamp from Eton to his elder sister, when her character and position were once being discussed. 'She's a heroine, and would shoot a fellow as soon as look at him.' In that scamp's family, Lucinda was ever afterwards called the heroine.

The manner in which Lord George de Bruce Carruthers had attached himself to these ladies was a mystery;—but then Lord George was always mysterious. He was a young man,— so considered,—about forty-five years of age, who had never done anything in the manner of other people. He hunted a great deal, but he did not fraternize with hunting men, and would appear now in this county and now in that, with an utmost disregard of grass, fences, friendships, or foxes. Leicester, Essex, Ayrshire, or the Baron*had equal delights for him; and in all counties he was quite at home. He had never owned a fortune, and had never been known to earn a shilling. It was said that early in life he had been apprenticed to an attorney at Aberdeen as George Carruthers. His third cousin, the Marquis of Killiecrankie, had been killed out hunting; the second scion of the noble family had fallen at Balaclava; a third had perished in the Indian Mutiny; and a fourth, who did reign for a few months, died suddenly, leaving a large family of daughters. Within three years the four brothers vanished, leaving among them no male heir, and George's elder brother, who was then in a West India Regiment, was called home from Demerara to be Marquis of Killiecrankie. By a usual exercise of the courtesy of the Crown, all the brothers were made lords, and some twelve years before the date of our story George Carruthers, who had long since left the attorney's office at Aberdeen, became Lord George de Bruce Carruthers. How he lived no one knew. That his brother did much for him was presumed to be impossible, as the property entailed on the Killiecrankie title certainly was not large. He sometimes went into the City, and was supposed to know something about shares. Perhaps he played a little, and made a few bets. He generally lived with men of means;—or perhaps with one man of means at a time; but they, who knew him well, declared that he never borrowed a shilling from a friend, and never owed a guinea to a tradesman. He always had horses, but never had a home. When in London he lodged in a single room, and dined at his club. He was a Colonel of Volunteers,* having got up the regiment known as the Long Shore Riflemen,—the roughest regiment of Volunteers in all England,—and was reputed to be a bitter Radical.* He was suspected even of republican sentiments, and ignorant young men about London hinted that he was the grand centre of the British Fenians.* He had been invited to stand for the Tower Hamlets,* but had told the deputation which waited upon him that he knew a thing worth two of that. Would they guarantee his expenses, and then give him a salary? The deputation doubted its ability to promise so much. 'I more than doubt it,' said Lord George; and then the deputation went away.

In person he was a long-legged, long-bodied, long-faced man, with rough whiskers and a rough beard on his upper lip, but with a shorn chin. His eyes were very deep set in his head, and his cheeks were hollow and sallow, and yet he looked to be and was a powerful, healthy man. He had large hands, which seemed to be all bone, and long arms, and a neck which looked to be long; because he so wore his shirt that much of his throat was always bare. It was manifest enough that he liked to have good-looking women about him, and yet nobody presumed it probable that he would marry. For the last two or three years there had been friendship between him and Mrs. Carbuncle; and during the last season he had become almost intimate with our Lizzie. Lizzie thought that perhaps he might be the Corsair whom, sooner or later in her life, she must certainly encounter.

Sir Griffin Tewett, who at the present period of his existence was being led about by Lord George, was not exactly an amiable young baronet. Nor were his circumstances such as make a man amiable. He was nominally, not only the heir to, but actually the possessor of, a large property;—but he could not touch the principal, and of the income only so much as certain legal curmudgeons* would allow him. As Greystock had said, everybody was at law with him,—so successful had been his father, in mismanaging, and miscontrolling, and mis-appropriating the property. Tewett Hall had gone to rack and ruin for four years, and was now let almost for nothing. He was a fair, frail young man, with a bad eye, and a weak mouth, and a thin hand, who was fond of liqueurs, and hated to the death any acquaintance who won a five-pound note of him, or any tradesman who wished to have his bill paid. But he had this redeeming quality,—that having found Lucinda

Roanoke to be the handsomest woman he had ever seen, he did desire to make her his wife.

Such were the friends whom Lizzie Eustace received at Portray Castle on the first day of her grand hospitality,—together with John Eustace and Mr. Joseph Emilius, the fashionable preacher from Mayfair.

CHAPTER XXXVII
Lizzie's First Day

THE coming of John Eustace was certainly a great thing for Lizzie, though it was only for two days. It saved her from that feeling of desertion before her friends,—desertion by those who might naturally belong to her,—which would otherwise have afflicted her. His presence there for two days gave her a start. She could call him John, and bring down her boy to him, and remind him, with the sweetest smile,—with almost a tear in her eye,—that he was the boy's guardian. 'Little fellow! So much depends on that little life,—does it not, John?' she said, whispering the words into his ear.

'Lucky little dog!' said John, patting the boy's head. 'Let me see! of course he'll go to Eton.'

'Not yet,' said Lizzie with a shudder.

'Well; no; hardly;—when he's twelve.' And then the boy was done with and was carried away. She had played that card and had turned her trick. John Eustace was a thoroughly good-natured man of the world, who could forgive many faults, not expecting people to be perfect. He did not like Mrs. Carbuncle;—was indifferent to Lucinda's beauty;—was afraid of that Tartar, Lord George;—and thoroughly despised Sir Griffin. In his heart he believed Mr. Emilius to be an impostor, who might, for aught he knew, pick his pocket; and Miss Macnulty had no attraction for him. But he smiled, and was gay, and called Lady Eustace by her Christian name, and was content to be of use to her in showing her friends that she had not been altogether dropped by the Eustace people. 'I got such a nice affectionate letter from the dear bishop,' said Lizzie, 'but he couldn't come. He could not escape a previous engagement.'

'It's a long way,' said John, 'and he's not so young as he was once;—and then there are the Bobsborough parsons to look after.'

'I don't suppose anything of that kind stops him,' said Lizzie, who did not think it possible that a bishop's bliss should be alloyed by work. John was so very nice that she almost made up her mind to talk to him about the necklace; but she was cautious, and thought of it, and found that it would be better that she should abstain. John Eustace was certainly very good-natured, but perhaps he might say an ugly word to her if she were rash. She refrained, therefore, and after breakfast on the second day he took his departure without an allusion to things that were unpleasant.

'I call my brother-in-law a perfect gentleman,' said Lizzie with enthusiasm, when his back was turned.

'Certainly,' said Mrs. Carbuncle. 'He seems to me to be very quiet.'

'He didn't quite like his party,' said Lord George.

'I am sure he did,' said Lizzie.

'I mean as to politics. To him we are all turbulent demagogues and Bohemians.* Eustace is an old-world Tory, if there's one left anywhere. But you're right, Lady Eustace; he is a gentleman.'

'He knows on which side his bread is buttered as well as any man,' said Sir Griffin.

'Am I a demagogue,' said Lizzie, appealing to the Corsair, 'or a Bohemian? I didn't know it.'

'A little in that way, I think, Lady Eustace;—not a demagogue, but demagognical;—not a Bohemian, but that way given.'

'And is Miss Roanoke demagognical?'

'Certainly,' said Lord George. 'I hardly wrong you there, Miss Roanoke?'

'Lucinda is a democrat, but hardly a demagogue, Lord George,' said Mrs. Carbuncle.

'Those are distinctions which we hardly understand on this thick-headed side of the water. But demagogues, democrats, demonstrations, and Demosthenic oratory* are all equally odious to John Eustace. For a young man he's about the best Tory I know.'

'He is true to his colours,' said Mr. Emilius, who had been endeavouring to awake the attention of Miss Roanoke on the subject of Shakespeare's dramatic action, 'and I like men who are true to their colours.' Mr. Emilius spoke with the slightest possible tone of a foreign accent,—a tone so slight that it simply served to attract attention to him.

While Eustace was still in the house, there had come a letter from Frank Greystock, saying that he would reach Portray, by way of Glasgow, on Wednesday, the 5th of November. He must sleep in Glasgow on that night, having business, or friends, or pleasure demanding his attention in that prosperous mart of commerce. It had been impressed upon him that he should hunt, and he had consented. There was to be a meet out on the Kilmarnock side of the county on that Wednesday, and he would bring a horse with him from Glasgow. Even in Glasgow a hunter was to be hired, and could be sent forty or fifty miles out of the town in the morning and brought back in the evening. Lizzie had learned all about that, and had told him. If he would call at Mac-Farlane's stables in Buchanan Street, or even write to Mr. MacFarlane, he would be sure to get a horse that would carry him. MacFarlane was sending horses down into the Ayrshire country every day of his life. It was simply an affair of money. Three guineas for the horse, and then just the expense of the railway. Frank, who knew quite as much about it as did his cousin, and who never thought much of guineas or of railway tickets, promised to meet the party at the meet ready equipped. His things would go on by train, and Lizzie must send for them to Troon. He presumed a beneficent Providence would take the horse back to the bosom of Mr. MacFarlane. Such was the tenour of his letter. 'If he don't mind, he'll find himself astray,' said Sir Griffin. 'He'll have to go one way by rail and his horse another.' 'We can manage better for our cousin than that,' said Lizzie, with a rebuking nod.

But there was hunting from Portray before Frank Greystock came. It was specially a hunting party, and Lizzie was to be introduced to the glories of the field. In giving her her due, it must be acknowledged that she was fit for the work. She rode well, though she had not ridden to hounds, and her courage was cool. She looked well on horseback, and had that presence of mind which should never desert a lady when she is hunting. A couple of horses had been purchased for her, under Lord George's superintendence,—his conjointly with Mrs. Carbuncle's,—and had been at the castle for the last ten days—'eating their varra heeds off,' as Andy Gowran had said in sorrow. There had been practising even while John Eustace was there, and before her preceptors had slept three nights at the castle, she had ridden backwards and forwards, half-a-dozen times, over a stone wall. 'Oh yes,' Lucinda had said, in answer to a remark from Sir Griffin, 'It's easy enough,—till you come across something difficult.'

'Nothing difficult stops you,' said Sir Griffin;—to which compliment Lucinda vouchsafed no reply.

On the Monday Lizzie went out hunting for the first time in her life. It must be owned that, as she put her habit on, and afterwards breakfasted with all her guests in hunting gear around her, and then was driven with them in her own carriage to the meet, there was something of trepidation at her heart. And her feeling of cautious fear in regard to money had received a shock. Mrs. Carbuncle had told her that a couple of horses fit to carry her might perhaps cost her about £180. Lord George had received the commission, and the cheque required from her had been for £320. Of course she had written the cheque without a word, but it did begin to occur to her that hunting was an expensive amusement. Gowran had informed her that he had bought a rick of hay from a neighbour for £75 15s. 9d. 'God forgie me,' said Andy, 'but I b'lieve I've been o'er hard on the puir man in your leddyship's service.' £75 15s. 9d. did seem a great deal of money to pay; and could it be necessary that she should buy a whole rick? There were to be eight horses in the stable. To what friend could she apply to learn how much of a rick of hay one horse ought to eat in a month of hunting? In such a matter she might have trusted Andy Gowran implicitly; but how was she to know that? And then, what if at some desperate fence she were to be thrown off and break her nose and knock out her front teeth! Was the game worth the candle? She was by no means sure that she liked Mrs. Carbuncle very much. And though she liked Lord George very well, could it be possible that he bought the horses for £90 each and charged her £160? Corsairs do do these sort of things. The horses themselves were two sweet dears, with stars on their foreheads, and shining coats, and a delicious aptitude for jumping over everything at a moment's notice. Lord George had not, in truth, made a penny by them, and they were good hunters, worth the money;—but how was Lizzie to know that? But though she doubted, and was full of fears, she could smile and look as though she liked it. If the worst should come she could certainly get money for the diamonds.

On that Monday, the meet was comparatively near to them,—distant only twelve miles. On the following Wednesday it would be sixteen, and they would use the railway—having the carriage sent to meet them in the evening. The three ladies and Lord George filled the carriage, and Sir Griffin was perched upon the box. The ladies' horses had gone on with two grooms, and those for Lord George and Sir Griffin were to come to the meet. Lizzie felt somewhat proud of her establishment and her equipage;—but at the same time somewhat fearful. Hitherto she knew but very little of the county people, and was not sure how she might be received;—and then how would it be with her, if the fox should at once start away across country, and she should lack either the pluck or the power to follow? There was Sir Griffin to look after Miss Roanoke, and Lord George to attend to Mrs. Carbuncle. At last an idea so horrible struck her that she could not keep it down. 'What am I to do,' she said, 'if I find myself all alone in a field, and everybody else gone away!'

'We won't treat you quite in that fashion,' said Mrs. Carbuncle.

'The only possible way in which you can be alone in a field is that you will have cut everybody else down,' said Lord George.

'I suppose it will come right,' said Lizzie, plucking up her courage, and telling herself that a woman can die but once.

Everything was right,—as it usually is. The horses were there,—quite a throng of horses, as the two gentlemen had two each; and there was, moreover, a mounted groom to look after the three ladies. Lizzie had desired to have a groom to herself, but had been told that the expenditure in horseflesh was more than the stable could stand. 'All I ever want of a man is to carry for me my flask, and waterproof, and luncheon,' said Mrs. Carbuncle. 'I don't care if I never see a groom, except for that.'

'It's convenient to have a gate opened sometimes,' said Lucinda slowly.

'Will no one but a groom do that for you?' asked Sir Griffin.

'Gentlemen can't open gates,' said Lucinda. Now, as Sir Griffin thought that he had opened many gates during the last season for Miss Roanoke, he felt this to be hard.

But there were eight horses, and eight horses with three servants and a carriage made quite a throng. Among the crowd of Ayrshire hunting men,—a lord or two, a dozen lairds, two dozen farmers, and as many men of business out of Ayr, Kilmarnock, and away from Glasgow,—it was soon told that Lady Eustace and her party were among them. A good deal had been already heard of Lizzie, and it was at least known of her that she had, for her life, the Portray estate in her hands. So there was an undercurrent of whispering, and that sort of commotion which the appearance of new-comers does produce at a hunt-meet. Lord George knew one or two men, who were surprised to find him in Ayrshire, and Mrs. Carbuncle was soon quite at home with a young nobleman whom she had met in the vale with the Baron. Sir Griffin did not leave Lucinda's side, and for a while poor Lizzie felt herself alone in a crowd.

Who does not know that terrible feeling, and the all but necessity that exists for the sufferer to pretend that he is not suffering,—which again is aggravated by the conviction that the pretence is utterly vain? This may be bad with a man, but with a woman, who never looks to be alone in a crowd, it is terrible. For five minutes, during which everybody else was speaking to everybody,—for five minutes, which seemed to her to be an hour, Lizzie spoke to no one, and no one spoke to her. Was it for such misery as this that she was spending hundreds upon hundreds, and running herself into debt? For she was sure that there would be debt before she had parted with Mrs. Carbuncle. There are people, very many people, to whom an act of hospitality is in itself a good thing; but there are others who are always making calculations, and endeavouring to count up the thing purchased against the cost. Lizzie had been told that she was a rich woman,—as women go, very rich. Surely she was entitled to entertain a few friends; and if Mrs. Carbuncle and Miss Roanoke could hunt, it could not be that hunting was beyond her own means. And yet she was spending a great deal of money. She had seen a large waggon loaded with sacks of corn coming up the hill to the Portray stables, and she knew that there would be a long bill at the corn-chandler's. There had been found a supply of wine in the cellars at Portray,—which at her request had been inspected by her cousin Frank;—but it had been necessary, so he had told her, to have much more sent down from London,—champagne, and liqueurs, and other nice things that cost money. 'You won't like not to have them if these people are coming?' 'Oh, no;

certainly not,' said Lizzie with enthusiasm. What other rich people did, she would do. But now, in her five minutes of misery, she counted it all up, and was at a loss to find what was to be her return for her expenditure. And then, if on this her first day she should have a fall, with no tender hand to help her, and then find that she had knocked out her front teeth!

But the cavalcade began to move, and then Lord George was by her side. 'You mustn't be angry if I seem to stick too close to you,' he said. She gave him her sweetest smile as she told him that that would be impossible. 'Because, you know, though it's the easiest thing in the world to get along out hunting, and women never come to grief, a person is a little astray at first.'

'I shall be so much astray,' said Lizzie. 'I don't at all know how we are going to begin. Are we hunting a fox now?' At this moment they were trotting across a field or two, through a run of gates up to the first covert.*

'Not quite yet. The hounds haven't been put in yet.* You see that wood there? I suppose they'll draw*that.'

'What is drawing, Lord George? I want to know all about it, and I am so ignorant. Nobody else will tell me.' Then Lord George gave his lesson, and explained the theory and system of fox-hunting. 'We're to wait here, then, till the fox runs away? But it's ever so large, and if he runs away, and nobody sees him? I hope he will, because it will be nice to go on easily.'

'A great many people hope that, and a great many think it nice to go on easily. Only you must not confess to it.' Then he went on with his lecture, and explained the meaning of scent,* was great on the difficulty of getting away,* described the iniquity of heading the fox,* spoke of up wind*and down wind,* got as far as the trouble of 'carrying,'*and told her that a good ear was everything in a big wood,—when there came upon them the thrice-repeated note of an old hound's voice, and the quick scampering, and low, timid, anxious, trustful whinnying of a dozen comrade younger hounds, who

recognised the sagacity of their well-known and highly-appreci-
ated elder,—'That's a fox,' said Lord George.

'What shall I do now?' said Lizzie, all in a twitter.

'Sit just where you are and light a cigar, if you're given to
smoking.'

'Pray don't joke with me. You know I want to do it
properly.'

'And therefore you must sit just where you are, and not
gallop about. There's a matter of a hundred and twenty
acres here, I should say, and a fox doesn't always choose to
be evicted at the first notice. It's a chance whether he goes
at all from a wood like this. I like woods myself, because,
as you say, we can take it easy; but if you want to ride, you
should—— By George, they've killed him!'

'Killed the fox?'

'Yes; he's dead. Didn't you hear?'

'And is that a hunt?'

'Well;—as far as it goes, it is.'

'Why didn't he run away? What a stupid beast! I don't
see so very much in that. Who killed him? That man that was
blowing the horn?'

'The hounds chopped him.'*

'Chopped him!' Lord George was very patient, and explained to Lizzie, who was now indignant and disappointed,
the misfortune of chopping. 'And are we to go home now?
Is it all over?'

'They say the country is full of foxes,' said Lord George.
'Perhaps we shall chop half-a-dozen.'

'Dear me! Chop half-a-dozen foxes! Do they like to be
chopped? I thought they always ran away.'

Lord George was constant and patient, and rode at Lizzie's
side from covert to covert. A second fox they did kill in the
same fashion as the first; a third they couldn't hunt a yard;
a fourth got to ground*after five minutes, and was dug out*
ingloriously;—during which process a drizzling rain commenced. 'Where is the man with my waterproof?' demanded
Mrs. Carbuncle. Lord George had sent the man to see whether

there was shelter to be had in a neighbouring yard. And Mrs. Carbuncle was angry. 'It's my own fault,' she said, 'for not having my own man. Lucinda, you'll be wet.'

'I don't mind the wet,' said Lucinda. Lucinda never did mind anything.

'If you'll come with me, we'll get into a barn,' said Sir Griffin.

'I like the wet,' said Lucinda. All the while seven men were at work with picks and shovels, and the master and four or five of the more ardent sportsmen were deeply engaged in what seemed to be a mining operation on a small scale. The huntsman stood over giving his orders. One enthusiastic man, who had been lying on his belly, grovelling in the mud for five minutes, with a long stick in his hand, was now applying the point of it scientifically to his nose. An ordinary observer with a magnifying-glass might have seen a hair at the end of the stick. 'He's there,' said the enthusiastic man, covered with mud, after a long-drawn, eager sniff at the stick. The huntsman deigned to give one glance. 'That's rabbit,' said the huntsman. A conclave was immediately formed over the one visible hair that stuck to the stick, and three experienced farmers decided that it was rabbit. The muddy enthusiastic man, silenced but not convinced, retired from the crowd, leaving his stick behind him, and comforted himself with his brandy-flask.

'He's here, my lord,' said the huntsman to his noble master, 'only we ain't got nigh him yet.' He spoke almost in a whisper, so that the ignorant crowd should not hear the words of wisdom, which they wouldn't understand or perhaps believe. 'It's that full of rabbits that the holes is all hairs. They ain't got no terrier here, I suppose. They never has aught that is wanted in these parts. Work round to the right, there;——that's his line.' The men did work round to the right, and in something under an hour the fox was dragged out by his brush and hind legs, while the experienced whip who dragged him held the poor brute tight by the back of his neck. 'An old dog, my lord. There's such a many of 'em here,

that they'll be a deal better for a little killing.' Then the
hounds ate their third fox for that day.

Lady Eustace, in the meantime, and Mrs. Carbuncle, with
Lord George, had found their way to the shelter of a cattle-
shed. Lucinda had slowly followed, and Sir Griffin had
followed her. The gentlemen smoked cigars, and the ladies,
when they had eaten their luncheons and drank their sherry,
were cold and cross. 'If this is hunting,' said Lizzie, 'I really
don't think so much about it.'

'It's Scotch hunting,' said Mrs. Carbuncle.

'I have seen foxes dug out south of the Tweed,' suggested
Lord George.

'I suppose everything is slow after the Baron,' said Mrs.
Carbuncle, who had distinguished herself with the Baron's
stag-hounds last March.

'Are we to go home now?' asked Lizzie, who would have
been well-pleased to have received an answer in the affirmative.

'I presume they'll draw again,' exclaimed Mrs. Carbuncle,
with an angry frown on her brow. 'It's hardly two o'clock.'

'They always draw till seven, in Scotland,' said Lord
George.

'That's nonsense,' said Mrs. Carbuncle. 'It's dark at four.'

'They have torches in Scotland,' said Lord George.

'They have a great many things in Scotland that are very
far from agreeable,' said Mrs. Carbuncle. 'Lucinda, did you
ever see three foxes killed without five minutes' running,
before? I never did.'

'I've been out all day without finding at all,' said Lucinda,
who loved the truth.

'And so have I,' said Sir Griffin;—'often. Don't you
remember that day when we went down from London to
Bringher Wood, and they pretended to find at half-past
four? That's what I call a sell.'

'They're going on, Lady Eustace,' said Lord George. 'If
you're not tired, we might as well see it out.' Lizzie was
tired, but said that she was not, and she did see it out. They

found a fifth fox, but again there was no scent. 'Who the —— is to hunt a fox with people scurrying about like that!' said the huntsman, very angrily, dashing forward at a couple of riders. 'The hounds is behind you, only you ain't a looking. Some people never do look!' The two peccant* riders unfortunately were Sir Griffin and Lucinda.

The day was one of those from which all the men and women return home cross, and which induce some half-hearted folk to declare to themselves that they never will hunt again. When the master decided a little after three that he would draw no more, because there wasn't a yard of scent, our party had nine or ten miles to ride back to their carriages. Lizzie was very tired, and, when Lord George took her from her horse, could almost have cried from fatigue. Mrs. Carbuncle was never fatigued, but she had become damp,— soaking wet through, as she herself said,—during the four minutes that the man was absent with her waterproof jacket, and could not bring herself to forget the ill-usage she had suffered. Lucinda had become absolutely dumb, and any observer would have fancied that the two gentlemen had quarrelled with each other. 'You ought to go on the box now,' said Sir Griffin, grumbling. 'When you're my age, and I'm yours, I will,' said Lord George, taking his seat in the carriage. Then he appealed to Lizzie. 'You'll let me smoke, won't you?' She simply bowed her head. And so they went home,—Lord George smoking, and the ladies dumb. Lizzie, as she dressed for dinner, almost cried with vexation and disappointment.

There was a little conversation up-stairs between Mrs. Carbuncle and Lucinda, when they were free from the attendance of their joint maid. 'It seems to me,' said Mrs. Carbuncle, 'that you won't make up your mind about anything.'

'There is nothing to make up my mind about.'

'I think there is;—a great deal. Do you mean to take this man who is dangling after you?'

'He isn't worth taking.'

'Carruthers says that the property must come right, sooner

or later. You might do better, perhaps, but you won't trouble yourself. We can't go on like this for ever, you know.'

'If you hated it as much as I do, you wouldn't want to go on.'

'Why don't you talk to him? I don't think he's at all a bad fellow.'

'I've nothing to say.'

'He'll offer to-morrow, if you'll accept him.'

'Don't let him do that, Aunt Jane. I couldn't say Yes. As for loving him;—oh laws!'

'It won't do to go on like this, you know.'

'I'm only eighteen;—and it's my money, aunt.'

'And how long will it last? If you can't accept him, refuse him, and let somebody else come.'

'It seems to me,' said Lucinda, 'that one is as bad as another. I'd a deal sooner marry a shoemaker and help him to make shoes.'

'That's downright wickedness,' said Mrs. Carbuncle. And then they went down to dinner.

CHAPTER XXXVIii
Nappie's Grey Horse

DURING the leisure of Tuesday, our friends regained their good humour, and on the Wednesday morning they again started for the hunting-field. Mrs. Carbuncle, who probably felt that she had behaved ill about the groom and in regard to Scotland, almost made an apology, and explained that a cold shower always did make her cross. 'My dear Lady Eustace, I hope I wasn't very savage.' 'My dear Mrs. Carbuncle, I hope I wasn't very stupid,' said Lizzie with a smile. 'My dear Lady Eustace, and my dear Mrs. Carbuncle, and my dear Miss Roanoke, I hope I wasn't very selfish,' said Lord George.

'I thought you were,' said Sir Griffin.

'Yes, Griff; and so were you;—but I succeeded.'

'I am almost glad that I wasn't of the party,' said Mr. Emilius, with that musical foreign tone of his. 'Miss Macnulty and I did not quarrel; did we?'

'No, indeed,' said Miss Macnulty, who had liked the society of Mr. Emilius.

But on this morning there was an attraction for Lizzie which the Monday had wanted. She was to meet her cousin, Frank Greystock. The journey was long, and the horses had gone on over night. They went by railway to Kilmarnock, and there a carriage from the inn had been ordered to meet them. Lizzie, as she heard the order given, wondered whether she would have to pay for that, or whether Lord George and Sir Griffin would take so much off her shoulders. Young women generally pay for nothing: and it was very hard that she, who was quite a young woman, should have to pay for all. But she smiled, and accepted the proposition. 'Oh, yes; of course a carriage at the station. It is so nice to have some one to think of things, like Lord George.' The carriage met them, and everything went prosperously. Almost the first person they saw was Frank Greystock, in a black coat, indeed, but riding a superb grey horse, and looking quite as though he knew what he was about. He was introduced to Mrs. Carbuncle and Miss Roanoke and Sir Griffin. With Lord George he had some slight previous acquaintance.

'You've had no difficulty about a horse?' said Lizzie.

'Not the slightest. But I was in an awful fright this morning. I wrote to MacFarlane from London, and absolutely hadn't a moment to go to his place yesterday or this morning. I was staying over at Glenshiels, and had not a moment to spare in catching the train. But I found a horse-box on, and a lad from MacFarlane's just leaving as I came up.'

'Didn't he send a boy down with the horse?' asked Lord George.

'I believe there is a boy, and the boy'll be awfully bothered. I told him to book the horse for Kilmarnock.'

'They always do book for Kilmarnock for this meet,' said

a gentleman who had made acquaintance with some of Lizzie's party on the previous hunting-day;—'but Stewarton is ever so much nearer.'

'So somebody told me in the carriage,' continued Frank, 'and I contrived to get my box off at Stewarton. The guard was uncommon civil, and so was the porter. But I hadn't a moment to look for the boy.'

'I always make my fellow stick to his horses,' said Sir Griffin.

'But you see, Sir Griffin, I haven't got a fellow, and I've only hired a horse. But I shall hire a good many horses from Mr. MacFarlane if he'll always put me up like this.'

'I'm so glad you're here,' said Lizzie.

'So am I. I hunt about twice in three years, and no man likes it so much. I've still got to find out whether the beast can jump.'

'Any mortal thing alive, sir,' said one of those horsey-looking men who are to be found in all hunting-fields, who wear old brown breeches, old black coats, old hunting caps, who ride screws,* and never get thrown out.

'You know him, do you?' said Frank.

'I know him. I didn't know as Muster MacFarlane owned him. No more he don't,' said the horsey man, turning aside to one of his friends. 'That's Nappie's horse, from Jamaica Street.'

'Not possible,' said the friend.

'You'll tell me I don't know my own horse next.'

'I don't believe you ever owned one,' said the friend.

Lizzie was in truth delighted to have her cousin beside her. He had, at any rate, forgiven what she had said to him at his last visit, or he would not have been there. And then, too, there was a feeling of reality in her connection with him, which was sadly wanting to her,—unreal as she was herself,—in her acquaintance with the other people around her. And on this occasion three or four people spoke or bowed to her, who had only stared at her before; and the huntsman took off his cap, and hoped that he would do something better for her than on the previous Monday. And the huntsman

was very courteous also to Miss Roanoke, expressing the
same hope, cap in hand, and smiling graciously. A huntsman
at the beginning of any day or at the end of a good day is so
different from a huntsman at the end of a bad day! A huntsman often has a very bad time out hunting, and it is sometimes a marvel that he does not take the advice which Job
got from his wife.* But now all things were smiling, and it
was soon known that his lordship intended to draw Craigattan
Gorse. Now in those parts there is no surer find, and no
better chance of a run, than Craigattan Gorse affords.

'There is one thing I want to ask, Mr. Greystock,' said
Lord George, in Lizzie's hearing.

'You shall ask two,' said Frank.

'Who is to coach Lady Eustace to-day;—you or I?'

'Oh, do let me have somebody to coach me,' said Lizzie.

'For devotion in coachmanship,' said Frank,—'devotion,
that is, to my cousin, I defy the world. In point of skill I
yield to Lord George.'

'My pretensions are precisely the same,' said Lord George.
'I glow with devotion; my skill is naught.'

'I like you best, Lord George,' said Lizzie, laughing.

'That settles the question,' said Lord George.

'Altogether,' said Frank, taking off his hat.

'I mean as a coach,' said Lizzie.

'I quite understand the extent of the preference,' said
Lord George. Lizzie was delighted, and thought the game
was worth the candle. The noble master had told her that
they were sure of a run from Craigattan, and she wasn't in
the least tired, and they were not called upon to stand still
in a big wood, and it didn't rain, and, in every respect, the
day was very different from Monday. Mounted on a bright-
skinned, lively steed, with her cousin on one side and Lord
George de Bruce Carruthers on the other, with all the hunting world of her own county civil* around her, and a fox just
found in Craigattan Gorse, what could the heart of woman
desire more? This was to live. There was, however, just
enough of fear to make the blood run quickly to her heart.

'We'll be away at once now,' said Lord George with utmost earnestness; 'follow me close, but not too close. When the men see that I am giving you a lead, they won't come between. If you hang back, I'll not go ahead. Just check your horse as he comes to his fences, and, if you can, see me over before you go at them. Now then, down the hill;— there's a gate at the corner, and a bridge over the water. We couldn't be better. By George! there they are,—altogether. If they don't pull him down in the first two minutes, we shall have a run.'

Lizzie understood most of it,—more at least than would nine out of ten young women who had never ridden a hunt before. She was to go wherever Lord George led her, and she was not to ride upon his heels. So much at least she understood,—and so much she was resolved to do. That dread about her front teeth which had perplexed her on Monday was altogether gone now. She would ride as fast as Lucinda Roanoke. That was her prevailing idea. Lucinda, with Mrs. Carbuncle, Sir Griffin, and the ladies' groom, was at the other side of the covert. Frank had been with his cousin and Lord George, but had crept down the hill while the hounds were in the gorse. A man who likes hunting but hunts only once a year is desirous of doing the best he can with his day. When the hounds came out and crossed the brook at the end of the gorse, perhaps he was a little too forward. But, indeed, the state of affairs did not leave much time for waiting, or for the etiquette of the hunting-field. Along the opposite margin of the brook there ran a low paling, which made the water a rather nasty thing to face. A circuit of thirty or forty yards gave the easy riding of a little bridge, and to that all the crowd hurried. But one or two men with good eyes, and hearts as good, had seen the leading hounds across the brook turning up the hill away from the bridge, and knew that two most necessary minutes might be lost in the crowd. Frank did as they did, having seen nothing of any hounds, but with instinctive knowledge that they were men likely to be right in a hunting-field. 'If that ain't Nappie's horse, I'll eat him,' said one of the leading men to the other, as all the three were breasting the hill together. Frank only knew that he had been carried over water and timber without a mistake, and felt a glow of gratitude towards Mr. MacFarlane. Up the hill they went, and not waiting to inquire into the circumstances of a little gate, jumped a four foot wall and were away. 'How the mischief did he get a top of Nappie's horse?' said the horsey man to his friend.

'We're about right for it now,' said the huntsman, as he came up alongside of Frank. He had crossed the bridge, but had been the first across it, and knew how to get over his ground quickly. On they went, the horsey man leading on his thoroughbred screw, the huntsman second, and Frank third. The pace had already been too good for the other horsey man.

When Lord George and Lizzie had mounted the hill, there was a rush of horses at the little gate. As they topped the hill Lucinda and Mrs. Carbuncle were jumping the wall. Lord George looked back and asked a question without a word. Lizzie answered it as mutely, Jump it! She was already a little short of breath, but she was ready to jump anything that Lucinda Roanoke had jumped. Over went Lord George, and she followed him almost without losing the stride of her horse. Surely in all the world there was nothing equal to this! There was a large grass field before them, and for a moment she came up alongside of Lord George. 'Just steady him before he leaps,' said Lord George. She nodded her assent, and smiled her gratitude. She had plenty of breath for riding, but none for speaking. They were now very near to Lucinda, and Sir Griffin, and Mrs. Carbuncle. 'The pace is too good for Mrs. Carbuncle's horse,' said Lord George. Oh, if she could only pass them, and get up to those men whom she saw before her! She knew that one of them was her cousin Frank. She had no wish to pass them, but she did wish that he should see her. In the next fence Lord George spied a rail, which he thought safer than a blind hedge, and he made for it. His horse took it well, and so did Lizzie's; but

Lizzie jumped it a little too near him, as he had paused an instant to look at the ground. 'Indeed, I won't do it again,' she said, collecting all her breath for an apology. 'You are going admirably,' he said, 'and your horse is worth double the money.' She was so glad now that he had not spared for price in mounting her. Looking to the right she could see that Mrs. Carbuncle had only just floundered through the hedge. Lucinda was still ahead, but Sir Griffin was falling behind, as though divided in duty between the niece and the aunt. Then they passed through a gate, and Lord George stayed his horse to hold it for her. She tried to thank him but he stopped her. 'Don't mind talking, but come along; and take it easy.' She smiled again, and he told himself that she was wondrous pretty. And then her pluck was so good! And then she had four thousand a year! 'Now for the gap!—don't be in a hurry. You first, and I'll follow you to keep off these two men. Keep to the left, where the other horses have been.' On they went, and Lizzie was in heaven. She could not quite understand her feelings, because it had come to that with her that to save her life she could not have spoken a word. And yet she was not only happy but comfortable. The leaping was delightful, and her horse galloped with her as though his pleasure was as great as her own. She thought that she was getting nearer to Lucinda. For her, in her heart, Lucinda was the quarry. If she could only pass Lucinda! That there were any hounds she had altogether forgotten. She only knew that two or three men were leading the way, of whom her cousin Frank was one, that Lucinda Roanoke was following them closely, and that she was gaining upon Lucinda Roanoke. She knew she was gaining a little, because she could see now how well and squarely Lucinda sat upon her horse. As for herself, she feared that she was rolling;—but she need not have feared. She was so small, and lithe, and light, that her body adapted itself naturally to the pace of her horse. Lucinda was of a different build, and it behoved her to make for herself a perfect seat. 'We must have the wall,' said Lord George, who was again at her side for a moment. She would have 'had' a castle wall, moat included, turrets and all, if he would only have shown her the way. The huntsman and Frank had taken the wall. The horsey man's bit of blood, knowing his own powers to an inch, had declined,—not roughly, with a sudden stop and a jerk, but with a swerve to the left which the horsey man at once understood. What the brute lacked in jumping he could make up in pace, and the horsey man was along the wall and over a broken bank at the head of it, with the loss of not more than a minute. Lucinda's horse, following the ill example, balked the jump. She turned him round with a savage gleam in her eye which Lizzie was just near enough to see, struck him rapidly over the shoulders with her whip, and the animal flew with her into the next field. 'Oh, if I could do it like that!' thought Lizzie. But in that very minute she was doing it, not only as well but better. Not following Lord George, but close at his side, the little animal changed his pace, trotted for a yard or two, hopped up as though the wall were nothing, knocked off a top stone with his hind feet, and dropped on to the ground so softly that Lizzie hardly believed that she had gone over the big obstruction that had cost Lucinda such an effort. Lucinda's horse came down on all four legs, with a grunt and a groan, and she knew that she had bustled*him. At that moment Lucinda was very full of wrath against the horsey man with the screw who had been in her way. 'He touched it,' gasped Lizzie, thinking that her horse had disgraced himself. 'He's worth his weight in gold,' said Lord George. 'Come along. There's a brook with a ford. Morgan is in it.' Morgan was the huntsman. 'Don't let them get before you.' Oh, no. She would let no one get before her. She did her very best, and just got her horse's nose on the broken track leading down into the brook before Lucinda. 'Pretty good, isn't it? said Lucinda. Lizzie smiled sweetly. She could smile, though she could not speak. 'Only they do balk one so at one's fences!' said Lucinda. The horsey man had all but regained his place, and was immediately behind Lucinda, within hearing—as Lucinda knew.

On the further side of the field, beyond the brook, there was a little spinny, and for half a minute the hounds came to a check. 'Give 'em time, sir, give 'em time,' said Morgan to Frank, speaking in full good humour, with no touch of Monday's savagery. 'Wind him, Bolton; Beaver's got it. Very good thing, my lady, isn't it? Now, Carstairs, if you're a going to 'unt the fox, you'd better 'unt him.' Carstairs was the horsey man,—and one with whom Morgan very often quarrelled. 'That's it, my hearties,' and Morgan was across a broken wall in a moment, after the leading hounds. 'Are we to go on?' said Lizzie, who feared much that Lucinda would get ahead of her. There was a matter of three dozen horsemen up now, and, as far as Lizzie saw, the whole thing might have to be done again. In hunting, to have ridden is the pleasure; —and not simply to have ridden well, but to have ridden better than others. 'I call it very awkward ground,' said Mrs. Carbuncle, coming up. 'It can't be compared to the Baron's country.' 'Stone walls four feet and a half high, and well built, are awkward,' said the noble master.

But the hounds were away again, and Lizzie had got across the gap before Lucinda, who, indeed, made way for her hostess with a haughty politeness which was not lost upon Lizzie. Lizzie could not stop to beg pardon, but she would remember to do it in her prettiest way on their journey home. They were now on a track of open country, and the pace was quicker even than before. The same three men were still leading, Morgan, Greystock, and Carstairs. Carstairs had slightly the best of it; and of course Morgan swore afterwards that he was among the hounds the whole run. 'The scent was that good, there wasn't no putting of 'em off;—no thanks to him,' said Morgan. 'I 'ate to see 'em galloping, galloping, galloping, with no more eye to the 'ounds than a pig. Any idiot can gallop, if he's got it under him.' All which only signified that Jack Morgan didn't like to see any of his field before him. There was need, indeed, now for galloping, and it may be doubted whether Morgan himself was not doing his best. There were about five or six in the second flight, and

among these Lord George and Lizzie were well placed. But
Lucinda had pressed again ahead. 'Miss Roanoke had better
have a care, or she'll blow her horse,' Lord George said.
Lizzie didn't mind what happened to Miss Roanoke's horse,
so that it could be made to go a little slower and fall behind.
But Lucinda still pressed on, and her animal went with a
longer stride than Lizzie's horse.

They now crossed a road, descending a hill, and were
again in a close country. A few low hedges seemed as nothing
to Lizzie. She could see her cousin gallop over them ahead of
her, as though they were nothing; and her own horse, as he
came to them, seemed to do exactly the same. On a sudden
they found themselves abreast with the huntsman. 'There's
a biggish brook below there, my lord,' said he. Lizzie was
charmed to hear it. Hitherto she had jumped all the big
things so easily, that it was a pleasure to hear of them. 'How
are we to manage it?' asked Lord George. 'It is rideable, my
lord; but there's a place about half a mile down. Let's see
how'll they head. Drat it, my lord, they've turned up, and
we must have it or go back to the road.' Morgan hurried on,
showing that he meant to 'have' it, as did also Lucinda.
'Shall we go to the road?' said Lord George. 'No, no!' said
Lizzie. Lord George looked at her and at her horse, and then
galloped after the huntsman and Lucinda. The horsey man,
with the well-bred screw, was first over the brook. The
little animal could take almost any amount of water, and his
rider knew the spot. 'He'll do it like a bird,' he had said to
Greystock, and Greystock had followed him. Mr. Mac-
Farlane's hired horse did it like a bird. 'I know him, sir,'
said Carstairs. 'Mr. Nappie gave £250 for him down in
Northamptonshire last February;—bought him of Mr. Percival. You know Mr. Percival, sir?' Frank knew neither Mr.
Percival nor Mr. Nappie, and at this moment cared nothing
for either of them. To him, at this moment, Mr. MacFarlane,
of Buchanan Street, Glasgow, was the best friend he ever
had.

Morgan, knowing well the horse he rode, dropped him into

the brook, floundered and half swam through the mud and water, and scrambled out safely on the other side. 'He wouldn't have jumped it with me, if I'd asked him ever so,' he said afterwards. Lucinda rode at it, straight as an arrow, but her brute came to a dead balk, and, but that she sat well, would have thrown her into the stream. Lord George let Lizzie take the leap before he took it, knowing that, if there were misfortune, he might so best render help. To Lizzie it seemed as though the river were the blackest, and the deepest, and the broadest that ever ran. For a moment her heart quailed;—but it was but for a moment. She shut her eyes, and gave the little horse his head. For a moment she thought that she was in the water. Her horse was almost upright on the bank, with his hind-feet down among the broken ground, and she was clinging to his neck. But she was light, and the beast made good his footing, and then she knew that she had done it. In that moment of the scramble her heart had been so near her mouth that she was almost choked. When she looked round, Lord George was already by her side. 'You hardly gave him powder enough,' he said, 'but still he did it beautifully. Good heavens! Miss Roanoke is in the river.' Lizzie looked back, and there, in truth, was Lucinda struggling with her horse in the water. They paused a moment, and then there were three or four men assisting her. 'Come on,' said Lord George;—'there are plenty to take her out, and we couldn't get to her if we stayed.'

'I ought to stop,' said Lizzie.

'You couldn't get back if you gave your eyes for it,' said Lord George. 'She's all right.' So instigated, Lizzie followed her leader up the hill, and in a minute was close upon Morgan's heels.

The worst of doing a big thing out hunting is the fact that in nine cases out of ten they who don't do it are as well off as they who do. If there were any penalty for riding round, or any mark given to those who had ridden straight,—so that justice might in some sort be done,—it would perhaps be better. When you have nearly broken your neck to get to hounds, or made your horse exert himself beyond his proper power, and then find yourself, within three minutes, over-taking the hindmost ruck of horsemen on a road because of some iniquitous turn that the fox has taken, the feeling is not pleasant. And some man who has not ridden at all, who never did ride at all, will ask you where you have been; and his smile will give you the lie in your teeth if you make any at-tempt to explain the facts. Let it be sufficient for you at such a moment to feel that you are not ashamed of yourself. Self-respect will support a man even in such misery as this.

The fox on this occasion, having crossed the river, had not left its bank, but had turned from his course up the stream, so that the leading spirits who had followed the hounds over the water came upon a crowd of riders on the road in a space something short of a mile. Mrs. Carbuncle, among others, was there, and had heard of Lucinda's mishap. She said a word to Lord George in anger, and Lord George answered her. 'We were over the river before it happened, and if we had given our eyes we couldn't have got to her. Don't you make a fool of yourself!' The last words were spoken in a whisper, but Lizzie's sharp ears caught them.

'I was obliged to do what I was told,' said Lizzie apolo-getically.

'It will be all right, dear Lady Eustace. Sir Griffin is with her. I am so glad you are going so well.'

They were off again now, and the stupid fox absolutely went back across the river. But, whether on one side or on the other, his struggle for life was now in vain. Two years of happy, free existence amidst the wilds of Craigattan had been allowed him. Twice previously had he been 'found', and the kindly storm or not less beneficent brightness of the sun had enabled him to baffle his pursuers. Now there had come one glorious day, and the common lot of mortals must be his. A little spurt there was, back towards his own home,—just enough to give something of selectness to the few who saw him fall,—and then he fell. Among the few were Frank, and Lord George, and our Lizzie. Morgan was there, of course, and one of his whips. Of Ayrshire folk, perhaps five or six, and among them our friend, Mr. Carstairs. They had run him down close to the outbuildings of a farm-yard, and they broke him up in the home paddock.

'What do you think of hunting?' said Frank to his cousin.

'It's divine!'

'My cousin went pretty well, I think,' he said to Lord George.

'Like a celestial bird of Paradise. No one ever went better; —or I believe so well. You've been carried rather nicely yourself.'

'Indeed I have,' said Frank, patting his still palpitating horse, 'and he's not to say tired now.'

'You've taken it pretty well out of him, sir,' said Carstairs. 'There was a little bit of hill that told when we got over the brook. I know'd you'd find he'd jump a bit.'

'I wonder whether he's to be bought?' asked Frank in his enthusiasm.

'I don't know the horse that isn't,' said Mr. Carstairs, —'so long as you don't stand at the figure.'

They were collected on the farm road, and now, as they were speaking, there was a commotion among the horses. A man, driving a little buggy, was forcing his way along the road, and there was a sound of voices, as though the man in the buggy were angry. And he was very angry. Frank, who was on foot by his horse's head, could see that the man was dressed for hunting, with a bright red coat and a flat hat, and that he was driving the pony with a hunting-whip. The man was talking as he approached, but what he said did not much matter to Frank. It did not much matter to Frank till his new friend, Mr. Carstairs, whispered a word in his ear. 'It's Nappie, by gum!' Then there crept across Frank's mind an idea that there might be trouble coming.

'There he is,' said Nappie, bringing his pony to a dead stop with a chuck, and jumping out of the buggy. 'I say, you sir; you've stole my 'orse!' Frank said not a word, but stood his ground with his hand on the nag's bridle. 'You've stole

my 'orse; you've stole him off the rail. And you've been a-
riding him all day. Yes, you 'ave. Did ever anybody see the
like of this? Why, the poor beast can't a'most stand!'

'I got him from Mr. MacFarlane.'

'MacFarlane be blowed! You didn't do nothing of the
kind. You stole him off the rail at Stewarton. Yes, you did;
—and him booked to Kilmarnock. Where's a police? Who's
to stand the like o' this? I say, my lord,—just look at this.'
A crowd had now been formed round poor Frank, and the
master had come up. Mr. Nappie was a Huddersfield man,
who had come to Glasgow in the course of the last winter,
and whose popularity in the hunting-field was not as yet
quite so great as it perhaps might have been.

'There's been a mistake, I suppose,' said the master.

'Mistake, my lord! Take a man's 'orse off the rail at
Stewarton, and him booked to Kilmarnock, and ride him to
a standstill! It's no mistake at all. It's 'orse-nobbling; that's
what it is. Is there any police here, sir?' This he said, turning
round to a farmer. The farmer didn't deign any reply.
'Perhaps you'll tell me your name, sir? if you've got a name.
No gen'leman ever took a gen'leman's 'orse off the rail like
that.'

'Oh, Frank, do come away,' said Lizzie, who was standing
by.

'We shall be all right in two minutes,' said Frank.

'No, we shan't,' said Mr. Nappie,—'nor yet in two hours.
I've asked what's your name?'

'My name is—Greystock.'

'Greystockings,' said Mr. Nappie more angrily than ever.
'I don't believe in no such name. Where do you live?' Then
somebody whispered a word to him. 'Member of Parliament,
—is he? I don't care a—— A member of Parliament isn't
to steal my 'orse off the rail, and him booked to Kilmarnock.
Now, my lord, what'd you do if you was served like that?'
This was another appeal to the noble master.

'I should express a hope that my horse had carried the
gentleman as he liked to be carried,' said the master.

'And he has,—carried me remarkably well,' said Frank;—whereupon there was a loud laugh among the crowd.

'I wish he'd broken the infernal neck of you, you scoundrel, you,—that's what I do!' said Mr. Nappie. 'There was my man, and my 'orse, and myself all booked from Glasgow to Kilmarnock;—and when I got there what did the guard say to me?—why, just that a man in a black coat had taken my horse off at Stewarton; and now I've been driving all about the country in that gig there for three hours!' When Mr. Nappie had got so far as this in his explanation he was almost in tears. 'I'll make 'im pay, that I will. Take your hand off my horse's bridle, sir. Is there any gentleman here as would like to give two hundred and eighty guineas for a horse, and then have him rid to a standstill by a fellow like that down from London. If you're in Parliament, why don't you stick to Parliament? I don't suppose he's worth fifty pound this moment.'

Frank had all the while been endeavouring to explain the accident; how he had ordered a horse from Mr. MacFarlane, and the rest of it,—as the reader will understand; but quite in vain. Mr. Nappie in his wrath would not hear a word. But now that he spoke about money, Frank thought that he saw an opening. 'Mr. Nappie,' he said, 'I'll buy the horse for the price you gave for him.'

'I'll see you——; extremely well——first,' said Mr. Nappie.

The horse had now been surrendered to Mr. Nappie, and Frank suggested that he might as well return to Kilmarnock in the gig, and pay for the hire of it. But Mr. Nappie would not allow him to set a foot upon the gig. 'It's my gig for the day,' said he, 'and you don't touch it. You shall foot it all the way back to Kilmarnock, Mr. Greystockings.' But Mr. Nappie, in making this threat, forgot that there were gentlemen there with second horses. Frank was soon mounted on one belonging to Lord George, and Lord George's servant, at the corner of the farmyard, got into the buggy, and was driven back to Kilmarnock by the man who had accompanied poor Mr. Nappie in their morning's hunt on wheels after the hounds.

'Upon my word, I was very sorry,' said Frank as he rode back with his friends to Kilmarnock; 'and when I first really understood what had happened, I would have done anything. But what could I say? It was impossible not to laugh, he was so unreasonable.'

'I should have put my whip over his shoulder,' said a stout farmer, meaning to be civil to Frank Greystock.

'Not after using it so often over his horse,' said Lord George.

'I never had to touch him once,' said Frank.

'And are you to have it all for nothing?' asked the thoughtful Lizzie.

'He'll send a bill in, you'll find,' said a bystander.

'Not he,' said Lord George. 'His grievance is worth more to him than his money.'

No bill did come to Frank, and he got his mount for nothing. When Mr. MacFarlane was applied to, he declared that no letter ordering a horse had been delivered in his establishment. From that day to this Mr. Nappie's grey horse has had a great character in Ayrshire; but all the world there says that its owner never rides him as Frank Greystock rode him that day.

THE EUSTACE DIAMONDS

VOLUME II

CHAPTER XXXIX
Sir Griffin takes an Unfair Advantage

WE must return to the unfortunate Lucinda, whom we last saw struggling with her steed in the black waters of the brook which she attempted to jump. A couple of men were soon in after her, and she was rescued and brought back to the side from which she had taken off without any great difficulty. She was neither hurt nor frightened, but she was wet through; and for a while she was very unhappy, because it was not found quite easy to extricate her horse. During the ten minutes of her agony, while the poor brute was floundering in the mud, she had been quite disregardful of herself, and had almost seemed to think that Sir Griffin, who was with her, should go into the water after her steed. But there were already two men in the water, and three on the bank, and Sir Griffin thought that duty required him to stay by the young lady's side. 'I don't care a bit about myself,' said Lucinda, 'but if anything can be done for poor Warrior!' Sir Griffin assured her that 'poor Warrior' was receiving the very best attention; and then he pressed upon her the dangerous condition in which she herself was standing,—quite wet through, covered, as to her feet and legs, with mud, growing colder and colder every minute. She touched her lips with a little brandy that somebody gave her, and then declared again that she cared for nothing but poor Warrior. At last poor Warrior was on his legs, with the water dripping from his black flanks, with his nose stained with mud, with one of his legs a little cut,— and, alas! with the saddle wet through. Nevertheless, there was nothing to be done better than to ride into Kilmarnock. The whole party must return to Kilmarnock,* and, perhaps, if they hurried, she might be able to get her clothes dry before they would start by the train. Sir Griffin, of course, accompanied her, and they two rode into the town alone. Mrs. Carbuncle did hear of the accident soon after the occurrence, but had not seen her niece; nor when she heard of it, could she have joined Lucinda.

If anything would make a girl talk to a man, such a ducking as Lucinda had had would do so. Such sudden events, when they come in the shape of misfortune, or the reverse, generally have the effect of abolishing shyness for the time. Let a girl be upset with you in a railway train, and she will talk like a Rosalind,* though before the accident she was as mute as death. But with Lucinda Roanoke the accustomed change did not seem to take place. When Sir Griffin had placed her on her saddle, she would have trotted all the way into Kilmarnock without a word if he would have allowed her. But he, at least, understood that such a joint misfortune should create confidence,—for he, too, had lost the run, and he did not intend to lose his opportunity also. 'I am so glad that I was near you,' he said.

'Oh, thank you, yes; it would have been bad to be alone.'

'I mean that I am glad that it was I,' said Sir Griffin. 'It's very hard even to get a moment to speak to you.' They were now trotting along on the road, and there were still three miles before them.

'I don't know,' said she. 'I'm always with the other people.'

'Just so.' And then he paused. 'But I want to find you when you're not with the other people. Perhaps, however, you don't like me.'

As he paused for a reply, she felt herself bound to say something. 'Oh, yes, I do,' she said,—'as well as anybody else.'

'And is that all?'

'I suppose so.'

After that he rode on for the best part of another mile before he spoke to her again. He had made up his mind that he would do it. He hardly knew why it was that he wanted her. He had not determined that he was desirous of the charms or comfort of domestic life. He had not even thought where he would live were he married. He had not suggested to himself that Lucinda was a desirable companion, that her temper would suit his, that her ways and his were sympathetic, or that she would be a good mother to the future Sir Griffin Tewett. He had seen that she was a very handsome girl, and therefore he had thought that he would like to possess her. Had she fallen like a ripe plum into his mouth, or shown herself ready so to fall, he would probably have closed his lips and backed out of the affair. But the difficulty no doubt added something to the desire. 'I had hoped,' he said, 'that after knowing each other so long there might have been more than that.'

She was again driven to speak because he paused. 'I don't know that that makes much difference.'

'Miss Roanoke, you can't but understand what I mean.'

'I'm sure I don't,' said she.

'Then I'll speak plainer.'

'Not now, Sir Griffin, because I'm so wet.'

'You can listen to me even if you will not answer me. I am sure that you know that I love you better than all the world. Will you be mine?' Then he moved on a little forward so that he might look back into her face. 'Will you allow me to think of you as my future wife?'

Miss Roanoke was able to ride at a stone wall or at a river, and to ride at either the second time when her horse balked the first. Her heart was big enough for that. But her heart was not big enough to enable her to give Sir Griffin an answer. Perhaps it was that, in regard to the river and the stone wall, she knew what she wanted; but that, as to Sir Griffin, she did not. 'I don't think this is a proper time to ask,' she said.

'Why not?'

'Because I am wet through and cold. It is taking an unfair advantage.'

'I didn't mean to take any unfair advantage,' said Sir Griffin scowling—'I thought we were alone——'

'Oh, Sir Griffin, I am so tired!' As they were now entering Kilmarnock, it was quite clear he could press her no further. They clattered up, therefore, to the hotel, and he busied himself in getting a bedroom fire lighted, and in obtaining the services of the landlady. A cup of tea was ordered and toast, and in two minutes Lucinda Roanoke was relieved from the presence of the baronet. 'It's a kind of thing a fellow doesn't quite understand,' said Griffin to himself. 'Of course she means it, and why the devil can't she say so?' He had no idea of giving up the chase, but he thought that perhaps he would take it out of her when she became Lady Tewett.

They were an hour at the inn before Mrs. Carbuncle and Lady Eustace arrived, and during that hour Sir Griffin did not see Miss Roanoke. For this there was, of course, ample reason. Under the custody of the landlady, Miss Roanoke was being made dry and clean, and was by no means in a condition to receive a lover's vows. The baronet sent up half-a-dozen messages as he sauntered about the yard of the inn, but he got no message in return. Lucinda, as she sat drinking her tea and drying her clothes, did no doubt think about him,—but she thought about him as little as she could. Of course, he would come again, and she could make up her mind then. It was no doubt necessary that she should do something. Her fortune, such as it was, would soon be spent in the adventure of finding a husband. She also had her ideas about love, and had enough of sincerity about her to love a man thoroughly; but it had seemed to her that all the men who came near her were men whom she could not fail to dislike. She was hurried here and hurried there, and knew nothing of real social intimacies. As she told her aunt in her wickedness, she would almost have preferred a shoemaker,— if she could have become acquainted with a shoemaker in a manner that should be unforced and genuine. There was a savageness of antipathy in her to the mode of life which her circumstances had produced for her. It was that very savageness which made her ride so hard, and which forbade her to smile and be pleasant to people whom she could not like. And yet she knew that something must be done. She could not afford to wait as other girls might do. Why not Sir Griffin as well as any other fool? It may be doubted whether she knew how obstinate, how hard, how cruel to a woman a fool can be.

Her stockings had been washed and dried, and her boots and trousers were nearly dry, when Mrs. Carbuncle, followed by Lizzie, rushed into the room. 'Oh, my darling, how are you?' said the aunt, seizing her niece in her arms.

'I'm only dirty now,' said Lucinda.

'We've got off the biggest of the muck, my lady,' said the landlady.

'Oh, Miss Roanoke,' said Lizzie, 'I hope you don't think I behaved badly in going on.'

'Everybody always goes on, of course,' said Lucinda.

'I did so pray Lord George to let me try and jump back to you. We were over, you know, before it happened. But he said it was quite impossible. We did wait till we saw you were out.'

'It didn't signify at all, Lady Eustace.'

'And I was so sorry when I went through the wall at the corner of the wood before you. But I was so excited I hardly knew what I was doing.' Lucinda, who was quite used to these affairs in the hunting-field, simply nodded her acceptance of this apology. 'But it was a glorious run; wasn't it?'

'Pretty well,' said Mrs. Carbuncle.

'Oh, it was glorious,—but then I got over the river. And oh, if you had been there afterwards. There was such an adventure between a man in a gig and my cousin Frank.' Then they all went to the train, and were carried home to Portray.

CHAPTER XL

'You are not angry?'

ON their journey back to Portray, the ladies were almost too tired for talking; and Sir Griffin was sulky. Sir Griffin had as yet heard nothing about Greystock's adventure, and did not care to be told. But when once they were at the castle, and had taken warm baths, and glasses of sherry, and got themselves dressed and had come down to dinner, they were all very happy. To Lizzie it had certainly been the most triumphant day of her life. Her marriage with Sir Florian had been triumphant, but that was only a step to something good that was to come after. She then had at her own disposal her little wits and her prettiness, and a world before her in which, as it then seemed to her, there was a deal of pleasure if she could only reach it. Up to this period of her career she had hardly reached any pleasure; but this day had been very pleasant. Lord George de Bruce Carruthers had in truth been her Corsair, and she had found the thing which she liked to do, and would soon know how to do. How glorious it was to jump over that black, yawning stream, and then to see Lucinda fall into it! And she could remember every jump, and her feeling of ecstasy as she landed on the right side. And she had by heart every kind word that Lord George had said to her,—and she loved the sweet, pleasant, Corsair-like intimacy that had sprung up between them. She wondered whether Frank was at all jealous. It wouldn't be amiss that he should be a little jealous. And then somebody had brought home in his pocket the fox's brush*which the master of the hounds had told the huntsman to give her. It was all delightful;—and so much more delightful because Mrs. Carbuncle had not gone quite so well as she liked to go, and because Lucinda had fallen into the water.

They did not dine till past eight, and the ladies and gentlemen all left the room together. Coffee and liqueurs were to be brought into the drawing-room, and they were all to be intimate, comfortable, and at their ease;—all except Sir Griffin Tewett, who was still very sulky. 'Did he say anything?' Mrs. Carbuncle had asked. 'Yes.' 'Well?' 'He proposed; but of course I could not answer him when I was wet through.' There had been but a moment, and in that moment this was all that Lucinda would say.

'Now I don't mean to stir again,' said Lizzie, throwing herself into a corner of a sofa, 'till somebody carries me to bed. I never was so tired in all my life.' She was tired, but there is a fatigue which is delightful as long as all the surroundings are pleasant and comfortable.

'I didn't call it a very hard day,' said Mrs. Carbuncle.

'You only killed one fox,' said Mr. Emilius, pretending a delightfully clerical ignorance, 'and on Monday you killed four. Why should you be tired?'

'I suppose it was nearly twenty miles,' said Frank, who was also ignorant.

'About ten, perhaps,' said Lord George. 'It was an hour and forty minutes, and there was a good bit of slow hunting after we had come back over the river.'

'I'm sure it was thirty,' said Lizzie, forgetting her fatigue in her energy.

'Ten is always better than twenty,' said Lord George, 'and five generally better than ten.'

'It was just whatever is best,' said Lizzie. 'I know Frank's friend, Mr. Nappie, said it was twenty. By-the-bye, Frank, oughtn't we to have asked Mr. Nappie home to dinner?'

'I thought so,' said Frank; 'but I couldn't take the liberty myself.'

'I really think poor Mr. Nappie was very badly used,' said Mrs. Carbuncle.

'Of course he was,' said Lord George;—'no man ever worse since hunting was invented. He was entitled to a dozen dinners, and no end of patronage; but you see he took it out in calling your cousin Mr. Greystockings.'

'I felt that blow,' said Frank.

'I shall always call you Cousin Greystockings,' said Lizzie.

'It was hard,' continued Lord George, 'and I understood it all so well when he got into a mess in his wrath about booking the horse to Kilmarnock. If the horse had been on the roadside, he or his men could have protected him. He is put under the protection of a whole railway company, and the company gives him up to the first fellow that comes and asks for him.'

'It was cruel,' said Frank.

'If it had happened to me, I should have been very angry,' said Mrs. Carbuncle.

'But Frank wouldn't have had a horse at all,' said Lizzie, 'unless he had taken Mr. Nappie's.'

Lord George still continued his plea for Mr. Nappie. 'There's something in that, certainly; but, still, I agree with Mrs. Carbuncle. If it had happened to me, I should,—just have committed murder and suicide. I can't conceive anything so terrible. It's all very well for your noble master to talk of being civil, and hoping that the horse had carried him well, and all that. There are circumstances in which a man can't be civil. And then everybody laughed at him! It's the way of the world. The lower you fall, the more you're kicked.'

'What can I do for him?' asked Frank.

'Put him down at your club, and order thirty dozen of grey shirtings from Nappie and Co., without naming the price.'

'He'd send you grey stockings instead,' said Lizzie.

But though Lizzie was in heaven, it behoved her to be careful. The Corsair was a very fine specimen of the Corsair breed;—about the best Corsair she had ever seen, and had been devoted to her for the day. But these Corsairs are known to be dangerous, and it would not be wise that she should sacrifice any future prospect of importance on behalf of a feeling, which, no doubt, was founded on poetry, but which might too probably have no possible beneficial result. As far as she knew, the Corsair had not even an island of his own in the Ægean Sea.* And, if he had, might not the island too probably have a Medora or two of its own? In a ride across the country the Corsair was all that a Corsair should be; but knowing, as she did, but very little of the Corsair, she could not afford to throw over her cousin for his sake. As she was leaving the drawing-room, she managed to say one word to her cousin. 'You were not angry with me because I got Lord George to ride with me instead of you?'

'Angry with you?'

'I knew I should only be a hindrance to you.'

'It was a matter of course. He knows all about it, and I know nothing. I am very glad that you liked it so much.'

'I did like it;—and so did you. I was so glad you got that poor man's horse. You were not angry then?' They had now passed across the hall, and were on the bottom stair.

'Certainly not.'

'And you are not angry for what happened before?' She did not look into his face as she asked this question, but stood with her eyes fixed on the stair-carpet.

'Indeed no.'

'Good·night, Frank.'

'Good night, Lizzie.' Then she went, and he returned to a room below which had been prepared for purposes of tobacco and soda-water and brandy.

'Why, Griff, you're rather out of sorts to-night,' said Lord George to his friend, before Frank had joined them.

'So would you be out of sorts if you'd lost your run and had to pick a young woman out of the water. I don't like young women when they're damp and smell of mud.'

'You mean to marry her, I suppose?'

'How would you like me to ask you questions? Do you mean to marry the widow? And, if you do, what'll Mrs. Carbuncle say? And if you don't, what do you mean to do; and all the rest of it?'

'As for marrying the widow, I should like to know the facts first. As to Mrs. C., she wouldn't object in the least. I generally have my horses so bitted*that they can't very well object. And as to the other question, I mean to stay here for the next fortnight, and I advise you to make it square with Miss Roanoke. Here's my lady's cousin; for a man who doesn't ride often, he went very well to-day.'

'I wonder if he'd take a twenty-pound note if I sent it to him,' said Frank, when they broke up for the night. 'I don't like the idea of riding such a fellow's horse for nothing.'

'He'll bring an action against the railway, and then you can offer to pay if you like.' Mr. Nappie did bring an action against the railway, claiming exorbitant damages;—but with what result, we need not trouble ourselves to inquire.

CHAPTER XLI

'Likewise the bears in couples agree'

FRANK GREYSTOCK stayed till the following Monday at Portray, but could not be induced to hunt on the Saturday,—on which day the other sporting men and women went to the meet. He could not, he said, trust to that traitor MacFarlane, and he feared that his friend Mr. Nappie would not give him another mount on the grey horse. Lizzie offered him one of her two darlings,—an offer which he, of course, refused; and Lord George also proposed to put him up. But Frank averred that he had ridden his hunt for that season, and would not jeopardise the laurels*he had gained. 'And, moreover,' said he, 'I should not dare to meet Mr. Nappie in the field.' So he remained at the castle and took a walk with Mr. Emilius. Mr. Emilius asked a good many questions about Portray, and exhibited the warmest sympathy with Lizzie's widowed condition. He called her a 'sweet, gay, unsophisticated, light-hearted young thing.' 'She is very young,' replied her cousin. 'Yes,' he continued, in answer to further questions; 'Portray is certainly very nice. I don't know what the income is. Well; yes. I should think it is over a thousand. Eight! No, I never heard it said that it was as much as that.' When Mr. Emilius put it down in his mind as five, he was not void of acuteness, as very little information had been given to him.

There was a joke throughout the castle that Mr. Emilius had fallen in love with Miss Macnulty. They had been a great deal together on those hunting days; and Miss Macnulty was unusually enthusiastic in praise of his manner and conversation. To her, also, had been addressed questions as to Portray and its income, all of which she had answered to the best of her ability;—not intending to betray any secret, for she had no secret to betray; but giving ordinary information on that commonest of all subjects, our friends' incomes. Then there had risen a question whether there was a vacancy for such promotion to Miss Macnulty. Mrs. Carbuncle had certainly heard that there was a Mrs. Emilius. Lucinda was sure that there was not,—an assurance which might have been derived from a certain eagerness in the reverend gentleman's demeanour to herself on a former occasion. To Lizzie, who at present was very good-natured, the idea of Miss Macnulty having a lover, whether he were a married man or not, was very delightful. 'I'm sure I don't know what you mean,' said Miss Macnulty. 'I don't suppose Mr. Emilius had any idea of the kind.' Upon the whole, however, Miss Macnulty liked it.

On the Saturday nothing especial happened. Mr. Nappie was out on his grey horse, and condescended to a little conversation with Lord George. He wouldn't have minded, he said, if Mr. Greystock had come forward; but he did think Mr. Greystock hadn't come forward as he ought to have done. Lord George professed that he had observed the same thing; but then, as he whispered into Mr. Nappie's ear, Mr. Greystock was particularly known as a bashful man. 'He didn't ride my 'orse anyway bashful,' said Mr. Nappie;—all of which was told at dinner in the evening, amidst a great deal of laughter. There had been nothing special in the way of sport, and Lizzie's enthusiasm for hunting, though still high, had gone down a few degrees below fever heat. Lord George had again coached her; but there had been no great need for coaching, no losing of her breath, no cutting down of Lucinda, no river, no big wall,—nothing, in short, very fast. They had been much in a big wood; but Lizzie, in giving an account of the day to her cousin, had acknowledged that she had not quite understood what they were doing at any time. 'It was a blowing of horns and a galloping up and down all the day,' she said; 'and then Morgan got cross again and scolded all the people. But there was one nice paling, and Dandy flew over it beautifully. Two men tumbled down, and one of them was a good deal hurt. It was very jolly;—but not at all like Wednesday.'

Nor had it been like Wednesday to Lucinda Roanoke, who did not fall into the water, and who did accept Sir Griffin when he again proposed to her in Sarkie wood. A great deal had been said to Lucinda on the Thursday and the Friday by Mrs. Carbuncle,—which had not been taken at all in good part by Lucinda. On those days Lucinda kept as much as she could out of Sir Griffin's way, and almost snapped at the baronet when he spoke to her. Sir Griffin swore to himself that he wasn't going to be treated that way. He'd have her, by George! There are men in whose love a good deal of hatred is mixed;—who love as the huntsman loves the fox, towards the killing of which he intends to use all his energies and intellects. Mrs. Carbuncle, who did not quite understand the sort of persistency by which a Sir Griffin can be possessed, feared greatly that Lucinda was about to lose her prize, and spoke out accordingly. 'Will you, then, just have the kindness to tell me what it is you propose to yourself?' asked Mrs. Carbuncle.

'I don't propose anything.'

'And where will you go when your money's done?'

'Just where I am going now!' said Lucinda. By which it may be feared that she indicated a place to which she should not on such an occasion have made an allusion.

'You don't like anybody else?' suggested Mrs. Carbuncle.

'I don't like anybody or anything,' said Lucinda.

'Yes, you do;—you like horses to ride, and dresses to wear.'

'No I don't. I like hunting because, perhaps, some day I may break my neck. It's no use your looking like that, Aunt Jane. I know what it all means. If I could break my neck it would be the best thing for me.'

'You'll break my heart, Lucinda.'

'Mine's broken long ago.'

'If you'll accept Sir Griffin, and just get a home round yourself, you'll find that everything will be happy. It all comes from the dreadful uncertainty. Do you think I have suffered nothing? Carbuncle is always threatening that he'll go back to New York, and as for Lord George, he treats me that way I'm sometimes afraid to show my face.'

'Why should you care for Lord George?'

'It's all very well to say, why should I care for him. I don't care for him, only one doesn't want to quarrel with one's friends. Carbuncle says he owes him money.'

'I don't believe it,' said Lucinda.

'And he says Carbuncle owes him money.'

'I do believe that,' said Lucinda.

'Between it all, I don't know which way to be turning. And now, when there's this great opening for you, you won't know your own mind.'

'I know my mind well enough.'

'I tell you you'll never have such another chance. Good looks isn't everything. You've never a word to say to anybody; and when a man does come near you, you're as savage and cross as a bear.'

'Go on, Aunt Jane.'

'What with your hatings and dislikings, one would suppose you didn't think God Almighty made men at all.'

'He made some of 'em very bad,' said Lucinda. 'As for some others, they're only half made. What can Sir Griffin do, do you suppose?'

'He's a gentleman.'

'Then if I were a man, I should wish not to be a gentleman; that's all. I'd a deal sooner marry a man like that huntsman, who has something to do and knows how to do it.' Again she said, 'Don't worry any more, Aunt Jane. It doesn't do any good. It seems to me that to make myself Sir Griffin's wife would be impossible; but I'm sure your talking won't do it.' Then her aunt left her, and, having met Lord George, at his bidding went and made civil speeches to Lizzie Eustace.

That was on the Friday afternoon. On the Saturday afternoon Sir Griffin, biding his time, found himself, in a ride with Lucinda, sufficiently far from other horsemen for his purpose. He wasn't going to stand any more nonsense. He was entitled to an answer, and he knew that he was entitled, by his rank and position, to a favourable answer. Here was a girl who, as far as he knew, was without a shilling, of whose birth and parentage nobody knew anything, who had nothing but her beauty to recommend her,—nothing but that and a certain capacity for carrying herself in the world as he thought ladies should carry themselves,—and she was to give herself airs with him, and expect him to propose to her half a dozen times! By George!—he had a very good mind to go away and let her find out her mistake. And he would have done so,—only that he was a man who always liked to have all that he wanted. It was intolerable to him that anybody should refuse him anything. 'Miss Roanoke,' he said; and then he paused.

'Sir Griffin,' said Lucinda, bowing her head.

'Perhaps you will condescend to remember what I had the honour of saying to you as we rode into Kilmarnock last Wednesday.'

'I had just been dragged out of a river, Sir Griffin, and I don't think any girl ought to be asked to remember what was said to her in that condition.'

'If I say it again now, will you remember?'

'I cannot promise, Sir Griffin.'

'Will you give me an answer?'

'That must depend.'

'Come;—I will have an answer. When a man tells a lady that he admires her, and asks her to be his wife, he has a right to an answer. Don't you think that in such circumstances a man has a right to expect an answer?'

Lucinda hesitated for a moment, and he was beginning again to remonstrate impatiently, when she altered her tone, and replied to him seriously, 'In such circumstances a gentleman has a right to expect an answer.'

'Then give me one. I admire you above all the world, and I ask you to be my wife. I'm quite in earnest.'

'I know that you are in earnest, Sir Griffin. I would do neither you nor myself the wrong of supposing that it could be otherwise.'

'Very well then. Will you accept the offer that I make you?'

Again she paused. 'You have a right to an answer,—of course; but it may be so difficult to give it. It seems to me that you have hardly realised how serious a question it is.'

'Haven't I, though! By George, it is serious!'

'Will it not be better for you to think it over again?'

He now hesitated for a moment. Perhaps it might be better. Should she take him at his word there would be no going back from it. But Lord George knew that he had proposed before. Lord George had learned this from Mrs. Carbuncle, and had shown that he knew it. And then, too,—he had made up his mind about it. He wanted her, and he meant to have her. 'It requires no more thinking with me, Lucinda. I'm not a man who does things without thinking; and when I have thought I don't want to think again. There's my hand;—will you have it?'

'I will,' said Lucinda, putting her hand into his. He no sooner felt her assurance than his mind misgave him that he had been precipitate, that he had been rash, and that she had taken advantage of him. After all, how many things are there in the world more precious than a handsome girl. And she had never told him that she loved him.

'I suppose you love me?' he asked.

'H'sh!—here they all are.' The hand was withdrawn, but not before both Mrs. Carbuncle and Lady Eustace had seen it.

Mrs. Carbuncle, in her great anxiety, bided her time, keeping close to her niece. Perhaps she felt that if the two were engaged, it might be well to keep the lovers separated for awhile, lest they should quarrel before the engagement should have been so confirmed by the authority of friends as to be beyond the power of easy annihilation. Lucinda rode quite demurely with the crowd. Sir Griffin remained near her, but without speaking. Lizzie whispered to Lord George that there had been a proposal. Mrs. Carbuncle sat in stately dignity on her horse, as though there were nothing which at that moment especially engaged her attention. An hour almost had passed before she was able to ask the important question, 'Well;— what have you said to him?'

'Oh;—just what you would have me.'

'You have accepted him?'

'I suppose I was obliged. At any rate I did. You shall know

one thing, Aunt Jane, at any rate, and I hope it will make you comfortable. I hate a good many people; but of all the people in the world I hate Sir Griffin Tewett the worst.'

'Nonsense, Lucinda.'

'It shall be nonsense, if you please; but it's true. I shall have to lie to him,—but there shall be no lying to you, however much you may wish it. I hate him!'

This was very grim, but Mrs. Carbuncle quite understood that to persons situated in great difficulty things might be grim. A certain amount of grimness must be endured. And she knew, too, that Lucinda was not a girl to be driven without showing something of an intractable spirit in harness. Mrs. Carbuncle had undertaken the driving of Lucinda, and had been not altogether unsuccessful. The thing so necessary to be done was now effected. Her niece was engaged to a man with a title, to a man reported to have a fortune, to a man of family, and a man of the world. Now that the engagement was made, the girl could not go back from it, and it was for Mrs. Carbuncle to see that neither should Sir Griffin go back. Her first steps must be taken at once. The engagement should be made known to all the party, and should be recognised by some word spoken between herself and the lover. The word between herself and the lover must be the first thing. She herself, personally, was not very fond of Sir Griffin; but on such an occasion as this she could smile and endure the bear. Sir Griffin was a bear,—but so also was Lucinda. 'The rabbits and hares All go in pairs; And likewise the bears In couples agree.'*Mrs. Carbuncle consoled herself with the song, and assured herself that it would all come right. No doubt the she-bears were not as civil to the he-bears as the turtle doves are to each other. It was, perhaps, her misfortune that her niece was not a turtle dove; but, such as she was, the best had been done for her. 'Dear Sir Griffin,' she said on the first available opportunity, not caring much for the crowd, and almost desirous that her very words should be overheard, 'my darling girl has made me so happy by what she has told me.'

'She hasn't lost any time,' said Sir Griffin.

'Of course she would lose no time. She is the same to me as a daughter. I have no child of my own, and she is everything to me. May I tell you that you are the luckiest man in Europe?'

'It isn't every girl that would suit me, Mrs. Carbuncle.'

'I am sure of that. I have noticed how particular you are. I won't say a word of Lucinda's beauty. Men are better judges of that than women: but for high, chivalrous spirit, for true principle and nobility, and what I call downright worth, I don't think you will easily find her superior. And she is as true as steel.'

'And about as hard, I was beginning to think.'

'A girl like that, Sir Griffin, does not give herself away easily. You will not like her the less for that now that you are the possessor. She is very young, and has known my wish that she should not engage herself to any one quite yet. But, as it is, I cannot regret anything.'

'I daresay not,' said Sir Griffin.

That the man was a bear was a matter of course, and bears probably do not themselves know how bearish they are. Sir Griffin, no doubt, was unaware of the extent of his own rudeness. And his rudeness mattered but little to Mrs. Carbuncle, so long as he acknowledged the engagement. She had not expected a lover's raptures from the one more than from the other. And was not there enough in the engagement to satisfy her? She allowed, therefore, no cloud to cross her brow as she rode up alongside of Lord George. 'Sir Griffin has proposed, and she has accepted him,' she said in a whisper. She was not now desirous that any one should hear her but he to whom she spoke.

'Of course she has,' said Lord George.

'I don't know about that, George. Sometimes I thought she would, and sometimes that she wouldn't. You have never understood Lucinda.'

'I hope Griff will understand her,—that's all. And now that the thing is settled, you'll not trouble me about it any more. Their woes be on their own head. If they come to blows Lucinda will thrash him, I don't doubt. But while it's simply a matter of temper and words, she won't find Tewett so easy-going as he looks.'

'I believe they'll do very well together.'

'Perhaps they will. There's no saying who may do well together. You and Carbuncle get on à merveille.* When is it to be?'

'Of course nothing is settled yet.'

'Don't be too hard about settlements, or, maybe, he'll find a way of wriggling out. When a girl without a shilling asks very much, the world supports a man for breaking his engagement. Let her pretend to be indifferent about it;—that will be the way to keep him firm.'

'What is his income, George?'

'I haven't an idea. There never was a closer man about money. I believe he must have the bulk of the Tewett property some day. He can't spend above a couple of thousand now.'

'He's not in debt, is he?'

'He owes me a little money,—twelve hundred or so, and I mean to have it. I suppose he is in debt, but not much, I think. He makes stupid bets, and the devil won't break him of it.'

'Lucinda has two or three thousand pounds, you know.'

'That's a flea-bite. Let her keep it. You're in for it now, and you'd better say nothing about money. He has a decent solicitor, and let him arrange about the settlements. And look here, Jane;—get it done as soon as you can.'

'You'll help me?'

'If you don't bother me, I will.'

On their way home Mrs. Carbuncle was able to tell Lady Eustace. 'You know what has occurred?'

'Oh dear, yes,' said Lizzie laughing.

'Has Lucinda told you?'

'Do you think I've got no eyes? Of course it was going to be. I knew that from the very moment Sir Griffin reached Portray. I am so glad that Portray has been useful.'

'Oh, so useful, dear Lady Eustace! Not but what it must have come off anywhere, for there never was a man so much in love as Sir Griffin. The difficulty has been with Lucinda.'

'She likes him, I suppose?'

'Oh yes, of course,' said Mrs. Carbuncle with energy.

'Not that girls ever really care about men now. They've got to be married, and they make the best of it. She's very handsome, and I suppose he's pretty well off.'

'He will be very rich indeed. And they say he's such an excellent young man when you know him.'

'I dare say most young men are excellent,—when you come to know them. What does Lord George say?'

'He's in raptures. He is very much attached to Lucinda, you know.' And so that affair was managed. They hadn't been home a quarter of an hour before Frank Greystock was told. He asked Mrs. Carbuncle about the sport, and then she whispered to him, 'An engagement has been made.'

'Sir Griffin?' suggested Frank. Mrs. Carbuncle smiled and nodded her head. It was well that everybody should know it.

CHAPTER XLII
Sunday morning

'So, miss, you've took him?' said the joint abigail*of the Carbuncle establishment that evening to the younger of her two mistresses. Mrs. Carbuncle had resolved that the thing should be quite public. 'Just remember this,' replied Lucinda, 'I don't want to have a word said to me on the subject.' 'Only just to wish you joy, miss.' Lucinda turned round with a flash of anger at the girl. 'I don't want your wishing. That'll do. I can manage by myself. I won't have you come near me if you can't hold your tongue when you're told.' 'I can hold my tongue as well as anybody,' said the abigail with a toss of her head.

This happened after the party had separated for the evening. At dinner Sir Griffin had, of course, given Lucinda his arm; but so he had always done since they had been at Portray. Lucinda hardly opened her mouth at table, and had retreated to bed with a headache when the men, who on that day lingered a few minutes after the ladies, went into the drawing-room. This Sir Griffin felt to be almost an affront, as there was a certain process of farewell for the night which he had anticipated. If she was going to treat him like that, he would cut up rough, and she should know it. 'Well, Griff, so it's all settled,' said Lord George in the smoking-room. Frank Greystock was there, and Sir Griffin did not like it.

'What do you mean by settled? I don't know that any-thing is settled.'

'I thought it was. Weren't you told so?'—and Lord George turned to Greystock.

'I thought I heard a hint,' said Frank.

'I'm——if I ever knew such people in my life!' said Sir Griffin. 'They don't seem to have an idea that a man's own affairs may be private.'

'Such an affair as that never is private,' said Lord George. 'The women take care of that. You don't suppose they're going to run down their game, and let nobody know it.'

'If they take me for game——'

'Of course you're game. Every man's game. Only some men are such bad game that they ain't worth following. Take it easy, Griff; you're caught.'

'No; I ain't.'

'And enjoy the satisfaction of knowing that she's about the handsomest girl out. As for me, I'd sooner have the widow. I beg your pardon, Mr. Greystock.' Frank merely bowed. 'Simply, I mean, because she rides about two stone lighter. It'll cost you something to mount Lady Tewett.'*

'I don't mean that she shall hunt,' said Sir Griffin. It will be seen, therefore, that the baronet made no real attempt to deny his engagement.

On the following day, which was a Sunday, Sir Griffin having ascertained that Miss Roanoke did not intend to go to church, stayed at home also. Mr. Emilius had been engaged to preach at the nearest episcopal place of worship,* and the remainder of the party all went to hear him. Lizzie was very particular about her Bible and Prayer-book, and Miss Macnulty wore a brighter ribbon on her bonnet than she had ever been known to carry before. Lucinda, when she had heard of the arrangement, had protested to her aunt that she would not go down-stairs till they had all returned; but Mrs. Carbuncle, fearing the anger of Sir Griffin, doubting whether, in his anger, he might not escape them altogether, said a word or two which even Lucinda found to be rational. 'As you have accepted him, you shouldn't avoid him, my dear. That is only making things worse for the future. And then it's cowardly, is it not?' No word that could have been spoken was more likely to be efficacious. At any rate, she would not be cowardly.

As soon then as the wheels of the carriage were no longer heard grating upon the road, Lucinda, who had been very careful in her dress,—so careful as to avoid all appearance of care,—with slow majestic step descended to a drawing-room which they were accustomed to use on mornings. It was probable that Sir Griffin was smoking somewhere about the grounds, but it could not be her duty to go after him out of doors. She would remain there, and, if he chose, he might come to her. There could be no ground of complaint on his side if she allowed herself to be found in one of the ordinary sitting-rooms of the house. In about half an hour he sauntered upon the terrace, and flattened his nose against the window. She bowed and smiled to him,—hating herself for smiling. It was perhaps the first time that she had endeavoured to put on a pleasant face wherewithal to greet him. He said nothing then, but passed round the house, threw away the end of his cigar, and entered the room. Whatever happened, she would not be a coward. The thing had to be done. Seeing that she had accepted him on the previous day, had not run away in the night or taken poison, and had come down to undergo the interview, she would undergo it at least with courage. What did it matter, even though he should embrace her? It was her lot to undergo misery, and as she had not chosen to take poison, the misery must be endured. She rose as he entered and gave him her hand. She had thought what she would do, and was collected and dignified. He had not, and was very awkward. 'So you haven't gone to church, Sir Griffin,—as you ought,' she said, with another smile.

'Come; I've gone as much as you.'

'But I had a headache. You stayed away to smoke cigars.'

'I stayed to see you, my girl.' A lover may call his lady love his girl, and do so very prettily. He may so use the word that she will like it, and be grateful in her heart for the sweetness of the sound. But Sir Griffin did not do it nicely. 'I've got ever so much to say to you.'

'I won't flatter you by saying that I stayed to hear it.'

'But you did;—didn't you now?' She shook her head, but there was something almost of playfulness in her manner of doing it. 'Ah, but I know you did. And why shouldn't you speak out, now that we are to be man and wife? I like a girl to speak out. I suppose if I want to be with you, you want as much to be with me; eh?'

'I don't see that that follows.'

'By——, if it doesn't, I'll be off!'

'You must please yourself about that, Sir Griffin.'

'Come; do you love me? You have never said you loved me.' Luckily perhaps for her he thought that the best assurance of love was a kiss. She did not revolt, or attempt to struggle with him; but the hot blood flew over her entire face, and her lips were very cold to his, and she almost trembled in his grasp. Sir Griffin was not a man who could ever have been the adored of many women, but the instincts of his kind were strong enough within him to make him feel that she did not return his embrace with passion. He had found her to be very beautiful;—but it seemed to him that she had never been so little beautiful as when thus pressed close to his bosom. 'Come,' he said, still holding her; 'you'll give me a kiss?'

'I did do it,' she said.

'No;—nothing like it. Oh, if you won't, you know——'

On a sudden she made up her mind, and absolutely did kiss him. She would sooner have leaped at the blackest, darkest, dirtiest river in the county. 'There,' she said, 'that will do,' gently extricating herself from his arms. 'Some girls are

different, I know; but you must take me as I am, Sir Griffin;
—that is if you do take me.'

'Why can't you drop the Sir?'

'Oh yes;—I can do that.'

'And you do love me?' There was a pause, while she tried
to swallow the lie. 'Come;—I'm not going to marry any girl
who is ashamed to say that she loves me. I like a little flesh
and blood. You do love me?'

'Yes,' she said. The lie was told; and for the moment he
had to be satisfied. But in his heart he didn't believe her. It
was all very well for her to say that she wasn't like other girls.
Why shouldn't she be like other girls? It might, no doubt, suit
her to be made Lady Tewett;—but he wouldn't make her
Lady Tewett if she gave herself airs with him. She should lie
on his breast and swear that she loved him beyond all the
world;—or else she should never be Lady Tewett. Different

from other girls indeed! She should know that he was different from other men. Then he asked her to come and take a walk about the grounds. To that she made no objection. She would get her hat and be with him in a minute.

But she was absent more than ten minutes. When she was alone she stood before her glass looking at herself, and then she burst into tears. Never before had she been thus polluted. The embrace had disgusted her. It made her odious to herself. And if this, the beginning of it, were so bad, how was she to drink the cup to the bitter dregs? Other girls, she knew, were fond of their lovers,—some so fond of them that all moments of absence were moments, if not of pain, at any rate of regret. To her as she stood there ready to tear herself because of the vileness of her own condition, it now seemed as though no such love as that were possible to her. For the sake of this man who was to be her husband, she hated all men. Was not everything around her base, and mean, and sordid? She had understood thoroughly the quick divulgings of Mrs. Car-buncle's tidings, the working of her aunt's anxious mind. The man, now that he had been caught, was not to be allowed to escape. But how great would be the boon if he would escape. How should she escape? And yet she knew that she meant to go on and bear it all. Perhaps by study and due practice she might become as were some others,—a beast of prey, and nothing more. The feeling that had made these few minutes so inexpressibly loathsome to her might, perhaps, be driven from her heart. She washed the tears from her eyes with savage energy and descended to her lover with a veil fastened closely under her hat. 'I hope I haven't kept you waiting,' she said.

'Women always do,' he replied laughing. 'It gives them importance.'

'It is not so with me, I can assure you. I will tell you the truth. I was agitated,—and I cried.'

'Oh, ay; I dare say.' He rather liked the idea of having reduced the haughty Lucinda to tears. 'But you needn't have been ashamed of my seeing it. As it is I can see nothing. You must take that off presently.'

'Not now, Griffin.' Oh, what a name it was. It seemed to blister her tongue as she used it without the usual prefix.

'I never saw you tied up in that way before. You don't do it out hunting. I've seen you when the snow has been driving in your face, and you didn't mind it,—not so much as I did.'

'You can't be surprised that I should be agitated now.'

'But you're happy;—ain't you?'

'Yes,' she said. The lie once told must of course be continued.

'Upon my word I don't quite understand you,' said Sir Griffin. 'Look here, Lucinda, if you want to back out of it, you can, you know.'

'If you ask me again I will.' This was said with the old savage voice, and it at once reduced Sir Griffin to thraldom. To be rejected now would be the death of him. And should there come a quarrel he was sure that it would seem to be that he had been rejected.

'I suppose it's all right,' he said, 'only when a man is only thinking how he can make you happy, he doesn't like to find nothing but crying.' After this there was but little more said between them, before they returned to the castle.

CHAPTER XLIII
Life at Portray

On the Monday Frank took his departure. Everybody at the castle had liked him except Sir Griffin, who, when he had gone, remarked to Lucinda that he was an insufferable legal prig, and one of those chaps who think themselves somebody because they are in Parliament. Lucinda had liked Frank, and said so very boldly. 'I see what it is,' replied Sir Griffin, 'you always like the people I don't.' When he was going, Lizzie left her hand in his for a moment, and gave one look up into his eyes. 'When is Lucy to be made blessed?' she asked. 'I don't know that Lucy will ever be made blessed,' he replied, 'but I am sure I hope she will.' Not a word more was said, and he returned to London.

After that Mrs. Carbuncle and Lucinda remained at Portray Castle till after Christmas, greatly overstaying the original time fixed for their visit. Lord George and Sir Griffin went and returned, and went again and returned again. There was much hunting and a great many love passages, which need not be recorded here. More than once during these six or seven weeks there arose a quarrel, bitter, loud, and pronounced, between Sir Griffin and Lucinda; but Lord George and Mrs. Carbuncle between them managed to throw oil upon the waters,* and when Christmas came the engagement was still an engagement. The absolute suggestion that it should be broken, and abandoned, and thrown to the winds, always came from Lucinda; and Sir Griffin, when he found that Lucinda was in earnest, would again be moved by his old desires, and would determine that he would have the thing he wanted. Once he behaved with such coarse brutality that nothing but an abject apology would serve the turn. He made the abject apology, and after that became conscious that his wings were clipped, and that he must do as he was bidden. Lord George took him away, and brought him back again, and blew him up;—and at last, under pressure from Mrs. Carbuncle, made him consent to the fixing of a day. The marriage was to take place during the first week in April. When the party moved from Portray, he was to go up to London and see his lawyer. Settlements were to be arranged, and something was to be fixed as to future residence.

In the midst of all this Lucinda was passive as regarded the making of the arrangements, but very troublesome to those around her as to her immediate mode of life. Even to Lady Eustace she was curt and uncivil. To her aunt she was at times ferocious. She told Lord George more than once to his face that he was hurrying her to perdition. 'What the d—— is it you want?' Lord George said to her. 'Not to be married to this man.' 'But you have accepted him. I didn't ask you to take him. You don't want to go into a workhouse, I suppose?'

Then she rode so hard that all the Ayrshire lairds were startled out of their propriety, and there was a general fear that she would meet some terrible accident. And Lizzie, instigated by jealousy, learned to ride as hard, and as they rode against each other every day, there was a turmoil in the hunt. Morgan, scratching his head, declared that he had known 'drunken rampaging men,' but had never seen ladies so wicked. Lizzie did come down rather badly at one wall, and Lucinda got herself jammed against a gate-post. But when Christmas was come and gone, and Portray Castle had been left empty, no very bad accident had occurred.

A great friendship had sprung up between Mrs. Carbuncle and Lizzie, so that both had become very communicative. Whether both or either had been candid may, perhaps, be doubted. Mrs. Carbuncle had been quite confidential in discussing with her friend the dangerous varieties of Lucinda's humours, and the dreadful aversion which she still seemed to entertain for Sir Griffin. But then these humours and this aversion were so visible, that they could not well be concealed;—and what can be the use of confidential communications if things are kept back which the confidante would see even if they were not told? 'She would be just like that whoever the man was,' said Mrs. Carbuncle.

'I suppose so,' said Lizzie, wondering at such a phenomenon in female nature. But, with this fact understood between them to be a fact,—namely, that Lucinda would be sure to hate any man whom she might accept,—they both agreed that the marriage had better go on.

'She must take a husband, some day, you know,' said Mrs. Carbuncle.

'Of course,' said Lizzie.

'With her good looks, it would be out of the question that she shouldn't be married.'

'Quite out of the question,' repeated Lizzie.

'And I really don't see how she's to do better. It's her nature, you know. I have had enough of it, I can tell you. And at the pension,* near Paris, they couldn't break her in at all.*

Nobody ever could break her in. You see it in the way she rides.'

'I suppose Sir Griffin must do it,' said Lizzie laughing.

'Well;—that, or the other thing, you know.' But there was no doubt about this;—whoever might break or be broken, the marriage must go on. 'If you don't persevere with one like her, Lady Eustace, nothing can be done.' Lizzie quite concurred. What did it matter to her who should break, or who be broken, if she could only sail her own little bark without dashing it on the rocks? Rocks there were. She didn't quite know what to make of Lord George, who certainly was a Corsair,—who had said some very pretty things to her, quite à la Corsair. But in the meantime, from certain rumours that she heard, she believed that Frank had given up, or at least, was intending to give up, the little chit who was living with Lady Linlithgow. There had been something of a quarrel,— so, at least, she had heard through Miss Macnulty, with whom Lady Linlithgow still occasionally corresponded in spite of their former breaches. From Frank Lizzie heard repeatedly, but Frank in his letters never mentioned the name of Lucy Morris. Now, if there should be a division between Frank and Lucy, then, she thought, Frank would return to her. And if so, for a permanent holding rock of protection in the world, her cousin Frank would be at any rate safer than the Corsair.

Lizzie and Mrs. Carbuncle had quite come to understand each other comfortably about money. It suited Mrs. Carbuncle very well to remain at Portray. It was no longer necessary that she should carry Lucinda about in search of game to be run down. The one head of game needed had been run down, such as it was,—not, indeed, a very noble stag; but the stag had been accepted; and a home for herself and her niece, which should have about it a sufficient air of fashion to satisfy public opinion,—out of London,—better still, in Scotland, belonging to a person with a title, enjoying the appurtenances of wealth, and one to which Lord George and Sir Griffin could have access,—was very desirable. But it was out of the question that Lady Eustace should bear all the expense. Mrs. Carbuncle undertook to find the stables, and did pay for that rick of hay and for the cart-load of forage*which had made Lizzie's heart quake as she saw it dragged up the hill towards her own granaries. It is very comfortable when all these things are clearly understood. Early in January they were all to go back to London. Then for a while,—up to the period of Lucinda's marriage,—Lizzie was to be Mrs. Carbuncle's guest at the small house in Mayfair;—but Lizzie was to keep the carriage. There came at last to be some little attempt, perhaps, at a hard bargain at the hand of each lady, in which Mrs. Carbuncle, as the elder, probably got the advantage. There was a question about the liveries in London. The footman there must appertain to Mrs. Carbuncle, whereas the coachman would as necessarily be one of Lizzie's retainers. Mrs. Carbuncle assented at last to finding the double livery, —but, like a prudent woman, arranged to get her quid pro quo. 'You can add something, you know, to the present you'll have to give Lucinda. Lucinda shall choose something up to forty pounds.' 'We'll say thirty,' said Lizzie, who was beginning to know the value of money. 'Split the difference,' said Mrs. Carbuncle, with a pleasant little burst of laughter,—and the difference was split. That the very neat and even dandified appearance of the groom who rode out hunting with them should be provided at the expense of Mrs. Carbuncle was quite understood; but it was equally well understood that Lizzie was to provide the horse on which he rode on every third day. It adds greatly to the comfort of friends living together when these things are accurately settled.

Mr. Emilius remained longer than had been anticipated, and did not go till Lord George and Sir Griffin took their departure. It was observed that he never spoke of his wife; and yet Mrs. Carbuncle was almost sure that she had heard of such a lady. He had made himself very agreeable, and was, either by art or nature, a courteous man,—one who paid compliments to ladies. It was true, however, that he sometimes startled his hearers by things which might have been considered to border on coarseness if they had not been said by a clergyman. Lizzie had an idea that he intended to marry Miss Macnulty. And Miss Macnulty certainly received his attentions with pleasure. In these circumstances his prolonged stay at the castle was not questioned;—but when towards the end of November Lord George and Sir Griffin took their departure, he was obliged to return to his flock.

On the great subject of the diamonds Lizzie had spoken her mind freely to Mrs. Carbuncle early in the days of their friendship,—immediately, that is, after the bargainings had been completed. 'Ten thousand pounds!' ejaculated Mrs. Carbuncle, opening wide her eyes. Lizzie nodded her head thrice, in token of reiterated assurance. 'Do you mean that you really know their value?' The ladies at this time were closeted together, and were discussing many things in the closest confidence.

'They were valued for me by jewellers.'

'Ten thousand pounds! And Sir Florian gave them to you?'

'Put them round my neck, and told me they were to be mine,—always.'

'Generous man!'

'Ah, if you had but known him!' said Lizzie, just touching her eye with her handkerchief.

'I daresay. And now the people claim them. I'm not a bit surprised at that, my dear. I should have thought a man couldn't give away so much as that,—not just as one makes a present that costs forty or fifty pounds.' Mrs. Carbuncle could not resist the opportunity of showing that she did not think so very much of that coming thirty-five pound 'gift' for which the bargain had been made.

'That's what they say. And they say ever so many other things besides. They mean to prove that it's an—heirloom.'

'Perhaps it is.'

'But it isn't. My cousin Frank, who knows more about law than any other man in London, says that they can't make a necklace an heirloom. If it was a brooch or a ring it would be different. I don't quite understand it, but it is so.'

'It's a pity Sir Florian didn't say something about it in his will,' suggested Mrs. Carbuncle.

'But he did;—at least, not just about the necklace.' Then Lady Eustace explained the nature of her late husband's will, as far as it regarded chattels to be found in the Castle of Portray at the time of his death; and added the fiction, which had now become common to her, as to the necklace having been given to her in Scotland.

'I shouldn't let them have it,' said Mrs. Carbuncle.

'I don't mean,' said Lizzie.

'I should—sell them,' said Mrs. Carbuncle.

'But why?'

'Because there are so many accidents. A woman should be very rich indeed before she allows herself to walk about with ten thousand pounds upon her shoulders. Suppose somebody broke into the house and stole them. And if they were sold, my dear, so that some got to Paris, and others to St. Petersburg, and others to New York, they'd have to give it up then.' Before the discussion was over, Lizzie tripped up-stairs and brought the necklace down, and put it on Mrs. Carbuncle's neck. 'I shouldn't like to have such property in my house, my dear,' continued Mrs. Carbuncle. 'Of course, diamonds are very nice. Nothing is so nice. And if a person had a proper place to keep them, and all that——'

'I've a very strong iron case,' said Lizzie.

'But they should be at the bank, or at the jewellers, or somewhere quite—quite safe. People might steal the case and all. If I were you, I should sell them.' It was explained to Mrs. Carbuncle on that occasion that Lizzie had brought them down with her in the train from London, and that she intended to take them back in the same way. 'There's nothing the thieves would find easier than to steal them on the way,' said Mrs. Carbuncle.

It was some days after this that there came down to her by post some terribly frightful documents, which were the first results, as far as she was concerned, of the filing of a bill in Chancery;*—which hostile proceeding was, in truth, effected by the unaided energy of Mr. Camperdown, although Mr. Camperdown put himself forward simply as an instrument used by the trustees of the Eustace property. Within eight days she was to enter an appearance,* or go through some preliminary ceremony, towards showing why she should not surrender her diamonds to the Lord Chancellor, or to one of those satraps of his, the Vice-Chancellors,* or to some other terrible myrmidon. Mr. Camperdown in his letter explained that the service of this document upon her in Scotland would amount to nothing,—even were he to send it down by a messenger; but that, no doubt, she would send it to her attorney, who would see the expedience of avoiding exposure by accepting the service. Of all which explanation Lizzie did not understand one word. Messrs. Camperdowns' letter and the document which it contained did frighten her considerably, although the matter had been discussed so often that she had accustomed herself to declare that no such bugbears as that should have any influence on her. She had asked Frank whether, in the event of such missiles reaching her, she might send them to him. He had told her that they should be at once placed in the hands of her attorney;—and consequently she now sent them to Messrs. Mowbray and Mopus, with a very short note from herself. 'Lady Eustace presents her compliments to Messrs. Mowbray and Mopus, and encloses some papers she has received about her diamonds. They are her own diamonds, given to her by her late husband. Please do what is proper, but Mr. Camperdown ought to be made to pay all the expenses.'

She had, no doubt, allowed herself to hope that no further steps would be taken in the matter; and the very name of the Vice-Chancellor did for a few hours chill the blood at her heart. In those few hours she almost longed to throw the necklace into the sea, feeling sure that, if the diamonds were absolutely lost, there must be altogether an end of the matter. But, by degrees, her courage returned to her, as she remembered that her cousin had told her that, as far as he could see, the necklace was legally her own. Her cousin had, of course, been deceived by the lies which she had repeated to him; but lies which had been efficacious with him might be efficacious with others. Who could prove that Sir Florian had not taken the diamonds to Scotland, and given them to her there, in that very house which was now her own?

She told Mrs. Carbuncle of the missiles which had been hurled at her from the London courts of law, and Mrs. Carbuncle evidently thought that the diamonds were as good as gone. 'Then I suppose you can't sell them?' said she.

'Yes I could;—I could sell them to-morrow. What is to hinder me? Suppose I took them to jewellers in Paris.'

'The jewellers would think you had stolen them.'

'I didn't steal them,' said Lizzie; 'they're my very own. Frank says that nobody can take them away from me. Why shouldn't a man give his wife a diamond necklace as well as a diamond ring? That's what I can't understand. What may he give her so that men shan't come and worry her life out of her in this way? As for an heirloom, anybody who knows anything, knows that it can't be an heirloom. A pot or a pan may be an heirloom;—but a diamond necklace cannot be an heirloom. Everybody knows that, that knows anything.'

'I daresay it will all come right,' said Mrs. Carbuncle, who did not in the least believe Lizzie's law about the pot and pan.

In the first week in January Lord George and Sir Griffin returned to the castle with the view of travelling up to London with the three ladies. This arrangement was partly thrown over by circumstances, as Sir Griffin was pleased to leave Portray two days before the others and to travel by himself. There was a bitter quarrel between Lucinda and her lover, and it was understood afterwards by Lady Eustace that Sir Griffin had had a few words with Lord George;—but what those few words were, she never quite knew. There was no open rupture between the two gentlemen, but Sir Griffin showed his displeasure to the ladies, who were more likely to bear patiently his ill-humour in the present circumstances than was Lord George. When a man has shown himself to be so far amenable to feminine authority as to have put himself in the way of matrimony, ladies will bear a great deal from him. There was nothing which Mrs. Carbuncle would not endure from Sir Griffin,—just at present; and, on behalf of Mrs. Carbuncle, even Lizzie was long-suffering. It cannot, however, be said that this Petruchio*had as yet tamed his own peculiar shrew. Lucinda was as savage as ever, and would snap and snarl, and almost bite. Sir Griffin would snarl too, and say very bearish things. But when it came to the point of actual quarrelling, he would become sullen, and in his sullenness would yield.

'I don't see why Carruthers should have it all his own way,' he said, one hunting morning, to Lucinda.

'I don't care twopence who have their way,' said Lucinda, 'I mean to have mine;—that's all.'

'I'm not speaking about you. I call it downright interference on his part. And I do think you give way to him. You never do anything that I suggest.'

'You never suggest anything that I like to do,' said Lucinda.

'That's a pity,' said Sir Griffin, 'considering that I shall have to suggest so many things that you will have to do.'

'I don't know that at all,' said Lucinda.

Mrs. Carbuncle came up during the quarrel, meaning to throw oil upon the waters. 'What children you are!' she said laughing. 'As if each of you won't have to do what the other suggests.'

'Mrs. Carbuncle,' began Sir Griffin, 'if you will have the great kindness not to endeavour to teach me what my conduct should be now or at any future time, I shall take it as a kindness.'

'Sir Griffin, pray don't quarrel with Mrs. Carbuncle,' said Lizzie.

'Lady Eustace, if Mrs. Carbuncle interferes with me, I shall quarrel with her. I have borne a great deal more of this kind of thing than I like. I'm not going to be told this and told that because Mrs. Carbuncle happens to be the aunt of the future Lady Tewett,—if it should come to that. I'm not going to marry a whole family; and the less I have of this kind of thing the more likely it is that I shall come up to scratch when the time is up.'

Then Lucinda rose and spoke. 'Sir Griffin Tewett,' she said, 'there is not the slightest necessity that you should come up,—"to scratch." I wonder that I have not as yet been able to make you understand that if it will suit your convenience to break off our match, it will not in the least interfere with mine. And let me tell you this, Sir Griffin,—that any repetition of your unkindness to my aunt will make me utterly refuse to see you again.'

'Of course, you like her better than you do me.'

'A great deal better,' said Lucinda.

'If I stand that I'll be——,' said Sir Griffin, leaving the room. And he left the castle, sleeping that night at the inn at Kilmarnock. The day, however, was passed in hunting; and though he said nothing to either of the three ladies, it was understood by them as they returned to Portray that there was to be no quarrel. Lord George and Sir Griffin had discussed the matter, and Lord George took upon himself to say that there was no quarrel. On the morning but one following, there came a note from Sir Griffin to Lucinda,—just as they were leaving home for their journey up to London,—in which Sir Griffin expressed his regret if he had said anything displeasing to Mrs. Carbuncle.

CHAPTER XLIV
A Midnight Adventure

SOMETHING as to the jewels had been told to Lord George;— and this was quite necessary, as Lord George intended to travel with the ladies from Portray to London. Of course, he had heard of the diamonds,—as who had not? He had heard too of Lord Fawn, and knew why it was that Lord Fawn had peremptorily refused to carry out his engagement. But, till he was told by Mrs. Carbuncle, he did not know that the diamonds were then kept within the castle, nor did he understand that it would be part of his duty to guard them on their way back to London. 'They are worth ever so much; ain't they?' he said to Mrs. Carbuncle, when she first gave him the information.

'Ten thousand pounds,' said Mrs. Carbuncle, almost with awe.

'I don't believe a word of it,' said Lord George.

'She says that they've been valued at that, since she's had them.'

Lord George owned to himself that such a necklace was worth having,—as also, no doubt, were Portray Castle and the income arising from the estate, even though they could be held in possession only for a single life. Hitherto in his very chequered career he had escaped the trammels of matrimony, and among his many modes of life had hardly even suggested to himself the expediency of taking a wife with a fortune, and then settling down for the future, if submissively, still comfortably. To say that he had never looked forward to such a marriage as a possible future arrangement, would probably be incorrect. To men such as Lord George it is too easy a result of a career to be altogether banished from the mind. But no attempt had ever yet been made, nor had any special lady ever been so far honoured in his thoughts as to be connected in them with any vague ideas which he might have formed on the subject. But now it did occur to him that Portray Castle was a place in which he could pass two or three months annually without ennui. And that if he were to marry, little Lizzie Eustace would do as well as any other woman with money whom he might chance to meet. He did not say all this to anybody, and therefore cannot be accused of vanity. He was the last man in the world to speak on such a subject to any one. And as our Lizzie certainly bestowed upon him many of her smiles, much of her poetry, and some of her confidence, it cannot be said that he was not justified in his views. But then she was such an—'infernal little liar.' Lord George was quite able to discover so much of her.

'She does lie, certainly,' said Mrs. Carbuncle, 'but then who doesn't?'

On the morning of their departure the box with the diamonds was brought down into the hall just as they were about to depart. The tall London footman again brought it down, and deposited it on one of the oak hall-chairs, as though it were a thing so heavy that he could hardly stagger along with it. How Lizzie did hate the man as she watched him, and regret that she had not attempted to carry it down herself. She had been with her diamonds that morning, and had seen them out of the box and into it. Few days passed on which she did not handle them and gaze at them. Mrs. Carbuncle had suggested that the box, with all her diamonds in it, might be stolen from her,—and as she thought of this her heart almost sank within her. When she had them once again in London she would take some steps to relieve herself from this embarrassment of carrying about with her so great a burthen of care. The man, with a vehement show of exertion, deposited the box on a chair, and then groaned aloud. Lizzie knew very well that she could lift the box by her own unaided exertions, and that the groan was at any rate unnecessary.

'Supposing somebody were to steal that on the way,' said Lord George to her, not in his pleasantest tone.

'Do not suggest anything so horrible,' said Lizzie, trying to laugh.

'I shouldn't like it at all,' said Lord George.

'I don't think it would make me a bit unhappy. You've heard about it all. There never was such a persecution. I often say that I should be well pleased to take the bauble and fling it into the ocean waves.'

'I should like to be a mermaid and catch it,' said Lord George.

'And what better would you be? Such things are all vanity and vexation of spirit.* I hate the shining thing.'*And she hit the box with the whip she held in her hand.

It had been arranged that the party should sleep at Carlisle. It consisted of Lord George, the three ladies, the tall man servant, Lord George's own man, and the two maids. Miss

Macnulty, with the heir and the nurses, were to remain at Portray for yet a while longer. The iron box was again put into the carriage; and was used by Lizzie as a footstool. This might have been very well, had there been no necessity for changing their train. At Troon the porter behaved well, and did not struggle much as he carried it from the carriage on to the platform. But at Kilmarnock, where they met the train from Glasgow, the big footman interfered again, and the scene was performed under the eyes of a crowd of people. It seemed to Lizzie that Lord George almost encouraged the struggling, as though he were in league with the footman to annoy her. But there was no further change between Kilmarnock and Carlisle, and they managed to make themselves very comfortable. Lunch had been provided;—for Mrs. Carbuncle was a woman who cared for such things, and Lord George also liked a glass of champagne in the middle of the day. Lizzie professed to be perfectly indifferent on such matters; but nevertheless she enjoyed her lunch, and allowed Lord George to press upon her a second, and perhaps a portion of a third glass of wine. Even Lucinda was roused up from her general state of apathy, and permitted herself to forget Sir Griffin for a while.

During this journey to Carlisle Lizzie Eustace almost made up her mind that Lord George was the very Corsair she had been expecting ever since she had mastered Lord Bryon's great poem. He had a way of doing things and of saying things, of proclaiming himself to be master, and at the same time of making himself thoroughly agreeable to his dependants,—and especially to the one dependant whom he most honoured at the time,—which exactly suited Lizzie's ideas of what a man should be. And then he possessed that utter indifference to all conventions and laws, which is the great prerogative of Corsairs. He had no reverence for aught divine or human,—which is a great thing. The Queen and Parliament, the bench of bishops, and even the police, were to him just so many fungi and parasites, and noxious vapours, and false hypocrites. Such were the names by which he ventured to call these bugbears of the world. It was so delightful to live with a man, who himself had a title of his own, but who could speak of dukes and marquises as being quite despicable by reason of their absurd position. And as they became gay and free after their luncheon he expressed almost as much contempt for honesty as for dukes, and showed clear'y that he regarded matrimony and marquises to be equally vain and useless. 'How dare you say such things in our hearing!' exclaimed Mrs. Carbuncle.

'I assert that if men and women were really true, no vows would be needed;—and if no vows, then no marriage vows. Do you believe such vows are kept?'

'Yes,' said Mrs. Carbuncle enthusiastically.

'I don't,' said Lucinda.

'Nor I,' said the Corsair. 'Who can believe that a woman will always love her husband because she swears she will? The oath is false on the face of it.'

'But women must marry,' said Lizzie. The Corsair declared freely that he did not see any such necessity.

And then, though it could hardly be said that this Corsair was a handsome man, still he had fine Corsair's eyes, full of expression and determination, eyes that could look love and bloodshed almost at the same time; and then he had those manly properties,—power, bigness, and apparent boldness,—which belong to a Corsair. To be hurried about the world by such a man, treated sometimes with crushing severity, and at others with the tenderest love, not to be spoken to for one fortnight, and then to be embraced perpetually for another, to be cast every now and then into some abyss of despair by his rashness, and then raised to a pinnacle of human joy by his courage,—that, thought Lizzie, would be the kind of life which would suit her poetical temperament. But then, how would it be with her, if the Corsair were to take to hurrying about the world without carrying her with him;—and were to do so always at her expense! Perhaps he might hurry about the world and take somebody else with him. Medora,* if Lizzie remembered rightly, had had no jointure or private fortune. But yet a woman must risk something if the spirit of poetry is to be allowed any play at all! 'And now these weary diamonds again,' said Lord George, as the carriage was stopped against the Carlisle platform. 'I suppose they must go into your bedroom, Lady Eustace?'

'I wish you'd let the man put the box in yours;—just for this night,' said Lizzie.

'No;—not if I know it,' said Lord George. And then he explained. Such property would be quite as liable to be stolen when in his custody as it would in hers;—but if stolen while in his would entail upon him a grievous vexation which would by no means lessen the effect of her loss. She did not understand him, but finding that he was quite in earnest she directed that the box should be again taken to her own chamber. Lord George suggested that it should be entrusted to the landlord; and for a moment or two Lizzie submitted to the idea. But she stood for that moment thinking of it, and then decided that the box should go to her own room. 'There's no knowing what that Mr. Camperdown mightn't do,' she whispered to Lord George. The porter and the tall footman, between them, staggered along under their load, and the iron box was again deposited in the bedroom of the Carlisle inn.

The evening at Carlisle was spent very pleasantly. The ladies agreed that they would not dress;*—but of course they did so with more or less of care. Lizzie made herself to look very pretty, though the skirt of the gown in which she came down was that which she had worn during the journey. Pointing this out with much triumph, she accused Mrs. Carbuncle and Lucinda of great treachery, in that they had not adhered to any vestige of their travelling raiment. But the rancour was not vehement, and the evening was passed pleasantly. Lord George was infinitely petted by the three Houris*around him, and Lizzie called him a Corsair to his face. 'And you are the Medora,' said Mrs. Carbuncle.

'Oh no. That is your place,—certainly,' said Lizzie.

'What a pity Sir Griffin isn't here,' said Mrs. Carbuncle, 'that we might call him the Giaour.' Lucinda shuddered, without an attempt at concealing her shudder. 'That's all very well, Lucinda, but I think Sir Griffin would make a very good Giaour.'

'Pray don't, aunt. Let one forget it all just for a moment.'

'I wonder what Sir Griffin would say if he was to hear this!' said Lord George.

Late in the evening Lord George strolled out, and of course the ladies discussed his character in his absence. Mrs. Carbuncle declared that he was the soul of honour. In regard to her own feeling for him, she averred that no woman had ever had a truer friend. Any other sentiment was of course out of the question,—for was she not a married woman? Had it not been for that accident, Mrs. Carbuncle really thought that she could have given her heart to Lord George. Lucinda declared that she always regarded him as a kind of supplementary father. 'I suppose he is a year or two older than Sir Griffin,' said Lizzie. 'Lady Eustace, why should you make me unhappy?' said Lucinda. Then Mrs. Carbuncle explained, that whereas Sir Griffin was not yet thirty, Lord George was over forty. 'All I can say is, he doesn't look it,' urged Lady Eustace enthusiastically. 'Those sort of men never do,' said Mrs. Carbuncle. Lord George, when he returned, was greeted with an allusion to angels' wings,—and would have been a good deal spoilt among them were it in the nature of such an article to receive injury. As soon as the clock had struck ten the ladies all went away to their beds.

Lizzie, when she was in her own room, of course found her maid waiting for her. It was necessarily part of the religion of such a woman as Lizzie Eustace that she could not go to bed, or change her clothes, or get up in the morning, without the assistance of her own young woman. She would not like to have it thought that she could stick a pin into her own belongings without such assistance. Nevertheless it was often the case with her, that she was anxious to get rid of her girl's attendance. It had been so on this morning, and before dinner, and was so now again. She was secret in her movements, and always had some recess in her boxes and bags and dressing

apparatuses to which she did not choose that Miss Patience
Crabstick should have access. She was careful about her letters,
and very careful about her money. And then as to that iron
box in which the diamonds were kept! Patience Crabstick had
never yet seen the inside of it. Moreover, it may be said,—
either on Lizzie's behalf or to her discredit, as the reader
may be pleased to take it,—that she was quite able to dress
herself, to brush her own hair, to take off her own clothes;
and that she was not, either by nature or education, an incapable
young woman. But that honour and glory demanded it, she
would almost as lief have had no Patience Crabstick to pry
into her most private matters. All which Crabstick knew, and
would often declare her missus to be 'of all missusses the
most slyest and least come-at-able.' On this present night she
was very soon despatched to her own chamber. Lizzie, however, took one careful look at the iron box before the girl was
sent away.

Crabstick, on this occasion, had not far to go to seek her
own couch. Alongside of Lizzie's larger chamber there was
a small room,—a dressing-room with a bed in it, which, for
this night, was devoted to Crabstick's accommodation. Of
course, she departed from attendance on her mistress by the
door which opened from the one room to the other; but this
had no sooner been closed than Crabstick descended to complete the amusements of the evening. Lizzie, when she was
alone, bolted both the doors on the inside, and then quickly
retired to rest. Some short prayer she said, with her knees
close to the iron box. Then she put certain articles of property
under her pillow,—her watch and chain, and the rings from
her fingers, and a packet which she had drawn from her
travelling-desk,—and was soon in bed, thinking that, as she
fell away to sleep, she would revolve in her mind that question
of the Corsair;—would it be good to trust herself and all her
belongings to one who might perhaps take her belongings
away, but leave herself behind? The subject was not unpleasant,
and while she was considering it, she fell asleep.

It was, perhaps, about two in the morning when a man,

very efficient at the trade which he was then following, knelt outside Lady Eustace's door, and, with a delicately-made saw, aided, probably, by some other equally well-finished tools, absolutely cut out that portion of the bedroom door on which the bolt was fastened. He must have known the spot exactly, for he did not doubt a moment as he commenced his work; and yet there was nothing on the exterior of the door to show where the bolt was placed. The bit was cut out without the slightest noise, and then, when the door was opened, was placed, just inside, upon the floor. The man then with perfectly noiseless step entered the room, knelt again,—just where poor Lizzie had knelt as she said her prayers,—so that he might the more easily raise the iron box without a struggle, and left the room with it in his arms without disturbing the lovely sleeper. He then descended the stairs, passed into the coffee-room at the bottom of them, and handed the box through an open window to a man who was crouching on the outside in the dark. He then followed the box, pulled down the window, put on a pair of boots which his friend had ready for him; and the two, after lingering a few moments in the shade of the dark wall, retreated with their prize round a corner. The night itself was almost pitch-dark, and very wet. It was as nearly black with darkness as a night can be. So far, the enterprising adventurers had been successful, and we will now leave them in their chosen retreat, engaged on the longer operation of forcing open the iron safe. For it had been arranged between them that the iron safe should be opened then and there. Though the weight to him who had taken it out of Lizzie's room had not been oppressive, as it had oppressed the tall serving-man, it might still have been an encumbrance to gentlemen intending to travel by railway with as little observation as possible. They were, however, well supplied with tools, and we will leave them at their work.

On the next morning Lizzie was awakened earlier than she had expected, and found, not only Patience Crabstick in her bedroom, but also a chambermaid, and the wife of the manager of the hotel. The story was soon told to her. Her room had been broken open, and her treasure was gone. The party had intended to breakfast at their leisure, and proceed to London by a train leaving Carlisle in the middle of the day; but they were soon disturbed from their rest. Lady Eustace had hardly time to get her slippers on her feet, and to wrap herself in her dressing-gown, to get rid of her dishevelled nightcap, and make herself just fit for public view, before the manager of the hotel, and Lord George, and the tall footman, and the boots were in her bedroom. It was too plainly manifest to them all that the diamonds were gone. The superintendent of the Carlisle police was there almost as soon as the others;—and following him very quickly came the important gentleman* who was the head of the constabulary of the county.

Lizzie, when she first heard the news, was awe-struck, rather than outwardly demonstrative of grief. 'There has been a regular plot,' said Lord George. Captain Fitzmaurice, the gallant chief, nodded his head. 'Plot enough,' said the superintendent,—who did not mean to confide his thoughts to any man, or to exempt any human being from his suspicion. The manager of the hotel was very angry, and at first did not restrain his anger. Did not everybody know that if articles of value were brought into an hotel they should be handed over to the safe keeping of the manager? He almost seemed to think that Lizzie had stolen her own box of diamonds. 'My dear fellow,' said Lord George, 'nobody is saying a word against you, or your house.'

'No, my lord;—but——'

'Lady Eustace is not blaming you, and do not you blame anybody else,' said Lord George. 'Let the police do what is right.'

At last the men retreated, and Lizzie was left with Patience and Mrs. Carbuncle. But even then she did not give way to her grief, but sat upon the bed awe-struck, and mute. 'Perhaps I had better get dressed,' she said at last.

'I feared how it might be,' said Mrs. Carbuncle, holding Lizzie's hand affectionately.

'Yes;—you said so.'

'The prize was so great.'

'I always was a-telling my lady——' began Crabstick.

'Hold your tongue!' said Lizzie angrily. 'I suppose the police will do the best they can, Mrs. Carbuncle?'

'Oh yes;—and so will Lord George.'

'I think I'll lie down again for a little while,' said Lizzie. 'I feel so sick I hardly know what to do. If I were to lie down for a little I should be better.' With much difficulty she got them to leave her. Then, before she again undressed herself, she bolted the door that still had a bolt, and turned the lock in the other. Having done this, she took out from under her pillow the little parcel which had been in her desk,—and, untying it, perceived that her dear diamond necklace was perfect, and quite safe.

The enterprising adventurers had, indeed, stolen the iron case, but they had stolen nothing else. The reader must not suppose that because Lizzie had preserved her jewels, she was therefore a consenting party to the abstraction of the box. The theft had been a genuine theft, planned with great skill, carried out with much ingenuity, one in the perpetration of which money had been spent,—a theft which for a while baffled the police of England, and which was supposed to be very creditable to those who had been engaged in it. But the box, and nothing but the box, had fallen into the hands of the thieves.

Lizzie's silence when the abstraction of the box was made known to her,—her silence as to the fact that the necklace was at that moment within the grasp of her own fingers,—was not at first the effect of deliberate fraud. She was ashamed to tell them that she brought the box empty from Portray, having the diamonds in her own keeping because she had feared that the box might be stolen. And then it occurred to her, quick as thought could flash, that it might be well that Mr. Camperdown should be made to believe that they had been stolen. And so she kept her secret. The reflections of the next half-hour told her how very great would now be her difficulties. But, as she had not disclosed the truth at first, she could hardly disclose it now.

CHAPTER XLV
The Journey to London

WHEN we left Lady Eustace alone in her bedroom at the Carlisle hotel after the discovery of the robbery, she had very many cares upon her mind. The necklace was, indeed, safe under her pillow in the bed; but when all the people were around her,—her own friends, and the police, and they who were concerned with the inn,—she had not told them that it was so, but had allowed them to leave her with the belief that the diamonds had gone with the box. Even at this moment, as she knew well, steps were being taken to discover the thieves, and to make public the circumstances of the robbery. Already, no doubt, the fact that her chamber had been entered in the night, and her jewel-box withdrawn, was known to the London police officers. In such circumstances how could she now tell the truth? But it might be that already had the thieves been taken. In that case would not the truth be known, even though she should not tell it? Then she thought for a while that she would get rid of the diamonds altogether, so that no one should know aught of them. If she could only think of a place fit for such purpose she would so hide them that no human ingenuity could discover them. Let the thieves say what they might, her word would, in such case, be better than that of the thieves. She would declare that the jewels had been in the box when the box was taken. The thieves would swear that the box had been empty. She would appeal to the absence of the diamonds, and the thieves,—who would be known as thieves—would be supposed, even by their own friends and associates, to have disposed of the diamonds before they had been taken. There would be a mystery in all this, and a cunning cleverness, the idea of which had in itself a certain charm for Lizzie Eustace. She would have all the world at a loss. Mr. Camperdown could do nothing further to harass her; and would have been, so far, overcome. She would be saved from the feeling of public defeat in the affair of the necklace, which would be very dreadful to her. Lord Fawn might probably be again at her feet. And in all the fuss and rumour which such an affair would make in London, there would be nothing of which she need be ashamed. She liked the idea, and she had grown to be very sick of the necklace.

But what should she do with it? It was, at this moment, between her fingers beneath the pillow. If she were minded, —and she thought she was so minded,—to get rid of it altogether, the sea would be the place. Could she make up her mind absolutely to destroy so large a property, it would be best for her to have recourse to 'her own broad waves,' as she called them even to herself. It was within the 'friendly depths of her own rock-girt ocean' that she should find a grave for her great trouble. But now her back was to the sea, and she could hardly insist on returning to Portray without exciting a suspicion that might be fatal to her.

And then might it not be possible to get altogether quit of the diamonds and yet to retain the power of future possession? She knew that she was running into debt, and that money would, some day, be much needed. Her acquaintance with Mr. Benjamin, the jeweller, was a fact often present to her mind. She might not be able to get ten thousand pounds from Mr. Benjamin;—but if she could get eight, or six, or even five, how pleasant would it be! If she could put away the diamonds for three or four years,—if she could so hide them that no human eyes could see them till she should again produce them to the light,—surely, after so long an interval, they might be made available! But where should be found such hiding-place? She understood well how great was the peril while the necklace was in her own immediate keeping. Any accident might discover it, and if the slightest suspicion were aroused, the police would come upon her with violence and discover it. But surely there must be some such hiding-place,—if only she could think of it! Then her mind reverted to all the stories she had ever heard of mysterious villanies. There must be some way of accomplishing this thing, if she could only bring her mind to work upon it exclusively. A hole dug deep into the ground;—would not that be the place? But then, where should the hole be dug? In what spot should she trust the earth? If anywhere, it must be at Portray. But now she was going from Portray to London. It seemed to her to be certain that she could dig no hole in London that would be secret to herself. Nor could she trust herself, during the hour or two that remained to her, to find such a hole in Carlisle.

What she wanted was a friend;—some one that she could trust. But she had no such friend. She could not dare to give the jewels up to Lord George. So tempted, would not any Corsair appropriate the treasure? And if, as might be possible, she were mistaken about him and he was no Corsair, then would he betray her to the police? She thought of all her dearest friends,—Frank Greystock, Mrs Carbuncle, Lucinda, Miss Macnulty,—even of Patience Crabstick,—but there was no friend whom she could trust. Whatever she did she must do alone! She began to fear that the load of thought required would be more than she could bear. One thing, however, was certain to her;—she could not now venture to tell them all that the necklace was in her possession, and that the stolen box had been empty.

Thinking of all this, she went to sleep,—still holding the packet tight between her fingers,—and in this position was awakened at about ten by a knock at the door from her friend Mrs. Carbuncle. Lizzie jumped out of bed, and admitted her friend, admitting also Patience Crabstick. 'You had better get up now, dear,' said Mrs. Carbuncle. 'We are all going to breakfast.' Lizzie declared herself to be so fluttered, that she must have her breakfast up-stairs. No one was to wait for her. Crabstick would go down and fetch for her a cup of tea,—and just a morsel of something to eat. 'You can't be surprised that I shouldn't be quite myself,' said Lizzie.

Mrs. Carbuncle's surprise did not run at all in that direction. Both Mrs. Carbuncle and Lord George had been astonished to find how well she bore her loss. Lord George gave her credit for real bravery. Mrs. Carbuncle suggested, in a whisper, that perhaps she regarded the theft as an easy way out of a lawsuit. 'I suppose you know, George, they would have got it from her.' Then Lord George whistled, and, in another whisper, declared that, if the little adventure had all been arranged by Lady Eustace herself with the view of getting the better of Mr. Camperdown, his respect for that lady would be very greatly raised. 'If,' said Lord George, 'it turns out that she has had a couple of bravos in her pay, like an old Italian marquis,* I shall think very highly of her indeed.' This had occurred before Mrs. Carbuncle came up to Lizzie's room;—but neither of them for a moment suspected that the necklace was still within the hotel.

The box had been found, and a portion of the fragments were brought into the room while the party were still at breakfast. Lizzie was not in the room, but the news was at once taken up to her by Crabstick, together with a pheasant's wing and some buttered toast. In a recess beneath an archway running under the railroad, not distant from the hotel above a hundred and fifty yards, the iron box had been found. It had been forced open, so said the sergeant of police, with tools of the finest steel, peculiarly made for such purpose. The sergeant of police was quite sure that the thing had been done by London men who were at the very top of their trade. It was manifest that nothing had been spared. Every motion of the party must have been known to them, and probably one of the adventurers had travelled in the same train with them. And the very doors of the bedroom in the hotel had been measured by the man who had cut out the bolt. The sergeant of police was almost lost in admiration;—but the superintendent of police, whom Lord George saw more than once, was discreet and silent. To the superintendent of police it was by no means sure that Lord George himself might not be fond of diamonds. Of a suspicion flying so delightfully high as this, he breathed no word to any one; but simply suggested that he should like to retain the companionship of one of the party. If Lady Eustace could dispense with the services of the tall footman, the tall footman might be found useful at

Carlisle. It was arranged, therefore, that the tall footman should remain;—and the tall footman did remain, though not with his own consent.

The whole party, including Lady Eustace herself and Patience Crabstick, were called upon to give their evidence to the Carlisle magistrates before they could proceed to London. This Lizzie did, having the necklace at that moment locked up in her desk at the inn. The diamonds were supposed to be worth ten thousand pounds. There was to be a lawsuit about them. She did not for a moment doubt that they were her property. She had been very careful about the diamonds because of the lawsuit. Fearing that Mr. Camperdown might wrest them from her possession, she had caused the iron box to be made. She had last seen the diamonds on the evening before her departure from Portray. She had then herself locked them up, and she now produced the key. The lock was still so far uninjured that the key would turn it. That was her evidence. Crabstick, with a good deal of reticence, supported her mistress. She had seen the diamonds, no doubt, but had not seen them often. She had seen them down at Portray; but not for ever so long. Crabstick had very little to say about them; but the clever superintendent was by no means sure that Crabstick did not know more than she said. Mrs. Carbuncle and Lord George had also seen the diamonds at Portray. There was no doubt whatever as to the diamonds having been in the iron box;—nor was there, said Lord George, any doubt but that this special necklace had acquired so much public notice from the fact of the threatened lawsuit, as might make its circumstances and value known to London thieves. The tall footman was not examined; but was detained by the police under a remand*given by the magistrates.

Much information as to what had been done oozed out in spite of the precautions of the discreet superintendent. The wires*had been put into operation in every direction, and it had been discovered that one man whom nobody knew had left the down mail train at Annan, and another at Dumfries. These men had taken tickets by the train leaving Carlisle between four and five a.m., and were supposed to have been the two thieves. It had been nearly seven before the theft had been discovered, and by that time not only had the men reached the towns named, but had had time to make their way back again or farther on into Scotland. At any rate, for the present, all trace of them was lost. The sergeant of police did not doubt but that one of these men was making his way up to London with the necklace in his pocket. This was told to Lizzie by Lord George; and though she was awe-struck by the danger of her situation, she nevertheless did feel some satisfaction in remembering that she and she only held the key of the mystery. And then as to those poor thieves! What must have been their consternation when they found, after all the labour and perils of the night, that the box contained no diamonds,—that the treasure was not there, and that they were nevertheless bound to save themselves by flight and stratagem from the hands of the police! Lizzie, as she thought of this, almost pitied the poor thieves. What a consternation there would be among the Camperdowns and Garnetts, among the Mopuses and Benjamins, when the news was heard in London! Lizzie almost enjoyed it. As her mind went on making fresh schemes on the subject, a morbid desire of increasing the mystery took possession of her. She was quite sure that nobody knew her secret, and that nobody as yet could even guess it. There was great danger, but there might be delight and even profit if she could safely dispose of the jewels before suspicion against herself should be aroused. She could understand that a rumour should get to the police that the box had been empty, even if the thieves were not taken;—but such rumour would avail nothing if she could only dispose of the diamonds. As she first thought of all this, the only plan hitherto suggested to herself would require her immediate return to Portray. If she were at Portray she could find a spot in which she could bury the necklace. But she was obliged to allow herself now to be hurried up to London. When she got into the train the little parcel was in her desk,* and the key of her desk was fastened round her neck.

They had secured a compartment for themselves from Carlisle to London, and of course filled four seats. 'As I am alive,' said Lord George as soon as the train had left the station, 'that head-policeman thinks that I am the thief!' Mrs. Carbuncle laughed. Lizzie protested that this was absurd. Lucinda declared that such a suspicion would be vastly amusing. 'It's a fact,' continued Lord George. 'I can see it in the fellow's eye, and I feel it to be a compliment. They are so very 'cute*that they delight in suspicions. I remember, when the altar-plate was stolen from Barchester Cathedral*some years ago, a splendid idea occurred to one of the police, that the Bishop had taken it!'

'Really?' asked Lizzie.

'Oh, yes;—really. I don't doubt but that there is already a belief in some of their minds that you have stolen your own diamonds for the sake of getting the better of Mr. Camperdown.'

'But what could I do with them if I had?' asked Lizzie.

'Sell them, of course. There is always a market for such goods.'

'But who would buy them?'

'If you have been so clever, Lady Eustace, I'll find a purchaser for them. One would have to go a good distance to do it,—and there would be some expense. But the thing could be done. Vienna, I should think, would be about the place.'

'Very well, then,' said Lizzie. 'You won't be surprised if I ask you to take the journey for me.' Then they all laughed, and were very much amused. It was quite agreed among them that Lizzie bore her loss very well.

'I shouldn't care the least for losing them,' said Lizzie,—'only that Florian gave them to me. They have been such a vexation to me that to be without them will be a comfort.' Her desk had been brought into the carriage and was now used as a foot-stool in place of the box which was gone.

They arrived at Mrs. Carbuncle's house in Hertford Street* quite late, between ten and eleven;—but a note had been sent from Lizzie to her cousin Frank's address from the Euston

Square*station by a commissionaire. Indeed, two notes were sent,—one to the House of Commons, and the other to the Grosvenor Hotel. 'My necklace has been stolen. Come to me early to-morrow at Mrs. Carbuncle's house, No. —, Hertford Street.' And he did come,—before Lizzie was up. Crabstick brought her mistress word that Mr. Greystock was in the parlour soon after nine o'clock. Lizzie again hurried on her clothes so that she might see her cousin, taking care as she did so that though her toilet might betray haste, it should not be other than charming. And as she dressed she endeavoured to come to some conclusion. Would it not be best for her that she should tell everything to her cousin, and throw herself upon his mercy, trusting to his ingenuity to extricate her from her difficulties? She had been thinking of her position almost through the entire night, and had remembered that at Carlisle she had committed perjury. She had sworn that the diamonds had been left by her in the box. And should they be found with her it might be that they would put her in gaol for stealing them. Little mercy could she expect from Mr. Camperdown should she fall into that gentleman's hands! But Frank, if she would even yet tell him everything honestly, might probably save her.

'What is this about the diamonds?' he asked as soon as he saw her. She had flown almost into his arms as though carried there by the excitement of the moment. 'You don't really mean that they have been stolen?'

'I do, Frank.'

'On the journey?'

'Yes, Frank;—at the inn at Carlisle.'

'Box and all?' Then she told him the whole story;—not the true story, but the story as it was believed by all the world. She found it to be impossible to tell him the true story. 'And the box was broken open, and left in the street?'

'Under an archway,' said Lizzie.

'And what do the police think?'

'I don't know what they think. Lord George says that they believe he is the thief.'

'He knew of them,' said Frank, as though he imagined that the suggestion was not altogether absurd.

'Oh, yes;—he knew of them.'

'And what is to be done?'

'I don't know. I've sent for you to tell me.' Then Frank averred that information should be immediately given to Mr. Camperdown. He would himself call on Mr. Camperdown, and would also see the head of the London police.* He did not doubt but that all the circumstances were already known in London at the police office;—but it might be well that he should see the officer. He was acquainted with the gentleman, and might perhaps learn something. Lizzie at once acceded, and Frank went direct to Mr. Camperdown's offices. 'If I had lost ten thousand pounds in that way,' said Mrs. Carbuncle, 'I think I should have broken my heart.' Lizzie felt that her heart was bursting rather than being broken, because the ten thousand pounds' worth of diamonds was not really lost.

CHAPTER XLVI
Lucy Morris in Brook Street

LUCY MORRIS went to Lady Linlithgow early in October, and was still with Lady Linlithgow when Lizzie Eustace returned to London in January. During these three months she certainly had not been happy. In the first place, she had not once seen her lover. This had aroused no anger or suspicion in her bosom against him, because the old countess had told her that she would have no lover come to the house, and that, above all, she would not allow a young man with whom she herself was connected to come in that guise to her companion. 'From all I hear,' said Lady Linlithgow, 'it's not at all likely to be a match;—and at any rate it can't go on here.' Lucy thought that she would be doing no more than standing up properly for her lover by asserting her conviction that it would be a match;—and she did assert it bravely; but she made no petition for his presence, and bore that trouble

bravely. In the next place Frank was not a satisfactory correspondent. He did write to her occasionally;—and he wrote
also to the old countess immediately on his return to town
from Bobsborough a letter which was intended as an answer
to that which she had written to Mrs. Greystock. What was
said in that letter Lucy never knew;—but she did know that
Frank's few letters to herself were not full and hearty,—were
not such thorough-going love-letters as lovers write to each
other when they feel unlimited satisfaction in the work. She
excused him,—telling herself that he was overworked, that
with his double trade of legislator and lawyer he could hardly
be expected to write letters,—that men, in respect of letter-
writing, are not as women are, and the like; but still there
grew at her heart a little weed of care, which from week to
week spread its noxious, heavy-scented leaves, and robbed
her of her joyousness. To be loved by her lover, and to feel
that she was his,—to have a lover of her own to whom she
could thoroughly devote herself,—to be conscious that she
was one of those happy women in the world who find a mate
worthy of worship as well as love,—this to her was so great a
joy that even the sadness of her present position could not
utterly depress her. From day to day she assured herself that
she did not doubt and would not doubt,—that there was no
cause for doubt;—that she would herself be base were she to
admit any shadow of suspicion. But yet his absence,—and the
shortness of those little notes, which came perhaps once a
fortnight, did tell upon her in opposition to her own convictions. Each note as it came was answered,—instantly; but she
would not write except when the notes came. She would not
seem to reproach him by writing oftener than he wrote. When
he had given her so much, and she had nothing but her confidence to give in return, would she stint him in that? There
can be no love, she said, without confidence, and it was the
pride of her heart to love him.

The circumstances of her present life were desperately
weary to her. She could hardly understand why it was that
Lady Linlithgow should desire her presence. She was required

to do nothing. She had no duties to perform, and, as it seemed to her, was of no use to any one. The countess would not even allow her to be of ordinary service in the house. Lady Linlithgow, as she had said of herself, poked her own fires, carved her own meat, lit her own candles, opened and shut the doors for herself, wrote her own letters,—and did not even like to have books read to her. She simply chose to have some one sitting with her to whom she could speak and make little cross-grained, sarcastic, and ill-natured remarks. There was no company at the house in Brook Street, and when the countess herself went out, she went out alone. Even when she had a cab to go shopping, or to make calls, she rarely asked Lucy to go with her,—and was benevolent chiefly in this,—that if Lucy chose to walk round the square, or as far as the park, her ladyship's maid was allowed to accompany her for protection. Poor Lucy often told herself that such a life would be unbearable,—were it not for the supreme satisfaction she had in remembering her lover. And then the arrangement had been made only for six months. She did not feel quite assured of her fate at the end of those six months, but she believed that there would come to her a residence in a sort of outer garden to that sweet Elysium in which she was to pass her life. The Elysium would be Frank's house; and the outer garden was the deanery at Bobsborough.

Twice during the three months Lady Fawn, with two of the girls, came to call upon her. On the first occasion she was unluckily out, taking advantage of the protection of her ladyship's maid in getting a little air. Lady Linlithgow had also been away, and Lady Fawn had seen no one. Afterwards, both Lucy and her ladyship were found at home, and Lady Fawn was full of graciousness and affection. 'I daresay you've got something to say to each other,' said Lady Linlithgow, 'and I'll go away.'

'Pray don't let us disturb you,' said Lady Fawn.

'You'd only abuse me if I didn't,' said Lady Linlithgow.

As soon as she was gone Lucy rushed into her friend's arms.

'It is so nice to see you again.'

'Yes, my dear, isn't it? I did come before, you know.'

'You have been so good to me! To see you again is like the violets and primroses.' She was crouching close to Lady Fawn, with her hand in that of her friend Lydia. 'I haven't a word to say against Lady Linlithgow, but it is like winter here, after dear Richmond.'

'Well;—we think we're prettier at Richmond,' said Lady Fawn.

'There were such hundreds of things to do there,' said Lucy. 'After all, what a comfort it is to have things to do.'

'Why did you come away?' said Lydia.

'Oh, I was obliged. You mustn't scold me now that you have come to see me.'

There were a hundred things to be said about Fawn Court and the children, and a hundred more things about Lady Linlithgow and Bruton Street. Then, at last, Lady Fawn asked the one important question. 'And now, my dear, what about Mr. Greystock?'

'Oh,—I don't know;—nothing particular, Lady Fawn. It's just as it was, and I am—quite satisfied.'

'You see him sometimes?'

'No, never. I have not seen him since the last time he came down to Richmond. Lady Linlithgow doesn't allow—followers.' There was a pleasant little spark of laughter in Lucy's eye as she said this, which would have told to any bystander the whole story of the affection which existed between her and Lady Fawn.

'That's very ill-natured,' said Lydia.

'And he's a sort of cousin too,' said Lady Fawn.

'That's just the reason why,' said Lucy, explaining. 'Of course, Lady Linlithgow thinks that her sister's nephew can do better than marry her companion. It's a matter of course she should think so. What I am most afraid of is that the dean and Mrs. Greystock should think so too.'

No doubt the dean and Mrs. Greystock would think so;—Lady Fawn was very sure of that. Lady Fawn was one of the best women breathing,—unselfish, motherly, affectionate, appreciative, and never happy unless she was doing good to somebody. It was her nature to be soft, and kind, and beneficent. But she knew very well that if she had had a son,—a second son,—situated as was Frank Greystock, she would not wish him to marry a girl without a penny, who was forced to earn her bread by being a governess. The sacrifice on Mr. Greystock's part would, in her estimation, be so great, that she did not believe that it would be made. Woman-like, she regarded the man as being so much more important than the woman, that she could not think that Frank Greystock would devote himself simply to such a one as Lucy Morris. Had Lady Fawn been asked which was the better creature of the two, her late governess or the rising barrister who had declared himself to be that governess's lover, she would have said that no man could be better than Lucy. She knew Lucy's worth and goodness so well that she was ready herself to do any act of friendship on behalf of one so sweet and excellent. For herself and her girls Lucy was a companion and friend in every way satisfactory. But was it probable that a man of the world, such as was Frank Greystock, a rising man, a member of Parliament, one who, as everybody knew, was especially in want of money,—was it probable that such a man as this would make her his wife just because she was good, and worthy, and sweet-natured? No doubt the man had said that he would do so,—and Lady Fawn's fears betrayed on her ladyship's part a very bad opinion of men in general. It may seem to be a paradox to assert that such bad opinion sprung from the high idea which she entertained of the importance of men in general;—but it was so. She had but one son, and of all her children he was the least worthy; but he was more important to her than all her daughters. Between her own girls and Lucy she hardly made any difference;—but when her son had chosen to quarrel with Lucy it had been necessary to send Lucy to eat her meals up-stairs. She could not believe that Mr. Greystock should think so much of such a little girl as to marry her. Mr. Greystock would no doubt behave very badly in not doing so;—but then men do so often behave very badly! And at the bottom of her heart she almost thought that they might be excused for doing so. According to her view of things, a man out in the world had so many things to think of, and was so very important, that he could hardly be expected to act at all times with truth and sincerity.

Lucy had suggested that the dean and Mrs. Greystock would dislike the marriage, and upon that hint Lady Fawn spoke. 'Nothing is settled, I suppose, as to where you are to go when the six months are over?'

'Nothing as yet, Lady Fawn.'

'They haven't asked you to go to Bobsborough?'

Lucy would have given the world not to blush as she answered, but she did blush. 'Nothing is fixed, Lady Fawn.'

'Something should be fixed, Lucy. It should be settled by this time;—shouldn't it, dear? What will you do without a home, if at the end of the six months Lady Linlithgow should say that she doesn't want you any more?'

Lucy certainly did not look forward to a condition in which Lady Linlithgow should be the arbitress of her destiny. The idea of staying with the countess was almost as bad to her as that of finding herself altogether homeless. She was still blushing, feeling herself to be hot and embarrassed. But Lady Fawn sat, waiting for an answer. To Lucy there was only one answer possible. 'I will ask Mr. Greystock what I am to do.' Lady Fawn shook her head. 'You don't believe in Mr. Greystock, Lady Fawn; but I do.'

'My darling girl,' said her ladyship, making the special speech for the sake of making which she had travelled up from Richmond,—'it is not exactly a question of belief, but one of common prudence. No girl should allow herself to depend on a man before she is married to him. By doing so she will be apt to lose even his respect.'

'I didn't mean for money,' said Lucy, hotter than ever, with her eyes full of tears.

'She should not be in any respect at his disposal till he has bound himself to her at the altar. You may believe me, Lucy, when I tell you so. It is only because I love you so that I say so.'

'I know that, Lady Fawn.'

'When your time here is over, just put up your things and come back to Richmond. You need fear nothing with us. Frederic quite liked your way of parting with him at last, and all that little affair is forgotten. At Fawn Court you'll be safe;—and you shall be happy too, if we can make you happy. It's the proper place for you.'

'Of course you'll come,' said Diana Fawn.

'You'll be the worst little thing in the world if you don't,' said Lydia. 'We don't know what to do without you. Do we, mamma?'

'Lucy will please us all by coming back to her old home,' said Lady Fawn. The tears were now streaming down Lucy's face, so that she was hardly able to say a word in answer to all this kindness. And she did not know what word to say. Were she to accept the offer made to her, and acknowledge that she could do nothing better than creep back under her old friend's wing,—would she not thereby be showing that she doubted her lover? And yet she could not go to the dean's house unless the dean and his wife were pleased to take her; and, suspecting as she did, that they would not be pleased, would it become her to throw upon her lover the burthen of finding for her a home with people who did not want her? Had she been welcome at Bobsborough, Mrs. Greystock would surely have so told her before this. 'You needn't say a word, my dear,' said Lady Fawn. 'You'll come, and there's an end of it.'

'But you don't want me any more,' said Lucy, from amidst her sobs.

'That's just all that you know about it,' said Lydia. 'We do want you,—more than anything.'

'I wonder whether I may come in now,' said Lady Linlithgow, entering the room. As it was the countess's own drawing-room, as it was now mid-winter, and as the fire in the dining-room had been allowed, as was usual, to sink almost to two hot coals, the request was not unreasonable. Lady Fawn was profuse in her thanks, and immediately began to account for Lucy's tears, pleading their dear friendship, and their long absence, and poor Lucy's emotional state of mind. Then she took her leave, and Lucy, as soon as she had been kissed by her friends outside the drawing-room door, took herself to her bedroom, and finished her tears in the cold.

'Have you heard the news?' said Lady Linlithgow to her companion about a month after this. Lady Linlithgow had been out, and asked the question immediately on her return. Lucy, of course, had heard no news. 'Lizzie Eustace has just come back to London, and has had all her jewels stolen on the road.'

'The diamonds?' asked Lucy, with amaze.

'Yes,—the Eustace diamonds! And they didn't belong to her any more than they did to you. They've been taken, any-way; and from what I hear I shouldn't be at all surprised if she had arranged the whole matter herself.'

'Arranged that they should be stolen?'

'Just that, my dear. It would be the very thing for Lizzie Eustace to do. She's clever enough for anything.'

'But, Lady Linlithgow——'

'I know all about that. Of course, it would be very wicked, and if it were found out she'd be put in the dock and tried for her life. It is just what I expect she'll come to some of these days. She has gone and got up a friendship with some dis-reputable people, and was travelling with them. There was a man who calls himself Lord George de Bruce Carruthers. I know him, and can remember when he was errand-boy to a disreputable lawyer at Aberdeen.' This assertion was a falsehood on the part of the countess; Lord George had never been an errand-boy, and the Aberdeen lawyer,—as provincial Scotch lawyers go,—had been by no means disreputable. 'I'm told that the police think that he has got them.'

'How very dreadful!'

'Yes;—it's dreadful enough. At any rate, men got into Lizzie's room at night and took away the iron box and

diamonds and all. It may be she was asleep at the time;—
but she's one of those who pretty nearly always sleep with
one eye open.'

'She can't be so bad as that, Lady Linlithgow.'

'Perhaps not. We shall see. They had just begun a lawsuit
about the diamonds,—to get them back. And then all at once,
—they're stolen. It looks what the men call—fishy. I'm told
that all the police in London are up about it.'

On the very next day who should come to Brook Street,
but Lizzie Eustace herself. She and her aunt had quarrelled,
and they hated each other;—but the old woman had called
upon Lizzie, advising her, as the reader will perhaps remember, to give up the diamonds, and now Lizzie returned the
visit. 'So you're here, installed in poor Macnulty's place,'
began Lizzie to her old friend, the countess at the moment
being out of the room.

'I am staying with your aunt for a few months,—as her
companion. Is it true, Lizzie, that all your diamonds have
been stolen?' Lizzie gave an account of the robbery, true
in every respect, except in regard to the contents of the box.
Poor Lizzie had been wronged in that matter by the countess,
for the robbery had been quite genuine. The man had opened
her room and taken her box, and she had slept through it all.
And then the broken box had been found, and was in the
hands of the police, and was evidence of the fact.

'People seem to think it possible,' said Lizzie, 'that Mr.
Camperdown the lawyer arranged it all.' As this suggestion
was being made Lady Linlithgow came in, and then Lizzie
repeated the whole story of the robbery. Though the aunt
and niece were open and declared enemies, the present circumstances were so peculiar and full of interest that conversation, for a time almost amicable, took place between them.
'As the diamonds were so valuable, I thought it right, Aunt
Susanna, to come and tell you myself.'

'It's very good of you, but I'd heard it already. I was telling
Miss Morris yesterday what very odd things there are being
said about it.'

'Weren't you very much frightened?' asked Lucy.

'You see, my child, I knew nothing about it till it was all over. The man cut the bit out of the door in the most beautiful way, without my ever hearing the least sound of the saw.'

'And you that sleep so light,' said the countess.

'They say that perhaps something was put into the wine at dinner to make me sleep.'

'Ah,' ejaculated the countess, who did not for a moment give up her own erroneous suspicion;—'very likely.'

'And they do say these people can do things without making the slightest tittle of noise. At any rate, the box was gone.'

'And the diamonds?' asked Lucy.

'Oh yes;—of course. And now there is such a fuss about it! The police keep on coming to me almost every day.'

'And what do the police think?' asked Lady Linlithgow. 'I'm told that they have their suspicions.'

'No doubt they have their suspicions,' said Lizzie.

'You travelled up with friends, I suppose.'

'Oh yes,—with Lord George de Bruce Carruthers; and with Mrs. Carbuncle,—who is my particular friend, and with Lucinda Roanoke, who is just going to be married to Sir Griffin Tewett. We were quite a large party.'

'And Macnulty?'

'No. I left Miss Macnulty at Portray with my darling. They thought he had better remain a little longer in Scotland.'

'Ah yes;—perhaps Lord George de Bruce Carruthers does not care for babies. I can easily believe that. I wish Macnulty had been with you.'

'Why do you wish that?' said Lizzie, who already was beginning to feel that the countess intended, as usual, to make herself disagreeable.

'She's a stupid, dull, pig-headed creature; but one can believe what she says.'

'And don't you believe what I say?' demanded Lizzie.

'It's all true, no doubt, that the diamonds are gone.'

'Indeed it is.'

'But I don't know much about Lord George de Bruce Carruthers.'

'He's the brother of a marquis, anyway,' said Lizzie, who thought that she might thus best answer the mother of a Scotch Earl.

'I remember when he was plain George Carruthers, running about the streets of Aberdeen, and it was well with him when his shoes weren't broken at the toes and down at heel. He earned his bread then, such as it was;—nobody knows how he gets it now. Why does he call himself de Bruce, I wonder.'

'Because his godfathers and godmothers gave him that name when he was made a child of Christ, and an inheritor of the kingdom of heaven,' said Lizzie, ever so pertly.

'I don't believe a bit of it.'

'I wasn't there to see, Aunt Susanna; and therefore I can't swear to it. That's his name in all the peerages,* and I suppose they ought to know.'

'And what does Lord George de Bruce say about the diamonds?'

Now it had come to pass that Lady Eustace herself did not feel altogether sure that Lord George had not had a hand in this robbery. It would have been a trick worthy of a genuine Corsair to arrange and carry out such a scheme for the appropriation of so rich a spoil. A watch or a brooch would, of course, be beneath the notice of a good genuine Corsair,—of a Corsair who was written down in the peerage as a marquis's brother;—but diamonds worth ten thousand pounds are not to be had every day. A Corsair must live, and if not by plunder rich as that,—how then? If Lord George had concocted this little scheme, he would naturally be ignorant of the true event of the robbery till he should meet the humble executors of his design, and would, as Lizzie thought, have remained unaware of the truth till his arrival in London. That he had been ignorant of the truth during the journey was evident to her. But they had now been three days in London, during which she had seen him once. At that interview, he had been sullen, and almost cross,—and had said next to nothing about the robbery. He made but one remark about it. 'I have told the chief man here,' he said, 'that I shall be ready to give any evidence in my power when called upon. Till then I shall take no further steps in the matter. I have been asked questions that should not have been asked.' In saying this he had used a tone which prevented further conversation on the subject, but Lizzie, as she thought of it all, remembered his jocular remark, made in the railway carriage, as to the suspicion which had already been expressed on the matter in regard to himself. If he had been the perpetrator, and had then found that he had only stolen the box, how wonderful would be the mystery! 'He hasn't got anything to say,' replied Lizzie to the question of the countess.

'And who is your Mrs. Carbuncle?' asked the old woman.

'A particular friend of mine with whom I am staying at present. You don't go about a great deal, Aunt Linlithgow, but surely you must have met Mrs. Carbuncle.'

'I'm an ignorant old woman, no doubt. My dear, I'm not at all surprised at your losing your diamonds. The pity is that they weren't your own.'

'They were my own.'

'The loss will fall on you, no doubt, because the Eustace people will make you pay for them. You'll have to give up half your jointure for your life. That's what it will come to. To think of your travelling about with those things in a box!'

'They were my own, and I had a right to do what I liked with them. Nobody accuses you of taking them.'

'That's quite true. Nobody will accuse me. I suppose Lord George has left England for the benefit of his health. It would not at all surprise me if I were to hear that Mrs. Carbuncle had followed him;—not in the least.'

'You're just like yourself, Aunt Susanna,' said Lizzie, getting up and taking her leave. 'Good-bye, Lucy,—I hope you're happy and comfortable here. Do you ever see a certain friend of ours now?'

'If you mean Mr. Greystock, I haven't seen him since I left Fawn Court,' said Lucy with dignity.

When Lizzie was gone, Lady Linlithgow spoke her mind freely about her niece. 'Lizzie Eustace won't come to any good. When I heard that she was engaged to that prig,* Lord Fawn, I had some hopes that she might be kept out of harm. That's all over, of course. When he heard about the necklace he wasn't going to put his neck into that scrape. But now she's getting among such a set that nothing can save her. She has taken to hunting, and rides about the country like a mad woman.'

'A great many ladies hunt,' said Lucy.

'And she's got hold of this Lord George, and of that horrid American woman that nobody knows anything about. They've got the diamonds between them, I don't doubt. I'll bet you sixpence that the police find out all about it, and that there is some terrible scandal. The diamonds were no more hers than they were mine, and she'll be made to pay for them.'

The necklace, the meanwhile, was still locked up in Lizzie's desk,—with a patent Bramah key,*—in Mrs. Carbuncle's house, and was a terrible trouble to our unhappy friend.

CHAPTER XLVII
Matching Priory

BEFORE the end of January everybody in London had heard of the great robbery at Carlisle,—and most people had heard also that there was something very peculiar in the matter,—something more than a robbery. Various rumours were afloat. It had become widely known that the diamonds were to be the subject of litigation between the young widow and the trustees of the Eustace estate; and it was known also that Lord Fawn had engaged himself to marry the widow, and had then retreated from his engagement simply on account of this litigation. There were strong parties formed in the matter,—whom we may call Lizzieites and anti-Lizzieites. The Lizzieites were of opinion that poor Lady Eustace was being very ill-treated;—that the diamonds did probably belong to her, and that Lord Fawn, at any rate, clearly ought to be her own. It was worthy of remark that these Lizzieites were all of them Conservatives. Frank Greystock had probably set the party on foot;—and it was natural that political opponents should believe that a noble young Under-Secretary of State on the liberal side,—such as Lord Fawn,—had misbehaved himself. When the matter at last became of such importance as to demand leading articles in the newspapers, those journals which had devoted themselves to upholding the conservative politicians of the day were very heavy indeed upon Lord Fawn. The whole force of the Government, however, was anti-Lizzieite; and as the controversy advanced, every good Liberal became aware that there was nothing so wicked, so rapacious, so bold, or so cunning but that Lady Eustace might have done it, or caused it to be done, without delay, without difficulty, and without scruple. Lady Glencora Palliser for a while endeavoured to defend Lizzie in liberal circles,—from generosity rather than from any real belief, and instigated, perhaps, by a feeling that any woman in society who was capable of doing anything extraordinary ought to be defended. But even Lady Glencora was forced to abandon her generosity, and to confess, on behalf of her party, that Lizzie Eustace was—a very wicked young woman, indeed. All this, no doubt, grew out of the diamonds, and chiefly arose from the robbery; but there had been enough of notoriety attached to Lizzie before the affair at Carlisle to make people fancy that they had understood her character long before that.

The party assembled at Matching Priory, a country house belonging to Mr. Palliser in which Lady Glencora took much delight, was not large, because Mr. Palliser's uncle, the Duke of Omnium, who was with them, was now a very old man, and one who did not like very large gatherings of people. Lord and Lady Chiltern were there,—that Lord Chiltern who had been known so long and so well in the hunting-counties of England, and that Lady Chiltern who had been so popular in London as the beautiful Violet Effingham; and Mr. and Mrs. Grey were there, very particular friends of Mr. Palliser's. Mr. Grey was now sitting for the borough of Silverbridge, in which the Duke of Omnium was still presumed to have a controlling influence, in spite of all Reform bills, and Mrs. Grey was in some distant way connected with Lady Glencora. And Madame Max Goesler was there,—a lady whose society was still much affected by the old duke; and Mr. and Mrs. Bonteen,—who had been brought there, not, perhaps altogether because they were greatly loved, but in order that the gentleman's services might be made available by Mr. Palliser in reference to some great reform* about to be introduced in monetary matters. Mr. Palliser, who was now Chancellor of the Exchequer, was intending to alter the value of the penny. Unless the work should be too much for him, and he should die before he had accomplished the self-imposed task, the future penny was to be made, under his auspices, to contain five farthings, and the shilling ten pennies. It was thought that if this could be accomplished, the arithmetic of the whole world would be so simplified that henceforward the name of Palliser would be blessed by all school-boys, clerks, shop-keepers, and financiers. But the difficulties were so great that Mr. Palliser's hair was already grey from toil, and his shoulders bent by the burthen imposed upon them. Mr. Bonteen, with two private secretaries from the Treasury, was now at Matching to assist Mr. Palliser;—and it was thought that both Mr. and Mrs. Bonteen were near to madness under the pressure of the five-farthing penny. Mr. Bonteen had remarked to many of his political friends that those two extra farthings that could not be made to go into the shilling would put him into his cold grave before the world would know what he had done,—or had rewarded him for it with a handle to his name, and a pension. Lord Fawn was also at Matching,—a suggestion having been made to Lady Glencora by some leading Liberals that he should be supported in his difficulties by her hospitality.

The mind of Mr. Palliser himself was too deeply engaged to admit of its being interested in the great necklace affair; but, of all the others assembled, there was not one who did not listen anxiously for news on the subject. As regarded the old duke, it had been found to be quite a godsend; and from post to post as the facts reached Matching they were communicated to him. And, indeed, there were some there who would not wait for the post, but had the news about poor Lizzie's diamonds down by the wires. The matter was of the greatest moment to Lord Fawn, and Lady Glencora was, perhaps, justified, on his behalf, in demanding a preference for her affairs over the messages which were continually passing between Matching and the Treasury respecting those two ill-conditioned farthings.

'Duke,' she said, entering rather abruptly the small warm luxurious room in which her husband's uncle was passing his morning, 'duke, they say now that after all the diamonds were not in the box when it was taken out of the room at Carlisle.' The duke was reclining in an easy-chair, with his head leaning forward on his breast, and Madame Goesler was reading to him. It was now three o'clock, and the old man had been brought down to this room after his breakfast. Madame Goesler was reading the last famous new novel, and the duke was dozing. That, probably, was the fault neither of the reader nor of the novelist; as the duke was wont to doze in these days. But Lady Glencora's tidings awakened him completely. She had the telegram in her hand,—so that he could perceive that the very latest news was brought to him.

'The diamonds not in the box!' he said,—pushing his head a little more forward in his eagerness, and sitting with the extended fingers of his two hands touching each other.

'Barrington Erle says that Major Mackintosh is almost sure the diamonds were not there.' Major Mackintosh was an officer very high in the police force, whom everybody trusted implicitly, and as to whom the outward world believed that he could discover the perpetrators of any iniquity, if he would only take the trouble to look into it. Such was the pressing nature of his duties that he found himself compelled in one way or another to give up about sixteen hours a day to them; —but the outer world accused him of idleness. There was nothing he couldn't find out;—only he would not give himself the trouble to find out all the things that happened. Two or three newspapers had already been very hard upon him in regard to the Eustace diamonds. Such a mystery as that, they said, he ought to have unravelled long ago. That he had not unravelled it yet was quite certain.

'The diamonds not in the box!' said the duke.

'Then she must have known it,' said Madame Goesler.

'That doesn't quite follow, Madame Max,' said Lady Glencora.

'But why shouldn't the diamonds have been in the box?' asked the duke. As this was the first intimation given to Lady Glencora of any suspicion that the diamonds had not been taken with the box, and as this had been received by telegraph, she could not answer the duke's question with any clear exposition of her own. She put up her hands and shook her head. 'What does Plantagenet think about it?' asked the duke. Plantagenet Palliser was the full name of the duke's nephew and heir. The duke's mind was evidently much disturbed.

'He doesn't think that either the box or the diamonds were ever worth five farthings,' said Lady Glencora.

'The diamonds not in the box!' repeated the duke. 'Madame Max, do you believe that the diamonds were not in the box?' Madame Goesler shrugged her shoulders and made no answer; but the shrugging of her shoulders was quite satisfactory to the duke, who always thought that Madame Goesler did everything better than anybody else. Lady Glencora stayed with her uncle for the best part of an hour, and every word spoken was devoted to Lizzie and her necklace; but as this new idea had been broached, and as they had no other information than that conveyed in the telegram, very little light could be thrown upon it. But on the next morning there came a letter from Barrington Erle to Lady Glencora, which told so much, and hinted so much more, that it will be well to give it to the reader.

'My dear Lady Glencora,

'I hope you got my telegram yesterday. I had just seen Mackintosh,—on whose behalf, however, I must say that he told me as little as he possibly could. It is leaking out, however, on every side, that the police believe that when the box was taken out of the room at Carlisle, the diamonds were not in it. As far as I can learn, they ground this suspicion on the fact that they cannot trace the stones. They say that, if such a lot of diamonds had been through the thieves' market in London, they would have left some track behind them. As far as I can judge, Mackintosh thinks that Lord George has them, but that her ladyship gave them to him; and that this little game of the robbery at Carlisle was planned to put John Eustace and the lawyers off the scent. If it should turn out that the box was opened before it left Portray, that the door of her ladyship's room was cut by her ladyship's self, or by his lordship with her ladyship's aid, and that the fragments of the box were carried out of the hotel by his lordship in person, it will altogether have been so delightful a plot, that all concerned in it ought to be canonised,—or, at least, allowed to keep their plunder. One of the old detectives told me that the opening of the box under the arch of the railway, in an exposed place, could hardly have been executed so neatly as was done;—that no thief so situated would have given the time necessary to it; and that, if there had been thieves at all at work, they would have been traced. Against this, there is the certain fact,—as I have heard from various men engaged in the inquiry,—that certain persons among the community of thieves are very much at loggerheads with each other,— the higher, or creative department in thiefdom, accusing the lower or mechanical department of gross treachery in having appropriated to its own sole profit plunder, for the taking of which it had undertaken to receive a certain stipulated price. But then it may be the case that his lordship and her ladyship have set such a rumour abroad for the sake of putting the police off the scent. Upon the whole, the little mystery is quite delightful; and has put the ballot, and poor Mr. Palliser's five-farthinged penny, quite out of joint. Nobody now cares for anything except the Eustace diamonds. Lord George, I am told, has offered to fight everybody or anybody, beginning with Lord Fawn, and ending with Major Mackintosh. Should he be innocent, which, of course, is possible, the thing must be annoying. I should not at all wonder myself, if it should turn out that her ladyship left them in Scotland. The place there, however, has been searched, in compliance with an order from the police and by her ladyship's consent.

'Don't let Mr. Palliser quite kill himself. I hope the Bonteen plan answers. I never knew a man who could find more farthings in a shilling than Mr. Bonteen. Remember me very kindly to the duke, and pray enable poor Fawn to keep up his spirits. If he likes to arrange a meeting with Lord George, I shall be only too happy to be his friend. You remember our last duel. Chiltern is with you, and can put Fawn up to the proper way of getting over to Flanders,*—and of returning, should he chance to escape.

'Yours always most faithfully,
'BARRINGTON ERLE.

'Of course, I'll keep you posted in everything respecting the necklace till you come to town yourself.'

The whole of this letter Lady Glencora read to the duke, to Lady Chiltern, and to Madame Goesler;—and the principal contents of it she repeated to the entire company. It was certainly the general belief at Matching that Lord George had the diamonds in his possession,—either with or without the assistance of their late fair possessor.

The duke was struck with awe when he thought of all the circumstances. 'The brother of a marquis!' he said to his nephew's wife. 'It's such a disgrace to the peerage!'

'As for that, duke,' said Lady Glencora, 'the peerage is used to it by this time.'

'I never heard of such an affair as this before.'

'I don't see why the brother of a marquis shouldn't turn thief as well as anybody else. They say he hasn't got anything of his own;—and I suppose that is what makes men steal other people's property. Peers go into trade, and peeresses gamble on the Stock Exchange. Peers become bankrupt, and the sons of peers run away;—just like other men. I don't see why all enterprises should not be open to them. But to think of that little purring cat, Lady Eustace, having been so very—very clever! It makes me quite envious.'

All this took place in the morning;—that is, about two o'clock; but after dinner the subject became general. There might be some little reticence in regard to Lord Fawn's feelings,—but it was not sufficient to banish a subject so interesting from the minds and lips of the company. 'The Tewett marriage is to come off, after all,' said Mrs. Bonteen. 'I've a letter from dear Mrs. Rutter, telling me so as a fact.'

'I wonder whether Miss Roanoke will be allowed to wear one or two of the diamonds at the wedding,' suggested one of the private secretaries.

'Nobody will dare to wear a diamond at all next season,' said Lady Glencora. 'As for my own, I shan't think of having them out. I should always feel that I was being inspected.'

'Unless they unravel the mystery,' said Madame Goesler.

'I hope they won't do that,' said Lady Glencora. 'The play is too good to come to an end so soon. If we hear that Lord George is engaged to Lady Eustace, nothing, I suppose, can be done to stop the marriage.'

'Why shouldn't she marry if she pleases?' asked Mr. Palliser.

'I've not the slightest objection to her being married. I hope she will, with all my heart. I certainly think she should have her husband after buying him at such a price. I suppose Lord Fawn won't forbid the banns.' These last words were only whispered to her next neighbour, Lord Chiltern; but poor Lord Fawn saw the whisper, and was aware that it must have had reference to his condition.

On the next morning there came further news. The police had asked permission from their occupants to search the rooms in which lived Lady Eustace and Lord George, and in each case the permission had been refused. So said Barrington Erle in his letter to Lady Glencora. Lord George had told the applicant, very roughly, that nobody should touch any article belonging to him without a search-warrant. If any magistrate would dare to give such a warrant, let him do it. 'I'm told that Lord George acts the indignant madman uncommonly well,' said Barrington Erle in his letter. As for poor Lizzie, she had fainted when the proposition was made to her. The request was renewed as soon as she had been brought to herself; and then she refused,—on the advice, as she said, of her cousin, Mr. Greystock. Barrington Erle went on to say that the police were very much blamed. It was believed that no information could be laid before a magistrate sufficient to justify a search-warrant;—and, in such circumstances, no search should have been attempted. Such was the public verdict, as declared in Barrington Erle's last letter to Lady Glencora.

Mr. Palliser was of opinion that the attempt to search the lady's house was iniquitous. Mr. Bonteen shook his head, and rather thought that, if he were Home Secretary, he would have had the search made. Lady Chiltern said that, if policemen came to her, they might search everything she had in the world. Mrs. Grey reminded them that all they really knew of the unfortunate woman was, that her jewel-box had been stolen out of her bedroom at her hotel. Madame Goesler was of opinion that a lady who could carry such a box about the country with her, deserved to have it stolen. Lord Fawn felt himself obliged to confess that he agreed altogether with Madame Goesler. Unfortunately, he had been acquainted with the lady, and now was constrained to say that her conduct had been such as to justify the suspicions of the police. 'Of course, we all suspect her,' said Lady Glencora; 'and, of course, we suspect Lord George too, and Mrs. Carbuncle and Miss Roanoke. But then, you know, if I were to lose my diamonds, people would suspect me just the same,—or perhaps Plantagenet. It is so delightful to think that a woman has stolen her own property, and put all the police into a state of ferment.' Lord Chiltern declared himself to be heartily sick of the whole subject; and Mr. Grey, who was a very just man, suggested that the evidence, as yet, against anybody, was very slight. 'Of course, it's slight,' said Lady Glencora. 'If it were more than slight, it would be just like any other robbery, and there would be nothing in it.' On the same morning Mrs. Bonteen received a second letter from her friend Mrs. Rutter. The Tewett marriage had been certainly broken off. Sir Griffin had been very violent, misbehaving himself grossly in Mrs. Carbuncle's house, and Miss Roanoke had declared that, under no circumstances, would she ever speak to him again. It was Mrs. Rutter's opinion, however, that this violence had been 'put on' by Sir Griffin, who was desirous of escaping from the marriage because of the affair of the diamonds. 'He's very much bound up with Lord George,' said Mrs. Rutter, 'and is afraid that he may be implicated.'

'In my opinion he's quite right,' said Lord Fawn.

All these matters were told to the duke by Lady Glencora and Madame Goesler in the recesses of his grace's private room; for the duke was now infirm, and did not dine in company unless the day was very auspicious to him. But in the evening he would creep into the drawing-room, and on this occasion he had a word to say about the Eustace diamonds to every one in the room. It was admitted by them all that the robbery had been a godsend in the way of amusing the duke. 'Wouldn't have her boxes searched, you know,' said the duke; 'that looks uncommonly suspicious. Perhaps, Lady Chiltern, we shall hear to-morrow morning something more about it.'

'Poor dear duke,' said Lady Chiltern to her husband.

'Doting old idiot!' he replied.

CHAPTER XLVIII
Lizzie's Condition

WHEN such a man as Barrington Erle undertakes to send information to such a correspondent as Lady Glencora in reference to such a matter as Lady Eustace's diamonds, he is bound to be full rather than accurate. We may say, indeed, that perfect accuracy would be detrimental rather than otherwise, and would tend to disperse that feeling of mystery which is so gratifying. No suggestion had in truth been made to Lord George de Bruce Carruthers as to the searching of his lordship's boxes and desks. That very eminent detective officer, Mr. Bunfit, had, however, called upon Lord George more than once, and Lord George had declared very plainly that he did not like it. 'If you'll have the kindness to explain to me what it is you want, I'll be much obliged to you,' Lord George had said to Mr. Bunfit.

'Well, my lord,' said Bunfit, 'what we want is these diamonds.'

'Do you believe that I've got them?'

'A man in my situation, my lord, never believes anything. We has to suspect, but we never believes.'

'You suspect that I stole them?'

'No, my lord;—I didn't say that. But things are very queer; aren't they?' The immediate object of Mr. Bunfit's visit on this morning had been to ascertain from Lord George whether it was true that his lordship had been with Messrs. Harter and Benjamin, the jewellers, on the morning after his arrival in town. No one from the police had as yet seen either Harter or Benjamin in connection with this robbery; but it may not be too much to say that the argus eyes* of Major Mackintosh were upon Messrs. Harter and Benjamin's whole establishment, and it was believed that, if the jewels were in London, they were locked up in some box within that house. It was thought more than probable by Major Mackintosh and his myrmidons that the jewels were already at

Hamburg; and by this time, as the major had explained to Mr. Camperdown, every one of them might have been reset,—or even recut. But it was known that Lord George had been at the house of Messrs. Harter and Benjamin early on the morning after his return to town, and the ingenuous Mr. Bunfit, who, by reason of his situation, never believed anything and only suspected, had expressed a very strong opinion to Major Mackintosh that the necklace had in truth been transferred to the Jews on that morning. That there was nothing 'too hot or too heavy' for Messrs. Harter and Benjamin was quite a creed with the police of the west end of London. Might it not be well to ask Lord George what he had to say about the visit? Should Lord George deny the visit, such denial would go far to confirm Mr. Bunfit. The question was asked, and Lord George did not deny the visit. 'Unfortunately, they hold acceptances*of mine,' said Lord George, 'and I am often there.' 'We know as they have your lordship's name to paper,' said Mr. Bunfit,—thanking Lord George, however, for his courtesy. It may be understood that all this would be unpleasant to Lord George, and that he should be indignant almost to madness.

But Mr. Erle's information, though certainly defective in regard to Lord George de Bruce Carruthers, had been more correct when he spoke of the lady. An interview that was very terrible to poor Lizzie did take place between her and Mr. Bunfit in Mrs. Carbuncle's house on Tuesday, the 30th of January.* There had been many interviews between Lizzie and various members of the police force in reference to the diamonds, but the questions put to her had always been asked on the supposition that she might have mislaid the necklace. Was it not possible that she might have thought that she locked it up, but have omitted to place it in the box? As long as these questions had reference to a possible oversight in Scotland,—to some carelessness which she might have committed on the night before she left her home,— Lizzie upon the whole seemed rather to like the idea. It certainly was possible. She believed thoroughly that the diamonds had been locked by her in the box,—but she acknowledged that it might be the case that they had been left on one side. This had happened when the police first began to suspect that the necklace had not been in the box when it was carried out of the Carlisle hotel, but before it had occurred to them that Lord George had been concerned in the robbery, and possibly Lady Eustace herself. Men had been sent down from London, of course at considerable expense, and Portray Castle had been searched, with the consent of its owner, from the weathercock to the foundation-stone,—much to the consternation of Miss Macnulty, and to the delight of Andy Gowran. No trace of the diamonds was found, and Lizzie had so far fraternized with the police. But when Mr. Bunfit called upon her, perhaps for the fifth or sixth time, and suggested that he should be allowed, with the assistance of the female whom he had left behind him in the hall, to search all her ladyship's boxes, drawers, presses, and receptacles in London, the thing took a very different aspect. 'You see, my lady,' said Mr. Bunfit, excusing the peculiar nature of his request, 'it may have got anywhere among your ladyship's things, unbeknownst.' Lady Eustace and Mrs. Carbuncle were at the time sitting together, and Mrs. Carbuncle was the first to protest. If Mr. Bunfit thought that he was going to search her things, Mr. Bunfit was very much mistaken. What she had suffered about this necklace no man or woman knew,—and she meant that there should be an end of it. It was her opinion that the police should have discovered every stone of it days and days ago. At any rate, her house was her own, and she gave Mr. Bunfit to understand that his repeated visits were not agreeable to her. But when Mr. Bunfit, without showing the slightest displeasure at the evil things said of him, suggested that the search should be confined to the rooms used exclusively by Lady Eustace, Mrs. Carbuncle absolutely changed her views, and recommended that he should be allowed to have his way.

At that moment the condition of poor Lizzie Eustace was very sad. He who recounts these details has scorned to have a secret between himself and his readers. The diamonds were at this moment locked up within Lizzie's desk. For the last three weeks they had been there,—if it may not be more truly said that they were lying heavily on her heart. For three weeks had her mind with constant stretch been working on that point,—whither should she take the diamonds, and what should she do with them? A certain very wonderful strength she did possess, or she could not have endured the weight of so terrible an anxiety; but from day to day the thing became worse and worse with her, as gradually she perceived that suspicion was attached to herself. Should she confide the secret to Lord George, or to Mrs. Carbuncle, or to Frank Greystock? She thought she could have borne it all, if only some one would have borne it with her. But when the moments came in which such confidence might be made, her courage failed her. Lord George she saw frequently; but he was unsympathetic and almost rough with her. She knew that he also was suspected, and she was almost disposed to think that he had planned the robbery. If it were so, if the robbery had been his handiwork, it was not singular that he should be unsympathetic with the owner and probable holder of the prey which he had missed. Nevertheless Lizzie thought that if he would have been soft with her, like a dear, good, genuine Corsair, for half an hour, she would have told him all, and placed the necklace in his hands. And there were moments in which she almost resolved to tell her secret to Mrs. Carbuncle. She had stolen nothing;—so she averred to herself. She had intended only to defend and save her own property. Even the lie that she had told, and the telling of which was continued from day to day, had in a measure been forced upon her by circumstances. She thought that Mrs. Carbuncle would sympathise with her in that feeling which had prevented her from speaking the truth when first the fact of the robbery was made known to herself in her own bedroom. Mrs. Carbuncle was a lady who told many lies, as Lizzie knew well,—and surely could not be horrified at a lie told in such circumstances. But it was not in Lizzie's nature to trust a woman. Mrs.

Carbuncle would tell Lord George,—and that would destroy everything. When she thought of confiding everything to her cousin, it was always in his absence. The idea became dreadful to her as soon as he was present. She could not dare to own to him that she had sworn falsely to the magistrate at Carlisle. And so the burthen had to be borne, increasing every hour in weight, and the poor creature's back was not broad enough to bear it. She thought of the necklace every waking minute, and dreamed of it when she slept. She could not keep herself from unlocking her desk and looking at it twenty times a day, although she knew the peril of such nervous solicitude. If she could only rid herself of it altogether, she was sure now that she would do so. She would throw it into the ocean fathoms deep, if only she could find herself alone upon the ocean. But she felt that, let her go where she might, she would be watched. She might declare to-morrow her intention of going to Ireland,—or, for that matter, to America. But, were she to do so, some horrid policeman would be on her track. The iron box had been a terrible nuisance to her;—but the iron box had been as nothing compared to the necklace locked up in her desk. From day to day she meditated a plan of taking the thing out into the streets, and dropping it in the dark; but she was sure that, were she to do so, some one would have watched her while she dropped it. She was unwilling to trust her old friend Mr. Benjamin; but in these days her favourite scheme was to offer the diamonds for sale to him at some very low price. If he would help her they might surely be got out of their present hiding-place into his hands. Any man would be powerful to help, if there were any man whom she could trust. In furtherance of this scheme she went so far as to break a brooch,—a favourite brooch of her own,—in order that she might have an excuse for calling at the jewellers'. But even this she postponed from day to day. Circumstances, as they had occurred, had taught her to believe that the police could not insist on breaking open her desk unless some evidence could be brought against her. There was no evidence, and her desk was so far safe. But the same circumstances had made her understand that she was already suspected of some intrigue with reference to the diamonds,—though of what she was suspected she did not clearly perceive. As far as she could divine the thoughts of her enemies, they did not seem to suppose that the diamonds were in her possession. It seemed to be believed by those enemies that they had passed into the hands of Lord George. As long as her enemies were on a scent so false, might it not be best that she should remain quiet?

But all the ingenuity, the concentrated force, and trained experience of the police of London would surely be too great and powerful for her in the long run. She could not hope to keep her secret and the diamonds till they should acknowledge themselves to be baffled. And then she was aware of a morbid desire on her own part to tell the secret,—of a desire that amounted almost to a disease. It would soon burst her bosom open, unless she could share her knowledge with some one. And yet, as she thought of it all, she told herself that she had no friend so fast and true as to justify such confidence. She was ill with anxiety, and,—worse than that,— Mrs. Carbuncle knew that she was ill. It was acknowledged between them that this affair of the necklace was so terrible as to make a woman ill. Mrs. Carbuncle at present had been gracious enough to admit so much as that. But might it not be probable that Mrs. Carbuncle would come to suspect that she did not know the whole secret? Mrs. Carbuncle had already, on more than one occasion, said a little word or two which had been unpleasant.

Such was Lizzie's condition when Mr. Bunfit came, with his authoritative request to be allowed to inspect Lizzie's boxes, —and when Mrs. Carbuncle, having secured her own privacy, expressed her opinion that Mr. Bunfit should be allowed to do as he desired.

CHAPTER XLIX
Bunfit and Gager

As soon as the words were out of Mrs. Carbuncle's mouth,
—those ill-natured words in which she expressed her
assent to Mr. Bunfit's proposition that a search should be
made after the diamonds among all the possessions of Lady
Eustace which were now lodged in her own house,—poor
Lizzie's courage deserted her entirely. She had been very
courageous; for, though her powers of endurance had sometimes nearly deserted her, though her heart had often failed
her, still she had gone on and had endured and been silent.
To endure and to be silent in her position did require great
courage. She was all alone in her misery, and could see no
way out of it. The diamonds were heavy as a load of lead
within her bosom. And yet she had persevered. Now, as she
heard Mrs. Carbuncle's words, her courage failed her. There
came some obstruction in her throat, so that she could not

speak. She felt as though her heart were breaking. She put out both her hands and could not draw them back again. She knew that she was betraying herself by her weakness. She could just hear the man explaining that the search was merely a thing of ceremony,—just to satisfy everybody that there was no mistake;—and then she fainted. So far, Barrington Erle was correct in the information given by him to Lady Glencora. She pressed one hand against her heart, gasped for breath, and then fell back upon the sofa. Perhaps she could have done nothing better. Had the fainting been counterfeit, the measure would have shown ability. But the fainting was altogether true. Mrs. Carbuncle first, and then Mr. Bunfit, hurried from their seats to help her. To neither of them did it occur for a moment that the fit was false.

'The whole thing has been too much for her,' said Mrs. Carbuncle severely, ringing the bell at the same time for further aid.

'No doubt,—mum; no doubt. We has to see a deal of this sort of thing. Just a little air if you please, mum,—and as much water as 'd go to christen a babby. That's always best, mum.'

'If you'll have the kindness to stand on one side,' said Mrs. Carbuncle, as she stretched Lizzie on the sofa.

'Certainly, mum,' said Bunfit, standing erect by the wall, but not showing the slightest disposition to leave the room.

'You had better go,' said Mrs. Carbuncle,—loudly and very severely.

'I'll just stay and see her come to, mum. I won't do her a morsel of harm, mum. Sometimes they faints at the very fust sight of such as we; but we has to bear it. A little more air, if you could, mum;—and just dash the water on in drops like. They feels a drop more than they would a bucketful,—and then when they comes to they hasn't to change theirselves.'

Bunfit's advice, founded on much experience, was good, and Lizzie gradually came to herself and opened her eyes. She immediately clutched at her breast, feeling for her key. She found it unmoved, but before her finger had recognised the touch, her quick mind had told her how wrong the movement had been. It had been lost upon Mrs. Carbuncle, but not on Mr. Bunfit. He did not at once think that she had the diamonds in her desk; but he felt almost sure that there was something in her possession,—probably some document,—which, if found, would place him on the track of the diamonds. But he could not compel a search. 'Your ladyship'll soon be better,' said Bunfit graciously. Lizzie endeavoured to smile as she expressed her assent to this proposition. 'As I was a saying to the elder lady——'

'Saying to who, sir?' exclaimed Mrs. Carbuncle, rising up in wrath. 'Elder, indeed!'

'As I was a venturing to explain, these fits of fainting come often in our way. Thieves, mum,—that is, the regulars,— don't mind us a bit, and the women is more hardeneder than the men; but when we has to speak to a lady, it is so often that she goes off like that! I've known 'em do it just at being looked at.'

'Don't you think, sir, that you'd better leave us now?' said Mrs. Carbuncle.

'Indeed you had,' said Lizzie. 'I'm fit for nothing just at present.'

'We won't disturb your ladyship the least in life,' said Mr. Bunfit, 'if you'll only just let us have your keys. Your servant can be with us, and we won't move one tittle of anything.' But Lizzie, though she was still suffering that ineffable sickness which always accompanies and follows a real fainting-fit, would not surrender her keys. Already had an excuse for not doing so occurred to her. But for a while she seemed to hesitate. 'I don't demand it, Lady Eustace,' said Mr. Bunfit, 'but if you'll allow me to say so, I do think it will look better for your ladyship.'

'I can take no step without consulting my cousin, Mr. Greystock,' said Lizzie; and having thought of this she adhered to it. The detective supplied her with many reasons for giving up her keys, alleging that it would do no harm, and that her refusal would create infinite suspicions. But Lizzie had formed her answer and stuck to it. She always consulted her cousin, and always acted upon his advice. He had already cautioned her not to take any steps without his sanction. She would do nothing till he consented. If Mr. Bunfit would see Mr. Greystock, and if Mr. Greystock would come to her and tell her to submit,—she would submit. Ill as she was, she could be obstinate, and Bunfit left the house without having been able to finger that key which he felt sure that Lady Eustace carried somewhere on her person.

As he walked back to his own quarters in Scotland Yard, Bunfit was by no means dissatisfied with his morning's work. He had not expected to find anything with Lady Eustace, and, when she had fainted, had not hoped to be allowed to search. But he was now sure that her ladyship was possessed, at any rate, of some guilty knowledge. Bunfit was one of those who, almost from the first, had believed that the box was empty when taken out of the hotel. 'Stones like them must turn up more or less,' was Bunfit's great argument. That the police should already have found the stones themselves was not perhaps probable; but had any ordinary thieves had them in their hands, they could not have been passed on without leaving a trace behind them. It was his opinion that the box had been opened and the door cut by the instrumentality and concurrence of Lord George de Bruce Carruthers,—with the assistance of some well-skilled mechanical thief. Nothing could be made out of the tall footman;—indeed, the tall footman had already been set at liberty, although he was known to have evil associates, and the tall footman was now loud in demanding compensation for the injury done to him. Many believed that the tall footman had been concerned in the matter,—many, that is, among the experienced craftsmen of the police force. Bunfit thought otherwise. Bunfit believed that the diamonds were now either in the possession of Lord George or of Harter and Benjamin, that they had been handed over to Lord George to save them from Messrs. Camperdown and the lawsuit, and that Lord George and the lady were lovers. The lady's conduct at their last interview, her fit of fainting, and her clutching for the key, all confirmed Bunfit in his opinion. But unfortunately for Bunfit he was almost alone in his opinion. There were men in the force,—high in their profession as detectives,—who avowed that certainly two very experienced and well-known thieves had been concerned in the business. That a certain Mr. Smiler had been there,—a gentleman for whom the whole police of London entertained a feeling which approached to veneration, and that most diminutive of full-grown thieves, Billy Cann,—most diminutive but at the same time most expert,—was not doubted by some minds which were apt to doubt till conviction had become certainty. The traveller who had left the Scotch train at Dumfries had been a very small man, and it was a known fact that Mr. Smiler had left London, by train, from the Euston Square station, on the day before that on which Lizzie and her party had reached Carlisle. If it were so, if Mr. Smiler and Billy Cann had both been at work at the hotel, then,—so argued they who opposed the Bunfit theory,—it was hardly conceivable that the robbery should have been arranged by Lord George. According to the Bunfit theory, the only thing needed by the conspirators had been that the diamonds should be handed over by Lady Eustace to Lord George in such a way as to escape suspicion that such transfer had been made. This might have been done with very little trouble,— by simply leaving the box empty, with the key in it. The door of the bedroom had been opened by skilful professional men, and the box had been forced by the use of tools which none but professional gentlemen would possess. Was it probable that Lord George would have committed himself with such men, and incurred the very heavy expense of paying for their services, when he was,—according to the Bunfit theory,—able to get at the diamonds without any such trouble, danger, and expenditure? There was a young detective in the force, very clever,—almost too clever, and certainly a little too fast,—Gager by name, who declared that the Bunfit theory, 'warn't on the cards.' According to Gager's information, Smiler was at this moment a broken-hearted man,—

ranging between mad indignation and suicidal despondency, because he had been treated with treachery in some direction. Mr. Gager was as fully convinced as Bunfit that the diamonds had not been in the box. There was bitter, raging, heart-breaking disappointment about the diamonds in more quarters than one. That there had been a double robbery Gager was quite sure;—or rather a robbery in which two sets of thieves had been concerned, and in which one set had been duped by the other set. In this affair Mr. Smiler and poor little Billy Cann had been the dupes. So far Gager's mind had arrived at certainty. But then how had they been duped, and who had duped them? And who had employed them? Such a robbery would hardly have been arranged and executed except on commission. Even Mr. Smiler would not have burthened himself with such diamonds without knowing what to do with them, and what he should get for them. That they were intended ultimately for the hands of Messrs. Harter and Benjamin, Gager almost believed. And Gager was inclined to think that Messrs. Harter and Benjamin,—or rather Mr. Benjamin, for Mr. Harter himself was almost too old for work requiring so very great mental activity,—that Mr. Benjamin, fearing the honesty of his executive officer Mr. Smiler, had been splendidly treacherous to his subordinate. Gager had not quite completed his theory; but he was very firm on one great point,—that the thieves at Carlisle had been genuine thieves thinking that they were stealing the diamonds, and finding their mistake out when the box had been opened by them under the bridge. 'Who have 'em, then?' asked Bunfit of his younger brother, in a disparaging whisper.

'Well; yes; who 'ave 'em? It's easy to say, who 'ave 'em? Suppose 'e 'ave 'em.' The 'he' alluded to by Gager was Lord George de Bruce Carruthers. 'But, laws, Bunfit, they're gone —weeks ago. You know that, Bunfit.' This had occurred before the intended search among poor Lizzie's boxes, but Bunfit's theory had not been shaken. Bunfit could see all round his own theory. It was whole, and the motives as well as the operations of the persons concerned were explained by it. But the Gager theory only went to show what had not been done, and offered no explanation of the accomplished scheme. Then Bunfit went a little further in his theory, not disdaining to accept something from Gager. Perhaps Lord George had engaged these men, and had afterwards found it practicable to get the diamonds without their assistance. On one great point all concerned in the inquiry were in unison,—that the diamonds had not been in the box when it was carried out of the bedroom at Carlisle. The great point of difference consisted in this, that whereas Gager was sure that the robbery when committed had been genuine, Bunfit was of opinion that the box had been first opened, and then taken out of the hotel in order that the police might be put on a wrong track.

The matter was becoming very important. Two or three of the leading newspapers had first hinted at and then openly condemned the incompetence and slowness of the police. Such censure, as we all know, is very common, and in nine cases out of ten it is unjust. They who write it probably know but little of the circumstances;—and, in speaking of a failure here and a failure there, make no reference to the numerous successes, which are so customary as to partake of the nature of routine. It is the same in regard to all public matters,— army matters, navy matters, poor-law matters, and post office matters. Day after day, and almost every day, one meets censure which is felt to be unjust;—but the general result of all this injustice is increased efficiency. The coach does go the faster because of the whip in the coachman's hand, though the horses driven may never have deserved the thong. In this matter of the Eustace diamonds the police had been very active; but they had been unsuccessful, and had consequently been abused. The robbery was now more than three weeks old. Property to the amount of ten thousand pounds had been abstracted, and as yet the police had not even formed an assured opinion on the subject! Had the same thing occurred in New York or Paris every diamond would by this time have been traced. Such were the assertions made, and the police were instigated to new exertions. Bunfit would have jeopardised his right hand, and Gager his life, to get at the secret. Even Major Mackintosh was anxious.

The facts of the claim made by Mr. Camperdown, and of the bill which had been filed in Chancery for the recovery of the diamonds, were of course widely known, and added much to the general interest and complexity. It was averred that Mr. Camperdown's determination to get the diamonds had been very energetic, and Lady Eustace's determination to keep them equally so. Wonderful stories were told of Lizzie's courage, energy, and resolution. There was hardly a lawyer of repute but took up the question, and had an opinion as to Lizzie's right to the necklace. The Attorney and Solicitor-General were dead against her, asserting that the diamonds certainly did not pass to her under the will, and could not have become hers by gift. But they were members of a liberal government, and of course anti-Lizzieite. Gentlemen who were equal to them in learning, who had held offices equally high, were distinctly of a different opinion. Lady Eustace might probably claim the jewels as paraphernalia properly appertaining to her rank;—in which claim the bestowal of them by her husband would no doubt assist her. And to these gentlemen,—who were Lizzieites and of course Conservatives in politics,—it was by no means clear that the diamonds did not pass to her by will. If it could be shown that the diamonds had been lately kept in Scotland, the ex-Attorney-General thought that they would so pass. All which questions, now that the jewels had been lost, were discussed openly, and added greatly to the anxiety of the police. Both Lizzieites and anti-Lizzieites were disposed to think that Lizzie was very clever.

Frank Greystock in these days took up his cousin's part altogether in good faith. He entertained not the slightest suspicion that she was deceiving him in regard to the diamonds. That the robbery had been a bona-fide robbery, and that Lizzie had lost her treasure, was to him beyond doubt. He had gradually convinced himself that Mr. Camperdown

was wrong in his claim, and was strongly of opinion that
Lord Fawn had disgraced himself by his conduct to the lady.
When he now heard, as he did hear, that some undefined
suspicion was attached to his cousin,—and when he heard
also, as unfortunately he did hear,—that Lord Fawn had encouraged that suspicion, he was very irate, and said grievous
things of Lord Fawn. It seemed to him to be the extremity of
cruelty that suspicion should be attached to his cousin because
she had been robbed of her jewels. He was among those who
were most severe in their denunciation of the police,—and
was the more so, because he had heard it asserted that the
necklace had not in truth been stolen. He busied himself very
much in the matter, and even interrogated John Eustace as
to his intentions. 'My dear fellow,' said Eustace, 'if you hated
those diamonds as much as I do, you would never mention
them again.' Greystock declared that this expression of
aversion to the subject might be all very well for Mr. Eustace,
but that he found himself bound to defend his cousin. 'You
cannot defend her against me,' said Eustace, 'for I do not
attack her. I have never said a word against her. I went down
to Portray when she asked me. As far as I am concerned she
is perfectly welcome to wear the necklace, if she can get it
back again. I will not make or meddle in the matter one way
or the other.' Frank, after that, went to Mr. Camperdown,
but he could get no satisfaction from the attorney. Mr.
Camperdown would only say that he had a duty to do, and
that he must do it. On the matter of the robbery he refused to
give an opinion. That was in the hands of the police. Should
the diamonds be recovered, he would, of course, claim them on
behalf of the estate. In his opinion, whether the diamonds were
recovered or not, Lady Eustace was responsible to the estate
for their value. In opposition, first to the entreaties, and then
to the demands of her late husband's family, she had insisted
on absurdly carrying about with her an enormous amount of
property which did not belong to her. Mr. Camperdown
opined that she must pay for the lost diamonds out of her
jointure. Frank, in a huff, declared that, as far as he could see,

the diamonds belonged to his cousin;—in answer to which Mr. Camperdown suggested that the question was one for the decision of the Vice-Chancellor. Frank Greystock found that he could do nothing with Mr. Camperdown, and felt that he could wreak his vengeance only on Lord Fawn.

Bunfit, when he returned from Mrs. Carbuncle's house to Scotland Yard, had an interview with Major Mackintosh. 'Well, Bunfit, have you seen the lady?'

'Yes,—I did see her, sir.'

'And what came of it?'

'She fainted away, sir—just as they always do.'

'There was no search, I suppose?'

'No, sir;—no search. She wouldn't have it, unless her cousin, Mr. Greystock, permitted.'

'I didn't think she would.'

'Nor yet didn't I, sir. But I'll tell you what it is, major. She knows all about it.'

'You think she does, Bunfit?'

'She does, sir; and she's got something locked up somewhere in that house as'd elucidate the whole of this aggravating mystery, if only we could get at it. Major,——'

'Well, Bunfit?'

'I ain't noways sure as she ain't got them very diamonds themselves locked up, or, perhaps, tied round her person.'

'Neither am I sure that she has not,' said the major.

'The robbery at Carlisle was no robbery,' continued Bunfit. 'It was a got-up plant,* and about the best as I ever knowed. It's my mind that it was a got-up plant between her ladyship and his lordship; and either the one or the other is just keeping the diamonds till it's safe to take 'em into the market.'

CHAPTER L
In Hertford Street

During all this time Lucinda Roanoke was engaged to marry Sir Griffin Tewett, and the lover was an occasional visitor in Hertford Street. Mrs. Carbuncle was as anxious as ever that the marriage should be celebrated on the appointed day, and though there had been repeated quarrels, nothing had as yet taken place to make her despond. Sir Griffin would make some offensive speech; Lucinda would tell him that she had no desire ever to see him again; and then the baronet, usually under the instigation of Lord George, would make some awkward apology. Mrs. Carbuncle,—whose life at this period was not a pleasant one,—would behave on such occasions with great patience, and sometimes with great courage. Lizzie, who in her present emergency could not bear the idea of losing the assistance of any friend, was soft and graceful, and even gracious, to the bear. The bear himself certainly seemed to desire the marriage, though he would so often give offence which made any prospect of a marriage almost impossible. But with Sir Griffin, when the prize seemed to be lost, it again became valuable. He would talk about his passionate love to Mrs. Carbuncle, and to Lizzie,—and then, when things had been made straight for him, he would insult them, and neglect Lucinda. To Lucinda herself, however, he would rarely dare to say such words as he used daily to the other two ladies in the house. What could have been the man's own idea of his future married life, how can any reader be made to understand, or any writer adequately describe! He must have known that the woman despised him, and hated him. In the very bottom of his heart he feared her. He had no idea of other pleasure from her society than what might arise to him from the pride of having married a beautiful woman. Had she shown the slightest fondness for him, the slightest fear that she might lose him, the slightest feeling that she had won a valuable prize in getting him, he would have scorned her, and jilted her without the slightest remorse. But the scorn came from her, and it beat him down. 'Yes;—you hate me, and would fain be rid of me; but you have said that you will be my wife, and you cannot now escape me.' Sir Griffin did not exactly speak such words as these, but he acted them. Lucinda would bear his presence,—sitting apart from him, silent, imperious, but very beautiful. People said that she became more handsome from day to day, and she did so, in spite of her agony. Hers was a face which could stand such condition of the heart without fading or sinking under it. She did not weep, or lose her colour, or become thin. The pretty softness of a girl,—delicate feminine weakness, or laughing eyes and pouting lips, no one expected from her. Sir Griffin, in the early days of their acquaintance, had found her to be a woman with a character for beauty,—and she was now more beautiful than ever. He probably thought that he loved her; but, at any rate, he was determined that he would marry her.

He had expressed himself more than once as very angry about this affair of the jewels. He had told Mrs. Carbuncle that her inmate, Lady Eustace, was suspected by the police, and that it might be well that Lady Eustace should be,—be made to go, in fact. But it did not suit Mrs. Carbuncle that Lady Eustace should be made to go;—nor did it suit Lord George de Bruce Carruthers. Lord George, at Mrs. Carbuncle's instance, had snubbed Sir Griffin more than once, and then it came to pass that he was snubbed yet again more violently than before. He was at the house in Hertford Street on the day of Mr. Bunfit's visit, some hours after Mr. Bunfit was gone, when Lizzie was still lying on her bed up-stairs, nearly beaten by the great danger which had oppressed her. He was told of Mr. Bunfit's visit, and then again said that he thought that the continued residence of Lady Eustace beneath that roof was a misfortune. 'Would you wish us to turn her out because her necklace has been stolen?' asked Mrs. Carbuncle.

'People say very queer things,' said Sir Griffin.

'So they do, Sir Griffin,' continued Mrs. Carbuncle. 'They

say such queer things that I can hardly understand that they should be allowed to say them. I am told that the police absolutely suggest that Lord George stole the diamonds.'

'That's nonsense.'

'No doubt, Sir Griffin. And so is the other nonsense. Do you mean to tell us that you believe that Lady Eustace stole her own diamonds?'

'I don't see the use of having her here. Situated as I am, I have a right to object to it.'

'Situated as you are, Sir Griffin!' said Lucinda.

'Well;—yes, of course; if we are to be married, I cannot but think a good deal of the persons you stay with.'

'You were very glad to stay yourself with Lady Eustace at Portray,' said Lucinda.

'I went there to follow you,' said Sir Griffin gallantly.

'I wish with all my heart you had stayed away,' said Lucinda. At that moment Lord George was shown into the room, and Miss Roanoke continued speaking, determined that Lord George should know how the bear was conducting himself. 'Sir Griffin is saying that my aunt ought to turn Lady Eustace out of the house.'

'Not quite that,' said Sir Griffin with an attempt at laughter.

'Quite that,' said Lucinda. 'I don't suppose that he suspects poor Lady Eustace, but he thinks that my aunt's friend should be like Caesar's wife,* above the suspicion of others.'

'If you would mind your own business, Tewett,' said Lord George, 'it would be a deal better for us all. I wonder Mrs. Carbuncle does not turn you out of the room for making such a proposition here. If it were my room, I would.'

'I suppose I can say what I please to Mrs. Carbuncle? Miss Roanoke is not going to be your wife.'

'It is my belief that Miss Roanoke will be nobody's wife, —at any rate, for the present,' said that young lady;—upon which Sir Griffin left the room, muttering some words which might have been, perhaps, intended for an adieu. Immediately after this, Lizzie came in, moving slowly, but without a sound, like a ghost, with pale cheeks, and dishevelled hair, and that weary, worn look of illness which was become customary with her. She greeted Lord George with a faint attempt at a smile, and seated herself in a corner of a sofa. She asked whether he had been told the story of the proposed search, and then bade her friend Mrs. Carbuncle describe the scene.

'If it goes on like this it will kill me,' said Lizzie.

'They are treating me in precisely the same way,' said Lord George.

'But think of your strength and of my weakness, Lord George.'

'By heavens, I don't know!' said Lord George. 'In this matter your weakness is stronger than any strength of mine. I never was so cut up in my life. It was a good joke when we talked of the suspicions of that fellow at Carlisle as we came up by the railway,—but it is no joke now. I've had men with me, almost asking to search among my things.'

'They have quite asked me!' said Lizzie piteously.

'You;—yes. But there's some reason in that. These infernal diamonds did belong to you, or, at any rate, you had them. You are the last person known to have seen them. Even if you had them still, you'd only have what you call your own.' Lizzie looked at him with all her eyes and listened to him with all her ears. 'But what the mischief can I have had to do with them?'

'It's very hard upon you,' said Mrs. Carbuncle.

'Unless I stole them,' continued Lord George.

'Which is so absurd, you know,' said Lizzie.

'That a pig-headed provincial fool should have taken me for a midnight thief, did not disturb me much. I don't think I am very easily annoyed by what other people think of me. But these fellows, I suppose, were sent here by the head of the metropolitan police; and everybody knows that they have been sent. Because I was civil enough to you women to look after you coming up to town, and because one of you was careless enough to lose her jewels, I—I am to be talked about all over London as the man who took them!' This was not spoken with much courtesy to the ladies present. Lord George had dropped that customary chivalry of manner which, in ordinary life, makes it to be quite out of the question that a man shall be uncivil to a woman. He had escaped from conventional usage into rough, truthful speech, under stress from the extremity of the hardship to which he had been subjected. And the women understood it and appreciated it and liked it rather than otherwise. To Lizzie it seemed fitting that a Corsair so circumstanced should be as uncivil as he pleased; and Mrs. Carbuncle had long been accustomed to her friend's moods.

'They can't really think it,' said Mrs. Carbuncle.

'Somebody thinks it. I am told that your particular friend, Lord Fawn,'—this he said, specially addressing Lizzie,—'has expressed a strong opinion that I carry about the necklace always in my pocket. I trust to have the opportunity of wringing his neck some day.'

'I do so wish you would,' said Lizzie.

'I shall not lose a chance if I can get it. Before all this occurred I should have said of myself that nothing of the kind could put me out. I don't think there is a man in the world cares less what people say of him than I do. I am as indifferent to ordinary tittle-tattle as a rhinoceros. But, by George,— when it comes to stealing ten thousand pounds' worth of diamonds, and the delicate attentions of all the metropolitan police, one begins to feel that one is vulnerable. When I get up in the morning, I half feel that I shall be locked up before night, and I can see in the eyes of every man I meet that he takes me for the prince of burglars!'

'And it is all my fault,' said Lizzie.

'I wish the diamonds had been thrown into the sea,' said Mrs. Carbuncle.

'What do you think about them yourself?' asked Lucinda.

'I don't know what to think. I'm at a dead loss. You know that man, Mr. Benjamin, Lady Eustace?' Lizzie, with a little start, answered that she did,—that she had had dealings with him before her marriage, and had once owed him two or three hundred pounds. As the man's name had been mentioned, she thought it better to own as much. 'So he tells me. Now, in all London, I don't suppose there is a greater rascal than Benjamin.'

'I didn't know that,' said Lizzie.

'But I did; and with that rascal I have had money dealings for the last six or seven years. He has cashed bills for me, and has my name to bills now,—and Sir Griffin's too. I'm half inclined to think that he has got the diamonds.'

'Do you indeed?' said Mrs. Carbuncle.

'Mr. Benjamin!' said Lizzie.

'And he returns the compliment.'

'How does he return it?' asked Mrs. Carbuncle.

'He either thinks that I've got 'em, or he wants to make me believe that he thinks so. He hasn't dared to say it;—but that's his intention. Such an opinion from such a man on such a subject, would be quite a compliment. And I feel it. But yet it troubles me. You know that greasy, Israelitish smile of his, Lady Eustace.' Lizzie nodded her head and tried to smile. 'When I asked him yesterday about the diamonds, he leered at me and rubbed his hands. "It's a pretty little game;—ain't it, Lord George?" he said. I told him that I thought it a very bad game, and that I hoped the police would have the thief and the necklace soon. "It's been managed a deal too well for that, Lord George;—don't you think so?"' Lord George mimicked the Jew as he repeated the words, and the ladies, of course, laughed. But poor Lizzie's attempt at laughter was very sorry. 'I told him to his face that I thought he had them among his treasures. "No, no, no; Lord George," he said, and seemed quite to enjoy the joke. If he's got them himself, he can't think that I have them;—but if he has not, I don't doubt but he believes that I have. And I'll tell you another person who suspects me.'

'What fools they are,' said Lizzie.

'I don't know how that may be. Sir Griffin, Lucinda, isn't at all sure but what I have them in my pocket.'

'I can believe anything of him,' said Lucinda.

'And it seems he can believe anything of me. I shall begin

to think soon that I did take them, myself,—or, at any rate, that I ought to have done so. I wonder what you three women think of it. If you do think I've got 'em, don't scruple to say so. I'm quite used to it, and it won't hurt me any further.' The ladies again laughed. 'You must have your suspicions,' continued he.

'I suppose some of the London thieves did get them,' said Mrs. Carbuncle.

'The police say the box was empty,' said Lord George.

'How can the police know?' asked Lucinda. 'They weren't there to see. Of course, the thieves would say that they didn't take them.'

'What do you think, Lady Eustace?'

'I don't know what to think. Perhaps Mr. Camperdown did it.'

'Or the Lord Chancellor,' said Lord George. 'One is just as likely as the other. I wish I could get at what you really think. The whole thing would be so complete if all you three suspected me. I can't get out of it all by going to Paris or Kamschatka,* as I should have half a dozen detectives on my heels wherever I went. I must brazen it out here; and the worst of it is, that I feel that a look of guilt is creeping over me. I have a sort of conviction growing upon me that I shall be taken up and tried, and that a jury will find me guilty. I dream about it; and if,—as is probable,—it drives me mad, I'm sure that I shall accuse myself in my madness. There's a fascination about it that I can't explain or escape. I go on thinking how I would have done it if I did do it. I spend hours in calculating how much I would have realised, and where I would have found my market. I couldn't keep myself from asking Benjamin the other day how much they would be worth to him.'

'What did he say?' asked Lizzie, who sat gazing upon the Corsair, and who was now herself fascinated. Lord George was walking about the room, then sitting for a moment in one chair and again in another, and after a while leaning on the mantelpiece. In his speaking he addressed himself almost exclusively to Lizzie, who could not keep her eyes from his.

'He grinned greasily,' said the Corsair, 'and told me they had already been offered to him once before by you.'

'That's false,' said Lizzie.

'Very likely. And then he said that no doubt they'd fall into his hands some day. "Wouldn't it be a game, Lord George," he said, "if, after all, they should be no more than paste?" That made me think he had got them, and that he'd get paste diamonds put into the same setting,—and then give them up with some story of his own making. "You'd know whether they were paste or not; wouldn't you, Lord George?" he asked.' The Corsair, as he repeated Mr. Benjamin's words, imitated the Jew's manner so well, that he made Lizzie shudder. 'While I was there, a detective named Gager came in.'

'The same man who came here, perhaps,' suggested Mrs. Carbuncle.

'I think not. He seemed to be quite intimate with Mr. Benjamin, and went on at once about the diamonds. Benjamin said that they'd made their way over to Paris, and that he'd heard of them. I found myself getting quite intimate with Mr. Gager, who seemed hardly to scruple at showing that he thought that Benjamin and I were confederates. Mr. Camperdown has offered four hundred pounds reward for the jewels, —to be paid on their surrender to the hands of Mr. Garnett, the jeweller. Gager declared that, if any ordinary thief had them, they would be given up at once for that sum.'

'That's true, I suppose,' said Mrs. Carbuncle.

'How would the ordinary thief get his money without being detected? Who would dare to walk into Garnett's shop with the diamonds in his hands and ask for the four hundred pounds? Besides, they have been sold to some one,—and, as I believe, to my dear friend, Mr. Benjamin. "I suppose you ain't a going anywhere just at present, Lord George?" said that fellow Gager. "What the devil's that to you?" I asked him. He just laughed and shook his head. I don't doubt but that there's a policeman about waiting till I leave this house;— or looking at me now with a magnifying glass from the windows at the other side. They've photographed me while I'm going about, and published a list of every hair on my face in the "Hue and Cry."*I dined at the club yesterday, and found a strange waiter. I feel certain that he was a policeman done up in livery all for my sake. I turned sharp round in the street yesterday, and found a man at a corner. I am sure that man was watching me, and was looking at my pockets to see whether the jewel case was there. As for myself, I can think of nothing else. I wish I had got them. I should have something then to pay me for all this nuisance.'

'I do wish you had,' said Lizzie.

'What I should do with them I cannot even imagine. I am always thinking of that, too,—making plans for getting rid of them, supposing I had stolen them. My belief is, that I should be so sick of them that I should chuck them over the bridge into the river,—only that I should fear that some policeman's eye would be on me as I did it. My present position is not comfortable,—but if I had got them, I think that the weight of them would crush me altogether. Having a handle to my name, and being a lord, or, at least, called a lord, makes it all the worse. People are so pleased to think that a lord should have stolen a necklace.'

Lizzie listened to it all with a strange fascination. If this strong man were so much upset by the bare suspicion, what must be her condition? The jewels were in her desk up-stairs, and the police had been with her also,—were even now probably looking after her and watching her. How much more difficult must it be for her to deal with the diamonds than it would have been for this man. Presently Mrs. Carbuncle left the room, and Lucinda followed her. Lizzie saw them go, and did not dare to go with them. She felt as though her limbs would not have carried her to the door. She was now alone with her Corsair; and she looked up timidly into his deep-set eyes, as he came and stood over her. 'Tell me all that you know about it,' he said, in that deep low voice which, from her first acquaintance with him, had filled her with interest, and almost with awe.

CHAPTER LI
Confidence

LIZZIE EUSTACE was speechless as she continued to look up into the Corsair's face. She ought to have answered him briskly, either with indignation or with a touch of humour. But she could not answer him at all. She was desired to tell him all that she knew about the robbery, and she was unable to declare that she knew nothing. How much did he suspect? What did he believe? Had she been watched by Mrs. Carbuncle, and had something of the truth been told to him? And then would it not be better for her that he should know it all? Unsupported and alone she could not bear the trouble which was on her. If she were driven to tell her secret to any one, had she not better tell it to him? She knew that if she did so, she would be a creature in his hands to be dealt with as he pleased;—but would there not be a certain charm in being so mastered? He was but a pinchbeck lord. She had wit enough to know that; but then she had wit enough also to feel that she herself was but a pinchbeck lady. He would be fit for her, and she for him,—if only he would take her. Since her day-dreams first began, she had been longing for a Corsair; and here he was, not kneeling at her feet, but standing over her,—as became a Corsair. At any rate he had mastered her now, and she could not speak to him.

He waited perhaps a minute, looking at her, before he renewed his question; and the minute seemed to her to be an age. During every second her power beneath his gaze sank lower and lower. There gradually came a grim smile over his face, and she was sure that he could read her very heart. Then he called her by her Christian name,—as he had never called her before. 'Come, Lizzie,' he said, 'you might as well tell me all about it. You know.'

'Know what?' The words were audible to him, though they were uttered in the lowest whisper.

'About this d—— necklace. What is it all? Where are they? And how did you manage it?'

'I didn't manage anything!'

'But you know where they are?' He paused again, still gazing at her. Gradually there came across his face, or she fancied that it was so, a look of ferocity which thoroughly frightened her. If he should turn against her, and be leagued with the police against her, what chance would she have? 'You know where they are,' he said, repeating his words. Then at last she nodded her head, assenting to his assertion. 'And where are they? Come;—out with it! If you won't tell me, you must tell some one else. There has been a deal too much of this already.'

'You won't betray me?'

'Not if you deal openly with me.'

'I will; indeed I will. And it was all an accident. When I took them out of the box, I only did it for safety.'

'You did take them out of the box then?' Again she nodded her head. 'And have got them now?' There was another nod. 'And where are they? Come; with such a spirit of enterprise as yours you ought to be able to speak. Has Benjamin got them?'

'Oh no.'

'And he knows nothing about them?'

'Nothing.'

'Then I have wronged in my thoughts that son of Abraham?'

'Nobody knows anything,' said Lizzie.

'Not even Jane or Lucinda?'

'Nothing at all.'

'Then you have kept your secret marvellously. And where are they?'

'Up-stairs.'

'In your bed-room?'

'In my desk in the little sitting-room.'

'The Lord be good to us!' ejaculated Lord George. 'All the police in London, from the chief downwards, are agog about this necklace. Every well-known thief in the town is envied by every other thief because he is thought to have had a finger in the pie. I am suspected, and Mr. Benjamin is suspected; Sir Griffin is suspected, and half the jewellers in London and Paris are supposed to have the stones in their keeping. Every man and woman is talking about it, and people are quarrelling about it till they almost cut each other's throats; and all the while you have got them locked up in your desk! How on earth did you get the box broken open and then conveyed out of your room at Carlisle?'

Then Lizzie in a frightened whisper, with her eyes often turned on the floor, told the whole story. 'If I'd had a minute to think of it,' she said, 'I would have confessed the truth at Carlisle. Why should I want to steal what was my own? But they came to me all so quickly, and I didn't like to say that I had them under my pillow.'

'I daresay not.'

'And then I couldn't tell anybody afterwards. I always meant to tell you,—from the very first; because I knew you would be good to me. They are my own. Surely I might do what I liked with my own?'

'Well;—yes; in one way. But you see there was a lawsuit in Chancery going on about them; and then you committed perjury at Carlisle. And altogether,—it's not quite straight sailing, you know.'

'I suppose not.'

'Hardly. Major Mackintosh, and the magistrates, and Messrs. Bunfit and Gager won't settle down, peaceable and satisfied, when they hear the end of the story. And I think Messrs. Camperdown will have a bill against you. It's been uncommonly clever, but I don't see the use of it.'

'I've been very foolish,' said Lizzie,—'but you won't desert me!'

'Upon my word I don't know what I'm to do.'

'Will you have them,—as a present?'

'Certainly not.'

'They're worth ever so much;—ten thousand pounds! And they are my own, to do just what I please with them.'

'You are very good;—but what should I do with them?'

'Sell them.'

'Who'd buy them? And before a week was over I should be in prison, and in a couple of months should be standing at the Old Bailey at my trial. I couldn't just do that, my dear.'

'What will you do for me? You are my friend;—ain't you?' The diamond necklace was not a desirable possession in the eyes of Lord George de Bruce Carruthers;—but Portray Castle, with its income, and the fact that Lizzie Eustace was still a very young woman, was desirable. Her prettiness too was not altogether thrown away on Lord George,—though, as he was wont to say to himself, he was too old now to sacrifice much for such a toy as that. Something he must do, —if only because of the knowledge which had come to him. He could not go away and leave her, and neither say nor do anything in the matter. And he could not betray her to the police. 'You will not desert me!' she said, taking hold of his hand, and kissing it as a suppliant.

He passed his arm round her waist, but more as though she were a child than a woman, as he stood thinking. Of all the affairs in which he had ever been engaged it was the most difficult. She submitted to his embrace, and leaned upon his shoulder, and looked up into his face. If he would only tell her that he loved her, then he would be bound to her,— then must he share with her the burthen of the diamonds,— then must he be true to her. 'George!' she said, and burst into a low suppressed wailing, with her face hidden upon his arm.

'That's all very well,' said he, still holding her,—for she was pleasant to hold,—'but what the d—— is a fellow to do? I don't see my way out of it. I think you'd better go to Camperdown, and give them up to him, and tell him the truth.' Then she sobbed more violently than before, till her quick ear caught the sound of a footstep on the stairs, and in a moment she was out of his arms and seated on the sofa, with hardly a trace of tears in her eyes. It was the footman, who desired to know whether Lady Eustace would want the carriage that afternoon. Lady Eustace, with her cheeriest voice, sent her love to Mrs. Carbuncle, and her assurance that she would not want the carriage before the evening. 'I don't know that you can do anything else,' continued Lord George, 'except just give them up and brazen it out. I don't suppose they'd prosecute you.'

'Prosecute me!' ejaculated Lizzie.

'For perjury, I mean.'

'And what could they do to me?'

'Oh, I don't know. Lock you up for five years, perhaps.'

'Because I had my own necklace under the pillow in my own room?'

'Think of all the trouble you've given.'

'I'll never give them up to Mr. Camperdown. They are mine;—my very own. My cousin, Mr. Greystock, who is much more of a lawyer than Mr. Camperdown, says so. Oh, George, do think of something! Don't tell me that I must give them up! Wouldn't Mr. Benjamin buy them?'

'Yes;—for half nothing; and then go and tell the whole story and get money from the other side. You can't trust Benjamin.'

'But I can trust you.' She clung to him and implored him, and did get from him a renewed promise that he would not reveal her secret. She wanted him to take the terrible packet from her there and then, and use his own judgment in disposing of it. But this he positively refused to do. He protested that they were safer with her than they could be with him. He explained to her that if they were found in his hands, his offence in having them in his possession would be much greater than hers. They were her own,—as she was ever so ready to assert; or if not her own, the ownership was so doubtful that she could not be accused of having stolen them. And then he needed to consider it all,—to sleep upon it,—before he could make up his mind what he would do.

But there was one other trouble on her mind as to which he was called upon to give her counsel before he was allowed to leave her. She had told the detective officer that she would submit her boxes and desks to be searched if her cousin Frank should advise it. If the policeman were to return with her cousin while the diamonds were still in her desk, what should she do? He might come at any time; and then she would be bound to obey him. 'And he thinks that they were stolen at Carlisle?' asked Lord George. 'Of course he thinks so,' said Lizzie, almost indignantly. 'They would never ask to search your person,' suggested Lord George. Lizzie could not say. She had simply declared that she would be guided by her cousin. 'Have them about you when he comes. Don't take them out with you; but keep them in your pocket while you are in the house during the day. They will hardly bring a woman with them to search you.'

'But there was a woman with the man when he came before.'

'Then you must refuse in spite of your cousin. Show yourself angry with him and with everybody. Swear that you did not intend to submit yourself to such indignity as that. They can't do it without a magistrate's order, unless you permit it. I don't suppose they will come at all; and if they do they will only look at your clothes and your boxes. If they ask to do more, be stout with them and refuse. Of course they'll suspect you, but they do that already. And your cousin will suspect you;—but you must put up with that. It will be very bad;—but I see nothing better. But, of all things, say nothing of me.'

'Oh no,' said Lizzie, promising to be obedient to him. And then he took his leave of her. 'You will be true to me;—will you not?' she said, still clinging to his arm. He promised her that he would. 'Oh, George,' she said, 'I have no friend now but you. You will care for me?' He took her in his arms and kissed her, and promised her that he would care for her. How was he to save himself from doing so? When he was gone, Lizzie sat down to think of it all, and felt sure that at last she had found her Corsair.

CHAPTER LII

Mrs. Carbuncle goes to the Theatre

MRS. CARBUNCLE and Lizzie Eustace did not, in these days, shut themselves up because there was trouble in the household. It would not have suited the creed of Mrs. Carbuncle on social matters to be shut up from the amusements of life. She had sacrificed too much in seeking them for that, and was too conscious of the price she paid for them. It was still mid-winter, but nevertheless there was generally some amusement arranged for every evening. Mrs. Carbuncle was very fond of the play, and made herself acquainted with every new piece as it came out. Every actor and actress of note on the stage was known to her, and she dealt freely in criticisms on their respective merits. The three ladies had a box at the Haymarket taken for this very evening, at which a new piece, 'The Noble Jilt,'*from the hand of a very eminent author, was to be produced. Mrs. Carbuncle had talked a great deal about 'The Noble Jilt,' and could boast that she had discussed the merits of the two chief characters with the actor and actress who were to undertake them. Miss Talbot had assured her that the Margaret was altogether impracticable, and Mrs. Carbuncle was quite of the same opinion. And as for the hero, Steinmark,—it was a part that no man could play so as to obtain the sympathy of an audience. There was a second hero,—a Flemish Count,—tame as rain-water, Mrs. Carbuncle said. She was very anxious for the success of the piece, which, as she said, had its merits; but she was sure that it wouldn't do. She had talked about it a great deal, and now, when the evening came, she was not going to be deterred from seeing it by any trouble in reference to a diamond necklace. Lizzie, when she was left by Lord George, had many doubts on the subject,—whether she would go or stay at home. If he would have come to her, or her cousin Frank, or if, had it been possible, Lord Fawn would have come, she would have given up the play very willingly. But to be alone,

107

—with her necklace in the desk up-stairs, or in her pocket, was terrible to her. And then, they could not search her or her boxes while she was at the theatre. She must not take the necklace with her there. He had told her to leave it in her desk, when she went from home.

Lucinda, also, was quite determined that she would see the new piece. She declared to her aunt, in Lizzie's presence, without a vestige of a smile, that it might be well to see how a jilt could behave herself, so as to do her work of jilting in any noble fashion. 'My dear,' said her aunt, 'you let things weigh upon your heart a great deal too much.' 'Not upon my heart, Aunt Jane,' the young lady had answered. She also intended to go, and when she had made up her mind to anything, nothing would deter her. She had no desire to stay at home in order that she might see Sir Griffin. 'I daresay the play may be very bad,' she said, 'but it can hardly be so bad as real life.'

Lizzie, when Lord George had left her, crept up-stairs, and sat for awhile thinking of her condition, with the key of her desk in her hand. Should there come a knock at the door, the case of diamonds would be in her pocket in a moment. Her own room door was bolted on the inside, so that she might have an instant for her preparation. She was quite resolved that she would carry out Lord George's recommendation, and that no policeman or woman should examine her person, unless it were done by violence. There she sat, almost expecting that at every moment her cousin would be there with Bunfit and the woman. But nobody came, and at six she went down to dinner. After much consideration she then left the diamonds in the desk. Surely no one would come to search at such an hour as that. No one had come when the carriage was announced, and the three ladies went off together.

During the whole way Mrs. Carbuncle talked of the terrible situation in which poor Lord George was placed by the robbery, and of all that Lizzie owed him on account of his trouble. 'My dear,' said Mrs. Carbuncle, 'the least you can do for him is to give him all that you've got to give.' 'I don't know that he wants me to give him anything,' said Lizzie. 'I think that's quite plain,' said Mrs. Carbuncle, 'and I'm sure I wish it may be so. He and I have been dear friends,—very dear friends, and there is nothing I wish so much as to see him properly settled. Ill-natured people like to say all manner of things because everybody does not choose to live in their own heart-less, conventional form. But I can assure you there is nothing between me and Lord George which need prevent him from giving his whole heart to you.' 'I don't suppose there is,' said Lizzie, who loved an opportunity of giving Mrs. Car-buncle a little rap.

The play, as a play, was a failure; at least so said Mrs. Carbuncle. The critics, on the next morning, were somewhat divided,—not only in judgment, but as to facts. To say how a play has been received is of more moment than to speak of its own merits or of the merits of the actors. Three or four of the papers declared that the audience was not only eulo-gistic, but enthusiastic. One or two others averred that the piece fell very flatly. As it was not acted above four or five dozen times consecutively, it must be regarded as a failure. On their way home Mrs. Carbuncle declared that Minnie Talbot had done her very best with such a part as Margaret, but that the character afforded no scope for sympathy. 'A noble jilt, my dears,' said Mrs. Carbuncle eloquently, 'is a contradiction in terms. There can be no such thing. A woman, when she has once said the word, is bound to stick to it. The delicacy of the female character should not admit of hesitation between two men. The idea is quite revolting.'

'But may not one have an idea of no man at all?'—asked Lucinda. 'Must that be revolting also?'

'Of course a young woman may entertain such an idea; though for my part I look upon it as unnatural. But when she has once given herself there can be no taking back without the loss of that aroma which should be the apple of a young woman's eye.'

'If she finds that she has made a mistake—?' said Lucinda fiercely. 'Why shouldn't a young woman make a mistake as well as an old woman? Her aroma won't prevent her from having been wrong and finding it out.'

'My dear, such mistakes, as you call them, always arise from fantastic notions. Look at this piece. Why does the lady jilt her lover? Not because she doesn't like him. She's just as fond of him as ever.'

'He's a stupid sort of a fellow, and I think she was quite right,' said Lizzie. 'I'd never marry a man merely because I said I would. If I found I didn't like him, I'd leave him at the altar. If I found I didn't like him, I'd leave him even after the altar. I'd leave him any time I found I didn't like him. It's all very well to talk of aroma, but to live with a man you don't like—is the devil!'

'My dear, those whom God has joined together shouldn't be separated,—for any mere likings or dislikings.' This Mrs. Carbuncle said in a high tone of moral feeling, just as the carriage stopped at the door in Hertford Street. They at once perceived that the hall-door was open, and Mrs. Carbuncle, as she crossed the pavement, saw that there were two policemen in the hall. The footman had been with them to the theatre, but the cook and housemaid, and Mrs. Carbuncle's own maid, were with the policemen in the passage. She gave a little scream, and then Lizzie, who had followed her, seized her by the arm. She turned round and saw by the gas-light that Lizzie's face was white as a sheet, and that all the lines of her countenance were rigid and almost distorted. 'Then she does know all about it!' said Mrs. Carbuncle to herself. Lizzie didn't speak, but still hung on to Mrs. Carbuncle's arm, and Lucinda, having seen how it was, was also supporting her. A policeman stepped forward and touched his hat. He was not Bunfit;—neither was he Gager. Indeed, though the ladies had not perceived the difference, he was not at all like Bunfit or Gager. This man was dressed in a policeman's uniform, whereas Bunfit and Gager always wore plain clothes. 'My lady,' said the policeman, addressing Mrs. Carbuncle, 'there's been a robbery here.'

'A robbery!' ejaculated Mrs. Carbuncle.

'Yes, my lady. The servants all out,—all to one; and she's off. They've taken jewels, and, no doubt, money, if there was any. They don't mostly come unless they know what they comes for.'

With a horrid spasm across her heart, which seemed ready to kill her, so sharp was the pain, Lizzie recovered the use of her legs and followed Mrs. Carbuncle into the dining-room. She had been hardly conscious of hearing; but she had heard, and it had seemed to her that the robbery spoken of was something distinct from her own affair. The policemen did not speak of having found the diamonds. It was of something lost that they spoke. She seated herself in a chair against the wall, but did not utter a word. 'We've been up-stairs, my lady, and they've been in most of the rooms. There's a desk broke open,'—Lizzie gave an involuntary little scream;— 'Yes, mum, a desk,' continued the policeman turning to Lizzie, 'and a bureau, and a dressing-case. What's gone your lady-ship can tell when you sees. And one of the young women is off. It's she as done it.' Then the cook explained. She and the housemaid, and Mrs. Carbuncle's lady's maid, had just stepped out, only round the corner, to get a little air, leaving Patience Crabstick in charge of the house, and when they came back, the area gate was locked against them, the front door was locked, and finding themselves unable to get in after many knockings, they had at last obtained the assistance of a policeman. He had got into the place over the area gate, had opened the front door from within, and then the robbery had been discovered. It was afterwards found that the servants had all gone out to what they called a tea-party, at a public-house in the neighbourhood, and that by previous agreement Patience Crabstick had remained in charge. When they came back Patience Crabstick was gone, and the desk, and bureau, and dressing-case, were found to have been opened. 'She had a reg'lar thief along with her, my lady,' said the policeman, still addressing himself to Mrs. Carbuncle,—''cause of the way the things was opened.'

'I always knew that young woman was downright bad,' said Mrs. Carbuncle in her first expression of wrath.

But Lizzie sat in her chair without saying a word, still pale, with that almost awful look of agony in her face. Within ten minutes of their entering the house, Mrs. Carbuncle was making her way up-stairs, with the two policemen following her. That her bureau and her dressing-case should have been opened was dreadful to her, though the value that she could thus lose was very small. She also possessed diamonds,—but her diamonds were paste; and whatever jewellery she had of any value,—a few rings, and a brooch, and such like,—had been on her person in the theatre. What little money she had by her was in the drawing-room, and the drawing-room, as it seemed, had not been entered. In truth, all Mrs. Carbuncle's possessions in the house were not sufficient to have tempted a well-bred, well-instructed thief. But it behoved her to be indignant; and she could be indignant with grace, as the thief was discovered to be, not her maid, but Patience Crabstick. The policemen followed Mrs. Carbuncle, and the maids followed the policemen; but Lizzie Eustace kept her seat in the chair by the wall. 'Do you think they have taken much of yours?' said Lucinda, coming up to her and speaking very gently. Lizzie made a motion with her two hands upon her heart, and struggled, and gasped,—as though she wished to speak but could not. 'I suppose it is that girl who has done it all,' said Lucinda. Lizzie nodded her head, and tried to smile. The attempt was so ghastly that Lucinda, though not timid by nature, was frightened. She sat down and took Lizzie's hand, and tried to comfort her. 'It is very hard upon you,' she said, 'to be twice robbed.' Lizzie again nodded her head. 'I hope it is not much now. Shall we go up and see?' The poor creature did get upon her legs, but she gasped so terribly that Lucinda feared that she was dying. 'Shall I send for some one?' she said. Lizzie made an effort to speak, was shaken convulsively while the other supported her, and then burst into a flood of tears.

When that had come she was relieved, and could again act her part. 'Yes,' she said, 'we will go with them. It is so dreadful;—is it not?'

'Very dreadful;—but how much better that we weren't at home! Shall we go now?' Then together they followed the others, and on the stairs Lizzie explained that in her desk, of which she always carried the key round her neck, there was what money she had by her;—two ten-pound notes, and four five-pound notes, and three sovereigns;—in all, forty-three pounds. Her other jewels,—the jewels which she had possessed over and above the fatal diamond necklace,—were in her dressing-case. Patience, she did not doubt, had known that the money was there, and certainly knew of her jewels. So they went up-stairs. The desk was open and the money gone. Five or six rings and a bracelet had been taken also from Lizzie's dressing-case, which she had left open. Of Mrs. Carbuncle's property sufficient had been stolen to make a long list in that lady's handwriting. Lucinda Roanoke's room had not been entered,—as far as they could judge. The girl had taken the best of her own clothes, and a pair of strong boots belonging to the cook. A superintendent of police was there before they went to bed, and a list was made out. The superintendent was of opinion that the thing had been done very cleverly, but was of opinion that the thieves had expected to find more plunder. 'They don't care so much about bank-notes, my lady, because they fetches such a low price with them as they deal with. The three sovereigns is more to them than all the forty pounds in notes.' The superintendent had heard of the diamond necklace, and expressed an opinion that poor Lady Eustace was especially marked out for misfortune. 'It all comes of having such a girl as that about her,' said Mrs. Carbuncle. The superintendent, who intended to be consolatory to Lizzie, expressed his opinion that it was very hard to know what a young woman was. 'They looks as soft as butter, and they're as sly as foxes, and as quick, as quick,— as quick as greased lightning, my lady.' Such a piece of business as this which had just occurred, will make people intimate at a very short notice.

And so the diamond necklace, known to be worth ten thousand pounds, had at last been stolen in earnest! Lizzie, when the policemen were gone, and the noise was over, and the house was closed, slunk away to her bedroom, refusing any aid in lieu of that of the wicked Patience. She herself had examined the desk beneath the eyes of her two friends and of the policemen, and had seen at once that the case was gone. The money was gone too, as she was rejoiced to find. She perceived at once that had the money been left,—the very leaving of it would have gone to prove that other prize had been there. But the money was gone,—money of which she had given a correct account;—and she could now honestly allege that she had been robbed. But she had at last really lost her great treasure;—and if the treasure should be found, then would she infallibly be exposed. She had talked twice of giving away her necklace, and had seriously thought of getting rid of it by burying it deep in the sea. But now that it was in very truth gone from her, the loss of it was horrible to her. Ten thousand pounds, for which she had struggled so much and borne so many things, which had come to be the prevailing fact of her life, gone from her for ever! Nevertheless it was not that sorrow, that regret which had so nearly overpowered her in the dining-parlour. At that moment she hardly knew, had hardly thought, whether the diamonds had or had not been taken. But the feeling came upon her at once that her own disgrace was every hour being brought nearer to her. Her secret was no longer quite her own. One man knew it, and he had talked to her of perjury and of five years' imprisonment. Patience must have known it, too; and now some one else also knew it. The police, of course, would find it out, and then horrid words would be used against her. She hardly knew what perjury was. It sounded like forgery and burglary. To stand up before a judge and be tried,—and then to be locked up for five years in prison——! What an end would this be to all her glorious success? And what evil had she done to merit all this terrible punishment? When they came to her in her bedroom at Carlisle she had simply been too much frightened to tell them all that the necklace was at that moment under her pillow.

She tried to think of it all, and to form some idea in her mind of what might be the truth. Of course, Patience Crabstick had known her secret, but how long had the girl known it? And how had the girl discovered it? She was almost certain, from certain circumstances, from words which the girl had spoken, and from signs which she had observed, that Patience had not even suspected that the necklace had been brought with them from Carlisle to London. Of course, the coming of Bunfit and the woman would have set the girl's mind to work in that direction; but then Bunfit and the woman had only been there on that morning. The Corsair knew the facts, and no one but the Corsair. That the Corsair was a Corsair, the suspicions of the police had proved to her. She had offered the necklace to the Corsair; but when so offered, he had refused to take it. She could understand that he should see the danger of accepting the diamonds from her hand, and yet should be desirous of having them. And might not he have thought that he could best relieve her from the burthen of their custody in this manner? She felt no anger against the Corsair as she weighed the probability of his having taken them in this fashion. A Corsair must be a Corsair. Were he to come to her and confess the deed, she would almost like him the better for it,—admiring his skill and enterprise. But how very clever he must have been, and how brave! He had known, no doubt, that the three ladies were all going to the theatre; but in how short a time had he got rid of the other women and availed himself of the services of Patience Crabstick!

But in what way would she conduct herself when the police should come to her on the following morning,—the police and all the other people who would crowd to the house? How should she receive her cousin Frank? How should she look when the coincidence of the double robbery should be spoken of in her hearing? How should she bear herself when, as of course would be the case, she should again be taken before the magistrates, and made to swear as to the loss of her property? Must she commit more perjury, with the certainty that various people must know that her oath was false? All the world would suspect her. All the world would soon know the truth. Might it not be possible that the diamonds were at this moment in the hands of Messrs. Camperdown, and that they would be produced before her eyes, as soon as her second false oath had been registered against her? And yet how could she tell the truth? And what would the Corsair think of her,—the Corsair, who would know everything? She made one resolution during the night. She would not be taken into court. The magistrates and the people might come to her, but she would not go before them. When the morning came she said that she was ill, and refused to leave her bed. Policemen, she knew, were in the house early. At about nine Mrs. Carbuncle and Lucinda were up and in her room. The excitement of the affair had taken them from their beds,—but she would not stir. If it were absolutely necessary, she said, the men must come into her room. She had been so overset*by what had occurred on the previous night, that she could not leave her room. She appealed to Lucinda as to the fact of her illness. The trouble of these robberies was so great upon her that her heart was almost broken. If her deposition must be taken, she would make it in bed. In the course of the day the magistrate did come into her room and the deposition was taken. Forty-three pounds had been taken from her desk, and certain jewels, which she described, from her dressing-case. As far as she was aware, no other property of hers was missing. This she said in answer to a direct question from the magistrate, which, as she thought, was asked with a stern voice and searching eye. And so, a second time, she had sworn falsely. But this at least was gained,—that Lord George de Bruce Carruthers was not looking at her as she swore.

Lord George was in the house for a great part of the day, but he did not ask to be admitted to Lizzie's room;—nor did she ask to see him. Frank Greystock was there late in the afternoon, and went up at once to his cousin. The moment that she saw him she stretched out her arms to him, and burst into tears. 'My poor girl,' said he, 'what is the meaning of it all?'

'I don't know. I think they will kill me. They want to kill me. How can I bear it all? The robbers were here last night, and magistrates and policemen and people have been here all day.' Then she fell into a fit of sobbing and wailing, which was, in truth, hysterical. For,—if the readers think of it,— the poor woman had a great deal to bear.

Frank, into whose mind no glimmer of suspicion against his cousin had yet entered, and who firmly believed that she had been made a victim because of the value of her diamonds,— and who had a theory of his own about the robbery at Carlisle, to the circumstances of which he was now at some pains to make these latter circumstances adhere,—was very tender with his cousin, and remained in the house for more than an hour. 'Oh, Frank, what had I better do?' she asked him.

'I would leave London, if I were you.'

'Yes;—of course. I will. Oh yes, I will!'

'If you don't fear the cold of Scotland——'

'I fear nothing,—nothing but being where these policemen can come to me. Oh!'—and then she shuddered and was again hysterical. Nor was she acting the condition. As she remembered the magistrates, and the detectives, and the policemen in their uniforms,—and reflected that she might probably see much more of them before the game was played out, the thoughts that crowded on her were almost more than she could bear.

'Your child is there, and it is your own house. Go there till all this passes by.' Whereupon she promised him that, as soon as she was well enough, she would at once go to Scotland.

In the meantime, the Eustace diamonds were locked up in a small safe fixed into the wall at the back of a small cellar beneath the establishment of Messrs. Harter and Benjamin, in Minto Lane,* in the City. Messrs. Harter and Benjamin always kept a second place of business. Their great shop was at the West-end; but they had accommodation in the City.

The chronicler states this at once, as he scorns to keep from his reader any secret that is known to himself.

CHAPTER LIII
Lizzie's Sick-Room

WHEN the Hertford Street robbery was three days old, and was still the talk of all the town, Lizzie Eustace was really ill. She had promised to go down to Scotland in compliance with the advice given to her by her cousin Frank, and at the moment of promising would have been willing enough to be transported at once to Portray, had that been possible—so as to be beyond the visits of policemen and the authority of lawyers and magistrates; but as the hours passed over her head, and as her presence of mind returned to her, she remembered that even at Portray she would not be out of danger, and that she could do nothing in furtherance of her plans if once immured there. Lord George was in London, Frank Greystock was in London, and Lord Fawn was in London. It was more than ever necessary to her that she should find a husband among them,—a husband who would not be less her husband when the truth of that business at Carlisle should be known to all the world. She had, in fact, stolen nothing. She endeavoured to comfort herself by repeating to herself over and over again that assurance. She had stolen nothing; and she still thought that if she could obtain the support of some strong arm on which to lean, she might escape punishment for those false oaths which she had sworn. Her husband might take her abroad, and the whole thing would die away. If she should succeed with Lord George, of course he would take her abroad, and there would be no need for any speedy return. They might roam among islands in pleasant warm suns, and the dreams of her youth might be realised. Her income was still her own. They could not touch that. So she thought, at least,—oppressed by some slight want of assurance in that respect. Were she to go at once to Scotland, she must for the present give up that game altogether. If Frank would pledge himself to become her husband in three or four, or even in six months, she would go at once. She had more confidence in Frank than even in Lord George. As for love,—she would sometimes tell herself that she was violently in love; but she hardly knew with which. Lord George was certainly the best representative of that perfect Corsair which her dreams had represented to her; but, in regard to working life, she thought that she liked her cousin Frank better than she had ever yet liked any other human being. But, in truth, she was now in that condition, as she acknowledged to herself, that she was hardly entitled to choose. Lord Fawn had promised to marry her, and to him as a husband she conceived that she still had a right. Nothing had as yet been proved against her which could justify him in repudiating his engagement. She had, no doubt, asserted with all vehemence to her cousin that no consideration would now induce her to give her hand to Lord Fawn;—and when making that assurance she had been, after her nature, sincere. But circumstances were changed since that. She had not much hope that Lord Fawn might be made to succumb,—though evidence had reached her before the last robbery which induced her to believe that he did not consider himself to be quite secure. In these circumstances she was unwilling to leave London though she had promised, and was hardly sorry to find an excuse in her recognised illness.

And she was ill. Though her mind was again at work with schemes on which she would not have busied herself without hope, yet she had not recovered from the actual bodily prostration to which she had been compelled to give way when first told of the robbery on her return from the theatre. There had been moments, then, in which she thought that her heart would have broken,—moments in which, but that the power of speech was wanting, she would have told everything to Lucinda Roanoke. When Mrs. Carbuncle was marching up-stairs with the policemen at her heels she would have willingly sold all her hopes, Portray Castle, her lovers, her necklace, her income, her beauty, for any assurance of the humblest security. With that quickness of intellect, which was her peculiar gift, she had soon understood, in the midst of her sufferings, that her necklace had been taken by thieves whose robbery might assist her for a while in keeping her secret, rather than lead to the immediate divulging of it. Neither Camperdown nor Bunfit had been at work among the boxes. Her secret had been discovered, no doubt, by Patience Crabstick, and the diamonds were gone. But money also was taken, and the world need not know that the diamonds had been there. But Lord George knew. And then there arose to her that question. Had the diamonds been taken in consequence of that revelation to Lord George? It was not surprising that in the midst of all this Lizzie should be really ill.

She was most anxious to see Lord George; but, if what Mrs. Carbuncle said to her was true, Lord George refused to see her. She did not believe Mrs. Carbuncle, and was, therefore, quite in the dark about her Corsair. As she could only communicate with him through Mrs. Carbuncle, it might well be the case that he should have been told that he could not have access to her. Of course there were difficulties. That her cousin Frank should see her in her bedroom,—her cousin Frank, with whom it was essentially necessary that she should hold counsel as to her present great difficulties, was a matter of course. There was no hesitation about that. A fresh night-cap, and a clean pocket-handkerchief with a bit of lace round it, and, perhaps, some pretty covering to her shoulders if she were to be required to sit up in bed, and the thing was arranged. He might have spent the best part of his days in her bedroom if he could have spared the time. But the Corsair was not a cousin,—nor as yet an acknowledged lover. There was difficulty, even, in framing a reason for her request, when she made it to Mrs. Carbuncle; and the very reason which she gave was handed back to her as the Corsair's reason for not coming to her. She desired to see him because he had been so much mixed up in the matter of these terrible robberies. But Mrs. Carbuncle declared to her that Lord George would not come to her because his name had been so frequently mentioned in connection with the diamonds. 'You see, my dear,' said Mrs. Carbuncle, 'there can be no real reason

for his seeing you up in your bedroom. If there had been anything between you, as I once thought there would——'
There was something in the tone of Mrs. Carbuncle's voice which grated on Lizzie's ear,—something which seemed to imply that all that prospect was over.

'Of course,' said Lizzie querulously, 'I am very anxious to know what he thinks. I care more about his opinion than anybody else's. As to his name being mixed up in it,—that is all a joke.'

'It has been no joke to him, I can assure you,' said Mrs. Carbuncle. Lizzie could not press her request. Of course, she knew more about it than did Mrs. Carbuncle. The secret was in her own bosom,—the secret as to the midnight robbery at Carlisle, and that secret she had told to Lord George. As to the robbery in London she knew nothing,—except that it had been perpetrated through the treachery of Patience Crabstick. Did Lord George know more about it than she knew?— and if so, was he now deterred by that knowledge from visiting her? 'You see, my dear,' said Mrs. Carbuncle, 'that a gentleman visiting a lady with whom he has no connection in her bedroom, is in itself something very peculiar.' Lizzie made a motion of impatience under the bedclothes. Any such argument was trash to her, and she knew that it was trash to Mrs. Carbuncle also. What was one man in her bedroom more than another? She could see a dozen doctors if she pleased, and if so, why not this man, whose real powers of doctoring her would be so much more efficacious? 'You would want to see him alone, too,' continued Mrs. Carbuncle, 'and, of course, the police would hear of it. I am not at all surprised that he should stay away.' Lizzie's condition did not admit of much argument on her side, and she only showed her opposition to Mrs. Carbuncle by being cross and querulous.

Frank Greystock came to her with great constancy almost every day, and from him she did hear about the robbery all that he knew or heard. When three days had passed,—when six days, and even when ten days were gone, nobody had been as yet arrested. The police, according to Frank, were much on the alert, but were very secret. They either would not, or could not, tell anything. To him the two robberies, that at Carlisle and the last affair in Hertford Street, were of course distinct. There were those who believed that the Hertford Street thieves and the Carlisle thieves were not only the same, but that they had been in quest of the same plunder,—and had at last succeeded. But Frank was not one of these. He never for a moment doubted that the diamonds had been taken at Carlisle, and explained the second robbery by the supposition that Patience Crabstick had been emboldened by success. The iron box had no doubt been taken by her assistance, and her familiarity with the thieves, then established, had led to the second robbery. Lizzie's loss in that second robbery had amounted to some hundred pounds. This was Frank Greystock's theory, and of course it was one very comfortable to Lizzie.

'They all seem to think that the diamonds are at Paris,' he said to her one day.

'If you only knew how little I care about them. It seems as though I had almost forgotten them in these after troubles.'

'Mr. Camperdown cares about them. I'm told he says that he can make you pay for them out of your jointure.'

'That would be very terrible, of course,' said Lizzie, to whose mind there was something consolatory in the idea that the whole affair of the robbery might perhaps remain so mysterious as to remove her from the danger of other punishment than this.

'I feel sure that he couldn't do it,' said Frank,' and I don't think he'll try it. John Eustace would not let him. It would be persecution.'

'Mr. Camperdown has always chosen to persecute me,' said Lizzie.

'I can understand that he shouldn't like the loss of the diamonds. I don't think, Lizzie, you ever realised their true value.'

'I suppose not. After all, a necklace is only a necklace. I cared nothing for it,—except that I could not bear the idea that

that man should dictate to me. I would have given it up at once, at the slightest word from you.' He did not care to remind her then, as she lay in bed, that he had been very urgent in his advice to her to abandon the diamonds,—and not the less urgent because he had thought that the demand for them was unjust. 'I told you often,' she continued, 'that I was tempted to throw them among the waves. It was true; —quite true. I offered to give them to you, and should have been delighted to have been relieved from them.'

'That was, of course, simply impossible.'

'I know it was;—impossible on your part; but I would have been delighted. Of what use were they to me? I wore them twice because that man,'—meaning Lord Fawn,— 'disputed my right to them. Before that I never even looked at them. Do you think I had pleasure in wearing them, or pleasure in looking at them? Never. They were only a trouble to me. It was a point of honour with me to keep them, because I was attacked. But I am glad they are gone,—thoroughly glad.' This was all very well, and was not without its effect on Frank Greystock. It is hardly expected of a woman in such a condition, with so many troubles on her mind, who had been so persecuted, that every word uttered by her should be strictly true. Lizzie, with her fresh nightcap, and her laced handkerchief, pale, and with her eyes just glittering with tears, was very pretty. 'Didn't somebody once give some one a garment which scorched him up when he wore it,—some woman who sent it because she loved the man so much?'

'The shirt, you mean, which Dejanira sent to Hercules.* Yes;—Hercules was a good deal scorched.'

'And that necklace, which my husband gave me because he loved me so well, has scorched me horribly. It has nearly killed me. It has been like the white elephant* which the Eastern king gives to his subject when he means to ruin him. Only poor Florian didn't mean to hurt me. He gave it all in love. If these people bring a lawsuit against me, Frank, you must manage it for me.'

'There will be no lawsuit. Your brother-in-law will stop it.'

'I wonder who will really get the diamonds after all, Frank? They were very valuable. Only think that the ten thousand pounds should disappear in such a way!' The subject was a very dangerous one, but there was a fascination about it which made it impossible for her to refrain from it.

'A dishonest dealer in diamonds will probably realise the plunder,—after some years. There would be something very alluring in the theft of articles of great value, were it not that when got, they at once become almost valueless by the difficulty of dealing with them. Supposing I had the necklace!'

'I wish you had, Frank.'

'I could do nothing with it. Ten sovereigns would go further with me,—or ten shillings. The burthen of possessing it would in itself be almost more than I could bear. The knowledge that I had the thing, and might be discovered in having it, would drive me mad. By my own weakness I should be compelled to tell my secret to some one. And then I should never sleep for fear my partner in the matter should turn against me.' How well she understood it all! How probable it was that Lord George should turn against her! How exact was Frank's description of that burthen of a secret so heavy that it cannot be borne alone! 'A little reflection,' continued Frank, 'soon convinces a man that rough downright stealing is an awkward, foolish trade; and it therefore falls into the hands of those who want education for the higher efforts of dishonesty. To get into a bank at midnight and steal what little there may be in the till, or even an armful of bank-notes, with the probability of a policeman catching you as you creep out of the chimney and through a hole, is clumsy work; but to walk in amidst the smiles and bows of admiring managers and draw out money over the counter by thousands and tens of thousands, which you have never put in and which you can never repay; and which, when all is done, you have only borrowed;—that is a great feat.'

'Do you really think so?'

'The courage, the ingenuity, and the self-confidence needed are certainly admirable. And then there is a cringing and almost contemptible littleness about honesty, which hardly allows it to assert itself. The really honest man can never say a word to make those who don't know of his honesty believe that it is there. He has one foot in the grave before his neighbours have learned that he is possessed of an article for the use of which they would so willingly have paid, could they have been made to see that it was there. The dishonest man almost doubts whether in him dishonesty is dishonest, let it be practised ever so widely. The honest man almost doubts whether his honesty be honest, unless it be kept hidden. Let two unknown men be competitors for any place, with nothing to guide the judges but their own words and their own looks, and who can doubt but the dishonest man would be chosen rather than the honest? Honesty goes about with a hang-dog look about him, as though knowing that he cannot be trusted till he be proved. Dishonesty carries his eyes high, and assumes that any question respecting him must be considered to be unnecessary.'

'Oh, Frank, what a philosopher you are.'

'Well, yes; meditating about your diamonds has brought my philosophy out. When do you think you will go to Scotland?'

'I am hardly strong enough for the journey yet. I fear the cold so much.'

'You would not find it cold there by the sea-side. To tell you the truth, Lizzie, I want to get you out of this house. I don't mean to say a word against Mrs. Carbuncle; but after all that has occurred, it would be better that you should be away. People talk about you and Lord George.'

'How can I help it, Frank?'

'By going away;—that is, if I may presume one thing. I don't want to pry into your secrets.'

'I have none from you.'

'Unless there be truth in the assertion that you are engaged to marry Lord George Carruthers.'

'There is no truth in it.'

'And you do not wish to stay here in order that there may

be an engagement? I am obliged to ask you home*questions, Lizzie, as I could not otherwise advise you.'

'You do, indeed, ask home questions.'

'I will desist at once, if they be disagreeable.'

'Frank, you are false to me!' As she said this she rose in her bed, and sat with her eyes fixed upon his, and her thin hands stretched out upon the bedclothes. 'You know that I cannot wish to be engaged to him or to any other man. You know, better almost than I can know myself, how my heart stands. There has, at any rate, been no hypocrisy with me in regard to you. Everything has been told to you;—at what cost I will not now say. The honest woman, I fear, fares worse even than the honest man of whom you spoke. I think you admitted that he would be appreciated at last. She to her dying day must pay the penalty of her transgressions. Honesty in a woman the world never forgives.' When she had done speaking, he sat silent by her bedside, but, almost unconsciously, he stretched out his left hand and took her right hand in his. For a few seconds she admitted this, and she lay there with their hands clasped. Then with a start she drew back her arm, and retreated as it were from his touch. 'How dare you,' she said, 'press my hand, when you know that such pressure from you is treacherous and damnable!'

'Damnable, Lizzie!'

'Yes;—damnable. I will not pick my words for you. Coming from you, what does such pressure mean?'

'Affection.'

'Yes;—and of what sort? You are wicked enough to feed my love by such tokens, when you know that you do not mean to return it. O Frank, Frank, will you give me back my heart? What was it that you promised me when we sat together upon the rocks at Portray?'

It is inexpressibly difficult for a man to refuse the tender of a woman's love. We may almost say that a man should do so as a matter of course,—that the thing so offered becomes absolutely valueless by the offer,—that the woman who can make it has put herself out of court by her own abandonment

of the privileges due to her as a woman,—that stern rebuke
and even expressed contempt are justified by such conduct,—
and that the fairest beauty and most alluring charms of
feminine grace should lose their attraction when thus tendered
openly in the market. No doubt such is our theory as to love
and love-making. But the action to be taken by us in matters
as to which the plainest theory prevails for the guidance of
our practice, depends so frequently on accompanying circumstances and correlative issues, that the theory, as often as not,
falls to the ground. Frank could not despise this woman, and
could not be stern to her. He could not bring himself to tell
her boldly that he would have nothing to say to her in the way
of love. He made excuses for her, and persuaded himself that
there were peculiar circumstances in her position justifying
unwomanly conduct, although, had he examined himself on the
subject, he would have found it difficult to say what those
circumstances were. She was rich, beautiful, clever,—and he
was flattered. Nevertheless he knew that he could not marry
her;—and he knew also that much as he liked her he did not
love her. 'Lizzie,' he said, 'I think you hardly understand
my position.'

'Yes, I do. That little girl has cozened you out of a promise.'

'If it be so, you would not have me break it.'

'Yes, I would, if you think she is not fit to be your wife.
Is a man, such as you are, to be tied by the leg for life, have all
his ambition clipped, and his high hopes shipwrecked, because
a girl has been clever enough to extract a word from him?
Is it not true that you are in debt?'

'What of that? At any rate, Lizzie, I do not want help from
you.'

'That is so like a man's pride! Do we not all know that in
such a career as you have marked out for yourself, wealth, or
at any rate an easy income, is necessary? Do you think that I
cannot put two and two together? Do you believe so meanly
of me as to imagine that I should have said to you what I
have said, if I did not know that I could help you? A man, I
believe, cannot understand that love which induces a woman to

sacrifice her pride simply for his advantage. I want to see you prosper. I want to see you a great man and a lord, and I know that you cannot become so without an income. Ah, I wish I could give you all that I have got, and save you from the encumbrance that is attached to it!'

It might be that he would then have told her of his engagement to Lucy, and of his resolution to adhere to that promise, had not Mrs. Carbuncle at the moment entered the room. Frank had been there for above an hour, and as Lizzie was still an invalid, and to some extent under the care of Mrs. Carbuncle, it was natural that that lady should interfere. 'You know, my dear, you should not exhaust yourself altogether. Mr. Emilius is to come to you this afternoon.'

'Mr. Emilius!' said Greystock.

'Yes;—the clergyman. Don't you remember him at Portray? A dark man with eyes close together! You used to be very wicked, and say that he was once a Jew-boy in the streets.' Lizzie, as she spoke of her spiritual guide, was evidently not desirous of doing him much honour.

'I remember him well enough. He made sheep's eyes at Miss Macnulty, and drank a great deal of wine at dinner.'

'Poor Macnulty! I don't believe a word about the wine; and as for Macnulty, I don't see why she should not be converted as well as another. He is coming here to read to me. I hope you don't object.'

'Not in the least;—if you like it.'

'One does have solemn thoughts sometimes, Frank,— especially when one is ill.'

'Oh, yes. Well or ill, one does have solemn thoughts;— ghosts, as it were, which will appear. But is Mr. Emilius good at laying such apparitions?'

'He is a clergyman, Mr. Greystock,' said Mrs. Carbuncle, with something of rebuke in her voice.

'So they tell me. I was not present at his ordination, but I daresay it was done according to rule. When one reflects what a deal of harm a bishop may do, one wishes that there was some surer way of getting bishops.'

'Do you know anything against Mr. Emilius?' asked Lizzie.

'Nothing at all but his looks, and manners, and voice,—unless it be that he preaches popular sermons, and drinks too much wine, and makes sheep's eyes at Miss Macnulty. Look after your silver spoons, Mrs. Carbuncle,—if the last thieves have left you any. You were asking after the fate of your diamonds, Lizzie. Perhaps they will endow a Protestant church in Mr. Emilius's native land.'

Mr. Emilius did come and read to Lady Eustace that afternoon. A clergyman is as privileged to enter the bedroom of a sick lady as is a doctor or a cousin. There was another clean cap, and another laced handkerchief, and on this occasion a little shawl over Lizzie's shoulders. Mr. Emilius first said a prayer, kneeling at Lizzie's bedside; then he read a chapter in the Bible;—and after that he read the first half of the fourth canto of Childe Harold so well, that Lizzie felt for the moment that after all, poetry was life and life was poetry.

CHAPTER LIV
'I suppose I may say a Word'

THE second robbery to which Lady Eustace had been subjected by no means decreased the interest which was attached to her and her concerns in the fashionable world. Parliament had now met, and the party at Matching Priory,—Lady Glencora Palliser's party in the country,—had been to some extent broken up. All those gentlemen who were engaged in the service of Her Majesty's Government had necessarily gone to London, and they who had wives at Matching had taken their wives with them. Mr. and Mrs. Bonteen had seen the last of their holiday; Mr. Palliser himself was, of course, at his post; and all the private secretaries were with the public secretaries on the scene of action. On the 13th of February Mr. Palliser made his first great statement in Parliament on the matter of the five-farthinged penny, and pledged himself to do his very best to carry that stupendous measure through Parliament in the present session. The City men who were in the House that night,— and all the Directors of the Bank of England were in the gallery, and every chairman of a great banking company, and every Baring*and every Rothschild,* if there be Barings and Rothschilds who have not been returned by constituencies, and have not seats in the House by right,—agreed in declaring that the job in hand was too much for any one member or any one session. Some said that such a measure never could be passed, because the unfinished work of one session could not be used in lessening the labours of the next. Everything must be recommenced; and therefore,—so said these hopeless ones, —the penny with five farthings, the penny of which a hundred would make ten shillings, the halcyon penny, which would make all future pecuniary calculations easy to the meanest British capacity, could never become the law of the land. Others, more hopeful, were willing to believe that gradually the thing would so sink into the minds of members of Parliament, of writers of leading articles, and of the active public generally, as to admit of certain established axioms being taken as established, and placed, as it were, beyond the procrastinating power of debate. It might, for instance, at last be taken for granted that a decimal system was desirable, —so that a month or two of the spring need not be consumed on that preliminary question. But this period had not as yet been reached, and it was thought by the entire City that Mr. Palliser was much too sanguine. It was so probable, many said, that he might kill himself by labour which would be herculean in all but success, and that no financier after him would venture to face the task. It behoved Lady Glencora to see that her Hercules did not kill himself.

In this state of affairs Lady Glencora,—into whose hands the custody of Mr. Palliser's uncle, the duke, had now alto-gether fallen,—had a divided duty between Matching and London. When the members of Parliament went up to London, she went there also, leaving some half-dozen friends whom she could trust to amuse the duke; but she soon returned, knowing that there might be danger in a long absence. The duke, though old, was his own master; he much affected the company of Madame Goesler, and that lady's kindness to him was considerate and incessant; but there might still be danger, and Lady Glencora felt that she was responsible that the old nobleman should do nothing, in the feebleness of age, to derogate from the splendour of his past life. What, if some day his grace should be off to Paris and insist on making Madame Goesler a duchess in the chapel of the Embassy! Madame Goesler had hitherto behaved very well;—would probably continue to behave well. Lady Glencora really loved Madame Goesler. But then the interests at stake were very great! So circumstanced, Lady Glencora found herself compelled to be often on the road between Matching and London.

But though she was burthened with great care, Lady Glencora by no means dropped her interest in the Eustace diamonds; and when she 'learned that on the top of the great Carlisle robbery a second robbery had been superadded, and that this had been achieved while all the London police were yet astray about the former operation, her solicitude was of course enhanced. The duke himself, too, took the matter up so strongly, that he almost wanted to be carried up to London, with some view, as it was supposed by the ladies who were so good to him, of seeing Lady Eustace personally. 'It's out of the question, my dear,' Lady Glencora said to Madame Goesler, when the duke's fancy was first mentioned to her by that lady. 'I told him that the trouble would be too much for him.' 'Of course it would be too much,' said Lady Glencora. 'It is quite out of the question.' Then, after a moment, she added in a whisper, 'Who knows but what he'd insist on marrying her! It isn't every woman that can resist temptation.' Madame Goesler smiled, and shook her head, but made no answer to Lady Glencora's suggestion. Lady Glencora assured her uncle that everything should be told to him. She would write about it daily, and send him the latest news by the wires if the post should be too slow. 'Ah;—yes,' said the duke; 'I like telegrams best. I think, you know, that that Lord George Carruthers has had something to do with it. Don't you, Madame Goesler?' It had long been evident that the duke was anxious that one of his own order should be proved to have been the thief, as the plunder taken was so lordly.

In regard to Lizzie herself, Lady Glencora, on her return to London, took it into her head to make a diversion in our heroine's favour. It had hitherto been a matter of faith with all the liberal party that Lady Eustace had had something to do with stealing her own diamonds. That esprit de corps, which is the glorious characteristic of English statesmen, had caused the whole Government to support Lord Fawn, and Lord Fawn could only be supported on the supposition that Lizzie Eustace had been a wicked culprit. But Lady Glencora, though very true as a politician, was apt to have opinions of her own, and to take certain flights in which she chose that others of the party should follow her. She now expressed an opinion that Lady Eustace was a victim, and all the Mrs. Bonteens, with some even of the Mr. Bonteens, found themselves compelled to agree with her. She stood too high among her set to be subject to that obedience which restrained others,—too high, also, for others to resist her leading. As a member of a party she was erratic and dangerous, but from her position and peculiar temperament she was powerful. When she declared that poor Lady Eustace was a victim, others were obliged to say so too. This was particularly hard upon Lord Fawn, and the more so as Lady Glencora took upon her to assert that Lord Fawn had no right to jilt the young woman. And Lady Glencora had this to support her views,—that, for the last week past, indeed ever since the depositions which had been taken after the robbery in Hertford Street, the police had expressed no fresh suspicions in regard to Lizzie Eustace. She heard daily from Barrington Erle that Major Mackintosh and Bunfit and Gager were as active as ever in their inquiries, that all Scotland Yard was determined to unravel the mystery, and that there were emissaries at work tracking the diamonds at Hamburg, Paris, Vienna, and New York. It had been whispered to Mr. Erle that the whereabouts of Patience Crabstick had been discovered, and that many of the leading thieves in London were assisting the police;—but nothing more was done in the way of fixing any guilt upon Lizzie Eustace. 'Upon my word, I am beginning to think that she has been more sinned against than sinning.' This was said to Lady Glencora on the morning after Mr. Palliser's great speech about the five farthings, by Barrington Erle, who, as it seemed, had been specially told off by the party to watch this investigation.

'I am sure she has had nothing to do with it. I have thought so ever since the last robbery. Sir Simon Slope told me yesterday afternoon that Mr. Camperdown has given it up altogether.' Sir Simon Slope was the Solicitor-General of that day.

'It would be absurd for him to go on with his bill in Chancery now that the diamonds are gone,—unless he meant to make her pay for them.'

'That would be rank persecution. Indeed she has been persecuted. I shall call upon her.' Then she wrote the following letter to the duke;—

'February 14, 18—.
'My dear Duke,

'Plantagenet was on his legs last night for three hours and three quarters, and I sat through it all. As far as I could observe through the bars I was the only person in the House who listened to him. I'm sure Mr. Gresham was fast asleep. It was quite piteous to see some of them yawning. Plantagenet did it very well, and I almost think I understood him. They seem to say that nobody on the other side will take trouble enough to make a regular opposition, but that there are men in the City who will write letters to the newspapers, and get up a sort of Bank clamour. Plantagenet says nothing about it, but there is a do-or-die manner with him which is quite tragical. The House was up at eleven, when he came home and eat three oysters, drank a glass of beer, and slept well. They say the real work will come when it's in Committee;*—that is, if it gets there. The bill is to be brought in, and will be read the first time next Monday week.

'As to the robberies, I believe there is no doubt that the police have got hold of the young woman. They don't arrest her, but deal with her in a friendly sort of way. Barrington Erle says that a sergeant is to marry her in order to make quite sure of her. I suppose they know their business; but that wouldn't strike me as being the safest way. They seem to think the diamonds went to Paris but have since been sent on to New York.

'As to the little widow, I do believe she has been made a victim. She first lost her diamonds, and now her other jewels and her money have gone. I cannot see what she was to gain by treachery, and I think she has been ill-used. She is staying at the house of that Mrs. Carbuncle, but all the same I shall go and call on her. I wish you could see her, because she is such a little beauty;—just what you would like; not so much colour as our friend, but perfect features, with infinite play,— not perhaps always in the very best taste; but then we can't have everything; can we, dear duke?

'As to the real thief;—of course you must burn this at once, and keep it strictly private as coming from me;—I fancy that delightful Scotch lord managed it entirely. The idea is, that he did it on commission for the Jew jewellers. I don't suppose he had money enough to carry it out himself. As to the second robbery, whether he had or had not a hand in that, I can't make up my mind. I don't see why he shouldn't. If a man does go into a business, he ought to make the best of it. Of course, it was a poor thing after the diamonds; but still it was worth having. There is some story about a Sir Griffin Tewett. He's a real Sir Griffin, as you'll find by the peerage. He was to marry a young woman, and our Lord George insists that he shall marry her. I don't understand all about it, but the girl lives in the same house with Lady Eustace, and if I call I shall find out. They say that Sir Griffin knows all about the neck-lace, and threatens to tell unless he is let off marrying. I rather think the girl is Lord George's daughter, so that there is a thorough complication.

'I shall go down to Matching on Saturday. If anything turns up before that, I'll write again, or send a message. I don't know whether Plantagenet will be able to leave London. He says he must be back on Monday, and that he loses too much time on the road. Kiss my little darlings for me,'—the darlings were Lady Glencora's children, and the duke's playthings,—'and give my love to Madame Max. I suppose you don't see much of the others.

'Most affectionately yours,
'GLENCORA.'

On the next day Lady Glencora actually did call in Hertford Street, and saw our friend Lizzie. She was told by the servant that Lady Eustace was in bed; but, with her usual persistence, she asked questions, and when she found that Lizzie did receive visitors in her room, she sent up her card. The compliment was one much too great to be refused. Lady Glencora stood so high in the world, that her countenance would be almost as valuable as another lover. If Lord George would keep her secret, and Lady Glencora would be her friend, might she not still be a successful woman? So Lady Glencora Palliser was shown up to Lizzie's chamber. Lizzie was found with her nicest nightcap, and prettiest handkerchief, with a volume of Tennyson's poetry, and a scent-bottle. She knew that it behoved her to be very clever at this interview. Her instinct told her that her first greeting should show more of surprise than of gratification. Accordingly, in a pretty, feminine, almost childish way, she was very much surprised. 'I'm doing the strangest thing in the world, I know, Lady Eustace,' said Lady Glencora with a smile.

'I'm sure you mean to do a kind thing.'

'Well;—yes, I do. I think we have not met since you were at my house near the end of last season.'

'No, indeed. I have been in London six weeks, but have not been out much. For the last fortnight I have been in bed.

I have had things to trouble me so much that they have made me ill.'

'So I have heard, Lady Eustace, and I have just come to offer you my sympathy. When I was told that you did see people, I thought that perhaps you would admit me.'

'So willingly, Lady Glencora!'

'I have heard, of course, of your terrible losses.'

'The loss has been as nothing to the vexation that has accompanied it. I don't know how to speak of it. Ladies have lost their jewels before now, but I don't know that any lady before me has ever been accused of stealing them herself.'

'There has been no accusation, surely.'

'I haven't exactly been put in prison, Lady Glencora, but I have had policemen here wanting to search my things;— and then, you know yourself, what reports have been spread.'

'Oh, yes; I do. Only for that, to tell you plainly, I should hardly have been here now.' Then Lady Glencora poured out her sympathy,—perhaps with more eloquence and grace than discretion. She was, at any rate, both graceful and eloquent. 'As for the loss of the diamonds, I think you bear it wonderfully,' said Lady Glencora.

'If you could imagine how little I care about it!' said Lizzie with enthusiasm. 'They had lost the delight which I used to feel in them as a present from my husband. People had talked about them, and I had been threatened because I chose to keep what I knew to be my own. Of course, I would not give them up. Would you have given them up, Lady Glencora?'

'Certainly not.'

'Nor would I. But when once all that had begun, they became an irrepressible burthen to me. I often used to say that I would throw them into the sea.'

'I don't think I would have done that,' said Lady Glencora.

'Ah,—you have never suffered as I have suffered.'

'We never know where each other's shoes pinch each other's toes.'

'You have never been left desolate. You have a husband and friends.'

'A husband that wants to put five farthings into a penny! All is not gold that glistens, Lady Eustace.'

'You can never have known trials such as mine,' continued Lizzie, not understanding in the least her new friend's allusion to the great currency question. 'Perhaps you may have heard that in the course of last summer I became engaged to marry a nobleman, with whom I am aware that you are acquainted.' This she said in her softest whisper.

'Oh, yes;—Lord Fawn. I know him very well. Of course I heard of it. We all heard of it.'

'And you have heard how he has treated me?'

'Yes,—indeed.'

'I will say nothing about him,—to you, Lady Glencora. It would not be proper that I should do so. But all that came of this wretched necklace. After that, can you wonder that I should say that I wish these stones had been thrown into the sea?'

'I suppose Lord Fawn will,—will come all right again now?' said Lady Glencora.

'All right!' exclaimed Lizzie in astonishment.

'His objection to the marriage will now be over.'

'I'm sure I do not in the least know what are his lordship's views,' said Lizzie in scorn, 'and, to tell the truth, I do not very much care.'

'What I mean is, that he didn't like you to have the Eustace diamonds——'

'They were not Eustace diamonds. They were my diamonds.'

'But he did not like you to have them; and as they are now gone,—for ever——'

'Oh, yes;—they are gone for ever.'

'His objection is gone too. Why don't you write to him, and make him come and see you? That's what I should do.'

Lizzie, of course, repudiated vehemently any idea of forcing Lord Fawn into a marriage which had become distasteful to

137

him,—let the reason be what it might. 'His lordship is perfectly free, as far as I am concerned,' said Lizzie with a little show of anger. But all this Lady Glencora took at its worth. Lizzie Eustace had been a good deal knocked about, and Lady Glencora did not doubt but that she would be very glad to get back her betrothed husband. The little woman had suffered hardships,—so thought Lady Glencora,—and a good thing would be done by bringing her into fashion, and setting the marriage up again. As to Lord Fawn,—the fortune was there, as good now as it had been when he first sought it; and the lady was very pretty, a baronet's widow too!—and in all respects good enough for Lord Fawn. A very pretty little baronet's widow she was, with four thousand a year, and a house in Scotland, and a history. Lady Glencora determined that she would remake the match.

'I think, you know, friends who have been friends, should be brought together. I suppose I may say a word to Lord Fawn?'

Lizzie hesitated for a moment before she answered, and then remembered that revenge, at least, would be sweet to her. She had sworn that she would be revenged upon Lord Fawn. After all, might it not suit her best to carry out her oath by marrying him? But whether so or otherwise, it would not but be well for her that he should be again at her feet. 'Yes,—if you think good will come of it.' The acquiescence was given with much hesitation;—but the circumstances required that it should be so, and Lady Glencora fully understood the circumstances. When she took her leave, Lizzie was profuse in her gratitude. 'Oh, Lady Glencora, it has been so good of you to come. Pray come again, if you can spare me another moment.' Lady Glencora said that she would come again.

During the visit she had asked some question concerning Lucinda and Sir Griffin, and had been informed that that marriage was to go on. A hint had been thrown out as to Lucinda's parentage;—but Lizzie had not understood the hint, and the question had not been pressed.

CHAPTER LV
Quints or Semitenths

THE task which Lady Glencora had taken upon herself was not a very easy one. No doubt Lord Fawn was a man subservient to the leaders of his party, much afraid of the hard judgment of those with whom he was concerned, painfully open to impression from what he would have called public opinion, to a certain extent a coward, most anxious to do right so that he might not be accused of being in the wrong,— and at the same time gifted with but little of that insight into things which teaches men to know what is right and what is wrong. Lady Glencora, having perceived all this, felt that he was a man upon whom a few words from her might have an effect. But even Lady Glencora might hesitate to tell a gentleman that he ought to marry a lady, when the gentleman had already declared his intention of not marrying, and had attempted to justify his decision almost publicly by a reference to the lady's conduct. Lady Glencora almost felt that she had undertaken too much as she turned over in her mind the means she had of performing her promise to Lady Eustace.

The five-farthing bill had been laid upon the table*on a Tuesday, and was to be read the first time on the following Monday week. On the Wednesday Lady Glencora had written to the duke, and had called in Hertford Street. On the following Sunday she was at Matching, looking after the duke;— but she returned to London on the Tuesday, and on the Wednesday there was a little dinner at Mr. Palliser's house, given avowedly with the object of further friendly discussion respecting the new Palliser penny. The prime minister was to be there, and Mr. Bonteen, and Barrington Erle, and those special members of the government who would be available for giving special help to the financial Hercules of the day. A question, perhaps of no great practical importance, had occurred to Mr. Palliser,—but one which, if overlooked, might be fatal to the ultimate success of the measure. There is so much in a name,—and then an ounce of ridicule is often more potent than a hundredweight of argument. By what denomination should the fifth part of a penny be hereafter known? Some one had, ill-naturedly, whispered to Mr. Palliser that a farthing meant a fourth, and at once there arose a new trouble, which for a time bore very heavy on him. Should he boldly disregard the original meaning of the useful old word; or should he venture on the dangers of new nomenclature? October, as he said to himself, is still the tenth month of the year, November the eleventh, and so on, though by these names they are so plainly called the eighth and ninth. All France tried to rid itself of this absurdity, and failed. Should he stick by the farthing; or should he call it a fifthing, a quint, or a semi-tenth? 'There's the "Fortnightly Review"*comes out but once a month,' he said to his friend Mr. Bonteen, 'and I'm told that it does very well.' Mr. Bonteen, who was a rational man, thought the 'Review' would do better if it were called by a more rational name, and was very much in favour of 'a quint.' Mr. Gresham had expressed an opinion, somewhat offhand, that English people would never be got to talk about quints, and so there was a difficulty. A little dinner was therefore arranged, and Mr. Palliser, as was his custom in such matters, put the affair of the dinner into his wife's hands. When he was told that she had included Lord Fawn among the guests he opened his eyes. Lord Fawn, who might be good enough at the India Office, knew literally nothing about the penny. 'He'll take it as the greatest compliment in the world,' said Lady Glencora. 'I don't want to pay Lord Fawn a compliment,' said Mr. Palliser. 'But I do,' said Lady Glencora. And so the matter was arranged.

It was a very nice little dinner. Mrs. Gresham and Mrs. Bonteen were there, and the great question of the day was settled in two minutes, before the guests went out of the drawing-room. 'Stick to your farthing,' said Mr. Gresham.

'I think so,' said Mr. Palliser.

'Quint's a very easy word,' said Mr. Bonteen.

'But squint is an easier,' said Mr. Gresham, with all a prime minister's jocose authority.

'They'd certainly be called cock-eyes,' said Barrington Erle.

'There's nothing of the sound of a quarter in farthing,' said Mr. Palliser.

'Stick to the old word,' said Mr. Gresham. And so the matter was decided, while Lady Glencora was flattering Lord Fawn as to the manner in which he had finally arranged the affair of the Sawab of Mygawb. Then they went down to dinner, and not a word more was said that evening about the new penny by Mr. Palliser.

Before dinner Lady Glencora had exacted a promise from Lord Fawn that he would return to the drawing-room. Lady Glencora was very clever at such work, and said nothing then of her purpose. She did not want her guests to run away, and therefore Lord Fawn,—Lord Fawn especially,—must stay. If he were to go there would be nothing spoken of all the evening, but that weary new penny. To oblige her he must remain;

—and, of course, he did remain. 'Whom do you think I saw the other day?' said Lady Glencora, when she got her victim into a corner. Of course, Lord Fawn had no idea whom she might have seen. Up to that moment no suspicion of what was coming upon him had crossed his mind. 'I called upon poor Lady Eustace, and found her in bed.' Then did Lord Fawn blush up to the roots of his hair, and for a moment he was stricken dumb. 'I do feel for her so much! I think she has been so hardly used!'

He was obliged to say something. 'My name has, of course, been much mixed up with hers.'

'Yes, Lord Fawn, I know it has. And it is because I am so sure of your high-minded generosity and,—and thorough devotion, that I have ventured to speak to you. I am sure there is nothing you would wish so much as to get at the truth.'

'Certainly, Lady Glencora.'

'All manner of stories have been told about her, and, as I believe, without the slightest foundation. They tell me now that she had an undoubted right to keep the diamonds;—that even if Sir Florian did not give them to her, they were hers under his will. Those lawyers have given up all idea of proceeding against her.'

'Because the necklace has been stolen.'

'Altogether independently of that. Do you see Mr. Eustace, and ask him if what I say is not true. If it had not been her own she would have been responsible for the value, even though it were stolen; and with such a fortune as hers they would never have allowed her to escape. They were as bitter against her as they could be;—weren't they?'

'Mr. Camperdown thought that the property should be given up.'

'Oh yes;—that's the man's name; a horrid man. I am told that he was really most cruel to her. And then, because a lot of thieves had got about her,—after the diamonds, you know, like flies round a honey-pot,—and took first her necklace and then her money, they were impudent enough to say that she had stolen her own things!'

'I don't think they quite said that, Lady Glencora.'

'Something very much like it, Lord Fawn. I have no doubt in my own mind who did steal all the things.'

'Who was it?'

'Oh,—one musn't mention names in such an affair without evidence. At any rate, she has been very badly treated, and I shall take her up. If I were you I would go and call upon her; —I would indeed. I think you owe it to her. Well, duke, what do you think of Plantagenet's penny now? Will it ever be worth two halfpence?' This question was asked of the Duke of St. Bungay, a great nobleman whom all Liberals loved, and a member of the Cabinet. He had come in since dinner, and had been asking a question or two as to what had been decided.

'Well, yes; if properly invested I think it will. I'm glad that it is not to contain five semitenths. A semitenth would never have been a popular form of money in England. We hate new names so much that we have not yet got beyond talking of fourpenny bits.'

'There's a great deal in a name;—isn't there? You don't think they'll call them Pallisers, or Palls, or anything of that sort;—do you? I shouldn't like to hear that under the new régime two lollypops were to cost three Palls. But they say it never can be carried this session,—and we shan't be in, in the next year.'

'Who says so? Don't be such a prophetess of evil, Lady Glencora. I mean to be in for the next three sessions, and I mean to see Palliser's measure carried through the House of Lords next session. I shall be paying for my mutton chops at the club at so many quints a chop yet. Don't you think so, Fawn?'

'I don't know what to think,' said Lord Fawn, whose mind was intent on other matters. After that he left the room as quickly as he could, and escaped out into the street. His mind was very much disturbed. If Lady Glencora was determined to take up the cudgels for the woman he had rejected, the comfort and peace of his life would be over. He knew well enough how strong was Lady Glencora.

CHAPTER LVI
Job's Comforters

MRS. CARBUNCLE and Lady Eustace had now been up in town between six and seven weeks, and the record of their doings has necessarily dealt chiefly with robberies and the rumours of robberies. But at intervals the minds of the two ladies had been intent on other things. The former was still intent on marrying her niece, Lucinda Roanoke, to Sir Griffin, and the latter had never for a moment forgotten the imperative duty which lay upon her of revenging herself upon Lord Fawn. The match between Sir Griffin and Lucinda was still to be a match. Mrs. Carbuncle persevered in the teeth both of the gentleman and of the lady, and still promised herself success. And our Lizzie, in the midst of all her troubles, had not been idle. In doing her justice we must acknowledge that she had almost abandoned the hope of becoming Lady Fawn. Other hopes and other ambitions had come upon her. Latterly the Corsair had been all in all to her,—with exceptional moments in which she told herself that her heart belonged exclusively to her cousin Frank. But Lord Fawn's offences were not to be forgotten, and she continually urged upon her cousin the depth of the wrongs which she had suffered.

On the part of Frank Greystock there was certainly no desire to let the Under-Secretary escape. It is hoped that the reader, to whom every tittle of this story has been told without reserve, and every secret unfolded, will remember that others were not treated with so much open candour. The reader knows much more of Lizzie Eustace than did her cousin Frank. He, indeed, was not quite in love with Lizzie; but to him she was a pretty, graceful young woman, to whom he was bound by many ties, and who had been cruelly injured. Dangerous she was doubtless, and perhaps a little artificial. To have had her married to Lord Fawn would have been a good thing,—and would still be a good thing. According to all the rules known in such matters Lord Fawn was bound to marry her. He had become engaged to her, and Lizzie had done nothing to forfeit her engagement. As to the necklace,—the plea made for jilting her on that ground was a disgraceful pretext. Everybody was beginning to perceive that Mr. Camperdown would never have succeeded in getting the diamonds from her, even if they had not been stolen. It was 'preposterous,' as Frank said over and over again to his friend Herriot, that a man when he was engaged to a lady, should take upon himself to judge her conduct as Lord Fawn had done,—and then ride out of his engagement on a verdict found by himself. Frank had therefore willingly displayed alacrity in persecuting his lordship, and had not been altogether without hope that he might drive the two into a marriage yet,—in spite of the protestations made by Lizzie at Portray.

Lord Fawn had certainly not spent a happy winter. Between Mrs. Hittaway on one side and Frank Greystock on the other, his life had been a burthen to him. It had been suggested to him by various people that he was behaving badly to the lady,—who was represented as having been cruelly misused by fortune and by himself. On the other hand it had been hinted to him, that nothing was too bad to believe of Lizzie Eustace, and that no calamity could be so great as that by which he would be overwhelmed were he still to allow himself to be forced into that marriage. 'It would be better,' Mrs. Hittaway had said, 'to retire to Ireland at once, and cultivate your demesne in Tipperary.' This was a grievous sentence, and one which had greatly excited the brother's wrath;—but it had shown how very strong was his sister's opinion against the lady to whom he had unfortunately offered his hand. Then there came to him a letter from Mr. Greystock, in which he was asked for his 'written explanation.' If there be a proceeding which an official man dislikes worse than another, it is a demand for a written explanation. 'It is impossible,' Frank had said, 'that your conduct to my cousin should be allowed to drop without further notice. Hers has been without reproach. Your engagement with her has been made public,—

chiefly by you, and it is out of the question that she should be treated as you are treating her, and that your lordship should escape without punishment.' What the punishment was to be he did not say; but there did come a punishment on Lord Fawn from the eyes of every man whose eyes met his own, and in the tones of every voice that addressed him. The looks of the very clerks in the India Office accused him of behaving badly to a young woman, and the doorkeeper at the House of Lords seemed to glance askance at him. And now Lady Glencora, who was the social leader of his own party, the feminine pole-star of the liberal heavens, the most popular and the most daring woman in London, had attacked him personally, and told him that he ought to call on Lady Eustace!

Let it not for a moment be supposed that Lord Fawn was without conscience in the matter, or indifferent to moral obligations. There was not a man in London less willing to behave badly to a young woman than Lord Fawn; or one who would more diligently struggle to get back to the right path, if convinced that he was astray. But he was one who detested interference in his private matters, and who was nearly driven mad between his sister and Frank Greystock. When he left Lady Glencora's house he walked towards his own abode with a dark cloud upon his brow. He was at first very angry with Lady Glencora. Even her position gave her no right to meddle with his most private affairs as she had done. He would resent it, and would quarrel with Lady Glencora. What right could she have to advise him to call upon any woman? But by degrees this wrath died away, and gave place to fears, and qualms, and inward questions. He, too, had found a change in general opinion about the diamonds. When he had taken upon himself with a high hand to dissolve his own engagement, everybody had, as he thought, acknowledged that Lizzie Eustace was keeping property which did not belong to her. Now people talked of her losses as though the diamonds had been undoubtedly her own. On the next morning Lord Fawn took an opportunity of seeing Mr. Camperdown.

'My dear lord,' said Mr. Camperdown, 'I shall wash my hands of the matter altogether. The diamonds are gone, and the questions now are, who stole them, and where are they? In our business we can't meddle with such questions as those.'

'You will drop the bill in Chancery then?'

'What good can the bill do us when the diamonds are gone? If Lady Eustace had anything to do with the robbery——'

'You suspect her, then?'

'No, my lord; no. I cannot say that. I have no right to say that. Indeed it is not Lady Eustace that I suspect. She has got into bad hands, perhaps; but I do not think that she is a thief.'

'You were suggesting that,—if she had anything to do with the robbery——'

'Well;—yes;—if she had, it would not be for us to take steps against her in the matter. In fact, the trustees have decided that they will do nothing more, and my hands are tied. If the minor, when he comes of age, claims the property from them, they will prefer to replace it. It isn't very likely; but that's what they say.'

'But if it was an heirloom——' suggested Lord Fawn, going back to the old claim.

'That's exploded,' said Mr. Camperdown. 'Mr. Dove was quite clear about that.'

This was the end of the filing of that bill in Chancery as to which Mr. Camperdown had been so very enthusiastic! Now it certainly was the case that poor Lord Fawn in his conduct towards Lizzie had trusted greatly to the support of Mr. Camperdown's legal proceeding. The world could hardly have expected him to marry a woman against whom a bill in Chancery was being carried on for the recovery of diamonds which did not belong to her. But that support was now altogether withdrawn from him. It was acknowledged that the necklace was not an heirloom,—clearly acknowledged by Mr. Camperdown! And even Mr. Camperdown would not express an opinion that the lady had stolen her own diamonds.

How would it go with him, if after all, he were to marry her? The bone of contention between them had at any rate been made to vanish. The income was still there, and Lady Glencora Palliser had all but promised her friendship. As he entered the India Office on his return from Mr. Camperdown's chambers, he almost thought that that would be the best way out of his difficulty. In his room he found his brother-in-law, Mr. Hittaway, waiting for him. It is always necessary that a man should have some friend whom he can trust in delicate affairs, and Mr. Hittaway was selected as Lord Fawn's friend. He was not at all points the man whom Lord Fawn would have chosen, but for their close connection. Mr. Hittaway was talkative, perhaps a little loud, and too apt to make capital out of every incident of his life. But confidential friends are not easily found, and one does not wish to increase the circle to whom one's family secrets must become known. Mr. Hittaway was at any rate zealous for the Fawn family, and then his character as an official man stood high. He had been asked on the previous evening to step across from the Civil Appeal Office to give his opinion respecting that letter from Frank Greystock demanding a written explanation. The letter had been sent to him; and Mr. Hittaway had carried it home and shown it to his wife. 'He's a cantankerous Tory, and determined to make himself disagreeable,' said Mr. Hittaway, taking the letter from his pocket and beginning the conversation. Lord Fawn seated himself in his great arm-chair, and buried his face in his hands. 'I am disposed, after much consideration, to advise you to take no notice of the letter,' said Mr. Hittaway, giving his counsel in accordance with instructions received from his wife. Lord Fawn still buried his face. 'Of course the thing is painful,—very painful. But out of two evils one should choose the least. The writer of this letter is altogether unable to carry out his threat.' 'What can the man do to him?' Mrs. Hittaway had asked, almost snapping at her husband as she did so. 'And then,' continued Mr. Hittaway, 'we all know that public opinion is with you altogether. The conduct of Lady Eustace is notorious.'

'Everybody is taking her part,' said Lord Fawn almost crying. 'Surely not.'

'Yes;—they are. The bill in Chancery has been withdrawn, and it's my belief that if the necklace were found to-morrow, there would be nothing to prevent her keeping it,—just as she did before.'

'But it was an heirloom?'

'No, it wasn't. The lawyers were all wrong about it. As far as I can see, lawyers always are wrong. About those nine lacs of rupees for the Sawab, Finlay was all wrong. Camperdown owns that he was wrong. If, after all, the diamonds were hers, I'm sure I don't know what I am to do. Thank you, Hittaway, for coming over. That'll do for the present. Just leave that ruffian's letter, and I'll think about it.'

This was considered by Mrs. Hittaway to be a very bad state of things, and there was great consternation in Warwick Square when Mr. Hittaway told his wife this new story of her brother's weakness. She was not going to be weak. She did not intend to withdraw her opposition to the marriage. She was not going to be frightened by Lizzie Eustace and Frank Greystock,—knowing as she did that they were lovers, and very improper lovers, too. 'Of course she stole them herself,' said Mrs. Hittaway; 'and I don't doubt but she stole her own money afterwards. There's nothing she wouldn't do. I'd sooner see Frederic in his grave than married to such a woman as that. Men don't know how sly women can be;—that's the truth. And Frederic has been so spoilt among them down at Richmond, that he has no real judgment left. I don't suppose he means to marry her.'

'Upon my word I don't know,' said Mr. Hittaway. Then Mrs. Hittaway made up her mind that she would at once write a letter to Scotland.

There was an old lord about London in those days,—or, rather, one who was an old Liberal but a young lord,—one Lord Mount Thistle, who had sat in the Cabinet, and had lately been made a peer when his place in the Cabinet was wanted. He was a pompous, would-be important, silly old man, well acquainted with all the traditions of his party, and perhaps, on that account, useful,—but a bore, and very apt to meddle when he was not wanted. Lady Glencora, on the day after her dinner-party, whispered into his ear that Lord Fawn was getting himself into trouble, and that a few words of caution, coming to him from one whom he respected so much as he did Lord Mount Thistle, would be of service to him. Lord Mount Thistle had known Lord Fawn's father, and declared himself at once to be quite entitled to interfere. 'He is really behaving badly to Lady Eustace,' said Lady Glencora, 'and I don't think that he knows it.' Lord Mount Thistle, proud of a commission from the hands of Lady Glencora, went almost at once to his old friend's son. He found him at the House that night, and whispered his few words of caution in one of the lobbies.

'I know you will excuse me, Fawn,' Lord Mount Thistle said, 'but people seem to think that you are not behaving quite well to Lady Eustace.'

'What people?' demanded Lord Fawn.

'My dear fellow, that is a question that cannot be answered. You know that I am the last man to interfere if I didn't think it my duty as a friend. You were engaged to her?'—Lord Fawn only frowned. 'If so,' continued the late cabinet minister, 'and if you have broken it off, you ought to give your reasons. She has a right to demand as much as that.'

On the next morning, Friday, there came to him the note which Lady Glencora had recommended Lizzie to write. It was very short. 'Had you not better come and see me? You can hardly think that things should be left as they are now. L.E.—Hertford Street, Thursday.' He had hoped,—he had ventured to hope,—that things might be left, and that they would arrange themselves; that he could throw aside his engagement without further trouble, and that the subject would drop. But it was not so. His enemy, Frank Greystock, had demanded from him a 'written explanation' of his conduct. Mr. Camperdown had deserted him. Lady Glencora Palliser, with whom he had not the honour of any intimate acquaintance, had taken upon herself to give him advice. Lord Mount Thistle had found fault with him. And now there had come a note from Lizzie Eustace herself, which he could hardly venture to leave altogether unnoticed. On that Friday he dined at his club, and then went to his sister's house in Warwick Square. If assistance might be had anywhere, it would be from his sister;—she, at any rate, would not want courage in carrying on the battle on his behalf.

'Ill-used!' she said, as soon as they were closeted together. 'Who dares to say so?'

'That old fool, Mount Thistle, has been with me.'

'I hope, Frederic, you don't mind what such a man as that says. He has probably been prompted by some friend of hers. And who else?'

'Camperdown turns round now and says that they don't mean to do anything more about the necklace. Lady Glencora Palliser told me the other day that all the world believes that the thing was her own.'

'What does Lady Glencora Palliser know about it? If Lady Glencora Palliser would mind her own affairs it would be much better for her. I remember when she had troubles enough of her own, without meddling with other people's.'

'And now I've got this note.' Lord Fawn had already shown Lizzie's few scrawled words to his sister. 'I think I must go and see her.'

'Do no such thing, Frederic.'

'Why not? I must answer it, and what can I say?'

'If you go there, that woman will be your wife, and you'll never have a happy day again as long as you live. The match is broken off, and she knows it. I shouldn't take the slightest notice of her, or of her cousin, or of any of them. If she chooses to bring an action against you, that is another thing.'

Lord Fawn paused for a few moments before he answered. 'I think I ought to go,' he said.

'And I am sure that you ought not. It is not only about the diamonds,—though that was quite enough to break off any engagement. Have you forgotten what I told you that the man saw at Portray?'

'I don't know that the man spoke the truth.'

'But he did.'

'And I hate that kind of espionage. It is so very likely that mistakes should be made.'

'When she was sitting in his arms,—and kissing him! If you choose to do it, Frederic, of course you must. We can't prevent it. You are free to marry any one you please.'

'I'm not talking of marrying her.'

'What do you suppose she wants you to go there for? As for political life, I am quite sure it would be the death of you. If I were you I wouldn't go near her. You have got out of the scrape, and I would remain out.'

'But I haven't got out,' said Lord Fawn.

On the next day, Saturday, he did nothing in the matter. He went down, as was his custom, to Richmond, and did not once mention Lizzie's name. Lady Fawn and her daughters never spoke of her now,—neither of her, nor, in his presence, of poor Lucy Morris. But on his return to London on the Sunday evening he found another note from Lizzie. 'You will hardly have the hardihood to leave my note unanswered. Pray let me know when you will come to me.' Some answer must, as he felt, be made to her. For a moment he thought of asking his mother to call;—but he at once saw that by doing so he might lay himself open to terrible ridicule. Could he induce Lord Mount Thistle to be his Mercury? It would, he felt, be quite impossible to make Lord Mount Thistle understand all the facts of his position. His sister, Mrs. Hittaway, might have gone, were it not that she herself was violently opposed to any visit. The more he thought of it the more convinced he became that, should it be known that he had received two such notes from a lady and that he had not answered or noticed them, the world would judge him to have behaved badly. So, at last, he wrote,—on that Sunday evening,—fixing a somewhat distant day for his visit to Hertford Street. His note was as follows:—

'Lord Fawn presents his compliments to Lady Eustace. In accordance with the wish expressed in Lady Eustace's two notes of the 23rd instant and this date, Lord Fawn will do himself the honour of waiting upon Lady Eustace on Saturday next, March 3rd, at 12, noon. Lord Fawn had thought that under circumstances as they now exist, no further personal interview could lead to the happiness of either party; but as Lady Eustace thinks otherwise, he feels himself constrained to comply with her desire.

'Sunday evening, 25 February, 18—.'*

'I am going to see her in the course of this week,' he said, in answer to a further question from Lady Glencora, who, chancing to meet him in society, had again addressed him on the subject. He lacked the courage to tell Lady Glencora to mind her own business and to allow him to do the same. Had she been a little less great than she was,—either as regarded herself or her husband,—he would have done so. But Lady Glencora was the social queen of the party to which he belonged, and Mr. Palliser was Chancellor of the Exchequer, and would some day be Duke of Omnium.

'As you are great, be merciful, Lord Fawn,' said Lady Glencora. 'You men, I believe, never realise what it is that women feel when they love. It is my belief that she will die unless you are re-united to her. And then she is so beautiful!'

'It is a subject that I cannot discuss, Lady Glencora.'

'I daresay not. And I'm sure I am the last person to wish to give you pain. But you see,—if the poor lady has done nothing to merit your anger, it does seem rather a strong measure to throw her off and give her no reason whatever. How would you defend yourself, suppose she published it all?' Lady Glencora's courage was very great,—and perhaps we may say her impudence also. This last question Lord Fawn left unanswered, walking away in great dudgeon.

In the course of the week he told his sister of the interview which he had promised, and she endeavoured to induce him to postpone it till a certain man should arrive from Scotland. She had written for Mr. Andrew Gowran,—sending down funds for Mr. Gowran's journey,—so that her brother might hear Mr. Gowran's evidence out of Mr. Gowran's own mouth. Would not Frederic postpone the interview till he should have seen Mr. Gowran? But to this request Frederic declined to accede. He had fixed a day and an hour. He had made an appointment;—of course he must keep it.

CHAPTER LVII
Humpty Dumpty

THE robbery at the house in Hertford Street took place on the 30th of January, and on the morning of the 28th of February Bunfit and Gager were sitting together in a melancholy, dark little room in Scotland Yard, discussing the circumstances of that nefarious act. A month had gone by, and nobody was yet in custody. A month had passed since that second robbery; but nearly eight weeks had passed since the robbery at Carlisle, and even that was still a mystery. The newspapers had been loud in their condemnation of the police. It had been asserted over and over again that in no other civilised country in the world could so great an amount of property have passed through the hands of thieves without leaving some clue by which the police would have made their way to the truth. Major Mackintosh had been declared to be altogether incompetent, and all the Bunfits and Gagers of the force had been spoken of as drones and moles and ostriches. They were idle and blind, and so stupid as to think that, when they saw nothing, others saw less. The major, who was a broad-shouldered, philosophical man, bore all this as though it were, of necessity, a part of the burthen of his profession;— but the Bunfits and Gagers were very angry, and at their wits' ends. It did not occur to them to feel animosity against the newspapers which abused them. The thieves who would not be caught were their great enemies; and there was common to them a conviction that men so obstinate as these thieves, —men to whom a large amount of grace and liberty for in-

dulgence had accrued,—should be treated with uncommon
severity when they were caught. There was this excuse always
on their lips,—that had it been an affair simply of thieves,
such as thieves ordinarily are, everything would have been
discovered long since;—but when lords and ladies with titles
come to be mixed up with such an affair,—folk in whose
house a policeman can't have his will at searching and brow-
beating,—how is a detective to detect anything?

Bunfit and Gager had both been driven to recast their
theories as to the great Carlisle affair by the circumstances of
the later affair in Hertford Street. They both thought that
Lord George had been concerned in the robbery;—that, indeed, had now become the general opinion of the world at
large. He was a man of doubtful character, with large expenses, and with no recognised means of living. He had
formed a great intimacy with Lady Eustace at a period in
which she was known to be carrying these diamonds about
with her, had been staying with her at Portray Castle when
the diamonds were there, and had been her companion on the
journey during which the diamonds were stolen. The only men
in London supposed to be capable of dealing advantageously
with such a property, were Harter and Benjamin,—as to
whom it was known that they were conversant with the
existence of the diamonds, and known, also, that they were
in the habit of having dealings with Lord George. It was,
moreover, known that Lord George had been closeted with
Mr. Benjamin on the morning after his arrival in London.
These things put together made it almost a certainty that
Lord George had been concerned in the matter. Bunfit had
always been sure of it. Gager, though differing much from
Bunfit as to details, had never been unwilling to suspect Lord
George. But the facts known could not be got to dovetail
themselves pleasantly. If Lord George had possessed himself
of the diamonds at Carlisle,—or with Lizzie's connivance
before they reached Carlisle,—then, why had there been a
second robbery? Bunfit, who was very profound in his theory,
suggested that the second robbery was an additional plant,

got up with the view of throwing more dust into the eyes of the police. Patience Crabstick had, of course, been one of the gang throughout, and she had now been allowed to go off with her mistress's money and lesser trinkets,—so that the world of Scotland Yard might be thrown more and more into the mire of ignorance and darkness of doubt. To this view Gager was altogether opposed. He was inclined to think that Lord George had taken the diamonds at Carlisle with Lizzie's connivance;—that he had restored them in London to her keeping, finding the suspicion against him too heavy to admit of his dealing with them,—and that now he had stolen them a second time, again with Lizzie's connivance; but in this latter point, Gager did not pretend to the assurance of any conviction.

But Gager at the present moment had achieved a triumph in the matter which he was not at all disposed to share with his elder officer. Perhaps, on the whole, more power is lost than gained by habits of secrecy. To be discreet is a fine thing, —especially for a policeman; but when discretion is carried to such a length in the direction of self-confidence as to produce a belief that no aid is wanted for the achievement of great results, it will often militate against all achievement. Had Scotland Yard been less discreet and more confidential, the mystery might, perhaps, have been sooner unravelled. Gager at this very moment had reason to believe that a man whom he knew could,—and would, if operated upon duly,— communicate to him, Gager, the secret of the present whereabouts of Patience Crabstick! That belief was a great possession, and much too important, as Gager thought, to be shared lightly with such an one as Mr. Bunfit—a thick-headed sort of man, in Gager's opinion, although, no doubt, he had by means of industry been successful in some difficult cases.

''Is lordship ain't stirred,' said Bunfit.

'How do you mean,—stirred, Mr. Bunfit?'

'Ain't moved nowheres out of London.'

'What should he move out of London for? What could he get by cutting? There ain't nothing so bad when anything's

up against one as letting on that one wants to bolt. He knows
all that. He'll stand his ground. He won't bolt.'

'I don't suppose as he will, Gager. It's a rum go; ain't it?
—the rummest as I ever see.' This remark had been made so
often by Mr. Bunfit, that Gager had become almost weary of
hearing it.

'Oh,—rum; rum be b—— What's the use of all that?
From what the governor told me this morning, there isn't a
shadow of doubt where the diamonds are.'

'In Paris,—of course,' said Bunfit.

'They never went to Paris. They were taken from here to
Hamburg in a commercial man's kit,—a fellow as travels in
knives and scissors. Then they was recut. They say the
cutting was the quickest bit of work ever done by one man in
Hamburg. And now they're in New York. That's what has
come of the diamonds.'

'Benjamin, in course,' said Bunfit, in a low whisper, just
taking the pipe from between his lips.

'Well;—yes. No doubt it was Benjamin. But how did
Benjamin get 'em?'

'Lord George,—in course,' said Bunfit.

'And how did he get 'em?'

'Well;—that's where it is; isn't it?' Then there was a
pause, during which Bunfit continued to smoke. 'As sure as
your name's Gager, he got 'em at Carlisle.'

'And what took Smiler down to Carlisle?'

'Just to put a face on it,' said Bunfit.

'And who cut the door?'

'Billy Cann did,' said Bunfit.

'And who forced the box?'

'Them two did,' said Bunfit.

'And all to put a face on it?'

'Yes;—just that. And an uncommon good face they did put
on it between 'em;—the best as I ever see.'

'All right,' said Gager. 'So far, so good. I don't agree with
you, Mr. Bunfit; because the thing, when it was done,
wouldn't be worth the money. Lord love you, what would all

that have cost? And what was to prevent the lady and Lord George together taking the diamonds to Benjamin and getting their price. It never does to be too clever, Mr. Bunfit. And when that was all done, why did the lady go and get herself robbed again? No;—I don't say but what you're a clever man, in your way, Mr. Bunfit; but you've not got a hold of the thing here. Why was Smiler going about like a mad dog, —only that he found himself took in?'

'Maybe he expected something else in the box,—more than the necklace,—as was to come to him,' suggested Bunfit.

'Gammon.'*

'I don't see why you say Gammon, Gager. It ain't polite.'

'It is gammon,—running away with ideas like them, just as if you was one of the public. When they two opened that box at Carlisle, which they did as certain as you sit there, they believed as the diamonds were there. They were not there.'

'I don't think as they was,' said Bunfit.

'Very well;—where were they? Just walk up to it, Mr. Bunfit, making your ground good as you go. They two men cut the door, and took the box, and opened it,—and when they'd opened it, they didn't get the swag. Where was the swag?'

'Lord George,' said Bunfit again.

'Very well,—Lord George. Like enough. But it comes to this. Benjamin, and they two men of his, had laid themselves out for the robbery. Now, Mr. Bunfit, whether Lord George and Benjamin were together in that first affair, or whether they weren't, I can't see my way just at present, and I don't know as you can see yours;—not saying but what you're as quick as most men, Mr. Bunfit. If he was,—and I rayther think that's about it,—then he and Benjamin must have had a few words, and he must have got the jewels from the lady over night.'

'Of course he did,—and Smiler and Billy Cann knew as they weren't there.'

'There you are, all back again, Mr. Bunfit, not making

your ground good as you go. Smiler and Cann did their job according to order,—and precious sore hearts they had when they'd got the box open. Those fellows at Carlisle,—just like all the provincials,—went to work open-mouthed, and before the party had left Carlisle it was known that Lord George was suspected.'

'You can't trust them fellows any way,' said Mr. Bunfit.

'Well;—what happens next? Lord George, he goes to Benjamin, but he isn't goin' to take the diamonds with him. He has had words with Benjamin or he has not. Any ways he isn't goin' to take the necklace with him on that morning. He hasn't been goin' to keep the diamonds about him, not since what was up at Carlisle. So he gives the diamonds back to the lady.'

'And she had 'em all along?'

'I don't say it was so,—but I can see my way upon that hy—pothesis.'

'There was something as she had to conceal, Gager. I've said that all through. I knew it in a moment when I see'd her faint.'

'She's had a deal to conceal, I don't doubt. Well, there they are,—with her still,—and the box is gone, and the people as is bringing the lawsuit, Mr. Camperdown and the rest of 'em, is off their tack. What's she to do with 'em?'

'Take 'em to Benjamin,' said Bunfit, with confidence.

'That's all very well, Mr. Bunfit. But there's a quarrel up already with Benjamin. Benjamin was to have had 'em before. Benjamin has spent a goodish bit of money, and has been thrown over rather. I daresay Benjamin was as bad as Smiler, or worse. No doubt Benjamin let on to Smiler, and thought as Smiler was too many for him. I daresay there was a few words between him and Smiler. I wouldn't wonder if Smiler didn't threaten to punch Benjamin's head,—which well he could do it,—and if there wasn't a few playful remarks between 'em about penal servitude for life. You see, Mr. Bunfit, it couldn't have been pleasant for any of 'em.'

'They'd 've split,' said Bunfit.

'But they didn't,—not downright. Well,—there we are.

The diamonds is with the lady. Lord George has done it all. Lord George and Lady Eustace,—they're keeping company, no doubt, after their own fashion. He's a robbing of her, and she has to do pretty much as she's bid. The diamonds is with the lady, and Lord George is pretty well afraid to look at 'em. After all that's being done, there isn't much to wonder at in that. Then comes the second robbery.'

'And Lord George planned that too?' asked Bunfit.

'I don't pretend to say I know, but just put it this way, Mr. Bunfit. Of course the thieves were let in by the woman Crabstick.'

'Not a doubt.'

'Of course they was Smiler and Billy Cann.'

'I suppose they was.'

'She was always about the lady,—a doing for her in every thing. Say she goes to Benjamin and tells him as how her lady still has the necklace,—and then he puts up the second robbery. Then you'd have it all round.'

'And Lord George would have lost 'em. It can't be. Lord George and he are thick as thieves up to this day.'

'Very well. I don't say anything against that. Lord George knows as she has 'em;—indeed he'd given 'em back to her to keep. We've got as far as that, Mr. Bunfit.'

'I think she did 'ave 'em.'

'Very well. What does Lord George do then? He can't make money of 'em. They're too hot for his fingers, and so he finds when he thinks of taking 'em into the market. So he puts Benjamin up to the second robbery.'

'Who's drawing it fine, now, Gager;—eh?'

'Mr. Bunfit, I'm not saying as I've got the truth beyond this,—that Benjamin and his two men were clean done at Carlisle, that Lord George and his lady brought the jewels up to town between 'em, and that the party who didn't get 'em at Carlisle tried their hand again and did get 'em in Hertford Street.' In all of which the ingenious Gager would have been right, if he could have kept his mind clear from the alluring conviction that a lord had been the chief of the thieves.

'We shall never make a case of it now,' said Bunfit despondently.

'I mean to try it on all the same. There's Smiler about town as bold as brass, and dressed to the nines. He had the cheek to tell me he was going down to the Newmarket Spring to look after a horse he's got a share in.'

'I was talking to Billy only yesterday,' added Bunfit. 'I've got it on my mind that they didn't treat Billy quite on the square. He didn't let on anything about Benjamin; but he told me out plain, as how he was very much disgusted. "Mr. Bunfit," said he, "there's that roguery about, that a plain man like me can't touch it. There's them as'd pick my eyes out while I was sleeping, and then swear it against my very self." Them were his words, and I knew as how Benjamin hadn't been on the square with him.'

'You didn't let on anything, Mr. Bunfit?'

'Well,—I just reminded him as how there was five hundred pounds going a-begging from Mr. Camperdown.'

'And what did he say to that, Mr. Bunfit?'

'Well he said a good deal. He's a sharp little fellow, is Billy, as has read a deal. You've heard of 'Umpty Dumpty, Gager? 'Umpty Dumpty was a hegg.'

'All right.'

'As had a fall, and was smashed,—and there's a little poem about him.'

'I know.'

'Well;—Billy says to me: "Mr. Camperdown don't want no hinformation; he wants the diamonds. Them diamonds is like 'Umpty Dumpty, Mr. Bunfit. All the king's horses and all the king's men couldn't put 'Umpty Dumpty up again."'

'Billy was about right there,' said the younger officer rising from his seat.

Late on the afternoon of the same day, when London had already been given over to the gaslights, Mr. Gager, having dressed himself especially for the occasion of the friendly visit which he intended to make, sauntered into a small public-house at the corner of Meek Street and Pineapple Court,* which locality,—as all men well versed with London are aware,—lies within one minute's walk of the top of Gray's Inn Lane. Gager, during his conference with his colleague Bunfit, had been dressed in plain black clothes; but in spite of his plain clothes he looked every inch a policeman. There was a stiffness about his limbs, and, at the same time, a sharpness in his eyes, which, in the conjunction with the locality in which he was placed, declared his profession beyond the possibility of mistake. Nor, in that locality, would he have desired to be taken for anything else. But as he entered the 'Rising Sun' in Meek Street, there was nothing of the policeman about him. He might probably have been taken for a betting man, with whom the world had latterly gone well enough to enable him to maintain that sleek, easy, greasy appearance, which seems to be the beau-ideal of a betting man's personal ambition. 'Well, Mr. Howard,' said the lady at the bar, 'a sight of you is good for sore eyes.'

'Six penn'orth of brandy,—warm, if you please, my dear,' said the pseudo-Howard, as he strolled easily into an inner room, with which he seemed to be quite familiar. He seated himself in an old-fashioned wooden arm-chair, gazed up at the gas lamp, and stirred his liquor slowly. Occasionally he raised the glass to his lips, but he did not seem to be at all intent upon his drinking. When he entered the room, there had been a gentleman and a lady there, whose festive moments seemed to be disturbed by some slight disagreement; but Howard, as he gazed at the lamp, paid no attention to them whatever. They soon left the room, their quarrel and their drink finished together, and others dropped in and out. Mr. Howard's 'warm' must almost have become cold, so long did he sit there, gazing at the gas lamps, rather than attending to his brandy and water. Not a word did he speak to any one for more than an hour, and not a sign did he show of impatience. At last he was alone;—but had not been so for above a minute when in stepped a jaunty little man, certainly not more than five feet high, about three or four and twenty years of age, dressed with great care, with his trousers sticking to his legs, with a French chimney-pot hat on his head, very much peeked fore and aft and closely turned up at the sides. He had a bright-coloured silk handkerchief round his neck, and a white shirt, of which the collar and wristbands were rather larger and longer than suited the small dimensions of the man. He wore a white greatcoat tight buttoned round his waist, but so arranged as to show the glories of the coloured handkerchief; and in his hand he carried a diminutive cane with a little silver knob. He stepped airily into the room, and as he did so he addressed our friend the policeman with much cordiality. 'My dear Mr. 'Oward,' he said, 'this is a pleasure. This is a pleasure. This is a pleasure.'

'What is it to be?' asked Gager.

'Well;—ay, what? Shall I say a little port wine negus,* with the nutmeg in it rayther strong?' This suggestion he made to a young lady from the bar, who had followed him into the room. The negus was brought and paid for by Gager, who then requested that they might be left there undisturbed for five minutes. The young lady promised to do her best, and then closed the door. 'And now, Mr. 'Oward, what can I do for you?' said Mr. Cann, the burglar.

Gager, before he answered, took a pipe-case out of his pocket, and lit the pipe. 'Will you smoke, Billy?' said he.

'Well;—no, I don't know that I will smoke. A very little tobacco goes a long way with me, Mr. 'Oward. One cigar before I turn in;—that's about the outside of it. You see, Mr. 'Oward, pleasures should never be made necessities, when the circumstances of a gentleman's life may perhaps require that they shall be abandoned for prolonged periods. In your line of life, Mr. 'Oward,—which has its objections,— smoking may be pretty well a certainty.' Mr. Cann, as he made these remarks, skipped about the room, and gave point to his argument by touching Mr. Howard's waistcoat with the end of his cane.

'And now, Billy, how about the young woman?'

'I haven't set eyes on her these six weeks, Mr. 'Oward. I never see her but once in my life, Mr. 'Oward;—or, maybe, twice, for one's memory is deceitful; and I don't know that I ever wish to see her again. She ain't one of my sort, Mr. 'Oward. I likes 'em soft, and sweet, and coming. This one,— she has her good p'ints about her,—as clean a foot and ankle as I'd wish to see;—but, laws, what a nose, Mr. 'Oward! And then for manner;—she's no more manner than a stable dog.'

'She's in London, Billy?'

'How am I to know, Mr. 'Oward?'

'What's the good, then, of your coming here?' asked Gager, with no little severity in his voice.

'I don't know as it is good. I 'aven't said nothing about any good, Mr. 'Oward. What you wants to find is them diamonds?'

'Of course I do.'

'Well;—you won't find 'em. I knows nothing about 'em, in course, except just what I'm told. You know my line of life, Mr. 'Oward?'

'Not a doubt about it.'

'And I know yours. I'm in the way of hearing about these things,—and for the matter of that, so are you too. It may be, my ears are the longer. I 'ave 'eard. You don't expect me to tell you more than just that. I 'ave 'eard. It was a pretty thing, wasn't it? But I wasn't in it myself, more's the pity. You can't expect fairer than that, Mr. 'Oward?'

'And what have you heard?'

'Them diamonds is gone where none of you can get at 'em. That five hundred pounds as the lawyers 'ave offered is just nowhere. If you want information, Mr. 'Oward, you should say information.'

'And you could give it;—eh, Billy?'

'No—; no—' He uttered these two negatives in a low voice, and with much deliberation. 'I couldn't give it. A man can't give what he hasn't got;—but perhaps I could get it.'

'What an ass you are, Billy. Don't you know that I know all about it?'

'What an ass you are, Mr. 'Oward. Don't I know that you don't know;—or you wouldn't come to me. You guess. You're always a-guessing. And because you know how to guess, they pays you for guessing. But guessing ain't knowing. You don't know;—nor yet don't I. What is it to be, if I find out where that young woman is?'

'A tenner, Billy.'

'Five quid now, and five when you've seen her.'

'All right, Billy.'

'She's a-going to be married to Smiler next Sunday as ever is down at Ramsgate;—and at Ramsgate she is now. You'll find her, Mr. 'Oward, if you'll keep your eyes open, somewhere about the "Fiddle with One String."'

This information was so far recognised by Mr. Howard as correct, that he paid Mr. Cann five sovereigns down for it at once.

CHAPTER LVIII
'The Fiddle with One String'

M R. GAGER reached Ramsgate by the earliest train on the following morning, and was not long in finding out the 'Fiddle with One String.' The 'Fiddle with One String' was a public-house, very humble in appearance, in the outskirts of the town, on the road leading to Pegwell Bay. On this occasion Mr. Gager was dressed in his ordinary plain clothes, and though the policeman's calling might not be so manifestly declared by his appearance at Ramsgate as it was in Scotland Yard,—still, let a hint in that direction have ever been given, and the ordinary citizens of Ramsgate would at once be convinced that the man was what he was. Gager had doubtless considered all the circumstances of his day's work carefully, and had determined that success would more probably attend him with this than with any other line of action. He walked at once into the house, and asked whether a young woman was not lodging there. The man of the house was behind the bar, with his wife, and to him Gager whispered a few words. The man stood dumb for a moment, and then his wife spoke. 'What's up now?' said she. 'There's no young women here. We don't have no young women.' Then the man whispered a word to his wife, during which Gager stood among the customers before the bar with an easy, unembarrassed air. 'Well, what's the odds?' said the wife. 'There ain't anything wrong with us.'

'Never thought there was, ma'am,' said Gager. 'And there's nothing wrong as I know of with the young woman.' Then the husband and wife consulted together, and Mr. Gager was asked to take a seat in a little parlour, while the woman ran up-stairs for half an instant. Gager looked about him quickly, and took in at a glance the system of the construction of the 'Fiddle with One String.' He did sit down in the little parlour, with the door open, and remained there for perhaps a couple of minutes. Then he went to the front door, and glanced up at the roof. 'It's all right,' said the keeper of the house, following him. 'She ain't a-going to get away. She ain't just very well, and she's a-lying down.'

'You tell her, with my regards,' said Gager, 'that she needn't be a bit the worse because of me.' The man looked at him suspiciously. 'You tell her what I say. And tell her, too, the quicker the better. She has a gentleman a-looking after her, I daresay. Perhaps I'd better be off before he comes.' The message was taken up to the lady, and Gager again seated himself in the little parlour.

We are often told that all is fair in love and war, and, perhaps, the operation on which Mr. Gager was now intent may be regarded as warlike. But he now took advantage of a certain softness in the character of the lady whom he wished to meet, which hardly seems to be justifiable even in a policeman. When Lizzie's tall footman had been in trouble about the necklace, a photograph had been taken from him which had not been restored to him. This was a portrait of Patience Crabstick, which she, poor girl, in a tender moment, had given to him, who, had not things gone roughly with them, was to have been her lover. The little picture had fallen into Gager's hands, and he now pulled it from his pocket. He, himself, had never visited the house in Hertford Street till after the second robbery, and, in the flesh, had not as yet seen Miss Crabstick; but he had studied her face carefully, expecting, or, at any rate, hoping, that he might some day enjoy the pleasure of personal acquaintance. That pleasure was now about to come to him, and he prepared himself for it by making himself intimate with the lines of the lady's face as the sun had portrayed them. There was even yet some delay, and Mr. Gager more than once testified uneasiness. 'She ain't a-going to get away,' said the mistress of the house, 'but a lady as is going to see a gentleman can't jump into her things as a man does.' Gager intimated his acquiescence in all this, and again waited.

'The sooner she comes the less trouble for her,' said Gager to the woman; 'if you'll only make her believe that.' At last, when he had been somewhat over an hour in the house, he was asked to walk up-stairs, and then, in a little sitting-room over the bar, he had the opportunity, so much desired, of making personal acquaintance with Patience Crabstick.

It may be imagined that the poor waiting-woman had not been in a happy state of mind since she had been told that a gentleman was waiting to see her down-stairs, who had declared himself to be a policeman immediately on entering the shop. To escape was of course her first idea, but she was soon made to understand that this was impracticable. In the first place there was but one staircase, at the bottom of which was the open door of the room in which the policeman was sitting; and then, the woman of the house was very firm in declaring that she would connive at nothing which might cost her and her husband their licence. 'You've got to face it,' said the woman. 'I suppose they can't make me get out of bed unless I pleases,' said Patience firmly. But she knew that even that resource would fail her, and that a policeman, when aggravated, can take upon him all the duties of a lady's maid. She had to face it,—and she did face it. 'I've just got to have a few words with you, my dear,' said Gager.

'I suppose, then, we'd better be alone,' said Patience; whereupon the woman of the house discreetly left the room.

The interview was so long that the reader would be fatigued were he asked to study a record of all that was said on the occasion. The gentleman and lady were closeted together for more than an hour, and so amicably was the conversation carried on that when the time was half over Gager stepped down-stairs and interested himself in procuring Miss Crabstick's breakfast. He even condescended himself to pick a few shrimps and drink a glass of beer in her company. A great deal was said, and something was even settled, as may be learned from a few concluding words of that very memorable conversation. 'Just don't you say anything about it, my dear, but leave word for him that you've gone up to town on business.'

'Lord love you, Mr. Gager, he'll know all about it.'

'Let him know. Of course he'll know—if he comes down. It's my belief he'll never show himself at Ramsgate again.'

'But, Mr. Gager——'

'Well, my dear?'

'You aren't a perjuring of yourself?'

'What;—about making you my wife? That I ain't. I'm upright, and always was. There's no mistake about me, when you've got my word. As soon as this work is off my mind, you shall be Mrs. Gager, my dear. And you'll be all right. You've been took in, that's what you have.'

'That I have, Mr. Gager,' said Patience, wiping her eyes.

'You've been took in, and you must be forgiven.'

'I didn't get,—not nothing out of the necklace; and as for the other things, they've frighted me so, that I let 'em all go for just what I tell you. And as for Mr. Smiler,—I never didn't care for him; that I didn't. He ain't the man to touch my heart,—not at all; and it was not likely either. A plain fellow,—very, Mr. Gager.'

'He'll be plainer before long, my dear.'

'But I've been that worrited among 'em, Mr. Gager, since first they made their wicked prepositions, that I've been jest, —I don't know how I've been. And though my lady was not a lady as any girl could like, and did deserve to have her things took if anybody's things ever should be took, still, Mr. Gager, I knows I did wrong. I do know it,—and I'm a-repenting of it in sackcloth and ashes;—so I am. But you'll be as good as your word, Mr. Gager?'

It must be acknowledged that Mr. Gager had bidden high for success, and had allowed himself to be carried away by his zeal almost to the verge of imprudence. It was essential to him that he should take Patience Crabstick back with him to London,—and that he should take her as a witness and not as a criminal. Mr. Benjamin was the game at which he was flying, —Mr. Benjamin, and, if possible, Lord George; and he conceived that his net might be big enough to hold Smiler as well as the other two greater fishes, if he could induce Patience Crabstick and Billy Cann to co-operate with him cordially in his fishing.

But his mind was still disturbed on one point. Let him press his beloved Patience as closely as he might with questions, there was one point on which he could not get from her what he believed to be the truth. She persisted that Lord George de Bruce Carruthers had had no hand in either robbery, and Gager had so firmly committed himself to a belief on this matter, that he could not throw the idea away from him, even on the testimony of Patience Crabstick.

On that evening he returned triumphant to Scotland Yard with Patience Crabstick under his wing; and that lady was housed there with every comfort she could desire, except that of personal liberty.

I N the meantime Mrs. Hittaway was diligently spreading a report that Lizzie Eustace either was engaged to marry her cousin Frank,—or ought to be so engaged. This she did, no doubt, with the sole object of saving her brother; but she did it with a zeal that dealt as freely with Frank's name as with Lizzie's. They, with all their friends, were her enemies, and she was quite sure that they were, altogether, a wicked, degraded set of people. Of Lord George and Mrs. Carbuncle, of Miss Roanoke and Sir Griffin Tewett, she believed all manner of evil. She had theories of her own about the jewels, stories,—probably of her own manufacture in part, although no doubt she believed them to be true,—as to the manner of living at Portray, little histories of Lizzie's debts, and the great fact of the scene which Mr. Gowran had seen with his own eyes. Lizzie Eustace was an abomination to her, and this abominable woman her brother was again in danger of marrying! She was very loud in her denunciations, and took care that they should reach even Lady Linlithgow, so that poor Lucy Morris might know of what sort was the lover in whom she trusted. Andy Gowran had been sent for to town, and was on his journey while Mr. Gager was engaged at Ramsgate. It was at present the great object of Mrs. Hittaway's life to induce her brother to see Mr. Gowran before he kept his appointment with Lady Eustace.

Poor Lucy received the wound which was intended for her. The enemy's weapons had repeatedly struck her, but hitherto they had alighted on the strong shield of her faith. But let a shield be never so strong, it may at last be battered out of all form and service. On Lucy's shield there had been much of such batterings, and the blows which had come from him in whom she most trusted had not been the lightest. She had not seen him for months, and his letters were short, unsatisfactory, and rare. She had declared to herself and to her friend Lady Fawn, that no concurrence of circumstances, no absence, however long, no rumours that might reach her ears, would make her doubt the man she loved. She was still steadfast in the same resolution; but, in spite of her resolution, her heart began to fail her. She became weary, unhappy, and ill at ease, and though she would never acknowledge to herself that she doubted, she did doubt.

'So, after all, your Mr. Greystock is to marry my niece, Lizzie Greystock.' This good-natured speech was made one morning to poor Lucy by her present patroness, Lady Linlithgow.

'I rather think not,' said Lucy plucking up her spirits and smiling as she spoke.

'Everybody says so. As for Lizzie, she has become quite a heroine. What with her necklace, and her two robberies, and her hunting, and her various lovers,—two lords and a member of Parliament, my dear,—there is nothing to equal her. Lady Glencora Palliser has been calling on her. She took care to let me know that. And I'm now told that she certainly is engaged to her cousin.'

'According to your own showing, Lady Linlithgow, she has got two other lovers. Couldn't you oblige me by letting her marry one of the lords?'

'I'm afraid, my dear, that Mr. Greystock is to be the chosen one.' Then after a pause the old woman became serious. 'What is the use, Miss Morris, of not looking the truth in the face? Mr. Greystock is neglecting you.'

'He is not neglecting me. You won't let him come to see me.'

'Certainly not;—but if he were not neglecting you, you would not be here. And there he is with Lizzie Eustace every day of his life. He can't afford to marry you, and he can afford to marry her. It's a deal better that you should look it all in the face and know what it must all come to.'

'I shall just wait,—and never believe a word till he speaks it.'

'You hardly know what men are, my dear.'

'Very likely not, Lady Linlithgow. It may be that I shall have to pay dear for learning. Of course, I may be mistaken as well as another,—only I don't believe I am mistaken.'

When this little scene took place, only a month remained of the time for which Lucy's services were engaged to Lady Linlithgow, and no definite arrangement had been made as to her future residence. Lady Fawn was prepared to give her a home, and to Lady Fawn, as it seemed, she must go. Lady Linlithgow had declared herself unwilling to continue the existing arrangement because, as she said, it did not suit her that her companion should be engaged to marry her late sister's nephew. Not a word had been said about the deanery for the last month or two, and Lucy, though her hopes in that direction had once been good, was far too high-spirited to make any suggestion herself as to her reception by her lover's family. In the ordinary course of things she would have to look out for another situation, like any other governess in want of a place; but she could do this only by consulting Lady Fawn; and Lady Fawn when consulted would always settle the whole matter by simply bidding her young friend to come to Fawn Court.

There must be some end of her living at Fawn Court. So much Lucy told herself over and over again. It could be but a temporary measure. If—if it was to be her fate to be taken away from Fawn Court a happy, glorious, triumphant bride, then the additional obligation put upon her by her dear friends would not be more than she could bear. But to go to Fawn Court, and, by degrees, to have it acknowledged that another place must be found for her, would be very bad. She would infinitely prefer any intermediate hardship. How, then, should she know? As soon as she was able to escape from the countess, she went up to her own room, and wrote the following letter. She studied the words with great care as she wrote them,— sitting and thinking before she allowed her pen to run on the paper.

'MY DEAR FRANK,

'It is a long time since we met;—is it not? I do not write this as a reproach; but because friends tell me that I should not continue to think myself engaged to you. They say that, situated as you are, you cannot afford to marry a penniless girl, and that I ought not to wish you to sacrifice yourself. I do understand enough of your affairs to know that an imprudent marriage may ruin you, and I certainly do not wish to be the cause of injury to you. All I ask is that you should tell me the truth. It is not that I am impatient; but that I must decide what to do with myself when I leave Lady Linlithgow.

'Your most affectionate friend,

'March 2, 18—.'   'LUCY MORRIS.

She read this letter over and over again, thinking of all that it said and of all that it omitted to say. She was at first half disposed to make protestations of forgiveness,—to assure him that not even within her own heart would she reproach him, should he feel himself bound to retract the promise she had made him. She longed to break out into love, but so to express her love that her lover should know that it was strong enough even to sacrifice itself for his sake. But though her heart longed to speak freely, her judgment told her that it would be better that she should be reticent and tranquil in her language. Any warmth on her part would be in itself a reproach to him. If she really wished to assist him in extricating himself from a difficulty into which he had fallen in her behalf, she would best do so by offering him his freedom in the fewest and plainest words which she could select.

But even when the letter was written she doubted as to the wisdom of sending it. She kept it that she might sleep upon it. She did sleep upon it,—and when the morning came she would not send it. Had not absolute faith in her lover been the rock on which she had declared to herself that she would build the house of her future hopes? Had not she protested again and again that no caution from others should induce her to waver in her belief? Was it not her great doctrine to trust, —to trust implicitly, even though all should be lost if her trust should be misplaced? And was it well that she should depart from all this, merely because it might be convenient for her to make arrangements as to the coming months? If it were to be her fate to be rejected, thrown over, and deceived, of what use to her could be any future arrangements? All to her would be ruin, and it would matter to her nothing whither she should be taken. And then, why should she lie to him as she would lie in sending such a letter? If he did throw her over he would be a traitor, and her heart would be full of reproaches. Whatever might be his future lot in life, he owed it to her to share it with her, and if he evaded his debt he would be a traitor and a miscreant. She would never tell him so. She would be far too proud to condescend to spoken or written reproaches. But she would know that it would be so, and why should she lie to him by saying that it would not be so? Thinking of all this, when the morning came, she left the letter lying within her desk.

Lord Fawn was to call upon Lady Eustace on the Saturday, and on Friday afternoon Mr. Andrew Gowran was in Mrs. Hittaway's back parlour in Warwick Square. After many efforts, and with much persuasion, the brother had agreed to see his sister's great witness. Lord Fawn had felt that he would lower himself by any intercourse with such a one as Andy Gowran in regard to the conduct of the woman whom he had proposed to make his wife, and had endeavoured to avoid the meeting. He had been angry, piteous, haughty, and sullen by turns; but Mrs. Hittaway had overcome him by dogged perseverance; and poor Lord Fawn had at last consented. He was to come to Warwick Square as soon as the House was up on Friday evening, and dine there. Before dinner he was to be introduced to Mr. Gowran. Andy arrived at the house at half-past five, and after some conversation with Mrs. Hittaway, was left there all alone to await the coming of Lord Fawn. He was in appearance and manners very different from the Andy Gowran familiarly known among the braes and crofts of Portray. He had a heavy stiff hat, which he carried in his hand. He wore a black swallow-tail coat and black trousers, and a heavy red waistcoat buttoned up nearly to his throat, round which was tightly tied a dingy black silk handkerchief. At Portray no man was more voluble, no man more self-confident, no man more equal to his daily occupations than Andy Gowran; but the un-accustomed clothes, and the journey to London, and the town houses overcame him, and for a while almost silenced him. Mrs. Hittaway found him silent, cautious, and timid. Not knowing what to do with him, fearing to ask him to go and eat in the kitchen, and not liking to have meat and unlimited drink brought for him into the parlour, she directed the servant to supply him with a glass of sherry and a couple of biscuits. He had come an hour before the time named, and there, with nothing to cheer him beyond these slight creature-comforts, he was left to wait all alone till Lord Fawn should be ready to see him.

Andy had seen lords before. Lords are not rarer in Ayr-shire than in other Scotch counties; and then, had not Lord George de Bruce Carruthers been staying at Portray half the winter? But Lord George was not to Andy a real lord,—and then a lord down in his own county was so much less to him than a lord up in London. And this lord was a lord of Parlia-ment, and a government lord, and might probably have the power of hanging such a one as Andy Gowran were he to commit perjury, or say anything which the lord might choose to call perjury. What it was that Lord Fawn wished him to say, he could not make himself sure. That the lord's sister wished him to prove Lady Eustace to be all that was bad, he knew very well. But he thought that he was able to perceive that the brother and sister were not at one, and more than once during his journey up to London he had almost made up his mind that he would turn tail and go back to Portray. No doubt there was enmity between him and his mistress; but then his mistress did not attempt to hurt him even though he had insulted her grossly; and were she to tell him to leave her service, it would be from Mr. John Eustace, and not from Mrs. Hittaway, that he must look for the continuation of his employment. Nevertheless he had taken Mrs Hittaway's money and there he was.

At half-past seven Lord Fawn was brought into the room by his sister, and Andy Gowran, rising from his chair, three times ducked his head. 'Mr. Gowran,' said Mrs. Hittaway, 'my brother is desirous that you should tell him exactly what you have seen of Lady Eustace's conduct down at Portray. You may speak quite freely, and I know you will speak truly.' Andy again ducked his head. 'Frederic,' continued the lady, 'I am sure that you may implicitly believe all that Mr. Gowran will say to you.' Then Mrs. Hittaway left the room,—as her brother had expressly stipulated that she should do.

Lord Fawn was quite at a loss how to begin, and Andy was by no means prepared to help him. 'If I am rightly informed,' said the lord, 'you have been for many years employed on the Portray property?'

'A' my life,—so please your lairdship.'

'Just so;—just so. And, of course, interested in the welfare of the Eustace family?'

'Nae doobt, my laird,—nae doobt; vera interasted indeed.'

'And being an honest man, have felt sorrow that the Portray property should,—should,—should—; that anything bad should happen to it.' Andy nodded his head, and Lord Fawn perceived that he was nowhere near the beginning of his matter. 'Lady Eustace is at present your mistress?'

'Just in a fawshion, my laird,—as a mon may say. That is she is,—and she is nae. There's a mony things at Portray as ha' to be lookit after.'

'She pays you your wages,' said Lord Fawn shortly.

'Eh;—wages! Yes, my laird, she does a' that.'

'Then she's your mistress.' Andy again nodded his head, and Lord Fawn again struggled to find some way in which he might approach his subject. 'Her cousin, Mr. Greystock, has been staying at Portray lately?'

'More coothie than coosinly,' said Andy, winking his eye.

It was dreadful to Lord Fawn that the man should wink his

eye at him. He did not quite understand what Andy had last said, but he did understand that some accusation as to indecent familiarity with her cousin was intended to be brought by this Scotch steward against the woman to whom he had engaged himself. Every feeling of his nature revolted against the task before him, and he found that on trial it became absolutely impracticable. He could not bring himself to inquire minutely as to poor Lizzie's flirting down among the rocks. He was weak, and foolish, and, in many respects, ignorant,— but he was a gentleman. As he got nearer to the point which it had been intended that he should reach, the more he hated Andy Gowran,—and the more he hated himself for having submitted to such contact. He paused a moment, and then he declared that the conversation was at an end. 'I think that will do, Mr. Gowran,' he said. 'I don't know that you can tell me anything I want to hear. I think you had better go back to Scotland.' So saying, he left Andy alone and stalked up to the drawing-room. When he entered it, both Mr. Hittaway and his sister were there. 'Clara,' he said very sternly, 'you had better send some one to dismiss that man. I shall not speak to him again.'

Lord Fawn did not speak to Andy Gowran again, but Mrs. Hittaway did. After a faint and futile endeavour made by her to ascertain what had taken place in the parlour downstairs, she descended and found Andy seated in his chair, still holding his hat in his hand, as stiff as a wax figure. He had been afraid of the lord, but as soon as the lord had left him he was very angry with the lord. He had been brought up all that way to tell his story to the lord, and the lord had gone away without hearing a word of it,—had gone away and had absolutely insulted him, had asked him who paid him his wages, and had then told him that Lady Eustace was his mistress. Andy Gowran felt strongly that this was not that kind of confidential usage which he had had a right to expect. And after his experience of the last hour and a half, he did not at all relish his renewed solitude in that room. 'A drap of puir thin liquor,—poored out, too, in a weeny glass nae deeper than an egg-shell,—and two cookies; that's what she ca'ed—rafrashment!' It was thus that Andy afterwards spoke to his wife of the hospitalities offered to him in Warwick Square, regarding which his anger was especially hot, in that he had been treated like a child or a common labourer, instead of having the decanter left with him to be used at his own discretion. When, therefore, Mrs. Hittaway returned to him, the awe with which new circumstances and the lord had filled him was fast vanishing, and giving place to that stubborn indignation against people in general which was his normal condition. 'I suppose I'm jist to gang bock again to Portrae, Mrs. Heetaway, and that'll be a' you'll want o' me?' This he said the moment the lady entered the room.

But Mrs. Hittaway did not want to lose his services quite so soon. She expressed regret that her brother should have found himself unable to discuss a subject that was naturally so very distasteful to him, and begged Mr. Gowran to come to her again the next morning. 'What I saw wi' my ain twa e'es, Mrs. Heetaway, I saw,—and nane the less because his lairdship may nae find it jist tastefu', as your leddyship was saying. There were them twa, a' colloguing, and a seetting ilk in ither's laps a' o'er, and a keessing,—yes, my leddy, a keessing as females, not to say males, ought nae to keess, unless they be mon and wife,—and then not amang the rocks, my leddy; and if his lairdship does nae care to hear tell o' it, and finds it nae tastefu', as your leddyship was saying, he should nae ha' sent for Andie Gowran a' the way from Portray, jist to tell him what he wanna hear, now I'm come to tell't to him!'

All this was said with so much unction that even Mrs. Hittaway herself found it to be not 'tasteful.' She shrunk and shivered under Mr. Gowran's eloquence, and almost repented of her zeal. But women, perhaps, feel less repugnance than do men at using ignoble assistance in the achievement of good purposes. Though Mrs. Hittaway shrunk and shivered under the strong action with which Mr. Gowran garnished his strong words, still she was sure of the excellence of her purpose; and, believing that useful aid might still be obtained from Andy Gowran, and, perhaps, prudently anxious to get value in return for the cost of the journey up from Ayrshire, she made the man promise to return to her on the following morning.

CHAPTER LX
'Let it be as though it had never been'

BETWEEN her son, and her married daughter, and Lucy Morris, poor Lady Fawn's life had become a burthen to her. Everything was astray, and there was no happiness or tranquillity at Fawn Court. Of all simply human creeds the strongest existing creed for the present in the minds of the Fawn ladies was that which had reference to the general iniquity of Lizzie Eustace. She had been the cause of all these sorrows, and she was hated so much the more because she had not been proved to be iniquitous before all the world. There had been a time when it seemed to be admitted that she was so wicked in keeping the diamonds in opposition to the continued demands made for them by Mr. Camper-down, that all people would be justified in dropping her, and Lord Fawn among the number. But, since the two robberies, public opinion had veered round three or four points in Lizzie's favour, and people were beginning to say that she had been ill-used. Then had come Mrs. Hittaway's evidence as to Lizzie's wicked doings down in Scotland,—the wicked doings which Andy Gowran had described with a vehemence so terribly moral; and that which had been at first, as it were, added to the diamonds, as a supplementary weight thrown into the scale, so that Lizzie's iniquities might bring her absolutely to the ground, had gradually assumed the position of being the first charge against her. Lady Fawn had felt no aversion to discussing the diamonds. When Lizzie was called a 'thief,' and a 'robber,' and a 'swindler' by one or another of the ladies of the family,—who, in using those strong terms, whispered the words as ladies are wont to do when they desire

179

to lessen the impropriety of the strength of their language by the gentleness of the tone in which the words are spoken,—when Lizzie was thus described in Lady Fawn's hearing in her own house, she had felt no repugnance to it. It was well that the fact should be known, so that everybody might be aware that her son was doing right in refusing to marry so wicked a lady. But when the other thing was added to it; when the story was told of what Mr. Gowran had seen among the rocks, and when gradually that became the special crime which was to justify her son in dropping the lady's acquaintance, then Lady Fawn became very unhappy, and found the subject to be, as Mrs. Hittaway had described it, very distasteful.

And this trouble hit Lucy Morris as hard as it did Lord Fawn. If Lizzie Eustace was unfit to marry Lord Fawn because of these things, then was Frank Greystock not only unfit to marry Lucy, but most unlikely to do so, whether fit or unfit. For a week or two Lady Fawn had allowed herself to share Lucy's joy, and to believe that Mr. Greystock would prove himself true to the girl whose heart he had made all his own;—but she had soon learned to distrust the young member of Parliament who was always behaving insolently to her son, who spent his holidays down with Lizzie Eustace, who never visited and rarely wrote to the girl he had promised to marry, and as to whom all the world agreed in saying that he was far too much in debt to marry any woman who had not means to help him. It was all sorrow and vexation together; and yet when her married daughter would press the subject upon her, and demand her co-operation, she had no power of escaping. 'Mamma,' Mrs. Hittaway had said, 'Lady Glencora Palliser has been with her, and everybody is taking her up, and if her conduct down in Scotland isn't proved, Frederic will be made to marry her.' 'But what can I do, my dear?' Lady Fawn had asked, almost in tears. 'Insist that Frederic shall know the whole truth,' replied Mrs. Hittaway with energy. 'Of course, it is very disagreeable. Nobody can feel it more than I do. It is horrible to have to talk about such things,—and to think of them.' 'Indeed it is, Clara,—very horrible.' 'But anything, mamma, is better than that Frederic should be allowed to marry such a woman as that. It must be proved to him,—how unfit she is to be his wife.' With the view of carrying out this intention, Mrs. Hittaway had, as we have seen, received Andy Gowran at her own house; and with the same view she took Andy Gowran the following morning down to Richmond.

Mrs. Hittaway, and her mother, and Andy were closeted together for half an hour, and Lady Fawn suffered grievously. Lord Fawn had found that he couldn't hear the story, and he had not heard it. He had been strong enough to escape, and had, upon the whole, got the best of it in the slight skirmish which had taken place between him and the Scotchman; but poor old Lady Fawn could not escape. Andy was allowed to be eloquent, and the whole story was told to her, though she would almost sooner have been flogged at a cart's tail* than have heard it. Then 'rafrashments' were administered to Andy of a nature which made him prefer Fawn Court to Warwick Square, and he was told that he might go back to Portray as soon as he pleased.

When he was gone, Mrs. Hittaway opened her mind to her mother altogether. 'The truth is, mamma, that Frederic will marry her.'

'But why? I thought that he had declared that he would give it up. I thought that he had said so to herself.'

'What of that, if he retracts what he said? He is so weak. Lady Glencora Palliser has made him promise to go and see her; and he is to go to-day. He is there now, probably,—at this very moment. If he had been firm, the thing was done. After all that has taken place, nobody would ever have supposed that his engagement need go for anything. But what can he say to her now that he is with her, except just do the mischief all over again? I call it quite wicked in that woman's interfering. I do, indeed! She's a nasty, insolent, impertinent creature;—that's what she is! After all the trouble I've taken, she comes and undoes it all with one word.'

'What can we do, Clara?'

'Well;—I do believe that if Frederic could be made to act as he ought to do, just for a while, she would marry her cousin, Mr. Greystock, and then there would be an end of it altogether. I really think that she likes him best, and from all that I can hear, she would take him now, if Frederic would only keep out of the way. As for him, of course he is doing his very best to get her. He has not one shilling to rub against another, and is over head and ears in debt.'

'Poor Lucy!' ejaculated Lady Fawn.

'Well;—yes; but really that is a matter of course. I always thought, mamma, that you and Amelia were a little wrong to coax her up in that belief.'

'But, my dear, the man proposed for her in the plainest possible manner. I saw his letter.'

'No doubt;—men do propose. We all know that. I'm sure I don't know what they get by it, but I suppose it amuses them. There used to be a sort of feeling that if a man behaved badly something would be done to him; but that's all over now. A man may propose to whom he likes, and if he chooses to say afterwards that it doesn't mean anything, there's nothing in the world to bring him to book.'

'That's very hard,' said the elder lady, of whom everybody said that she did not understand the world as well as her daughter.

'The girls,—they all know that it is so, and I suppose it comes to the same thing in the long run. The men have to marry, and what one girl loses another girl gets.'

'It will kill Lucy.'

'Girls ain't killed so easy, mamma;—not now-a-days. Saying that it will kill her won't change the man's nature. It wasn't to be expected that such a man as Frank Greystock, in debt, and in Parliament, and going to all the best houses, should marry your governess. What was he to get by it? That's what I want to know.'

'I suppose he loved her.'

'Laws,* mamma, how antediluvian you are! No doubt he

did like her,—after his fashion; though what he saw in her, I never could tell. I think Miss Morris would make a very nice wife for a country clergyman who didn't care how poor things were. But she has no style;—and as far as I can see, she has no beauty. Why should such a man as Frank Greystock tie himself by the leg for ever to such a girl as that? But, mamma, he doesn't mean to marry Lucy Morris. Would he have been going on in that way with his cousin down in Scotland had he meant it? He means nothing of the kind. He means to marry Lady Eustace's income if he can get it;—and she would marry him before the summer if only we could keep Frederic away from her.'

Mrs. Hittaway demanded from her mother that in season and out of season she should be urgent with Lord Fawn, impressing upon him the necessity of waiting, in order that he might see how false Lady Eustace was to him; and also that she should teach Lucy Morris how vain were all her hopes. If Lucy Morris would withdraw her claims altogether the thing might probably be more quickly and more surely managed. If Lucy could be induced to tell Frank that she withdrew her claim, and that she saw how impossible it was that they should ever be man and wife, then,—so argued Mrs. Hittaway,—Frank would at once throw himself at his cousin's feet, and all the difficulty would be over. The abominable, unjustifiable, and insolent interference of Lady Glencora just at the present moment would be the means of undoing all the good that had been done, unless it could be neutralised by some such activity as this. The necklace had absolutely faded away into nothing. The sly creature was almost becoming a heroine on the strength of the necklace. The very mystery with which the robberies were pervaded was acting in her favour. Lord Fawn would absolutely be made to marry her,—forced into it by Lady Glencora and that set,—unless the love affair between her and her cousin, of which Andy Gowran was able to give such sufficient testimony, could in some way be made available to prevent it.

The theory of life and system on which social matters

should be managed, as displayed by her married daughter, was very painful to poor old Lady Fawn. When she was told that under the new order of things promises from gentlemen were not to be looked upon as binding, that love was to go for nothing, that girls were to be made contented by being told that when one lover was lost another could be found, she was very unhappy. She could not disbelieve it all, and throw herself back upon her faith in virtue, constancy, and honesty. She rather thought that things had changed for the worse since she was young, and that promises were not now as binding as they used to be. She herself had married into a liberal family, had a liberal son, and would have called herself a Liberal;* but she could not fail to hear from others, her neighbours, that the English manners, and English principles, and English society were all going to destruction in consequence of the so-called liberality of the age. Gentlemen, she thought, certainly did do things which gentlemen would not have done forty years ago; and as for ladies,—they, doubtless, were changed altogether. Most assuredly she could not have brought an Andy Gowran to her mother to tell such tales in their joint presence as this man had told!

Mrs. Hittaway had ridiculed her for saying that poor Lucy would die when forced to give up her lover. Mrs. Hittaway had spoken of the necessity of breaking up that engagement without a word of anger against Frank Greystock. According to Mrs. Hittaway's views Frank Greystock had amused himself in the most natural way in the world when he asked Lucy to be his wife. A governess like Lucy had been quite foolish to expect that such a man as Greystock was in earnest. Of course she must give up her lover; and if there must be blame, she must blame herself for her folly! Nevertheless, Lady Fawn was so soft-hearted that she believed that the sorrow would crush Lucy, even if it did not kill her.

But not the less was it her duty to tell Lucy what she thought to be the truth. The story of what had occurred among the rocks at Portray was very disagreeable, but she believed it to be true. The man had been making love to his

184

cousin after his engagement to Lucy. And then, was it not quite manifest that he was neglecting poor Lucy in every way? He had not seen her for nearly six months. Had he intended to marry her, would he not have found a home for her at the deanery? Did he in any respect treat her as he would treat the girl whom he intended to marry? Putting all these things together, Lady Fawn thought that she saw that Lucy's case was hopeless;—and, so thinking, wrote to her the following letter.

'Fawn Court, 3rd March, 18—.

'DEAREST LUCY,

'I have so much to say to you that I did think of getting Lady Linlithgow to let you come to us here for a day, but I believe it will perhaps be better that I should write. I think you leave Lady Linlithgow after the first week in April, and it is quite necessary that you should come to some fixed arrangement as to the future. If that were all, there need not be any trouble, as you will come here, of course. Indeed, this is your natural home, as we all feel; and I must say that we have missed you most terribly since you went,—not only for Cecilia and Nina, but for all of us. And I don't know that I should write at all if it wasn't for something else, that must be said, sooner or later;—because, as to your coming here in April, that is so much a matter of course. The only mistake was, that you should ever have gone away. So we shall expect you here on whatever day you may arrange with Lady Linlithgow as to leaving her.' The poor, dear lady went on repeating her affectionate invitation, because of the difficulty she encountered in finding words with which to give the cruel counsel which she thought that it was her duty to offer.

'And now, dearest Lucy, I must say what I believe to be the truth about Mr. Greystock. I think that you should teach yourself to forget him,—or, at any rate, that you should teach yourself to forget the offer which he made to you last autumn. Whether he was or was not in earnest then, I think that he has now determined to forget it. I fear there is no doubt that he has been making love to his cousin, Lady

Eustace. You well know that I should not mention such a thing, if I had not the strongest possible grounds to convince me that I ought to do so. But, independent of this, his conduct to you during the last six months has been such as to make us all feel sure that the engagement is distasteful to him. He has, probably, found himself so placed that he cannot marry without money, and has wanted the firmness, or perhaps you will say the hardness of heart, to say so openly. I am sure of this, and so is Amelia, that it will be better for you to give the matter up altogether, and to come here and recover the blow among friends who will be as kind to you as possible. I know all that you will feel, and you have my fullest sympathy; but even such sorrows as that are cured by time, and by the mercy of God, which is not only infinite, but all-powerful.

> 'Your most affectionate friend,
> 'C. FAWN.'

Lady Fawn, when she had written her letter, discussed it with Amelia, and the two together agreed that Lucy would never surmount the ill effects of the blow which was thus prophesied. 'As to saying it will kill her, mamma,' said Amelia, 'I don't believe in that. If I were to break my leg, the accident might shorten my life, and this may shorten hers. It won't kill her in any other way. But it will alter her altogether. Nobody ever used to make herself happy so easily as Lucy Morris; but all that will be gone now.'

When Lucy received the letter, the immediate effect upon her, the effect which came from the first reading of it, was not very great. She succeeded for some half-hour in putting it aside, as referring to a subject on which she had quite made up her mind in a direction contrary to that indicated by her correspondent's advice. Lady Fawn told her that her lover intended to be false to her. She had thought the matter over very carefully within the last day or two, and had altogether made up her mind that she would continue to trust her lover. She had abstained from sending to him the letter which she had written, and had abstained on that resolution. Lady Fawn, of course, was as kind and friendly as a friend could be. She loved Lady Fawn dearly. But she was not bound to think Lady Fawn right, and in this instance she did not think Lady Fawn right. So she folded up the letter and put it in her pocket.

But by putting the letter into her pocket she could not put it out of her mind. Though she had resolved, of what use to her was a resolution in which she could not trust? Day had passed by after day, week after week, and month after month, and her very soul within her had become sad for want of seeing this man, who was living almost in the next street to her. She was ashamed to own to herself how many hours she had sat at the window, thinking that, perhaps, he might walk before the house in which he knew that she was immured. And, even had it been impossible that he should come to her, the post was open to him. She had scorned to write to him oftener than he would write to her, and now their correspondence had dwindled almost to nothing. He knew as well as did Lady Fawn when the period of her incarceration in Lady Linlithgow's dungeon would come to an end; and he knew, too, how great had been her hope that she might be accepted as a guest at the deanery, when that period should arrive. He knew that she must look for a new home, unless he would tell her where she should live. Was it likely,—was it possible, that he should be silent so long if he still intended to make her his wife? No doubt he had come to remember his debts, to remember his ambition, to think of his cousin's wealth,—and to think also of his cousin's beauty. What right had she ever had to hope for such a position as that of his wife,—she who had neither money nor beauty,—she who had nothing to give him in return for his name and the shelter of his house beyond her mind and her heart? As she thought of it all, she looked down upon her faded grey frock, and stood up that she might glance at her features in the glass; and she saw how small she was and insignificant, and reminded herself that all she had in the world was a few pounds which she had saved and was still saving in order that she might go to him with decent clothes upon her back. Was it reasonable that she should expect it?

But why had he come to her and made her thus wretched? She could acknowledge to herself that she had been foolish, vain, utterly ignorant of her own value in venturing to hope; perhaps unmaidenly in allowing it to be seen that she had hoped;—but what was he in having first exalted her before all her friends, and then abasing her so terribly and bringing her to such utter shipwreck? From spoken or written reproaches she could, of course, abstain. She would neither write nor speak any;—but from unuttered reproaches how could she abstain? She had called him a traitor once in playful, loving irony, during those few hours in which her love had been to her a luxury that she could enjoy. But now he was a traitor indeed. Had he left her alone she would have loved him in silence, and not have been wretched in her love. She would, she knew, in that case, have had vigour enough and sufficient strength of character to bear her burthen without outward signs of suffering, without any inward suffering that would have disturbed the current of her life. But now everything was over with her. She had no thought of dying, but her future life was a blank to her.

She came down-stairs to sit at lunch with Lady Linlithgow, and the old woman did not perceive that anything was amiss with her companion. Further news had been heard of Lizzie Eustace, and of Lord Fawn, and of the robberies, and the countess declared how she had read in the newspaper that one man was already in custody for the burglary at the house in Hertford Street. From that subject she went on to tidings which had reached her from her old friend Lady Clantantram that the Fawn marriage was on again. 'Not that I believe it, my dear; because I think that Mr. Greystock has made it quite safe in that quarter.' All this Lucy heard, and never showed by a single sign, or by a motion of a muscle, that she was in pain. Then Lady Linlithgow asked her what she meant to do after the 5th of April. 'I don't see at all why you shouldn't stay here, if you like it, Miss Morris;—that is, if you have abandoned the stupid idea of an engagement with Frank Greystock.' Lucy smiled, and even thanked the countess, and said that she had made up her mind to go back to Richmond for a month or two, till she could get another engagement as a governess. The she returned to her room and sat again at her window, looking out upon the street.

What did it matter now where she went? And yet she must go somewhere, and do something. There remained to her the wearisome possession of herself, and while she lived she must eat, and have clothes, and require shelter. She could not dawdle out a bitter existence under Lady Fawn's roof, eating the bread of charity, hanging about the rooms and shrubberies useless and idle. How bitter to her was that possession of herself, as she felt that there was nothing good to be done with the thing so possessed! She doubted even whether ever again she could become serviceable as a governess, and whether the energy would be left to her of earning her bread by teaching adequately the few things that she knew. But she must make the attempt,—and must go on making it, till God in his mercy should take her to himself.

And yet but a few months since life had been so sweet to her! As she felt this she was not thinking of those short days of excited, feverish bliss in which she had believed that all the good things of the world were to be showered into her lap; but of previous years in which everything had been with her as it was now,—with the one exception that she had not then been deceived. She had been full of smiles, and humour, and mirth, absolutely happy among her friends, though conscious of the necessity of earning her bread by the exercise of a most precarious profession,—while elated by no hope. Though she had loved the man and had been hopeless, she was happy. But now, surely, of all maidens and of all women, she was the most forlorn.

Having once acceded to the truth of Lady Fawn's views, she abandoned all hope. Everybody said so, and it was so. There was no word from any side to encourage her. The thing was done and over, and she would never mention his name again. She would simply beg of all the Fawns that no allusion might be made to him in her presence. She would never blame him, and certainly she would never praise him. As far as she could rule her tongue, she would never have his name upon her lips again.

She thought for a time that she would send the letter which she had already written. Any other letter she could not bring herself to write. Even to think of him was an agony to her; but to communicate her thoughts to him was worse than agony. It would be almost madness. What need was there for any letter? If the thing was done, it was done. Perhaps there remained with her,—staying by her without her own knowledge, some faint spark of hope, that even yet he might return to her. At last she resolved that there should be no letter, and she destroyed that which she had written.

But she did write a note to Lady Fawn, in which she gratefully accepted her old friend's kindness, till such time as she could 'find a place.' 'As to that other subject,' she said, 'I know that you are right. Please let it all be as though it had never been.'

CHAPTER LXI
Lizzie's great Friend

THE Saturday morning came at last for which Lord Fawn had made his appointment with Lizzie, and a very important day it was in Hertford Street,—chiefly on account of his lordship's visit, but also in respect to other events which crowded themselves into the day. In the telling of our tale, we have gone a little in advance of this, as it was not till the subsequent Monday that Lady Linlithgow read in the newspaper, and told Lucy, how a man had been arrested on account of the robbery. Early on the Saturday morning Sir Griffin Tewett was in Hertford Street, and, as Lizzie afterwards understood, there was a terrible scene between both him and Lucinda and him and Mrs. Carbuncle. She saw nothing of it herself, but Mrs. Carbuncle brought her the tidings. For the last few days Mrs. Carbuncle had been very affectionate in her manner to Lizzie, thereby showing a great change; for during nearly the whole of February the lady who in fact owned the house, had hardly been courteous to her remunerative guest, expressing more than once a hint that the arrangement which had brought them together had better come to an end. 'You see, Lady Eustace,' Mrs. Carbuncle had once said, 'the trouble about these robberies is almost too much for me.' Lizzie, who was ill at the time, and still trembling with constant fear on account of the lost diamonds, had taken advantage of her sick condition, and declined to argue the question of her removal. Now she was supposed to be convalescent, but Mrs. Carbuncle had returned to her former ways of affection. No doubt there was cause for this,— cause that was patent to Lizzie herself. Lady Glencora Palliser had called,—which thing alone was felt by Lizzie to alter her position altogether. And then, though her diamonds were gone, and though the thieves who had stolen them were undoubtedly aware of her secret as to the first robbery, though she had herself told that secret to Lord George, whom she had not seen since she had done so,—in spite of all these causes for trouble, she had of late gradually found herself to be emerging from the state of despondency into which she had fallen while the diamonds were in her own custody. She knew that she was regaining her ascendancy; and, therefore, when Mrs. Carbuncle came to tell her of the grievous things which had been said down-stairs between Sir Griffin and his mistress, and to consult her as to the future, Lizzie was not surprised. 'I suppose the meaning of it is that the match must be off,' said Lizzie.

'Oh dear no;—pray don't say anything so horrid after all that I have gone through. Don't suggest anything of that kind to Lucinda.'

'But surely after what you've told me now, he'll never come here again.'

'Oh yes, he will. There's no danger about his coming back. It's only a sort of a way he has.'

'A very disagreeable way,' said Lizzie.

'No doubt, Lady Eustace. But then you know you can't have it all sweet. There must be some things disagreeable. As far as I can learn, the property will be all right after a few years,—and it is absolutely indispensable that Lucinda should do something. She has accepted him, and she must go on with it.'

'She seems to me to be very unhappy, Mrs. Carbuncle.'

'That was always her way. She was never gay and cheery like other girls. I have never known her once to be what you would call happy.'

'She likes hunting.'

'Yes,—because she can gallop away out of herself. I have done all I can for her, and she must go on with the marriage now. As for going back, it is out of the question. The truth is, we couldn't afford it.'

'Then you must keep him in a better humour.'

'I am not so much afraid about him; but, dear Lady Eustace, we want you to help us a little.'

'How can I help you?'

'You can, certainly. Could you lend me two hundred and fifty pounds, just for six weeks?' Lizzie's face fell and her eyes became very serious in their aspect. Two hundred and fifty pounds! 'You know you would have ample security. You need not give Lucinda her present till I've paid you, and that will be forty-five pounds.'

'Thirty-five,' said Lizzie with angry decision.

'I thought we agreed upon forty-five when we settled about the servants' liveries;—and then you can let the man at the stables know that I am to pay for the carriage and horses. You wouldn't be out of the money hardly above a week or so, and it might be the salvation of Lucinda just at present.'

'Why don't you ask Lord George?'

'Ask Lord George! He hasn't got it. It's much more likely that he should ask me. I don't know what's come to Lord

George this last month past. I did believe that you and he were to come together. I think these two robberies have upset him altogether. But, dear Lizzie;—you can let me have it, can't you?'

Lizzie did not at all like the idea of lending money, and by no means appreciated the security now offered to her. It might be very well for her to tell the man at the stables that Mrs. Carbuncle would pay him her bill, but how would it be with her, if Mrs. Carbuncle did not pay the bill? And as for her present to Lucinda,—which was to have been a present, and regarded by the future Lady Tewett as a voluntary offering of good-will and affection,—she was altogether averse to having it disposed of in this fashion. And yet she did not like to make an enemy of Mrs. Carbuncle. 'I never was so poor in my life before,—not since I was married,' said Lizzie.

'You can't be poor, dear Lady Eustace.'

'They took my money out of my desk, you know,—ever so much.'

'Forty-three pounds,' said Mrs. Carbuncle, who was, of course, well instructed in all the details of the robbery.

'And I don't suppose you can guess what the autumn cost me at Portray. The bills are only coming in now, and really they sometimes so frighten me that I don't know what I shall do. Indeed, I haven't got the money to spare.'

'You'll have every penny of it back in six weeks,' said Mrs. Carbuncle, upon whose face a glow of anger was settling down. She quite intended to make herself very disagreeable to her 'dear Lady Eustace' or her 'dear Lizzie' if she did not get what she wanted; and she knew very well how to do it. It must be owned that Lizzie was afraid of the woman. It was almost impossible for her not to be afraid of the people with whom she lived. There were so many things against her; —so many sources of fear! 'I am quite sure you won't refuse me such a trifling favour as this,' said Mrs. Carbuncle, with the glow of anger reddening more and more upon her brow.

'I don't think I have so much at the bankers,' said Lizzie.

'They'll let you overdraw,—just as much as you please.

If the cheque comes back that will be my look out.' Lizzie
had tried that game before, and knew that the bankers would
allow her to overdraw. 'Come, be a good friend and do it at
once,' said Mrs. Carbuncle.

'Perhaps I can manage a hundred and fifty,' said Lizzie,
trembling. Mrs. Carbuncle fought hard for the greater sum;
but at last consented to take the less, and the cheque was
written.

'This, of course, won't interfere with Lucinda's present,'
said Mrs. Carbuncle,—'as we can make all this right by the
horse and carriage account.' To this proposition, however,
Lady Eustace made no answer.

Soon after lunch, at which meal Miss Roanoke did not
show herself, Lady Glencora Palliser was announced, and sat
for about ten minutes in the drawing-room. She had come,
she said, especially to give the Duke of Omnium's compliments to Lady Eustace, and to express a wish on the part
of the duke that the lost diamonds might be recovered. 'I
doubt,' said Lady Glencora, 'whether there is any one in
England except professed jewellers who knows so much about
diamonds as his grace.'

'Or who has so many,' said Mrs. Carbuncle, smiling
graciously.

'I don't know about that. I suppose there are family
diamonds, though I have never seen them. But he sym-
pathises with you completely, Lady Eustace. I suppose there
is hardly hope now of recovering them.' Lizzie smiled and
shook her head. 'Isn't it odd that they never should have
discovered the thieves? I'm told they haven't at all given it
up,—only, unfortunately, they'll never get back the necklace.'
She sat there for about a quarter of an hour, and then, as she
took her leave, she whispered a few words to Lizzie. 'He is
to come and see you;—isn't he?' Lizzie assented with a smile,
but without a word. 'I hope it will be all right,' said Lady
Glencora, and then she went.

Lizzie liked this friendship from Lady Glencora amazingly.
Perhaps, after all, nothing more would ever be known about

the diamonds, and they would simply be remembered as having added a peculiar and not injurious mystery to her life. Lord George knew,—but then she trusted that a benevolent, true-hearted Corsair, such as was Lord George, would never tell the story against her. The thieves knew,—but surely they, if not detected, would never tell. And if the story were told by thieves, or even by a Corsair, at any rate half the world would not believe it. What she had feared,—had feared till the dread had nearly overcome her,—was public exposure at the hands of the police. If she could escape that, the world might still be bright before her. And the interest taken in her by such persons as the Duke of Omnium and Lady Glencora, was evidence not only that she had escaped it hitherto, but also that she was in a fair way to escape it altogether. Three weeks ago she would have given up half her income to have been able to steal out of London without leaving a trace behind her. Three weeks ago Mrs. Carbuncle was treating her with discourtesy, and she was left alone nearly the whole day in her sick bedroom. Things were going better with her now. She was recovering her position. Mr. Camperdown, who had been the first to attack her, was, so to say, 'nowhere.' He had acknowledged himself beaten. Lord Fawn, whose treatment to her had been so great an injury, was coming to see her that very day. Her cousin Frank, though he had never offered to marry her, was more affectionate to her than ever. Mrs. Carbuncle had been at her feet that morning borrowing money. And Lady Glencora Palliser,— the very leading star of fashion,—had called upon her twice! Why should she succumb? She had an income of four thousand pounds a year, and she thought that she could remember that her aunt, Lady Linlithgow, had but seven hundred pounds. Lady Fawn with all her daughters had not near so much as she had. And she was beautiful, too, and young, and perfectly free to do what she pleased. No doubt the last eighteen months of her life had been made wretched by those horrid diamonds;—but they were gone, and she had fair reason to hope that the very knowledge of them was gone also.

In this condition, would it be expedient for her to accept Lord Fawn when he came? She could not, of course, be sure that any renewed offer would be the result of his visit;—but she thought it probable that with care she might bring him to that. Why should he come to her if he himself had no such intention? Her mind was quite made up on this point,—that he should be made to renew his offer; but whether she would renew her acceptance was quite another question. She had sworn to her cousin Frank, that she would never do so, and she had sworn also that she would be revenged on this wretched lord. Now would be her opportunity of accomplishing her revenge, and of proving to Frank that she had been in earnest. And she positively disliked the man. That, probably, did not go for much, but it went for something, even with Lizzie Eustace. Her cousin she did like,—and Lord George. She hardly knew which was her real love;—though, no doubt, she gave the preference greatly to her cousin, because she could trust him. And then Lord Fawn was very poor. The other two men were poor also; but their poverty was not so objectionable in Lizzie's eyes as were the respectable, close-fisted economies of Lord Fawn. Lord Fawn, no doubt, had an assured income and a real peerage, and could make her a peeress. As she thought of it all, she acknowledged that there was a great deal to be said on each side, and that the necessity of making up her mind then and there was a heavy burthen upon her.

Exactly at the hour named Lord Fawn came, and Lizzie was, of course, found alone. That had been carefully provided. He was shown up, and she received him very gracefully. She was sitting, and she rose from her chair, and put out her hand for him to take. She spoke no word of greeting, but looked at him with a pleasant smile, and stood for a few seconds with her hand in his. He was awkward, and much embarrassed, and she certainly had no intention of lessening his embarrassment. 'I hope you are better than you have been,' he said at last.

'I am getting better, Lord Fawn. Will you not sit down?' He then seated himself, placing his hat beside him on the floor, but at the moment could not find words to speak. 'I have been very ill.'

'I have been so sorry to hear it.'

'There has been much to make me ill,—has there not?'

'About the robbery, you mean?'

'About many things. The robbery has been by no means the worst, though, no doubt, it frightened me much. There were two robberies, Lord Fawn.'

'Yes,—I know that.'

'And it was very terrible. And then, I had been threatened with a lawsuit. You have heard that, too?'

'Yes,—I had heard it.'

'I believe they have given that up now. I understand from my cousin, Mr. Greystock, who has been my truest friend in all my troubles, that the stupid people have found out at last that they had not a leg to stand on. I daresay you have heard that, Lord Fawn?'

Lord Fawn certainly had heard, in a doubtful way, the gist

of Mr. Dove's opinion, namely, that the necklace could not be
claimed from the holder of it as an heirloom attached to the
Eustace family. But he had heard at the same time that Mr.
Camperdown was as confident as ever that he could recover
the property by claiming it after another fashion. Whether or
no that claim had been altogether abandoned, or had been
allowed to fall into abeyance because of the absence of the
diamonds, he did not know, nor did any one know,—Mr.
Camperdown himself having come to no decision on the subject. But Lord Fawn had been aware that his sister had of late
shifted the ground of her inveterate enmity to Lizzie Eustace,
making use of the scene which Mr. Gowran had witnessed,
in lieu of the lady's rapacity in regard to the necklace. It might
therefore be assumed, Lord Fawn thought and feared, that his
strong ground in regard to the necklace had been cut from
under his feet. But still, it did not behove him to confess that
the cause which he had always alleged as the ground for his
retreat from the engagement was no cause at all. It might go
hard with him should an attempt be made to force him to
name another cause. He knew that he would lack the courage
to tell the lady that he had heard from his sister that one Andy
Gowran had witnessed a terrible scene down among the rocks
at Portray. So he sat silent, and made no answer to Lizzie's
first assertion respecting the diamonds.

But the necklace was her strong point, and she did not
intend that he should escape the subject. 'If I remember right,
Lord Fawn, you yourself saw that wretched old attorney once
or twice on the subject?'

'I did see Mr. Camperdown, certainly. He is my own family
lawyer.'

'You were kind enough to interest yourself about the
diamonds,—were you not?' She asked him this as a question,
and then waited for a reply. 'Was it not so?'

'Yes, Lady Eustace; it was so.'

'They were of great value, and it was natural,' continued
Lizzie. 'Of course you interested yourself. Mr. Camperdown
was full of awful threats against me;—was he not? I don't

know what he was not going to do. He stopped me in the street as I was driving to the station in my own carriage, when the diamonds were with me;—which was a very strong measure, I think. And he wrote me ever so many,—oh, such horrid letters. And he went about telling everybody that it was an heirloom;—didn't he? You know all that, Lord Fawn?'

'I know that he wanted to recover them.'

'And did he tell you that he went to a real lawyer,—somebody who really knew about it, Mr. Turbot, or Turtle, or some such name as that, and the real lawyer told him that he was all wrong, and that the necklace couldn't be an heirloom at all, because it belonged to me, and that he had better drop his lawsuit altogether? Did you hear that?'

'No;—I did not hear that.'

'Ah, Lord Fawn, you dropped your inquiries just at the wrong place. No doubt you had too many things to do in Parliament and the Government to go on with them; but if you had gone on, you would have learned that Mr. Camperdown had just to give it up,—because he had been wrong from beginning to end.' Lizzie's words fell from her with extreme rapidity, and she had become almost out of breath from the effects of her own energy.

Lord Fawn felt strongly the necessity of clinging to the diamonds as his one great and sufficient justification. 'I thought,' said he, 'that Mr. Camperdown had abandoned his action for the present because the jewels had been stolen.'

'Not a bit of it,' said Lizzie, rising suddenly to her legs. 'Who says so? Who dares to say so? Whoever says so is,— is a storyteller. I understand all about that. The action could go on just the same, and I could be made to pay for the necklace out of my own income if it hadn't been my own. I am sure, Lord Fawn, such a clever man as you, and one who has always been in the Government and in Parliament, can see that. And will anybody believe that such an enemy as Mr. Camperdown has been to me, persecuting me in every possible way, telling lies about me to everybody,—who tried to prevent my dear, darling husband from marrying me,—that he wouldn't go on with it if he could?'

'Mr. Camperdown is a very respectable man, Lady Eustace.'

'Respectable! Talk to me of respectable after all that he has made me suffer! As you were so fond of making inquiries, Lord Fawn, you ought to have gone on with them. You never would believe what my cousin said.'

'Your cousin always behaved very badly to me.'

'My cousin, who is a brother rather than a cousin, has known how to protect me from the injuries done to me,—or, rather, has known how to take my part when I have been injured. My lord, as you have been unwilling to believe him, why have you not gone to that gentleman who, as I say, is a real lawyer? I don't know, my lord, that it need have concerned you at all, but as you began, you surely should have gone on with it. Don't you think so?' She was still standing up, and, small as was her stature, was almost menacing the unfortunate Under-Secretary of State, who was still seated in his chair. 'My lord,' continued Lizzie, 'I have had great wrong done me.'

'Do you mean by me?'

'Yes, by you. Who else has done it?'

'I do not think that I have done wrong to any one. I was obliged to say that I could not recognise those diamonds as the property of my wife.'

'But what right had you to say so? I had the diamonds when you asked me to be your wife.'

'I did not know it.'

'Nor did you know that I had this little ring upon my finger. Is it fit that you, or that any man should turn round upon a lady and say to her that your word is to be broken, and that she is to be exposed before all her friends, because you have taken a fancy to dislike her ring or her brooch? I say, Lord Fawn, it was no business of yours, even after you were engaged to me. What jewels I might have, or not have, was no concern of yours till after I had become your wife. Go and ask all the world if it is not so? You say that my cousin affronts you because he takes my part,—like a brother. Ask any one else. Ask any lady you may know. Let us name some one to decide between us which of us has been wrong. Lady Glencora Palliser is a friend of yours, and her husband is in the Government. Shall we name her? It is true, indeed, that her uncle, the Duke of Omnium, the grandest and greatest of English noblemen, is specially interested on my behalf.' This was very fine in Lizzie. The Duke of Omnium she had never seen; but his name had been mentioned to her by Lady Glencora, and she was quick to use it.

'I can admit of no reference to any one,' said Lord Fawn.

'And I then,—what am I to do? I am to be thrown over simply because your lordship—chooses to throw me over. Your lordship will admit no reference to any one! Your lordship makes inquiries as long as an attorney tells you stories against me, but drops them at once when the attorney is made to understand that he is wrong. Tell me this, sir. Can you justify yourself,—in your own heart?'

Unfortunately for Lord Fawn, he was not sure that he could justify himself. The diamonds were gone, and the action was laid aside, and the general opinion which had prevailed a month or two since, that Lizzie had been disreputably concerned in stealing her own necklace, seemed to have been laid aside. Lady Glencora and the duke went for almost as much with Lord Fawn as they did with Lizzie. No doubt the misbehaviour down among the rocks was left to him; but he had that only on the evidence of Andy Gowran,—and even Andy Gowran's evidence he had declined to receive otherwise than second-hand. Lizzie, too, was prepared with an answer to this charge,—an answer which she had already made more than once, though the charge was not positively brought against her, and which consisted in an assertion that Frank Greystock was her brother rather than her cousin. Such brotherhood was not altogether satisfactory to Lord Fawn, when he came once more to regard Lizzie Eustace as his possible future wife; but still the assertion was an answer, and one that he could not altogether reject.

It certainly was the case that he had again begun to think what would be the result of a marriage with Lady Eustace. He must sever himself altogether from Mrs. Hittaway, and must relax the closeness of his relations with Fawn Court. He would have a wife respecting whom he himself had spread evil tidings, and the man whom he most hated in the world would be his wife's favourite cousin, or, so to say,—brother. He would, after a fashion, be connected with Mrs. Carbuncle, Lord George de Bruce Carruthers, and Sir Griffin Tewett, all of whom he regarded as thoroughly disreputable. And, moreover, at his own country house at Portray, as in such case it would be, his own bailiff or steward would be the man who had seen,—what he had seen. These were great objections; but how was he to avoid marrying her? He was engaged to her. How, at any rate, was he to escape from the renewal of his engagement at this moment? He had more than once positively stated that he was deterred from marrying her, only by her possession of the diamonds. The diamonds were now gone.

Lizzie was still standing, waiting for an answer to her question,—Can you justify yourself in your own heart? Having paused for some seconds, she repeated her question in a stronger and more personal form. 'Had I been your sister, Lord Fawn, and had another man behaved to me as you have now done, would you say that he had behaved well, and that she had no ground for complaint? Can you bring yourself to answer that question honestly?'

'I hope I shall answer no question dishonestly.'

'Answer it then. No; you cannot answer it, because you would condemn yourself. Now, Lord Fawn, what do you mean to do?'

'I had thought, Lady Eustace, that any regard which you might ever have entertained for me——'

'Well;—what had you thought of my regard?'

'That it had been dissipated.'

'Have I told you so? Has any one come to you from me with such a message?'

'Have you not received attentions from any one else?'

'Attentions,—what attentions? I have received plenty of attentions,—most flattering attentions. I was honoured even this morning by a most gratifying attention on the part of his grace the Duke of Omnium.'

'I did not mean that.'

'What do you mean, then? I am not going to marry the Duke of Omnium because of his attention,—nor any one else. If you mean, sir, after the other inquiries you have done me the honour to make, to throw it in my face now, that I have— have in any way rendered myself unworthy of the position of your wife because people have been civil and kind to me in my sorrow, you are a greater dastard than I took you to be. Tell me at once, sir, whom you mean.'

It is hardly too much to say that the man quailed before her. And it certainly is not too much to say that, had Lizzie Eustace been trained as an actress, she would have become a favourite with the town. When there came to her any fair scope for acting, she was perfect. In the ordinary scenes of ordinary life, such as befell her during her visit to Fawn Court, she could not acquit herself well. There was no reality about her, and the want of it was strangely plain to most unobservant eyes. But give her a part to play that required exaggerated strong action, and she hardly ever failed. Even in that terrible moment, when, on her return from the theatre, she thought that the police had discovered her secret about the diamonds, though she nearly sank through fear, she still carried on her acting in the presence of Lucinda Roanoke; and when she had found herself constrained to tell the truth to Lord George Carruthers, the power to personify a poor, weak, injured creature was not wanting to her. The reader will not think that her position in society at the present moment was very well established,—will feel, probably, that she must still have known herself to be on the brink of social ruin. But she had now fully worked herself up to the necessities of the occasion, and was as able to play her part as any actress that ever walked the boards. She had called him a dastard, and now stood looking him in the face. 'I didn't mean anybody in particular,' said Lord Fawn.

'Then what right can you have to ask me whether I have received attentions? Had it not been for the affectionate attention of my cousin, Mr. Greystock, I should have died beneath the load of sorrow you have heaped upon me!' This she said quite boldly, and yet the man she named was he of whom Andy Gowran told his horrid story, and whose love-making to Lizzie had, in Mrs. Hittaway's opinion, been sufficient to atone for any falling off of strength in the matter of the diamonds.

'A rumour reached me,' said Lord Fawn, plucking up his courage, 'that you were engaged to marry your cousin.'

'Then rumour lied, my lord. And he or she who repeated the rumour to you, lied also. And any he or she who repeats it again will go on with the lie.' Lord Fawn's brow became very black. The word 'lie,' itself, was offensive to him,— offensive, even though it might not be applied directly to himself; but he still quailed, and was unable to express his indignation,—as he had done to poor Lucy Morris, his mother's governess. 'And now let me ask, Lord Fawn, on what ground you and I stand together. When my friend, Lady Glencora, asked me, only this morning, whether my engagement with you was still an existing fact, and brought me the kindest possible message on the same subject from her uncle, the duke, I hardly knew what answer to make to her.' It was not surprising that Lizzie in her difficulties should use her new friend, but perhaps she over-did the friendship a little. 'I told her that we were engaged, but that your lord-ship's conduct to me had been so strange, that I hardly knew how to speak of you among my friends.'

'I thought I explained myself to your cousin.'

'My cousin certainly did not understand your explanation.'

Lord Fawn was certain that Greystock had understood it well; and Greystock had in return insulted him,—because the engagement was broken off. But it is impossible to argue on facts with a woman who has been ill-used. 'After all that has passed, perhaps we had better part,' said Lord Fawn.

'Then I shall put the matter into the hands of the Duke of Omnium,' said Lizzie boldly. 'I will not have my whole life ruined, my good name blasted——'

'I have not said a word to injure your good name.'

'On what plea, then, have you dared to take upon yourself to put an end to an engagement which was made at your own pressing request,—which was, of course, made at your own request? On what ground do you justify such conduct? You are a Liberal, Lord Fawn; and everybody regards the Duke of Omnium as the head of the liberal nobility in England. He is my friend, and I shall put the matter into his hands.' It was, probably, from her cousin Frank that Lizzie had learned that Lord Fawn was more afraid of the leaders of his own party than of any other tribunal upon earth,—or, perhaps, elsewhere.

Lord Fawn felt the absurdity of the threat, and yet it had effect upon him. He knew that the Duke of Omnium was a worn-out old debauchee, with one foot in the grave, who was looked after by two or three women who were only anxious that he should not disgrace himself by some absurdity before he died. Nevertheless, the Duke of Omnium, or the duke's name, was a power in the nation. Lady Glencora was certainly very powerful, and Lady Glencora's husband was Chancellor of the Exchequer. He did not suppose that the duke cared in the least whether Lizzie Eustace was or was not married;— but Lady Glencora had certainly interested herself about Lizzie, and might make London almost too hot to hold him if she chose to go about everywhere saying that he ought to marry the lady. And in addition to all this prospective grief, there was the trouble of the present moment. He was in Lizzie's own room,—fool that he had been to come there,— and he must get out as best he could. 'Lady Eustace,' he said, 'I am most anxious not to behave badly in this matter.'

'But you are behaving badly,—very badly.'

'With your leave I will tell you what I would suggest. I will submit to you in writing my opinion on this matter;'— Lord Fawn had been all his life submitting his opinion in writing, and thought that he was rather a good hand at the work. 'I will then endeavour to explain to you the reasons which make me think that it will be better for us both that our engagement should be at an end. If, after reading it, you shall disagree with me, and still insist on the right which I gave you when I asked you to become my wife,—I will then perform the promise which I certainly made.' To this most foolish proposal on his part, Lizzie, of course, acquiesced. She acquiesced, and bade him farewell with her sweetest smile. It was now manifest to her that she could have her husband,—or her revenge, just as she might prefer.

This had been a day of triumph to her, and she was talking f it in the evening triumphantly to Mrs. Carbuncle, when she was told that a policeman wanted to see her down-stairs! Oh, those wretched police! Again all the blood rushed to her head, and nearly killed her. She descended slowly; and was then informed by a man, not dressed, like Bunfit, in plain clothes, but with all the paraphernalia of a policeman's uniform, that her late servant, Patience Crabstick, had given herself up as Queen's evidence, and was now in custody in Scotland Yard. It had been thought right that she should be so far informed; but the man was able to tell her nothing further.

CHAPTER LXII
'You know where my Heart is'

ON the Sunday following Frank, as usual, was in Hertford Street. He had become almost a favourite with Mrs. Carbuncle; and had so far ingratiated himself even with Lucinda Roanoke that, according to Lizzie's report, he might, if so inclined, rob Sir Griffin of his prize without much difficulty. On this occasion he was unhappy and in low spirits; and when questioned on the subject made no secret of the fact that he was harassed for money. 'The truth is I have overdrawn my bankers by five hundred pounds, and they have, as they say, ventured to remind me of it. I wish they were not venturesome quite so often; for they reminded me of the same fact about a fortnight ago.'

'What do you do with your money, Mr. Greystock?' asked Mrs. Carbuncle, laughing.

'Muddle it away, paying my bills with it,—according to the very, very old story. The fact is, I live in that detestable no-man's land, between respectability and insolvency, which has none of the pleasure of either. I am fair game for every creditor, as I am supposed to pay my way,—and yet I never can pay my way.'

'Just like my poor dear father,' said Lizzie.

'Not exactly, Lizzie. He managed much better, and never paid anybody. If I could only land on terra-firma,—one side or the other,—I shouldn't much care which. As it is I have all the recklessness, but none of the carelessness of the hopelessly insolvent man. And it is so hard with us. Attorneys owe us large sums of money, and we can't dun them very well. I have a lot of money due to me from rich men, who don't pay me simply because they don't think that it matters. I talk to them grandly, and look big, as though money was the last thing I thought of, when I am longing to touch my hat and ask them as a great favour to settle my little bill.' All this time Lizzie was full of matter which she must impart to her cousin, and could impart to him only in privacy.

It was absolutely necessary that she should tell him what she had heard of Patience Crabstick. In her heart of hearts she wished that Patience Crabstick had gone off safely with her plunder to the Antipodes. She had no wish to get back what had been lost, either in the matter of the diamonds or of the smaller things taken. She had sincerely wished that the police might fail in all their endeavours, and that the thieves might enjoy perfect security with their booty. She did not even begrudge Mr. Benjamin the diamonds,—or Lord George, if in

truth Lord George had been the last thief. The robbery had
enabled her to get the better of Mr. Camperdown, and apparently of Lord Fawn; and had freed her from the custody of
property which she had learned to hate. It had been a very
good robbery. But now these wretched police had found
Patience Crabstick, and would disturb her again!

Of course she must tell her cousin. He must hear the news,
and it would be better that he should hear it from her than
from others. This was Sunday, and she thought he would be
sure to know the truth on the following Monday. In this she
was right; for on the Monday old Lady Linlithgow saw it
stated in the newspapers that an arrest had been made. 'I
have something to tell you,' she said, as soon as she had
succeeded in finding herself alone with him.

'Anything about the diamonds?'

'Well, no; not exactly about the diamonds;—though perhaps it is. But first, Frank, I want to say something else to
you.'

'Not about the diamonds?'

'Oh no;—not at all. It is this. You must let me lend you
that five hundred pounds you want.'

'Indeed you shall do no such thing. I should not have mentioned it to you if I had not thought that you were one of the
insolvent yourself. You were in debt yourself when we last
talked about money.'

'So I am;—and that horrid woman, Mrs. Carbuncle, has
made me lend her one hundred and fifty pounds. But it is so
different with you, Frank.'

'Yes;—my needs are greater than hers.'

'What is she to me?—while you are everything! Things
can't be so bad with me but what I can raise five hundred
pounds. After all, I am not really in debt, for a person with
my income; but if I were, still my first duty would be to help
you if you want help.'

'Be generous first, and just afterwards. That's it;—isn't it,
Lizzie? But indeed under no circumstances could I take a
penny of your money. There are some persons from whom a

man can borrow, and some from whom he cannot. You are clearly one of those from whom I cannot borrow.'

'Why not?'

'Ah,—one can't explain these things. It simply is so. Mrs. Carbuncle was quite the natural person to borrow your money, and it seems that she has complied with nature. Some Jew,* who wants thirty per cent., is the natural person for me. All these things are arranged, and it is of no use disturbing the arrangements and getting out of course. I shall pull through. And now let me know your own news.'

'The police have taken Patience.'

'They have,—have they? Then at last we shall know all about the diamonds.' This was gall to poor Lizzie. 'Where did they get her?'

'Ah!—I don't know that.'

'And who told you?'

'A policeman came here last night and said so. She is going to turn against the thieves, and tell all that she knows. Nasty, mean creature.'

'Thieves are nasty, mean creatures generally. We shall get it all out now,—as to what happened at Carlisle and what happened here. Do you know that everybody believes, up to this moment, that your dear friend Lord George de Bruce sold the diamonds to Mr. Benjamin, the jeweller?'

Lizzie could only shrug her shoulders. She herself, among many doubts, was upon the whole disposed to think as everybody thought. She did believe,—as far as she believed anything in the matter, that the Corsair had determined to become possessed of the prize from the moment that he saw it in Scotland, that the Corsair arranged the robbery in Carlisle, and that again he arranged the robbery in the London house as soon as he learned from Lizzie where the diamonds were placed. To her mind this had been the most ready solution of the mystery, and when she found that other people almost regarded him as the thief, her doubts became a belief. And she did not in the least despise or dislike him or condemn him for what he had done. Were he to come to her and confess it all, telling his story in such a manner as to make her seem to be safe for the future, she would congratulate him and accept him at once as her own dear, expected Corsair. But, if so, he should not have bungled the thing. He should have managed his subordinates better than to have one of them turn evidence against him. He should have been able to get rid of a poor weak female like Patience Crabstick. Why had he not sent her to New York, or—or,—or anywhere? If Lizzie were to hear that Lord George had taken Patience out to sea in a yacht,—somewhere among the bright islands of which she thought so much,—and dropped the girl overboard, tied up in a bag, she would regard it as a proper Corsair arrangement. Now she was angry with Lord George, because her trouble was coming back upon her. Frank had suggested that Lord George was the robber in chief, and Lizzie merely shrugged her shoulders. 'We shall know all about it now,' said he triumphantly.

'I don't know that I want to know any more about it. I have been so tortured about these wretched diamonds, that I never wish to hear them mentioned again. I don't care who has got them. My enemies used to think that I loved them so well that I could not bear to part with them. I hated them always, and never took any pleasure in them. I used to think that I would throw them into the sea, and when they were gone I was glad of it.'

'Thieves ought to be discovered, Lizzie,—for the good of the community.'

'I don't care for the community. What has the community ever done for me? And now I have something else to tell you. Ever so many people came yesterday as well as that wretched policeman. Dear Lady Glencora was here again.'

'They'll make a Radical of you among them, Lizzie.'

'I don't care a bit about that. I'd just as soon be a Radical as a stupid old Conservative. Lady Glencora has been most kind, and she brought me the dearest message from the Duke of Omnium. The duke had heard how ill I had been treated.'

'The duke is doting.'

'It is so easy to say that when a man is old. I don't think you know him, Frank.'

'Not in the least;—nor do I wish.'

'It is something to have the sympathy of men high placed in the world. And as to Lady Glencora, I do love her dearly. She just comes up to my beau-ideal of what a woman should be,—disinterested, full of spirit, affectionate, with a dash of romance about her.'

'A great dash of romance, I fancy.'

'And a determination to be something in the world. Lady Glencora Palliser is something.'

'She is awfully rich, Lizzie.'

'I suppose so. At any rate, that is no disgrace. And then, Frank, somebody else came.'

'Lord Fawn was to have come.'

'He did come.'

'And how did it go between you?'

'Ah,—that will be so difficult to explain. I wish you had been behind the curtain to hear it all. It is so necessary that you should know, and yet it is so hard to tell. I spoke up to him, and was quite high-spirited.'

'I daresay you were.'

'I told him out, bravely, of all the wrong he had done me. I did not sit and whimper, I can assure you. Then he talked about you,—of your attentions.'

Frank Greystock, of course, remembered the scene among the rocks, and Mr. Gowran's wagging head and watchful eyes. At the time he had felt certain that some use would be made of Andy's vigilance, though he had not traced the connection between the man and Mrs. Hittaway. If Lord Fawn had heard of the little scene, there might, doubtless, be cause for him to talk of 'attentions.' 'What did it matter to him?' asked Frank. 'He is an insolent ass,—as I have told him once, and shall have to tell him again.'

'I think it did matter, Frank.'

'I don't see it a bit. He had resigned his rights,—whatever they were.'

'But I had not accepted his resignation,—as they say in the newspapers;—nor have I now.'

'You would still marry him?'

'I don't say that, Frank. This is an important business, and let us go through it steadily. I would certainly like to have him again at my feet. Whether I would deign to lift him up again is another thing. Is not that natural, after what he has done to me?'

'Woman's nature.'

'And I am a woman. Yes, Frank. I would have him again at my disposal,—and he is so. He is to write me a long letter; —so like a Government-man, isn't it? And he has told me already what he is to put into the letter. They always do, you know. He is to say that he'll marry me if I choose.'

'He has promised to say that?'

'When he said that he would come, I made up my mind that he should not go out of the house till he had promised that. He couldn't get out of it. What had I done?' Frank thought of the scene among the rocks. He did not, of course, allude to it, but Lizzie was not so reticent. 'As to what that old rogue saw down in Scotland, I don't care a bit about it, Frank. He has been up in London, and telling them all, no doubt. Nasty, dirty eavesdropper! But what does it come to? Psha! When he mentioned your name I silenced him at once. What could I have done, unless I had had some friend? At any rate, he is to ask me again in writing,—and then what shall I say?'

'You must consult your own heart.'

'No, Frank;—I need not do that. Why do you say so?'

'I know not what else to say.'

'A woman can marry without consulting her heart. Women do so every day. This man is a lord, and has a position. No doubt I despise him thoroughly,—utterly. I don't hate him, because he is not worth being hated.'

'And yet you would marry him?'

'I have not said so. I will tell you this truth, though, per-haps, you will say it is not feminine. I would fain marry some one. To be as I have been for the last two years is not a happy condition.'

'I would not marry a man I despised.'

'Nor would I,—willingly. He is honest and respectable; and in spite of all that has come and gone would, I think, behave well to a woman when she was once his wife. Of course, I would prefer to marry a man that I could love. But if that is impossible, Frank——'

'I thought that you had determined that you would have nothing to do with this lord.'

'I thought so too. Frank, you have known all that I have thought, and all that I have wished. You talk to me of marrying where my heart has been given. Is it possible that I should do so?'

'How am I to say?'

'Come, Frank, be true with me. I am forcing myself to speak truth to you. I think that between you and me, at any rate, there should be no words spoken that are not true. Frank, you know where my heart is.' As she said this, she stood over him, and laid her hand upon his shoulder. 'Will you answer me one question?'

'If I can, I will.'

'Are you engaged to marry Lucy Morris?'

'I am.'

'And you intend to marry her?' To this question he made no immediate answer. 'We are old enough now, Frank, to know that something more than what you call heart is wanted to make us happy when we marry. I will say nothing hard of Lucy, though she be my rival.'

'You can say nothing hard of her. She is perfect.'

'We will let that pass, though it is hardly kind of you, just at the present moment. Let her be perfect. Can you marry this perfection without a sixpence,—you that are in debt, and who never could save a sixpence in your life? Would it be for her good,—or for yours? You have done a foolish thing, sir, and you know that you must get out of it.'

'I know nothing of the kind.'

213

'You cannot marry Lucy Morris. That is the truth. My present need makes me bold. Frank, shall I be your wife? Such a marriage will not be without love, at any rate, on one side,—though there be utter indifference on the other!'

'You know I am not indifferent to you,' said he, with wicked weakness.

'Now, at any rate,' she continued, 'you must understand what must be my answer to Lord Fawn. It is you that must answer Lord Fawn. If my heart is to be broken, I may as well break it under his roof as another.'

'I have no roof to offer you,' he said.

'But I have one for you,' she said, throwing her arm round his neck. He bore her embrace for a minute, returning it with the pressure of his arm; and then, escaping from it, seized his hat and left her standing in the room.

CHAPTER LXIII
The Corsair is Afraid

ON the following morning,—Monday morning,—there appeared in one of the daily newspapers the paragraph of which Lady Linlithgow had spoken to Lucy Morris. 'We are given to understand,'—newspapers are very frequently given to understand,—'that a man well-known to the London police as an accomplished housebreaker, has been arrested in reference to the robbery which was effected on the 30th of January last at Lady Eustace's house in Hertford Street. No doubt the same person was concerned in the robbery of her ladyship's jewels at Carlisle on the night of the 8th of January. The mystery which has so long enveloped these two affairs, and which has been so discreditable to the metropolitan police, will now probably be cleared up.' There was not a word about Patience Crabstick in this; and, as Lizzie observed, the news brought by the policeman on Saturday night referred only to Patience, and said nothing of the arrest of any burglar. The ladies in Hertford Street scanned the sentence with the greatest care, and Mrs. Carbuncle was very angry because the house was said to be Lizzie's house. 'It wasn't my doing,' said Lizzie.

'The policeman came to you about it.'

'I didn't say a word to the man,—and I didn't want him to come.'

'I hope it will be all found out now,' said Lucinda.

'I wish it were all clean forgotten,' said Lizzie.

'It ought to be found out,' said Mrs. Carbuncle. 'But the police should be more careful in what they say. I suppose we shall all have to go before the magistrates again.'

Poor Lizzie felt that fresh trouble was certainly coming upon her. She had learned now that the crime for which she might be prosecuted and punished was that of perjury,—that even if everything was known, she could not be accused of stealing, and that if she could only get out of the way till the wrath of the magistrate and policemen should have evaporated, she might, possibly, escape altogether. At any rate, they could not take her income away from her. But how could she get out of the way, and how could she endure to be cross-examined, and looked at, and inquired into, by all those who would be concerned in the matter? She thought that, if only she could have arranged her matrimonial affairs before the bad day came upon her, she could have endured it better. If she might be allowed to see Lord George, she could ask for advice,—could ask for advice, not as she was always forced to do from her cousin, on a false statement of facts, but with everything known and declared.

On that very day Lord George came to Hertford Street. He had been there more than once, perhaps half a dozen times, since the robbery; but on all these occasions Lizzie had been in bed, and he had declined to visit her in her chamber. In fact, even Lord George had become somewhat afraid of her since he had been told the true story as to the necklace at Carlisle. That story he had heard from herself, and he had also heard from Mr. Benjamin some other little details as to her former life. Mr. Benjamin, whose very close attention had been drawn to the Eustace diamonds, had told Lord George how he had valued them at her ladyship's request, and had caused an iron case to be made for them, and how her ladyship had, on one occasion, endeavoured to sell the necklace to him. Mr. Benjamin, who certainly was intimate with Lord George, was very fond of talking about the diamonds, and had once suggested to his lordship that, were they to become his lordship's by marriage, he, Benjamin, might be willing to treat with his lordship. In regard to treating with her ladyship,—Mr. Benjamin acknowledged that he thought it would be too hazardous. Then came the robbery of the box, and Lord George was all astray. Mr. Benjamin was for a while equally astray, but neither friend believed in the other friend's innocence. That Lord George should suspect Mr. Benjamin was quite natural. Mr. Benjamin hardly knew what to think; —hardly gave Lord George credit for the necessary courage, skill, and energy. But at last, as he began to put two and two together, he divined the truth, and was enabled to set the docile Patience on the watch over her mistress's belongings. So it had been with Mr. Benjamin, who at last was able to satisfy Mr. Smiler and Mr. Cann that he had been no party to their cruel disappointment at Carlisle. How Lord George had learned the truth has been told;—the truth as to Lizzie's hiding the necklace under her pillow and bringing it up to London in her desk. But of the facts of the second robbery he knew nothing up to this morning. He almost suspected that Lizzie had herself again been at work,—and he was afraid of her. He had promised her that he would take care of her,— had, perhaps, said enough to make her believe that some day he would marry her. He hardly remembered what he had said; —but he was afraid of her. She was so wonderfully clever that, if he did not take care, she would get him into some mess from which he would be unable to extricate himself.

He had never whispered her secret to any one; and had still been at a loss about the second robbery, when he too saw the paragraph in the newspaper. He went direct to Scotland Yard and made inquiry there. His name had been so often used in the affair, that such inquiry from him was justified. 'Well, my lord; yes; we have found out something,' said Bunfit. 'Mr. Benjamin is off,*you know.'

'Benjamin off?'

'Cut the painter, my lord, and started.* But what's the good, now we has the wires?'

'And who were the thieves?'

'Ah, my lord, that's telling. Perhaps I don't know. Perhaps I do. Perhaps two or three of us knows. You'll hear all in good time, my lord.' Mr. Bunfit wished to appear communicative because he knew but little himself. Gager, in the meanest possible manner, had kept the matter very close; but the fact that Mr. Benjamin had started suddenly on foreign travel had become known to Mr. Bunfit.

Lord George had been very careful, asking no question about the necklace;—no question which would have shown that he knew that the necklace had been in Hertford Street when the robbery took place there; but it seemed to him now that the police must be aware that it was so. The arrest had been made because of the robbery in Hertford Street, and because of that arrest Mr. Benjamin had taken his departure. Mr. Benjamin was too big a man to have concerned himself deeply in the smaller matters which had then been stolen.

From Scotland Yard Lord George went direct to Hertford Street. He was in want of money, in want of a settled home, in want of a future income, and altogether unsatisfied with his present mode of life. Lizzie Eustace, no doubt, would take him,—unless she had told her secret to some other lover. To have his wife, immediately on her marriage, or even before it, arraigned for perjury, would not be pleasant. There was very much in the whole affair of which he would not be proud as he led his bride to the altar;—but a man does not expect to get four thousand pounds a year for nothing. Lord George, at any rate, did not conceive himself to be in a position to do so. Had there not been something crooked about Lizzie,—a screw loose, as people say,—she would never have been within his reach. There are men who always ride lame horses, and yet see as much of the hunting as others. Lord George, when he had begun to think that, after the tale which he had forced her to tell him, she had caused the diamonds to be stolen by her own maid out of her own desk, became almost afraid of her. But now, as he looked at the matter again and again, he believed that the second robbery had been genuine. He did not quite make up his mind, but he went to Hertford Street resolved to see her.

He asked for her, and was shown at once into her own sitting-room. 'So you have come at last,' she said.

'Yes;—I've come at last. It would not have done for me to come up to you when you were in bed. Those women down-stairs would have talked about it everywhere.'

'I suppose they would,' said Lizzie almost piteously.

'It wouldn't have been at all wise after all that has been said. People would have been sure to suspect that I had got the things out of your desk.'

'Oh no;—not that.'

'I wasn't going to run the risk, my dear.' His manner to her was anything but civil, anything but complimentary. If this was his Corsair humour, she was not sure that a Corsair might be agreeable to her. 'And now tell me what you know about this second robbery.'

'I know nothing, Lord George.'

'Oh yes, you do. You know something. You know, at any rate, that the diamonds were there.'

'Yes;—I know that.'

'And that they were taken?'

'Of course they were taken.'

'You are sure of that?' There was something in his manner absolutely insolent to her. Frank was affectionate, and even Lord Fawn treated her with deference. 'Because, you know, you have been very clever. To tell you the truth, I did not think at first that they had been really stolen. It might, you know, have been a little game to get them out of your own hands,—between you and your maid.'

'I don't know what you take me for, Lord George.'

'I take you for a lady who, for a long time, got the better of the police and the magistrates, and who managed to shift all the trouble off your own shoulders on to those of other people. You have heard that they have taken one of the thieves?'

'And they have got the girl.'

'Have they? I didn't know that. That scoundrel, Benjamin, has levanted*too.'

'Levanted!' said Lizzie, raising both her hands.

'Not an hour too soon, my lady. And now what do you mean to do?'

'What ought I to do?'

'Of course the whole truth will come out.'

'Must it come out?'

'Not a doubt of that. How can it be helped?'

'You won't tell. You promised that you would not.'

'Psha;—promised! If they put me in a witness-box of course I must tell. When you come to this kind of work, promises don't go for much. I don't know that they ever do. What is a broken promise?'

'It's a story,' said Lizzie, in innocent amazement.

'And what was it you told when you were upon your oath at Carlisle; and again when the magistrate came here?'

'Oh, Lord George;—how unkind you are to me!'

'Patience Crabstick will tell it all, without any help from me. Don't you see that the whole thing must be known? She'll say where the diamonds were found;—and how did they come there, if you didn't put them there? As for telling, there'll be telling enough. You've only two things to do.'

'What are they, Lord George?'

'Go off, like Mr. Benjamin; or else make a clean breast of it. Send for John Eustace and tell him the whole. For his brother's sake he'll make the best of it. It will all be published, and then, perhaps, there will be an end of it.'

'I couldn't do that, Lord George!' said Lizzie, bursting into tears.

'You ask me, and I can only tell you what I think. That

you should be able to keep the history of the diamonds a secret, does not seem to me to be upon the cards. No doubt people who are rich, and are connected with rich people, and have great friends,—who are what the world call swells,— have great advantages over their inferiors when they get into trouble. You are the widow of a baronet, and you have an uncle a bishop, and another a dean, and a countess for an aunt. You have a brother-in-law and a first-cousin in Parliament, and your father was an admiral. The other day you were engaged to marry a peer.'

'Oh yes,' said Lizzie, 'and Lady Glencora Palliser is my particular friend.'

'She is; is she? So much the better. Lady Glencora, no doubt, is a very swell among swells.'

'The Duke of Omnium would do anything for me,' said Lizzie with enthusiasm.

'If you were nobody, you would, of course, be indicted for perjury, and would go to prison. As it is, if you will tell all your story to one of your swell friends, I think it very likely that you may be pulled through. I should say that Mr. Eustace, or your cousin Greystock, would be the best.'

'Why couldn't you do it? You know it all. I told you because,—because,—because I thought you would be the kindest to me.'

'You told me, my dear, because you thought it would not matter much with me, and I appreciate the compliment. I can do nothing for you. I am not near enough to those who wear wigs.'

Lizzie did not above half understand him,—did not at all understand him when he spoke of those who wore wigs, and was quite dark to his irony about her great friends;—but she did perceive that he was in earnest in recommending her to confess. She thought about it for a moment in silence, and the more she thought the more she felt that she could not do it. Had he not suggested a second alternative,—that she should go off, like Mr. Benjamin? It might be possible that she should go off, and yet be not quite like Mr. Benjamin. In that case ought she not to go under the protection of her Corsair? Would not that be the proper way of going? 'Might I not go abroad,—just for a time?' she asked.

'And so let it blow over?'

'Just so, you know.'

'It is possible that you might,' he said. 'Not that it would blow over altogether. Everybody would know it. It is too late now to stop the police, and if you meant to be off, you should be off at once;—to-day or to-morrow.'

'Oh dear!'

'Indeed, there's no saying whether they will let you go. You could start now, this moment;—and if you were at Dover could get over to France. But when once it is known that you had the necklace all that time in your own desk, any magistrate, I imagine, could stop you. You'd better have some lawyer you can trust;—not that blackguard Mopus.'

Lord George had certainly brought her no comfort. When he told her that she might go at once if she chose, she remembered, with a pang of agony, that she had already overdrawn her account at the bankers. She was the actual possessor of an income of four thousand pounds a year, and now, in her terrible strait, she could not stir because she had not money with which to travel. Had all things been well with her, she could, no doubt, have gone to her bankers and have arranged this little difficulty. But as it was, she could not move, because her purse was empty.

Lord George sat looking at her, and thinking whether he would make the plunge and ask her to be his wife,—with all her impediments and drawbacks about her. He had been careful to reduce her to such a condition of despair, that she would, undoubtedly, have accepted him, so that she might have some one to lean upon in her trouble;—but, as he looked at her, he doubted. She was such a mass of deceit, that he was afraid of her. She might say that she would marry him, and then, when the storm was over, refuse to keep her word. She might be in debt,—almost to any amount. She might be already married, for anything that he knew. He did know that she was subject to all manner of penalties for what she had done. He looked at her, and told himself that she was very pretty. But, in spite of her beauty, his judgment went against her. He did not dare to share even his boat with so dangerous a fellow-passenger. 'That's my advice,' he said, getting up from his chair.

'Are you going?'

'Well;—yes; I don't know what else I can do for you.'

'You are so unkind!' He shrugged his shoulders, just touched her hand, and left the room without saying another word to her.

CHAPTER LXIV
Lizzie's Last Scheme

LIZZIE, when she was left alone, was very angry with the Corsair,—in truth, more sincerely angry than she had ever been with any of her lovers, or, perhaps, with any human being. Sincere, true, burning wrath was not the fault to which she was most exposed. She could snap and snarl, and hate, and say severe things; she could quarrel, and fight, and be malicious;—but to be full of real wrath was uncommon with her. Now she was angry. She had been civil, more than civil, to Lord George. She had opened her house to him, and her heart. She had told him her great secret. She had implored his protection. She had thrown herself into his arms. And now he had rejected her. That he should have been rough to her was only in accordance with the poetical attributes which she had attributed to him. But his roughness should have been streaked with tenderness. He should not have left her roughly. In the whole interview he had not said a loving word to her. He had given her advice,—which might be good or bad,— but he had given it as to one whom he despised. He had spoken to her throughout the interview exactly as he might have spoken to Sir Griffin Tewett. She could not analyse her feelings thoroughly, but she felt, that because of what had passed between them, by reason of his knowledge of her secret, he had robbed her of all that observance which was due to her as a woman and a lady. She had been roughly used before,—by people of inferior rank, who had seen through her ways. Andrew Gowran had insulted her. Patience Crabstick had argued with her. Benjamin, the employer of thieves, had been familiar with her. But hitherto, in what she was pleased to call her own set, she had always been treated with that courtesy which ladies seldom fail to receive. She understood it all. She knew how much of mere word-service there often is in such complimentary usage. But, nevertheless, it implies respect, and an acknowledgement of the position of her who is so respected. Lord George had treated her as one schoolboy treats another.

And he had not spoken to her one word of love. Love will excuse roughness. Spoken love will palliate even spoken roughness. Had he once called her his own Lizzie, he might have scolded her as he pleased,—might have abused her to the top of his bent.* But as there had been nothing of the manner of a gentleman to a lady, so also had there been nothing of the lover to his mistress. That dream was over. Lord George was no longer a Corsair, but a brute.

But what should she do? Even a brute may speak truth. She was to have gone to a theatre that evening with Mrs. Carbuncle, but she stayed at home thinking over her position. She heard nothing throughout the day from the police; and she made up her mind, that, unless she were stopped by the police, she would go to Scotland on the day but one following. She thought that she was sure that she would do so; but, of course, she must be guided by events as they occurred. She wrote, however, to Miss Macnulty saying that she would come, and she told Mrs. Carbuncle of her proposed journey as that lady was leaving the house for the theatre. On the following morning, however, news came which again made her journey doubtful. There was another paragraph in the newspaper about the robbery, acknowledging the former paragraph to have been in some respect erroneous. The

'accomplished housebreaker' had not been arrested. A con-
federate of the 'accomplished housebreaker' was in the hands
of the police, and the police were on the track of the 'accomplished housebreaker' himself. Then there was a line or two
alluding in a very mysterious way to the disappearance of a
certain jeweller. Taking it altogether, Lizzie thought that
there was ground for hope,—and that, at any rate, there
would be delay. She would, perhaps, put off going to Scotland
for yet a day or two. Was it not necessary that she should
wait for Lord Fawn's answer; and would it not be incumbent
on her cousin Frank to send her some account of himself after
the abrupt manner in which he had left her?

If in real truth she should be driven to tell her story to any
one,—and she began to think that she was so driven,—she
would tell it to him. She believed more in his regard for her
than that of any other human being. She thought that he
would, in truth, have been devoted to her, had he not become
entangled with that wretched little governess. And she thought
that if he could see his way out of that scrape, he would marry
her even yet,—would marry her, and be good to her, so that
her dream of a poetical phase of life should not be altogether
dissolved. After all, the diamonds were her own. She had not
stolen them. When perplexed in the extreme by magistrates
and policemen, with nobody near her whom she trusted to
give her advice,—for Lizzie now of course declared to herself
that she had never for a moment trusted the Corsair,—she
had fallen into an error, and said what was not true. As she
practised it before the glass, she thought that she could tell
her story in a becoming manner, with becoming tears, to
Frank Greystock. And, were it not for Lucy Morris, she
thought that he would take her with all her faults and all her
burthens.

As for Lord Fawn, she knew well enough that, let him write
what he would, and renew his engagement in what most
formal manner might be possible, he would be off again when
he learned the facts as to that night at Carlisle. She had
brought him to succumb, because he could no longer justify

his treatment of her by reference to the diamonds. But when once all the world should know that she had twice perjured herself, his justification would be complete,—and his escape would be certain. She would use his letter simply to achieve that revenge which she had promised herself. Her effort,— her last final effort must be made to secure the hand and heart of her cousin Frank. 'Ah, 'tis his heart I want!' she said to herself.

She must settle something before she went to Scotland,—if there was anything that could be settled. If she could only get a promise from Frank before all her treachery had been exposed, he probably would remain true to his promise. He would not desert her as Lord Fawn had done. Then, after much thinking of it, she resolved upon a scheme, which, of all her schemes, was the wickedest. Whatever it might cost her, she would create a separation between Frank Greystock and Lucy Morris. Having determined upon this, she wrote to Lucy, asking her to call in Hertford Street at a certain hour.

'DEAR LUCY,

'I particularly want to see you,—on business. Pray come to me at twelve to-morrow. I will send the carriage for you, and it will take you back again. Pray do this. We used to love one another, and I am sure I love you still.

'Your affectionate old friend,

'LIZZIE.'

As a matter of course Lucy went to her. Lizzie, before the interview, studied the part she was to play with all possible care,—even to the words which she was to use. The greeting was at first kindly, for Lucy had almost forgotten the bribe that had been offered to her, and had quite forgiven it. Lizzie Eustace never could be dear to her; but,—so Lucy had thought during her happiness,—this former friend of hers was the cousin of the man who was to be her husband, and was dear to him. Of course she had forgiven the offence. 'And now, dear, I want to ask you a question,' Lizzie said;

'or rather, perhaps, not a question. I can do it better than that. I think that my cousin Frank once talked of,—of making you his wife.' Lucy answered not a word, but she trembled in every limb, and the colour came to her face. 'Was it not so, dear?'

'What if it was? I don't know why you should ask me any question like that, about myself.'

'Is he not my cousin?'

'Yes,—he is your cousin. Why don't you ask him? You see him every day, I suppose?'

'Nearly every day.'

'Why do you send for me, then?'

'It is so hard to tell you, Lucy. I have sent to you in good faith, and in love. I could have gone to you,—only for the old vulture, who would not have let us have a word in peace. I do see him—constantly. And I love him dearly.'

'That is nothing to me,' said Lucy. Anybody hearing them, and not knowing them, would have said that Lucy's manner was harsh in the extreme.

'He has told me everything.' Lizzie, when she said this, paused, looking at her victim. 'He has told me things which he could not mention to you. It was only yesterday,—the day before yesterday,—that he was speaking to me of his debts. I offered to place all that I have at his disposal, so as to free him, but he would not take my money.'

'Of course he would not.'

'Not my money alone. Then he told me that he was engaged to you. He had never told me before, but yet I knew it. It all came out then. Lucy, though he is engaged to you, it is me that he loves.'

'I don't believe it,' said Lucy.

'You can't make me angry, Lucy, because my heart bleeds for you.'

'Nonsense! trash! I don't want your heart to bleed. I don't believe you've got a heart. You've got money; I know that.'

'And he has got none. If I did not love him, why should I wish to give him all that I have? Is not that disinterested?'

'No. You are always thinking of yourself. You couldn't be disinterested.'

'And of whom are you thinking? Are you doing the best for him,—a man in his position, without money, ambitious, sure to succeed if want of money does not stop him,—in wishing him to marry a girl with nothing? Cannot I do more for him than you can?'

'I could work for him on my knees, I love him so truly!'

'Would that do him any service? He cannot marry you. Does he ever see you? Does he write to you as though you were to be his wife? Do you not know that it is all over?— that it must be over? It is impossible that he should marry you. But if you will give him back his word, he shall be my husband, and shall have all that I possess. Now, let us see who loves him best!'

'I do!' said Lucy.

'How will you show it?'

'There is no need that I should show it. He knows it. The only one in the world to whom I wish it to be known, knows it already well enough. Did you send for me for this?'

'Yes;—for this.'

'It is for him to tell me the tidings;—not for you. You are nothing to me;—nothing. And what you say to me now is all for yourself,—not for him. But it is true that he does not see me. It is true that he does not write to me. You may tell him from me,—for I cannot write to him myself,—that he may do whatever is best for him. But if you tell him that I do not love him better than all the world, you will lie to him. And if you say that he loves you better than he does me, that also will be a lie. I know his heart.'

'But Lucy——'

'I will hear no more. He can do as he pleases. If money be more to him than love and honesty, let him marry you. I shall never trouble him; he may be sure of that. As for you, Lizzie, I hope that we may never meet again.'

She would not get into the Eustace-Carbuncle carriage, which was waiting for her at the door, but walked back to

Bruton Street. She did not doubt but that it was all over with her now. That Lizzie Eustace was an inveterate liar, she knew well; but she did believe that the liar had on this occasion been speaking truth. Lady Fawn was not a liar, and Lady Fawn had told her the same. And, had she wanted more evidence, did not her lover's conduct give it? 'It is because I am poor,' she said to herself,—'for I know well that he loves me!'

CHAPTER LXV

Tribute

LIZZIE put off her journey to Scotland from day to day, though her cousin Frank continually urged upon her the expediency of going. There were various reasons, he said, why she should go. Her child was there, and it was proper that she should be with her child. She was living at present with people whose reputation did not stand high,—and as to whom all manner of evil reports were flying about the town. It was generally thought,—so said Frank,—that that Lord George de Bruce Carruthers had assisted Mr. Benjamin in stealing the diamonds, and Frank himself did not hesitate to express his belief in the accusation. 'Oh no, that cannot be,' said Lizzie, trembling. But, though she rejected the supposition, she did not reject it very firmly. 'And then, you know,' continued Lizzie, 'I never see him. I have actually only set eyes on him once since the second robbery, and then just for a minute. Of course, I used to know him,—down at Portray,— but now we are strangers.' Frank went on with his objections. He declared that the manner in which Mrs. Carbuncle had got up the match between Lucinda Roanoke and Sir Griffin was shameful,—all the world was declaring that it was shameful,—that she had not a penny, that the girl was an adventurer, and that Sir Griffin was an obstinate, pig-headed ruined idiot. It was expedient on every account that Lizzie should take herself away from that 'lot'.* The answer that Lizzie desired to make was very simple. Let me go as your betrothed bride, and I will start to-morrow,—to Scotland or elsewhere, as you may direct. Let that little affair be settled, and I shall be quite as willing to get out of London as you can be to send me. But I am in such a peck of troubles that something must be settled. And as it seems that after all the police are still astray about the necklace, perhaps I needn't run away from them for a little while even yet. She did not say this. She did not even in so many words make the first proposition. But she did endeavour to make Frank understand that she would obey his dictation if he would earn the right to dictate. He either did not or would not understand her, and then she became angry with him,—or pretended to be angry. 'Really, Frank,' she said, 'you are hardly fair to me.'

'In what way am I unfair?'

'You come here and abuse all my friends, and tell me to go here and go there, just as though I were a child. And,—and,—and——'

'And what, Lizzie?'

'You know what I mean. You are one thing one day and one another. I hope Miss Lucy Morris was quite well when you last heard from her.'

'You have no right to speak to me of Lucy,—at least, not in disparagement.'

'You are treating her very badly, you know that.'

'I am.'

'Then why don't you give it up? Why don't you let her have her chances,—to do what she can with them? You know very well that you can't marry her. You know that you ought not to have asked her. You talk of Miss Roanoke and Sir Griffin Tewett. There are people quite as bad as Sir Griffin, —or Mrs. Carbuncle either. Don't suppose I am speaking for myself. I've given up all that idle fancy long ago. I shall never marry a second time myself. I have made up my mind to that. I have suffered too much already.' Then she burst into tears.

He dried her tears and comforted her, and forgave all the injurious things she had said of him. It is almost impossible for a man,—a man under forty and unmarried, and who is not a philosopher,—to have familiar and affectionate intercourse with a beautiful young woman, and carry it on as he might do with a friend of the other sex. In his very heart Greystock despised this woman; he had told himself over and over again that were there no Lucy in the case he would not marry her, that she was affected, unreal,—and, in fact, a liar in every word and look and motion which came from her with premeditation. Judging, not from her own account, but from circumstances as he saw them and such evidence as had reached him, he did not condemn her in reference to the diamonds. He had never for a moment conceived that she had secreted them. He acquitted her altogether from those special charges which had been widely circulated against her; but, nevertheless, he knew her to be heartless and bad. He had told himself a dozen times that it would be well for him that she should be married and taken out of his hands. And yet he loved her after a fashion, and was prone to sit near her, and was fool enough to be flattered by her caresses. When she would lay her hand on his arm, a thrill of pleasure went through him. And yet he would willingly have seen any decent man take her and marry her, making a bargain that he should never see her again. Young or old, men are apt to become Merlins when they encounter Viviens.* On this occasion he left her, disgusted indeed, but not having told her that he was disgusted. 'Come again, Frank, to-morrow, won't you?' she said. He made her no promise as he went, nor had she expected it. He had left her quite abruptly the other day, and he now went away almost in the same fashion. But she was not surprised. She understood that the task she had in hand was one very difficult to be accomplished,—and she did perceive, in some dark way, that, good as her acting was, it was not quite good enough. Lucy held her ground because she was real. You may knock about a diamond, and not even scratch it; whereas paste in rough usage betrays itself. Lizzie, with all her self-assuring protestations, knew that she was paste, and knew that Lucy was real stone. Why could she not force herself to act a little better, so that the paste*might be as good as the stone,—might at least seem to be as good? 'If he despises me now, what will he say when he finds it all out?' she asked herself.

As for Frank Greystock himself, though he had quite made up his mind about Lizzie Eustace, he was still in doubt about the other girl. At the present moment he was making over two thousand pounds a year, and yet was more in debt now than he had been a year ago. When he attempted to look at his affairs, he could not even remember what had become of his money. He did not gamble. He had no little yacht, costing him about six hundred a year. He kept one horse in London, and one only. He had no house. And when he could spare time from his work, he was generally entertained at the houses of his friends. And yet from day to day his condition seemed to become worse and worse. It was true that he never thought of half-a-sovereign; that in calling for wine at his club he was never influenced by the cost; that it seemed to him quite rational to keep a cab waiting for him half the day; that in going or coming he never calculated expense; that in giving an order to a tailor he never dreamed of anything beyond his own comfort. Nevertheless, when he recounted with pride his great economies, reminding himself that he, a successful man, with a large income and no family, kept neither hunters, nor yacht, nor moor, and that he did not gamble, he did think it very hard that he should be embarrassed. But he was embarrassed, and in that condition could it be right for him to marry a girl without a shilling?

In these days Mrs. Carbuncle was very urgent with her friend not to leave London till after the marriage. Lizzie had given no promise,—had only been induced to promise that the loan of one hundred and fifty pounds should not be held to have any bearing on the wedding present to be made to Lucinda. That could be got on credit from Messrs. Harter and Benjamin; for though Mr. Benjamin was absent,—on a little tour through Europe in search of precious stones in the cheap markets, old Mr. Harter suggested,—the business went on the same as ever. There was a good deal of consultation about the present, and Mrs. Carbuncle at last decided, no doubt with the concurrence of Miss Roanoke, that it should consist simply of silver forks and spoons,—real silver as far as the money would go. Mrs. Carbuncle herself went with her friend to select the articles,—as to which, perhaps, we shall do her no injustice in saying that a ready sale, should such a lamentable occurrence ever become necessary, was one of the objects which she had in view. Mrs. Carbuncle's investigations as to the quality of the metal quite won Mr. Harter's respect; and it will probably be thought that she exacted no more than justice,—seeing that the thing had become a matter of bargain,—in demanding that the thirty-five pounds should be stretched to fifty, because the things were bought on long credit. 'My dear Lizzie,' Mrs. Carbuncle said, 'the dear girl won't have an ounce more than she would have got, had you gone into another sort of shop with thirty-five sovereigns in your hand.' Lizzie growled, but Mrs. Carbuncle's final argument was conclusive. 'I'll tell you what we'll do,' said she; 'we'll take thirty pounds down in ready money.' There was no answer to be made to so reasonable a proposition.

The presents to be made to Lucinda were very much thought of in Hertford Street at this time, and Lizzie,—independently of any feeling that she might have as to her own contribution,—did all she could to assist the collection of tribute. It was quite understood that as a girl can only be married once,—for a widow's chance in such matters amounts to but little,—everything should be done to gather toll from the tax-payers of society. It was quite fair on such an occasion that men should be given to understand that something worth having was expected,—no trumpery thirty-shilling piece of crockery, no insignificant glass bottle, or fantastic paper-knife of no real value whatever, but got up just to put money into the tradesmen's hands. To one or two elderly gentlemen upon whom Mrs. Carbuncle had smiled, she ventured to suggest in plain words that a cheque was the most convenient cadeau. 'What do you say to a couple of sovereigns?' one sarcastic old gentleman replied, upon whom probably Mrs. Carbuncle had not smiled enough. She laughed and congratulated her sarcastic friend upon his joke;—but the two sovereigns were left upon the table, and went to swell the spoil.

'You must do something handsome for Lucinda,' Lizzie said to her cousin.

'What do you call handsome?'

'You are a bachelor and a Member of Parliament. Say fifteen pounds.'

'I'll be —— if I do!' said Frank, who was beginning to be very much disgusted with the house in Hertford Street. 'There's a five-pound note, and you may do what you please with it.' Lizzie gave over the five-pound note,—the identical bit of paper that had come from Frank; and Mrs. Carbuncle, no doubt, did do what she pleased with it.

There was almost a quarrel because Lizzie, after much consideration, declared that she did not see her way to get a present from the Duke of Omnium. She had talked so much to Mrs. Carbuncle about the duke, that Mrs. Carbuncle was almost justified in making the demand. 'It isn't the value, you know,' said Mrs. Carbuncle; 'neither I nor Lucinda would think of that; but it would look so well to have the dear duke's name on something.' Lizzie declared that the duke was unapproachable on such subjects. 'There you're wrong,' said Mrs. Carbuncle. 'I happen to know there is nothing his grace likes so much as giving wedding presents.' This was the harder upon Lizzie as she actually did succeed in saying such kind things about Lucinda, that Lady Glencora sent Miss Roanoke the prettiest smelling-bottle in the world. 'You don't mean to say you've given a present to the future Lady Tewett,' said Madame Max Goesler to her friend. 'Why not? Sir Griffin can't hurt me. When one begins to be good-natured, why shouldn't one be good-natured all round?' Madame Max remarked that it might, perhaps, be preferable to put an end to good-nature altogether. 'There I daresay you're right, my dear,' said Lady Glencora. 'I've long felt that making presents means nothing. Only if one has a lot of money and people like it, why shouldn't one? I've made so many to people I hardly ever saw that one more to Lady Tewett can't hurt.'

Perhaps the most wonderful affair in that campaign was the spirited attack which Mrs. Carbuncle made on a certain Mrs. Hanbury Smith, who for the last six or seven years had not been among Mrs. Carbuncle's more intimate friends. Mrs. Hanbury Smith lived with her husband in Paris, but before her marriage had known Mrs. Carbuncle in London. Her father, Mr. Bunbury Jones, had, from certain causes, chosen to show certain civilities to Mrs. Carbuncle just at the period of his daughter's marriage, and Mrs. Carbuncle being perhaps, at that moment, well supplied with ready money, had presented a marriage present. From that to this present day Mrs. Carbuncle had seen nothing of Mrs. Hanbury Smith, nor of Mr. Bunbury Jones, but she was not the woman to waste the return-value of such a transaction. A present so given was seed sown in the earth,—seed, indeed, that could not be expected to give back twenty-fold, or even ten-fold, but still seed from which a crop should be expected. So she wrote to Mrs. Hanbury Smith, explaining that her darling niece Lucinda was about to be married to Sir Griffin Tewett, and that, as she had no child of her own, Lucinda was the same to her as a daughter. And then, lest there might be any want of comprehension, she expressed her own assurance that her friend would be glad to have an opportunity of reciprocating the feelings which had been evinced on the occasion of her own marriage. 'It is no good mincing matters now-a-days,' Mrs. Carbunc' would have said, had any friend pointed out to her that she was taking strong measures in the exaction of toll. 'People have come to understand that a spade is a spade, and £10, £10,' she would have said. Had Mrs. Hanbury Smith not noticed the application, there might, perhaps, have been an end of it, but she was silly enough to send over from Paris a little trumpery bit of finery, bought in the Palais

Royal for ten francs. Whereupon Mrs. Carbuncle wrote the following letter;—

'MY DEAR MRS. HANBURY SMITH,

'Lucinda has received your little brooch, and is much obliged to you for thinking of her; but you must remember that, when you were married, I sent you a bracelet which cost £10. If I had a daughter of my own, I should, of course, expect that she would reap the benefit of this on her marriage;—and my niece is the same to me as a daughter. I think that this is quite understood now among people in society. Lucinda will be disappointed much if you do not send her what she thinks she has a right to expect. Of course you can deduct the brooch if you please.

'Yours very sincerely,
'JANE CARBUNCLE.'

Mr. Hanbury Smith was something of a wag, and caused his wife to write back as follows;—

'DEAR MRS. CARBUNCLE,

'I quite acknowledge the reciprocity system, but don't think it extends to descendants,—certainly not to nieces. I acknowledge, too, the present quoted at £10. I thought it had been £7 10s.'—'The nasty mean creature,' said Mrs. Carbuncle, when showing the correspondence to Lizzie, 'must have been to the tradesman to inquire! The price named was £10, but I got £2 10s. off for ready money.'—'At your second marriage I will do what is needful; but I can assure you I haven't recognised nieces with any of my friends.

'Yours very truly,
'CAROLINE HANBURY SMITH.'

The correspondence was carried no further, for not even can a Mrs. Carbuncle exact payment of such a debt in any established court; but she inveighed bitterly against the meanness of Mrs. Smith, telling the story openly, and never feeling that she told it against herself. In her set it was generally thought that she had done quite right.

She managed better with old Mr. Cabob, who had certainly received many of Mrs. Carbuncle's smiles, and who was very rich. Mr. Cabob did as he was desired, and sent a cheque,—a cheque for £20; and added a message that he hoped Miss Roanoke would buy with it any little thing that she liked. Miss Roanoke,—or her aunt for her,—liked a thirty-guinea ring, and bought it, having the bill for the balance sent in to Mr. Cabob. Mr. Cabob, who probably knew that he must pay well for his smiles, never said anything about it.

Lady Eustace went into all this work, absolutely liking it. She had felt nothing of anger even as regarded her own contribution,—much as she had struggled to reduce the amount. People, she felt, ought to be sharp;—and it was nice to look at pretty things, and to be cunning about them. She would have applied to the Duke of Omnium had she dared, and was very triumphant when she got the smelling-bottle from Lady Glencora. But Lucinda herself took no part whatever in all these things. Nothing that Mrs. Carbuncle could say would induce her to take any interest in them, or even in the trousseau, which, without reference to expense, was being supplied chiefly on the very indifferent credit of Sir Griffin. What Lucinda had to say about the matter was said solely to her aunt. Neither Lady Eustace, nor Lord George, nor even the maid who dressed her, heard any of her complaints. But complain she did, and that with terrible energy. 'What is the use of it, Aunt Jane? I shall never have a house to put them into.'

'What nonsense, my dear! Why shouldn't you have a house as well as others?'

'And if I had, I should never care for them. I hate them. What does Lady Glencora Palliser or Lord Fawn care for me?' Even Lord Fawn had been put under requisition, and had sent a little box full of stationery.

'They are worth money, Lucinda; and when a girl marries she always gets them.'

'Yes;—and when they come from people who love her, and who pour them into her lap with kisses, because she has given herself to a man she loves, then it must be nice. Oh,—

if I were marrying a poor man, and a poor friend had given me a gridiron to help me to cook my husband's dinner, how I could have valued it!'

'I don't know that you like poor things and poor people better than anybody else,' said Aunt Jane.

'I don't like anything or anybody,' said Lucinda.

'You had better take the good things that come to you, then; and not grumble. How I have worked to get all this arranged for you, and now what thanks have I?'

'You'll find you have worked for very little, Aunt Jane. I shall never marry the man yet.' This, however, had been said so often that Aunt Jane thought nothing of the threat.

CHAPTER LXVI

The Aspirations of Mr. Emilius

IT was acknowledged by Mrs. Carbuncle very freely that in the matter of tribute no one behaved better than Mr. Emilius, the fashionable foreign ci-devant Jew preacher, who still drew great congregations in the neighbourhood of Mrs. Carbuncle's house. Mrs. Carbuncle, no doubt, attended regularly at Mr. Emilius's church, and had taken a sitting for thirteen Sundays at something like ten shillings a Sunday. But she had not as yet paid the money, and Mr. Emilius was well aware that if his tickets were not paid for in advance, there would be considerable defalcations in his income. He was, as a rule, very particular as to such payments, and would not allow a name to be put on a sitting till the money had reached his pockets; but with Mrs. Carbuncle he had descended to no such commercial accuracy. Mrs. Carbuncle had seats for three,—for one of which Lady Eustace paid her share in advance,—in the midst of the very best pews in the most conspicuous part of the house,—and hardly a word had been said to her about money. And now there came to them from Mr. Emilius the prettiest little gold salver that ever was seen.

'I send Messrs. Clerico's docket,' wrote Mr. Emilius, 'as Miss Roanoke may like to know the quality of the metal.' 'Ah,' said Mrs. Carbuncle inspecting the little dish, and putting two and two together; 'he's got it cheap, no doubt,—at the place where they commissioned him to buy the plate and candlesticks for the church; but at £3 16s. 3d. the gold is worth nearly twenty pounds.' Mr. Emilius no doubt had had his outing in the autumn through the instrumentality of Mrs. Carbuncle's kindness; but that was past and gone, and such lavish gratitude for a past favour could hardly be expected from Mr. Emilius. 'I'll be hanged if he isn't after Portray Castle,' said Mrs. Carbuncle to herself.

Mr. Emilius was after Portray Castle, and had been after Portray Castle in a silent, not very confident, but yet not altogether hopeless, manner ever since he had seen the glories of that place, and learned something of truth as to the widow's income. Mrs. Carbuncle was led to her conclusion not simply by the wedding present, but in part also by the diligence displayed by Mr. Emilius in removing the doubts which had got abroad respecting his condition in life. He assured Mrs. Carbuncle that he had never been married. Shortly after his ordination, which had been effected under the hands of that great and good man the late Bishop of Jerusalem, he had taken to live with him a lady who was—, Mrs. Carbuncle did not quite recollect who the lady was, but remembered that she was connected in some way with a step-mother of Mr. Emilius who lived in Bohemia. This lady had for awhile kept house for Mr. Emilius;—but ill-natured things had been said, and Mr. Emilius, having respect to his cloth, had sent the poor lady back to Bohemia. The consequence was that he now lived in a solitude which was absolute, and, as Mr. Emilius added, somewhat melancholy. All this Mr. Emilius explained very fully, not to Lizzie herself, but to Mrs. Carbuncle. If Lady Eustace chose to entertain such a suitor, why should he not come? It was nothing to Mrs. Carbuncle.

Lizzie laughed when she was told that she might add the reverend gentleman to the list of her admirers. 'Don't you remember,' she said, 'how we used to chaff Miss Macnulty about him?'

'I knew better than that,' replied Mrs. Carbuncle.

'There is no saying what a man may be after,' said Lizzie, 'I didn't know but what he might have thought that Macnulty's connections would increase his congregation.'

'He's after you, my dear, and your income. He can manage a congregation for himself.'

Lizzie was very civil to him, but it would be unjust to her to say that she gave him any encouragement. It is quite the proper thing for a lady to be on intimate, and even on affectionate, terms with her favourite clergyman, and Lizzie certainly had intercourse with no clergyman who was a greater favourite with her than Mr. Emilius. She had a dean for an uncle, and a bishop for an uncle-in-law; but she was at no pains to hide her contempt for these old fogies of the Church. 'They preach now and then in the cathedral,' she said to Mr. Emilius, 'and everybody takes the opportunity of going to sleep.' Mr. Emilius was very much amused at this description of the eloquence of the dignitaries. It was quite natural to him that people should go to sleep in church who take no trouble in seeking eloquent preachers. 'Ah,' he said, 'the Church in England, which is my Church,—the Church which I love,—is beautiful. She is as a maiden, all glorious with fine raiment.* But alas! she is mute. She does not sing. She has no melody. But the time cometh in which she shall sing. I, myself,—I am a poor singer in the great choir.' In saying which Mr. Emilius, no doubt, intended to allude to his eloquence as a preacher.

He was a man who could listen as well as sing, and he was very careful to hear well that which was being said in public about Lady Eustace and her diamonds. He had learned thoroughly what was her condition in reference to the Portray estate, and was rejoiced rather than otherwise to find that she enjoyed only a life-interest in the property. Had the thing been better than it was, it would have been the further removed from his reach. And in the same way, when rumours reached him prejudicial to Lizzie in respect of the diamonds, he perceived that such prejudice might work weal for him. A gentleman once, on ordering a mackerel for dinner, was told that a fresh mackerel would come to a shilling. He could have a stale mackerel for sixpence. 'Then bring me a stale mackerel,' said the gentleman. Mr. Emilius coveted fish, but was aware that his position did not justify him in expecting the best fish on the market. The Lord Fawns and the Frank Greystocks of the world would be less likely to covet Lizzie, should she, by any little indiscretion, have placed herself under a temporary cloud. Mr. Emilius had carefully observed the heavens, and knew how quickly such clouds will disperse themselves when they are tinged with gold. There was nothing which Lizzie had done, or would be likely to do, which could materially affect her income. It might indeed be possible that the Eustaces should make her pay for the necklace; but, even in that case, there would be quite enough left for that modest, unambitious comfort which Mr. Emilius desired. It was by preaching, and not by wealth, that he must make himself known in the world!—but for a preacher to have a pretty wife with a title and a good income,—and a castle in Scotland,—what an Elysium it would be! In such a condition he would envy no dean, no bishop,—no archbishop! He thought a great deal about it, and saw no positive bar to his success.

She told him that she was going to Scotland. 'Not immediately!' he exclaimed.

'My little boy is there,' she said.

'But why should not your little boy be here? Surely, for people who can choose, the great centre of the world offers attractions which cannot be found in secluded spots.'

'I love seclusion,' said Lizzie, with rapture.

'Ah; yes; I can believe that.' Mr. Emilius had himself witnessed the seclusion of Portray Castle, and had heard, when there, many stories of the Ayrshire hunting. 'It is your nature;—but, dear Lady Eustace, will you allow me to say that our nature is implanted in us in accordance with the Fall?'

'Do you mean to say that it is wicked to like to be in Scotland better than in this giddy town?'

'I say nothing about wicked, Lady Eustace; but this I do say, that nature alone will not lead us always aright. It is good to be at Portray part of the year, no doubt; but are there not blessings in such a congregation of humanity as this London which you cannot find at Portray?'

'I can hear you preach, Mr. Emilius, certainly.'

'I hope that is something, too, Lady Eustace;—otherwise a great many people who kindly come to hear me must sadly waste their time. And your example to the world around;— is it not more serviceable amidst the crowds of London than in the solitudes of Scotland? There is more good to be done, Lady Eustace, by living among our fellow-creatures than by deserting them. Therefore I think you should not go to Scotland before August, but should have your little boy brought to you here.'

'The air of his native mountains is everything to my child,' said Lizzie. The child had, in fact, been born at Bobsborough, but that probably would make no real difference.

'You cannot wonder that I should plead for your stay,' said Mr. Emilius, throwing all his soul into his eyes. 'How dark would everything be to me if I missed you from your seat in the house of praise and prayer!'

Lizzie Eustace, like some other ladies who ought to be more appreciative, was altogether deficient in what may perhaps be called good taste in reference to men. Though she was clever, and though, in spite of her ignorance, she at once knew an intelligent man from a fool, she did not know the difference between a gentleman and a—'cad'.* It was in her estimation something against Mr. Emilius that he was a clergyman, something against him that he had nothing but what he earned, something against him that he was supposed to be a renegade Jew, and that nobody knew whence he came, nor who he was. These deficiences or drawbacks Lizzie recognised. But it was nothing against him in her judgment that he was a greasy, fawning, pawing, creeping, black-browed rascal, who could not look her full in the face, and whose every word sounded like a lie. There was a twang in his voice which ought to have told her that he was utterly untrustworthy. There was an oily pretence at earnestness in his manner which ought to have told that he was not fit to associate with gentlemen. There was a foulness of demeanour about him which ought to have given to her, as a woman at any rate brought up among ladies, an abhorrence of his society. But all this Lizzie did not feel. She ridiculed to Mrs. Carbuncle the idea of the preacher's courtship. She still thought that in the teeth of all her misfortunes she could do better with herself than marry Mr. Emilius. She conceived that the man must be impertinent if Mrs. Carbuncle's assertions were true;—but she was neither angry nor disgusted, and she allowed him to talk to her, and even to make love to her, after his nasty pseudo-clerical fashion.

She could surely still do better with herself than marry Mr. Emilius! It was now the twentieth of March, and a fortnight had gone since an intimation had been sent to her from the headquarters of the police that Patience Crabstick was in their hands. Nothing further had occurred, and it might be that Patience Crabstick had told no tale against her. She could not bring herself to believe that Patience had no tale to tell, but it might be that Patience, though she was in the hands of the police, would find it to her interest to tell no tale against her late mistress. At any rate, there was silence and quiet, and the affair of the diamonds seemed almost to be passing out of people's minds. Greystock had twice called in Scotland Yard, but had been able to learn nothing. It was feared, they said, that the people really engaged in the robbery had got away scot-free. Frank did not quite believe them, but he could learn nothing from them. Thus encouraged, Lizzie determined that she would remain in London till after Lucinda's marriage,—till after she should have received the promised letter from Lord Fawn, as to which, though it was so long in coming, she did not doubt that it would come at last. She could do nothing with Frank,—who was a fool! She could do nothing with Lord George,—who was a brute! Lord Fawn would still be within her reach, if only the secret about the diamonds could be kept a secret till after she should have become his wife.

About this time Lucinda spoke to her respecting her proposed journey. 'You were talking of going to Scotland a week ago, Lady Eustace.'

'And am still talking of it.'

'Aunt Jane says that you are waiting for my wedding. It is very kind of you;—but pray don't do that.'

'I shouldn't think of going now till after your marriage. It only wants ten or twelve days.'

'I count them. I know how many days it wants. It may want more than that.'

'You can't put it off now, I should think,' said Lizzie; 'and as I have ordered my dress for the occasion I shall certainly stay and wear it.'

'I am very sorry for your dress. I am very sorry for it all. Do you know;—I sometimes think I shall——murder him.'

'Lucinda,—how can you say anything so horrible! But I see you are only joking.' There did come a ghastly smile over that beautiful face, which was so seldom lighted up by any expression of mirth or good humour. 'But I wish you would not say such horrible things.'

'It would serve him right;—and if he were to murder me, that would serve me right. He knows that I detest him, and yet he goes on with it. I have told him so a score of times, but nothing will make him give it up. It is not that he loves me, but he thinks that that will be his triumph.'

'Why don't you give it up, if it makes you unhappy?'

'It ought to come from him,—ought it not?'

'I don't see why,' said Lizzie.

'He is not bound to anybody as I am bound to my aunt. No one can have exacted an oath from him. Lady Eustace, you don't quite understand how we are situated. I wonder whether you would take the trouble to be good to me?'

Lucinda Roanoke had never asked a favour of her before;—

had never, to Lizzie's knowledge, asked a favour of any one.
'In what way can I be good to you?' she said.

'Make him give it up. You may tell him what you like of
me. Tell him that I shall only make him miserable, and more
despicable than he is;—that I shall never be a good wife to
him. Tell him that I am thoroughly bad, and that he will
repent it to the last day of his life. Say whatever you like,—
but make him give it up.'

'When everything has been prepared!'

'What does all that signify compared to a life of misery?
Lady Eustace, I really think that I should—kill him, if he
really were,—were my husband.' Lizzie at last said that she
would, at any rate, speak to Sir Griffin.

And she did speak to Sir Griffin, having waited three or
four days for an opportunity to do so. There had been some
desperately sharp words between Sir Griffin and Mrs. Carbuncle, with reference to money. Sir Griffin had been given
to understand that Lucinda had, or would have, some few
hundred pounds, and insisted that the money should be
handed over to him on the day of his marriage. Mrs. Carbuncle had declared that the money was to come from property to be realised in New York, and had named a day which
had seemed to Sir Griffin to be as the Greek Kalends.* He
expressed an opinion that he was swindled, and Mrs. Carbuncle, unable to restrain herself, had turned upon him full
of wrath. He was caught by Lizzie as he was descending the
stairs, and in the dining-room he poured out the tale of his
wrongs. 'That woman doesn't know what fair dealing means,'
said he.

'That's a little hard, Sir Griffin, isn't it?' said Lizzie.

'Not a bit. A trumpery six hundred pounds! And she hasn't
a shilling of fortune, and never will have, beyond that! No
fellow ever was more generous or more foolish than I have
been.' Lizzie, as she heard this, could not refrain from thinking of the poor departed Sir Florian. 'I didn't look for fortune,
or say a word about money, as almost every man does,—but
just took her as she was. And now she tells me that I can't

have just the bit of money that I wanted for our tour. It would serve them both right if I were to give it up.'

'Why don't you?' said Lizzie. He looked quickly, sharply, and closely into her face as she asked the question. 'I would, if I thought as you do.'

'And lay myself in for all manner of damages,' said Sir Griffin.

'There wouldn't be anything of that kind, I'm sure. You see, the truth is, you and Miss Roanoke are always having,—having little tiffs together. I sometimes think you don't really care a bit for her.'

'It's the old woman I'm complaining of,' said Sir Griffin, 'and I'm not going to marry her. I shall have seen the last of her when I get out of the church, Lady Eustace.'

'Do you think she wishes it?'

'Who do you mean?' asked Sir Griffin.

'Why;—Lucinda?'

'Of course she does. Where'd she be now if it wasn't to go on? I don't believe they've money enough between them to pay the rent of the house they're living in.'

'Of course, I don't want to make difficulties, Sir Griffin, and no doubt the affair has gone very far now. But I really think Lucinda would consent to break it off if you wish it. I have never thought that you were really in love with her.'

He again looked at her very sharply and very closely. 'Has she sent you to say all this?'

'Has who sent me? Mrs. Carbuncle didn't.'

'But Lucinda?'

She paused for a moment before she replied;—but she could not bring herself to be absolutely honest in the matter. 'No; —she didn't send me. But from what I see and hear, I am quite sure she does not wish to go on with it.'

'Then she shall go on with it,' said Sir Griffin. 'I'm not going to be made a fool of in that way. She shall go on with it; and the first thing I mean to tell her, as my wife, is, that she shall never see that woman again. If she thinks she's going to be master, she's very much mistaken.' Sir Griffin, as he said this, showed his teeth, and declared his purpose to be masterful by his features as well as by his words;—but Lady Eustace was, nevertheless, of opinion that when the two came to an absolute struggle for mastery, the lady would get the better of it.

Lizzie never told Miss Roanoke of her want of success, or even of the effort she had made; nor did the unhappy young woman come to her for any reply. The preparations went on, and it was quite understood that, on this peculiar occasion, Mrs. Carbuncle intended to treat her friends with profuse hospitality. She proposed to give a breakfast; and as the house in Hertford Street was very small, rooms had been taken at an hotel in Albemarle Street. Thither, as the day of the marriage drew near, all the presents were taken,—so that they might be viewed by the guests, with the names of the donors attached to them. As some of the money given had been very much wanted indeed, so that the actual cheques could not be conveniently spared just at the moment to pay for the presents which ought to have been bought,—a few very pretty things were hired, as to which, when the donors should see their names attached to them, they should surely think that the money given had been laid out to great advantage.

CHAPTER LXVII
The Eye of the Public

It took Lord Fawn a long time to write his letter, but at last he wrote it. The delay must not be taken as throwing any slur on his character as a correspondent or a man of business, for many irritating causes sprang up sufficient to justify him in pleading that it arose from circumstances beyond his own control. It is, moreover, felt by us all that the time which may fairly be taken in the performance of any task depends, not on the amount of work, but on the performance of it when done. A man is not expected to write a cheque for a couple

of thousand pounds as readily as he would one for five,—
unless he be a man to whom a couple of thousand pounds is a
mere nothing. To Lord Fawn the writing of this letter was
everything. He had told Lizzie, with much exactness, what
he would put into it. He would again offer his hand,—acknowledging himself bound to do so by his former offer,—but
would give reasons why she should not accept it. If anything
should occur in the meantime which would, in his opinion,
justify him in again repudiating her, he would, of course, take
advantage of such circumstance. If asked himself what was
his prevailing motive in all that he did or intended to do, he
would have declared that it was above all things necessary
that he should 'put himself right in the eye of the British
public.'

But he was not able to do this without interference from
the judgment of others. Both Mr. and Mrs. Hittaway interfered; and he could not prevent himself from listening to them
and believing them, though he would contradict all they said,
and snub all their theories. Frank Greystock also continued
to interfere, and Lady Glencora Palliser. Even John Eustace
had been worked upon to write to Lord Fawn, stating his
opinion, as trustee for his late brother's property, that the
Eustace family did not think that there was ground of complaint against Lady Eustace in reference to the diamonds
which had been stolen. This was a terrible blow to Lord
Fawn, and had come, no doubt, from a general agreement
among the Eustace faction,—including the bishop, John
Eustace, and even Mr. Camperdown,—that it would be a
good thing to get the widow married and placed under some
decent control.

Lady Glencora absolutely had the effrontery to ask him
whether the marriage was not going to take place, and when
a day would be fixed. He gathered up his courage to give her
ladyship a rebuke. 'My private affairs do seem to be uncommonly interesting,' he said.

'Why yes, Lord Fawn,' said Lady Glencora, whom nothing
could abash;—'most interesting. You see, dear Lady Eustace

is so very popular, that we all want to know what is to be her fate.'

'I regret to say that I cannot answer your ladyship's question with any precision,' said Lord Fawn.

But the Hittaway persecution was by far the worst. 'You have seen her, Frederic?' said his sister.

'Yes,—I have.'

'You have made her no promise?'

'My dear Clara, this is a matter in which I must use my own judgment.'

'But the family, Frederic?'

'I do not think that any member of our family has a just right to complain of my conduct since I have had the honour of being its head. I have endeavoured so to live that my actions should encounter no private or public censure. If I fail to meet with your approbation, I shall grieve; but I cannot, on that account, act otherwise than in accordance with my own judgment.'

Mrs. Hittaway knew her brother well, and was not afraid of him. 'That's all very well; and I am sure you know, Frederic, how proud we all are of you. But this woman is a nasty, low, scheming, ill-conducted, dishonest little wretch; and if you make her your wife you'll be miserable all your life. Nothing would make me and Orlando so unhappy as to quarrel with you. But we know that it is so, and to the last minute I shall say so. Why don't you ask her to her face about that man down in Scotland?'

'My dear Clara, perhaps I know what to ask her and what not to ask her better than you can tell me.'

And his brother-in-law was quite as bad. 'Fawn,' he said, 'in this matter of Lady Eustace, don't you think you ought to put your conduct into the hands of some friend?'

'What do you mean by that?'

'I think it is an affair in which a man would have so much comfort in being able to say that he was guided by advice. Of course, her people want you to marry her. Now, if you could just tell them that the whole thing was in the hands of,

—say me,—or any other friend, you would be relieved, you know, of so much responsibility. They might hammer away at me ever so long, and I shouldn't care twopence.'

'If there is to be any hammering, it cannot be borne vicariously,' said Lord Fawn,—and as he said it, he was quite pleased by his own sharpness and wit.

He had, indeed, put himself beyond protection by vicarious endurance of hammering when he promised to write to Lady Eustace, explaining his own conduct and giving reasons. Had anything turned up in Scotland Yard which would have justified him in saying,—or even in thinking,—that Lizzie had stolen her own diamonds, he would have sent word to her that he must abstain from any communication till that matter had been cleared up; but, since the appearance of that mysterious paragraph in the newspapers, nothing had been heard of the robbery, and public opinion certainly seemed to be in favour of Lizzie's innocence. He did think that the Eustace faction was betraying him, as he could not but remember how eager Mr. Camperdown had been in asserting that the widow was keeping an enormous amount of property and claiming it as her own, whereas, in truth, she had not the slightest title to it. It was, in a great measure, in consequence of the assertions of the Eustace faction, almost in obedience to their advice, that he had resolved to break off the match; and now they turned upon him, and John Eustace absolutely went out of his way to write him a letter which was clearly meant to imply that he, Lord Fawn, was bound to marry the woman to whom he had once engaged himself! Lord Fawn felt that he was ill-used, and that a man might have to undergo a great deal of bad treatment who should strive to put himself right in the eye of the public.

At last he wrote his letter,—on a Wednesday, which with him had something of the comfort of a half-holiday, as on that day he was not required to attend Parliament.

'My dear Lady Eustace, 'India Office, 28th March, 18—.

'In accordance with the promise which I made to you when I did myself the honour of waiting upon you in Hertford

Street, I take up my pen with the view of communicating to you the result of my deliberations respecting the engagement of marriage which, no doubt, did exist between us last summer.

'Since that time I have no doubt taken upon myself to say that that engagement was over; and I am free to admit that I did so without any assent or agreement on your part to that effect. Such conduct no doubt requires a valid and strong defence. My defence is as follows;—

'I learned that you were in possession of a large amount of property, vested in diamonds, which was claimed by the executors under your late husband's will as belonging to his estate; and as to which they declared, in the most positive manner, that you had no right or title to it whatever. I consulted friends and I consulted lawyers, and I was led to the conviction that this property certainly did not belong to you. Had I married you in these circumstances, I could not but have become a participator in the lawsuit which I was assured would be commenced. I could not be a participator with you, because I believed you to be in the wrong. And I certainly could not participate with those who would in such case be attacking my own wife.

'In this condition of things I requested you,—as you must, I think, yourself own, with all deference and good feeling,—to give up the actual possession of the property, and to place the diamonds in neutral hands,'—Lord Fawn was often called upon to be neutral in reference to the condition of outlying Indian principalities,—'till the law should have decided as to their ownership. As regards myself, I neither coveted nor rejected the possession of that wealth for my future wife. I desired simply to be free from an embarrassment which would have overwhelmed me. You declined my request,—not only positively, but perhaps I may add peremptorily; and then I was bound to adhere to the decision I had communicated to you.

'Since that time the property has been stolen, and, as I believe, dissipated. The lawsuit against you has been withdrawn; and the bone of contention, so to say, is no longer existing. I am no longer justified in declining to keep my engagement because of the prejudice to which I should have been subjected by your possession of the diamonds;—and, therefore, as far as that goes, I withdraw my withdrawal.' This Lord Fawn thought was rather a happy phrase, and he read it aloud to himself more than once.

'But now there arises the question whether, in both our interests, this marriage should go on, or whether it may not be more conducive to your happiness and to mine that it should be annulled for causes altogether irrespective of the diamonds. In a matter so serious as marriage, the happiness of the two parties is that which requires graver thought than any other consideration.

'There has no doubt sprung up between us a feeling of mutual distrust, which has led to recrimination, and which is hardly compatible with that perfect confidence which should exist between a man and his wife. This first arose, no doubt, from the different views which we took as to that property of which I have spoken,—and as to which your judgment may possibly have been better than mine. On that head I will add nothing to what I have already said; but the feeling has arisen; and I fear it cannot be so perfectly allayed as to admit of that reciprocal trust without which we could not live happily together. I confess that for my own part I do not now desire a union which was once the great object of my ambition,— and that I could not go to the altar with you without fear and trembling. As to your own feelings, you best know what they are. I bring no charge against you;—but if you have ceased to love me, I think you should cease to wish to be my wife, and that you should not insist upon a marriage simply because by doing so you would triumph over a former objection.' Before he finished this paragraph, he thought much of Andy Gowran and of the scene among the rocks of which he had heard. But he could not speak of it. He had found himself unable to examine the witness who had been brought to him, and had honestly told himself that he could not take that charge as proved. Andy Gowran might have lied. In his heart he believed that Andy Gowran had lied. The matter was distasteful to him, and he would not touch it. And yet he knew that the woman did not love him, and he longed to tell her so.

'As to what we might each gain or each lose in a worldly point of view, either by marrying or not marrying, I will not say a word. You have rank and wealth, and, therefore, I can comfort myself by thinking that if I dissuade you from this marriage I shall rob you of neither. I acknowledge that I wish to dissuade you, as I believe that we should not make each other happy. As, however, I do consider that I am bound to keep my engagement to you if you demand that I shall do so, I leave the matter in your hands for decision.

'I am, and shall remain,

'Your sincere friend,

'FAWN.'

He read the letter and copied it, and gave himself great credit for the composition. He thought that it was impossible that any woman after reading it should express a wish to become the wife of the man who wrote it; and yet,—so he believed,—no man or woman could find fault with him for writing it. There certainly was one view of the case, which was very distressing. How would it be with him if, after all, she should say that she would marry him? After having given her her choice,—having put it all in writing,—he could not again go back from it. He would be in her power, and of what use would his life be to him? Would Parliament, or the India Office, or the eye of the public be able to comfort him then in the midst of his many miseries? What could he do with a wife whom he married with a declaration that he disliked her? With such feelings as were his, how could he stand before a clergyman and take an oath that he would love her and cherish her? Would she not ever be as an adder to him,*—as an adder whom it would be impossible that he should admit into his bosom? Could he live in the same house with her; and, if so, could he ask his mother and sisters to visit her? He remembered well what Mrs. Hittaway had called her;—a nasty, low, scheming, ill-conducted, dishonest little wretch! And he believed that she was so! Yet he was once again offering to marry her, should she choose to accept him.

Nevertheless, the letter was sent. There was, in truth, no alternative. He had promised that he would write such a letter, and all that had remained to him was the power of cramming into it every available argument against the marriage. This he had done, and, as he thought, had done well. It was impossible that she should desire to marry him after reading such a letter as that!

Lizzie received it in her bedroom, where she breakfasted, and told of its arrival to her friend Mrs. Carbuncle as soon as they met each other. 'My lord has come down from his high horse at last,' she said, with the letter in her hand.

'What,—Lord Fawn?'

'Yes; Lord Fawn. What other lord? There is no other lord for me. He is my lord, my peer of Parliament, my Cabinet minister, my right honourable, my member of the Government,—my young man, too, as the maid-servants call them.'

'What does he say?'

'Say;—what should he say?—just that he has behaved very badly, and that he hopes I shall forgive him.'

'Not quite that; does he?'

'That's what it all means. Of course, there is ever so much of it,—pages of it. It wouldn't be Lord Fawn if he didn't spin it all out like an Act of Parliament, with "whereas" and "wherein," and "whereof." It is full of all that; but the meaning of it is that he's at my feet again, and that I may pick him up if I choose to take him. I'd show you the letter, only perhaps it wouldn't be fair to the poor man.

'What excuse does he make?'

'Oh,—as to that he's rational enough. He calls the necklace the—bone of contention. That's rather good for Lord Fawn; isn't it? The bone of contention, he says, has been removed; and, therefore, there is no reason why we shouldn't marry if we like it. He shall hear enough about the bone of contention if we do "marry." '

'And what shall you do now?'

'Ah; yes; that's easily asked; is it not? The man's a good sort of man in his way, you know. He doesn't drink or gamble; and I don't think there is a bit of the King David*about him, —that I don't.'

'Virtue personified, I should say.'

'And he isn't extravagant.'

'Then why not have him and have done with it?' asked Mrs. Carbuncle.

'He is such a lumpy man,' said Lizzie;—'such an ass; such a load of Government waste-paper.'

'Come, my dear;—you've had troubles.'

'I have, indeed,' said Lizzie.

'And there's no quite knowing yet how far they're over.'

'What do you mean by that, Mrs. Carbuncle?'

'Nothing very much;—but still, you see, they may come again. As to Lord George, we all know that he has not got a penny-piece in the world that he can call his own.'

'If he had as many pennies as Judas,* Lord George would be nothing to me,' said Lizzie.

'And your cousin really doesn't seem to mean anything.'

'I know very well what my cousin means. He and I understand each other thoroughly; but cousins can love one another very well without marrying.'

'Of course you know your own business, but if I were you I would take Lord Fawn. I speak in true kindness,—as one woman to another. After all, what does love signify? How much real love do we ever see among married people? Does Lady Glencora Palliser really love her husband, who thinks of nothing in the world but putting taxes on and off?'

'Do you love your husband, Mrs. Carbuncle?'

'No;—but that is a different kind of thing. Circumstances have caused me to live apart from him. The man is a good man, and there is no reason why you should not respect him, and treat him well. He will give you a fixed position,—which really you want badly, Lady Eustace.'

'Tooriloo, tooriloo, tooriloo, looriloo,' said Lizzie, in contemptuous disdain of her friend's caution.

'And then all this trouble about the diamonds and the robberies will be over,' continued Mrs. Carbuncle. Lizzie looked at her very intently. What should make Mrs. Carbuncle suppose that there need be, or, indeed, could be, any further trouble about the diamonds?

'So;—that's your advice,' said Lizzie. 'I'm half inclined to take it, and perhaps I shall. However, I have brought him round, and that's something, my dear. And either one way or the other, I shall let him know that I like my triumph. I was determined to have it, and I've got it.'

Then she read the letter again very seriously. Could she possibly marry a man who in so many words told her that he didn't want her? Well;—she thought she could. Was not everybody treating everybody else much in the same way? Had she not loved her Corsair truly,—and how had he treated her? Had she not been true, disinterested, and most affectionate to Frank Greystock; and what had she got from him? To manage her business wisely, and put herself upon firm ground;—that was her duty at present. Mrs. Carbuncle was right there. The very name of Lady Fawn would be a rock to her,—and she wanted a rock. She thought upon the whole that she could marry him;—unless Patience Crabstick and the police should again interfere with her prosperity.

CHAPTER LXVIII
The Major

LADY EUSTACE did not intend to take as much time in answering Lord Fawn's letter as he had taken in writing it; but even she found that the subject was one which demanded a good deal of thought. Mrs. Carbuncle had very freely recommended her to take the man, supporting her advice by arguments which Lizzie felt to be valid; but then Mrs. Carbuncle did not know all the circumstances. Mrs. Carbuncle had not actually seen his lordship's letter; and, though the great part of the letter, the formal repetition, namely, of the writer's offer of marriage, had been truly told to her, still, as the reader will have perceived, she had been kept in the dark as to some of the details. Lizzie did sit at her desk with the object of putting a few words together in order that she might see how they looked, and she found that there was a difficulty. 'My dear Lord Fawn. As we have been engaged to marry each other, and as all our friends have been told, I think that the thing had better go on.' That, after various attempts, was, she thought, the best letter that she could send,—if she should make up her mind to be Lady Fawn. But, on the morning of the 30th of March she had not sent her letter. She had told herself that she would take two days to think of her reply,—and, on the Friday morning the few words she had prepared were still lying in her desk.

What was she to get by marrying a man she absolutely disliked? That he also absolutely disliked her was not a matter much in her thoughts. The man would not ill-treat her because he disliked her; or, it might perhaps be juster to say, that the ill-treatment which she might fairly anticipate would not be of a nature which would much affect her comfort grievously. He would not beat her, nor rob her, nor lock her up, nor starve her. He would either neglect her, or preach sermons to her. For the first she could console herself by the attention of others; and should he preach, perhaps she could preach too,—as sharply if not as lengthily as his lordship. At any rate, she was not afraid of him. But what would she gain? It is very well to have a rock, as Mrs. Carbuncle had said, but a rock is not everything. She did not know whether she cared much for living upon a rock. Even stability may be purchased at too high a price. There was not a grain of poetry in the whole composition of Lord Fawn, and poetry was what her very soul craved;—poetry, together with houses, champagne, jewels, and admiration. Her income was still her own, and she did not quite see that the rock was so absolutely necessary to her. Then she wrote another note to Lord Fawn, a specimen of a note, so that she might have the opportunity of comparing the two. This note took her much longer than the one first written.

'My Lord,—I do not know how to acknowledge with sufficient humility the condescension and great kindness of your lordship's letter. But perhaps its manly generosity is more conspicuous than either. The truth is, my Lord, you want to escape from your engagement, but are too much afraid of the consequences to dare to do so by any act of your own;—therefore you throw it upon me. You are quite successful. I don't think you ever read poetry, but perhaps you may understand the two following lines;—

> "I am constrained to say, your lordship's scullion
> Should sooner be my husband than yourself."

'I see through you, and despise you thoroughly.

'E. EUSTACE.'

She was comparing the two answers together, very much in doubt as to which should be sent, when there came a message to her by a man, whom she knew to be a policeman, though he did not announce himself as such, and was dressed in plain clothes. Major Mackintosh sent his compliments to her, and would wait upon her that afternoon at three o'clock, if she would have the kindness to receive him. At the first moment of seeing the man she felt that after all the rock was what she wanted. Mrs. Carbuncle was right. She had had troubles and might have more, and the rock was the thing. But then the more certainly did she become convinced of this by the presence of the major's messenger, the more clearly did she see the difficulty of attaining the security which the rock offered. If this public exposure should fall upon her, Lord Fawn's renewed offer, as she knew well, would stand for nothing. If once it were known that she had kept the necklace, —her own necklace,—under her pillow at Carlisle, he would want no further justification in repudiating her, were it for the tenth time.

She was very uncivil to the messenger, and the more so because she found that the man bore her rudeness without turning upon her and rending her. When she declared that the police had behaved very badly, and that Major Mackintosh was inexcusable in troubling her again, and that she had ceased to care two-pence about the necklace,—the man made no remonstrance to her petulance. He owned that the trouble was very great, and the police very inefficient. He almost owned that the major was inexcusable. He did not care what he owned so that he achieved his object. But, when Lizzie said that she could not see Major Mackintosh at three, and objected equally to two, four, or five; then the courteous messenger from Scotland Yard did say a word to make her understand that there must be a meeting,—and he hinted also that the major was doing a most unusually good-natured thing in coming to Hertford Street. Of course, Lizzie made the appointment. If the major chose to come, she would be at home at three.

As soon as the policeman was gone, she sat alone, with a manner very much changed from that which she had worn since the arrival of Lord Fawn's letter,—with a fresh weight of care upon her, greater perhaps than she had ever hitherto borne. She had had bad moments,—when, for instance, she had been taken before the magistrates at Carlisle, when she found the police in her house on her return from the theatre, and when Lord George had forced her secret from her. But at each of these periods hope had come renewed, before despair had crushed her. Now it seemed to her that the thing was done and that the game was over. This chief man of the London police no doubt knew the whole story. If she could only already have climbed upon some rock, so that there might be a man bound to defend her,—a man at any rate bound to put himself forward on her behalf and do whatever might be done in her defence, she might have endured it!

What should she do now,—at this minute? She looked at her watch and found that it was already past one. Mrs. Carbuncle, as she knew, was closeted up-stairs with Lucinda, whose wedding was fixed for the following Monday. It was now Friday. Were she to call upon Mrs. Carbuncle for aid, no aid would be forthcoming unless she were to tell the whole truth. She almost thought that she would do so. But then, how great would have been her indiscretion if, after all, when the major should come, she should discover that he did not know the truth himself! That Mrs. Carbuncle would keep her secret she did not for a moment think. She longed for the comfort of some friend's counsel, but she found at last that she could not purchase it by telling everything to a woman.

Might it not be possible that she should still run away? She did not know much of the law, but she thought that they could not punish her for breaking an appointment even with a man so high in authority as Major Mackintosh. She could leave a note saying that pressing business called her out. But whither should she go? She thought of taking a cab to the House of Commons, finding her cousin, and telling him everything. It would be so much better that he should see the major. But then, again, it might be that she should be mistaken as to the amount of the major's information. After a while, she almost determined to fly off at once to Scotland, leaving word that she was obliged to go instantly to her child. But there was no direct train to Scotland before eight or nine in the evening, and during the intervening hours the police would have ample time to find her. What, indeed, could she do with herself during these intervening hours? Ah, if she had but a rock now, so that she need not be dependent altogether on the exercise of her own intellect!

Gradually the minutes passed by, and she became aware that she must face the major. Well! What had she done? She had stolen nothing. She had taken no person's property. She had, indeed, been wickedly robbed, and the police had done nothing to get back for her her property, as they were bound to have done. She would take care to tell the major what she thought about the negligence of the police. The major should not have the talk all to himself.

If it had not been for one word with which Lord George had stunned her ears, she could still have borne it well. She had told a lie;—perhaps two or three lies. She knew that she had lied. But then people lie every day. She would not have minded it much if she were simply to be called a liar. But he had told her that she would be accused of—perjury. There was something frightful to her in the name. And there were, she knew not what, dreadful penalties attached to it. Lord

George had told her that she might be put in prison,—whether he had said for years or for months she had forgotten. And she thought she had heard of people's property being confiscated to the Crown when they had been made out to be guilty of certain great offences. Oh, how she wished that she had a rock!

When three o'clock came, she had not started for Scotland or elsewhere, and at last she received the major. Could she have thoroughly trusted the servant, she would have denied herself at the last moment, but she feared that she might be betrayed, and she thought that her position would be rendered even worse than it was at present by a futile attempt. She was sitting alone, pale, haggard, trembling, when Major Mackintosh was shown into her room. It may be as well explained at once that, at this moment, the major knew, or thought that he knew, every circumstance of the two robberies, and that his surmises were in every respect right. Miss Crabstick and Mr. Cann were in comfortable quarters, and were prepared to tell all that they could tell. Mr. Smiler was in durance,* and Mr. Benjamin was at Vienna, in the hands of the Austrian police, who were prepared to give him up to those who desired his society in England, on the completion of certain legal formalities. That Mr. Benjamin and Mr. Smiler would be prosecuted, the latter for the robbery and the former for conspiracy to rob, and for receiving stolen goods, was a matter of course. But what was to be done with Lady Eustace? That, at the present moment, was the prevailing trouble with the police. During the last three weeks every precaution had been taken to keep the matter secret, and it is hardly too much to say, that Lizzie's interests were handled not only with consideration but with tenderness.

'Lady Eustace,' said the major, 'I am very sorry to trouble you. No doubt the man who called on you this morning explained to you who I am.'

'Oh yes, I know who you are,—quite well.' Lizzie made a great effort to speak without betraying her consternation; but she was nearly prostrated. The major, however, hardly observed her, and was by no means at ease himself in his effort to save her from unnecessary annoyance. He was a tall, thin, gaunt man of about forty, with large, good-natured eyes;—but it was not till the interview was half over that Lizzie took courage to look even into his face.

'Just so; I am come, you know, about the robbery which took place here,—and the other robbery at Carlisle.'

'I have been so troubled about these horrid robberies! Sometimes I think they'll be the death of me.'

'I think, Lady Eustace, we have found out the whole truth.'

'Oh, I daresay. I wonder why—you have been so long—finding it out.'

'We have had very clever people to deal with, Lady Eustace;—and I fear that, even now, we shall never get back the property.'

'I do not care about the property, sir;—although it was all my own. Nobody has lost anything but myself; and I really don't see why the thing should not die out, as I don't care about it. Whoever it is, they may have it now.'

'We were bound to get to the bottom of it all, if we could; and I think that we have,—at last. Perhaps, as you say, we ought to have done it sooner.'

'Oh,—I don't care.'

'We have two persons in custody, Lady Eustace, whom we shall use as witnesses, and I am afraid we shall have to call upon you also,—as a witness.' It occurred to Lizzie that they could not lock her up in prison and make her a witness too, but she said nothing. Then the major continued his speech, —and asked her the question which was, in fact, alone material. 'Of course, Lady Eustace, you are not bound to say anything to me unless you like it,—and you must understand that I by no means wish you to criminate yourself.'

'I don't know what that means.'

'If you yourself have done anything wrong, I don't want to ask you to confess it.'

'I have had all my diamonds stolen, if you mean that. Perhaps it was wrong to have diamonds.'

'But to come to my question,—I suppose we may take it for granted that the diamonds were in your desk when the thieves made their entrance into this house, and broke the desk open, and stole the money out of it?' Lizzie breathed so hardly, that she was quite unable to speak. The man's voice was very gentle and very kind,—but then how could she admit that one fact? All depended on that one fact. 'The woman Crabstick,' said the major, 'has confessed, and will state on her oath that she saw the necklace in your hands in Hertford Street, and that she saw it placed in the desk. She then gave information of this to Benjamin,—as she had before given information as to your journey up from Scotland,—and she was introduced to the two men whom she let into the house. One of them, indeed, who will also give evidence for us, she had before met at Carlisle. She then was present when the necklace was taken out of the desk. The man who opened the desk and took it out, who also cut the door at Carlisle, will give evidence to the same effect. The man who carried the necklace out of the house, and who broke open the box at Carlisle, will be tried,—as will also Benjamin, who disposed of the diamonds. I have told you the whole story, as it has been told to me by the woman Crabstick. Of course, you will deny the truth of it, if it be untrue.' Lizzie sat with her eyes fixed upon the floor, but said nothing. She could not speak. 'If you will allow me, Lady Eustace, to give you advice,— really friendly advice——'

'Oh, pray do.'

'You had better admit the truth of the story, if it is true.'

'They were my own,' she whispered.

'Or, at any rate, you believed that they were. There can be no doubt, I think, as to that. No one supposes that the robbery at Carlisle was arranged on your behalf.'

'Oh, no.'

'But you had taken them out of the box before you went to bed at the inn?'

'Not then.'

'But you had taken them?'

'I did it in the morning before I started from Scotland. They frightened me by saying the box would be stolen.'

'Exactly;—and then you put them into your desk here, in this house?'

'Yes,—sir.'

'I should tell you, Lady Eustace, that I had not a doubt about this before I came here. For some time past I have thought that it must be so; and latterly the confessions of two of the accomplices have made it certain to me. One of the housebreakers and the jeweller will be tried for the felony, and I am afraid that you must undergo the annoyance of being one of the witnesses.'

'What will they do to me, Major Mackintosh?' Lizzie now for the first time looked up into his eyes, and felt that they were kind. Could he be her rock? He did not speak to her like an enemy;—and then, too, he would know better than any man alive how she might best escape from her trouble.

'They will ask you to tell the truth.'

'Indeed I will do that,' said Lizzie,—not aware that, after so many lies, it might be difficult to tell the truth.

'And you will probably be asked to repeat it, this way and that, in a manner that will be troublesome to you. You see that here in London, and at Carlisle, you have—given incorrect versions.'

'I know I have. But the necklace was my own. There was nothing dishonest;—was there, Major Mackintosh? When they came to me at Carlisle I was so confused that I hardly knew what to tell them. And when I had once—given an incorrect version, you know, I didn't know how to go back.'

The major was not so well acquainted with Lizzie as is the reader, and he pitied her. 'I can understand all that,' he said.

How much kinder he was than Lord George had been when she confessed the truth to him. Here would be a rock! And such a handsome man as he was, too,—not exactly a Corsair, as he was great in authority over the London police,—but a powerful, fine fellow, who would know what to do with swords and pistols as well as any Corsair;—and one, too, no doubt, who would understand poetry! Any such dream, however, was altogether unavailing, as the major had a wife at home and seven children. 'If you will only tell me what to do, I will do it,' she said, looking up into his face with entreaty, and pressing her hands together in supplication.

Then at great length, and with much patience, he explained to her what he would have her do. He thought that, if she were summoned and used as a witness, there would be no attempt to prosecute her for the—incorrect versions—of which she had undoubtedly been guilty. The probability was, that she would receive assurance to this effect before she would be asked to give her evidence, preparatory to the committal of Benjamin and Smiler. He could not assure her that it would be so, but he had no doubt of it. In order, however, that things might be made to run as smooth as possible, he recommended her very strongly to go at once to Mr. Camperdown and make a clean breast of it to him. 'The whole family should be told,' said the major, 'and it will be better for you that they should know it from yourself than from us.' When she hesitated, he explained to her that the matter could no longer be kept as a secret, and that her evidence would certainly appear in the papers. He proposed that she should be summoned for that day week,—which would be the Friday after Lucinda's marriage, and he suggested that she should go to Mr. Camperdown's on the morrow. 'What!—to-morrow?' exclaimed Lizzie, in dismay.

'My dear Lady Eustace,' said the major, 'the sooner you get back into straight running, the sooner you will be comfortable.' Then she promised that she would go on the Tuesday,—the day after the marriage. 'If he learns it in the meantime, you must not be surprised,' said the major.

'Tell me one thing, Major Mackintosh,' she said, as she gave him her hand at parting,—'they can't take away from me anything that is my own;—can they?'

'I don't think they can,' said the major, escaping rather quickly from the room.

CHAPTER LXIX
'*I cannot do it*'

THE Saturday and the Sunday Lizzie passed in outward tranquillity, though, doubtless, her mind was greatly disturbed. She said nothing of what had passed between her and Major Mackintosh, explaining that his visit had been made solely with the object of informing her that Mr. Benjamin was to be sent home from Vienna, but that the diamonds were gone for ever. She had, as she declared to herself, agreed with Major Mackintosh that she would not go to Mr. Camperdown till the Tuesday,—justifying her delay by her solicitude in reference to Miss Roanoke's marriage; and therefore these two days were her own. After them would come a totally altered phase of existence. All the world would know the history of the diamonds,—cousin Frank, and Lord Fawn, and John Eustace, and Mrs. Carbuncle, and the Bobsborough people, and Lady Glencora, and that old vulturess, her aunt, the Countess of Linlithgow. It must come now;—but she had two days in which she could be quiet and think of her position. She would, she thought, send one of her letters to Lord Fawn before she went to Mr. Camperdown;—but which should she send? Or should she write a third explaining the whole matter in sweetly piteous feminine terms, and swearing that the only remaining feeling in her bosom was a devoted affection to the man who had now twice promised to be her husband?

In the meantime the preparations for the great marriage went on. Mrs. Carbuncle spent her time busily between Lucinda's bedchamber and the banqueting hall in Albemarle Street. In spite of pecuniary difficulties the trousseau was to be a wonder; and even Lizzie was astonished at the jewellery which that indefatigable woman had collected together for a preliminary show in Hertford Street. She had spent hours at Howell and James's, and had made marvellous bargains there and elsewhere. Things were sent for selection, of which the greater portion were to be returned, but all were kept for the show. The same things which were shown to separate friends in Hertford Street as part of the trousseau on Friday and Saturday, were carried over to Albemarle Street on the Sunday, so as to add to the quasi-public exhibition of presents on the Monday. The money expended had gone very far. The most had been made of a failing credit. Every particle of friendly generosity had been so manipulated as to add to the external magnificence. And Mrs. Carbuncle had done all this without any help from Lucinda,—in the midst of most contemptuous indifference on Lucinda's part. She could hardly be got to allow the milliners to fit the dresses to her body, and positively refused to thrust her feet into certain golden-heeled boots with brightly-bronzed toes, which were a great feature among the raiment. Nobody knew it except Mrs. Carbuncle and the maid,—even Lizzie Eustace did not know it;—but once the bride absolutely ran a muck among the finery, scattering the laces here and there, pitching the glove-boxes under the bed, chucking the golden-heeled boots into the fire-place, and exhibiting quite a tempest of fury against one of the finest shows of petticoats ever arranged with a view to the admiration and envy of female friends. But all this Mrs. Carbuncle bore, and still persevered. The thing was so nearly done now that she could endure to persevere though the provocation to abandon it was so great. She had even ceased to find fault with her niece,—but went on in silence counting the hours till the trouble should be taken off her own shoulders and placed on those of Sir Griffin. It was a great thing to her, almost more than she had expected, that neither Lucinda nor Sir Griffin should have positively declined the marriage. It was impossible that either should retreat from it now.

Luckily for Mrs. Carbuncle Sir Griffin took delight in the show. He did this after a bearish fashion, putting his finger upon little flaws with an intelligence for which Mrs. Carbuncle had not hitherto given him credit. As to certain ornaments, he observed that the silver was plated and the gold ormolu.* A 'rope' of pearls he at once detected as being false, —and after fingering certain lace he turned up his nose and shook his head. Then, on the Sunday, in Albemarle Street, he pointed out to Mrs. Carbuncle sundry articles which he had seen in the bedroom on the Saturday. 'But, my dear Sir Griffin,—that's of course,' said Mrs. Carbuncle. 'Oh;—that's of course, is it?' said Sir Griffin, turning up his nose again. 'Where did that Delph bowl come from?' 'It is one of Mortlock's finest Etruscan vases,' said Mrs. Carbuncle. 'Oh,—I thought that Etruscan vases came from—from somewhere in Greece or Italy,' said Sir Griffin. 'I declare that you are shocking,' said Mrs. Carbuncle, struggling to maintain her good humour.

He passed hours of the Sunday in Hertford Street, and Lord George also was there for some time. Lizzie, who could hardly devote her mind to the affairs of the wedding, remained alone in her own sitting-room during the greater part of the day;—but she did show herself while Lord George was there. 'So I hear that Mackintosh has been here,' said Lord George.

'Yes,—he was here.'

'And what did he say?' Lizzie did not like the way in which the man looked at her, feeling it to be not only unfriendly, but absolutely cruel. It seemed to imply that he knew that her secret was about to be divulged. And what was he to her now that he should be impertinent to her? What he knew, all the world would know before the end of the week. And that other man who knew it already, had been kind to her, had said nothing about perjury, but had explained to her that what she would have to bear would be trouble, and not imprisonment and loss of money. Lord George, to whom she had been so civil, for whom she had spent money, to whom she had almost offered herself and all that she possessed,—Lord George, whom she had selected as the first repository of her secret, had spoken no word to comfort her, but had made things look worse for her than they were. Why should she submit to be questioned by Lord George? In a day or two the secret which he knew would be no secret. 'Never mind what he said, Lord George,' she replied.

'Has he found it all out?'

'You had better go and ask himself,' said Lizzie. 'I am sick of the subject, and I mean to have done with it.'

Lord George laughed, and Lizzie hated him for his laugh.

'I declare,' said Mrs. Carbuncle, 'that you two who were such friends, are always snapping at each other now.'

'The fickleness is all on her ladyship's part,—not on mine,' said Lord George; whereupon Lady Eustace walked out of the room and was not seen again till dinner-time.

Soon afterwards Lucinda also endeavoured to escape, but to this Sir Griffin objected. Sir Griffin was in a very good humour, and bore himself like a prosperous bridegroom. 'Come, Luce,' he said, 'get off your high horse for a little. To-morrow, you know, you must come down altogether.'

'So much the more reason for my remaining up to-day.'

'I'll be shot if you shall,' said Sir Griffin. 'Luce, sit in my lap, and give me a kiss.'

At this moment Lord George and Mrs. Carbuncle were in the front drawing-room, and Lord George was telling her the true story as to the necklace. It must be explained on his behalf that in doing this he did not consider that he was betraying the trust reposed in him. 'They know all about it in Scotland Yard,' he said; 'I got it from Gager. They were bound to tell me, as up to this week past every man in the police thought that I had been the master-mind among the thieves. When I think of it I hardly know whether to laugh or cry.'

'And she had them all the time?' exclaimed Mrs. Carbuncle.

'Yes;—in this house! Did you ever hear of such a little cat? I could tell you more than that. She wanted me to take them and dispose of them.'

'No!'

'She did though;—and now see the way she treats me! Never mind. Don't say a word to her about it till it comes out of itself. She'll have to be arrested, no doubt.'

'Arrested!' Mrs. Carbuncle's further exclamations were stopped by Lucinda's struggles in the other room. She had

declined to sit upon the bridegroom's lap, but had acknowledged that she was bound to submit to be kissed. He had
kissed her, and then had striven to drag her on to his knee.
But she was strong, and had resisted violently, and, as he
afterwards said, had struck him savagely. 'Of course I struck
him,' said Lucinda.

'By —— you shall pay for it!' said Sir Griffin. This took
place in the presence of Lord George and Mrs. Carbuncle,
and yet they were to be married to-morrow.

'The idea of complaining that a girl hit you,—and the girl
who is to be your wife!' said Lord George, as they walked
off together.

'I know what to complain of, and what not,' said Sir
Griffin. 'Are you going to let me have that money?'

'No;—I am not,' said Lord George,—'so there's an end
of that.' Nevertheless, they dined together at their club afterwards, and in the evening Sir Griffin was again in Hertford
Street.

This happened on the Sunday, on which day none of the
ladies had gone to church. Mr. Emilius well understood the
cause of their absence, and felt nothing of a parson's anger
at it. He was to marry the couple on the Monday morning,
and dined with the ladies on the Sunday. He was peculiarly
gracious and smiling, and spoke of the Hymeneals*as though
they were even more than ordinarily joyful and happy in their
promise. To Lizzie he was almost affectionate, and Mrs. Carbuncle he flattered to the top of her bent. The power of the
man in being sprightly under such a load of trouble as oppressed the household, was wonderful. He had to do with
three women who were worldly, hard, and given entirely to
evil things. Even as regarded the bride, who felt the horror
of her position, so much must be in truth admitted. Though
from day to day and hour to hour she would openly declare
her hatred of the things around her,—yet she went on. Since
she had entered upon life she had known nothing but falsehood and scheming wickedness;—and, though she rebelled
against the consequences, she had not rebelled against the

wickedness. Now to this unfortunate young woman and her two companions, Mr. Emilius discoursed with an unctuous mixture of celestial and terrestrial glorification, which was proof, at any rate, of great ability on his part. He told them how a good wife was a crown, or rather a chaplet of aetherial roses, to her husband, and how high rank and great station in the world made such a chaplet more beautiful and more valuable. His work in the vineyard, he said, had fallen lately among the wealthy and nobly born; and though he would not say that he was entitled to take glory on that account, still he gave thanks daily in that he had been enabled to give his humble assistance towards the running of a godly life to those who, by their example, were enabled to have so wide an effect upon their poorer fellow-creatures. He knew well how difficult it was for a camel to go through the eye of a needle. They had the highest possible authority for that. But Scripture never said that the camel,*—which, as he explained it, was simply a thread larger than ordinary thread,—could not go through the needle's eye. The camel which succeeded, in spite of the difficulties attending its exalted position, would be peculiarly blessed. And he went on to suggest that the three ladies before him, one of whom was about to enter upon a new phase of life to-morrow, under auspices peculiarly propitious, were, all of them, camels of this description. Sir Griffin, when he came in, received for a while the peculiar attention of Mr. Emilius. 'I think, Sir Griffin,' he commenced, 'that no period of a man's life is so blessed, as that upon which you will enter to-morrow.' This he said in a whisper, but it was a whisper audible to the ladies.

'Well;—yes; it's all right, I daresay,' said Sir Griffin.

'Well, after all, what is life till a man has met and obtained the partner of his soul? It is a blank,—and the blank becomes every day more and more intolerable to the miserable solitary.'

'I wonder you don't get married yourself,' said Mrs. Carbuncle, who perceived that Sir Griffin was rather astray for an answer.

'Ah!—if one could always be fortunate when one loved!' said Mr. Emilius, casting his eyes across to Lizzie Eustace. It was evident to them all that he did not wish to conceal his passion.

It was the object of Mrs. Carbuncle that the lovers should not be left alone together, but that they should be made to think that they were passing the evening in affectionate intercourse. Lucinda hardly spoke, hardly had spoken since her disagreeable struggle with Sir Griffin. He said but little, but with Mrs. Carbuncle was better humoured than usual. Every now and then she made little whispered communications to him, telling that they would be sure to be at the church at eleven to the moment, explaining to him what would be the extent of Lucinda's boxes for the wedding tour, assuring him that he would find Lucinda's new maid a treasure in regard to his own shirts and pocket-handkerchiefs. She toiled marvellously at little subjects, always making some allusion to Lucinda, and never hinting that aught short of Elysium was in store for him. The labour was great; the task was terrible; but now it was so nearly over! And to Lizzie she was very courteous, never hinting by a word or a look that there was any new trouble impending on the score of the diamonds. She, too, as she received the greasy compliments of Mr. Emilius with pretty smiles, had her mind full enough of care.

At last Sir Griffin went, again kissing his bride as he left. Lucinda accepted his embrace without a word and almost without a shudder. 'Eleven to the moment, Sir Griffin,' said Mrs. Carbuncle, with her best good-humour. 'All right,' said Sir Griffin as he passed out of the door. Lucinda walked across the room, and kept her eyes fixed on his retreating figure as he descended the stairs. Mr. Emilius had already departed, with many promises of punctuality, and Lizzie now withdrew for the night. 'Dear Lizzie, good night,' said Mrs. Carbuncle, kissing her.

'Good night, Lady Eustace,' said Lucinda. 'I suppose I shall see you to-morrow?'

'See me!—Of course you will see me. I shall come into your room with the girls, after you have had your tea.' The girls mentioned were the four bridesmaids, as to whom there had been some difficulty, as Lucinda had neither sister nor cousins, and had contracted no peculiarly tender friendships. But Mrs. Carbuncle had arranged it, and four properly-equipped young ladies were to be in attendance at ten on the morrow.

Then Lucinda and Mrs. Carbuncle were alone. 'Of one thing I feel sure,' said Lucinda in a low voice.

'What is that, dear?'

'I shall never see Sir Griffin Tewett again.'

'You talk in that way on purpose to break me down at the last moment,' said Mrs. Carbuncle.

'Dear Aunt Jane, I would not break you down if I could help it. I have struggled so hard,—simply that you might be freed from me. We have been very foolish, both of us; but I would bear all the punishment,—if I could.'

'You know that this is nonsense now.'

'Very well. I only tell you. I know that I shall never see him again. I will never trust myself alone in his presence. I could not do it. When he touches me my whole body is in agony. To be kissed by him is madness.'

'Lucinda, this is very wicked. You are working yourself up to a paroxysm of folly.'

'Wicked;—yes, I know that I am wicked. There has been enough of wickedness certainly. You don't suppose that I mean to excuse myself?'

'Of course you will marry Sir Griffin to-morrow.'

'I shall never be married to him. How I shall escape from him,—by dying, or going mad,—or by destroying him, God only knows.' Then she paused, and her aunt looking into her face almost began to fear that she was in earnest. But she would not take it as at all indicating any real result for the morrow. The girl had often said nearly the same thing before, and had still submitted. 'Do you know, Aunt Jane, I don't think I could feel to any man as though I loved him. But for this man, —— Oh God, how I do detest him! I cannot do it.'

'You had better go to bed, Lucinda, and let me come to you in the morning.'

'Yes;—come to me in the morning;—early.'

'I will,—at eight.'

'I shall know then, perhaps.'

'My dear, will you come to my room to-night, and sleep with me?'

'Oh, no. I have ever so many things to do. I have papers to burn, and things to put away. But come to me at eight. Good night, Aunt Jane.' Mrs. Carbuncle went up to her room with her, kissed her affectionately, and then left her.

She was now really frightened. What would be said of her if she should press the marriage forward to a completion, and if after that some terrible tragedy should take place between the bride and bridegroom? That Lucinda, in spite of all that had been said, would stand at the altar, and allow the ceremony to be performed, she still believed. Those last words about burning papers and putting things away, seemed to imply that the girl still thought that she would be taken away from her present home on the morrow. But what would come afterwards? The horror which the bride expressed was, as Mrs. Carbuncle well knew, no mock feeling, no pretence at antipathy. She tried to think of it, and to realise what might in truth be the girl's action and ultimate fate when she should find herself in the power of this man whom she so hated. But had not other girls done the same thing, and lived through it all, and become fat, indifferent, and fond of the world? It is only the first step that signifies.

At any rate, the thing must go on now;—must go on, whatever might be the result to Lucinda or to Mrs. Carbuncle herself. Yes; it must go on. There was, no doubt, very much of bitterness in the world for such as them,—for persons doomed by the necessities of their position to a continual struggle. It always had been so, and always would be so. But each bitter cup must be drained in the hope that the next might be sweeter. Of course the marriage must go on; though, doubtless, this cup was very bitter.

More than once in the night Mrs. Carbuncle crept up to the door of her niece's room, endeavouring to ascertain what might be going on within. At two o'clock, while she was on the landing-place, the candle was extinguished, and she could hear that Lucinda put herself to bed. At any rate, so far, things were safe. An indistinct, incompleted idea of some possible tragedy had flitted across the mind of the poor woman, causing her to shake and tremble, forbidding her, weary as she was, to lie down;—but now she told herself at last that this was an idle phantasy, and she went to bed. Of course Lucinda must go through with it. It had been her own doing, and Sir Griffin was not worse than other men. As she said this to herself, Mrs. Carbuncle hardened her heart by remembering that her own married life had not been peculiarly happy.

Exactly at eight on the following morning she knocked at her niece's door, and was at once bidden to enter. 'Come in, Aunt Jane.' The words cheered her wonderfully. At any rate, there had been no tragedy as yet, and as she turned the handle of the door, she felt that, as a matter of course, the marriage would go on just like any other marriage. She found Lucinda up and dressed,—but so dressed as certainly to show no preparation for a wedding-toilet. She had on an ordinary stuff morning frock, and her hair was close tucked up and pinned, as it might have been had she already prepared herself for a journey. But what astonished Mrs. Carbuncle more than the dress was the girl's manner. She was sitting at a table with a book before her, which was afterwards found to be the Bible, and she never turned her head as her aunt entered the room. 'What, up already,' said Mrs. Carbuncle,—'and dressed?'

'Yes; I am up,—and dressed. I have been up ever so long. How was I to lie in bed on such a morning as this? Aunt Jane, I wish you to know as soon as possible that no earthly consideration will induce me to leave this room to-day.'

'What nonsense, Lucinda!'

'Very well;—all the same you might as well believe me.

I want you to send to Mr. Emilius, and to those girls,—and to the man. And you had better get Lord George to let the other people know. I'm quite in earnest.'

And she was in earnest,—quite in earnest, though there was a flightiness about her manner which induced Mrs. Carbuncle for awhile to think that she was less so than she had been on the previous evening. The unfortunate woman remained with her niece for an hour and a half, imploring, threatening, scolding, and weeping. When the maids came to the door, first one maid and then another, they were refused entrance. It might still be possible, Mrs. Carbuncle thought, that she would prevail. But nothing now could shake Lucinda or induce her even to discuss the subject. She sat there looking steadfastly at the book,—hardly answering, never defending herself, but protesting that nothing should induce her to leave the room on that day. 'Do you want to destroy me?' Mrs. Carbuncle said at last.

'You have destroyed me,' said Lucinda.

At half-past nine Lizzie Eustace came to the room, and Mrs. Carbuncle, in her trouble, thought it better to take other counsel. Lizzie, therefore, was admitted. 'Is anything wrong?' asked Lizzie.

'Everything is wrong,' said the aunt. 'She says that—she won't be married.'

'Oh, Lucinda!'

'Pray speak to her, Lady Eustace. You see it is getting so late, and she ought to be nearly dressed now. Of course she must allow herself to be dressed.'

'I am dressed,' said Lucinda.

'But, dear Lucinda,—everybody will be waiting for you,' said Lizzie.

'Let them wait,—till they're tired. If Aunt Jane doesn't choose to send, it is not my fault. I shan't go out of this room to-day unless I am carried out. Do you want to hear that I have murdered the man?'

They brought her tea, and endeavoured to induce her to eat and drink. She would take the tea, she said, if they would promise to send to put the people off. Mrs. Carbuncle so far gave way as to undertake to do so, if she would name the next day or the day following for the wedding. But, on hearing this, she arose almost in a majesty of wrath. Neither on this day, or on the next, or on any following day, would she yield herself to the wretch whom they had endeavoured to force upon her. 'She must do it, you know,' said Mrs. Carbuncle, turning to Lizzie. 'You'll see if I must,' said Lucinda, sitting square at the table, with her eyes firmly fixed upon the book.

Then came up the servant to say that the four bridesmaids were all assembled in the drawing-room. When she heard this, even Mrs. Carbuncle gave way, and threw herself upon the bed and wept. 'Oh, Lady Eustace, what are we to do? Lucinda, you have destroyed me. You have destroyed me altogether, after all that I have done for you.'

'And what has been done to me, do you think?' said Lucinda.

Something must be settled. All the servants in the house by this time knew that there would be no wedding, and no doubt some tidings as to the misadventure of the day had already reached the four ladies in the drawing-room. 'What am I to do?' said Mrs. Carbuncle, starting up from the bed.

'I really think you had better send to Mr. Emilius,' said Lizzie;—'and to Lord George.'

'What am I to say? Who is there to go? Oh,—I wish that somebody would kill me this minute! Lady Eustace, would you mind going down and telling those ladies to go away?'

'And had I not better send Richard to the church?'

'Oh yes;—send anybody everywhere. I don't know what to do. Oh, Lucinda, this is the unkindest and the wickede, and the most horrible thing that anybody ever did! I sha never, never be able to hold up my head again.' Mrs. Carbuncle was completely prostrate, but Lucinda sat square at the table, firm as a rock, saying nothing, making no excuse for herself, with her eyes fixed upon the Bible.

Lady Eustace carried her message to the astonished and indignant bridesmaids, and succeeded in sending them back to their respective homes. Richard, glorious in new livery, forgetting that his flowers were still on his breast,—ready dressed to attend the bride's carriage,—went with his sad message, first to the church and then to the banqueting-hall in Albemarle Street.

'Not any wedding?' said the head-waiter at the hotel. 'I knew they was folks as would have a screw loose somewheres. There's lots to stand for the bill, anyways,' he added, as he remembered all the tribute.

CHAPTER LXX

Alas!

No attempt was made to send other messages from Hertford Street than those which were taken to the church and to the hotel. Sir Griffin and Lord George went together to the church in a brougham, and, on the way, the best man rather ridiculed the change in life which he supposed that his friend was about to make. 'I don't in the least know how you mean to get along,' said Lord George.

'Much as other men do, I suppose.'

'But you're always sparring, already.'

'It's that old woman that you're so fond of,' said Sir Griffin. 'I don't mean to have any ill-humour from my wife, I can tell you. I know who will have the worst of it if there is.'

'Upon my word, I think you'll have your hands full,' said Lord George. They got out at a sort of private door attached to the chapel, and were there received by the clerk, who wore a very long face. The news had already come, and had been communicated to Mr. Emilius, who was in the vestry. 'Are the ladies here yet?' asked Lord George. The woebegone clerk told them that the ladies were not yet there, and suggested that they should see Mr. Emilius. Into the presence of Mr. Emilius they were led, and then they heard the truth.

'Sir Griffin,' said Mr. Emilius, holding the baronet by the

278

hand, 'I'm sorry to have to tell you that there's something wrong in Hertford Street.'

'What's wrong?' asked Sir Griffin.

'You don't mean to say that Miss Roanoke is not to be here?' demanded Lord George. 'By George, I thought as much. I did indeed.'

'I can only tell you what I know, Lord George. Mrs. Carbuncle's servant was here ten minutes since, Sir Griffin,—before I came down, and he told the clerk that—that——'

'What the d—— did he tell him?' asked Sir Griffin.

'He said that Miss Roanoke had changed her mind, and didn't mean to be married at all. That's all that I can learn from what he says. Perhaps you will think it best to go up to Hertford Street?'

'I'll be —— if I do,' said Sir Griffin.

'I am not in the least surprised,' repeated Lord George. 'Tewett, my boy, we might as well go home to lunch, and the sooner you're out of town the better.'

'I knew that I should be taken in at last by that accursed woman,' said Sir Griffin.

'It wasn't Mrs. Carbuncle, if you mean that. She'd have given her left hand to have had it completed. I rather think you've had an escape, Griff; and if I were you, I'd make the best of it.' Sir Griffin spoke not another word, but left the church with his friend in the brougham that had brought them, and so he disappears from our story. Mr. Emilius looked after him with wistful eyes, regretful for his fee. Had the baronet been less coarse and violent in his language he would have asked for it; but he feared that he might be cursed in his own church, before his clerk, and abstained. Late in the afternoon Lord George, when he had administered comfort to the disappointed bridegroom in the shape of a hot lunch, Curaçoa,* and cigars, walked up to Hertford Street, calling at the hotel in Albemarle Street on the way. The waiter told him all that he knew. Some thirty or forty guests had come to the wedding-banquet, and had all been sent away with tidings that the marriage had been—postponed. 'You might have told 'em a trifle more than that,' said Lord George. 'Postponed was pleasantest, my lord,' said the waiter. 'Anyways, that was said, and we supposes, my lord, as the things ain't wanted now.' Lord George replied that, as far as he knew, the things were not wanted, and then continued his way up to Hertford Street.

At first he saw Lizzie Eustace, upon whom the misfortune of the day had had a most depressing effect. The wedding was to have been the one morsel of pleasing excitement which would come before she underwent the humble penance to which she was doomed. That was frustrated and abandoned, and now she could think only of Mr. Camperdown, her cousin Frank, and Lady Glencora Palliser. 'What's up now?' said Lord George, with that disrespect which had always accompanied his treatment of her since she had told him her secret. 'What's the meaning of all this?'

'I daresay that you know as well as I do, my lord.'

'I must know a good deal if I do. It seems that among you there is nothing but one trick upon another.'

'I suppose you are speaking of your own friends, Lord George. You doubtless know much more than I do of Miss Roanoke's affairs.'

'Does she mean to say that she doesn't mean to marry the man at all?'

'So I understand;—but really you had better send for Mrs. Carbuncle.'

He did send for Mrs. Carbuncle, and after some words with her, was taken up into Lucinda's room. There sat the unfortunate girl, in the chair from which she had not moved since the morning. There had come over her face a look of fixed but almost idiotic resolution; her mouth was compressed, and her eyes were glazed, and she sat twiddling her book before her with her fingers. She had eaten nothing since she had got up, and had long ceased to be violent when questioned by her aunt. But, nevertheless, she was firm enough when her aunt begged to be allowed to write a letter to Sir Griffin, explaining that all this had arisen from temporary indisposition. 'No; it isn't temporary. It isn't temporary at all. You can write to him; but I'll never come out of this room if I am told that I am to see him.'

'What is all this about, Lucinda?' said Lord George, speaking in his kindest voice.

'Is he there?' said she, turning round suddenly.

'Sir Griffin;—no indeed. He has left town.'

'You're sure he's not there. It's no good his coming. If he comes for ever and ever he shall never touch me again;—not alive; he shall never touch me again alive.' As she spoke she moved across the room to the fire-place and grasped the poker in her hand.

'Has she been like that all the morning?' whispered Lord George.

'No;—not like. She has been quite quiet. Lucinda!'

'Don't let him come here, then; that's all. What's the use? They can't make me marry him. And I won't marry him. Everybody has known that I hated him,—detested him. Oh, Lord George, it has been very, very cruel.'

'Has it been my fault, Lucinda?'

'She wouldn't have done it if you had told her not. But you won't bring him again;—will you?'

'Certainly not. He means to go abroad.'

'Ah;—yes; that will be best. Let him go abroad. He knew it, all the time,—that I hated him. Why did he want me to be his wife? If he has gone abroad, I will go down-stairs. But I won't go out of the house. Nothing shall make me go out of the house. Are the bridesmaids gone?'

'Long ago,' said Mrs. Carbuncle, piteously.

'Then I will go down.' And, between them, they led her into the drawing-room.

'It is my belief,' said Lord George to Mrs. Carbuncle, some minutes afterwards, 'that you have driven her mad.'

'Are you going to turn against me?'

'It is true. How you have had the heart to go on pressing it upon her, I could never understand. I am about as hard as a milestone, but I'll be shot if I could have done it. From day to day I thought that you would have given way.'

'That is so like a man,—when it is all over, to turn upon a woman and say that she did it.'

'Didn't you do it? I thought you did, and that you took a great deal of pride in the doing of it. When you made him offer to her down in Scotland, and made her accept him, you were so proud that you could hardly hold yourself. What will you do now? Go on just as though nothing had happened?'

'I don't know what we shall do. There will be so many things to be paid.'

'I should think there would,—and you can hardly expect Sir Griffin to pay for them. You'll have to take her away somewhere. You'll find that she can't remain here. And that other woman will be in prison before the week's over, I should say,—unless she runs away.'

There was not much of comfort to be obtained by any of them from Lord George, who was quite as harsh to Mrs. Carbuncle as he had been to Lizzie Eustace. He remained in Hertford Street for an hour, and then took his leave, saying that he thought that he also should go abroad. 'I didn't think,' he said, 'that anything could have hurt my character much; but, upon my word, between you and Lady Eustace, I begin to find that in every deep there may be a lower depth. All the town has given me credit for stealing her ladyship's necklace, and now I shall be mixed up in this mock marriage. I shouldn't wonder if Rooper were to send his bill in to me,'—Mr. Rooper was the keeper of the hotel in Albemarle Street,—'I think I shall follow Sir Griffin abroad. You have made England too hot to hold me.' And so he left them.

The evening of that day was a terrible time to the three ladies in Hertford Street,—and the following day was almost worse. Nobody came to see them, and not one of them dared to speak of the future. For the third day, the Wednesday, Lady Eustace had made her appointment with Mr. Camperdown, having written to the attorney, in compliance with the pressing advice of Major Mackintosh, to name an hour.

Mr. Camperdown had written again, sending his compliments, and saying that he would receive Lady Eustace at the time fixed by her. The prospect of this interview was very bad, but even this was hardly so oppressive as the actual existing wretchedness of that house. Mrs. Carbuncle, whom Lizzie had always known as high-spirited, bold, and almost domineering, was altogether prostrated by her misfortunes. She was querulous, lachrymose, and utterly despondent. From what Lizzie now learned, her hostess was enveloped in a mass of debt which would have been hopeless, even had Lucinda gone off as a bride, but she had been willing to face all that with the object of establishing her niece. She could have expected nothing from the marriage for herself. She well knew that Sir Griffin would neither pay her debts nor give her a home nor lend her money. But to have married the girl who was in her charge would have been in itself a success, and would have in some sort repaid her for her trouble. There would have been something left to show for her expenditure of time and money. But now there was nothing around her but failure and dismay. The very servants in the house seemed to know that ordinary respect was hardly demanded from them.

As to Lucinda, Lizzie felt, from the very hour in which she first saw her on the morning of the intended wedding, that her mind was astray. She insisted on passing the time up in her own room, and always sat with the Bible before her. At every knock at the door, or ring at the bell, she would look round suspiciously, and once she whispered into Lizzie's ear that, if ever 'he' should come there again, she would 'give him a kiss with a vengeance.' On the Tuesday, Lizzie recommended Mrs. Carbuncle to get medical advice,— and at last they sent for Mr. Emilius that they might ask counsel of him. Mr. Emilius was full of smiles and consolation, and still allowed his golden hopes as to some Elysian future to crop out;—but he did acknowledge at last, in a whispered conference with Lady Eustace, that somebody ought to see Miss Roanoke. Somebody did see Miss Roanoke,—and the doctor who was thus appealed to shook his head. Perhaps Miss Roanoke had better be taken into the country for a little while.

'Dear Lady Eustace,' said Mrs. Carbuncle, 'now you can be a friend indeed,'—meaning, of course, that an invitation to Portray Castle would do more than could anything else towards making straight the crooked things of the hour. Mrs. Carbuncle, when she made the request, of course knew of Lizzie's coming troubles;—but let them do what they could to Lizzie, they could not take away her house.

But Lizzie felt at once that this would not suit. 'Ah, Mrs. Carbuncle,' she said. 'You do not know the condition which I am in myself!'

CHAPTER LXXI
Lizzie is threatened with the Treadmill

EARLY on the Wednesday morning, two or three hours before the time fixed for Lizzie's visit to Mr. Camperdown, her cousin Frank came to call upon her. She presumed him to be altogether ignorant of all that Major Mackintosh had known, and therefore endeavoured to receive him as though her heart were light.

'Oh Frank,' she said, 'you have heard of our terrible misfortune here?'

'I have heard so much,' said he gravely, 'that I hardly know what to believe and what not to believe.'

'I mean about Miss Roanoke's marriage?'

'Oh yes;—I have been told that it is broken off.'

Then Lizzie, with affected eagerness, gave him a description of the whole affair, declaring how horrible, how tragic, the thing had been from its very commencement. 'Don't you remember, Frank, down at Portray, they never really cared for each other? They became engaged the very time you were there.'

'I have not forgotten it.'

'The truth is, Lucinda Roanoke did not understand what real love means. She had never taught herself to comprehend what is the very essence of love;——and as for Sir Griffin Tewett, though he was anxious to marry her, he never had any idea of love at all. Did not you always feel that, Frank?'

'I'm sorry you have had so much to do with them, Lizzie.'

'There's no help for spilt milk, Frank; and, as for that, I don't suppose that Mrs. Carbuncle can do me any harm. The man is a baronet, and the marriage would have been respectable. Miss Roanoke has been eccentric, and that has been the long and the short of it. What will be done, Frank, with all the presents that were bought?'

'I haven't an idea. They'd better be sold to pay the bills. But I came to you, Lizzie, about another piece of business.'

'What piece of business?' she asked, looking him in the face for a moment, trying to be bold, but trembling as she did so. She had believed him to be ignorant of her story, but she had soon perceived, from his manner to her, that he knew it all,—or, at least, that he knew so much that she would have to tell him all the rest. There could be no longer any secret with him. Indeed there could be no longer any secret with anybody. She must be prepared to encounter a world accurately informed as to every detail of the business which, for the last three months, had been to her a burden so oppressive that, at some periods, she had sunk altogether under the weight. She had already endeavoured to realise her position, and to make clear to herself the condition of her future life. Lord George had talked to her of perjury and prison, and had tried to frighten her by making the very worst of her faults. According to him she would certainly be made to pay for the diamonds, and would be enabled to do so by saving her income during a long term of incarceration. This was a terrible prospect of things; —and she had almost believed in it. Then the major had come to her. The major, she thought, was the truest gentleman she had ever seen, and her best friend. Ah;—if it had not been for the wife and seven children, there might still have been comfort! That which had been perjury with Lord George, had by the major been so simply, and yet so correctly, called an incorrect version of facts! And so it was,—and no more than that. Lizzie, in defending herself to herself, felt that, though cruel magistrates and hard-hearted lawyers and pig-headed jurymen might call her little fault by the name of perjury, it could not be real, wicked perjury, because the diamonds had been her own. She had defrauded nobody,—had wished to defraud nobody,—if only the people would have left her alone. It had suited her to give—an incorrect version of facts, because people had troubled themselves about her affairs; and now all this had come upon her! The major had comforted her very greatly; but still,—what would the world say? Even he, kind and comfortable as he had been, had made her understand that she must go into court and confess the incorrectness of her own version. She believed every word the major said. Ah, there was a man worthy to be believed;—a man of men! They could not take away her income or her castle. They could not make her pay for the diamonds. But still,—what would the world say? And what would her lovers say? What one of her lovers thought proper to say, she had already heard. Lord George had spoken out, and had made himself very disagreeable. Lord Fawn, she knew, would withdraw the renewal of his offer, let her answer to him be what it might. But what would Frank say? And now Frank was with her, looking into her face with severe eyes.

She was more than ever convinced that the life of a widow was not suited for her, and that, among her several lovers, she must settle her wealth and her heart upon some special lover. Neither her wealth nor her heart would be in any way injured by the confession which she was prepared to make. But then men are so timid, so false, and so blind! In regard to Frank, whom she now believed that she had loved with all the warmth of her young affections from the first moment in which she had seen him after Sir Florian's death,—she had been at great trouble to clear the way for him. She knew of his silly engagement to Lucy Morris, and was willing to forgive him that offence. She knew that he could not marry Lucy, because of her pennilessness and his indebtedness; and therefore she had taken the trouble to see Lucy with the view of making things straight on that side. Lucy had, of course, been rough with her, and ill-mannered, but Lizzie thought that, upon the whole, she had succeeded. Lucy was rough and ill-mannered, but was, at the same time, what the world calls good, and would hardly persevere after what had been said to her. Lizzie was sure that, a month since, her cousin would have yielded himself to her willingly, if he could only have freed himself from Lucy Morris. But now, just in this very nick of time, which was so momentous to her, the police had succeeded in unravelling her secret, and there sat Frank, looking at her with stern, ill-natured eyes, like an enemy rather than a lover.

'What piece of business?' she asked, in answer to his question. She must be bold,—if she could. She must brazen it out with him, if only she could be strong enough to put on her brass in his presence. He had been so stupidly chivalrous in believing all her stories about the robbery when nobody else had quite believed them, that she felt that she had before her a task that was very disagreeable and very difficult. She looked up at him, struggling to be bold, and then her glance sank before his gaze and fell upon the floor.

'I do not at all wish to pry into your secrets,' he said.

Secrets from him! Some such exclamation was on her lips, when she remembered that her special business, at the present moment, was to acknowledge a secret which had been kept from him. 'It is unkind of you to speak to me in that way,' she said.

'I am quite in earnest. I do not wish to pry into your secrets. But I hear rumours which seem to be substantiated; and though, of course, I could stay away from you——'

'Oh,—whatever happens, pray, pray do not stay away from me. Where am I to look for advice if you stay away from me?'

'That is all very well, Lizzie.'

'Ah, Frank! if you desert me, I am undone.'

'It is, of course, true that some of the police have been with you lately?'

'Major Mackintosh was here, about the end of last week,— a most kind man, altogether a gentleman, and I was so glad to see him.'

'What made him come?'

'What made him come?' How should she tell her story? 'Oh, he came, of course, about the robbery. They have found out everything. It was the jeweller, Benjamin, who concocted it all. That horrid sly girl I had, Patience Crabstick, put him up to it. And there were two regular housebreakers. They have found it all out at last.'

'So I hear.'

'And Major Mackintosh came to tell me about it.'

'But the diamonds are gone?'

'Oh yes;—those weary, weary diamonds. Do you know, Frank, that, though they were my own, as much as the coat you wear is your own, I am glad they are gone. I am glad that the police have not found them. They tormented me so that I hated them. Don't you remember that I told you how I longed to throw them into the sea, and to be rid of them for ever?'

'That, of course, was a joke.'

'It was no joke, Frank. It was solemn, serious truth.'

'What I want to know is,—where were they stolen?'

That, of course, was the question which hitherto Lizzie Eustace had answered by an incorrect version of facts, and now she must give the true version. She tried to put a bold face upon it, but it was very difficult. A face bold with brass she could not assume. Perhaps a little bit of acting might serve her turn, and a face that should be tender rather than bold. 'Oh, Frank!' she exclaimed, bursting out into tears.

'I always supposed that they were taken at Carlisle,' said Frank. Lizzie fell on her knees, at his feet, with her hands clasped together, and her one long lock of hair hanging down so as to touch his arm. Her eyes were bright with tears, but were not, as yet, wet and red with weeping. Was not this confession enough? Was he so hard-hearted as to make her tell her own disgrace in spoken words? Of course he knew well enough now, when the diamonds had been stolen. If he were possessed of any tenderness, any tact, any manliness, he would go on, presuming that question to have been answered.

'I don't quite understand it all,' he said, laying his hand softly upon her shoulder. 'I have been led to make so many statements to other people, which now seem to have been— incorrect! It was only the box that was taken at Carlisle?'

'Only the box.' She could answer that question.

'But the thieves thought that the diamonds were in the box?'

'I suppose so. But, oh, Frank! don't cross-question me about it. If you could know what I have suffered, you would not punish me any more. I have got to go to Mr. Camperdown's this very day. I offered to do that at once, and I shan't have strength to go through it if you are not kind to me now. Dear, dear Frank,—do be kind to me.'

And he was kind to her. He lifted her up to the sofa and did not ask her another question about the necklace. Of course she had lied to him and to all the world. From the very commencement of his intimacy with her, he had known that she was a liar, and what else could he have expected but lies? As it happened, this particular lie had been very big, very efficacious, and the cause of boundless troubles. It had been wholly unnecessary, and, from the first, though injurious to many, more injurious to her than to any other. He himself had been injured, but it seemed to him now that she had absolutely ruined herself. And all this had been done for nothing,—had been done, as he thought, that Mr. Camperdown might be kept in the dark, whereas all the light in the world would have assisted Mr. Camperdown nothing. He brought to mind, as he stood over her, all those scenes which she had so successfully performed in his presence since she had come to London,— scenes in which the robbery in Carlisle had been discussed between them. She had on these occasions freely expressed her opinion about the necklace, saying, in a low whisper, with a pretty little shrug of her shoulders, that she presumed it to be impossible that Lord George should have been concerned in the robbery. Frank had felt, as she said so, that some suspicion was intended by her to be attached to Lord George. She had wondered whether Mr. Camperdown had known anything about it. She had hoped that Lord Fawn would now be satisfied. She had been quite convinced that Mr. Benjamin had the diamonds. She had been indignant that the police had not traced the property. She had asked in another whisper,—a very low whisper indeed,—whether it was possible that Mrs. Carbuncle should know more about it than she was pleased to tell? And all the while the necklace had been lying in her own desk, and she had put it there with her own hands!

It was marvellous to him that the woman could have been so false and have sustained her falsehood so well. And this was his cousin, his well-beloved,—as a cousin, certainly well-beloved; and there had, doubtless, been times in which he had thought that he would make her his wife! He could not but smile as he stood looking at her, contemplating all the confusion which she had caused, and thinking how very little the disclosure of her iniquity seemed to confound herself. 'Oh, Frank, do not laugh at me,' she said.

'I am not laughing, Lizzie; I am only wondering,'

'And now, Frank, what had I better do?'

'Ah;—that is difficult; is it not? You see I hardly know all the truth yet. I do not want to know more,—but how can I advise you?'

'I thought you knew everything.'

'I don't suppose anybody can do anything to you.'

'Major Mackintosh says that nobody can. He quite understands that they were my own property, and that I had a right to keep them in my desk if I pleased. Why was I to tell everybody where they were? Of course I was foolish, and now they are lost. It is I that have suffered. Major Mackintosh quite understands that, and says that nobody can do anything to me; —only I must go to Mr. Camperdown.'

'You will have to be examined again before a magistrate.'

'Yes;—I suppose I must be examined. You will go with me, Frank,—won't you?' He winced, and made no immediate reply. 'I don't mean to Mr. Camperdown, but before the magistrate. Will it be in a court?'

'I suppose so.'

'The gentleman came here before. Couldn't he come here again?' Then he explained to her the difference of her present position, and in doing so he did say something of her iniquity. He made her understand that the magistrate had gone out of his way at the last inquiry, believing her to be a lady who had been grievously wronged, and one, therefore, to whom much consideration was due. 'And I have been grievously wronged,' said Lizzie. But now she would be required to tell the truth in opposition to the false evidence which she had formerly given; and she would herself be exempted from prosecution for perjury only on the ground that she would be called on to criminate herself in giving evidence against criminals whose crimes had been deeper than her own. 'I suppose they can't quite eat me,' she said, smiling through her tears.

'No;—they won't eat you,' he replied gravely.

'And you will go with me?'

'Yes;—I suppose I had better do so.'

'Ah;—that will be so nice.' The idea of the scene at the police-court was not at all 'nice' to Frank Greystock. 'I shall not mind what they say to me as long as you are by my side. Everybody will know that they were my own,—won't they?'

'And there will be the trial afterwards.'

'Another trial?' Then he explained to her the course of affairs,—that the men might not improbably be tried at Carlisle for stealing the box, and again in London for stealing the diamonds,—that two distinct acts of burglary had been committed, and that her evidence would be required on both occasions. He told her, also, that her attendance before the magistrate on Friday would only be a preliminary ceremony, and that, before the thing was over, she would, doubtless, be doomed to bear a great deal of annoyance, and to answer very many disagreeable questions. 'I shall care for nothing if you will only be at my side,' she exclaimed.

He was very urgent with her to go to Scotland as soon as her examination before the magistrates should be over, and was much astonished at the excuse she made for not doing so. Mrs. Carbuncle had borrowed all her ready money; but as she was now in Mrs. Carbuncle's house, she could repay herself a portion of the loan by remaining there and eating it out. She did not exactly say how much Mrs. Carbuncle had borrowed, but she left an impression on Frank's mind that it was about ten times the actual sum. With this excuse he was not satisfied, and told her that she must go to Scotland, if only for the sake of escaping from the Carbuncle connection. She promised to obey him if he would be her convoy. The Easter holidays were just now at hand, and he could not refuse on the plea of time. 'Oh, Frank, do not refuse me this;—only think how terribly forlorn is my position!' He did not refuse, but he did not quite promise. He was still tender-hearted towards her in spite of her enormities. One iniquity,—perhaps her worst iniquity, he did not yet know. He had not as yet heard of her disinterested appeal to Lucy Morris.

When he left her she was almost joyous for a few minutes; —till the thought of her coming interview with Mr. Camperdown again overshadowed her. She had dreaded two things chiefly,—her first interview with her cousin Frank after he should have learned the truth, and those perils in regard to perjury with which Lord George had threatened her. Both these bugbears had now vanished. That dear man, the major, had told her that there would be no such perils, and her cousin Frank had not seemed to think so very much of her lies and treachery! He had still been affectionate with her; he would support her before the magistrate; and would travel with her to Scotland. And after that who could tell what might come next? How foolish she had been to trouble herself as she had done,—almost to choke herself with an agony of fear, because she had feared detection. Now she was detected;—and what had come of it? That great officer of justice,

Major Mackintosh, had been almost more than civil to her; and her dear cousin Frank was still a cousin,—dear as ever. People, after all, did not think so very much of perjury,—of perjury such as hers, committed in regard to one's own property. It was that odious Lord George who had frightened her, instead of comforting, as he would have done, had there been a spark of the true Corsair poetry about him. She did not feel comfortably confident as to what might be said of her by Lady Glencora and the Duke of Omnium, but she was almost inclined to think that Lady Glencora would support her. Lady Glencora was no poor, mealy-mouthed thing, but a woman of the world who understood what was what. Lizzie, no doubt, wished that the trials and examinations were over;—but her money was safe. They could not take away Portray, nor could they rob her of four thousand a year. As for the rest, she could live it down.

She had ordered the carriage to take her to Mr. Camper-down's chambers, and now she dressed herself for the occasion. He should not be made to think, at any rate by her outside appearance, that she was ashamed of herself. But before she started she had just a word with Mrs. Carbuncle. 'I think I shall go down to Scotland on Saturday,' she said, proclaiming her news not in the most gracious manner.

'That is if they let you go,' said Mrs. Carbuncle.

'What do you mean? Who is to prevent me?'

'The police. I know all about it, Lady Eustace, and you need not look like that. Lord George informs me that you will probably,—be locked up to-day or to-morrow.'

'Lord George is a story-teller. I don't believe he ever said so. And if he did, he knows nothing about it.'

'He ought to know, considering all that you have made him suffer. That you should have gone on, with the necklace in your own box all the time, letting people think that he had taken them, and accepting his attentions all the while, is what I cannot understand! And however you were able to look those people at Carlisle in the face, passes me! Of course, Lady Eustace, you can't stay here after what has occurred.'

'I shall stay just as long as I like, Mrs. Carbuncle.'

'Poor dear Lucinda! I do not wonder that she should be driven beyond herself by so horrible a story. The feeling that she has been living all this time in the same house with a woman who had deceived all the police,—all the police,—has been too much for her. I know it has been almost too much for me.' And yet, as Lizzie at once understood, Mrs. Carbuncle knew nothing now which she had not known when she made her petition to be taken to Portray. And this was the woman, too, who had borrowed her money last week, whom she had entertained for months at Portray, and who had pretended to be her bosom-friend. 'You are quite right in getting off to Scotland as soon as possible,—if they will let you go,' continued Mrs. Carbuncle. 'Of course you could not stay here. Up to Friday night it can be permitted; but the servants had better wait upon you in your own rooms.'

'How dare you talk to me in that way?' screamed Lizzie.

'When a woman has committed perjury,' said Mrs. Carbuncle, holding up both her hands in awe and grief, 'nothing too bad can possibly be said to her. You are amenable to the outraged laws of the country, and it is my belief that they can keep you upon the treadmill and bread and water for months and months,—if not for years.' Having pronounced this terrible sentence, Mrs. Carbuncle stalked out of the room. 'That they can sequester your property for your creditors, I know,' she said, returning for a moment and putting her head within the door.

The carriage was ready, and it was time for Lizzie to start if she intended to keep her appointment with Mr. Camperdown. She was much flustered and weakened by Mrs. Carbuncle's ill-usage, and had difficulty in restraining herself from tears. And yet what the woman had said was false from beginning to end. The maid, who was the successor of Patience Crabstick, was to accompany her; and, as she passed through the hall, she so far recovered herself as to be able to conceal her dismay from the servants.

CHAPTER LXXII
Lizzie triumphs

Reports had, of course, reached Mr. Camperdown of the true story of the Eustace diamonds. He had learned that the Jew jeweller had made a determined set at them, having in the first place hired housebreakers to steal them at Carlisle, and having again hired the same housebreakers to steal them from the house in Hertford Street, as soon as he knew that Lady Eustace had herself secreted them. By degrees this information had reached him,—but not in a manner to induce him to declare himself satisfied with the truth. But now Lady Eustace was coming to him,—as he presumed, to confess everything.

When he first heard that the diamonds had been stolen at Carlisle, he was eager with Mr. Eustace in contending that the widow's liability in regard to the property was not at all the less because she had managed to lose it through her own pig-headed obstinacy. He consulted his trusted friend, Mr. Dove, on the occasion, making out another case for the barrister, and Mr. Dove had opined that, if it could be first proved that the diamonds were the property of the estate and not of Lady Eustace, and afterwards proved that they had been stolen through her laches,*—then could the Eustace estate recover the value from her estate. As she had carried the diamonds about with her in an absurd manner, her responsibility might probably be established;—but the non-existence of ownership by her must be first declared by a Vice-Chancellor,—with probability of appeal to the Lords Justices and to the House of Lords. A bill in Chancery must be filed, in the first place, to have the question of ownership settled; and then, should the estate be at length declared the owner, restitution of the property which had been lost through the lady's fault, must be sought at Common Law.

That had been the opinion of the Turtle Dove, and Mr. Camperdown had at once submitted to the law of his great legal mentor. But John Eustace had positively declared when he heard it that no more money should be thrown away in looking after property which would require two lawsuits to establish, and which, when established, might not be recovered. 'How can we make her pay ten thousand pounds? She might die first,' said John Eustace;—and Mr. Camperdown had been forced to yield. Then came the second robbery, and gradually there was spread about a report that the diamonds had been in Hertford Street all the time;—that they had not been taken at Carlisle, but certainly had been stolen at last.

Mr. Camperdown was again in a fever, and again had recourse to Mr. Dove and to John Eustace. He learned from the police all that they would tell him, and now the whole truth was to be divulged to him by the chief culprit herself. For, to the mind of Mr. Camperdown, the two housebreakers, and Patience Crabstick,—and even Mr. Benjamin himself, were white as snow as compared with the blackness of Lady Eustace. In his estimation no punishment could be too great for her,—and yet he began to understand that she would escape scot-free! Her evidence would be needed to convict the thieves, and she could not be prosecuted for perjury when once she had been asked for her evidence. 'After all, she has only told a fib about her own property,' said the Turtle Dove. 'About property not her own,' replied Mr. Camperdown stoutly. 'Her own,—till the contrary shall have been proved; her own, for all purposes of defence before a jury, if she were prosecuted now. Were she tried for the perjury, your attempt to obtain possession of the diamonds would be all so much in her favour.' With infinite regrets, Mr. Camperdown began to perceive that nothing could be done to her.

But she was to come to him and let him know from her own lips, facts of which nothing more than rumour had yet reached him. He had commenced his bill in Chancery,* and had hitherto stayed proceedings simply because it had been reported,—falsely, as it now appeared,—that the diamonds had been stolen at Carlisle. Major Mackintosh, in his desire to use Lizzie's evidence against the thieves, had recommended her to tell the whole truth openly to those who claimed the property on behalf of her husband's estate; and now, for the first time in her life, this odious woman was to visit him in his own chambers.

He did not think it expedient to receive her alone. He consulted his mentor, Mr. Dove, and his client, John Eustace, and the latter consented to be present. It was suggested to Mr. Dove that he might, on so peculiar an occasion as this, venture to depart from the established rule, and visit the attorney on his own quarter-deck; but he smiled, and explained that, though he was altogether superior to any such prejudice as that, and would not object at all to call on his friend, Mr. Camperdown, could any good effect arise from his doing so, he considered that, were he to be present on this occasion, he would simply assist in embarrassing the poor lady.

On this very morning, while Mrs. Carbuncle was abusing Lizzie in Hertford Street, John Eustace and Mr. Camperdown were in Mr. Dove's chambers, whither they had gone to tell him of the coming interview. The Turtle Dove was sitting back in his chair, with his head leaning forward as though it were going to drop from his neck, and the two visitors were listening to his words. 'Be merciful, I should say,' suggested the barrister. John Eustace was clearly of opinion that they ought to be merciful. Mr. Camperdown did not look merciful. 'What can you get by harassing the poor, weak, ignorant creature?' continued Mr. Dove. 'She has hankered after her bauble, and has told falsehoods in her efforts to keep it. Have you never heard of older persons, and more learned persons, and persons nearer to ourselves, who have done the same?' At that moment there was presumed to be great rivalry, not unaccompanied by intrigue, among certain leaders of the learned profession with reference to various positions of high honour and emolument, vacant or expected to be vacant. A Lord Chancellor was about to resign, and a Lord Justice had died. Whether a somewhat unpopular Attorney-General should be forced to satisfy himself with the one place, or allowed to wait for the other, had been debated in all the newspapers. It was agreed that there was a middle course in reference to a certain second-class Chief-Justiceship,—only that the present second-class Chief-Justice objected to shelve himself. There existed considerable jealousy, and some statements had been made which were not, perhaps, strictly founded on fact. It was understood, both by the attorney and by the Member of Parliament, that the Turtle Dove was referring to these circumstances when he spoke of baubles and falsehoods, and of learned persons near to themselves. He himself had hankered after no bauble,—but, as is the case with many men and women who are free from such hankerings, he was hardly free from that dash of malice which the possession of such things in the hands of others is so prone to excite. 'Spare her,' said Mr. Dove. 'There is no longer any material question as to the property, which seems to be gone irrecoverably. It is, upon the whole, well for the world, that property so fictitious as diamonds should be subject to the risk of such annihilation. As far as we are concerned, the property is annihilated, and I would not harass the poor, ignorant young creature.'

As Eustace and the attorney walked across from the Old to the New Square, the former declared that he quite agreed with Mr. Dove. 'In the first place, Mr. Camperdown, she is my brother's widow.' Mr. Camperdown with sorrow admitted the fact. 'And she is the mother of the head of our family. It should not be for us to degrade her;—but rather to protect her from degradation, if that be possible.' 'I heartily wish she had got her merits before your poor brother ever saw her,' said Mr. Camperdown.

Lizzie, in her fears, had been very punctual; and when the two gentlemen reached the door leading up to Mr. Camperdown's chambers, the carriage was already standing there. Lizzie had come up the stairs, and had been delighted at hearing that Mr. Camperdown was out, and would be back in a moment. She instantly resolved that it did not become her to wait. She had kept her appointment, had not found Mr.

Camperdown at home, and would be off as fast as her carriage-wheels could take her. But, unfortunately, while with a gentle murmur she was explaining to the clerk how impossible it was that she should wait for a lawyer who did not keep his own appointment, John Eustace and Mr. Camperdown appeared upon the landing, and she was at once convoyed into the attorney's particular room.

Lizzie, who always dressed well, was now attired as became a lady of rank, who had four thousand a year, and was the intimate friend of Lady Glencora Palliser. When last she saw Mr. Camperdown she had been arrayed for a summer, long, dusty journey down to Scotland, and neither by her outside garniture nor by her manner had she then been able to exact much admiration. She had been taken by surprise in the street, and was frightened. Now, in difficulty though she was, she resolved that she would hold up her head and be very brave. She was a little taken aback when she saw her brother-in-law, but she strove hard to carry herself with confidence. 'Ah, John,' she said, 'I did not expect to find you with Mr. Camperdown.'

'I thought it best that I should be here,—as a friend,' he said.

'It makes it much pleasanter for me, of course,' said Lizzie. 'I am not quite sure that Mr. Camperdown will allow me to regard him as a friend.'

'You have never had any reason to regard me as your enemy, Lady Eustace,' said Mr. Camperdown. 'Will you take a seat? I understand that you wish to state the circumstances under which the Eustace family diamonds were stolen while they were in your hands.'

'My own diamonds, Mr. Camperdown.'

'I cannot admit that for a moment, my lady.'

'What does it signify?' said Eustace. 'The wretched stones are gone for ever; and whether they were of right the property of my sister-in-law, or of her son, cannot matter now.'

Mr. Camperdown was irritated, and shook his head. It cut

him to the heart that everybody should take the part of the wicked, fraudulent woman who had caused him such infinite trouble. Lizzie saw her opportunity and was bolder than ever. 'You will never get me to acknowledge that they were not my own,' she said. 'My husband gave them to me, and I know that they were my own.'

'They have been stolen, at any rate,' said the lawyer.

Yes;—they have been stolen.'

'And now will you tell us how?'

Lizzie looked round upon her brother-in-law and sighed. She had never yet told the story in all its nakedness, although it had been three or four times extracted from her by admission. She paused, hoping that questions might be asked her which she could answer by easy monosyllables, but not a word was uttered to help her. 'I suppose you know all about it,' she said at last.

'I know nothing about it,' said Mr. Camperdown.

'We heard that your jewel-case was taken out of your room at Carlisle and broken open,' said Eustace.

'So it was. They broke into my room in the dead of night, when I was in bed, fast asleep, and took the case away. When the morning came, everybody rushed into my room, and I was so frightened that I did not know what I was doing. How would your daughter bear it, if two men cut away the locks and got into her bedroom when she was asleep? You don't think about that at all.'

'And where was the necklace?' asked Eustace.

Lizzie remembered that her friend the major had specially advised her to tell the whole truth to Mr. Camperdown,— suggesting that, by doing so, she would go far towards saving herself from any prosecution. 'It was under my pillow,' she whispered.

'And why did you not tell the magistrate that it had been under your pillow?'

Mr. Camperdown's voice, as he put to her this vital question, was severe, and almost justified the little burst of sobs which came forth as a prelude to Lizzie's answer. 'I did not know what I was doing. I don't know what you expect from me. You had been persecuting me ever since Sir Florian's death about the diamonds, and I didn't know what I was to do. They were my own, and I thought I was not obliged to tell everybody where I kept them. There are things which nobody tells. If I were to ask you all your secrets, would you tell them? When Sir Walter Scott was asked whether he wrote the novels, he didn't tell.'

'He was not upon his oath, Lady Eustace.'

'He did take his oath,—ever so many times. I don't know what difference an oath makes. People ain't obliged to tell their secrets, and I wouldn't tell mine.'

'The difference is this, Lady Eustace;—that if you give false evidence upon oath, you commit perjury.'

'How was I to think of that, when I was so frightened and confused that I didn't know where I was or what I was doing? There;—now I have told you everything.'

'Not quite everything. The diamonds were not stolen at Carlisle, but they were stolen afterwards. Did you tell the police what you had lost,—or the magistrate,—after the robbery in Hertford Street?'

'Yes; I did. There was some money taken, and rings, and other jewellery.'

'Did you tell them that the diamonds had been really stolen on that occasion?'

'They never asked me, Mr. Camperdown.'

'It is all as clear as a pike-staff, John,' said the lawyer.

'Quite clear, I should say,' replied Mr. Eustace.

'And I suppose I may go,' said Lizzie, rising from her chair.

There was no reason why she should not go; and, indeed, now that the interview was over, there did not seem to be any reason why she should have come. Though they had heard so much from her own mouth, they knew no more than they had known before. The great mystery had been elucidated, and Lizzie Eustace had been found to be the intriguing villain; but it was quite clear, even to Mr. Camperdown, that nothing could be done to her. He had never really thought that it would be expedient that she should be prosecuted for perjury, and he now found that she must go utterly scatheless, although, by her obstinacy and dishonesty, she had inflicted so great a loss on the distinguished family which had taken her to its bosom. 'I have no reason for wishing to detain you, Lady Eustace,' he said. 'If I were to talk for ever, I should not, probably, make you understand the extent of the injury you have done, or teach you to look in a proper light at the position in which you have placed yourself and all those who belong to you. When your husband died, good advice was given you, and given, I think, in a very kind way. You would not listen to it, and you see the result.'

'I ain't a bit ashamed of anything,' said Lizzie.

'I suppose not,' rejoined Mr. Camperdown.

'Good-bye, John.' And Lizzie put out her hand to her brother-in-law.

'Good-bye, Lizzie.'

'Mr. Camperdown, I have the honour to wish you good morning.' And Lizzie made a low curtsey to the lawyer, and was then attended to her carriage by the lawyer's clerk. She had certainly come forth from the interview without fresh wounds.

'The barrister who will have the cross-examining of her at the Central Criminal Court,' said Mr. Camperdown, as soon as the door was closed behind her, 'will have a job of work on his hand. There's nothing a pretty woman can't do when she has got rid of all sense of shame.'

'She is a very great woman,' said John Eustace,—'a very great woman; and, if the sex could have its rights, would make an excellent lawyer.' In the meantime Lizzie Eustace returned home to Hertford Street in triumph.

CHAPTER LXXIII
Lizzie's last Lover

Lizzie's interview with the lawyer took place on the Wednesday afternoon, and, on her return to Hertford Street, she found a note from Mrs. Carbuncle. 'I have made arrangements for dining out to-day, and shall not return till after ten. I will do the same to-morrow, and on every day till you leave town, and you can breakfast in your own room. Of course you will carry out your plan for leaving this house on Monday. After what has passed, I shall prefer not to meet you again. —J.C.' And this was written by a woman who, but a few days since, had borrowed £150 from her, and who at this moment had in her hands fifty pounds' worth of silver-plate, supposed to have been given to Lucinda, and which clearly ought to have been returned to the donor when Lucinda's marriage was—postponed, as the newspapers had said! Lucinda at this time had left the house in Hertford Street, but Lizzie had not been informed whither she had been taken. She could not apply to Lucinda for restitution of the silver,—which was, in fact, held at the moment by the Albemarle Street hotel-keeper as part security for his debt,—and she was quite sure that any application to Mrs. Carbuncle for either the silver or the debt would be unavailing. But she might, perhaps, cause annoyance by a letter, and could, at any rate, return insult for insult. She therefore wrote to her late friend.

'MADAM,

'I certainly am not desirous of continuing an acquaintance into which I was led by false representations, and in the course of which I have been almost absurdly hospitable to persons altogether unworthy of my kindness. You, and your niece, and your especial friend Lord George Carruthers, and that unfortunate young man your niece's lover, were entertained at my country-house as my guests for some

303

months. I am here, in my own right, by arrangement; and as
I pay more than a proper share of the expense of the establishment, I shall stay as long as I please, and go when I please.

'In the meantime, as we are about to part, certainly for
ever, I must beg you at once to repay me the sum of £150,—
which you have borrowed from me; and I must also insist
on your letting me have back the present of silver which was
prepared for your niece's marriage. That you should retain it
as a perquisite for yourself cannot for a moment be thought
of, however convenient it might be to yourself.

'Yours, &c.,
'E. EUSTACE.'

As far as the application for restitution went, or indeed in
regard to the insult, she might as well have written to a milestone. Mrs. Carbuncle was much too strong, and had fought
her battle with the world much too long, to regard such word-
pelting as that. She paid no attention to the note, and as she
had come to terms with the agent of the house by which she
was to evacuate it on the following Monday,—a fact which
was communicated to Lizzie by the servant,—she did not
much regard Lizzie's threat to remain there. She knew, moreover, that arrangements were already being made for the
journey to Scotland.

Lizzie had come back from the attorney's chambers in
triumph, and had been triumphant when she wrote her note
to Mrs. Carbuncle; but her elation was considerably repressed
by a short notice which she read in the fashionable evening
paper of the day. She always took the fashionable evening
paper, and had taught herself to think that life without it was
impossible. But on this afternoon she quarrelled with that
fashionable evening paper for ever. The popular and well-
informed organ of intelligence in question informed its
readers, that the Eustace diamonds—— &c., &c. In fact, it
told the whole story; and then expressed a hope that, as the
matter had from the commencement been one of great interest to the public, who had sympathised with Lady Eustace

deeply as to the loss of her diamonds, Lady Eustace would be able to explain that part of her conduct which certainly, at present, was quite unintelligible. Lizzie threw the paper from her with indignation, asking what right newspaper-scribblers could have to interfere with the private affairs of such persons as herself!

But on this evening the question of her answer to Lord Fawn was the one which most interested her. Lord Fawn had taken long in the writing of his letter, and she was justified in taking what time she pleased in answering it;—but, for her own sake, it had better be answered quickly. She had tried her hand at two different replies, and did not at all doubt but what she would send the affirmative answer, if she were sure that these latter discoveries would not alter Lord Fawn's decision. Lord Fawn had distinctly told her that, if she pleased, he would marry her. She would please;—having been much troubled by the circumstances of the past six months. But then, was it not almost a certainty that Lord Fawn would retreat from his offer on learning the facts which were now so well known as to have been related in the public papers? She thought that she would take one more night to think of it.

Alas! she took one night too many. On the next morning, while she was still in bed, a letter was brought to her from Lord Fawn, dated from his club the preceding evening. 'Lord Fawn presents his compliments to Lady Eustace. Lady Eustace will be kind enough to understand that Lord Fawn recedes altogether from the proposition made by him in his letter to Lady Eustace dated March 28th last. Should Lady Eustace think proper to call in question the propriety of this decision on the part of Lord Fawn, she had better refer the question to some friend, and Lord Fawn will do the same. Lord Fawn thinks it best to express his determination, under no circumstances, to communicate again personally with Lady Eustace on this subject,—or, as far as he can see at present, on any other.'

The letter was a blow to her, although she had felt quite certain that Lord Fawn would have no difficulty in escaping from her hands as soon as the story of the diamonds should be made public. It was a blow to her, although she had assured herself a dozen times that a marriage with such a one as Lord Fawn, a man who had not a grain of poetry in his composition, would make her unutterably wretched. What escape would her heart have had from itself in such a union? This question she had asked herself over and over again, and there had been no answer to it. But then why had she not been beforehand with Lord Fawn? Why had she not rejected his second offer with the scorn which such an offer had deserved? Ah,—there was her misfortune; there was her fault!

But, with Lizzie Eustace, when she could not do a thing which it was desirable that she should be known to have done, the next consideration was whether she could not so arrange as to seem to have done it. The arrival of Lord Fawn's note just as she was about to write to him, was unfortunate. But she would still write to him, and date her letter before the time that his was dated. He probably would not believe her date. She hardly ever expected to be really believed by anybody. But he would have to read what she wrote; and, writing on this pretence, she would avoid the necessity of alluding to his last letter.

Neither of the notes which she had by her quite suited the occasion,—so she wrote a third. The former letter in which she declined his offer was, she thought, very charmingly insolent, and the allusion to his lordship's scullion would have been successful, had it been sent on the moment, but now a graver letter was required,—and the graver letter was as follows:—

'Hertford Street, Wednesday, April 3.'

—The date, it will be observed, was the day previous to the morning on which she had received Lord Fawn's last very conclusive note.—

'MY LORD,

'I have taken a week to answer the letter which your lordship has done me the honour of writing to me, because I have thought it best to have time for consideration in a matter of such importance. In this I have copied your lordship's official caution.

'I think I never read a letter so false, so unmanly, and so cowardly, as that which you have found yourself capable of sending to me.

'You became engaged to me when, as I admit with shame, I did not know your character. You have since repudiated me and vilified my name, simply because, having found that I had enemies, and being afraid to face them, you wished to escape from your engagement. It has been cowardice from the beginning to the end. Your whole conduct to me has been one long, unprovoked insult, studiously concocted, because you have feared that there might possibly be some trouble for you to encounter. Nobody ever heard of anything so mean, either in novels or in real life.

'And now you again offer to marry me,—because you are again afraid. You think you will be thrashed, I suppose, if you decline to keep your engagement; and feel that if you offer to go on with it, my friends cannot beat you. You need not be afraid. No earthly consideration would induce me to be your wife. And if any friend of mine should look at you as though he meant to punish you, you can show him this letter and make him understand that it is I who have refused to be your wife, and not you who have refused to be my husband.

'E. EUSTACE.'

This epistle Lizzie did send, believing that she could add nothing to its insolence, let her study it as she might. And, she thought, as she read it for the fifth time, that it sounded as though it had been written before her receipt of the final note from himself, and that it would, therefore, irritate him the more.

This was to be the last week of her sojourn in town, and then she was to go down and bury herself at Portray, with no other companionship than that of the faithful Macnulty, who had been left in Scotland for the last three months as nurse-in-chief to the little heir! She must go and give her evidence before the magistrate on Friday, as to which she had already received an odious slip of paper;—but Frank would accompany her. Other misfortunes had passed off so lightly that she hardly dreaded this. She did not quite understand why she was to be so banished, and thought much on the subject. She had submitted herself to Frank's advice when first she had begun to fear that her troubles would be insuperable. Her troubles were now disappearing; and, as for Frank,—what was Frank to her, that she should obey him? Nevertheless, her trunks were being already packed, and she knew that she must go. He was to accompany her on her journey, and she would still have one more chance with him.

As she was thinking of all this, Mr. Emilius, the clergyman, was announced. In her loneliness she was delighted to receive any visitor, and she knew that Mr. Emilius would be at least courteous to her. When he had seated himself, he at once began to talk about the misfortune of the unaccomplished marriage, and in a very low voice hinted that, from the beginning to end, there had been something wrong. He had always feared that an alliance based on a footing that was so openly 'pecuniary,'—he declared that the word pecuniary expressed his meaning better than any other epithet,—could not lead to matrimonial happiness. 'We all know,' said he, 'that our dear friend, Mrs. Carbuncle, had views of her own quite distinct from her niece's happiness. I have the greatest possible respect for Mrs. Carbuncle,—and I may say esteem; but it is impossible to live long in any degree of intimacy with Mrs. Carbuncle without seeing that she is—mercenary.'

'Mercenary;—indeed she is,' said Lizzie.

'You have observed it? Oh yes; it is so, and it cast a shadow over a character which otherwise has so much to charm.'

'She is the most insolent and the most ungrateful woman that I ever heard of!' exclaimed Lizzie, with energy. Mr. Emilius opened his eyes, but did not contradict her assertion.

'As you have mentioned her name, Mr. Emilius, I must tell you. I have done everything for that woman. You know how I treated her down in Scotland.'

'With a splendid hospitality,' said Mr. Emilius.

'Of course she did not pay for anything there.'

'Oh no.' The idea of any one being called upon to pay for what one ate and drank at a friend's house, was peculiarly painful to Mr. Emilius.

'And I have paid for everything here. That is to say, we have made an arrangement, very much in her favour. And she has borrowed large sums of money from me.'

'I am not at all surprised at that,' said Mr. Emilius.

'And when that unfortunate girl, her niece, was to be married to poor Sir Griffin Tewett, I gave her a whole service of plate.'

'What unparalleled generosity!'

'Would you believe she has taken the whole for her own base purposes? And then what do you think she has done?'

'My dear Lady Eustace, hardly anything would astonish me.'

Lizzie suddenly found a difficulty in describing to her friend the fact that Mrs. Carbuncle was endeavouring to turn her out of the house, without also alluding to her own troubles about the robbery. 'She has actually told me,' she continued, 'that I must leave the house without a day's warning. But I believe the truth is, that she has run so much into debt that she cannot remain.'

'I know that she is very much in debt, Lady Eustace.'

'But she owed me some civility. Instead of that, she has treated me with nothing but insolence. And why, do you think? It is all because I would not allow her to take that poor insane young woman to Portray Castle.'

'You don't mean that she asked to go there?'

'She did, though.'

'I never heard such impertinence in my life,—never,' said Mr. Emilius, again opening his eyes and shaking his head.

'She proposed that I should ask them both down to Portray, for,—for,—of course it would have been almost for ever. I don't know how I should have got rid of them. And that poor young woman is mad, you know;—quite mad. She never recovered herself after that morning. Oh,—what I have suffered about that unhappy marriage, and the cruel, cruel way in which Mrs. Carbuncle urged it on. Mr. Emilius, you can't conceive the scenes which have been acted in this house during the last month. It has been dreadful. I wouldn't go though such a time again for anything that could be offered to me. It has made me so ill that I am obliged to go down to Scotland to recruit my health.'

'I heard that you were going to Scotland, and I wished to have an opportunity of saying—just a word to you, in private, before you go.' Mr. Emilius had thought a good deal about this interview, and had prepared himself for it with considerable care. He knew, with tolerable accuracy, the whole story of the necklace, having discussed it with Mrs. Carbuncle, who, as the reader will remember, had been told the tale by Lord George. He was aware of the engagement with Lord Fawn, and of the growing intimacy which had existed between Lord George and Lizzie. He had been watchful, diligent, patient, and had at last become hopeful. When he learned that his beloved was about to start for Scotland, he felt that it would be well that he should strike a blow before she went. As to a journey down to Ayrshire, that would be nothing to one so enamoured as was Mr. Emilius; and he would not scruple to show himself at the castle-door without invitation. Whatever may have been his deficiences, Mr. Emilius did not lack the courage needed to carry such an enterprise as this to a happy conclusion. As far as pluck and courage might serve a man, he was well served by his own gifts. He could, without a blush or a quiver in his voice, have asked a duchess to marry him, with ten times Lizzie's income. He had now considered deeply whether, with the view of prevailing, it would be better that he should allude to the lady's trespasses in regard to the diamonds, or that he should pretend to be in ignorance;

and he had determined that ultimate success might, with most probability, be achieved by a bold declaration of the truth. 'I know how desperately you must be in want of some one to help you through your troubles, and I know also that your grand lovers will avoid you because of what you have done, and therefore you had better take me at once. Take me, and I'll bring you through everything. Refuse me, and I'll help to crush you.' Such were the arguments which Mr. Emilius had determined to use, and such the language,—of course, with some modifications. He was now commencing his work, and was quite resolved to leave no stone unturned in carrying it to a successful issue. He drew his chair nearer to Lizzie as he announced his desire for a private interview, and leaned over towards her with his two hands closed together between his knees. He was a dark, hookey-nosed, well-made man, with an exuberance of greasy hair, who would have been considered handsome by many women, had there not been something, almost amounting to a squint, amiss with one of his eyes. When he was preaching, it could hardly be seen, but in the closeness of private conversation it was disagreeable.

'Oh,—indeed!' said Lizzie, with a look of astonishment, perfectly well assumed. She had already begun to consider whether, after all, Mr. Emilius——would do.

'Yes;—Lady Eustace; it is so. You and I have known each other now for many months, and I have received the most unaffected pleasure from the acquaintance,—may I not say from the intimacy which has sprung up between us?' Lizzie did not forbid the use of the pleasant word, but merely bowed. 'I think that, as a devoted friend and a clergyman, I shall not be thought to be intruding on private ground in saying that circumstances have made me aware of the details of the robberies by which you have been so cruelly persecuted.' So the man had come about the diamonds, and not to make an offer! Lizzie raised her eyebrows and bowed her head, with the slightest possible motion. 'I do not know how far your friends or the public may condemn you, but——'

'My friends don't condemn me at all, sir.'

'I am so glad to hear it!

'Nobody has dared to condemn me, except this impudent woman here, who wants an excuse for not paying me what she owes me.'

'I am delighted. I was going to explain that although I am aware you have infringed the letter of the law, and made yourself liable to proceedings which may, perhaps, be unpleasant——'

'I ain't liable to anything unpleasant at all, Mr. Emilius.'

'Then my mind is greatly relieved. I was about to remark, having heard in the outer world that there were those who ventured to accuse you of—of perjury——'

'Nobody has dared to accuse me of anything. What makes you come here and say such things?'

'Ah,—Lady Eustace. It is because these calumnies are spoken so openly behind your back.'

'Who speaks them? Mrs. Carbuncle, and Lord George Carruthers;—my enemies.'

Mr. Emilius was beginning to feel that he was not making progress. 'I was on the point of observing to you that according to the view of the matter which I, as a clergyman, have taken, you were altogether justified in the steps which you took for the protection of property which was your own, but which had been attacked by designing persons.'

'Of course I was justified,' said Lizzie.

'You know best, Lady Eustace, whether any assistance I can offer will avail you anything.'

'I don't want any assistance,—Mr. Emilius,—thank you.'

'I certainly have been given to understand that they who ought to stand by you with the closest devotion have, in this period of what I may, perhaps, call—tribulation, deserted your side with cold selfishness.'

'But there isn't any tribulation, and nobody has deserted my side.'

'I was told that Lord Fawn——'

'Lord Fawn is an idiot.'

'Quite so;—no doubt.'

'And I have deserted him. I wrote to him this very morning, in answer to a pressing letter from him to renew our engagement, to tell him that that was out of the question. I despise Lord Fawn, and my heart never can be given where my respect does not accompany it.'

'A noble sentiment, Lady Eustace, which I reciprocate completely. And now, to come to what I may call the inner purport of my visit to you this morning, the sweet cause of my attendance on you, let me assure you that I should not now offer you my heart, unless with my heart went the most perfect respect and esteem which any man ever felt for a woman.' Mr. Emilius had found the necessity of coming to the point by some direct road, as the lady had refused to allow him to lead up to it in the manner he had proposed to himself. He still thought that what he had said might be efficacious, as he did not for a moment believe her assertions as to her own friends, and the non-existence of any trouble as to the oaths which she had falsely sworn. But she carried the matter with a better courage than he had expected to find, and drove him out of his intended line of approach. He had, however, seized his opportunity without losing much time.

'What on earth do you mean, Mr. Emilius?' she said.

'I mean to lay my heart, my hand, my fortunes, my profession, my career at your feet. I make bold to say of myself that I have, by my own unaided eloquence and intelligence, won for myself a great position in this swarming metropolis. Lady Eustace, I know your great rank. I feel your transcendent beauty,—ah, too acutely. I have been told that you are rich. But I, myself, who venture to approach you, as a suitor for your hand, am also somebody in the world. The blood that runs in my veins is as illustrious as your own, having descended to me from the great and ancient nobles of my native country. The profession which I have adopted is the grandest which ever filled the heart of man with aspirations. I have barely turned my thirty-second year, and I am known as the greatest preacher of my day, though I preach in a language which is not my own. Your House of Lords would be open to me as a spiritual peer, would I condescend to come to terms with those who crave the assistance which I could give them. I can move the masses. I can touch the hearts of men. And in this great assemblage of mankind which you call London, I can choose my own society among the highest of the land. Lady Eustace, will you share with me my career and my fortunes? I ask you, because you are the only woman whom my heart has stooped to love.'

The man was a nasty, greasy, lying, squinting Jew preacher; an impostor, over forty years of age, whose greatest social success had been achieved when, through the agency of Mrs. Carbuncle, he made his way into Portray Castle. He was about as near an English mitre as had been that great man of a past generation, the Deputy Shepherd.* He was a creature to loathe,—because he was greasy, and a liar, and an impostor. But there was a certain manliness in him. He was not afraid of the woman; and in pleading his cause with her he could stand up for himself courageously. He had studied his speech, and having studied it, he knew how to utter the words. He did not blush, nor stammer, nor cringe. Of grandfather or grandmother belonging to himself he had probably never heard, but he could so speak of his noble ancestors as to produce belief in Lizzie's mind. And he almost succeeded in convincing her that he was, by the consent of mankind, the greatest preacher of the day. While he was making his speech she almost liked his squint. She certainly liked the grease and nastiness. Presuming, as she naturally did, that something of what he said was false, she liked the lies. There was a dash of poetry about him; and poetry, as she thought, was not compatible with humdrum truth. A man, to be a man in her eyes, should be able to swear that all his geese are swans;—should be able to reckon his swans by the dozen, though he have not a feather belonging to him, even from a goose's wing. She liked his audacity; and then, when he was making love, he was not afraid of talking out boldly about his heart. Nevertheless he was only Mr. Emilius, the clergyman; and she had means of knowing that his income was not generous. Though she admired his manner and his language, she was quite aware that he was in pursuit of her money. And from the moment in which she first understood his object, she was resolved that she would never become the wife of Mr. Emilius as long as there was a hope as to Frank Greystock.

'I was told, Mr. Emilius,' she said, 'that some time since you used to have a wife.'

'It was a falsehood, Lady Eustace. From motives of pure charity I gave a home to a distant cousin. I was then in a land of strangers, and my life was misinterpreted. I made no complaint, but sent the lady back to her native country. My compassion could supply her wants there as well as here.'

'Then you still support her?'

Mr. Emilius bethought himself for a moment. There might be danger in asserting that he was subject to such an encumbrance. 'I did do so,' he answered, 'till she found a congenial home as the wife of an honest man.'

'Oh, indeed. I'm quite glad to hear that.'

'And now, Lady Eustace, may I venture to hope for a favourable answer?'

Upon this, Lizzie made him a speech as long and almost as well turned as his own. Her heart had of late been subject to many vicissitudes. She had lost the dearest husband that a woman had ever worshipped. She had ventured, for purposes with reference to her child which she could not now explain, to think once again of matrimony with a man of high rank, but who had turned out to be unworthy of her. She had receded;—Lizzie, as she said this, acted the part of receding with a fine expression of scornful face;—and after that she was unwilling to entertain any further idea of marriage. Upon hearing this, Mr. Emilius bowed low, and before the street-door was closed against him had begun to calculate how much a journey to Scotland would cost him.

CHAPTER LXXIV
Lizzie at the Police-court

O N the Wednesday and Thursday Lizzie had been triumphant; for she had certainly come out unscathed from Mr.
Camperdown's chambers, and a lady may surely be said to
triumph when a gentleman lays his hand, his heart, his fortunes, and all that he has got, at her feet. But when the
Friday came, though she was determined to be brave, her
heart did sink within her bosom. She understood well that
she would be called upon to admit in public the falseness of
the oaths she had sworn upon two occasions; and that though
she would not be made amenable to any absolute punishment
for her perjury, she would be subject to very damaging remarks from the magistrate, and probably also from some
lawyers employed to defend the prisoners. She went to bed
in fairly good spirits, but in the morning she was cowed and

unhappy. She dressed herself from head to foot in black, and prepared for herself a heavy black veil. She had ordered from the livery stable a brougham for the occasion, thinking it wise to avoid the display of her own carriage. She breakfasted early, and then took a large glass of wine to support her. When Frank called for her at a quarter to ten, she was quite ready, and grasped his hand almost without a word. But she looked into his face with her eyes filled with tears. 'It will soon be over,' he said. She pressed his hand, and made him a sign to show that she was ready to follow him to the door. 'The case will come on at once,' he said, 'so that you will not be kept waiting.'

'Oh, you are so good;—so good to me.' She pressed his arm, and did not speak another word on their way to the police-court.

There was a great crowd about the office, which was in a little by-street, and so circumstanced that Lizzie's brougham could hardly make its way up to the door. But way was at once made for her when Frank handed her out of it, and the policemen about the place were as courteous to her as though she had been the Lord Chancellor's wife. Evil-doing will be spoken of with bated breath and soft words even by policemen, when the evil-doer comes in a carriage, and with a title. Lizzie was led at once into a private room, and told that she would be kept there only a very few minutes. Frank made his way into the court and found that two magistrates had just seated themselves on the bench. One would have sufficed for the occasion; but this was a case of great interest, and even police-magistrates are human in their interests. Greystock was allowed to get round to the bench, and to whisper a word or two to the gentleman who was to preside. The magistrate nodded his head, and then the case*began.

The unfortunate Mr. Benjamin had been sent back in durance vile*from Vienna, and was present in the court. With him, as joint malefactor, stood Mr. Smiler, the great housebreaker, a huge, ugly, resolute-looking scoundrel, possessed of enormous strength, who was very intimately known to the police, with whom he had had various dealings since he had been turned out upon the town to earn his bread some fifteen years ago. Indeed, long before that he had known the police. As far as his memory went back he had always known them. But the sportive industry of his boyish years was not now counted up against him. In the last fifteen years his biography was written with all the accuracy due to the achievements of a great man, and during those hundred and eighty months he had spent over one hundred in prison, and had been convicted twenty-three times. He was now growing old,—as a thief; and it was thought by his friends that he would be settled for life in some quiet retreat. Mr. Benjamin was a very respectable-looking man of about fifty with slightly grizzled hair, with excellent black clothes, showing, by a surprised air, his great astonishment at finding himself in such a position. He spoke constantly both to his attorney, and to the barrister who was to show cause why he should not be committed, and throughout the whole morning was very busy. Smiler, who was quite at home, and who understood his position, never said a word to any one. He stood, perfectly straight, looking at the magistrate, and never for a moment leaning on the rail before him during the four hours that the case consumed. Once, when his friend, Billy Cann, was brought into court to give evidence against him, dressed up to the eyes, serene and sleek as when we saw him once before at the 'Rising Sun', in Meek Street, Smiler turned a glance upon him which, to the eyes of all present, contained a threat of most bloody revenge. But Billy knew the advantages of his situation, and nodded at his old comrade, and smiled. His old comrade was very much stronger than he, and possessed of many natural advantages; but, perhaps, upon the whole, his old comrade had been the less intelligent thief of the two. It was thus that the bystanders read the meaning of Billy's smile.

The case was opened very shortly and very clearly by the gentleman who was employed for the prosecution. It would all, he said, have lain in a nutshell, had it not been complicated by a previous robbery at Carlisle. Were it necessary, he said, there would be no difficulty in convicting the prisoners for that offence also, but it had been thought advisable to confine the prosecution to the act of burglary committed in Hertford Street. He stated the facts of what had happened at Carlisle, merely for explanation, but would state nothing that could not be proved. Then he told all that the reader knows about the iron box. But the diamonds were not then in the box,—and he told that story also, treating Lizzie with great tenderness as he did so. Lizzie, all this time, was sitting behind her veil in the private room, and did not hear a word of what was going on. Then he came to the robbery in Hertford Street. He would prove by Lady Eustace that the diamonds were left by her in a locked desk,—were so deposited, though all her friends believed them to have been taken at Carlisle; and he would, moreover, prove by accomplices that they were stolen by two men,—the younger prisoner at the bar being one of them, and the witness who would be adduced, the other,—that they were given up by these men to the elder prisoner, and that a certain sum had been paid by him for the execution of the two robberies. There was much more of it;—but to the reader, who knows it all, it would be but a thrice-told tale. He then said that he first proposed to take the evidence of Lady Eustace, the lady who had been in possession of the diamonds when they were stolen. Then Frank Greystock left the court, and returned with poor Lizzie on his arm.

She was handed to a chair, and, after she was sworn, was told that she might sit down. But she was requested to remove her veil, which she had replaced as soon as she had kissed the book.* The first question asked her was very easy. Did she remember the night at Carlisle? Would she tell the history of what occurred on that night? When the box was stolen, were the diamonds in it? No; she had taken the diamonds out for security, and had kept them under her pillow. Then came a bitter moment, in which she had to confess her perjury before the Carlisle bench;—but even that seemed to pass off smoothly. The magistrate asked one severe question. 'Do you mean to say, Lady Eustace, that you gave false evidence on that occasion,—knowing it to be false?' 'I was in such a state, sir, from fear, that I did not know what I was saying,' exclaimed Lizzie, bursting into tears and stretching forth towards the bench her two clasped hands with the air of a suppliant. From that moment the magistrate was altogether on her side,—and so were the public. Poor ignorant, ill-used young creature;—and then so lovely! That was the general feeling. But she had not as yet come beneath the harrow of the learned gentleman on the other side, whose best talents were due to Mr. Benjamin. Then she told all she knew about the other robbery. She certainly had not said, when examined on that occasion, that the diamonds had then been taken. She had omitted to name the diamonds in her catalogue of the things stolen. But she was sure that she had never said that they were not then taken. She had said nothing about the diamonds, knowing them to be her own, and preferring to lose them to the trouble of again referring to the night at Carlisle. Such was her evidence for the prosecution, and then she was turned over to the very learned and very acute gentleman whom Mr. Benjamin had hired for his defence, —or rather, to show cause why he should not be sent for trial.

It must be owned that poor Lizzie did receive from his hands some of that punishment which she certainly deserved. This acute and learned gentleman seemed to possess for the occasion the blandest and most dulcet voice that ever was bestowed upon an English barrister. He addressed Lady Eustace with the softest words, as though he hardly dared to speak to a woman so eminent for wealth, rank, and beauty; but nevertheless he asked her some very disagreeable questions. 'Was he to understand that she went of her own will before the bench of magistrates at Carlisle, with the view of enabling the police to capture certain persons for stealing certain jewels, while she knew that the jewels were actually in her own possession?' Lizzie, confounded by the softness of his voice as joined to the harshness of the question, could hardly understand him, and he repeated it thrice, becoming every time more and more mellifluous. 'Yes,' said Lizzie at last. 'Yes?' he asked. 'Yes,' said Lizzie. 'Your ladyship did send the Cumberland police after men for stealing jewels which were in your ladyship's own hands when you swore the information?' 'Yes,' said Lizzie. 'And your ladyship knew that the information was untrue?' 'Yes,' said Lizzie. 'And the police were pursuing the men for many weeks?' 'Yes,' said Lizzie. 'On your information?' 'Yes,' said Lizzie, through her tears. 'And your ladyship knew all the time that the poor men were altogether innocent of taking the jewels?' 'But they took the box,' said Lizzie, through her tears. 'Yes,' said the acute and learned gentleman, 'somebody took your ladyship's iron box out of the room, and you swore that the diamonds had been taken. Was it not the fact that legal proceedings were being taken against you for recovery of the diamonds by persons who claimed the property?' 'Yes,' said Lizzie. 'And these persons withdrew their proceedings as soon as they heard that the diamonds had been stolen?'

Soft as he was in his manner, he nearly reduced Lizzie Eustace to fainting. It seemed to her that the questions would never end. It was in vain that the magistrate pointed out to the learned gentleman that Lady Eustace had confessed her own false swearing, both at Carlisle and in London, a dozen times. He continued his questions over and over again, harping chiefly on the affair at Carlisle, and saying very little as to the second robbery in Hertford Street. His idea was to make it appear that Lizzie had arranged the robbery with the view of defrauding Mr. Camperdown, and that Lord George Carruthers was her accomplice. He even asked her, almost in a whisper, and with the sweetest smile, whether she was not engaged to marry Lord George. When Lizzie denied this, he still suggested that some such alliance might be in contemplation. Upon this, Frank Greystock called upon the magistrate to defend Lady Eustace from such unnecessary vulgarity, and there was a scene in the court. Lizzie did not like the scene, but it helped to protect her from the contemplation of the public, who of course were much gratified by high words between two barristers.

Lady Eustace was forced to remain in the private room during the examination of Patience Crabstick and Mr. Cann; but she did not hear it. Patience was a most obdurate and difficult witness,—extremely averse to say evil of herself, and on that account unworthy of the good things which she had received. But Billy Cann was charming,—graceful, communicative, and absolutely accurate. There was no shaking him. The learned and acute gentleman who tried to tear him in pieces could do nothing with him. He was asked whether he had not been a professional thief for ten years. 'Ten or twelve,' he said. Did he expect that any jurymen would believe him on his oath? 'Not unless I am fully corroborated.' 'Can you look that man in the face,—that man who is at any rate so much honester than yourself' asked the learned gentleman with pathos. Billy said that he thought he could, and the way in which he smiled upon Smiler caused a roar through the whole court.

The two men were, as a matter of course, committed for trial at the Central Criminal Court, and Lizzie Eustace was bound by certain penalties to come forward when called upon, and give her evidence again. 'I am glad that it is over,' said Frank, as he left her at Mrs. Carbuncle's hall-door.

'O Frank, dearest Frank, where should I be if it were not for you?'

CHAPTER LXXV
Lord George gives his Reasons

LADY EUSTACE did not leave the house during the Saturday and Sunday, and engaged herself exclusively with preparing for her journey. She had no further interview with Mrs. Carbuncle, but there were messages between them, and even notes were written. They resulted in nothing. Lizzie was desirous of getting back the spoons and forks, and, if possible, some of her money. The spoons and forks were out of Mrs. Carbuncle's power, in Albemarle Street; and the money had of course been spent. Lizzie might have saved herself the trouble, had it not been that it was a pleasure to her to insult her late friend, even though in doing so new insults were heaped upon her own head. As for the trumpery spoons, they,—so said Mrs. Carbuncle,—were the property of Miss Roanoke, having been made over to her unconditionally long before the wedding, as a part of a separate pecuniary transaction. Mrs. Carbuncle had no power of disposing of Miss Roanoke's property. As to the money which Lady Eustace claimed, Mrs. Carbuncle asserted that, when the final accounts should be made up between them, it would be found that there was a considerable balance due to Mrs. Carbuncle. But even were there anything due to Lady Eustace, Mrs. Carbuncle would decline to pay it, as she was informed that all moneys possessed by Lady Eustace were now confiscated to the Crown by reason of the PERJURIES,—the word was doubly scored in Mrs. Carbuncle's note,—which Lady Eustace had committed. This, of course, was unpleasant; but Mrs. Carbuncle did not have the honours of the battle all to herself. Lizzie also said some unpleasant things,—which perhaps were the more unpleasant because they were true. Mrs. Carbuncle had come pretty nearly to the end of her career, whereas Lizzie's income, in spite of her perjuries, was comparatively untouched. The undoubted mistress of Portray Castle, and mother of the Sir Florian Eustace of the day, could still despise and look down upon Mrs. Carbuncle, although she were known to have told fibs about the family diamonds.

Lord George always came to Hertford Street on a Sunday, and Lady Eustace left word for him with the servant that she would be glad to see him before her journey into Scotland. 'Goes to-morrow, does she?' said Lord George to the servant. 'Well; I'll see her.' And he was shown up to her room before he went to Mrs. Carbuncle.

Lizzie, in sending to him, had some half-formed idea of a romantic farewell. The man, she thought, had behaved very badly to her;—had accepted very much from her hands, and had refused to give her anything in return; had become the first depository of her great secret, and had placed no mutual confidence in her. He had been harsh to her, and unjust. And then, too, he had declined to be in love with her! She was full of spite against Lord George and would have been glad to injure him. But, nevertheless, there would be some excitement in a farewell in which some mock affection might be displayed, and she would have an opportunity of abusing Mrs. Carbuncle.

'So you are off to-morrow?' said Lord George, taking his place on the rug before her fire, and looking down at her with his head a little on one side. Lizzie's anger against the man chiefly arose from a feeling that he treated her with all a Corsair's freedom without any of a Corsair's tenderness. She could have forgiven the want of deferential manner, had there been any devotion;—but Lord George was both impudent and indifferent.

'Yes,' she said. 'Thank goodness, I shall get out of this frightful place to-morrow, and soon have once more a roof of my own over my head. What an experience I have had since I have been here!'

'We have all had an experience,' said Lord George, still looking at her with that half-comic turn of his face,—almost as though he were investigating some curious animal of which so remarkable a specimen had never before come under his notice.

'No woman ever intended to show a more disinterested friendship than I have done; and what has been my return?'

'You mean to me?—disinterested friendship to me?' And Lord George tapped his breast lightly with his fingers. His head was still a little on one side, and there was still the smile upon his face.

'I was alluding particularly to Mrs. Carbuncle.'

'Lady Eustace, I cannot take charge of Mrs. Carbuncle's friendships. I have enough to do to look after my own. If you have any complaint to make against me,—I will at least listen to it.'

'God knows I do not want to make complaints,' said Lizzie, covering her face with her hands.

'They don't do much good;—do they? It's better to take people as you find 'em, and then make the best of 'em. They're a queer lot;—ain't they,—the sort of people one meets about in the world?'

'I don't know what you mean by that, Lord George.'

'Just what you were saying, when you talked of your experiences. These experiences do surprise one. I have knocked about the world a great deal, and would have almost said that nothing would surprise me. You are no more than a child to me, but you have surprised me.'

'I hope I have not injured you, Lord George.'

'Do you remember how you rode to hounds the day your cousin took that other man's horse? That surprised me.'

'Oh, Lord George, that was the happiest day of my life. How little happiness there is for people!'

'And when Tewett got that girl to say she'd marry him, the coolness with which you bore all the abomination of it in your house,—for people who were nothing to you;—that surprised me!'

'I meant to be so kind to you all.'

'And when I found that you always travelled with ten thousand pounds worth of diamonds in a box, that surprised me very much. I thought that you were a very dangerous companion.'

'Pray don't talk about the horrid necklace.'

'Then came the robbery, and you seemed to lose your diamonds without being at all unhappy about them. Of course, we understand that now.' On hearing this, Lizzie smiled, but did not say a word. 'Then I perceived that I—I was supposed to be the thief. You,—you yourself couldn't have suspected me of taking the diamonds, because—because you'd got them, you know, all safe in your pocket. But you might as well own the truth now. Didn't you think that it was I who stole the box?'

'I wish it had been you,' said Lizzie laughing.

'All that surprised me. The police were watching me every day as a cat watches a mouse, and thought that they surely had got the thief when they found that I had dealings with Benjamin. Well; you,—you were laughing at me in your sleeve all the time.'

'Not laughing, Lord George.'

'Yes you were. You had got the kernel yourself, and thought that I had taken all the trouble to crack the nut and had found myself with nothing but the shell. Then, when you found you couldn't eat the kernel; that you couldn't get rid of the swag without assistance, you came to me to help you. I began to think then that you were too many for all of us. By Jove, I did. Then I heard of the second robbery, and, of course, I thought you had managed that too.'

'Oh no,' said Lizzie

'Unfortunately you didn't; but I thought you did. And you thought that I had done it! Mr. Benjamin was too clever for us both, and now he is going to have penal servitude for the rest of his life. I wonder who will be the better of it all. Who'll have the diamonds at last?'

'I do not in the least care. I hate the diamonds. Of course I would not give them up, because they were my own.'

'The end of it seems to be that you have lost your property, and sworn ever so many false oaths, and have brought all your friends into trouble, and have got nothing by it. What was the good of being so clever?'

'You need not come here to tease me, Lord George.'

'I came here because you sent for me. There's my poor friend, Mrs. Carbuncle, declares that all her credit is destroyed, and her niece unable to marry, and her house taken away from her,—all because of her connection with you.'

'Mrs. Carbuncle is,—is,—is—— Oh, Lord George, don't you know what she is?'

'I know that Mrs. Carbuncle is in a very bad way, and that that girl has gone crazy, and that poor Griff has taken himself off to Japan, and that I am so knocked about that I don't know where to go; and somehow it seems all to have come from your little manœuvres. You see, we have, all of us, been made remarkable; haven't we?'

'You are always remarkable, Lord George.'

'And it is all your doing. To be sure you have lost your diamonds for your pains. I wouldn't mind it so much if anybody were the better for it. I shouldn't have begrudged even Benjamin the pull, if he'd got it.'

He stood there still looking down upon her, speaking with a sarcastic subrisive tone, and, as she felt, intending to be severe to her. She had sent for him, and now she didn't know what to say to him. Though she believed that she hated him, she would have liked to get up some show of an affectionate farewell, some scene in which there might have been tears, and tenderness, and poetry,—and, perhaps, a parting caress. But with his jeering words, and sneering face, he was as hard to her as a rock. He was now silent, but still looking down upon her as he stood motionless upon the rug,—so that she was compelled to speak again. 'I sent for you, Lord George, because I did not like the idea of parting with you for ever, without one word of adieu.'

'You are going to tear yourself away;—are you?'

'I am going to Portray on Monday.'

'And never coming back any more? You'll be up here before the season is over, with fifty more wonderful schemes in your little head. So Lord Fawn is done with; is he?'

'I have told Lord Fawn that nothing shall induce me ever to see him again.'

'And cousin Frank?'

'My cousin attends me down to Scotland.'

'Oh—h. That makes it altogether another thing. He attends you down to Scotland;—does he? Does Mr. Emilius go too?'

'I believe you are trying to insult me, sir.'

'You can't expect but what a man should be a little jealous, when he has been so completely cut out himself. There was a time, you know, when even cousin Frank wasn't a better fellow than myself.'

'Much you thought about it, Lord George.'

'Well;—I did. I thought about it a good deal, my lady. And I liked the idea of it very much.' Lizzie pricked up her ears. In spite of all his harshness, could it be that he should be the Corsair still? 'I am a rambling, uneasy, ill-to-do sort of man; but still I thought about it. You are pretty, you know,—uncommonly pretty.'

'Don't, Lord George.'

'And I'll acknowledge that the income goes for much. I suppose that's real at any rate?'

'Well;—I hope so. Of course it's real. And so is the prettiness, Lord George;—if there is any.'

'I never doubted that, Lady Eustace. But when it came to my thinking that you had stolen the diamonds, and you thinking that I had stolen the box——! I'm not a man to stand on trifles, but, by George, it wouldn't do then.'

'Who wanted it to do?' said Lizzie. 'Go away. You are very unkind to me. I hope I may never see you again. I believe you care more for that odious vulgar woman downstairs than you do for anybody else in the world.'

'Ah dear! I have known her for many years, Lizzie, and that both covers and discovers many faults. One learns to know how bad one's old friends are, but then one forgives them, because they are old friends.'

'You can't forgive me,—because I'm bad, and only a new friend.'

'Yes, I will. I forgive you all, and hope you may do well yet. If I may give you one bit of advice at parting, it is to caution you against being clever when there is nothing to get by it.'

'I ain't clever at all,' said Lizzie, beginning to whimper.

'Good-bye, my dear.'

'Good-bye,' said Lizzie. He took her hand in one of his; patted her on the head with the other, as though she had been a child, and then he left her.

CHAPTER LXXVI
Lizzie returns to Scotland

F RANK GREYSTOCK, the writer fears, will not have recommended himself to those readers of this tale who think the
part of lover to the heroine should be always filled by a young
man with heroic attributes. And yet the young member for
Bobsborough was by no means deficient in fine qualities, and
perhaps was quite as capable of heroism as the majority of
barristers and members of Parliament among whom he con-
sorted, and who were to him—the world. A man born to
great wealth may,—without injury to himself or friends,—do
pretty nearly what he likes in regard to marriage, always
presuming that the wife he selects be of his own rank. He
need not marry for money, nor need he abstain from marriage
because he can't support a wife without money. And the very
poor man, who has no pretension to rank, or standing, other
than that which honesty may give him, can do the same.
His wife's fortune will consist in the labour of her hands, and
in her ability to assist him in his home. But between these
there is a middle class of men, who, by reason of their education, are peculiarly susceptible to the charms of womanhood,
but who literally cannot marry for love, because their earnings will do no more than support themselves. As to this
special young man, it must be confessed that his earnings
should have done much more than that; but not the less did
he find himself in a position in which marriage with a penniless girl seemed to threaten him and her with ruin. All his
friends told Frank Greystock that he would be ruined were he
to marry Lucy Morris;—and his friends were people supposed
to be very good and wise. The dean, and the dean's wife, his
father and mother, were very clear that it would be so. Old
Lady Linlithgow had spoken of such a marriage as quite out
of the question. The Bishop of Bobsborough, when it was
mentioned in his hearing, had declared that such a marriage
would be a thousand pities. And even dear old Lady Fawn,

though she wished it for Lucy's sake, had many times prophesied that such a thing was quite impossible. When the rumour
of the marriage reached Lady Glencora, Lady Glencora told
her friend, Madame Max Goesler, that that young man was
going to blow his brains out. To her thinking the two actions
were equivalent. It is only when we read of such men that
we feel that truth to his sweetheart is the first duty of man.
I am afraid that it is not the advice which we give to our
sons.

But it was the advice which Frank Greystock had most per-
sistently given to himself since he had first known Lucy
Morris. Doubtless he had vacillated, but, on the balance of
his convictions as to his own future conduct, he had been
much nobler than his friends. He had never hesitated for a
moment as to the value of Lucy Morris. She was not beautiful. She had no wonderful gifts of nature. There was nothing
of a goddess about her. She was absolutely penniless. She
had never been what the world calls well-dressed. And yet
she had been everything to him. There had grown up a sympathy between them quite as strong on his part as on hers,
and he had acknowledged it to himself. He had never
doubted his own love,—and when he had been most near to
convincing himself that in his peculiar position he ought to
marry his rich cousin, because of her wealth, then, at those
moments, he had most strongly felt that to have Lucy Morris
close to him was the greatest charm in existence. Hitherto
his cousin's money, joined to flatteries and caresses,—
which, if a young man can resist, he is almost more than a
young man,—had tempted him; but he had combated the
temptation. On one memorable evening his love for Lucy
had tempted him. To that temptation he had yielded, and
the letter by which he became engaged to her had been
written. He had never meant to evade it;—had always told
himself that it should not be evaded; but, gradually, days
had been added to days, and months to months, and he had
allowed her to languish without seeing him, and almost without hearing from him.

She, too, had heard from all sides that she was deserted by him, and she had written to him to give him back his troth. But she had not sent her letters. She did not doubt that the thing was over,—she hardly doubted. And yet she would not send any letter. Perhaps it would be better that the matter should be allowed to drop without any letter-writing. She would never reproach him,—though she would ever think him to be a traitor. Would not she have starved herself for him, could she so have served him? And yet he could bear for her sake no touch of delay in his prosperity! Would she not have been content to wait, and always to wait,—so that he with some word of love would have told her that he waited also? But he would not only desert her,—but would give himself to that false, infamous woman, who was so wholly unfitted to be his wife. For Lucy, though to herself she would call him a traitor,—and would think him to be a traitor, still regarded him as the best of mankind, as one who, in marrying such a one as Lizzie Eustace, would destroy all his excellence, as a man might mar his strength and beauty by falling into a pit. For Lizzie Eustace Lucy Morris had now no forgiveness. Lucy had almost forgotten Lizzie's lies, and her proffered bribe, and all her meanness, when she made that visit to Hertford Street. Then, when Lizzie claimed this man as her lover, a full remembrance of all the woman's iniquities came back on Lucy's mind. The statement that Lizzie then made, Lucy did believe. She did think that Frank, her Frank, the man whom she worshipped, was to take this harpy to his bosom as his wife. And if it were to be so, was it not better that she should be so told? But, from that moment, poor Lizzie's sins were ranker to Lucy Morris than even to Mr. Camperdown or Mrs. Hittaway. She could not refrain from saying a word even to old Lady Linlithgow. The countess had called her niece a little liar. 'Liar!' said Lucy. 'I do not think Satan himself can lie as she does.' 'Heighty-tighty,' said the countess. 'I suppose, then, there's to be a match between Lady Satan and her cousin Frank?' 'They can do as they like about that,' said Lucy, walking out of the room.

Then came the paragraph in the fashionable evening news-paper, after that the report of the examination before the magistrate, and then certain information that Lady Eustace was about to proceed to Scotland together with her cousin Mr. Greystock, the Member for Bobsborough. 'It is a large income,' said the countess; 'but, upon my word, she's dear at the money.' Lucy did not speak, but she bit her lip till the blood ran into her mouth. She was going down to Fawn Court almost immediately, to stay there with her old friends till she should be able to find some permanent home for her-self. Once and once only would she endure discussion, and then the matter should be banished for ever from her tongue.

Early on the appointed morning Frank Greystock, with a couple of cabs, was at Mrs. Carbuncle's door in Hertford Street. Lizzie had agreed to start by a very early train,—at eight a.m.,—so that she might get through to Portray in one day. It had been thought expedient, both by herself and by her cousin, that for the present there should be no more sleeping at the Carlisle hotel. The robbery was probably still talked about in that establishment; and the report of the proceedings at the police-court had, no doubt, travelled as far north as the border city. It was to be a long day, and could hardly be other than sad. Lizzie, understanding this, feeling that though she had been in a great measure triumphant over her difficulties before the magistrate, she ought still to con-sider herself for a short while as being under a cloud, crept down into the cab and seated herself beside her cousin almost without a word. She was again dressed in black, and again wore the thick veil. Her maid, with the luggage, followed them, and they were driven to Euston Square almost without a word. On this occasion no tall footman accompanied them. 'Oh Frank; dear Frank,' she had said, and that was all. He had been active about the luggage and useful in giving orders; —but beyond his directions and inquiries as to the journey, he spoke not a word. Had she breakfasted? Would she have a cup of tea at the station? Should he take any luncheon for her? At every question she only looked into his face and shook her head. All thoughts as to creature-comforts were over with her now for ever. Tranquillity, a little poetry, and her darling boy, were all that she needed for the short remainder of her sojourn upon earth. These were the sentiments which she intended to convey when she shook her head and looked up into his eyes. The world was over for her. She had had her day of pleasure, and found how vain it was. Now she would devote herself to her child. 'I shall see my boy again to-night,' she said, as she took her seat in the carriage.

Such was the state of mind, or such rather the resolutions, with which she commenced her journey. Should he become bright, communicative, and pleasant, or even tenderly silent, or, perhaps, now at length affectionate and demonstrative, she, no doubt, might be able to change as he changed. He had been cousinly, but gloomy, at the police-court; in the same mood when he brought her home; and, as she saw with the first glance of her eye, in the same mood again when she met him in the hall this morning. Of course she must play his tunes. Is it not the fate of women to play the tunes which men dictate,—except in some rare case in which the woman can make herself the dictator? Lizzie loved to be a dictator; but at the present moment she knew that circumstances were against her.

She watched him,—so closely. At first he slept a good deal. He was never in bed very early, and on this morning had been up at six. At Rugby he got out and ate what he said was his breakfast. Would not she have a cup of tea? Again she shook her head and smiled. She smiled as some women smile when you offer them a third glass of champagne. 'You are joking with me, I know. You cannot think that I would take it.' That was the meaning of Lizzie's smile. He went into the refreshment-room, growled at the heat of the tea, and the abominable nastiness of the food provided, and then, after the allotted five minutes, took himself to a smoking-carriage. He did not rejoin his cousin till they were at Crewe. When he went back to his old seat, she only smiled again. He asked her whether she had slept, and again she shook her head. She had been repeating to herself the address to Ianthe's soul, and her whole being was pervaded with poetry.

It was absolutely necessary, as he thought, that she should eat something, and he insisted that she should dine upon the road somewhere. He, of course, was not aware that she had been nibbling biscuits and chocolate while he had been smoking, and had had recourse even to the comfort of a sherry-flask which she carried in her dressing-bag. When he talked of dinner she did more than smile and refuse. She expostulated. For she well knew that the twenty minutes for dinner were allowed at the Carlisle station; and even if there had been no chocolate and no sherry, she would have endured on, even up to absolute inanition, rather than step out upon this well-remembered platform. 'You must eat, or you'll be starved,' he said. 'I'll fetch you something.' So he bribed a special waiter, and she was supplied with cold chicken and more sherry. After this Frank smoked again, and did not reappear till they had reached Dumfries.

Hitherto there had been no tenderness,—nothing but the coldest cousinship. He clearly meant her to understand that he had submitted to the task of accompanying her back to Portray Castle as a duty, but that he had nothing to say to one who had so misbehaved herself. This was very irritating. She could have taken herself home to Portray without his company, and have made the journey more endurable without him than with him, if this were to be his conduct throughout. They had had the carriage to themselves all the way from Crewe to Carlisle, and he had hardly spoken a word to her. If he would have rated her soundly for her wickednesses, she could have made something of that. She could have thrown herself on her knees, and implored his pardon; or, if hard pressed, have suggested the propriety of throwing herself out of the carriage-window. She could have brought him round if he would only have talked to her, but there is no doing anything with a silent man. He was not her master. He had no power over her. She was the lady of Portray, and he could not interfere with her. If he intended to be sullen with her to the end, and to show his contempt for her, she would turn against him. 'The worm will turn,' she said to herself. And yet she did not think herself a worm.

A few stations beyond Dumfries they were again alone. It was now quite dark, and they had already been travelling over ten hours. They would not reach their own station till eight, and then again there would be the journey to Portray. At last he spoke to her. 'Are you tired, Lizzie?'

'Oh, so tired!'

'You have slept, I think.'

'No, not once; not a wink. You have slept.' This she said in a tone of reproach.

'Indeed I have.'

'I have endeavoured to read, but one cannot command one's mind at all times. Oh, I am so weary. Is it much further? I have lost all reckoning as to time and place.'

'We change at the next station but one. It will soon be over now. Will you have a glass of sherry? I have some in my flask.' Again she shook her head. 'It is a long way down to Portray, I must own.'

'Oh, I am so sorry that I have given you the trouble to accompany me.'

'I was not thinking of myself. I don't mind it. It was better that you should have somebody with you,—just for this journey.'

'I don't know why this journey should be different from any other,' said Lizzie crossly. She had not done anything that made it necessary that she should be taken care of,— like a naughty girl.

'I'll see you to the end of it now, anyway.'

'And you'll stay a few days with me, Frank? You won't go away at once? Say you'll stay a week. Dear, dear Frank; say you'll stay a week. I know that the House doesn't meet for ever so long. Oh, Frank, I do so wish you'd be more like yourself.' There was no reason why she should not make one other effort, and as she made it every sign of fatigue passed away from her.

'I'll stay over to-morrow certainly,' he replied.

'Only one day!'

'Days with me mean money, Lizzie, and money is a thing which is at present very necessary to me.'

'I hate money.'

'That's very well for you, because you have plenty of it.'

'I hate money. It is the only thing that one has that one cannot give to those one loves. I could give you anything else;—though it cost a thousand pounds.

'Pray don't. Most people like presents, but they only bore me.'

'Because you are so indifferent, Frank;—so cold. Do you remember giving me a little ring?'

'Very well indeed. It cost eight and sixpence.'

'I never thought what it cost;—but there it is.' This she said, drawing off her glove and showing him her finger. 'And when I am dead, there it will be. You say you want money, Frank. May I not give it you? Are not we brother and sister?'

'My dear Lizzie, you say you hate money. Don't talk about it.'

'It is you that talk about it. I only talk about it because I want to give it you;—yes, all that I have. When I first knew what was the real meaning of my husband's will, my only thought was to be of assistance to you.'

In real truth Frank was becoming very sick of her. It seemed to him now to have been almost impossible that he should ever soberly have thought of making her his wife. The charm was all gone, and even her prettiness had in his eyes lost its value. He looked at her, asking himself whether in truth she was pretty. She had been travelling all day, and perhaps the scrutiny was not fair. But he thought that even after the longest day's journey Lucy would not have been soiled, haggard, dishevelled, and unclean, as was this woman.

Travellers again entered the carriage, and they went on with a crowd of persons till they reached the platform at which they changed the carriage for Troon. Then they were again alone, for a few minutes, and Lizzie with infinite courage determined that she would make her last attempt. 'Frank,' she said, 'you know what it is that I mean. You cannot feel that I am ungenerous. You have made me love you. Will you have all that I have to give?' She was leaning over, close to him, and he was observing that her long lock of hair was out of curl and untidy,—a thing that ought not to have been there during such a journey as this.

'Do you not know,' he said, 'that I am engaged to marry Lucy Morris?'

'No;—I do not know it.'

'I have told you so more than once.'

'You cannot afford to marry her.'

'Then I shall do it without affording.' Lizzie was about to speak,—had already pronounced her rival's name in that tone of contempt which she so well knew how to use, when he stopped her. 'Do not say anything against her, Lizzie, in my hearing, for I will not bear it. It would force me to leave you at the Troon station, and I had better see you now to the end of the journey.' Lizzie flung herself back into the corner of her carriage, and did not utter another word till she reached Portray Castle. He handed her out of the railway carriage, and into her own vehicle which was waiting for them, attended to the maid, and got the luggage; but still she did not speak. It would be better that she should quarrel with him. That little snake, Lucy, would of course now tell him of the meeting between them in Hertford Street, after which anything but quarrelling would be impossible. What a fool the man must be, what an idiot, what a soft-hearted, mean-spirited fellow! Lucy, by her sly, quiet little stratagems, had got him once to speak the word, and now he had not courage enough to go back from it! He had less strength of will even than Lord Fawn! What she offered to him would be the making of him. With his position, his seat in Parliament, such a country house as Portray Castle, and the income which she would give him, there was nothing that he might not reach! And he was so infirm of purpose, that though he had hankered after it all, he would not open his hand to take it,—because he was afraid of such a little thing as Lucy Morris! It was thus that she thought of him, as she leaned back in the carriage without speaking. In giving her all that is due to her, we must acknowledge that she had less feeling of the injury done to her charms as a woman than might have been expected. That she hated Lucy was a matter of course;—and equally so that she should be very angry with Frank Greystock. But the anger arose from general disappointment, rather than from any sense of her own despised beauty. 'Ah, now I shall see my child,' she said, as the carriage stopped at the castle-gate.

When Frank Greystock went to his supper, Miss Macnulty brought to him his cousin's compliments with a message saying that she was too weary to see him again that night. The message had been intended to be curt and uncourteous, but Miss Macnulty had softened it,—so that no harm was done. 'She must be very weary,' said Frank.

'I suppose though that nothing would ever really tire Lady Eustace,' said Miss Macnulty. 'When she is excited nothing will tire her. Perhaps the journey has been dull.'

'Exceedingly dull,' said Frank, as he helped himself to the collops* which the Portray cook had prepared for his supper.

Miss Macnulty was very attentive to him, and had many questions to ask. About the necklace she hardly dared to speak, merely observing how sad it was that all those precious diamonds should have been lost for ever. 'Very sad indeed,' said Frank with his mouth full. She then went on to the marriage,—the marriage that was no marriage. Was not that very dreadful? Was it true that Miss Roanoke was really—out of her mind? Frank acknowledged that it was dreadful, but thought that the marriage had it been completed would have been more so. As for the young lady, he only knew that she had been taken somewhere out of the way. Sir Griffin, he had been told, had gone to Japan.

'To Japan!' said Miss Macnulty, really interested. Had Sir Griffin gone no further than Boulogne, her pleasure in the news would certainly have been much less. Then she asked some single question about Lord George, and from that came to the real marrow of her anxiety. Had Mr. Greystock lately seen the—the Rev. Mr. Emilius? Frank had not seen the clergyman, and could only say of him that had Lucinda Roanoke and Sir Griffin Tewett been made one, the knot would have been tied by Mr. Emilius.

'Would it indeed? Did you not think Mr. Emilius very clever when you met him down here?'

'I don't doubt but what he is a sharp sort of fellow.'

'Oh, Mr. Greystock, I don't think that that's the word for him at all. He did promise me when he was here that he would write to me occasionally, but I suppose that the increasing duties of his position have rendered that impossible.' Frank, who had no idea of the extent of the preacher's ambition, assured Miss Macnulty that among his multifarious clerical labours it was out of the question that Mr. Emilius should find time to write letters.

Frank had consented to stay one day at Portray, and did not now like to run away without again seeing his cousin. Though much tempted to go at once, he did stay the day, and had an opportunity of speaking a few words to Mr. Gowran. Mr. Gowran was very gracious, but said nothing of his journey up to London. He asked various questions concerning her 'leddyship's' appearance at the police-court, as to which tidings had already reached Ayrshire, and pretended to be greatly shocked at the loss of the diamonds. 'When they talk o' ten thoosand poond, that's a lee, nae doobt?' asked Andy.

'No lie at all, I believe,' said Greystock.

'And her leddyship wad tak' aboot wi' her ten thoosand poond—in a box?' Andy still showed much doubt by the angry glance of his eye and the close compression of his lips, and the great severity of his demeanour as he asked the question.

'I know nothing about diamonds myself, but that is what they say they were worth.'

'Her leddyship's her ain sell seems nae to ha' been in ain story aboot the box, Muster Greystock?' But Frank could not stand to be cross-questioned on this delicate matter, and walked off, saying that as the thieves had not yet been tried for the robbery, the less said about it the better.

At four o'clock on that afternoon he had not seen Lizzie, and then he received a message from her to the effect that she was still so unwell from the fatigue of her journey that she could bear no one with her but her child. She hoped that her cousin was quite comfortable, and that she might be able to see him after breakfast on the following day. But Frank was determined to leave Portray very early on the following day, and therefore wrote a note to his cousin. He begged that she would not disturb herself, that he would leave the castle the next morning before she could be up, and that he had only further to remind her that she must come up to London at once as soon as she should be summoned for the trial of Mr. Benjamin and his comrade. It had seemed to Frank that she had almost concluded that her labours connected with that disagreeable matter were at an end. 'The examination may be long, and I will attend you if you wish it,' said her cousin. Upon receiving this she thought it expedient to come down to him, and there was an interview for about a quarter of an hour in her own little sitting-room looking out upon the sea. She had formed a project, and at once suggested it to him. If she found herself ill when the day of the trial came, could they make her go up and give her evidence? Frank told her that they could, and that they would. She was very clever about it. 'They couldn't go back to what I said at Carlisle, you know; because they already have made me tell all that myself.' As she had been called upon to criminate herself, she could not now be tried for the crime. Frank, however, would not listen to this, and told her that she must come. 'Very well, Frank. I know you like to have your own way. You always did. And you think so little of my feelings! I shall make inquiry, and if I must,—why I suppose I must.'

'You'd better make up your mind to come.

'Very well. And now, Frank, as I am so very tired, if you please I'll say good-bye to you. I am very much obliged to you for coming with me. Good-bye.' And so they parted.

CHAPTER LXXVII
The Story of Lucy Morris is concluded

ON the day appointed, Lucy Morris went back from the house of the old countess to Fawn Court. 'My dear,' said Lady Linlithgow, 'I am sorry that you are going. Perhaps you'll think I haven't been very kind to you, but I never am kind. People have always been hard to me, and I'm hard. But I do like you.'

'I'm glad you like me, as we have lived together so long.'

'You may go on staying here, if you choose, and I'll try to make it better.'

'It hasn't been bad at all,—only that there's nothing particular to do. But I must go. I shall get another place as a governess somewhere, and that will suit me best.'

'Because of the money, you mean.'

'Well;—that in part.'

'I mean to pay you something,' said the countess, opening her pocket-book, and fumbling for two bank-notes which she had deposited there.

'Oh, dear no. I haven't earned anything.'

'I always gave Macnulty something, and she was not near so nice as you.' And then the countess produced two ten-pound notes. But Lucy would have none of her money, and when she was pressed, became proud and almost indignant in her denial. She had earned nothing, and she would take nothing, and it was in vain that the old lady spread the clean bits of paper before her. 'And so you'll go and be a governess again; will you?'

'When I can get a place.'

'I'll tell you what, my dear. If I were Frank Greystock, I'd stick to my bargain.' Lucy at once fell a-crying, but she smiled upon the old woman through her tears. 'Of course he's going to marry that little limb of the devil.'

'Oh, Lady Linlithgow,—if you can, prevent that!'

'How am I to prevent it, my dear? I've nothing to say to either of them.'

'It isn't for myself I'm speaking. If I can't,—if I can't,—can't have things go as I thought they would by myself, I will never ask any one to help me. It is not that I mean. I have given all that up.'

'You have given it up?'

'Yes;—I have. But nevertheless I think of him. She is bad, and he will never be happy if he marries her. When he asked me to be his wife, he was mistaken as to what would be good for him. He ought not to have made such a mistake. For my sake he ought not.'

'That's quite true, my dear.'

'But I do not wish him to be unhappy all his life. He is not bad, but she is very bad. I would not for worlds that any-body should tell him that he owed me anything; but if he could be saved from her,—oh, I should be so glad.'

'You won't have my money, then?'

'No,—Lady Linlithgow.'

'You'd better. It is honestly your own.'

'I will not take it, thank you.'

'Then I may as well put it up again.' And the countess replaced the notes in her pocket-book. When this conversation took place, Frank Greystock was travelling back alone from Portray to London. On the same day the Fawn carriage came to fetch Lucy away. As Lucy was in peculiar distress, Lady Fawn would not allow her to come by any other con-veyance. She did not exactly think that the carriage would console her poor favourite; but she did it as she would have ordered something specially nice to eat for any one who had broken his leg. Her soft heart had compassion for misery,

though she would sometimes show her sympathy by strange
expressions. Lady Linlithgow was almost angry about the
carriage. 'How many carriages and how many horses does
Lady Fawn keep?' she asked.

'One carriage and two horses.'

'She's very fond of sending them up into the streets of
London, I think.' Lucy said nothing more, knowing that it
would be impossible to soften the heart of this dowager in
regard to the other. But she kissed the old woman at parting,
and then was taken down to Richmond in state.

She had made up her mind to have one discussion with
Lady Fawn about her engagement,—the engagement which
was no longer an engagement,—and then to have done with
it. She would ask Lady Fawn to ask the girls never to mention Mr. Greystock's name in her hearing. Lady Fawn had
also made up her mind to the same effect. She felt that the
subject should be mentioned once,—and once only. Of course
Lucy must have another place, but there need be no hurry
about that. She fully recognised her young friend's feeling of
independence, and was herself aware that she would be wrong
to offer to the girl a permanent home among her own
daughters, and therefore she could not abandon the idea of a
future place; but Lucy would, of course, remain till a situation
should have been found for her that would be in every sense
unexceptionable. There need, however, be no haste,—and, in
the meantime, the few words about Frank Greystock must be
spoken. They need not, however, be spoken quite immediately. Let there be smiles, and joy, and a merry ring of
laughter on this the first day of the return of their old friend.
As Lucy had the same feelings on that afternoon, they did
talk pleasantly and were merry. The girls asked questions
about the Vulturess,—as they had heard her called by Lizzie
Eustace,—and laughed at Lucy to her face when she swore
that, after a fashion, she liked the old woman.

'You'd like anybody, then,' said Nina.

'Indeed I don't,' said Lucy, thinking at once of Lizzie
Eustace.

Lady Fawn planned out the next day with great precision. After breakfast, Lucy and the girls were to spend the morning in the old schoolroom, so that there might be a general explanation as to the doings of the last six months. They were to dine at three, and after dinner there should be the discussion. 'Will you come up to my room at four o'clock, my dear?' said Lady Fawn, patting Lucy's shoulder, in the breakfast-parlour. Lucy knew well why her presence was required. Of course she would come. It would be wise to get it over and have done with it.

At noon Lady Fawn, with her three eldest daughters, went out in the carriage, and Lucy was busy among the others with books and maps and sheets of scribbled music. Nothing was done on that day in the way of instruction; but there was much of half-jocose acknowledgement of past idleness, and a profusion of resolutions of future diligence. One or two of the girls were going to commence a course of reading that would have broken the back of any professor, and suggestions were made as to very rigid rules as to the talking of French and German. 'But as we can't talk German,' said Nina, 'we should simply be dumb.' 'You'd talk High Dutch, Nina, sooner than submit to that,' said one of the sisters.

The conclave was still sitting in full deliberation, when one of the maids entered the room with a very long face. There was a gentleman in the drawing room asking for Miss Morris! Lucy, who at the moment was standing at a table on which were spread an infinity of books, became at once as white as a sheet. Her fast friend, Lydia Fawn, who was standing by her, immediately took hold of her hand quite tightly. The face of the maid was fit for a funeral. She knew that Miss Morris had had a 'follower,'—that the follower had come,—and that then Miss Morris had gone away. Miss Morris had been allowed to come back; and now, on the very first day, just when my lady's back was turned, here was the follower again! Before she had come up with her message, there had been an unanimous expression of opinion in the kitchen that the fat would all be in the fire. Lucy was as white as marble, and felt such a sudden shock at her heart, that she could not speak. And yet she never doubted for a moment that Frank Greystock was the man. And with what purpose but one could he have come there? She had on the old, old frock in which, before her visit to Lady Linlithgow, she used to pass the morning amidst her labours with the girls,—a pale, grey, well-worn frock, to which must have been imparted some attraction from the milliner's art, because everybody liked it so well,—but which she had put on this very morning as a testimony, to all the world around her, that she had abandoned the idea of being anything except a governess. Lady Fawn had understood the frock well. 'Here is the dear little old woman just the same as ever,' Lydia had said, embracing her. 'She looks as if she'd gone to bed before the winter, and had a long sleep, like a dormouse,' said Cecilia. Lucy had liked it all, and thoroughly appreciated the loving-kindness; but she had known what it all meant. She had left them as the engaged bride of Mr. Greystock, the member for Bobsborough; and now she had come back as Lucy Morris, the governess, again. 'Just the same as ever,' Lucy had said, with the sweetest smile. They all understood that, in so saying, she renounced her lover.

And now there stood the maid, inside the room, who, having announced that there was a gentleman asking for Miss Morris, was waiting for an answer. Was the follower to be sent about his business, with a flea in his ear, having come slyly, craftily, and wickedly, in Lady Fawn's absence; or would Miss Morris brazen it out, and go and see him?

'Who is the gentleman?' asked Diana, who was the eldest of the Fawn girls present.

'It's he as used to come after Miss Morris before,' said the maid.

'It is Mr. Greystock,' said Lucy, recovering herself with an effort. 'I had better go down to him. Will you tell him, Mary, that I'll be with him almost immediately?'

'You ought to have put on the other frock, after all,' said Nina, whispering into her ear.

'He has not lost much time in coming to see you,' said Lydia.

'I suppose it was all because he didn't like Lady Linlithgow,' said Cecilia. Lucy had not a word to say. She stood for a minute among them, trying to think, and then she slowly left the room.

She would not condescend to alter her dress by the aid of a single pin, or by the adjustment of a ribbon. It might well be that, after the mingled work and play of the morning, her hair should not be smooth; but she was too proud to look at her hair. The man whom she had loved, who had loved her but had neglected her, was in the house. He would surely not have followed her thither did he not intend to make reparation for his neglect. But she would use no art with him; —nor would she make any entreaty. It might be that, after all, he had the courage to come and tell her, in a manly, straightforward way, that the thing must be all over,—that he had made a mistake, and would beg her pardon. If it were so, there should be no word of reproach. She would be quite quiet with him; but there should be no word of reproach. But if—— In that other case she could not be sure of her behaviour, but she knew well that he would not have to ask long for forgiveness. As for her dress,—he had chosen to love her in that frock before, and she did not think that he would pay much attention to her dress on the present occasion.

She opened the door very quietly and very slowly, intending to approach him in the same way. But in a moment, before she could remember that she was in the room, he had seized her in his arms, and was showering kisses upon her forehead, her eyes, and her lips. When she thought of it afterwards, she could not call to mind a single word that he had spoken before he held her in his embrace. It was she, surely, who had spoken first, when she begged to be released from his pressure. But she well remembered the first words that struck her ear. 'Dearest Lucy, will you forgive me?' She could only answer them through her tears by taking up his hand and kissing it.

When Lady Fawn came back with the carriage, she herself saw the figures of two persons, walking very close together, in the shrubberies. 'Is that Lucy?' she asked.

'Yes,' said Augusta, with a tone of horror. 'Indeed it is, and—Mr. Greystock.'

Lady Fawn was neither shocked nor displeased; nor was she disappointed; but a certain faint feeling of being ill-used by circumstances came over her. 'Dear me;—the very first day!' she said.

'It's because he wouldn't go to Lady Linlithgow's,' said Amelia. 'He has only waited, mamma.'

'But the very first day!' exclaimed Lady Fawn. 'I hope Lucy will be happy;—that's all.'

There was a great meeting of all the Fawns, as soon as Lady Fawn and the eldest girls were in the house. Mr. Greystock had been walking about the grounds with Lucy for the last hour and a half. Lucy had come in once to beg that Lady Fawn might be told directly she came in. 'She said you were to send for her, mamma,' said Lydia.

'But it's dinner-time, my dear. What are we to do with Mr. Greystock?'

'Ask him to lunch, of course,' said Amelia.

'I suppose it's all right,' said Lady Fawn.

'I'm quite sure it's all right,' said Nina.

'What did she say to you, Lydia?' asked the mother.

'She was as happy as ever she could be,' said Lydia. 'There's no doubt about its being all right, mamma. She looked just as she did when she got the letter from him before.'

'I hope she managed to change her frock,' said Augusta.

'She didn't then,' said Cecilia.

'I don't suppose he cares one halfpenny about her frock,' said Nina. 'I should never think about a man's coat if I was in love.'

'Nina, you shouldn't talk in that way,' said Augusta. Whereupon Nina made a face behind one of her sisters' backs. Poor Augusta was never allowed to be a prophetess among them.

The consultation was ended by a decision in accordance with which Nina went as an ambassador to the lovers. Lady Fawn sent her compliments to Mr. Greystock, and hoped he would come in to lunch. Lucy must come in to dinner, because dinner was ready.* 'And mamma wants to see you just for a minute,' added Nina, in a pretended whisper.

'Oh, Nina, you darling girl!' said Lucy, kissing her young friend in an ecstasy of joy.

'It's all right?' asked Nina in a whisper which was really intended for privacy. Lucy did not answer the question otherwise than by another kiss.

Frank Greystock was, of course, obliged to take his seat at the table, and was entertained with a profusion of civility. Everybody knew that he had behaved badly to Lucy,—everybody, except Lucy herself, who, from this time forward, altogether forgot that she had for some time looked upon him as a traitor, and had made up her mind that she had been deceived and ill-used. All the Fawns had spoken of him, in Lucy's absence, in the hardest terms of reproach, and declared that he was not fit to be spoken to by any decent person. Lady Fawn had known from the first that such a one as he was not to be trusted. Augusta had never liked him. Amelia had feared that poor Lucy Morris had been unwise, and too ambitious. Georgina had seen that, of course, it would never do. Diana had sworn that it was a great shame. Lydia was sure that Lucy was a great deal too good for him. Cecilia had wondered where he would go to;—a form of anathema which had brought down a rebuke from her mother. And Nina had always hated him like poison. But now nothing was too good for him. An unmarried man who is willing to sacrifice himself is, in feminine eyes, always worthy of ribbons and a chaplet. Among all these Fawns there was as little selfishness as can be found,—even among women. The lover was not the lover of one of themselves, but of their governess. And yet, though he desired neither to eat nor drink at that hour, something special had been cooked for him, and a special bottle of wine had been brought out of the cellar. All his sins were forgiven him. No single question was asked as to his gross misconduct during the last six months. No pledge or guarantee was demanded for the future. There he was, in the guise of a declared lover, and the fatted calf was killed.

After this early dinner it was necessary that he should return to town, and Lucy obtained leave to walk with him to the station. To her thinking now, there was no sin to be forgiven. Everything was, and had been, just as it ought to be. Had any human being hinted that he had sinned, she would have defended him to the death. Something was said between them about Lizzie, but nothing that arose from jealousy. Not till many months had passed did she tell him of Lizzie's message to herself, and of her visit to Hertford Street. But they spoke of the necklace, and poor Lucy shuddered as she was told the truth about those false oaths. 'I really do think that, after that, Lord Fawn is right,' she said, looking round at her lover. 'Yes; but what he did, he did before that,' said Frank. 'But are they not good and kind?' she said, pleading for her friends. 'Was ever anybody so well treated as they have treated me? I'll tell you what, sir, you mustn't quarrel with Lord Fawn any more. I won't allow it.' Then she walked back from the station alone, almost bewildered by her own happiness.

That evening something like an explanation was demanded by Lady Fawn, but no explanation was forthcoming. When questions were asked about his silence, Lucy, half in joke and half in earnest, fired up and declared that everything had been as natural as possible. He could not have come to Lady Linlithgow's house. Lady Linlithgow would not receive him. No doubt she had been impatient, but then that had been her fault. Had he not come to her the very first day after her return to Richmond? When Augusta said something as to letters which might have been written, Lucy snubbed her. 'Who says he didn't write? He did write. If I am contented, why should you complain?' 'Oh, I don't complain,' said Augusta.

Then questions were asked as to the future,—questions to which Lady Fawn had a right to demand an answer. What did Mr. Greystock propose to do now? Then Lucy broke down, sobbing, crying, triumphing, with mingled love and happiness. She was to go to the deanery. Frank had brought with him a little note to her from his mother, in which she was invited to make the deanery at Bobsborough her home for the present.

'And you are to go away just when you've come?' asked Nina.

'Stay with us a month, my dear,' said Lady Fawn, 'just to let people know that we are friends, and after that the deanery will be the best home for you.' And so it was arranged.

*   *   *   *   *   *

It need only be further said, in completing the history of Lucy Morris as far as it can be completed in these pages, that she did go to the deanery, and that there she was received with all the affection which Mrs. Greystock could show to an adopted daughter. Her quarrel had never been with Lucy personally,—but with the untoward fact that her son would not marry money. At the deanery she remained for fifteen happy months, and then became Mrs. Greystock, with a bevy of Fawn bridesmaids around her. As the personages of a chronicle such as this should all be made to operate backwards and forwards on each other from the beginning to the end, it would have been desirable that the chronicler should have been able to report that the ceremony was celebrated by Mr. Emilius. But as the wedding did not take place till the end of the summer, and as Mr. Emilius at that time never remained in town, after the season was over, this was impossible. It was the Dean of Bobsborough, assisted by one of the minor canons, who performed the service.

CHAPTER LXXVIII
The Trial

Having told the tale of Lucy Morris to the end, the chronicler must now go back to the more important persons of this history. It was still early in April when Lizzie Eustace was taken down to Scotland by her cousin, and the trial of Mr. Benjamin and Mr. Smiler was fixed to take place at the Central Criminal Court about the middle of May. Early in May the attorneys for the prosecution applied to Greystock, asking him whether he would make arrangements for his cousin's appearance on the occasion, informing him that she had already been formally summoned. Whereupon he wrote to Lizzie, telling her what she had better do, in the kindest manner,—as though there had been no cessation of their friendly intercourse; offering to go with her into court, —and naming an hotel at which he would advise her to stay during the very short time that she need remain in London. She answered this letter at once. She was sorry to say that she was much too ill to travel, or even to think of travelling. Such was her present condition that she doubted greatly whether she would ever again be able to leave the two rooms to which she was at present confined. All that remained to her in life was to watch her own blue waves from the casement of her dear husband's castle,—that casement at which he had loved to sit, and to make herself happy in the smiles of her child. A few months would see the last of it all, and then, perhaps, they who had trampled her to death would feel some pangs of remorse as they thought of her early fate. She had given her evidence once and had told all the truth,—though she was now aware that she need not have done so, as she had been defrauded of a vast amount of property through the gross negligence of the police. She was advised now by persons who seemed really to understand the law, that she could recover the value of the diamonds which her dear, dear husband had given her, from the freeholders of the parish in

which the robbery had taken place.* She feared that her
health did not admit of the necessary exertion. Were it
otherwise she would leave no stone unturned to recover the
value of her property,—not on account of its value, but
because she had been so ill treated by Mr. Camperdown, and
the police. Then she added a postscript to say that it was
quite out of the question that she should take any journey for
the next six months.

The reader need hardly be told that Greystock did not believe a word of what she said. He felt sure that she was not
ill. There was an energy in the letter hardly compatible with
illness. But he could not make her come. He certainly did
not intend to go down again to Scotland to fetch her,—and
even had he done so he could not have forced her to accompany him. He could only go to the attorneys concerned, and
read to them so much of the letter as he thought fit to communicate to them. 'That won't do at all,' said an old gentleman at the head of the firm. 'She has been very leniently
treated, and she must come.'

'You must manage it, then,' said Frank.

'I hope she won't give us trouble, because if she does we
must expose her,' said the second member.

'She has not even sent a medical certificate,' said the tyro
of the firm, who was not quite so sharp as he will probably
become when he has been a member of it for ten or twelve
years. You should never ask the ostler whether he greases his
oats. In this case Frank Greystock was not exactly in the
position of the ostler; but he did inform his cousin by letter
that she would lay herself open to all manner of pains and
penalties if she disobeyed such a summons as she had received, unless she did so by a very strong medical advice,
backed by a medical certificate.

Lizzie, when she received this, had two strings to her bow.
A writer from Ayr had told her that the summons sent to her
was not worth the paper on which it was printed in regard to
a resident in Scotland;—and she had also got a doctor from
the neighbourhood who was satisfied that she was far too ill to

travel up to London. Pulmonary debilitation was the complaint from which she was suffering, which, with depressed vitality in all the organs, and undue languor in all the bodily functions, would be enough to bring her to a speedy end if she so much as thought of making a journey up to London. A certificate to this effect was got in triplicate. One copy she sent to the attorneys, one to Frank, and one she kept herself.

The matter was very pressing indeed. It was considered that the trial could not be postponed till the next sitting at the Criminal Court, because certain witnesses in respect to the diamonds had been procured from Hamburgh and Vienna, at a very great cost; they were actually on their way to London when Lizzie's second letter was received. Mr. Camperdown had resolved to have the diamonds, still with a hope that they might be restored to the keeping of Messrs. Garnett, there to lie hidden and unused at any rate for the next twenty years. The diamonds had been traced first to Hamburgh, and then to Vienna;—and it was to be proved that they were now adorning the bosom of a certain enormously rich Russian princess. From the grasp of the Russian princess it was found impossible to rescue them; but the witnesses who, as it was hoped, might have aided Mr. Camperdown in his efforts, were to be examined at the trial.

A confidential clerk was sent down to Portray, but the confidential clerk altogether failed in making his way into Lizzie's presence. Word was brought to him that nothing but force could take Lady Eustace from her bed-chamber; and that force used to that effect might take her out dead, but certainly not alive. He made inquiry, however, about the doctor, and found that he certainly was a doctor. If a doctor will certify that a lady is dying, what can any judge do, or any jury? There are certain statements which, though they are false as hell, must be treated as though they were true as gospel. The clerk reported, when he got back to London, that, to his belief, Lady Eustace was enjoying an excellent state of health;—but that he was perfectly certain that she would not appear as a witness at the trial.

The anger felt by many persons as to Lizzie's fraudulent obstinacy was intense. Mr. Camperdown thought that she ought to be dragged up to London by cart ropes. The attorneys engaged for the prosecution were almost beside themselves. They did send down a doctor of their own, but Lizzie would not see the doctor,—would not see the doctor though threats of most frightful consequences were conveyed to her. She would be exposed, fined thousands of pounds, committed to gaol for contempt of court, and prosecuted for perjury into the bargain. But she was firm. She wrote one scrap of a note to the doctor who came from London, 'I shall not live to satisfy their rabid vengeance.' Even Frank Greystock felt almost more annoyed than gratified that she should be able thus to escape. People who had heard of the inquiry before the magistrate, had postponed their excitement and interest on the occasion, because they knew that the day of the trial would be the great day; and when they heard that they were to be robbed of the pleasure of Lady Eustace's cross-examination, there arose almost a public feeling of wrath that justice should be thus outraged. The doctor who had given the certificate was vilified in the newspapers, and long articles were written as to the impotence of the law. But Lizzie was successful, and the trial went on without her.

It appeared that though her evidence was very desirable it was not absolutely essential, as, in consequence of her certified illness, the statement which she had made at the police-court could be brought up and used against the prisoners. All the facts of the robbery were, moreover, proved by Patience Crabstick and Billy Cann. And the transfer of the diamonds by Mr. Benjamin to the man who recut them at Hamburgh, was also proved. Many other morsels of collateral evidence had also been picked up by the police,—so that there was no possible doubt as to any detail of the affair in Hertford Street. There was a rumour that Mr. Benjamin intended to plead guilty. He might, perhaps, have done so had it not been for the absence of Lady Eustace; but as that was thought to give him a possible chance of escape, he stood his ground.

Lizzie's absence was a great disappointment to the sight-seers of London, but nevertheless the court was crowded. It was understood that the learned serjeant who was retained on this occasion to defend Mr. Benjamin, and who was assisted by the acute gentleman who had appeared before the magistrate, would be rather severe upon Lady Eustace, even in her absence; and that he would ground his demand for an acquittal on the combined facts of her retention of the diamonds, her perjury, and of her obstinate refusal to come forward on the present occasion. As it was known that he could be very severe, many came to hear him,—and they were not disappointed. The reader shall see a portion of his address to the jury,—which we hope may have had some salutary effect on Lizzie, as she read it in her retreat at Portray, looking out upon her own blue waves.

'And now, gentlemen of the jury, let me recapitulate to you the history of this lady as far as it relates to the diamonds as to which my client is now in jeopardy. You have heard on the testimony of Mr. Camperdown that they were not hers at all, —that, at any rate, they were not supposed to be hers by those in whose hands was left the administration of her husband's estate, and that when they were first supposed to have been stolen at the inn at Carlisle, he had already commenced legal steps for the recovery of them from her clutches. A bill in Chancery had been filed because she had obstinately refused to allow them to pass out of her hands. It has been proved to you by Lord Fawn that though he was engaged to marry her, he broke his engagement because he supposed her possession of these diamonds to be fraudulent and dishonest.' This examination had been terrible to the unfortunate Under-Secretary;—and had absolutely driven him away from the India Board and from Parliament for a month. 'It has been proved to you that when the diamonds were supposed to have vanished at Carlisle, she there committed perjury. That she did so she herself stated on oath in that evidence which she gave before the magistrate when my client was committed, and which has, as I maintain, improperly and illegally been used against my client at this trial.' Here the judge looked over his spectacles and admonished the learned serjeant, that his argument on that subject had already been heard, and the matter decided. 'True, my lord; but my conviction of my duty to my client compels me to revert to it. Lady Eustace committed perjury at Carlisle, having the diamonds in her pocket at the very moment in which she swore that they had been stolen from her. And if justice had really been done in this case, gentlemen, it is Lady Eustace who should now be on her trial before you, and not my unfortunate client. Well,—what is the next that we hear of it? It seems that she brought the diamonds up to London; but how long she kept them there, nobody knows. It was, however, necessary to account for them. A robbery is got up between a young woman who seems to have been the confidential friend rather than the maid of Lady Eustace, and that other witness whom you have heard testifying against himself, and who is, of all the informers that ever came into my hands, the most flippant, the most hardened, the least conscientious, and the least credible. That they two were engaged in a conspiracy I cannot doubt. That Lady Eustace was engaged with them, I will not say. But I will ask you to consider whether such may not probably have been the case. At any rate, she then perjures herself again. She gives a list of the articles stolen from her, and omits the diamonds. She either perjures herself a second time,—or else the diamonds in regard to which my client is in jeopardy were not in the house at all, and could not then have been stolen. It may very probably have been so. Nothing more probable. Mr. Camperdown and the managers of the Eustace estate had gradually come to a belief that the Carlisle robbery was a hoax,—and, therefore, another robbery is necessary to account for the diamonds. Another robbery is arranged, and this young and beautiful widow, as bold as brass, again goes before the magistrate and swears. Either the diamonds were not stolen, or else again she commits a second perjury.

'And now, gentlemen, she is not here. She is sick forsooth

at her own castle in Scotland, and sends to us a medical certificate. But the gentlemen who are carrying on the prosecution
know their witness, and don't believe a word of her sickness.
Had she the feelings of woman in her bosom she ought
indeed to be sick unto death. But they know her better, and
send down a doctor of their own. You have heard his evidence,—and yet this wonderful lady is not before us. I say
again that she ought to be here in that dock,—in that dock
in spite of her fortune, in that dock in spite of her title, in that
dock in spite of her castle, her riches, her beauty, and her
great relatives. A most wonderful woman, indeed, is the
widow Eustace. It is she whom public opinion will convict as
the guilty one in this marvellous mass of conspiracy and intrigue. In her absence, and after what she has done herself,
can you convict any man either of stealing or of disposing of
these diamonds?' The vigour, the attitude, and the indignant tone of the man were more even than his words;—but,
nevertheless, the jury did find both Benjamin and Smiler
guilty, and the judge did sentence them to penal servitude
for fifteen years.

And this was the end of the Eustace diamonds as far as
anything was ever known of them in England. Mr. Camperdown altogether failed, even in his attempt to buy them back
at something less than their value, and was ashamed himself
to look at the figures when he found how much money he had
wasted for his clients in their pursuit. In discussing the
matter afterwards with Mr. Dove, he excused himself by
asserting his inability to see so gross a robbery perpetrated
by a little minx under his very eyes without interfering with
the plunder. 'I knew what she was,' he said, 'from the
moment of Sir Florian's unfortunate marriage. He had
brought a little harpy into the family, and I was obliged to
declare war against her.' Mr. Dove seemed to be of opinion
that the ultimate loss of the diamonds was upon the whole
desirable, as regarded the whole community. 'I should like
to have had the case settled as to right of possession,' he said,
'because there were in it one or two points of interest. We

none of us know, for instance, what a man can, or what a man cannot, give away by a mere word.'

'No such word was ever spoken,' said Mr. Camperdown in wrath.

'Such evidence as there is would have gone to show that it had been spoken. But the very existence of such property so to be disposed of, or so not to be disposed of, is in itself an evil. Thus, we have had to fight for six months about a lot of stones hardly so useful as the flags in the street, and then they vanish from us, leaving us nothing to repay us for our labour.' All which Mr. Camperdown did not quite understand. Mr. Dove would be paid for his labour,—as to which, however, Mr. Camperdown knew well that no human being was more indifferent than Mr. Dove.

There was much sorrow, too, among the police. They had no doubt succeeded in sending two scoundrels out of the social world, probably for life, and had succeeded in avoiding the reproach which a great robbery, unaccounted for, always entails upon them. But it was sad to them that the property should altogether have been lost, and sad also that they should have been constrained to allow Billy Cann to escape out of their hands. Perhaps the sadness may have been lessened to a certain degree in the breast of the great Mr. Gager, by the charms and graces of Patience Crabstick, to whom he kept his word by making her his wife. This fact,—or rather the prospect of this fact, as it then was,—had also come to the knowledge of the learned serjeant, and, in his hands, had served to add another interest to the trial. Mr. Gager, when examined on the subject, did not attempt to deny the impeachment, and expressed a strong opinion that, though Miss Crabstick had given way to temptation under the wiles of the Jew, she would make an honest and an excellent wife. In which expectation let us trust that he may not be deceived.

Amusement had, indeed, been expected from other sources which failed. Mrs. Carbuncle had been summoned, and Lord George; but both of them had left town before the summons could reach them. It was rumoured that Mrs. Carbuncle, with her niece, had gone to join her husband at New York. At any rate, she disappeared altogether from London, leaving behind her an amount of debts which showed how extremely liberal in their dealings the great tradesmen of London will occasionally be. There were milliners' bills which had been running for three years, and horse-dealers had given her credit year after year, though they had scarcely ever seen the colour of her money. One account, however, she had honestly settled. The hotel-keeper in Albemarle Street had been paid, and all the tribute had been packed and carried off from the scene of the proposed wedding banquet. What became of Lord George for the next six months, nobody ever knew; but he appeared at Melton*in the following November, and I do not know that any one dared to ask him questions about the Eustace diamonds.

Of Lizzie, and her future career, something further must be said in the concluding chapters of this work. She has been our heroine, and we must see her through her immediate troubles before we can leave her; but it may be as well to mention here, that although many threats had been uttered against her, not only by Mr. Camperdown and the other attorneys, but even by the judge himself, no punishment at all was inflicted upon her in regard to her recusancy, nor was any attempt made to punish her. The affair was over, and men were glad to avoid the necessity of troubling themselves further with the business. It was said that a case would be got up with the view of proving that she had not been ill at all, and that the Scotch doctor would be subjected to the loss of his degree, or whatever privileges in the healing art belonged to him;—but nothing was done, and Lizzie triumphed in her success.

CHAPTER LXXIX
Once more at Portray

ON the very day of the trial Mr. Emilius travelled from
London to Kilmarnock. The trial took place on a Monday,
so that he had at his command an entire week before he would
be required to appear again in his church. He had watched
the case against Benjamin and Smiler very closely, and had
known beforehand, almost with accuracy, what witnesses
would appear and what would not at the great coming event
at the Old Bailey. When he first heard of Lady Eustace's
illness, he wrote to her a most affectionately pastoral letter,
strongly adjuring her to think of her health before all things,
and assuring her that in his opinion, and in that of all his
friends, she was quite right not to come up to London. She
wrote him a very short, but a very gracious, answer, thanking
him for his solicitude, and explaining to him that her condition made it quite impossible that she should leave Portray.

'I don't suppose anybody knows how ill I am; but it does not matter. When I am gone, they will know what they have done.' Then Mr. Emilius resolved that he would go down to Scotland. Perhaps Lady Eustace was not as ill as she thought; but it might be that the trial, and the hard things lately said of her, and her loneliness, and the feeling that she needed protection, might, at such a moment as this, soften her heart. She should know at least that one tender friend did not desert her because of the evil things which men said of her.

He went to Kilmarnock, thinking it better to make his approaches by degrees. Were he to present himself at once at the castle and be refused admittance, he would hardly know how to repeat his application, or to force himself upon her presence. From Kilmarnock he wrote to her, saying that business connected with his ministrations during the coming autumn had brought him into her beautiful neighbourhood, and that he could not leave it without paying his respects to her in person. With her permission he would call upon her on the Thursday at about noon. He trusted that the state of her health would not prevent her from seeing him, and reminded her that a clergyman was often as welcome a visitor at the bedside of the invalid, as the doctor or the nurse. He gave her no address, as he rather wished to hinder her from answering him, but at the appointed hour he knocked at the castle-door.

Need it be said that Lizzie's state of health was not such as to preclude her from seeing so intimate a friend as Mr. Emilius? That she was right to avoid by any effort the castigation which was to have fallen upon her from the tongue of the learned serjeant, the reader who is not straight-laced, will be disposed to admit. A lone woman, very young, and delicately organised! How could she have stood up against such treatment as was in store for her? And is it not the case that false pretexts against public demands are always held to be justifiable by the female mind? What lady will ever scruple to avoid her taxes? What woman ever understood her duty to the State? And this duty which was required of her was so terrible, that it might well have reduced to falsehood a stouter heart than her own. It can hardly be reckoned among Lizzie's great sins that she did not make that journey up to London. An appearance of sickness she did maintain, even with her own domestics. To do as much as that was due even to the doctor whom she had cajoled out of the certificate, and who was afterwards frightened into maintaining it. But Mr. Emilius was her clergyman,—her own clergyman, as she took care to say to her maid,—her own clergyman, who had come all the way from London to be present with her in her sickness; and of course she would see him.

Lizzie did not think much of the coming autumnal ministration at Kilmarnock. She knew very well why Mr. Emilius had undertaken the expense of a journey into Scotland in the middle of the London season. She had been maimed fearfully in her late contests with the world, and was now lame and soiled and impotent. The boy with none of the equipments of the skilled sportsman can make himself master of a wounded bird. Mr. Emilius was seeking her in the moment of her weakness, fearing that all chance of success might be over for him should she ever again recover the full use of her wings. All this Lizzie understood, and was able to measure Mr. Emilius at his own value of himself. But then, again, she was forced to ask herself what was her value. She had been terribly mauled by the fowlers. She had been hit, so to say, on both wings, and hardly knew whether she would ever again be able to attempt a flight in public. She could not live alone in Portray Castle for the rest of her days. Ianthe's soul and the Corsair were not, in truth, able to console her for the loss of society. She must have somebody to depend upon;—ah, some one whom, if it were possible, she might love. She saw no reason why she should not love Mr. Emilius. She had been shockingly ill-treated by Lord Fawn, and the Corsair, and Frank Greystock. No woman had ever been so knocked about in her affections. She pitied herself with an exceeding pity when she thought of all the hardships which she had endured. Left an early widow, persecuted by her husband's family, twice robbed, spied upon by her own servants, unappreciated by the world at large, ill-used by three lovers, victimised by her selected friend, Mrs Carbuncle, and now driven out of society because she had lost her diamonds, was she not more cruelly treated than any woman of whom she had ever read or heard? But she was not going to give up the battle, even now. She still had her income, and she had great faith in income. And though she knew that she had been grievously wounded by the fowlers, she believed that time would heal her wounds. The world would not continue to turn its back altogether upon a woman with four thousand pounds a year, because she had told a fib about her necklace. She weighed all this; but the conviction strongest upon her mind was the necessity that she should have a husband. She felt that a woman by herself in the world can do nothing, and that an unmarried woman's strength lies only in the expectation that she may soon be married. To her it was essentially necessary that she should have the protection of a husband who might endure on her behalf some portion of those buffetings to which she seemed to be especially doomed. Could she do better with herself than take Mr. Emilius?

Might she have chosen from all the world, Mr. Emilius was not, perhaps, the man whom she would have selected. There were, indeed, attributes in the man, very objectionable in the sight of some people, which to her were not specially disagreeable. She thought him rather good-looking than otherwise, in spite of a slight defect in his left eye. His coal-black, glossy hair commanded and obtained her admiration, and she found his hooky nose to be handsome. She did not think much of the ancestral blood of which he had boasted, and hardly believed that he would ever become a bishop. But he was popular, and with a rich, titled wife, might become more so. Mr. Emilius and Lady Eustace would, she thought, sound very well, and would surely make their way in society. The man had a grasping ambition about him, and a capacity, too, which, combined, would enable him to preach himself into notoriety. And then in marrying Mr. Emilius, should she determine to do so, she might be sure, almost sure, of dictating her own terms as to settlement. With Lord Fawn, with Lord George, or even with her cousin Frank, there would have been much difficulty. She thought that with Mr. Emilius she might obtain the undisputed command of her own income. But she did not quite make up her mind. She would see him and hear what he had to say. Her income was her own, and should she refuse Mr. Emilius, other suitors would no doubt come.

She dressed herself with considerable care,—having first thought of receiving him in bed. But as the trial had now gone on without her, it would be convenient that her recovery should be commenced. So she had herself dressed in a white morning wrapper with pink bows, and allowed the curl to be made fit to hang over her shoulder. And she put on a pair of pretty slippers, with gilt bindings, and took a laced handkerchief and a volume of Shelley,—and so she prepared herself to receive Mr. Emilius. Lizzie, since the reader first knew her, had begun to use a little colouring in the arrangement of her face, and now, in honour of her sickness, she was very pale indeed. But still, through the paleness, there was the faintest possible tinge of pink colour shining through the translucent pearl powder. Any one who knew Lizzie would be sure that, when she did paint, she would paint well.

The conversation was at first, of course, confined to the lady's health. She thought that she was, perhaps, getting better, though, as the doctor had told her, the reassuring symptoms might too probably only be too fallacious. She could eat nothing,—literally nothing. A few grapes out of the hothouse had supported her for the last week. This statement was foolish on Lizzie's part, as Mr. Emilius was a man of an inquiring nature, and there was not a grape in the garden. Her only delight was in reading and in her child's society. Sometimes she thought that she would pass away with the boy in her arms and her favourite volume of Shelley in her

hand. Mr. Emilius expressed a hope that she would not pass
away yet, for ever so many years. 'Oh, my friend,' said
Lizzie, 'what is life, that one should desire it?' Mr. Emilius
of course reminded her that, though her life might be nothing
to herself, it was very much indeed to those who loved her.
'Yes;—to my boy,' said Lizzie. Mr. Emilius informed her,
with confidence, that it was not only her boy that loved her.
There were others:—or, at any rate, one other. She might be
sure of one faithful heart, if she cared for that. Lizzie only
smiled, and threw from her taper fingers a little paper pellet
into the middle of the room,—probably with the view of
showing at what value she priced the heart of which Mr.
Emilius was speaking.

The trial had occupied two days, Monday and Tuesday,
and this was now the Wednesday. The result had been tele-
graphed to Mr. Emilius,—of course without any record of
the serjeant's bitter speech,—and the suitor now gave the
news to his lady-love. Those two horrid men had at last
been found guilty, and punished with all the severity of the
law. 'Poor fellows,' said Lady Eustace,—'poor Mr. Benjamin! Those ill-starred jewels have been almost as unkind
to him as to me.'

'He'll never come back alive, of course,' said Mr. Emilius.
'It'll kill him.'

'And it will kill me too,' said Lizzie. 'I have a something
here which tells me that I shall never recover. Nobody will
ever believe what I have suffered about those paltry diamonds. But he coveted them. I never coveted them, Mr.
Emilius; though I clung to them because they were my
darling husband's last gift to me.' Mr. Emilius assured her
that he quite understood the facts, and appreciated all her
feelings.

And now, as he thought, had come the time for pressing his
suit. With widows, he had been told, the wooing should be
brisk. He had already once asked her to be his wife, and of
course she knew the motive of his journey to Scotland.
'Dearest Lady Eustace,' he said suddenly, 'may I be allowed

to renew the petition which I was once bold enough to make to you in London?'

'Petition!' exclaimed Lizzie.

'Ah yes; I can well understand that your indifference should enable you to forget it. Lady Eustace, I did venture to tell you—that—I loved you.'

'Mr. Emilius, so many men have told me that.'

'I can well believe it. Some have told you so, perhaps, from base, mercenary motives.'

'You are very complimentary, sir.'

'I shall never pay you any compliments, Lady Eustace. Whatever may be our future intercourse in life, you will only hear words of truth from my lips. Some have told you so from mercenary motives.'—Mr. Emilius repeated the words with severity, and then paused to hear whether she would dare to argue with him. As she was silent, he changed his voice, and went on with that sweet, oily tone, which had made his fortune for him.—'Some, no doubt, have spoken from the inner depths of their hearts. But none, Lady Eustace, have spoken with such adamantine truth, with so intense an anxiety, with so personal a solicitude for your welfare in this world and the next, as that,—or I should rather say those,—which glow within this bosom.' Lizzie was certainly pleased by the manner in which he addressed her. She thought that a man ought to dare to speak out, and that on such an occasion as this he should venture to do so with some enthusiasm and some poetry. She considered that men generally were afraid of expressing themselves, and were as dumb as dogs, from the want of becoming spirit. Mr. Emilius gesticulated, and struck his breast, and brought out his words as though he meant them.

'It is easy to say all that, Mr. Emilius,' she replied.

'The saying of it is hard enough, Lady Eustace. You can never know how hard it is to speak from a full heart. But to feel it, I will not say is easy;—only to me, not to feel it is impossible. Lady Eustace, my heart is devoted to your heart, and seeks its comrade. It is sick with love and will not be stayed. It forces from me words,—words which will return upon me with all the bitterness of gall, if they be not accepted by you as faithful, ay and of great value.'

'I know well the value of such a heart as yours, Mr. Emilius.'

'Accept it then, dearest one.'

'Love will not always go by command, Mr. Emilius.'

'No indeed;—nor at command will it stay away. Do you think I have not tried that? Do you believe that for a man it can be pleasant to be rebuffed;—that for one who up to this day has always walked on, triumphant over every obstacle, who has conquered every nay that has obstructed his path, it can have less of bitterness than the bitterness of death to encounter a no from the lips of a woman?'

'A poor woman's no should be nothing to you, Mr. Emilius.'

'It is everything to me,—death, destruction, annihilation, —unless I can overcome it. Darling of my heart, queen of my soul, empress presiding over the very spirit of my being, say,—shall I overcome it now?'

She had never been made love to after this fashion before. She knew, or half knew, that the man was a scheming hypocrite, craving her money, and following her in the hour of her troubles, because he might then have the best chance of success. She had no belief whatever in his love. And yet she liked it, and approved his proceedings. She liked lies, thinking them to be more beautiful than truth. To lie readily and cleverly, recklessly and yet successfully, was, according to the lessons which she had learned, a necessity in woman, and an added grace in man. There was that wretched Macnulty, who would never lie; and what was the result? She was unfit even for the poor condition of life which she pretended to fill. When poor Macnulty had heard that Mr. Emilius was coming to the castle, and had not even mentioned her name; and again, when he had been announced on this very morning, the unfortunate woman had been unable to control her absurd disappointment.

'Mr. Emilius,' Lizzie said, throwing herself back upon her couch, 'you press me very hard.'

'I would press you harder still to gain the glory I covet.' And he made a motion with his arms as though he had already got her tight within his grasp.

'You take advantage of my illness.'

'In attacking a fortress do not the besiegers take all advantages? Dear Lady Eustace, allow me to return to London with the right of protecting your name at this moment, in which the false and the thoughtless are attacking it. You need a defender now.'

'I can defend myself, sir, from all attacks. I do not know that any one can hurt me.'

'God forbid that you should be hurt. Heaven forbid that even the winds of heaven should blow too harshly on my beloved. But my beloved is subject to the malice of the world. My beloved is a flower all beautiful within and with-out, but one whose stalk is weak, whose petals are too delicate, whose soft bloom is evanescent. Let me be the strong staff against which my beloved may blow in safety.'

A vague idea came across Lizzie's mind that this glowing language had a taste of the Bible about it, and that, there-fore, it was in some degree impersonal, and intended to be pious. She did not relish piety at such a crisis as this, and was, therefore, for a moment inclined to be cold. But she liked being called a flower, and was not quite sure whether she remembered her Bible rightly. The words which struck her ear as familiar might have come from Juan and Haidee,* and if so, nothing could be more opportune. 'Do you expect me to give you answer now, Mr. Emilius?'

'Yes,—now.' And he stood before her in calm dignity, with his arms crossed upon his breast.

She did give him his answer then and there, but first she turned her face to the wall,—or rather to the back of the sofa, and burst into a flood of tears. It was a delicious moment to her, that in which she was weeping. She sobbed forth something about her child, something about her sorrows, something as to the wretchedness of her lot in life, something of her widowed heart,—something also of that duty to others which would compel her to keep her income in her own hands; and then she yielded herself to his entreaties.

* * * * * * *

That evening she thought it proper to tell Miss Macnulty what had occurred. 'He is a great preacher of the gospel,' she said, 'and I know no position in the world more worthy of a woman's fondest admiration.' Miss Macnulty was unable to answer a word. She could not congratulate her successful rival, even though her bread depended on it. She crept slowly out of the room, and went upstairs, and wept.

Early in the month of June, Lady Eustace was led to the hymeneal altar by her clerical bridegroom. The wedding took place at the Episcopal church at Ayr, far from the eyes of curious Londoners. It need only be further said that Mr. Emilius could be persuaded to agree to no settlements prejudical to that marital supremacy which should be attached to the husband; and that Lizzie, when the moment came, knowing that her betrothals had been made public to all the world, did not dare to recede from another engagement. It may be that Mr. Emilius will suit her as well as any husband that she could find,—unless it shall be found that his previous career has been too adventurous. After a certain fashion he will, perhaps, be tender to her; and he will have his own way in everything, and be no whit afraid when she is about to die in an agony of tears before his eyes. The writer of the present story may, however, declare that the future fate of this lady shall not be left altogether in obscurity.

CHAPTER LXXX
What was said about it all at Matching

THE Whitsuntide holidays were late this year, not taking place till the beginning of June, and were protracted till the 9th of that month. On the 8th Lizzie and Mr. Emilius became man and wife, and on that same day Lady Glencora Palliser entertained a large company of guests at Matching Priory. That the Duke of Omnium was there was quite a matter of course. Indeed, in these days, Lady Glencora seldom separated herself far, or for any long time, from her husband's uncle,—doing her duty to the head of her husband's family in the most exemplary manner. People indeed said that she watched him narrowly, but of persons in high station common people will say anything. It was at any rate certain that she made the declining years of that great nobleman's life comfortable and decorous. Madame Max Goesler was also at Matching, a lady whose society always gave gratification to the duke. And Mr. Palliser was also there, taking the rest that was so needful to him;—by which it must be understood that after having worked all day, he was able to eat his dinner, and then only write a few letters before going to bed, instead of attending the House of Commons till two or three o'clock in the morning. But his mind was still deep in quints and semitenths. His great measure was even now in committee. His hundred and second clause had been carried, with only nine divisions against him of any consequence. Seven of the most material clauses had, no doubt, been postponed, and the great bone of contention as to the two superfluous farthings still remained before him. Nevertheless he fondly hoped that he would be able to send his bill complete to the House of Lords before the end of July. What might be done in the way of amendments there he had hitherto refused to consider. 'If the peers choose to put themselves in opposition to the whole nation on a purely commercial question, the responsibility of all evils that may

follow must be at their doors.' This he had said, as a commoner. A year or two at the farthest,—or more probably
a few months,—would make him a peer; and then, no doubt,
he would look at the matter in a wholly different light. But
he worked at his great measure with a diligence which at
any rate deserved success; and he now had with him a whole
bevy of secretaries, private secretaries, chief clerks, and
accountants, all of whom Lady Glencora captivated by her
flattering ways, and laughed at behind their backs. Mr.
Bonteen was there with his wife, repeatedly declaring to
all his friends that England would achieve the glories of
decimal coinage by his blood and over his grave,—and
Barrington Erle, who took things much more easily, and
Lord Chiltern, with his wife, who would occasionally ask
her if she could explain to him the value of a quint, and
many others whom it may not be necessary to name. Lord
Fawn was not there. Lord Fawn, whose health had temporarily given way beneath the pressing labours of the India
Board, was visiting his estates in Tipperary.

'She is married to-day, duke, down in Scotland,'—said
Lady Glencora, sitting close to the duke's ear, for the duke
was a little deaf. They were in the duke's small morning
sitting-room, and no one else was present excepting Madame
Max Goesler.

'Married to-morrow,—down in Scotland. Dear, dear!
what is he?' The profession to which Mr. Emilius belonged
had been mentioned to the duke more than once before.

'He's some sort of a clergyman, duke. You went and
heard him preach, Madame Max. You can tell us what he's
like.'

'Oh, yes; he's a clergyman of our church,' said Madame
Goesler.

'A clergyman of our church;—dear, dear. And married in
Scotland! That makes it stranger. I wonder what made a
clergyman marry her?'

'Money, duke,' said Lady Glencora, speaking very loud.
'Oh, ah, yes; money. So he'd got money; had he?'

'Not a penny, duke; but she had.'

'Oh, ah, yes. I forgot. She was very well left; wasn't she? And so she has married a clergyman without a penny. Dear, dear! Did not you say she was very beautiful?'

'Lovely!'

'Let me see,—you went and saw her, didn't you?'

'I went to her twice,—and got quite scolded about it. Plantagenet said that if I wanted horrors I'd better go to Madame Tussaud.* Didn't he, Madame Max?' Madame Max smiled and nodded her head.

'And what's the clergyman like?' asked the duke.

'Now, my dear, you must take up the running,' said Lady Glencora, dropping her voice. 'I ran after the lady, but it was you who ran after the gentleman.' Then she raised her voice. 'Madame Max will tell you all about it, duke. She knows him very well.'

'You know him very well; do you? Dear, dear, dear!'

'I don't know him at all, duke, but I once went to hear him preach. He's one of those men who string words together, and do a good deal of work with a cambric pocket-handkerchief.'

'A gentleman?' asked the duke.

'About as like a gentleman as you're like an archbishop,' said Lady Glencora.

This tickled the duke amazingly. 'He, he, he;—I don't see why I shouldn't be like an archbishop. If I hadn't happened to be a duke, I should have liked to be an archbishop. Both the archbishops take rank of me. I never quite understood why that was, but they do. And these things never can be altered when they're once settled. It's quite absurd, now-a-days, since they've cut the archbishops down so terribly. They were princes once, I suppose, and had great power. But it's quite absurd now, and so they must feel it. I have often thought about that a good deal, Glencora.'

'And I think about poor Mrs. Arch, who hasn't got any rank at all.'

'A great prelate having a wife does seem to be an

absurdity,' said Madame Max, who had passed some years of her life in a Catholic country.

'And the man is a cad;—is he?' asked the duke.

'A Bohemian Jew, duke,—an impostor who has come over here to make a fortune. We hear that he has a wife in Prague, and probably two or three elsewhere. But he has got poor little Lizzie Eustace and all her money into his grasp, and they who know him say that he's likely to keep it.'

'Dear, dear, dear!'

'Barrington says that the best spec he knows out, for a younger son, would be to go to Prague for the former wife, and bring her back with evidence of the marriage. The poor little woman could not fail of being grateful to the hero who would liberate her.'

'Dear, dear, dear!' said the duke. 'And the diamonds never turned up after all. I think that was a pity, because I knew the late man's father very well. We used to be together a good deal at one time. He had a fine property, and we used to live;—but I can't just tell you how we used to live. He, he, he!'

'You had better tell us nothing about it, duke,' said Madame Max.

The affairs of our heroine were again discussed that evening in another part of the Priory. They were in the billiard-room in the evening, and Mr. Bonteen was inveighing against the inadequacy of the law as it had been brought to bear against the sinners who, between them, had succeeded in making away with the Eustace diamonds. 'It was a most unworthy conclusion to such a plot,' he said. 'It always happens that they catch the small fry, and let the large fish escape.'

'Whom did you specially want to catch?' asked Lady Glencora.

'Lady Eustace, and Lord George de Bruce Carruthers,—as he calls himself.'

'I quite agree with you, Mr. Bonteen, that it would be very nice to send the brother of a marquis to Botany Bay, or wherever they go now; and that it would do a deal of good to have the widow of a baronet locked up in the Penitentiary; but you see, if they didn't happen to be guilty, it would be almost a shame to punish them for the sake of the example.'

'They ought to have been guilty,' said Barrington Erle.

'They were guilty,' protested Mr. Bonteen.

Mr. Palliser was enjoying ten minutes of recreation before he went back to his letters. 'I can't say that I attended to the case very closely,' he observed, 'and perhaps, therefore, I am not entitled to speak about it.'

'If people only spoke about what they attended to, how very little there would be to say,—eh, Mr. Bonteen?' This observation came, of course, from Lady Glencora.

'But as far as I could hear,' continued Mr. Palliser, 'Lord George Carruthers cannot possibly have had anything to do with it. It was a stupid mistake on the part of the police.'

'I'm not quite so sure, Mr. Palliser,' said Bonteen.

'I know Coldfoot told me so.' Now Sir Harry Coldfoot was at this time Secretary of State for the Home affairs, and in a matter of such importance of course had an opinion of his own.

'We all know that he had money dealings with Benjamin, the Jew,' said Mrs. Bonteen.

'Why didn't he come forward as a witness when he was summoned?' asked Mr. Bonteen triumphantly. 'And as for the woman, does anybody mean to say that she should not have been indicted for perjury?'

'The woman, as you are pleased to call her, is my particular friend,' said Lady Glencora. When Lady Glencora made any such statement as this,—and she often did make such statements, no one dared to answer her. It was understood that Lady Glencora was not to be snubbed, though she was very much given to snubbing others. She had attained this position for herself by a mixture of beauty, rank, wealth, and courage;—but the courage had, of the four, been her greatest mainstay.

Then Lord Chiltern, who was playing billiards with Barrington Erle, rapt his cue down on the floor, and made a speech. 'I never was so sick of anything in my life as I am of Lady Eustace. People have talked about her now for the last six months.'

'Only three months, Lord Chiltern,' said Lady Glencora, in a tone of rebuke.

'And all that I can hear of her is, that she has told a lot of lies and lost a necklace.'

'When Lady Chiltern loses a necklace worth ten thousand pounds there will be talk of her,' said Lady Glencora.

At that moment Madame Max Goesler entered the room and whispered a word to the hostess. She had just come from the duke, who could not bear the racket of the billiard-room. 'Wants to go to bed, does he? Very well. I'll go to him.'

'He seems to be quite fatigued with his fascination about Lady Eustace.

'I call that woman a perfect God-send. What should we have done without her?' This Lady Glencora said almost to herself as she prepared to join the duke. The duke had only one more observation to make before he retired for the night. 'I'm afraid, you know, that your friend hasn't what I call a good time before her, Glencora.'

In this opinion of the Duke of Omnium's, the readers of this story will perhaps agree.

EXPLANATORY NOTES

I N preparing these notes to *The Eustace Diamonds* I have tried to meet the needs of various kinds of reader—the student of literature who may be unfamiliar with the historical context in which Trollope wrote, the general reader who may require information on literary convention as well as legal terminology, and the professional critic who may find here data to modify his preconceptions of Trollope. While I have taken the opportunity occasionally to expand on the argument advanced in the Introduction, the bulk of what follows is information rather than interpretation. I am aware that no one reader will require *all* of these annotations, but trust that each will find all that he or she needs.

I have had the advantage of consulting the notes in the Oxford Trollope edition (1950), and those in Stephen Gill and John Sutherland's Penguin edition (1969), and to these editors I am happy to make due acknowledgement. Kate Kent and Gwyneth Pitt have also assisted generously in preparing the notes that follow; to them I offer my warm thanks. Staff in the various libraries of the University of Leeds have, in their anonymous and self-effacing way, contributed the most practical assistance too.

VOLUME I

CHAPTER I

Page 2. (1) *termagant*: a violent, or overpowering, or quarrelsome person (now used all but exclusively of women).

(2) *Old Bond Street*: the southern part of what is commonly known as Bond Street (laid out 1686), still renowned for its fashionable shops, picture-dealers etc.; it links Piccadilly to Oxford Street.

(3) *Brook Street*: runs from Grosvenor Square to Hanover Square, a club-land area; see also note to p. I. 301.

Page 6. (1) *Algiers*: the north African city had become accessible to European invalids in the wake of French colonization of Algeria in the seventeen years after invasion (1830). At the time of the novel's serial publication, the republican Commune in Paris still survived, though France was locked in civil war. From the late 1860s, it was evident to Englishmen that France was heading for trouble, and the *Fortnightly Review* carried numerous articles on French politics—the issue containing the first instalment of *The Eustace Diamonds* included two, and these followed directly after Trollope's fiction. One of these compared the alleged atrocities of the Communards to events in Ceylon, Jamaica, and other British colonies. Algeria, like Ireland, was both a colony and officially an integral part of the metropolitan state. Sir Florian's refusal to take a cure in Algiers was perhaps more sensible than the suggestion.

(2) *hecatomb*: sacrifice of many victims.

CHAPTER II

Page 13. *Portray Castle*: Given the presentation of Lizzie Eustace as surrounded by artifice, fiction, and illusion, and given the novel's considerable emphasis on the falseness of art, it seems worth noting that Lady Eustace's castle is Portray (cf. portrait, etc.); the name may be modelled on that infinitely more august Scottish castle, Inveraray, seat of the Duke of Argyll, who became Secretary of State for India in December 1868.

Page 16. *Mount Street, near the park*: parallel to Brook Street, running from the edge of Hyde Park eastward to Berkeley Square.

Page 17. *chignon*: a large coil or bun of hair worn behind or on top of the head; without a chignon, a woman's hair is *loose*—cf. the description of Eva in her state of innocence in Milton's *Paradise Lost*.

Page 18. *cerulean*: of the colour of cloudless sky, pure blue.

CHAPTER III

Page 19. *Becky Sharp*: the heroine, or at least the central female character in W. M. Thackeray's *Vanity Fair* (1847–8); the resemblance between the two characters struck contemporary reviewers of *E.D.*, and Trollope himself wrote in his *Autobiography*:

As I wrote the book, the idea constantly presented itself to me that Lizzie Eustace was but a second Becky Sharpe; but in planning the character I had not thought of this, and I believe that Lizzie would have been just as she is though Becky Sharpe had never been described.

Page 22. (1) *filthy lucre*: see Saint Paul's *Epistle to Titus*, 1:2 and *I Epistle to Timothy*, 3:3 & 8.

(2) *£10,000 a year*: it is difficult to translate such an income into present-day terms—in relation to the cost of *necessities*, it was of course very ample indeed, though we should note that Lady Eustace's mode of living includes some penny pinching; it may be more helpful to place such a figure as being the sort of income enjoyed by a member of the middle gentry or a professional man well below the maximum earning range of his calling.

Page 23. (1) *croquet*: game played on a lawn, in which a ball is driven through iron hoops by means of a wooden mallet; introduced from France, initially to the north of Ireland, in the 1850s; Trollope's *Small House at Allington* (1862) provides a very early literary allusion.

(2) *piquet*: a game played by two persons with a pack of thirty-two cards.

Page 24. (1) *a Peer of Parliament and an Under-Secretary of State*: the rhythm of this is bombastic, with a falling away in the rather less than august dignity of an Under-Secretary.

(2) *blue-books*: reports and other publications of parliamentary committees, so called from their blue covers; in the nineteenth century blue-books came to signify the exhaustive powers of administration and inquiry at the disposal of parliament and the civil service.

(3) *the India Board*: in 1858, as a consequence of the events known in Britain as the Indian Mutiny, the East India Company was dissolved and its political and administrative functions assumed by the Crown; at the same time the Board of Control was dissolved; the transformation of the government of India into Empire is but one of the transitional aspects of the mid-Victorian period which form the background to *E.D.*

(4) *the Board of Civil Appeals*: there does not appear to have been such a body.

Page 25. *the Sawab of Mygawb*: both the title and the place-name are of course invented, the first perhaps modelled on 'nabob' or 'nawab' and the second on 'Mysore'—such invented terms underline the dismissive attitude towards the Indian prince whose complaint forms part of the dispute between Lord Fawn and Frank Greystock.

CHAPTER IV

Page 32. doing his duty to others: the catechism of the Anglican church inquires as to one's duty towards God (as laid down in the first four of the Ten Commandments) and to one's neighbour (the latter six commandments).

Page 33. (1) *as freemasons*: strictly, in the manner of members of masonic lodges, Free and Accepted Masons; but here suggesting an affable and inward looking fraternity, generally.

(2) *the changes that have been made*: the gist of this and the preceding twelve sentences is that all political change since the execution of Charles I in 1649 is to be deplored by Tories such as Frank Greystock. The various calamities are not listed chronologically, and rhythmically the passage conveys the whimsical nature of such despair, a despair which nonetheless insists that 'old' England remains unchanged despite these calamitous changes.

Page 35. (1) *apostacy*: the abandonment of one's (religious) principles, usually from cowardice or considerations of worldly advantage.

(2) *Gladstone as Apollyon*: William Ewart Gladstone (1809–98) in early life was an ardent Tory and High Churchman; in 1868 was Liberal Prime Minister and architect of radical reforms in the Irish Church Establishment; such evident apostasy identified him, in the eyes of Tories, with Apollyon, Satanic destroyer in the Book of Revelations (9: 3–11).

(3) *John Bright the Abomination of Desolation*: Bright (1811–89) was a political radical who voiced the interests of the manufacturing classes and as such was antagonistic to the old landowning Tories; in Matthew 24: 15 Christ (citing the prophet Daniel) declares that the appearance of 'the abomination of desolation' will signal the destruction of the world. In the serial text as published in the *Fortnightly Review*, the Abomination is given as Mr. Lowe (i.e. Robert Lowe, Chancellor of the Exchequer at the time, later Viscount Sherbrooke, 1811–92).

CHAPTER V

Page 40. *appanages*: specially appointed endowments or attributes; dependent properties; given the recurrent Irish references in the novel, cf. Sydney Smith's description of Ireland as 'the appanage of our empire' (see *OED*).

Page 44. *'if I had a Corsair . . . by the sea shore!'*: a corsair was a pirate, often one whose activities were approved by his home country; Byron's narrative poem 'The Corsair' (pub. 1814) provides Lizzie with a model for the hero she longs for; however, Byronic heroism is singularly lacking in all the men she meets.

Page 46. (1) *Hansom cab*: a low-slung, two-wheeled vehicle, carrying two passengers, with the driver mounted high at the back; named after the architect Joseph Aloysius Hansom (1803–82).

(2) *A peer can go*: a member of the House of Lords is entitled to attend (the House of Commons). It is likely that Fawn is here rather overemphasizing the point that he is not an *Irish* peer (who were entitled to election of the Commons); he later tells Lady Lizzie that his father had been an Irish peer until Melbourne's time, the irony being that Melbourne sat as Prime Minister in the Commons by virtue of his title being an Irish one. See note (2) to I p. 72.

CHAPTER VI

Page 51. *buckram, whalebone, paint, and false hair*: all these are materials used in cosmetics etc., that is, to create false appearances.

Page 53. *picking and stealing*: cf. 'To keep my hands from picking and stealing' in the Anglican catechism.

CHAPTER VII

Page 58. (1) *Mr. Burke's Speeches*: Edmund Burke (1729–97) was the outstanding parliamentarian of his age. An Irishman by birth and a Whig by party, his speeches became a handbook for Victorian Tories. In *E.D.*, the most relevant are those delivered during the impeachment of Warren Hastings for managerial and financial malpractice in the affairs of the East India Company; see note (3) to I p. 24.

(2) *to mingle mercy with justice*: a common notion; see Shakespeare *Merchant of Venice*, IV, i, 196; Milton *Paradise Lost*, X, 77; Du Bartas *Devine Weekes*, I, 1; and (in ironic form) Fielding *Tom Jones*, III, 10.

Pages 65–6. *speech to the electors of Bristol . . . Warren Hastings*: both are included in B. W. Hill (ed.), *Edmund Burke on Government, Politics and Society*, Fontana, 1975.

CHAPTER VIII

Page 71. *a bird in the hand is worth two in the bush*: commonplace proverb, traceable to Theocritus (c. 300–260 BC), and familiar in English literature from the Middle Ages onwards.

Page 72. (1) *My father's property was all Irish*: from the reign of Elizabeth to that of William and Mary, land in Ireland was put at the disposal of various adventurers, planters, and others deserving of reward, with the further intention of pacifying Ireland through a strong loyalist landlord element; many such landlords ceased after the first generation to reside in Ireland, and so there emerged in British society a group whose careers lay in one kingdom while their incomes derived from the other. The editors of the Penguin edition of *E.D.* find Lord Fawn's attempt to describe his financial position to Lizzie to be an example of Trollope's 'splendid sense of the absurd'; in point of fact, Fawn is struggling to articulate—none too successfully—an anomaly in British society more frequently left unarticulated.

(2) *Irish peer*: up to 1801, there was a distinctive Irish peerage, with a House of Lords in Dublin; though nominally independent, it was increasingly used in the late eighteenth century as a form of patronage at the Crown's disposal; thus, if Fawn's father's title was pre-1801, there is a possible imputation of office-serving. Moreover, after 1801, only a proportion of Irish title-holders (elected essentially from among their own number) could sit in the united House of Lords in Westminster; thus, not all Irish peers sat in parliament as peers.

(3) *no place on it*: no residence on the estate; not all absentee landlords failed to build a house on their Irish estates, but those who did so fail were held locally to have deprived their Irish tenants of an important element in their income.

EXPLANATORY NOTES

(4) *Tipperary*: one of the largest Irish counties, in the south midlands; in the 1867 Fenian rebellion, Tipperary was one of the few counties where conflict occurred, and in 1869 Jeremiah O'Donovan Rossa (1831–1915) was elected MP for Tipperary while still serving a jail sentence for his Fenian activities. A recent historian quotes Lord Kimberley's reaction as representative of British attitudes—'just what might be expected from the ruffians who inhabit that county . . . fitly represented by the rowdy felon they have chosen. What a descent from Grattan and O'Connell, or even Wolfe Tone and Emmet.' See E. D. Steele, *Irish Land and British Politics*, Cambridge University Press, 1974, 272.

CHAPTER IX

Page 74. *'climbing trees in the Hesperides'*: cf. Shakespeare, *Love's Labour's Lost*, IV, iii, 338–9—

For valour is not Love a Hercules,

Still climbing trees in the Hesperides?

The Hesperides were 'the Fortunate Islands' on which grew the golden apples Hercules had to gather as one of his labours.

Page 80. *forbid the banns*: prevent the announcement of intention to marry.

Page 82. *adhesion*: attachment to a person or party or viewpoint.

Page 83. *the French novels*: the work of Balzac and Flaubert is not in question here; by the term, the English public meant trashy and exciting fiction, for example the novels of Eugène Sue (1804–75); of course both the French and English publics were capable of reading *Madame Bovary* as a French novel in the English sense.

CHAPTER X

Page 90. *Killeagent*: it has been suggested that this place name should be read as a coded version of 'Kill Agent' and Killaud as 'Kill Lord'; however, the element 'kill' in Irish placenames often is simply the Gaelic word 'cill' = church.

Page 92. *Maltese cross*: a modified cross formée (in which the arms are narrow where they meet and gradually expand outward) with the outer side of each arm indented to produce a cross of eight points.

Page 95. *poltroon*: a spiritless coward (*OED*); a term sometimes used by politicians to describe a leader whom they follow and then desert.

CHAPTER XI

Page 100. *Golconda*: the old name for Hyderabad in British India, celebrated for its diamonds, and used as a synonym for 'a mine of wealth'; see Horace Walpole's *Letters* (ed. of 1858), VII, 438.

Page 102. *as there was no House*: as the House of Commons was not sitting (on a Saturday).

CHAPTER XIII

Page 116. *Temple*: a general name covering two of the four Inns of Court (Middle and Inner Temple), and lying south of Fleet Street.

Page 119. (1) *but goa where munny is!*: cf. ll. 19–20 of Tennyson's 'Northern Farmer, New Style'—

But I knawed a Quaäker feller as often 'as towd ma this:

'Doänt thou marry for munny, but goä wheer munny is!'

The poem was published in December 1869 in *The Holy Grail and Other Poems* (dated 1870).

(2) *the Belgrave-cum-Pimlico life*: the 1860s were a decade of rapid expansion in London building, especially in suburban housing, and the alternative districts which Frank considers as potential homes represent diverging attitudes to social life; Belgrave Square was within the purlieus of the fashionable district, while Pimlico lay further south near Victoria; the combination suggests a somewhat insecure man-about-town existence in which accommodation was rented by the season.

Page 120. (1) *somewhere north of Oxford Street*: in mid-century this was a rapidly expanding residential district of a distinctly suburban kind, in which houses were purchased rather than rented, and domesticity of a bourgeois kind is implied as distinct from the previous mode of merely renting accommodation in the city while having one's 'place' in the country.

(2) *loved as well as Romeo*: Trollope's allusions to Shakespeare are generally obvious; in *E.D.* two plays he draws on are *Romeo and Juliet*

(written 1591) and *Othello* (acted 1604); the first is a romantic tragedy of young love set in a violently divided society, and the second is a bitter domestic tragedy in which sexual difference and racial origin is exploited; both plays have a more than obvious relevance to the setting and psychology of this novel.

CHAPTER XIV

Page 124. (1) *Legge Wilson*: no individual of this name is traceable; Secretaries of State for India did indeed sit in the Cabinet.

(2) *two were one flesh*: see *Ephesians* 5: 31; the phrase is repeated in the Anglican marriage service.

CHAPTER XV

Page 132. *the pillar letter-box*: in his *Autobiography* Trollope recorded that his proposals as a post office administrator included the following:

That the public in little villages should be enabled to buy postage stamps; that they should have their letters delivered free and at an early hour; that pillar letter-boxes should be put up for them (of which accommodation in the streets and ways of England I was the originator, having, however, got authority for the erection of the first at St. Heliers in Jersey) . . .

Page 134. *The post-office, with that accuracy . . . conspicuous among all offices*: another instance of the author's referring puckishly to his own non-literary career; he had been a postal official from 1834 to 1867.

CHAPTER XVI

Page 146. *would not attempt any personal encounter*: i.e. would not challenge his rival to a duel.

Page 151. *indifferent*: impartial, neutral.

CHAPTER XVII

Page 152. *jointure*: the holding of property to the joint use of a husband and wife for life or in tail, as a provision for the latter, in the event of her widowhood; hence, by extension, a sole estate limited to the wife being 'a competent livelihood of freehold for the wife of lands and tenements, to take effect upon the death of the husband for the life of the wife at least'.

Page 153. (1) *'I don't know where it is she's lame'*: the language of course is that of the horse-racing or hunting fraternity, and means that the speaker cannot detect where Lizzie's defect lies.

(2) *'but she don't go flat all round'*: i.e. she does not perform evenly and properly (as a horse does when all four feet are in good condition); the reduction of Lizzie to the status of horse has an ironic side given the later hunting-scene in which she is the prize rather than the hunter.

Page 155. *Commoner*: member of the community below the rank of peer.

Page 159. (1) *quadrille*: a square dance, of French origin, usually performed by four couples.

(2) *garniture*: ornaments, decoration added to clothing.

CHAPTER XVIII

Page 166. (1) *Swiss Cottage*: in 1871 a suburban district, on the Finchley Road north of Oxford Street.

(2) *Elysium*: the state, or abode, of the dead, in Greek mythology.

Page 167. *the grouse can*: the legal shooting of grouse commences annually on 12 August, and the short-hand term 'the twelfth' meaning specifically the opening of the season dates from 1868; the analogy between girls and grouse, though whimsical, is one of a series which runs through the novel, culminating in the hunting scene of chapters 37 & 38.

Pages 167–8. *even an Othello*: the conventional view of Othello as the embodiment of jealousy, but see p. i. 120, note (2).

CHAPTER XIX

Page 173. *a volume of poetry*: it is clear from the summary which follows that Lizzie has been reading some of Tennyson's Arthurian poems, and *Idylls of the King* (1859; new ed. 1862) is the most likely volume; (see refs. to Lancelot and Arthur on p. I. 174); the idyll 'Lancelot and Elaine' resembles the plot of *E.D.* in several respects, not the least of them being summarized in these lines of Tennyson's:

'These jewels, whereupon I chanced
Divinely, are the kingdom's, not the King's—
For public use . . .' (ll. 58–60)

Tennyson's recreation of the chivalric world acknowledges the legal concept of heirloom and links it to the *possession* of love.

Page 179. *tire-woman*: a lady's maid who assists her in dressing.

Page 181. *'The king himself has followed her, When she has gone before'*: See Oliver Goldsmith's deliberately bathetic poem, 'An Elegy on that Glory of her Sex, Mrs. Mary Blaize', stanza 5:

Her love was sought, I do aver,
By twenty beaux and more;
The king himself has followed her,—
When she has walked before. (Original emphasis)

CHAPTER XX

Page 185. *the job-carriage*: carriage hired for an occasion.

Page 188. (1) *barrister*: a member of the legal profession, who has been called to the bar and so may plead for clients before the courts; the division of the profession in Britain into barristers and solicitors is seen in *E.D.* in its social aspects—the hero Frank Greystock, a reliable Tory MP and representative of a good family, is a barrister, whereas Mr. Camperdown, the Eustace family's solicitor, is seen as being without family connection and as being a shade too aggressive to be socially the equal of Greystock or Eustace.

(2) *attorney*: strictly speaking, 'a properly qualified legal agent practising in the Courts of Common Law (as a *solicitor* practised in Chancery)', but more generally used as the synonym of solicitor, one who instructs a barrister: the term solicitor came into more general use in 1875.

(3) *with the box still struggling*: this is an excellent instance of animation, the bestowing of animate qualities (to struggle, etc.) on an inanimate object; Dickens frequently employs the device to indicate the power which objects possess over men and women in industrialized society in the nineteenth century; Marx's *Das*

Kapital (vol. 1, pub. 1867) discusses 'the personfication of things and the reification of persons'.

CHAPTER XXI

Page 189. (1) *'Ianthe's soul'*: Ianthe is the heroine of P. B. Shelley's *Queen Mab* (1813)—see esp. I, 131; the editors of the Penguin *E.D.* remark that Lizzie reads Shelley when she wants to be thought intellectual and spiritual; it might be added that Shelley's presence in the novel highlights the absence of any idealism in the men around Lady Eustace, and that Shelley (like Byron whom she also reads) was distinctly radical in his politics. (For the relevance of the case Shelley v. Shelley to the question of heirlooms see my Introduction p. xix above.)

(2) *Troon*: small town in Ayrshire, Scotland, 390 miles from London.

Page 191. *green spot*: area of vivacity.

Page 193. (1) *Suttee*: (Sanskrit *satī* = a true wife) the rite of widow-burning as practised by certain castes of Hindus, and eminently by the Rajputs.

(2) *bombazine*: a twilled or corded dress material; in black it is much used in mourning.

Page 195. (1) *jobbed*: hired; (see note to p. i. 185).

(2) *Newgate*: celebrated London prison, synonymous with crime and its penalties, pulled down in 1902 and so available to Lizzie as a vision of retribution.

(3) *Lord Chancellor*: the highest legal officer in the land, though in modern times his functions have been absorbed into the area of political administration.

Page 197. (1) *'Instinct with inexpressible beauty and grace . . . Immortal amid ruin'*: Shelley *Queen Mab*, I, 134–8.

(2) *'All-beautiful in naked purity!'*: Ibid., I, 132.

CHAPTER XXII

Page 201. *'Fairy Queen'*: Edmund Spenser (1552?–99) published his great allegorical poem from 1589 onwards; its role in the literary allusiveness of the novel is of course ironic, in that Spenser's Lady Una does indeed possess both unsullied purity and a true and faithful knight, whereas Lizzie lacks both.

Page 205. (1) *auchteen*: Trollope's rendering of Scots pronunciation of 'eighteen'.

(2) *gentles'll*: i.e. 'gentlemen and ladies will', employing 'gentles', a word which has passed out of usage in standard English but is preserved in Scots.

Page 206. (1) *seddle*: i.e. 'saddle'.

(2) *briddle*: i.e. 'bridle'.

CHAPTER XXIII

Page 207. (1) *gillie*: (Gaelic: *gille, giolla*) an attendant (to a fisherman or hunter).

(2) *Fortnum and Mason's*: luxury store, specializing in high class groceries; founded 1770 in Piccadilly and still in business today.

(3) *Stone and Toddy's 'Digest of the Common Law'*: a non-existent work; Samuel Stone published a *Justice's Manual* in 1842 (28th ed. in 1895)—the name Toddy is a typical Trollopian absurdity, creating here a plausible legal authority (cf. Smith and Hogan's *Criminal Law*); R. A. Fisher published a common law digest in 1870, which became a standard work in the field.

Page 216. *Patient Grizel*: according to Brewer's *Reader's Handbook* (1885) Octavia, the wife of Mark Antony and sister of Augustus, is called the 'patient Grizel of Roman story'; the story of Griselda, the model of patience and submission, is in Boccaccio, Petrarch, Chaucer ('The Clerk's Tale'); see also Maria Edgeworth, *The Modern Griselda* (1804).

CHAPTER XXIV

Page 222. *supposing that to be correct in Ayrshire*: adding water to whisky is of course disapproved of throughout Scotland, except perhaps in those puritan areas where whisky itself is reprobated.

Page 223. *Prometheus*: Frank refers to the Prometheus of Greek mythology who was chained to a rock by Zeus (Jupiter or Jove in

Roman mythology) with an eagle (not a vulture) continuously pecking at his liver; as against this, Lizzie is familiar with Shelley, whose Prometheus is a heroic opponent of tyranny and superstition.

Page 224. (1) *the fox who had lost his tail*: according to the proverb, he attempted to persuade others to discard their tails.

(2) *Short commons*: insufficient rations (from 'commons', a meal provided for undergraduates in the ancient universities).

CHAPTER XXV

Page 225. (1) *Chancery Lane*: site of the old Inns of Chancery and, here, synonymous with the legal profession.

(2) *Lincoln's Inn*: one of the great Inns of Court which have the exclusive right to call persons to practise as barristers.

(3) *Temple*: see note to p. I. 116; here 'Temple' is synonymous with the legal profession at its most august.

Page 226. *Streatham*: a suburb south of London; Streatham Park (demolished 1863) was the home of Henry Thrale, Dr. Johnson's friend; much of the social tension lying behind *E.D.* is related to the growth of suburbia and its structural division of family life from gainful occupation—cf. 'Out at Streatham, where he lived, Mrs. Dove probably had her circle of acquaintance;—but Mr. Dove's domestic life and his forensic life were kept quite separate.'

Page 227. (1) *Exors. or Admors*: conventional abbreviations used in legal documents for 'executors or administrators'.

(2) *Littleton*: Sir Thomas Littleton (1422–81), author of a *Treatise on Tenures* which, with Coke's commentary, long remained a major authority on the English law of real property.

(3) *Brooke*: Sir Robert Brooke, author of an *Abridgement* (1568) of cases.

(4) *Coke*: Sir Edward Coke (1552–1634), the author of the *Institutes of the Laws of England*.

(5) *Spelman*: Sir Henry Spelman (1564?–1641) published a legal *Glossary* in 1626.

(6) *'Omne utensil robustius'*: all solid objects of use.

(7) *'Termes de Ley'*: legal work in old French published in 1624.

(8) *'Ascun parcel des ustensiles'*: each group of objects of use.

(9) *Coke upon Littleton*: the first part of Coke's *Institutes* is a commentary on Littleton: see notes (2) & (4) above.

(10) *pennons*: standards, banners, and ensigns carried in battle.

(11) *garter and collar of S.S.*: insignia of office, etc., the collar being made up of gold links each in the shape of the letter S. For the contemporary significance of this allusion see the remarks of Mac-Kinnon and others quoted in the Introduction above, pp. xviii–xix.

(12) *case of the Earl of Northumberland*: a case concerning a collar of SS; see *74 English Reports*, pp. 947–8.

(13) *Pusey horn*: 'a *horn*, which time out of mind had gone along with the plaintiff's estate . . . upon which horn was this inscription, *viz. pecote this horn to hold huy thy land*.'; see case cited in note (14) below, and cf. the relation between land (real property) and valorized object (heirloom) in Shelley v. Shelley as discussed in the Introduction above, pp. xix–xx.

(14) *Pusey v. Pusey*: see *23 English Reports*, pp. 465–6, and note (13) above.

(15) *Upton v. Lord Ferrers*: see *31 English Reports* (1799), p. 362 & (1801), pp. 866–9; the case did involve the Journal of the House of Lords as heirloom.

(16) *Carr v. Lord Errol*: see *33 English Reports* (1808), pp. 604–7.

(17) *14 Vesey*: i.e. the 14th volume of cases reported by Francis Vesey, junior.

(18) *Rowland v. Morgan*: see *41 English Reports* (1848), pp. 1139–42, and *67 English Reports* (1848), pp. 1247–51.

(19) *Lord Eldon*: John Scott, first earl of Eldon (1751–1838), Lord Chancellor from 1801 to 1827; he heard the case cited in note (20) below; for this remark see *37 English Reports* (1821), p. 793.

(20) *Ormonde case*: see 'Clarke v. the Earl of Ormonde', *37 English Reports* (1821), pp. 791–7.

Page 228. (1) *paraphernalia*: 'In older law, jewellery and ornaments given by a husband to his wife before or during marriage, disposable by the husband during his life but not by will, falling to the wife on the husband's death. In older Scots law, they were those goods which remained the sole property of a woman, notwithstanding marriage, and did not become her husband's property. They comprised clothing and jewellery. The concept is now obsolete.' (*Oxford Companion to Law*)

(2) *case of Lady Douglas*: see 'Lord Hastings against Sir Archibald Douglas' *79 English Reports* (1634), pp. 901–4.

(3) *Lord Keeper Finch*: Heneage Finch, first earl of Nottingham (1621–82), Lord Chancellor in 1674; he was the Amri of Dryden's 'Absalom and Achitophel'.

(4) *Lord Macclesfield*: Sir Thomas Parker, first earl of Macclesfield (1666?–1732), Lord Chancellor 1718–25, suspected of misappropriating the funds of suitors in his court; for the case 'Tipping *versus* Tipping' see *24 English Reports* (1721), p. 589.

(5) *Lord Talbot*: Charles Talbot, baron Talbot of Hensol (1685–1737), created Lord Chancellor in 1733.

(6) *Lord Hardwicke*: Philip Yorke, first earl of Hardwicke (1690–1764); as Lord Chancellor he ruled on jewels, etc. in the case of 'Northey *versus* Northey' *26 English Reports* (1740), pp. 447–8.

Page 231. *Dawlish*: sea-side town in south Devon, 215 miles from London.

CHAPTER XXVI

Page 232. (1) *gig*: a light, two-wheeled, one-horse carriage.

(2) *Prestwick*: small town in Ayrshire, four miles from Ayr.

Page 234. *peck of troubles*: a familiar expression dating back to the sixteenth century and meaning 'a great quantity of troubles'; cf. Thomas Hughes, *Tom Brown's Schooldays*, I, viii, 'a pretty peck of troubles'; (peck = a measure of dry goods, etc.)

Page 237. (1) *volume of Byron*: the three narrative poems contained in the book were written relatively early in Byron's career; William Ruddick has recently written that

> The analysis of social, political and moral pretence that one finds in Thackeray's work (or, less intensely worried over but still more broadly based in the political novels of Trollope) is clearly in a realistic tradition deriving from Byron's last poems. ('Byron and England: the Persistence of Byron's Political Ideas' in Paul Graham Trueblood (ed.), *Byron's Political and Cultural Influence in Nineteenth-Century Europe*, Macmillan, 1981, p. 18)

Trollope is therefore seen to be subjecting Lizzie's search for a Corsair to a Byronic criticism.

(2) *Lubin*: a peasant in Molière's play *George Dardin*, and a conventional name for a pastoral character.

CHAPTER XXVII

Page 245. *call him out*: to challenge him to a duel.

CHAPTER XXVIII

Page 253. *currish*: snappish, snarling, quarrelsome.

Page 254. (1) *coigns of legal vantage*: the phrase, meaning a position (properly a projecting corner) affording facility for observation or action, derives its currency from Walter Scott who uses it in *The Heart of Midlothian* (1818) and *Quentin Durward* (1823); cf. Shakespeare, *Macbeth* I, iv, 7:

> no jutty, frieze,
> Buttress, nor coign of vantage, but this bird
> Hath made his pendant bed . . .

(2) *Mors omnibus est communis*: (Lat.) Death is common to all.

Page 256. (1) *in vigours*: possessing mental or moral energies (an archaic usage).

(2) *catching fish in Connemara*: Connemara is a mountainous district in county Galway, Ireland, west of Galway city; from the middle of the nineteenth century it had become popular with tourists and anglers.

Page 258. *the more picturesque idea of maintaining chivalric associations*: what Dove is emphasizing in this paragraph is the Victorian interest in simulated antiquity and tabulated ancestry—viz. the mass of material appearing in the successive editions of Burke's *Peerage and Baronetage* (1826 onwards), *Landed Gentry* (1833 onwards), etc., and the various publications of John Burke (1787–1848) and his son Sir John Bernard Burke (1814–92) who annually re-edited the father's works to provide a vast corpus of cumulative, repetitive, and addictive data on family history.

Page 260. (1) *alienation*: (in law) the action of transferring ownership of anything to another; cf. Digby's *Real Property* (1876): 'By alienation is meant the intentional and voluntary transfer of a right.'

(2) *under the rose*: (Latin *sub rosa*) the phrase means 'in strict

confidence', and its origin (rather appropriately) remains obscure; Cupid is said to have bribed Harpocrates (the god of silence) with a rose so that he would not betray Venus's amours.

CHAPTER XXIX

Page 267. (1) *given me the lie*: accused me to my face of telling a lie.

(2) *Coventry*: it is said that the citizens of the town of Coventry had such a dislike of soldiers at one time that they refused to speak to them; hence 'to be sent to Coventry' means to be ostracized, ignored.

CHAPTER XXX

Page 274. (1) *quarrelled to the knife*: quarrelled to the extremity.

(2) *Jupiter*: supreme god of the Romans, equivalent to the Greeks' Zeus.

CHAPTER XXXI

Page 282. *underwood*: small trees or shrubs growing beneath higher timber in a forest.

Page 287. (1) *'Arabian Nights'*: Victorian translations (Torrens, 1838; Lane, 1839–41; Payne, 1882–4) of these ancient oriental tales were vastly popular; Sir Richard Burton's unexpurgated edition in 16 vols. appeared in 1885–8.

(2) *'And now, my gravest of Mentors, . . . trample on her too heavily?'*: Mentor is the aged and wise counsellor who advises the young Telemachus to search for his father Odysseus in Homer's *Odyssey*.

(3) *fainéant*: (Fr.) indolent, idle.

CHAPTER XXXII

Page 292. *Mr. Cook*: Thomas Cook (1808–92), tourist agent.

Page 293. (1) *both the alternate Prime Ministers*: from *Phineas Finn* onwards the Palliser novels refer frequently to two Prime Ministers—Mr. Gresham and Mr. Daubeny; because of the coincidence of initial letters, these are frequently 'identified' with Benjamin

Disraeli (PM briefly in 1868, and again in the 1870s) and W. E. Gladstone (PM 1868–73, and later); however, the interconnections of the entire Trollopian fiction are better authenticated by noting that Daubeny is MP for East Barsetshire and that Gresham is a member of the same family as Frank Gresham of *Doctor Thorne*.

(2) *which was inserted in the 'Morning Post'*: it was the custom for members of high society to ensure that their activities received approving notice in the press.

Page 294. (1) *Stackallan*: presumed to be a place in the region of Ayrshire, etc., though I do not find any reference to such a placename in Scotland; (there is a Stackallan in County Meath, Ireland, 5 miles from Navan).

(2) *a thing of beauty*: 'A thing of beauty is a joy forever', first line of John Keats's 'Endymion', a poet whom Lizzie does not elsewhere cite.

(3) *defalcation*: diminution or reduction by cutting away etc.; here used in the special sense of a reduction of a claim (fashion) by the amount of a counter-claim (duty).

Page 295. (1) *objurgations*: severe rebukes, actions of chiding, etc.

(2) *play old gooseberry*: make havoc; this late eighteenth-century/ early nineteenth-century idiom derives from the dice-players's name for the throw of two (Gooseberry), the unluckiest in the game.

CHAPTER XXXIII

Page 301. *Bruton Street*: evidently an error for Brook Street (see p. i. 2); however, Trollope had used Bruton Street in several other novels— e.g. Bishop Proudie's London house in *Barchester Towers*.

Page 304. *Croesus*: last king of Lydia (c. 560–46 BC), legendary for his wealth.

Page 305. *Ramsgate*: seaport and market town in Kent, 70 miles ESE of London.

CHAPTER XXXIV

Page 307. *runagate*: deserter, runaway, wanderer.

Page 308. *as poor as Job*: the biblical figure of Job has been used as the embodiment of poverty in English literature since the Middle Ages.

Page 310. *Tupper's great poem*: Martin Tupper (1810–89) published *Proverbial Philosophy* (1838) in verse, and gradually his name became synonymous with the commonplace.

Page 311. *unclean, frowzy structures on their head*: Gill and Sutherland's note in the Penguin edition can hardly be bettered:

> Trollope's tone is somewhat irritable towards the fluctuations of fashion, but his faithfulness in recording them is worth especial note. Other nineteenth-century novelists such as George Eliot, Thackeray and Dickens often avoid confrontation with the present by ante-dating the scene of their action.

Page 312. (1) *Miss Edgeworth's novels*: Maria Edgeworth (1767–1849), Irish novelist; Trollope's first two novels were in the tradition of her *Castle Rackrent* (1800) and *The Absentee* (1812).

(2) *'Pride and Prejudice'*: Jane Austen (1775–1817) was by the middle of the nineteenth century recognized as the doyenne of British novelists; *Pride and Prejudice* was published in 1813.

(3) *Mudie's*: a lending library specializing in three-volume novels, founded in 1842 by Charles Edward Mudie (1818–90), and famous for its vigilant protection of its readers' morality.

(4) *'Adam Bede'*: George Eliot's second novel (1859).

(5) *'Bandit Chief'*: anonymous four-volume romance (1818).

(6) *Books are cheap things*: at a constant price of one and a half guineas (£1.57½) throughout the Victorian period, the three-decker novel was far from cheap, and its high price was one of the factors encouraging such enterprises as Mudie's lending library; Trollope (with Dickens) belonged to a generation of novelists whose earnings were the equivalent of today's television personalities'; for *E.D.* in 1873 he received a total of £2,500; in his campaign for effective international copyright Trollope acted to protect this high earning power and so had a vested interest in declaring the price of books to be acceptably low.

Page 314. *as good as a play*: old and commonplace comparison, reflecting the experience of theatre as entertainment, and traceable to John Taylor (1580–1653) 'the water poet'.

CHAPTER XXXV

Page 316. *to get up*: to prepare (by studying).

Page 317. (1) *'It is good . . . on with the new'*: in ch. 7 of Dickens's *Old Curiosity Shop* (1840), Dick Swiveller refers to a proverb on this theme, and versions can be traced back to the sixteenth century.

(2) *Excalibur*: King Arthur's sword, familiar to Victorian readers through Tennyson's *Idylls of the King*, which began to appear in 1859.

Page 319. (1) *Ivanhoe*: the hero of Walter Scott's novel of the same name (1819).

(2) *Lord Evandale*: see Scott's *Old Mortality* (1817).

(3) *Edith Bellenden*: Evandale's beloved in Scott's *Old Mortality*.

(4) *Tresilian*: see Scott's *Kenilworth* (1821).

(5) *A 1.*: used of ships in first class condition, as to hull (A) and stores (1); phrase derives from terminology of shipping insurance through Lloyd's Register (1871), and so Trollope's use of it is remarkably early.

Page 323. *caracolling*: half-turning to left or right as one advances.

Page 325. *canonical habiliments*: pompous phrase for clerical dress.

CHAPTER XXXVI

Page 329. *Juno*: an early Italian goddess of women. Later, Jupiter's queen, tall, stately, imperious.

Page 330. (1) *Brinvilliers*: there has been much confusion concerning this allusion; Marie-Madeleine, Marquise de Brinvilliers (1630–76), a celebrated French poisoner, murdered her father and two brothers, and attempted to murder her husband, all from motives of cupidity; her lover died while experimenting with poison; having fled to England, she was subsequently abducted at Liège and brought back to France and execution (17 July 1676); in reminding men of the Marquise, Lucinda is seen as potentially fatal to all men around her and fatal to herself also.

(2) *Cleopatra*: like Brinvilliers and the Queen of Sheba, the comparison here is with an exotic *femme fatale*, and is of course a fairly conventional reading of Shakespeare's *Antony and Cleopatra*; these are fearsome as well as flattering comparisons for Lucinda in that both Brinvilliers and Cleopatra end up dead, and as a latter-day Queen of Sheba she can find no Solomon.

(3) *Queen of Sheba*: see 1 Kings 10 and 2 Chronicles 9.

(4) *Minerva*: the Roman goddess of wisdom, often represented in neo-classical art.

Page 332. (1) *the Baron*: the three-volume edition of *E.D.* was published in December 1872, and in Trollope's *Autobiography* we ead:

I got home [from 18 months' foreign travel] in December 1872, and in spite of any resolution to the contrary, my mind was full of hunting as I came back . . . At first I went back to Essex, my old country, but finding that to be inconvenient, I took my horses to Leighton Buzzard, and became one of that numerous herd of sportsmen who rode with the 'Baron' and Mr. Selby Lowndes. In those days Baron Meyer was alive, and the riding with his hounds was very good. I did not care so much for Mr. Lowndes. (Ch. 19)

'The Baron' was Meyer Amschel de Rothschild (1818–74).

(2) *Colonel of Volunteers*: Colonel Jonathan Peel established the ·National Volunteer Association in 1859, when a French invasion was feared; annual rallies were held throughout the 1860s and '70s.

(3) *a bitter Radical*: the Whig/Tory division of British politics frustrated the emergence of any distinctive party of advanced reformers, while the popularity of Queen Victoria made republicanism virtually unthinkable; consequently English radicals were stigmatized as either single-issue cranks (Charles Bradlaugh) or immoral (Sir Charles Dilke).

(4) *the British Fenians*: the Irish Republican Brotherhood, founded in 1858, was popularly known as the Fenian Brotherhood; it organized an abortive rising in Ireland in March 1867, and in December an attempt to rescue Fenian prisoners from Clerkenwell gaol in London resulted in several deaths; in the years after these events a massive campaign for amnesty was launched and this drew a certain amount of British radical and socialist support; on 24 October 1869 a mass rally was held in Trafalgar Square and Hyde Park, and in the letter of 5 March 1870 from Marx quoted above (p. xi) he describes his daughter Eleanor as one of the Fenians' head centres; Fenianism was a secret society whose leader was known as Head Centre, and the phrase conjured in the public mind notions of pervasive conspiracy.

Page 333. (1) *Tower Hamlets*: a constituency with a considerable working-class population in the east end of London, its MPs from

1857 to 1868 were A. S. Ayrton and C. S. Barber, both Liberals; in 1868 J. D. A. Samuda (also Liberal) replaced Barber; Edmond Beales was a candidate in 1868, representing a more radical element.

(2) *curmudgeons*: Johnson's dictionary defines a curmudgeon as 'an avaricious churlish fellow; a miser, a niggard'.

Page 335. Bohemians: those, often artists, who lead an irregular and unconventional life in society; dating from 1848 as English usage, the term connotes a rejection of bourgeois values.

Page 336. Demosthenic oratory: the Athenian statesman Demosthenes (384–22 BC) was considered the greatest of Greek orators.

Page 341. (1) *covert*: undergrowth, bushes which serve to shelter the fox or hunted game.

(2) *The hounds haven't been put in yet*: have not been released into the covert to seek the fox.

(3) *draw*: search for game in . . .

(4) *scent*: both as verb and noun the origin of the word lies in hunting; 'to scent' means to find or track game, prey by means of its smell; 'scent' is the hound's faculty of smelling, or secondly, the odour of the prey and the trail it so leaves behind.

(5) *getting away*: (in hunting) starting.

(6) *heading the fox*: going in front of the fox (and so reducing the sport of pursuit).

(7) *up wind*: against the wind, in a direction contrary to that of the wind.

(8) *down wind*: with the wind.

(9) *'carrying'*: clay, etc. is to 'carry' when it sticks to horses' hooves, thus impeding them.

Page 342. (1) *chopped*: seized by the hounds before it has been able to get clear of the covert.

(2) *got to ground*: went underground, in a burrow or hole.

(3) *dug out*: extracted (and so caught) by digging.

Page 345. peccant: offending.

CHAPTER XXXVIII

Page 348. screws: horses which are not properly sound (i.e. are awry in some regard).

EXPLANATORY NOTES

Page 349. (1) *the advice which Job got from his wife*: 'Then said his wife unto him, Dost thou still retain thine integrity? curse God, and die.' (Job 2: 9)

(2) *civil*: evidently used here with its distinctly modern meaning, 'polite'; alternatively the phrase 'county civil' may mean the county gentry or county families generally; the modern reading seems the more likely.

Page 353. *bustled*: caused him to move precipitously.

VOLUME II

CHAPTER XXXIX

Page 1. *Kilmarnock*: town in north Ayrshire, 25 miles SW of Glasgow.

Page 2. *Rosalind*: the resourceful lover in Shakespeare's *As You Like It* who, in disguise, teaches Orlando how to articulate his love for her.

CHAPTER XL

Page 6. *the fox's brush*: his tail, which is cut off as a trophy in ritual dismemberment of the victim.

Page 8. *Aegean Sea*: the action of Byron's 'Corsair' is set in the Aegean, east of the Greek mainland.

Page 9. *have my horses so bitted*: have my horses equipped with (or accustomed to) such bits that . . . (bit = metal bar, placed in the animal's mouth and linked to the reins).

CHAPTER XLI

Page 10. *the laurels*: leaves of the bay-laurel were emblematic of victory or distinction in Roman life.

Page 16. *'The rabbits and hares . . . In couples agree'*: this jingle remains irritatingly unidentified.

Page 18. *à merveille*: (Fr.) marvellously, wonderfully.

CHAPTER XLII

Pages 19. *the joint abigail*: the lady's maid who attended both on Lucinda and on Mrs. Carbuncle (hence 'joint').

Page 20. (1) *to mount Lady Tewett*: to provide her with a horse (a mount).

(2) *the nearest episcopal place of worship*: the Church of Scotland being presbyterian, the pious Anglican has to search diligently for an appropriate place to pray.

CHAPTER XLIII

Page 26. *to throw oil upon the waters*: reflecting a natural phenomenon, the phrase can be traced back to Bede's *Ecclesiastical History* (731).

Page 27. (1) *pension*: occasionally used, as here, to mean a boarding school, perhaps what is sometimes called a finishing school.

(2) *they couldn't break her in at all*: (in horse training) to break in = to tame, discipline the spirit of . . .

Page 29. *forage*: dry food (not grass) for horses and cattle.

Page 31. *a bill in Chancery*: written statement of a case, a pleading, in the court of the Lord Chancellor.

Page 32. (1) *to enter an appearance*: to indicate an attitude formally, to enter a plea, in relation to a case.

(2) *Vice-Chancellors*: the judges in the Court of Chancery, acting under the Lord Chancellor.

Page 34.(1) *Petruchio*: the principal male character, ultimately Katharine's husband, in Shakespeare's *The Taming of the Shrew* (c. 1594).

(2) *shrew*: even before Shakespeare's play, a scolding or meddlesome woman was compared to the shrew, that relatively unknown, long- and sharp-nosed little mammal of the genus *Sorex*.

CHAPTER XLIV

Page 37. (1) *all vanity and vexation of spirit*: cf. Ecclesiastes 1:14, 'I have seen all the works that are done under the sun; and, behold, all is vanity and vexation of spirit.'

(2) *the shining thing*: it is of course the diamond necklace, but Lizzie's hatred is directed either against its brilliance or its superficiality.

Page 39. *Medora*: the beloved of Conrad, hero of Byron's 'Corsair'; she dies of grief at the reported death of her lover.

Page 40.(1) *they would not dress*: i.e. they would not dress formally for the evening.

(2) *Houris*: in Muslim theology, the virgins of Paradise, whose beauty rewards the devout male.

Page 44. *the important gentleman*: the chief constable of a police force was usually a leading member of the gentry or the nobility of the area, that is, a layman.

CHAPTER XLV

Page 49. *a couple of bravos in her pay, like an old Italian marquis*: the old Italian nobleman is a stock character in many plays; he retains younger men to perform various tasks his age or rank prohibit.

Page 50. (1) *under remand*: (re)committed to custody (usually while awaiting trial).

(2) *wires*: telegraph wires; Trollope had earlier used this current idiom in ch. 18 of *Framley Parsonage* (1860).

Page 51. *desk*: a portable box or case, usually made of wood or leather, opening to provide a sloping surface for reading and writing on.

Page 52. (1) *'cute*: (aphetic form of *acute*); clever, sharp, keen-witted.

(2) *Barchester Cathedral*: yet another self-allusion by the author of the six Barsetshire novels.

(3) *Hertford Street*: lies to the north of Piccadilly, running east from Park Lane.

Page 53. *Euston Square*: the railway station at Euston was opened in the 1840s.

Page 54. *the head of London police*: the Metropolitan Police was founded in 1829 by Sir Robert Peel (hence 'peelers'); its area of jurisdiction was Greater London (excluding the City), and its chief officer was the Commissioner.

CHAPTER XLVI

Page 64. *peerages*: i.e. the various directories (many of them annual) of the nobility which were published throughout the Victorian period; see note to p. I. 258.

Page 66. (1) *prig*: (dates from seventeenth century) a spruce fellow, a fop; with undertones of moral unction.

(2) *a patent Bramah key*: keys invented by Joseph Bramah (1748–1814) are referred to in Dickens's *Sketches by Boz* (1836).

CHAPTER XLVII

Page 68. *some great reform*: the question of decimalization, though treated lightly and ironically throughout the Palliser novels, did have a topical interest in the 1870s; once again, the transitional nature of the period is underlined here as it is elsewhere in the novel in relation to suburban housing, fashion, and of course the relationship between wealth and land.

Page 72. *over to Flanders*: in ch. 38 of *Phineas Finn*, Lord Chiltern and Finn travel over to the continent to fight a duel; duelling was of course by this date illegal in Britain and discreet arrangements had to be made for extraterritorial encounters.

CHAPTER XLVIII

Page 76. *argus eyes*: after the death of Argus, his eyes were transformed by the goddess Hera into the tail of the peacock; hence, argus-eyed, etc.

Page 77. (1) *acceptances*: formal engagements to pay (bills).

(2) *Tuesday, the 30th of January*: such datings appear to offer the possibility of locating the action in a specific time; this particular date occurred in 1866 and in 1872; in the first instance a Tory government was in power, while the fictional context of *E.D.* has a Liberal government; in 1872, there was indeed a Liberal government, but Trollope can hardly have intended to *anticipate* events when he wrote *E.D.* between 4 December 1869 and 25 August 1870.

CHAPTER XLIX

Page 91. *plant*: = swindle (1825).

CHAPTER L

Page 94. *like Caesar's wife*: Julius Caesar divorced his wife, when she was cited in a scandal, not because he believed her guilty but because 'Caesar's wife should be above suspicion'; the story comes down from Suetonius, but the standard English formulation is found in Samuel Richardson's *Clarissa* (1748), Bk. III.

Page 98. *Kamschatka*: correctly, Kamchatka, a Siberian town.

Page 100. *'Hue and Cry'*: an official gazette in which details of crimes, etc. were published; in Trollope's time the popular name was a vigorous anachronism as the *Police Gazette* had dropped the phrase from its sub-title in 1839.

CHAPTER LII

Page 107. *'The Noble Jilt'*: in 1850 Trollope wrote an unproduceable play of this name, and the allusion here is another of the self-references which are dotted throughout *E.D.*; aspects of the plot are incorporated in *Can You Forgive Her?*; there is an account of the business in ch. 5 of the *Autobiography*.

Page 116. *overset*: upset, overcome.

Page 117. *Minto Lane*: in the first chapter we have been told that Messrs. Harter and Benjamin have their premises in Old Bond Street; the revelation of these second premises in the City does not simply fit the conventions of the crime story and the shady reputation of Lizzie's jewellers, it also contributes to the sense of increased mobility and instability in the novel's social base as the acknowledged and prosecuted crime of Patience Crabstick and her accomplices is substituted for that of Lady Elizabeth Eustace.

CHAPTER LIII

Page 123. (1) *which Dejanira sent to Hercules*: Deianira was married to Heracles; at a swollen stream, the centaur Nessus offered to carry

Deianira over, but then assaulted her; Heracles shot him with a poisoned arrow, and to avenge himself Nessus gave Deianira his blood-stained (and poisoned) tunic telling her that it had the power to reunite lovers; later, when Heracles was unfaithful, Deianira sent him the garment, which caused his death.

(2) *the white elephant*: a burdensome possession; a king of Siam was in the habit of loading courtiers he wanted to ruin with these 'expensive' presents.

Page 126. *home*: searching, pointed, close.

CHAPTER LIV

Page 130. (1) *Baring*: Sir Francis Baring (1740–1810) was the founder of Baring Brothers and Co., and a director of the East India Company; in 1784–90 and 1794–1806 he was an MP; as founder of one of Britain's great capitalist families he was succeeded by a son and two grandsons who, in addition to their commercial positions, also sat in the House of Commons; Sir Francis Thornhill Baring was raised to the peerage in 1866.

(2) *Rothschild*: the banking house of Rothschild was active in Britain from 1805 onwards; Lionel Nathan de Rothschild was elected Whig MP in 1847 but was refused access to the House on grounds of his being Jewish; finally allowed to sit in 1858, and re-elected three times (inc. 1869); his brother Meyer Amschel de R. (1818–74, known as 'Baron Meyer') was MP for Hythe 1859–74.

Page 134. *in Committee*: detailed discussion of a bill in the House of Commons takes place when the members 'sit in committee', that is, collectively examine a measure committed to them at an earlier stage.

Page 137. *All is not gold that glistens*: cf. Shakespeare, *Merchant of Venice*, II, 7, 65–6:

All that glisters is not gold,
Often have you heard that told.

CHAPTER LV

Page 140. (1) *laid upon the table*: a measure, bill, etc. is said to be 'laid on the table' when it is temporarily set aside, though further discussion is intended.

(2) *'Fortnightly Review'*: self-reference with a vengeance, as the serial of *E.D.* was appearing in this journal; in ch. 10 of the *Autobiography* Trollope describes his participation in the *Fortnightly*'s launching and early years.

CHAPTER LVI

Page 153. *'Sunday evening, 25 February, 18—'*: this date occurred in 1866 and 1872; see note (2) to p. II. 77.

CHAPTER LVII

Page 158. *'Gammon'*: 'Rubbish!'

Page 161. *Meek Street and Pineapple Court*: Meek Street is in Chelsea, running parallel to the King's Road and joining Lots Road to Ashburnham Road; the area was transformed in the 1880s by the development of the Cadogan estate which swept away a good deal of working class housing—it is this last aspect to which Trollope relates his conspirators.

Page 163. *negus*: a hot drink, made with port (or sherry), hot water, sugar, lemon, and spices; named after its inventor Colonel Francis Negus (died 1732).

CHAPTER LX

Page 181. *flogged at a cart's tail*: criminals sentenced to be flogged were sometimes drawn through the streets, tied to the back of a cart, receiving their lashes as they walked behind it.

Page 182. *Laws*: a mild exclamation, possibly a corruption of 'Laus' (Latin: praise!) or an euphemized blasphemy (Lord!)

Page 184. *Liberal*: the emergence of a Liberal party, as distinct from liberal opinions, occurs in the 1860s and is most conveniently observed in the change from the leadership of Lord Palmerston (died 1865) to that of W. E. Gladstone (PM 1868–74, etc.).

CHAPTER LXII

Page 209. *Some Jew*: the association of Jews with money-lending has of course a long history in English life, and its integration to political life is enacted in the growth of Rothschild's bank, etc.—see note (2) to II p. 130; Trollope's attitude to Victorian anti-semitism is ambivalent, being neither an insight into, nor an instance of, the prejudice—see John O. McCormick's introduction to *The Prime Minister*, The World's Classics, O.U.P., 1983.

CHAPTER LXIII

Page 217. (1) *off*: gone away, fled.

(2) *Cut the painter, my lord, and started*: departed in secret haste . . . bolted; (from 'painter' = a rope attaching a boat to a jetty).

Page 219. *levanted*: to levant = abscond, bolt, make off.

CHAPTER LXIV

Page 223. *to the top of his bent*: to the height of his capacity, as far as possible, etc.; cf. Shakespeare, *Hamlet*, III, 2, 375: 'They fool me to the top of my bent.'

CHAPTER LXV

Page 228. *'lot'*: group of people showing some common characteristics; used pejoratively from c. 1840s.

Page 230. *to become Merlins when they encounter Viviens*: in Tennyson's *Idylls* (1856, etc.) Vivien induces Merlin to take refuge in a tree and then binds him with a spell; a similar story occurs in Scott's *Lady of the Lake* (1810).

Page 231. *paste*: imitation gem, made of a hard composition of silica, etc.

CHAPTER LXVI

Page 239. *She is as a maiden, all glorious with fine raiment*: Emilius here employs a degenerate version of tropes used in the Song of Solomon, interpreted in the Authorized Version of the Bible as praise of Christ's church; the effect is to emphasize his sensuality and his Jewish origins (as stigmatized in the novel).

EXPLANATORY NOTES

Page 241. *'cad'*: originally a corruption of 'cadet' in the sense of townsman who frequents the precincts of University or Public School—hence 'not a gentleman.'

Page 244. *as the Greek Kalends*: the Latin phrase 'ad Graecas kalendas' humorously meant 'never' because the Greeks did not use the term 'kalends' in their calendar.

CHAPTER LXVII

Page 252. *as an adder to him*: i.e. treacherous, poisonous, fatal.

Page 254. (1) *King David*: the Old Testament king, one of whose best known characteristics was adultery (with Bathsheba); see 2 Samuel: 11, etc.

(2) *as many pennies as Judas*: Judas Iscariot was given 'thirty pieces of silver' as payment for betraying Christ; see Matthew 26: 15.

CHAPTER LXVIII

Page 261. *in durance*: imprisoned.

CHAPTER LXIX

Page 267. *the silver was plated and the gold ormolu*: neither was solid; silver plating dates from 1825, ormolu (Fr. *or moulu* = ground gold) from 1765.

Page 270. *Hymeneals*: rites of marriage; (from Hymen, god of marriage).

Page 271. *camel*: see Matthew 19: 24, 'It is easier for a camel to go through the eye of a needle, than for a rich man to enter into the kingdom of God.'

CHAPTER LXX

Page 279. *Curaçoa*: a liqueur with bitter orange added; (named after the island of C.).

Page 283. *to have married the girl*: to have found a husband for her.

CHAPTER LXXII

Page 295. *laches*: (legal term) unreasonable delay or negligence in pursuing a right or claim.

Page 296. *He had commenced his bill in Chancery*: Camperdown is seen to be launching the proceedings on *his*, rather than his client's, initiative, and his divergence from Dove's view is another indicator of the attorney's prosecution of the case against Lady Eustace; see also note (2) to p. I. 188.

Page 299. *particular*: personal, private.

CHAPTER LXXIII

Page 314. *the Deputy Shepherd*: in Charles Dickens's *Pickwick Papers*, Mr. Stiggins is referred to as 'the Deputy Shepherd', an inferior spiritual adviser even by comparison with 'a great fat chap in black . . . smilin' away like clockwork' (chs. 22 & 27).

CHAPTER LXXIV

Page 317. (1) *the case*: this is, of course, only the preliminary (or, police-court) hearing of the case proper concerning the theft; just as Camperdown tends to displace the Eustace family in the prosecution of the case against Lizzie (and so reflecting the imminent upgrading of attorneys to become solicitors—see also note (2) to p. I. 188) so the case against Benjamin, Smiler, and Crabstick displaces that against Lizzie.

(2) *in durance vile*: a quasi-legal phrase meaning 'imprisoned', but used by Trollope here to mean a manner of transporting the prisoner under police guard.

Page 319. *had kissed the book*: had taken the oath on the Bible.

CHAPTER LXXVI

Page 338. *collops*: Scottish collops is a dish of steak with onions.

CHAPTER LXXVII

Page 348. *he would come in to lunch. Lucy must . . . dinner was ready*: the present-day middle-class distinction between lunch (at midday) and dinner (in the evening) does not quite reflect the Victorian usage—lunch was a less ceremonious meal taken during the morning, and dinner might well be eaten in the middle of the day; the inference is that Lucy is fully at home in the family (and so eats dinner) while Frank is to be accommodated warmly though unexpectedly.

CHAPTER LXXVIII

Page 352. *from the freeholders . . . taken place*: by claiming compensation from the local authorities in whose jurisdiction the crime took place.

Page 359. *Melton*: Lord George, we have been told (see p. I. 333), had been approached with an offer of a nomination for parliament, and the implication here may be that he stood for election at Melton in November (there was a general election in November 1868); however, prior to 1885, there was no constituency called Melton, and the area in Leicestershire which came to form the Melton constituency was in any case predominantly conservative, and so unsuitable for 'a bitter radical'; another implication simply is that Lord George turned up in the context of some other social adventure at Melton, Leics., the following November.

CHAPTER LXXIX

Page 368. *Juan and Haidee*: characters in Byron's *Don Juan* (1819–25); Haidée, Juan's Greek lover, rescues him but is herself subsequently driven mad by his later sufferings.

CHAPTER LXXX

Page 372. *Madame Tussaud*: Marie Gresholtz (1760–1850), born Berne, settled in England in 1802 where she opened her famous wax-works museum (now in Baker Street, London); the museum also contained a chamber of horrors, alluded to here by Lady Glencora.

WHO'S WHO

IN

THE EUSTACE DIAMONDS

(*The page-numbers all refer to Vol. I, unless preceded by* 'ii.')

411

Eustace, John, y.b. of Sir Florian E., 6.

EUSTACE, Lady: Elizabeth ('Lizzie') Greystock, only child of Admiral G., widow of Sir Florian Eustace, q.v.; of Portray Castle, Ayrshire, 13; and Mount Street, 16; 'not twenty-three yet', 35; m. Joseph Emilius, q.v.
> See also *Ph.R., P.M.*

Eustace, ——, Bishop of Bobsborough, Sir Florian E.'s uncle, 11; his wife, and d. Margaretta, 79, 97.

FAWN, Lord: Frederic, about thirty-five, 24; Viscount Fawn of Richmond, 74; of Killeagent, Killaud, Tipperary (i.e. Kill-agent, Kill-lord), 74, 90; of Fawn Court, Richmond, and Victoria Street, 103; Under-Secretary for India in the Liberal Government, 24, 89.
> See also *Ph.F., Ph.R., P.M., D.C.*

Fawn, dowager Viscountess; one s., Lord F., q.v.; 8 dd.; Clara Hittaway, q.v., Augusta, Amelia, Georgina, Diana, Lydia, Cecilia, Nina, 62, 81; signs 'C. Fawn' (presumably Clara), ii. 186.

Finlay, a lawyer, ii. 149.

FITZGIBBON, Hon. LAURENCE, Liberal M.P., 158.
> See also *Ph.F., Ph.R., P.M.*

Fitzmaurice, Captain, chief of the Carlisle police, ii. 44.

Gager, a detective, ii. 86.

Garnett, Messrs., jewellers, 39.

GOESLER, Madame MAX, 78.
> See also *Ph.F., Ph.R., P.M., D.C.*

Gowran, Andy, bailiff at Portray Castle, 203.
> See also *Ph.R.*

GRESHAM, ——, Liberal Prime Minister, 157, ii. 141.
> See also *Ph.F., Ph.R., P.M.*

GREY, John, Liberal M.P. for Silverbridge; his wife ALICE, *née* VAVASOR; ii. 68.
> See also *C.Y.F.H., Ph.F., P.M., D.C.*

Greystock, ——, Dean of Bobsborough, Lady Eustace's uncle, 2; 1 s. Frank, q.v., 3 d., 28 (Ellinor, 14, Margaret, 30); Mrs. G. *née* Jackson, 270.

Greystock, Frank, o.s. of the Dean of Bobsborough, 21; thirty, 29, 32; Conservative M.P. for Bobsborough, 29; barrister, of 2 Bolt Court, Middle Temple, 116, 119, 121; of the Grosvenor Hotel, 166; marries Lucy Morris, ii. 350.

Griggs, Lt., a clubman, 153.

Harter and Benjamin, jewellers of Old Bond Street, 2; their second place of business in the City, ii. 117.

Herriot, Arthur, barrister, 202.

Hittaway, Orlando (82), of the Board of Civil Appeals (81); of Warwick Square, 24, 78; m. Clara, e.d. of Lady Fawn.

Howell and James, jewellers, ii. 266. (See *P.M.* ii. 412: 'I am to have my veil from H. and J.')

Jane, a maid at Fawn Court, 262.

Jones, 'a clergyman of the safe sort', 157.

Juniper, a gardener at Fawn Court, 306.

Killiecrankie, Marquis of: —— Carruthers, 332.

LEGGE WILSON, Liberal Secretary of State for India, 124.
    See also *Ph.F.*, *Ph.R.*, *P.M.* ('Wilson'), *Way we Live Now*.

Linlithgow, Earl of, 4; his mother, Penelope (51), or Susannah (324, ii. 64), dowager Countess; of Brook Street (ii. 54), or Bruton Street (304 and elsewhere).

Macallum, postmaster of Troon, 204.

MacFarlane, horse-dealer of Buchanan Street, Glasgow, 336.

MACKINTOSH, Major, of Scotland Yard, ii. 69.
    See also *Ph.R.*

Macnulty, Julia, companion to Lady Eustace, 27, 44, 49, 54.

Morgan, Jack, huntsman of the Ayrshire, 353.

Morris, Lucy, an orphan, governess at Fawn Court, 19.

MOUNT THISTLE, Lord, ii. 149.
    See 'Morecombe' in *Ph.F.*

Mowbray and Mopus, attorneys, 15, 38, 100.

Nappie, of Huddersfield and Glasgow, a hunting man, 348.

OMNIUM, Duke of, ii. 67.
    See also *Ph.F.*, *Ph.R.*

PALLISER, Lady GLENCORA, wife of Plantagenet P., q.v. 153.

PALLISER, PLANTAGENET, Liberal Chancellor of the Exchequer, 126; nephew and heir-presumptive of the Duke of Omnium; of Matching Priory, 353.
    See also *Small House at Allington*, *C.Y.F.H.*, *Ph.F.*, *Ph.R.*, *P.M.*, *D.C.*

Percival, a hunting man, 355.

Pierrepoint, Lady, of Dumdum House, Dumfries, 294.

Richard, Mr. Carbuncle's servant, ii. 277.

Roanoke, Lucinda, 280; Mrs. Carbuncle's niece, 329.

Rooper, hotel-keeper in Albemarle Street, ii. 282.

Rutter, Mrs., ii. 73.